# Noble Society in Scotlar

Do not be overawed when a man grows rich,
when the splendour of his house increases;
for he will take nothing with him when he dies,
his splendour will not descend with him.
Though while he lived he counted himself blessed –
and men praise you when you prosper –
he will join the generations of his fathers,
who will never see the light of life.

Psalm 49:16–19 (New International Version)

Brothers, think of what you were when you were called. Not many of you were wise by human standards; not many were influential; not many were of noble birth.

1 Corinthians 1:26 (New International Version)

# Noble Society in Scotland

## *Wealth, Family and Culture, from Reformation to Revolution*

Keith M. Brown

Edinburgh University Press

For Hugh and Joyce Brown


Edinburgh University Press Ltd
22 George Square, Edinburgh

First published in hardback 2000
Reprinted 2001 (twice)
Reprinted with corrections (hardback) 2004
First published in paperback 2004

Typeset in Ehrhardt
by Norman Tilley Graphics, Northampton
and printed and bound in Great Britain by
Antony Rowe Ltd, Chippenham

A CIP Record for this book is available
from the British Library

ISBN 0 7486 1300 5 (hardback)
ISBN 0 7486 1299 8 (paperback)

# Contents

# Acknowledgements

The origins of this book lie in being confronted as an undergraduate over twenty years ago with the work of Lawrence Stone who died recently. Sadly, I never met Professor Stone but, like many others, I owe him a great debt and I would like to think he might have found something of interest in the pages that follow. However, I have benefited from the advice and help of many other colleagues whose influence is more immediate in that I prevailed on them to read all, or some, of my earlier drafts. Thank you to Bruce Gordon, Rab Houston and Roger Mason for comments relating to Part 3, and to Michael Penman who acted as my research assistant in completing the typescript, saving me from many errors and helping compile the statistical information. Above all, I am grateful to Hamish Scott who patiently read every chapter, and whose immense knowledge of European nobilities proved invaluable in guiding my thinking and in directing my reading to yet another comparative study. Conversations with many colleagues at St Andrews and elsewhere over the years have also broadened my thinking. Much of the research for this book was carried out in the University Library at St Andrews, in the National Library of Scotland and the National Archives of Scotland, the staff of these institutions continuing to make it their purpose to facilitate scholarship rather than obstruct it. I was able to consult and cite the papers of the Scotts of Buccleuch by permission of the duke of Buccleuch and Queensberry KT, and I am also grateful to lord Elibank for permission to cite from his family papers. In the selection of the illustrations I was helped greatly by the staff at the Scottish Portrait Gallery, Historic Scotland and the National Museum of Scotland. I am grateful for permission to reproduce paintings in the Hamilton collection, the Goodwood collection and the collection of the earl of Mar and Kellie. The map was drawn by the Reprographic Services of the University of St Andrews and made use of information provided by Ian Morrison in P. G. B. McNeill and H. L. McQueen eds, *Atlas of Scottish History to 1707* (Scottish Medievalists, Edinburgh, 1996), 15. Thank you to John Davey, who has been an encouraging and unobtrusive editor. As always, my family have been supportive and distractive to varying degrees. The amusement of my children, Michelle and Mark, that I should 'still' not be finished has been a greater incentive to publish than any Research Assessment Exercise (RAE) panel. Thank you to my wife, Janice, who has tolerated the excessive hours I have spent in the company of long-dead Scottish nobles. If those nobles could speak, I imagine they might have found my earlier work on blood feuds unflattering of their self-conscious Renaissance image. Perhaps this broader attempt to recapture something of their society will redress the balance a little.

# Glossary

| | |
|---|---|
| **annual rent** | interest paid on a debt |
| **baron** | tenant-in-chief and lowest rank of nobility |
| **barony** | a legal jurisdiction and franchise of court powers granted to a landlord by the crown; the lowest level of the Scottish legal system |
| **bonnet laird** | small owner-occupier |
| **buannachan** | professional soldiers serving Highland chiefs |
| **calps** | death duty paid by tenants to Highland chiefs |
| **carriage** | customary service by tenants of transportation of landlord's goods |
| **chalder** | measure of grain, i.e. c.16 bolls where 1 boll = c.164 lb |
| **collegiate church** | church founded by patron in which a college of clerks held votive masses for the souls of the patron and family |
| **conjunct fee** | joint landholding by husband and wife under feudal law |
| **court of session** | college of justice, highest civil law court |
| **curators** | guardians appointed to oversee the lands and affairs of a minor or incapacitated landlord |
| **distraint** | legal process by which a superior seized a tenant's goods or income until the tenant fulfilled an obligation or paid a penalty |
| **factor** | an estate manager |
| **ferme** | land let at a fixed annual rent; or the rent itself; or barony rents paid in kind, usually grain |
| **feu-ferm (feuing)** | practice of land tenure which boomed from the early sixteenth century, whereby tenants made an annual payment for their land (feu or feu-duty), increasingly of money rather than goods |
| **grassum** | original down-payment for a tack or feu-ferm grant and the sum paid to renew the charter periodically |
| **jointure** | estate settled upon wife by husband for her use and support after his death |
| **kirk session** | lowest level of court in Protestant Church of Scotland |

| | |
|---|---|
| **laird** | a landed proprietor, possibly of baronial status |
| **lord lyon** | King of Arms or royal officer with supreme jurisdiction in matters armorial |
| **maill** | a rental, usually of money |
| **oxgang** | division of arable land, nominally as much as a plough team could work in a year (8 oxgangs = 1 ploughgate) |
| **rack-renting** | tendering of land by landlord to highest rental bidder, regardless of traditions of hereditary tenure |
| **regality** | legal jurisdiction granted by the crown to substantial landlords, which included exemption from royal intervention in judicial matters, saving the four pleas of the crown (murder, treason, arson, rape) |
| **relief** | feudal 'casualty' or sum due to a lord on entry, or succession of an heir to land |
| **retour** | the official findings of an inquest, made in response to instructions (by a brieve) from the crown, commonly regarding inheritance and property disputes |
| **reversion** | redemption of alienated lands by a superior at the end of a tenant's lease, or repossession by hereditary family line |
| **sasine** | infeftment, the formal taking/receiving possession of lands (marked by documentation of charter of sasine) |
| **tack** | a lease of lands |
| **tacksman** | a holder of a tack; a term applied in the Highlands, especially from the seventeenth century, to more important tenants charged by chiefs with military leadership over particular areas |
| **tailzie** | legal entail document determining the succession to heritable property |
| **teinds** | tithes; tenth of the produce of the lands of a church parish, nominally for the upkeep of the local church and clergy |
| **terce** | a one-third life rent interest in the heritable estates of a husband given to wife as dower |
| **thane** | Anglo-Saxon term denoting either landed status or a jurisdictional office similar to sheriff; introduced to Scotland by twelfth century at least |
| **wadset** | to grant away lands as security for a debt (or loan), to be held by the creditor (wadsetter) until the debt was cleared |
| **ward** | superior's rights of property during the minority of an heir; ward and marriage = superior's right to decide marriage and collect marriage casualty of that minor |

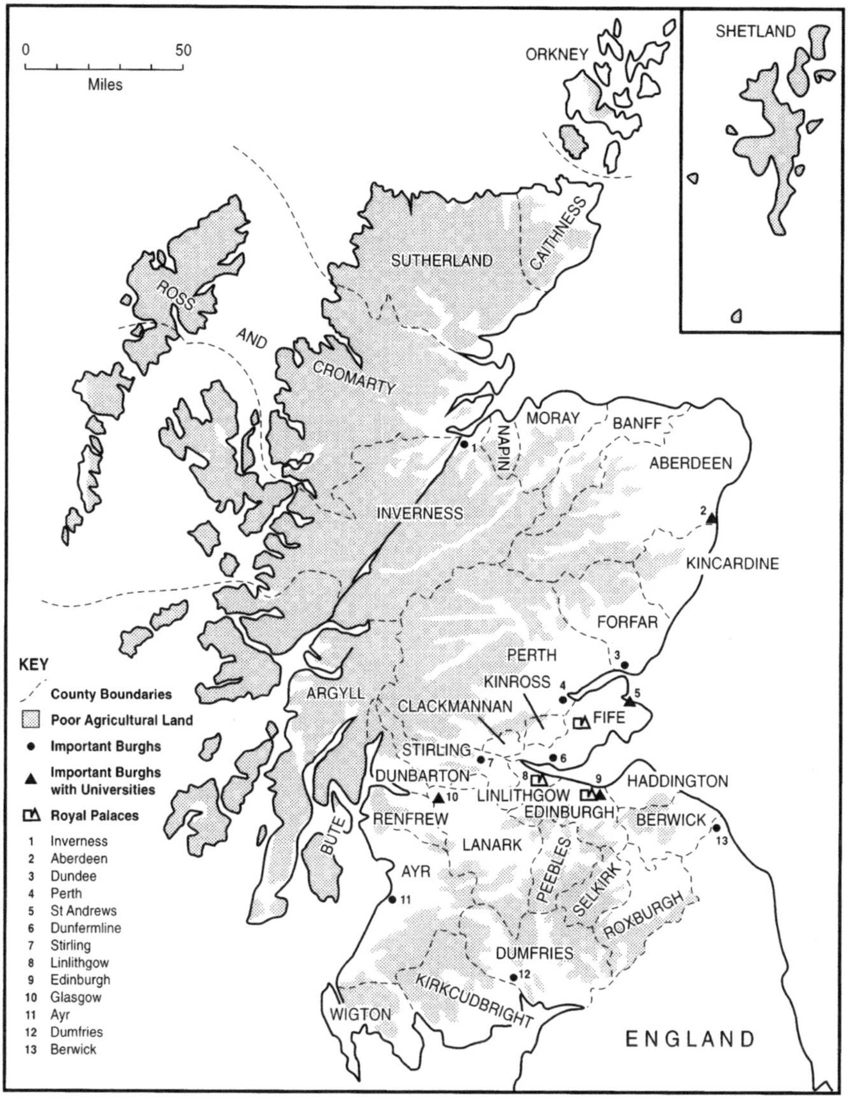


**Scotland c.1600.** The shaded areas represent medium- and poor-quality land. Based upon P. G. B. McNeill and H. L. MacQueen eds, *Atlas of Scottish History to 1707* (Scottish Medievalists, 1996), 15 (Ian Morrison).

# Introduction
# The Early Modern Scottish Nobility

## Contemporary Ideas about Nobility

The sixteenth-century British historian, William Camden, was reflecting a commonly held view of his world when he wrote that 'Men naturally favour Nobility'. But what was meant in his world when men thought, spoke and wrote about nobility? Clearly they were not envisaging a ruling class, a concept that in early modern society is anachronistic. While too much emphasis on contemporary opinion runs the risk of becoming an apologetic for early modern society, an estate society of orders is more appropriate for the sixteenth and seventeenth centuries when even the dead were ranked.[1] Medieval people found it just as perplexing as historians do to arrive at an adequate understanding of nobility, and arguments about the relative merits of ancestry and blood, as opposed to the Aristotelian idea of virtue, aroused passionate debate.[2] Early modern society was, perhaps, even further from arriving at a consensus. In France, the dispute about what constituted true nobility was particularly keen, fuelled by a dialogue between the *noblesse d'épée* and the *noblesse de robe* that historians often exaggerate, but which was nevertheless grounded in real differences of opinion. Here too a succession of writers failed to arrive at an acceptable and precise view of nobility, or of the routes into it. For example, among the Dutch, what constituted nobility differed from one province to another, so that in Guelders and Utrecht it continued to be a matter entirely of birth and descent, while in neighbouring Holland patents of nobility might be bought.[3] Almost every other European state experienced similar debates and similar inconsistencies, Scotland being neither an unusual nor an extreme case.

One answer to the search for nobility lay in function. The origins of European nobilities principally as knightly warriors ensured they retained to a greater or lesser extent some identification with martial pursuits. Of course, Scottish renaissance thinkers, most notably John Mair, joined those elsewhere in pouring scorn on the nobility's obsession with the warrior ideal, and in the later sixteenth century that theme was picked up by the Protestant clergy.[4] The extent to which sixteenth-century nobles were defined functionally by their military professions is debatable, but in France, the country with the greatest cultural influence on Scotland, this tradition was revived by the religious wars. Personal qualities like honour and bravery were embedded in notions of nobility, and the moral dimension of military leadership was as important as technical competency.[5] Certainly these ideas were prevalent in Scotland. Nobles who displayed personal bravery, strength and weapons skills, like the second earl of Moray, murdered in a feud in 1592, were praised, in his case as 'the maist weirlyk man bayth in curage and person'. The exemplification of martial qualities by Scottish lords was also expected and was practised – for example, nine earls and twelve lords of parliament were present at the battle of Langside in 1567 – even if it was only in the western Highland seaboard that the role of the professional soldier, or *buannachan*, was nurtured by lords within the affinity.[6] However, by the beginning of the seventeenth century, political and social changes, broadly comparable to those under way in France and England, made it less likely that lords would summon their followers to ride into combat either in pursuit of national political objectives or in the furtherance of a local bloodfeud.[7] Indeed, as early as the 1590s the crown was worrying about the kingdom's preparedness for war, and by the 1620s the absence of a military infrastructure was widely perceived.[8] Yet as was the case in almost every European state where governments subcontracted military enterprises, it was to nobles that the Scottish crown still turned for the expertise and resources to put down domestic rebellions, as on Orkney in 1614 and Islay in 1615, or to engage in war with France, singling out the sixth earl of Morton to raise men to serve in the duke of Buckingham's expedition to La Rochelle in 1627 because of 'the multitude of his kinsmen, allyes and freinds'. Scottish nobles also contracted in significant numbers to serve as mercenaries on the continent.[9] Kings might have wanted to contain the martial energies of their nobles, but the early modern crown could not afford to uncouple nobility from its functional warrior heritage.

A military tradition was nurtured in young nobles by an early conditioning for a martial life, their education requiring training in the use of weaponry, and many Scottish nobles travelled to the continent for exposure to the latest military knowledge. Respect for and interest in warfare was inspired by a lively chivalric culture, celebrated by the likes of Gavin Douglas, whose *Palice of Honour* eulogised a military ethos and ideas of honour rooted in personal and family glory won in war. Writers like David Hume of Godscroft in the early seventeenth century employed the history of great men like the 'Good' sir James Douglas who fought alongside Robert I, or the second earl of Douglas who died at Otterburn in 1388, as exemplars to inspire the nobility to martial deeds grounded in virtue. Nobles were seen as important patrons of soldiers, wishing to be associated in some way with the military life. Thus sir Thomas Kellie dedicated his 1627 manual on military technique, *Pallas Armata or Military Instructions for the Learned*, to the sixth earl of Rothes.[10] Many nobles retained their link with a military ethos in mercenary service, the house of Buccleuch being a good example of a family that earned its living in the Dutch Wars, while the Lindsays established themselves in Germany. All of the five legitimate and one illegitimate sons of the tenth lord Forbes served in the German wars, four of them being killed.[11] Even in their localities, particularly in the Highlands, nobles retained a military function, and in the 1620s the young thirteenth earl of Sutherland was advised to 'lead fourth your countreymen your selfe in persone; so shall they obey the more willingly, and fight with better courage'.[12] When civil war broke out after 1637, therefore, most nobles approached it as amateurs, but there was no question that they would assume the mantle of warriors just as their grandfathers had done in the civil warfare of the 1560s and 1570s.

If a martial ethos continued to be projected by the nobility as an integral facet of their identity, the most important pointer to a man's noble rank was the feudal title of his land. In Denmark, where the idea of nobility by descent alone was relatively weak, and where nobility was not automatically conferred by office, tangible evidence of land and tenure was particularly important in demonstrating nobility. In France, ownership of a lordship in itself conferred nobility until this practice was ended by the ordinance of Blois in 1579; the crucial factor here was legal, nobility being an '*ordre juridique*'.[13] Writing in the 1590s, sir Thomas Craig of Riccarton, the most prominent legal theorist of his day, argued that tenants-in-chief of the king, whose grant, or feu, included precedence and jurisdiction, were noble by dint of legal title. These tenants-in-chief were all barons, a style accorded to 'persons of rank generally'. By Riccarton's day, the barons included the peerage and those below that rank 'who possess the power of the sword, in other words that absolute form of jurisdiction which is implied in a grant "*furcae et fossae*"'. The titular lords of parliament, therefore, simply emerged from the barons, in effect becoming hereditary representatives of their rank. Even where noble rank was not explicitly conferred – that is, where the land was a simple feu, crown tenants 'if able for three or four generations successively to live on the revenues of their estate without engaging in manual labour or resorting to some form of trade, and meanwhile to discharge their feudal obligations to the prince with fidelity, may be held participants in dignity and precedence'. Therefore, 'a noble feu … endows the grantee with rank, and places him among the feudal nobility', so that whenever the king 'grants lands which have rank attached to them, he ennobles the grantee even though no express conferment of noble rank be made'.[14] Riccarton's judicial colleague, Thomas Hamilton, first earl of Melrose, writing in 1627, agreed, describing those who held the superiorities of their teinds as noblemen and gentlemen, while those paying teinds to superiors were simply 'gentrie', a lesser rank that did not equate with its English meaning.[15] Writing towards the end of the seventeenth century, the great jurist sir James Dalrymple of Stair confirmed this legal view, arguing that historically lesser barons were a product of the subdivision of fees, while the designation of greater baron had been reserved for those who held at least a hundred merk land from the king. Lordships and earldoms were 'but more noble titles of a barony, having the like feudal effects'.[16]

The issue here was not one of the title or designation held by the individual, but the legal title of his land. The lairds of Grant were not members of the parliamentary peerage, but as early as 1357 a charter described the then chief of the family as Patrick le Grant, '*dominus de Stratharthoc*'. With such a lineage, this family did not need to be created lords of parliament to know they ranked among the nobility.[17] Hugh Rose of Kilravock, who died in 1597, might conventionally be described as a laird. However, this man held over the course of his life the crown offices of sheriff of Inverness, sheriff and justice depute of Nairn, and constable of Inverness castle, and in addition was bailie of the lordship of Strathnairn and tutor of Calder. Kilravock was a man held in high esteem by all his neighbours, and by James VI who permitted him to keep his hat on in the royal presence, a privilege accorded only to nobles.[18] In spite of the superficial similarities that have fooled historians, baronial freeholders did not belong to the same rank as feu-holders who adopted the designation of laird over the course of the sixteenth century. This importance of superiority in determining nobility is equally evident when land was lost. In 1615 the third lord Ochiltree moved to Ireland, having sold all his land in Scotland. It was declared that since the family 'being as it wer deade in that our kingdome', the Ochiltree title should lapse. However, lord Ochiltree petitioned that a cousin, sir James Stewart of Killeith, who had purchased the lands, might succeed to the title, which the king was pleased to allow. Furthermore, parliament was extremely uneasy when in the 1620s the king created Scottish peerages for a handful of Englishmen who held no land in the country, and the practice was subsequently abolished by the Covenanters.[19]

Along with tenure, lineage was a good indicator of nobility. John Knox argued that noblemen were 'called Princes of the people ... not be reasson of your birth and progenye, (as the most part of men falslie do suppose,) but by ressoun of your office and dewtie'. Knox was wrong and, as he admitted, the majority of men believed differently. In so far as nobles were born to exercise hereditary office they were magistrates, but there was no ennoblement by virtue of holding royal office, as was the case in parts of Europe.[20] His swipe at lineage was in a long-established humanist tradition of attacking a nobility of birth, preferring the emphasis to be on virtue, but it is a mistake to dismiss the idea of a nobility based on blood as a vulgar notion manipulated to retain the obedience of the ignorant.[21] Lineage was neither vulgar nor intended for popular consumption; it lay at the heart of noble self-consciousness. At the Estates General in 1560, the count de Rochefort asserted that the only real qualification for nobility was birth, roundly rejecting Aristotle's less exclusive definition. Later sixteenth-century France might even have seen a growing emphasis on birth as writers argued that virtue was more likely to be nurtured in noble families where it became a hereditary quality. The Scots wrestled with these same problems. At the funeral of lady Jane Maitland in 1631, the preacher skilfully blended birth and virtue, advancing the thought that her pedigree was honourable 'since both blood and vertue joyned to make them noble: noble not onely in inheritance, but by purchase: Their greatnesse from their blood, their goodnes was from their vertue'. The early seventeenth-century poet, Patrick Hannay, argued that some commoners did acquire virtue and some born to high rank lost honour by failing to add to their inherited virtues. However, he still concluded, 'For virtue, though aye clear, yet clearest shines/When she doth dart her lights from noble lines'. James VI also subscribed to the idea that nobility was a natural quality, being conveyed through the lineage in the blood. In *Basilikon Doron* he argued that 'vertue followeth oftest noble blood: the worthinesse of their [noblemen's] antecessors craveth a reverent regard to be had unto them'. This mystical belief in the properties of noble blood was combined with a veneration for the long-standing association of a family with high rank. Sir James Balfour of Denmilne, the lyon king of arms under Charles I, argued that a man who wished to prove his status must show lineal descent from noble ancestors over four generations, demonstrate that throughout his life his parents behaved nobly, not engaging in any activity that might lead to derogation, and he should be recognised as noble within his own community. As Denmilne indicated, Scottish views on lineage were close to those of France where writers were not uncritical of a nobility based on ancestry, but the importance of birth and blood lines was reinvigorated by the inspiration of Aristotle and other classical writers who argued for a nobility of birth imbued with virtue.[22]

In the Highlands, pride in ancient mythological lineages was preserved by bards who provided oral evidence at suitable occasions. Elsewhere oral memorialisation had disappeared, but detailed genealogies and myths of ancient origin particular to each family were essential in authenticating nobility, some seeing this as its truest measure. Hence in 1574, sir Richard Maitland of Lethington, a baron and court of session judge, described his house as 'but new in respect of the grandeur of others, yet inferiour to few for the ancientness therof'. Riccarton agreed, writing: 'posterity is even more ambitious of precedence than of wealth'. In discussing the origins of the Douglases, Godscroft, a man whose life was spent in the clientele of that family, asserted that the heads of the Douglas house had been noble long before sir James Douglas, the companion of Robert I, made his dramatic entry into Scotland's history. Even the founder of the family, Sholto, was 'not to have bene a man of base and ignoble birth'. Godscroft insisted that the ancient and pre-eminent nobility of the Douglases was clear from their valour and virtue, 'truest markes of nobilitie', their styles and dignities from the rank of knight upwards, their public offices, 'the nobilitie of their blud and dicent', and 'the lustre of their fame and glorie'.[23] This nobility by descent extended at least to younger sons and grandsons, with Scottish heraldry permitting the former to display their arms according to a precise gradation, distinguishing their place in line, and even heiresses and bastards might have their own coat of arms.[24] Nor was maternal ancestry ignored; in a mid-seventeenth-century account of the life of sir George Douglas, his father's illegitimate descent from the houses of Angus and Morton was compensated for by his mother's lineage, she being a Dundas of a house 'both ancient and noble'. However, the son of a noblewoman could not inherit her rank if she had married a commoner.[25]

Family historians encouraged nobles to be self-consciously aware of their place as individuals within the lineage. When Lethington completed his carefully researched *History of the House of Seytoun* c.1561, dedicating it to the fifth lord Seton, he suggested that a man would be the more likely to conserve and maintain his house if he 'rememberis the gud begynnyng of his hous and surename, the lang standing thairof, the honorable and vertuous actis of his predecessouris'. This growing enthusiasm for family histories was, therefore, fed by a desire to inspire young nobles to emulate the virtuous qualities of their ancestors, thus advertising a family's fitness to serve the king in the present.[26] Important to this genre was antiquity. The earls of Argyll traced their origins to Fergus Leithderg, the son of Nemed, and to the Norman family of de Beauchamp, reinforcing their Gaelic and French roots. They also claimed king Arthur as an ancestor, indicating that the British dimension was not to be neglected.[27] Sir Robert Gordon of Gordonstoun was fascinated by the possibilities of an exotic origin story, locating the Gordons in Macedonia as the Gordunia before they migrated to France where Julius Caesar encountered them. A duke of Gordon was believed to have been instrumental in subduing the Bretons for Charlemagne, and the French branch continued to be represented in the seventeenth century by Gordons at Quercy. In this patriotic narrative there is no reference to migration from England, while martial deeds performed in war with the English were given prominence, a Bertram Gordon being credited with slaying Richard I at Caalac.[28] Patriotic themes like this were common. The Hamiltons were said to have owed their fortune in Scotland to sir Walter Hamilton of Cadzow, who migrated from England to join the Bruce family. An older patriotic origin story was preserved among the Crawford house of Auchinames in Ayrshire, who believed their fortune was founded in the thirteenth century by an ancestor who fought the Norse at the battle of Largs in 1263. The Murrays claimed an even more ancient validation, tracing their origins from a tribe who fought the Romans, having migrated from southern Britain in the face of the Roman advance. Even modest families like the Arbuthnotts produced histories that glorified their lineage; in this instance the writer was Alexander Arbuthnott, principal of King's College, Aberdeen, who finished his history c.1567. A cruder form of memorialising the family history was produced by captain Walter Scott of

Satchells, the illiterate compiler of a metrical 'True History' of the Scotts, glorifying the life of the first earl of Buccleuch.[29] Yet it is likely that many if not most nobles were becoming sceptical about these extravagant myths. In the family history he completed in 1652, Cromarty traced his ancestry back to Adam, a tongue-in-cheek claim that the present age would mock, the succeeding age would doubt, and the third age would be likely to believe.[30]

Throughout Europe, nobles were defined by their privileges. This was most transparent when these were juridical, as in Holland where the nobility enjoyed relatively few privileges. By contrast, French nobles enjoyed an extensive array of privileges, and while these were subject to changes in social convention or political circumstance, the importance of tax exemptions helped draw a clear line between nobles and non-nobles.[31] In discussing this issue, Denmilne noted only that nobles should be saluted in public places by commoners, that a nobleman's word should always be given more weight over that of a commoner, that nobles could not be tortured, except in specific cases such as *lèse majesté* or heresy, and they could not be punished like plebeians unless their behaviour had first led to the derogation of their nobility.[32] However, Denmilne was ignoring other forms of privilege. Scottish nobles, titled and untitled, derived seigneurial rights from their land, including rights to levy private taxes and services, exercise patrimonial justice, and administer obligations to the crown such as levying troops, and they enjoyed certain economic monopolies on their estates like brewing and operating a mill. On the other hand, the Scottish nobility had no formal right to appoint public officials and no rights of pre-emption and first sale, and they did not exercise control over their tenants' rights to migrate, marry, change occupation and hold land, although they had influence over them. Nobles had their own rights of political representation, these being greater for the peerage who received a personal summons to parliament and had greater access to the royal court, along with the reservation of certain state offices for nobles and a range of honorific rights, such as armorial bearings, that were widely employed, and others that were more exclusive to the peerage. However, the Scottish nobility did not enjoy tax exemption or any other fiscal privileges, including protection from creditors; land ownership was not the preserve of nobles; they had no indemnity from judicial and service obligations; they did not enjoy many trading concessions; the wearing of weapons appears to have been commonplace; hunting was not a noble privilege; and sumptuary legislation was rarely enforced. Noblewomen in Scotland could enjoy all the corporate privileges of their rank, and some of the honorific privileges in the absence of male heirs, including succeeding to a higher title like an earldom depending upon the terms of the patent.[33]

It has been suggested that due to the localised nature of late medieval Scottish society and the absence of a well-established legal profession, the Scots were 'remarkably poor at definition generally', a view with which Denmilne concurred. He was one of the few Scottish writers to engage with the debate on nobility, although his thoughts were never published. Yet even the head of Scotland's heraldic court admitted that defining nobility was too difficult, presenting him with an insoluble semantic problem, 'The word being too wyde'.[34] But it was not only in Scotland that nobility was understood without being satisfactorily defined, and historians might have to resort to description rather than definition. In general, the Scots shared with most other European nobilities a powerful connection with a military past and ethos, a landed estate was important although not essential, the importance of noble birth was recognised, nobles enjoyed a variety of privileges, and a noble lifestyle was cultivated. However, a title was not necessary, and the great majority of European nobles did not possess hereditary titles. The early modern European nobility was pyramid-shaped, but fluid in its dynamic with a small élite of nationally important magnate families, a broader number of middle-ranking noble houses who dominated their own localities and from time to time exerted influence at a national level, and many lesser noble families who rarely attracted any interest outside of their localities, perhaps not even there.[35] Nobles also held a world view and lived according to a noble lifestyle, nobility being as much an issue of lifestyle and reputation as of legal status.[36] In other words, nobility was to some extent about being able to live in noble society.

## Rank and Titles

Denmilne wrote in his unpublished essay, 'On Nobility', that as in continental areas like Germany, the Scottish nobility was composed of many ranks, so that 'some are called gentile, some honourable, some worshipfull, others noble'.[37] These distinctions of rank mattered. Hence when in August 1581 Esmé Stewart was raised from an earldom to a dukedom, a proclamation was issued publicly charging all the king's subjects 'to acknawlege and reverance his said dearest causing [cousin] according to the stile titill place before specified'.[38] These gradations of status were apparent to contemporaries and were underlined at every opportunity. In May 1567, queen Mary allegedly offered rewards on a sliding scale to anyone who killed one of the rebel lords, the slaying of an earl being worth four times the murder of a baron. A range of laws and regulations recognised ranking, from those governing attendance at wappinschaws (= weapon showings) or limiting retinues, to that establishing fees charged by crown offices.[39] Careful distinctions were also made between different ranks of nobles. In 1606, a commission for ranking the peerage tried to iron out the many points of contention between the titular nobility.[40] Visually this ranking was reinforced in heraldry so that, for example, different forms of the helmet were used for royalty, peers, knights and baronets, barons and esquires, while mere gentlemen were not permitted helmets until 1672.[41] Architecture too reflected a world of hierarchy, ranks and estates.[42] When in 1624 James VI created a new hereditary rank of Nova Scotia baronets, the crown was careful to draw attention to the privileges this rank would enjoy, claiming that those so honoured would 'know ther owne places at home, and likewyse sall have ther due abroad from the subjectis of our other countreyis'.[43]

In a society so conscious of rank, honorific titles were much valued, and it was rare to encounter a man like George Seton, fifth lord Seton, who refused an earldom from queen Mary in 1562 on the grounds that there was more honour in being the senior lord of parliament than in being a recently created earl.[44] The sixteenth and especially the seventeenth centuries saw throughout Europe a great expansion in the numbers of titled nobles along with a proliferation of titles as kings sought inexpensive ways to patronise their nobilities.[45] The rise in the size of the Scottish peerage from fifty-two in 1560 to 102 in 1637 was consistent with developments elsewhere. The sharpest rise took place between 1603 and 1625, there being only seventeen new titles and nine promotions within the peerage in the later sixteenth century compared to fifty-three new titles and forty promotions in the early seventeenth century. Nevertheless, James VI could be stingy in rewarding faithful servants. Sir Robert Melville of Murdocairny loyally served Mary and James in a public career that began in 1559, but it was 1616 before the eighty-nine-year-old Murdocairny was created lord Melville of Monimail.[46] Land was not directly linked to a title, but possession of a landed estate was *de facto* a recognition for acquiring a title, and some correlation was maintained between landed worth and rank. In 1589 James VI promised Alexander Lindsay, one of the gentlemen of his bedchamber and a younger son of the tenth earl of Crawford, 'you shall be a Lord', but before creating him lord Spynie the king provided land from a former ecclesiastical estate and married him to a rich widow. This secularisation of ecclesiastical property allowed the crown to create lordships from twenty-one abbeys, eleven priories, six nunneries and one preceptory by 1625.[47] The crown did not sell hereditary peerages in Scotland, although the new and not highly valued Nova Scotia baronetcies were dreamt up as a revenue-making device, being sold to better-off members of the lesser nobility. This was not unlike much of Europe where a limited market in noble rank and titles operated, but there was certainly not the same sense of debasement that arose from the selling of titles by the duke of Buckingham in England.[48] Neverthless, the burst of creations that followed the regal union in 1603 – twenty-nine new creations between 1603 and 1625 with a further fifteen by 1637 – changed expectations dramatically, and the press for titles became ever more frantic as ambitious barons like Alexander Fraser of Philorth and sir Colin Campbell of Glenorchy sought the favour of crown officers and courtiers in getting a title. Under Charles I there was a slowing down of new creations. Sir James Johnstone of that ilk was successful in being created a lord at the 1633 parliament, but within months he was lobbying for an earldom, only to be told that such a reward must be preceded by 'some new occasion and service donne by your selff'. Not only had many of the leading baronial families now entered the peerage, but royal restraint also added value, as the king himself noted in 1629: 'these preferrments are the cheef marks of a prince's favour, wherby both the present age and the posteritie tak notice of his judgement and of the subjects' meritt as they find them to be conferred'.[49]

The business of making a peer was an occasion early modern kings manipulated to project authority, although not every monarch enjoyed an absolute monopoly, the Swedish nobility, for example, having some control over the registration of new nobles.[50] In Scotland, prior to 1603, peers might be made in parliament in the presence of the king, but that assembly performed no vetting function. Denmilne followed a familiar line of argument among those sympathetic to absolutist ideas, asserting that 'The fountaine and spring of Nobility is ather vertew or authority of the prince', and since the former was a philosophical concept commonly acquired, then civil nobility was entirely derived from the king. That virtue might manifest itself in contrasting service 'by airmes ore letteres', so that 'a two-fold Nobility be constitute, ane that is purchessed by Airmes, Valor and Skill in Military affairs, the uther by knowledge and learninge'. But in either case, Denmilne insisted, it was the prince who authenticated nobility in a formal, civil ceremony.[51] Hence the emphasis on service in the ratification of sir George Hume's earldom of Dunbar in 1606, which described him as one who had from his youth 'dedicate his bodie, mynd and haill lyfe to his majesteis service'.[52] The ritual of these events was important with new peers being belted in the king's presence, as in October 1581 when the first duke of Lennox and the new earls of Arran, Morton and Gowrie underwent this ceremony at Holyrood palace. The making of knights was an intrinsic part of the ceremony, as in 1599 when knights were dubbed at the ceremony raising lord Hamilton and the sixth earl of Huntly to the rank of marquis. On occasion these rituals were staged to coincide with important state ceremonial, such as the queen's coronation on 17 May 1590, when sir John Maitland of Thirlestane was created a lord of parliament and twelve barons were knighted.[53] After the regal union, most peers were created in the absence of the king, often with minimal ceremonial. However, elaborate ritual did not disappear entirely, and the king's role was performed by royal officers like the commissioner or chancellor, as in 1616 when Robert Ker, first lord Roxburghe, was created an earl. Charles I's presence at the 1633 parliament, in the course of a royal visit in which the king created one marquis, ten earls, two viscounts and eight lords of parliament, and dubbed fifty-four knights, offered the opportunity for the crown's role in the making of a peer to be displayed in even more magnificent majesty.[54]

Throughout early modern Europe, kings were tightening up their control of access to noble status, seeking to institutionalise the process, and the act of issuing letters of nobility was seen as a mark of sovereignty. The Scottish king's determination to manage the honours system was apparent from the procedure by which heritable possession of titles was claimed. Normally claimants registered their right to succeed to land and titles without opposition, and difficulties only arose when there was no male heir or there was doubt over the line of succession.[55] But it was not only the financial potential that interested the crown, and archbishop Spottiswoode recounted that James VI 'was always most tender in the conveyance of honours'. In 1612, the succession of a fictive heir to the childless fifth earl of Eglinton provided the king with a case in which to test the principle that the crown alone was 'the fontane of all honour within his Majesteis dominionis'. With his own chancellor and privy council opposed to him, it is unsurprising that James lost the case in the court of session, but he won an important point of principle. It was conceded that in future no alienation, disposition or entail be made by a peer that altered the succession of honours, titles and dignities without having the king's own personal approval. Almost two decades later, a similar case arose over the Lothian succession, and the claims of the male heir were overturned. In 1632, Charles I's privy council asserted that the conferment of honours and dignities lay entirely in the king's hands, it being 'ane high and malapert presumptioun in a subject to usurpe suche auctoritie or to assume unto thameselffis anie title of dignitie not lawfullie conferred upon thame be his Majestie', but the court of session continued to have jurisdiction over peerage cases.[56]

However, the Scottish nobility was not simply the parliamentary peerage. What has led some historians to make this error is an appropriation of an English model (on which even English historians cannot agree) that the seventeenth-century diarist, John Evelyn, rightly claimed was unique to his country: 'nor indeed is there in any kingdome (save ours onely) that severe distinction of *minores* and *majores* amongst the Nobility, a difference which some think neither suits with true policy or justice'.[57] While there was a trend towards hereditary titles in most European states, some countries did not have a peerage at all, particularly in eastern Europe. In Sweden, titles outside the royal family only appeared in 1561; in Hungary they were introduced in 1608; and in Poland they were not recognised by the government at all prior to partition.[58] In Scotland, the foundation of an order of baronial landlords was laid in the twelfth and thirteenth centuries, and until the mid-fifteenth century the nobility was a landowning order of earls, barons and other freeholders, sometimes referred to as 'other nobles'. It was the emergence of a parliamentary peerage with honorific titles and often scattered estates, and whose principal distinction from the untitled nobility was the personal summons they received to parliament, that has led to the mistaken idea of a social and political division between nobles, meaning the parliamentary peerage, and lairds, meaning the barons or lesser nobility.[59] Certainly early modern Scots were aware of the evolutionary nature of honorific titles, and when the style of marquis made its first appearance in

1599, it was observed that it 'wes ane new styill in this kingdome of Scotland'. Men also had an informed view of the origins of titles, some of which were known to have originated in the late Roman empire, others, like that of thane, in the eleventh century. Of course, it was fashionable to describe titles in terms that suggested great age; thus sir James Melville of Halhill referred to the fifth earl Marischall in 1589 as 'ane ancien erle', when in fact the earldom was only created in 1458. Contemporaries knew well that the process of creating titles was a dynamic one, and the often modest origin of noble houses was public knowledge. By the middle of the sixteenth century, the lords Gray had held their title for a century, but bishop John Leslie recorded how in the reign of James I, in the early fifteenth century, Andrew Gray was a royal servant, although 'nocht of the lawest degrei', who was helped by his royal master to marry an heiress and to acquire the estate at Fowlis that was the beginning of the Gray fortune.[60]

For those historians who have gone in search of a Scottish gentry there certainly is some misleading sixteenth-century evidence in which the use of the terms nobility, barons and gentlemen appears to signify social distinctions.[61] Once in England, James VI even described the nobility as 'in credite and honnour nixt unto us', while lumping the barons and gentlemen together as 'the greatest pairt' of the commonweal. The term gentry gained some currency in the early seventeenth century, Charles I being described by one historian as 'among its most active promoters'.[62] There, of course, is an important clue, for that is exactly what one would expect from an anglicised imperialist. The shift in language is most apparent among crown officers. Between the privy councils of the regent Morton and Charles I there was a shift in language from 'the Nobill men, Baronis and Gentill men' of the 1570s, to the 'Nobilitie and Gentrie' of the 1620s.[63] However, the attractiveness of a new vocabulary in governing circles is not necessarily a reflection of real societal changes, a point that has been demonstrated for early modern Castile. Furthermore, the European norm in the late medieval period was not that of England with its tiny but powerful peerage as the sole possessors of nobility. Instead it was a large but stratified nobility. In discussing this issue of the boundaries of nobility in relation to fifteenth-century Europe, it has been suggested that the casual use of terms like gentleman should not mislead historians, these being common throughout the continent in countries that did not have a gentry in the sense in which there was one in England. A gentleman was not a rank but an ideal type, and in France the traditional nobility laid claim to the term in order to distinguish themselves from *noblesse de robe*.[64] When in 1597 James VI described sir Walter Scott of Buccleuch as 'a gentleman', he was not implying that this great border baron was anything other than a nobleman. Parliament also recognised this definition of nobility when in 1567 it recommended that 'the baronis of this realme aucht to haif voit in parliament as ane part of the nobilitie'. Riccarton's feudal analysis of Scottish society was unambiguous in recognising all untitled barons as noble, reserving for their vassals the designation of lesser nobility, and placing the gentry even lower in rank among the tenants of these vassals. In spite of James VI's later confusion once ensconced in England, he was clear in *Basilikon Doron*, a decade earlier, that 'the small Barrones are but an inferiour part of the Nobilitie and of their estate'. Denmilne agreed, writing that 'in ane Inferior degree of Nobility are Knights of severall degrees and orders according to the custome and previlidges of the places quhair thay live, and lastlie Barrons and Equuyres, and Gentlemen and Squyres'.[65] Both the king and the lord lyon king were describing a range of noble ranks that was commonplace in almost any European state apart from England. The large Spanish nobility comprehended a wide range of status and wealth, with those at the lower end, the impoverished *hidalguía*, being recognised as the 'common base of all nobility', a position occupied in Scotland by the baronage.[66] A title, therefore, was essentially an honour granted to a baron. The words lord and laird even had the same meaning so that in October 1571 sir William Drury, marshall of Berwick, wrote of the Scottish lairds 'whom they term barons', while the common usage in records from those of the privy council to private letters was to describe lairds as noble.[67]

The barons themselves were self-consciously noble, proclaiming their status at every opportunity – for example, in monumental inscriptions on tombs. The monument above the grave of the ninth earl of Angus and his wife (the earl died in 1591) contains a genealogical record of the lairds of Glenbervie that dates from the year 730. Here is a man who inherited one of the greatest titles in the kingdom only two years before his own death, but chose to be remembered as the head of a long and proud line of noblemen who had been barons of Glenbervie.[68] Another baronial family keen to state its nobility was that of Glenorchy, whose chief, sir Colin Campbell of Glenorchy, listed among his possessions thirty-four 'Pictures of the Lairdes and Laidies of Glenurquhy and other Noblemen come of the House of Glenurquhy'. These men also recognised differentiation in rank between one another. Sir Hugh Campbell of Loudon, sheriff of Ayr, complained to the privy council on 24 July 1600 at being asked to give surety to George Shaw of Glenmure for it 'hes not bene sene that assuiranceis [are made] betuix ane of the said complenaris rank and calling and the said George Shaw, quha is a meane gentilman'. Less than twelve months later, Loudon was created a lord of parliament, emphasising the already immense social distinction between these two 'lairds'. The pride invested in a baronial pedigree is even more emphatically underlined in an exchange that took place in 1567 when sir William Murray of Tullibardine told the fourth earl of Bothwell that he was 'his [Bothwell's] better in estate, and in antiquitie of house many degrees above him'. In a slightly more defensive mode, Robert Maule was indignant that people thought his nephew, sir Patrick Maule, was the first of his house to be ennobled when he was created earl of Panmure in

1646. In his account of the Maule history, the St Andrews commissary provided evidence of baronial status from the thirteenth century, claiming that in those days 'knychts wor al barons in the immediat rank to Earles'.[69] In the memory of the house of Panmure that noble status had been kept alive over the centuries when others around them acquired new, titular dignities.

## Size and Social Mobility

How large was the Scottish nobility? Sir James Melville of Halhill's lament about 'ther gret nomber' of noblemen was echoed by Riccarton's observation that 'in Scotland we have barons and baronies in plenty,' and by James VI who in 1612 complained that 'the great number of noblemen there [Scotland] doe more harme then goode to that state, and that they exceede and surpasse the number of the noblemen heere [England]'.[70] Regional descriptions also highlighted the 'mony noblemen' of a given locality, and an undated intelligence list from the last quarter of the sixteenth century included fifty-four named peers 'besides lairds, wherof many are barons and of equal credit and revenue with the lords'.[71] European estimates suggest a figure of 1 or 2 per cent of the population as a useful starting point for most of the continent, France being close to an average. Where a warrior ethos was more marked, such as in Hungary, Poland or Spain, nobilities made up a higher share of the population, while the number of nobles was insignificant in Scandinavia and most of the Balkans.[72] Since Scottish definitions of nobility were close to those of France, the nobility might be estimated at around 7500 people – that is, on the basis of 1 per cent of 750 000, including around 1000 heads of noble houses.

Can this estimate be substantiated? In an illustrated roll of barons showing their coats of arms, prepared for queen Mary and based on a 1532 armorial, 204 houses are listed, a relatively small number, even if it is four times larger than the peerage of the day. The beautifully crafted Seton armorial of 1591 contains the arms of fifty-two peers and 322 barons, while another armorial of the late sixteenth century contains the names of 379 barons and lairds with no peers at all. The author of an early seventeenth-century commonplace book, probably Patrick Hume of Polwarth, jotted down a list of people who mattered, beginning with the king of Scotland, the Holy Roman Emperor and other European rulers, before going on to list the Scottish peerage and the names of 494 baronial houses; here is a complete list of the 500 or so noble houses Polwarth regarded as the political élite of his day. John Monipenny's 1603 guide book to Scotland and its élite contained the names of fifty-eight peers, eighty-four knights and 926 barons, lairds and gentlemen as well as clan and border chieftains.[73] Local evidence suggests an even greater number. The band by the barons of the north pledging allegiance to the king and the regent Morton in September 1574 omits a number of important individuals, most notably the fifth earl of Huntly, but still adds up to eight peers, or their sons, and sixty-two barons. A similar band for Roxburgheshire contained the signatures of four peers, one commendator and a wide range of men from sir Walter Scott of Buccleuch to minor freeholders. In some localities, like Teviotdale and Liddesdale, there were no peers at all, but in February 1584 the privy council summoned from these shires thirty-eight barons.[74] More comprehensively, in 1590 the government began a survey of the landed proprietors throughout Scotland, completing it for twenty-one shires, largely those south of a line from Argyll to the Tay, accounting for perhaps two-thirds of the population of the country. Listed there are some 950 major landowners, those men who paid the land tax and were represented in parliament or sat there themselves. From this evidence one might suggest that the total size of the landed nobility was at least 1500 heads of houses, a figure still below the 2000 tenants-in-chief who signed the Ragman's Rolls in 1296, or the similar numbers of electors in the first half of the eighteenth century.[75]

The percentage share of nobles in the population appears to have been fairly constant but the stability of those noble houses was erratic, and the century and a half of stability in the upper ranks of the Scottish peerage that followed the turmoil of the mid-fifteenth century can be misleading.[76] Noble houses throughout Europe were constantly rising and falling, and whether in Poland or Castile commoners could move up into the ranks of the lesser nobility. Men became noble by ennoblement, office, landownership, assumption and marriage. Others dropped out of nobility by derogation, by contempt of service, as a punishment for treason, and as a consequence of a *mésalliance*. On the whole, therefore, noble society was permeable, open to men of talent and wealth as long as they conformed to the expectations of those from whom they craved acceptance.[77] In his prologue to the *History of the House of Seytoun*, written in the mid-sixteenth century, Lethington wrote:

> Thair is bot certane maneris of begynnyng of housis in this cuntrie of Scotland: ane is by gift of princeis or grit men, for trew and thankfull service; ane uther is be just conquest be ane mannis silver or geir; the third is be maryage of ladyis of heritage; and ferdlie, quhen be eventure heretage fallis to ane man be his mother, or sum uther famell his predecessour.[78]

Godscroft too conceded that men might rise, citing the motto of James Stewart, earl of Arran, *Sic fuit est & erit*, 'meaning it was an ordinary thing in all ages for meane men to rise to great fortunes; and that therefore it ought not either to be wondered at, or to be envied'. However, like Lethington, he stressed that the means by which men rose must be virtuous.[79]

It remains to ask whether the greater social mobility of the early seventeenth century, when the peerage was significantly expanded, added up to anything more meaningful than the seized opportunities of a handful of successful families. Should any credence be given to the over-quoted English observer who reported as early as 1572 that, 'I see the nobleman's great credit decay … and the barons, burghs and such-like take more upon them'?[80] At that time, Scotland was governed by the regent Morton, a man who was born the grandson of the fifth earl of Angus but whose younger years were spent in obscurity, finding employment as 'a serving man'. Even Godscroft, the family historian, concedes this point, admitting that marriage changed Morton's fortune. By 1573, an English intelligencer could report that 'no man doubts of his nobility and the antiquity therof'.[81] Morton's career demonstrates the dangers of underestimating the social mobility of this society. Nor should the distinction between the peerage and the baronage be overdrawn. Many of the new peerage houses of the fifteenth century, like that of the earls of Errol, never rose much above the landed wealth and power of their baronial neighbours. By contrast, the house of Huntly soon surpassed all in the region, successfully exploiting access to the king to persuade those neighbouring barons to offer their manrent.[82] This thin line between peers and barons is evident in most of the new peerage creations, none of which came from outside the landed nobility. In granting titles, the king was largely reinforcing the existing social hierarchy, promoting to the peerage men like Alexander Stewart of Garlies, created a lord of parliament in 1607 but already 'the grittest and first barrone in all that pairt quhair he dweltt'.[83] Much of the social mobility of the period was little more than a catching-up exercise as leading baronial houses received titles that brought them alongside those families favoured in the fifteenth century. While in the mid-sixteenth century the fifth lord Maxwell received the bonds of manrent of the barons of Drumlanrig, Garlies, Lochinvar and Johnstone, none of these houses granted bonds to Maxwell's heirs after 1550, and all four had reached the peerage by 1633.[84] These families were all territorial barons whose lordship was exactly like that of the Maxwells who had pulled ahead of them in 1455 in the fall-out over the destruction of the Black Douglases. Their catching up did not represent social change, and local society demonstrated a remarkable degree of continuity in the composition of its élites, as was the case in England or in northern France.[85] A more convincing case for dramatic upward mobility might be made for George Hume, earl of Dunbar, who was merely the third or fourth son of a minor baron raised to enormous wealth and power by royal service.[86] Such cases, however, were rare and were always the consequence of unusually generous royal largesse. There was social climbing facilitated by land acquisition in the highly volatile market of the sixteenth century and by feuing, but even those lairds who did particularly well did not reject traditional patterns of hierarchy. James Gordon of Lesmoir was one such man who expanded his estates to become one of the largest landowners in Aberdeenshire; he was appointed to various local offices by the king and acquired a Nova Scotia baronetcy in 1625. Yet throughout his long life,

Lesmoir remained a committed adherent of the sixth earl of Huntly, sharing in all his exploits and fortunes over six decades.[87]

The idea of a structural rivalry between higher and lower nobilities can be dismissed, but in a society so deeply conscious of rank, it is unsurprising to discover some resistance to the idea that men should move upwards. In part, this was a product of the natural conservatism of established élites to newcomers, accompanied by a desire to protect the currency of nobility. In some provinces of France the usurpation of nobility was relatively easy. Tax exemptions offered a powerful inducement to seek noble status and an equally powerful reason for the crown to attempt regulation. Hence the royal commissions to investigate claims to noble status and the appointment in 1615 of a *juge général des armes* to create a register of noble families and their arms. In the Habsburg lands similar efforts were made to weed out usurpations. In Flanders, legislation of 1616 outlawed the assumption of another family's coat of arms. In England, the college of arms was increasingly busy in regulating coats of arms and carrying out visitations to root out spurious cases.[88] The Scottish experience paralleled these developments as kings and their nobilities sought to control the honours system. In 1592, parliament forbade the use of arms without the authority of the lyon king, who was to conduct a visitation of the kingdom, drawing up a register of arms and fining any who had usurped them. The 1606 commission to investigate ranking among the peerage followed some of the procedures of the French *recherches*, the difference being that the Scottish investigation was only to establish precedence among the highest ranks of the nobility, not to establish nobility itself. In 1627, the privy council reiterated the need for the lyon king of arms and his heralds to examine and register coats of arms, and 'to putt inhibitioun to all the commoun sort of people not worthie be the law of armes to beare anie signes armorialls'. Three years later, there was another initiative mounted to stem the proliferation of unauthorised arms 'quhairby the nobilitie and gentrie of good ranke and qualitie ar verie farre wronged'.[89] As lyon king, Denmilne was critical of commoners who allegedly created for themselves an ancestry, manipulating their names for social advantage:

> This contagione and plague hath so corrupted this kingdome of Scotland that base locusts coming from the citey, and neir the barr of justice, with ther money wrunge from all sortes of cunning and oppression, and ther with purchassing the heritages of our ancient Gentrey: presently they must be named the laird, and have some fair coate erected such as them best lykes (for the servile printer dar not forsuith offend ther worschipes).[90]

As there was no loss to the state in the form of taxes, however, there is little evidence of men being formally charged with usurpation. One exceptional case to come to the attention of the privy council was in 1613 when, following complaints from tenants that he was illegally trying to exercise baronial jurisdiction, sir John Ker of Littledean was charged with assuming 'the title and styll of ane lord', and he was forbidden to assume the style of lord for himself or 'to tak the place or rank of a nobleman'.[91]

Yet perhaps the most effective counter to upward mobility was social pressure. During a heated exchange at court in 1595 between James VI and chancellor Thirlestane, the king delivered a devastating put-down, saying that the latter 'was but a cadet of a mean house', while his rival, the second earl of Mar, had a dozen barons of Thirlestane's rank in his following.[92] These prejudices mattered a great deal to a man like Alexander Hume, younger son of the laird of Polwarth, who was denied an audience with Elizabeth I in 1580 because he was not a nobleman.[93] What irritated contemporaries was an over-rapid rise in fortune, accompanied by immodest behaviour and a disregard for older noble houses. This was most evident in the criticisms opponents made of the Arran regime in which James Stewart of Bothwellhaugh and his colleagues were described as 'lewd persons of no desert or worthiness, and for the most part of base lineage, not born to any foot-land of ground'. Bothwellhaugh was a younger son of the second lord Ochiltree and a professional soldier who was raised to the earldom of Arran, arousing the jealousy of the first duke of Lennox, who told the king he found Arran's behaviour intolerable in one who was not 'a lord born', but whom 'from a simple gentleman you have raised to great honour and dignity'.[94] In fact, Lennox too was the beneficiary of royal patronage, being a minor French nobleman.

Lennox's snobbery perhaps reflects the fact that, as in France, quarrels over the relative rank of nobles were more common than over whether a man was noble or not. When the fourth earl of Bothwell refused to fight sir William Kirkcaldy of Grange at Carberry in 1567 it was on the grounds that Grange was only 'ane small barroun' and Bothwell 'wald not degraid the honour of his hous to fecht witht sic ane base man of degrie. Bot wald ony lord of ane antient hous fecht he wald fecht with him'. In contrast to Bothwell, the fifth earl of Huntly offered to duel with either the first earl of Moray, the bastard son of a king, or William Maitland, younger of Lethington, the secretary of state and eldest son of a baron and court of session judge. Huntly had fewer scruples than Bothwell, although he could not resist making the point that he issued his challenge, 'albeit that Lethingtoun be nouther of qualitie nor blude equal unto us'. Yet it was not only at the interface of peerage and barons that such tensions surfaced. During the civil war, in 1571, Grange's cartel was answered by Alexander Stewart, younger of Garlies, who ridiculed the former for seeking to behave like the greatest of the nobility, 'being of so base condition, that his father had but eight oxengang of land, and his progenitors, for the most part, saltmakers'. Garlies accepted the offer of a duel, but 'With protestatioun, that it sall not be prejudiciall to my honour, nor to my blood, to compare my self with so late a printed gentleman' when his own family were 'gentlemen of blood and armes'. A stream of insulting correspondence flew back and forth as the two men tried to gain some advantage that was designed more to humiliate the other than to arrange a combat. Grange scoffed at Garlies' claims to nobility, pointing out that his rival:

> was degenerated from the ancient state of his hous, and his blood stained, in that one of the principall branches of his hous was a preest's daughter; wheras, on the contrare, it sall not be found that anie of his branches of anie continuance have beene other than gentlemen, without matching ather with preest or merchant.

Garlies dealt with this slight to his mother's father, who had married a priest's daughter, by pointing out that the woman in question 'had brought in more old inheritance to him and his hous, than he [Grange] had in propertie of anie lands holdin of the kings of this realme'. Crucially, in all these exchanges it was lineage that was the most significant determinant of noble pedigree. Here in these robust verbal exchanges was the kind of assertion of noble power which was typical of a martial nobility functioning in a predominantly oral world.[95]

These attitudes did not disappear in the less martial world of the early seventeenth century when social mobility was more marked. In 1628, sir Archibald Napier of Merchiston, the treasurer depute and a man only months earlier created a lord of parliament, described his colleague, sir James Baillie of Lochend the receiver of rents, as 'basely borne, and had his education under a butcher'. Indeed, the third earl of Lothian, who acquired his earldom by marriage to the daughter of a house itself recently raised to the peerage, recorded the thought that 'men of noble birth are commonly envious towards newe men'. Even a social conservative like Denmilne, who claimed that old-established noble families were superior to newly created noble houses, was irritated by 'the insolency of some who bostes of ther antiquity of discent in nobility, despyssing uthers new come up'. He poured scorn on those haughty individuals, often lacking in any noble virtues, who behaved 'as if they wer beyond all begining them selves', and he cited the well-known ditty that 'When Adam delved and Eva span, Neither wes then a Gentleman'. In his inimicably provocative way, sir Thomas Urquhart of Cromarty even encouraged low-born men to strive towards nobility, suggesting that it was 'better to have a noble life then birth, to found a new nobility, then find it founded'.[96]

Of course, social mobility operates in two directions. All European nobilities of the late medieval and early modern period sustained what could be quite alarming extinction rates, but this phenomenon is often a product of how historians measure the process than of any real biological decay. While seventy peers who were in possession of a title between 1560 and 1637, approximately one-fifth of the total population of the higher nobility for the period, died without a direct male heir of their own body, few houses became extinct. Entails ensured that other male members of the lineage were able to continue the line, with daughters often being married to these more distant heirs as a means of reinforcing the legitimacy of the blood line. Only one of the fifty-two peerage houses in existence in 1560, the house of Carlyle, had disappeared completely by 1637 as a result of biological failure. Failure was more common among the new peerage houses where the terms of their patents, the absence of entails, the age at which these men were in a position to marry and the lack of kinsmen all made extinction more likely.[97] Birth rates among noble families were relatively high, five adult children being the average for the higher nobility, and the steps taken by fathers principally to protect the interests of male heirs – primogeniture was commonly practised, except in some Highland localities[98] – appear to have ensured that most lineages survived. Yet noble society was in a constant state of flux, houses rising while their neighbours were in decline, and this threat of decay was appreciated by contemporaries whose thought patterns encouraged them to believe that decomposition was an inevitable state of nature. Hence the constant striving for advantage. No one believed that wealth and status lasted for ever, and it was a commonplace idea that the lineage was under perennial threat from decay or from the chance of fortune. This suggests that for all the trumpeting of ancient blood ties, nobles faced with the inconstancies of succession, economic vagaries and political fortunes were acutely aware of the sand on which they built their houses.

Lethington wrote that:

> we may se be experience how mony grit housis hes bein in this realme, and now sa far decayit, that scantlie is left ony of thair posterite, and thair haill houssis and heritage is translatit fra thair surenames in to the princeis handis, or sum uther strangear.

Sixty years later, Gordonstoun conveyed a clear sense of the mutability of life in a letter of advice to his nephew, pointing out that the 'rysing, decay and continuance of all estates and famelies is in the hand of the Almightie everliving God'. While some families had enjoyed a long run of success, there were many who 'from the verie highest step of fortune, have so fallen to decay, either by ther own fault, or by the injurie of tyme, that there remaineth not so much as any memory of them'. And there were those familes who 'from small and obscure beginings, have upon an instant attained to such a measure of greatnes, that they may compare their families with the best'. Godscroft's *History of the House of Douglas and Angus* also has the theme of mutability threaded throughout it. He tells his noble readers that:

> Such is the course of humaine affairs that nothing is found constant, nothing permanent in one state and measure amongst creatures here below. But stil rysing, or decaying; stil increassing, or diminishing; al is subject to revolution; where by we remarke smal beginnings to be brought by tymes to heigest eminencie; and agane things of greatest name to be redacted by age.

Using the example of the fifteenth-century earls of Douglas, Godscroft encouraged men to 'remember the changes of the world, and the vicissitudes of Fortune, and let every man bear with patience, and hear with calmness, either what he is now, or what he was before'. Religious works and sermons, literature and popular culture were similarly suffused with the idea of impermanence. Thus the comedy *Philotus* ends with the notion that 'All is hazard that we have, here is nothing byding'. Sir William Alexander of Menstrie, who rose to acquire the earldom of Stirling, mused that:

> The bramble growis althocht it be obscure,
> Quhillis michty cederis feilis the busteous windis;
> And myld plebeyan spreitis may leif secure,
> Quhylis michty tempestis toss imperiall myndis.

William Drummond of Hawthornden also recognised the transience of noble dynasties: 'Possessions are not enduring; children lose their names, families glorying, like marigolds in the sunne, on the highest top of wealth and honour, no better than they which are not yet borne, leaving off to bee'. Indeed, throughout late medieval and early modern Europe the nostalgic idea that the nobility was in decline fed an enduring myth, always finding new examples that appeared to demonstrate what was never more than the misfortunes of a particular family at a particular time.[99]

# Part I

## Wealth

CHAPTER I

# Landlords

The relationship between nobilities and land throughout most of medieval and early modern European society was intimate. The possession of feudal superiority of land conferred nobility; it created an obligation between feudal superiors and vassals from the king down, and provided the means by which lords exercised power. The landless noble was not unknown, especially in those countries with proportionately large noble populations, but it was undesirable, and the road from being landless to slipping out of the bottom of noble society was a short one. It is with this role of the noble as landlord that the search to uncover the layers of noble society begins. The jurisdictional and political significance of the landed estate to the nobility must be examined elsewhere; the focus here is on the centrality of land to the management of a noble house's wealth and its family members.

What makes this particular period so interesting is the remarkably volatile nature of the land market in Scotland; an enormous amount of land changed hands, and some minor noble families made quite staggering inroads into the highest levels of landed society. On the whole, this was a good time for nobles, especially for those members of the higher nobility who wanted to provide for younger sons, and there was a massive transfer of land from the church into secular hands. In thinking about how best to maintain the integrity of their possessions, nobles also chose to place increasing emphasis on entails that favoured male successors at the expense of daughters. Not only were nobles successful in grabbing more land, but they were also making sure their houses would hold on to it. On a daily basis too, nobles were concerned with how best to manage their estates to meet the needs of the day, be these the more military requirements of the mid-sixteenth century, or the largely commercial demands of the early seventeenth century.

## The Value of Land

Sir Thomas Craig of Riccarton's *Jus Feudale*, written in the 1590s, described a feudal law that was all-pervasive, and yet the ideal of feudalism and its attendant social structures had long since declined. While all land was held from the king by his tenants-in-chief, the feudal dues the king received from his vassals were largely nominal by the sixteenth century. William Tweedie of Drummelzier paid only £15 per annum for his Peeblesshire lands, and was obliged to give four blasts of the horn to waken the king and his hunters when they were in the locality. Furthermore, while at the top of this 'system' was a landed monarchy, by the later sixteenth century those lands either directly administered, or leased, by Scottish kings were modest, especially when compared, for example, to queen Anne's homeland of Denmark, where 52 per cent of cultivated land was owned by the crown following the Reformation acquisitions.[1] Only occasional forfeitures brought the king a windfall in land, and even its distribution was hedged in by obligations to kinsmen or neighbours of rebels whose support was necessary to make such drastic action palatable. Sir Walter Scott of Buccleuch gained a large share of the Bothwell estates after his stepfather's forfeiture in 1592, while the forfeiture of Kintyre allowed the seventh earl of Argyll the opportunity to expand his territory under royal patronage.[2] More commonly, royal servants acquired landed gifts piecemeal over the course of a career in the king's service, and save for exceptional circumstances, such as when Thomas Erskine of Gogar was rewarded for his part in saving the king's life at Perth in 1600, James VI was not lavish in disposing of lands, rarely allowing rewards to outstrip status.[3]

Nevertheless, the king alone could transform conquest land into freehold, and throughout Scotland, including the Highlands, all nobles were tenants-in-chief of the king, holding land in free heritage by charters; James VI rightly observed that 'the king is overlord over the whole lands'. General retours, by which an heir was legally required to secure his inheritance, along with the parliamentary ratification of charters brought landlords additional peace of mind. However, no one could inherit an estate without testimony that the previous vassal died 'in loyalty and peace with the king', all vassals being required to demonstrate title to their land to the king's own officers under pain of non-entry.[4] The penalties of failing to ensure that titles were secure could be heavy. Both in 1557 and again in 1588 the crown made it difficult for the eighth and ninth earls of Angus to succeed to their lands, and on the latter occasion James VI was bought off with what was in effect an inheritance tax of 35 000 merks and some land.[5] One effect of this feudal framework to landholding was to act as a restraint on alienation since land held in ward was subject to recognisance in the event of the superior's consent not being obtained prior to a transaction. It was because ward and relief was burdened with casualties that sixteenth-century landlords tried to renegotiate to free blanche ferme with its fixed compositions.[6] Under Charles I, crown officials paralleled the unwelcome initiatives of the court of wards in England by seeking to squeeze more out of feudal casualties, switching back to the more exploitative and profitable ward and relief that was imposed on some lordships for the first time.[7] A similar exploitation of the crown's feudal rights to investigate lands alienated during a minority led in 1625 to Charles I's infamous revocation, a legal process that created the impression of wholesale confiscation and was 'the ground stone of all the mischeiffe that followed after, bothe to the Kinges governiment and family'.[8]

The most significant change in the pattern of landholding in early modern Scotland was not caused by crown actions, however, but by a combination of feuing – a means of alienating land in return for a perpetual but fixed rent, not unlike the French *rente foncière* – and the secularisation of the greatest corporate landlord in the kingdom which accompanied the Reformation. The period of most intense feuing of ecclesiastical lands was from the 1540s to the 1580s, and by the time of the 1587 act of annexation, the majority of church estates had been feued. Similar landed revolutions took place elsewhere in Protestant Europe; for example, the finances of the Dutch nobility were enhanced by their acquisition of church incomes. However, the dramatic pace and scale of land transfers in Scotland were greater than those of most other European states, almost every Lowland region being affected by this transformation.[9]

Some have seen in this rapid land turnover the rise of the lairds, but one near contemporary rightly observed that church 'estats and lands were divyded amongst the great men, by themselves, without right or law'.[10] Even before the Reformation, monastic estates were subject to lay commendators who established de facto proprietary rights over the monasteries, a process that was accelerated after 1560. During that decade, the first earl of Mar scooped up a basket of ecclesiastical lands, chiefly Cambuskenneth, Inchmahome and Dryburgh, which in 1606 were united by his son into the lordship and barony of Cardross.[11] After 1560, the bishoprics were plundered just as ruthlessly; for example, Caithness was asset-stripped by successive earls of Sutherland.[12] Finally, in addition to abbatial and bishopric lands, there were the teinds, those tithes due on ecclesiastical lands that might have amounted to as much as 25 per cent of the income of some landlords.[13] However, estates carved out of ecclesiastical ones were taxed by the crown at the higher ecclesiastical level, and the value of many of these land grants was often reduced by feus and pensions, as in the second duke of Lennox's grant of the superiority of the archbishoprics of St Andrews and Glasgow.[14] On the other hand, because such land was usually unentailed it could be more flexibly utilised, enhancing its commercial value, while its easy liquidity stimulated the land market just as the crown's sale of monastic land did in England. Peers were able to provide generously for younger sons, older baronial families were hoisted up the landholding league, and even middle-ranking privy councillors were catapulted into the strata of large landowners.[15]

The title to ecclesiastical lands remained less secure than other forms of freehold, in part because of the confused and unsettling conditions in which these land transfers took place. Nobles like the sixth earl of Cassillis expended a great deal of energy on using the courts to defend rights to former ecclesiastical lands, in his case the lands of Glenluce abbey and of Maybole kirk, while throughout the 1590s lord Hamilton campaigned to ensure the king would allow his son to inherit Arbroath abbey.[16] The 1587 act of annexation tried to halt the process of *seigneurialisation* at a time when a number of lordships had already been created at Scone, Newbattle, Deer and Paisley for the Ruthven, Ker, Keith and Hamilton families. Yet the pressure to reward nobles undermined the intention of the legislation, and in 1606 new lordships of erection founded on former abbatial estates came into being. By the end of James VI's reign, twenty-one of the thirty abbeys had become the hereditary property of secular lords.[17] Following problems in implementing Charles I's 1625 revocation, the teind commission emerged two years later, its underlying aim being to provide additional income for the church by renegotiating the rights of landowners to kirk lands such that they were deprived of their superiorities without interfering in directly managed land. The conservative heritors were unenthusiastic, while superiors set about manipulating the teind commission into placing the burden for the king's plans on the backs of their vassals.[18]

Undoubtedly the land market heated up from the mid-sixteenth century, but for at least a century land had been utilised as a commercial commodity and the kingdom had a sophisticated code of property law. Some sense of the dynamism of the land market is conveyed in the history of the barony of Tyninghame in East Lothian, which changed hands five times between 1555 and the later 1620s.[19] Land was a saleable commodity that could be traded for quick profit. In the autumn of 1606, David Crichton of Lugton sold a portfolio of lands for 19 500 merks to sir George Elphinstone of Blythswood, who sold them on to sir John Bruce of Airth for 26 000 merks in 1610, a 33 per cent profit in four years. However, it was not all profit in the land market. Airth in turn sold the lands in 1615 for 25 000 merks, taking a small loss on his investment. Perhaps the most successful estate speculator of the period was the first earl of Haddington, but he was a careful buyer. When the indebted sixth earl of Morton was off-loading land in 1624, Haddington beat the price down by 5000 merks to 125 000 merks before withdrawing from the deal after a thorough investigation into the security of the teinds. There were other factors that might put a buyer off or depress the price of land. For example, the second earl of Mar found it difficult to liquidate land in Renfrewshire in 1617 because of the reputation of the tenants, described by his agent as 'strange stuborn proud folkis and not to be delt with'.[20]

As has already been argued, land was crucial to the nobility's own sense of identity, its acquisition being driven by more than commercial considerations. In 1615, the twelfth earl of Sutherland advised his brother to snap up an attractive neighbouring estate that was about to come on the market, and 'albeit ye wer in debt, it is for ane honest caus', that being the consolidation of Sutherland's grip on the region. The third earl of Lothian was worried in 1637 that he had over-extended himself in buying up the entire lands of Jedburgh abbey for 36 000 merks. Nevertheless, he insisted that 'I have noe disreputation in this bargaine, and I have a greate increase of command by it in Tividale, and I hope it salbe proffitable also'. That the immediate profitability of the land was regarded as something of an afterthought to the political importance of dominating the locality is significant. Indeed, among the Highland nobility the principal usefulness of land was to provide social space within which a clan might settle and multiply. This pursuit of land by noble families was often carried on over several generations, and judgements about the economic strategy of noble houses are better made when examining the evidence of centuries rather than decades. The Dundases of Arniston first feued their property in 1571, but it was 1609 before they persuaded the feudal superior to sell them the land outright.[21] In this rapidly expanding land market of the sixteenth century, some nobles were prodigious buyers, and the foundations of the huge Queensberry, Buccleuch and Breadalbane estates were laid at this time by sir James Douglas of Drumlangrig, Walter Scott, first lord Buccleuch, and sir Duncan Campbell of Glenorchy. Others at the margins of noble society, like sir Thomas Hope of Craighall, who made his money in legal practice and bought a country estate outside Edinburgh, made a more modest impact.[22]

The absence of data on the wealth of the medieval and early modern Scottish nobility is frustrating, especially in the Highlands, and one has sympathy with the second earl of Buccleuch's estate official, who wrote of the rental and value of the lands of Hassindean c.1633 that 'thay can not be verie weill afirmat'. By the standards of some of the great prince nobles of Europe, like Anne de Montmorency, no Scottish noble was spectacularly rich, the average value of a Scottish peer's inventory in this period being £3865, the equivalent of a wealthier member of the Yorkshire gentry.[23] Nevertheless, sir James Melville of Halhill was right to tell James VI that one explanation for the weakness of the Scottish crown was 'the gret rentis of the nobilite and ther great nomber'. Nobles were, on the whole, the richer members of society, and that wealth was based on land ownership in a period when land offered a secure investment and a significant annual return, and its capitalisation value rose steadily. Population growth, a steep rise in food prices ahead of labour costs, the massive secularisation of church lands, the emergence of more owner-occupiers due to feuing, the greater availability of credit, the high incidence of debt secured on land, the operation of political patronage, and changes in the law regarding land ownership, all encouraged a buoyant land market.[24] Those landed families who were flexible and adaptable enough to cope with changing circumstances proved to be the most successful.

The extent to which noble landlords dominated territory varied across the continent. Yet while the share of noble land might have been declining in the

Dutch republic, and the peerage might have lessened its grip in England, the general trend throughout most of Europe was for nobles to accumulate land at the expense of the crown, the church and the peasantry – what in Spain has been described as 're-señorialisation'. This produced the enormous estates that characterised much of the continent, especially in territories like Spain and the Austrian Habsburg lands where there was an abundant supply of land. However, in the later seventeenth and eighteenth centuries English and French nobles were increasingly less interested in maintaining the huge, territorially cohesive estates of earlier centuries.[25] Territorial consolidation continued to be important to Scottish landowners, and when an English visitor passed through Ayrshire in 1636 he was astonished to discover that the sixth earl of Eglinton 'hath a dozen or sixteen halls or houses hereabouts, and sways much in these parts'.[26] This tourist mistook Eglinton's feudal superiority over cadet houses for the earl's own estates, but many nobles did pursue a policy of territorial consolidation. The house of Sutherland, for example, extended its grip on its northern territories, swallowing up ecclesiastical lands and either buying out other landlords or acquiring the superiorities of their lands. In 1566, the lands of the tenth earl were erected into a free earldom, and his heirs concentrated on creating a 'country' of Sutherland, even if this meant sacrificing more productive land in Aberdeenshire. His grandson, Gordonstoun, urged further buying of any lands in Sutherland not owned by a Gordon, advising the thirteenth earl to 'use all meanes possible to preserve still your old merches in everie corner of the countrey, not onlie with the nighbouring provinces, but also within this countrey betuix you and your vassals'.[27] Yet in the aftermath of the destruction of regional lordships in late medieval Scotland, the common pattern of landholding was a form of modified territorial control in which most nobles held only one barony while a handful of noble houses accumulated new landed empires based around a core, but with scattered possessions elsewhere. While the fifth earl of Glencairn's principal estates during the 1570s were in the west of Scotland, in north Ayrshire, west Renfrewshire and south Dumbartonshire, he also owned land in the sheriffdom of Edinburgh.[28]

Early seventeenth-century retours, which are neither complete nor wholly accurate, provide some indication of the spread of landed possessions. The ducal house of Lennox held land in fourteen shires, the house of Hamilton had possessions in thirteen shires, the houses of Mar and Morton's estates were scattered over twelve shires, the Hamilton cadet house of Abercorn had a landed presence in ten shires, and by the 1630s the first earl of Haddington had spread his interests over eight shires as a result of the most dramatic estate accumulation of the period. Another five noble houses owned property in seven shires, seven houses had land in six shires, ten houses were landlords in five shires, and twenty houses possessed estates in four shires. These forty-eight houses with land in four or more shires, two-thirds of whom owned land in one of the two Lothian shires of Edinburgh or Haddington, were composed of twenty-one old peerage houses, twelve new peerage creations, thirteen baronial houses and two others. A further fifty-three landlords held land in three shires, and 106 houses or individuals were possessed of land in two shires, many of these being neighbouring shires. One explanation for this greater scattering of estates that occurs from the mid-sixteenth century lay in the nature of the supply of available land, the greatest bulk of which was former ecclesiastical lands; for example, many of the Mar lands were former abbatial estates acquired with no territorial strategy in mind.[29]

This evidence indicates nothing about the size of landholdings or the value of the land, and efforts to estimate the extent to which early modern land ownership was dominated by nobles are fraught with technical difficulties. Counting baronies, like counting manors, cannot provide an accurate picture of landed worth, and is no more than a useful indicator in the absence of better information. While in 1559 the tenth earl of Crawford owned all or part of eleven baronies and their lands, the value of these possessions is unknown.[30] Nevertheless, some approximation of the pattern of land ownership in individual shires can be attempted. Not surprisingly, dominance by a small landed élite was most common in the Highlands and on the borders, both upland regions of low agricultural productivity. However, tiny Lowland Clackmannan, with only two baronies, was carved up between the second earl of Mar, whose estate was based on Alloway, and the Shaws of Abercromby who possessed the barony of Sauchie. By contrast, a large shire like Ayrshire was far more complex, containing some forty to forty-five baronies, the precise number being subject to change as nobles acquired new charters from the king. In terms of the new extent valuation used for assessing taxation, the most valuable barony was that of Cassillis, possessed by the earls of Cassillis, the only landlords to have superiority over three Ayrshire baronies. Few other nobles possessed more than one barony in Ayrshire, but eleven nobles owned land in other shires. The Ayrshire lands of the earls of Cassillis were valued at a little over £1000 new extent, the Cunningham lairds of Caprington, the lords Boyd and the dukes of Lennox possessed land valued at between £800 and £1000 new extent, eight nobles had lands valued at between £200 and £800 new extent, and another thirteen nobles possessed lands valued between £100 and £200 new extent. The laird of Caprington's presence in the top rank of Ayrshire landowners demonstrates that while there was often a correlation between status and wealth, some barons were 'of larger means than many of the nobility called earls and lords'. Neighbouring Renfrewshire had between twenty-five and thirty nobles of varying status and wealth. Here it might be useful to discuss land ownership in terms of parishes. In some cases entire parishes in Renfrewshire were owned by a single lord, such as Eastwood and Eaglesham by the earls of Eglinton, or Houston parish by the lairds of Houston. On the other hand, the parish of Mearns had been extensively feued by the lords Maxwell, while in Paisley, Renfrew or Erskine there were a number of significant landlords. The retour evidence here accounts for four peers and two barons whose lands were valued in excess of £200 new extent.[31] This evidence suggests that in Renfrewshire, as in Ayrshire, the peerage usually formed the most significant landlords in a spectrum that had at the other end modest, or 'small', barons whose lands lay in a single parish.

The sheer extent of the landed possessions of the higher nobility was awesome, but neither shire distribution of ownership, or the number of baronies owned or parishes dominated tells the full story. The house of Glamis possessed land in only three shires, but this was largely productive arable farmland. A small estate in a fertile locality like Fife, where the rental for the single parish of Monimail in the early seventeenth century was 17 550 merks, was different from the large but relatively poor lands of the earls of Sutherland which provided 'lytle anugh to manteyne the qualitie of ane earle'. The richest of all nobles in the sixteenth century were probably the Keith earls Marischal, the fifth earl having the 'revennew greatest of any Erle in Scotlande', based on the possession of large tracts of some of the most productive arable farming in the east of the country.[32] In the 1580s it was estimated that the peerage had incomes of between sixteen and twenty score chalders (= a measure of grain equivalent to eight quarters) of victual per annum, amounting in value to around £20 000, a figure not far from the £17 000 per annum which was the income of the second earl of Orkney in the 1590s. By the 1630s, inflation had raised rentals considerably, and those of the higher nobility ranged from a poor peer like the first lord Jedburgh's £12 534, to the £60 000 per annum of the third earl of Home, £68 000 per annum of the first earl of Haddington, and the second earl of Buccleuch's income of some £100 000 per annum.[33] Estate incomes for the higher nobility in the later sixteenth century perhaps averaged £20 000 per annum, or under £3000 sterling, rising in the early seventeenth century to around £60 000 per annum, or £5000 sterling, for the richer members of the expanded peerage.

## Inheritance

Family histories, such as that of the Setons, commonly made the connection between lineage and place, between the transient members of a noble house and the enduring piece of earth it had occupied for generations.[34] The stewardship of that territory was reflected in the care with which charters were secured and catalogued in anxiously preserved and sometimes elaborately decorated cartularies. When the death of the second earl of Home without heirs in February 1633 created a succession quarrel between rival claimants, it was the late earl's 'haill kists and coffers' the crown impounded until a thorough investigation could be initiated. To lose such documentation was catastrophic, as occurred in 1585 when the Maxwells attacked the laird of Johnston's castle at Lochwood and 'distroyit my chartour kist with my haill evedentis and wreittis', or in February 1592 when the papers of the earls of Moray were burned at Donibristle.[35] In the early 1620s, the second earl of Mar's lawyers undertook research into the Erskine family's rights to the lands of the ancient earldom of Mar, labouring against the fact that 'it is notoriously knowen that fire and sword had passed off throw the haill corners of Scotland and had destroyed the maist part of the haill evidents and muniments of Scotland'. Every effort was made to defy those losses, including employing an expensive lawyer, sir Thomas Hope, and writing to the fifth earl of Marischal, a noted scholar, asking if he could supply missing documents from the fourteenth century. The end product was a partial and yet thoroughly researched history of the earldom from the reign of Malcolm Canmore that ensured Mar won his case.[36]

Therefore, an important reason for the value placed on accurate genealogical trees in family archives was the practical necessity of determining nobility and clarifying lines of succession that could be complicated by female heirs, different kinds of collateral claimants, the division of land into heritage and conquest, and the terms of tailzied succession. An agreed genealogy reduced the likelihood of inheritance disputes, maintaining an authentic memory of the outlying cadet branches of the kindred, a particularly important consideration where distant male heirs took precedence over daughters. By the sixteenth century, Scots law had a well-developed set of principles, derived from civil and feudal law, that determined the many different and complex varieties of succession, favouring legitimate, male primogeniture. Riccarton argued that natural justice and the obligations of kinship lay behind the emphasis the law placed on succession. Thus 'the mainspring of all those efforts to accumulate the means of well-being, in which men wear out their lives, is not to be found in purely selfish motives, but in the over-mastering desire to promote the welfare of the coming generation'.[37]

Of course, there was no guarantee that a man's heirs would serve the longer-term interests of the lineage well. Sir Richard Maitland of Lethington emphasised the folly of sacrificing one's soul to create a great house:

> Som waitt not weill quhat thair airis will be;
> Nor quhat will come of thair posteritie;
> For som may be great fuilles naturall;
> Som may be waistouris and mak quyt of all;
> Som great drunkard and spend thair thrift at wyn;
> Som may commit sic deidis criminall,
> That may thame baith geir and landis tyn.

Similar doubts were raised by another poetic nobleman, William Drummond of Hawthornden: 'now wee seeke to enlarge our boundes, increase our treasure, living poorelie, to purchase what wee must leave to those wee shall never see, or, happelie, to a foole or a prodigall heire'. That process of providing for the next generation commonly began before death, and Gordonstoun wisely advised fathers to provide for their children during their own lifetimes, 'for otherwayes your lyff will seeme ther bondage ... so that portion you shall leave them they may thank death for it and not you'. Seventeenth-century religious writers too recognised the legitimacy of endowing children with the goods of parents who 'long for children to continue their kind by a certaine immortality'.[38]

Sixteenth-century Europe experienced an intense debate over the advantages and disadvantages of male primogeniture. Its attraction, especially when linked to entails providing a means by which wealth was passed down through a lineage without its individual members having the right to dispose permanently of any of the capital assets, was in creating a system of landed inheritance conducive to the creation and survival of large estates. By the sixteenth century some form of male primogeniture and entail was virtually universal, although there were significant variations.[39] Scottish laws of inheritance, including the use of entails, were well established by the mid-sixteenth century, although some customary variations survived in parts of the Highlands. The absence of political interference by the crown meant that there were no fundamental legal changes affecting land or succession, the acts of 1555, 1599 and especially the 1617 act anent the registration of reversions, sasines and other writs being concerned with administrative issues. The entail's purpose was principally to convey property to male heirs and to secure the succession, rather than to prevent the alienation of property. Until the introduction of the strict settlement in 1685, landlords retained significant powers over the disposition of property, and there was little of the bitter litigation over entails that occurred in England. Thus while some jurists were critical of the emphasis on male primogeniture, there was no significant public debate. This heavy weighting of Scots law in favour of legitimate eldest sons was defended by Riccarton on the conventional grounds that it prevented the permanent subdivision of estates, 'so preserving from destruction the position of our great families who alone, as props and pillars of the state, sustain the burden of national defence in the absence of a mercenary army'. Therefore, while fathers enjoyed some freedom in the disposition of conquest lands, and while entailed land might even be mortgaged, the greater part of their possessions was subject to unbarrable, perpetual entails and such land could not be conveyed by wills.[40]

The Scottish tailzie or entail, therefore, was not a special form of fee, as was the case in England, but a 'simple fee with a special line of succession'. Charters commonly established perpetual succession in male lines, such as that granted in 1567 by queen Mary to the eighth lord Glamis, the heirs of his body, whom failing to his brother and other heirs male 'bearing the armes and surname of Lyon'. Entailing might be inspired by more particular circumstances such as the fifth lord Yester's decision in 1584 to overturn an earlier charter made to his eldest son and his heirs in the interests of the heirs of line. Lord Yester died two years later, to be followed in 1591 by his eldest son whose six daughters' interests had been set aside in 1584 to allow his younger brother, James, to succeed to the estates and titles. Further evidence that male succession was tightening its grip comes from the Sutherland earldom. In 1583 the eleventh earl of Sutherland entailed his earldom lands to the heirs-male of his own body, and a generation later, in 1601, the twelfth earl tightened up the entail to strengthen significantly the rights of male heirs against those of his own daughters.[41]

These tailzies, therefore, were designed to prevent female succession, cutting off the direct line of succession, or collaterals, where females intervened, and the rise in the value of daughters' portions possibly reflects compensation for an increasingly hard-line approach in the enforcement of male succession. Riccarton thought entails were 'more familiar in Scotland than in any other country, for the reason that the pride of our old families and the wish to perpetuate their high position makes succession in the male line preferable to succession through females'. He observed that this determination by the nobility to impose these long, carefully worded charters was far from popular among lawyers, or the general populace, admitting that tailzies 'are regarded in our law as odious'.[42] However, this is what the landed nobility wanted, and it was not only female heirs who were sacrificed. When the second lord Melville died without heirs in 1635, his titles and lands were inherited by John Melville of Raith, the son of his father's eldest brother, thus merging the family holdings in that part of Fife. The decision to award the succession to the heir of conquest was not contested by James Melville of Halhill, who normally would have been the heir general. Here the second lord Melville ensured that his estates went to the senior branch of the house, that being the strategy most likely to ensure the long-standing durability of the Melville interest in Fife.[43]

Scots law, therefore, was fundamentally sympathetic to entails, on the one hand placing few restrictions on an heir's freedom to dispose of land, while on the other making them unbreakable, reflecting the determination of landlords to preserve the estate in the male line. The downside for fathers was that the entrenched rights of their heirs had implications for parental authority since sons could not be easily dispossessed. Nevertheless, as in England or France, fathers and their eldest sons usually cooperated, the marriages of the latter often being the occasion of a settlement that left the father as a life tenant in the estate, while his son, in effect the tenant in tail, received a maintenance grant. In 1619, the tenth lord Forbes made a written agreement, sharing out the estate income in an ordered and equitable manner with his eldest son and heir, Alexander, master of Forbes, following the latter's recent marriage. However, marriage was not always the trigger to

Table 1.1 Average birth/maturation/survival of peers' sons, 1560–1637

| | Average no. of sons | Average no. of adult sons | Average no. of surviving sons |
|---|---|---|---|
| 1560–1637 | 2.9 | 2.5 | 2.2 |
| 16th century | 3.2 | 2.9 | 2.5 |
| 17th century | 2.5 | 1.6 | 1.6 |

these settlements. In 1577 the chronically ill and elderly third lord Elphinstone made over all his lands to his eldest son, becoming a life renter with an income from the estate. By 1601 it was time for a new arrangement to be made, reallocating the family's landed resources among the surviving generations.[44]

Scottish nobles were remarkably successful at producing sons. Peers on average produced 2.9 sons, the figure being higher among the sixteenth-century sample at 3.2, falling to 2.5 among the smaller seventeenth-century sample (see Table 1.1). These included some impressive feats of reproduction, like the nine sons of the fourth earl of Huntly, all of whom survived childhood with only one of them predeceasing his father, or the eight sons of the second earl of Mar, seven of whom outlived their father. As these examples suggest, not all children reached adulthood, and even a high birth rate within a family could be harshly culled by nature and fate. Of the fourteen sons sired by the fourth lord Elphinstone, only five reached adulthood, and three of these died before their long-lived father. Therefore, removing those sons who died young reduces the average number of sons to 2.5 for the entire period, with 2.2 sons outliving their fathers, the seventeenth-century sample being slightly smaller in each case. Failure to produce male heirs was relatively low, and even after allowing for the impact of high mortality rates among children, only one in five of the higher nobility did not leave at least one son at the time of his own death. However, of these seventy-seven peers, forty-three were succeeded by grandsons, younger brothers and nephews, so that only one in ten noble houses throughout this period was unable to produce male heirs from the immediate family. Nor was this biological success confined to the peerage. Among nine Gordon cadet houses over the period 1560 to 1640, twenty-one out of twenty-six heads of the household were succeeded by their eldest son, one by a younger son, two by grandsons, one by a younger brother and one by an uncle.[45]

The existence of younger sons represented insurance against the death of the eldest son and heir, but they were also a potential threat to estate consolidation, creating a tension between the principles of primogeniture and making strategic, long-term use of younger children in the interests of the lineage. There was also the unpredictable impact of affection for particular children on the thinking of fathers. On the other hand, the extent to which nobles could provide for these younger sons was a measure of wealth, and the creation of durable cadet houses represented a potent accretion of power. Among the higher nobility, sixty-nine peers, 19 per cent of the total, were survived by three or more sons. One solution to what to do about these excess sons has been described as 'preferential partibility', by which the great majority of an estate was entailed, while outlying lands and newly acquired properties were left to be disposed of freely. The land and barony of Benholm in Aberdeenshire was deployed as a transferable asset by successive Keith earls Marischal to support younger sons and brothers during their lifetimes.[46] An over-generous father might create problems for his eldest son, who had to live with the consequences of a much reduced income. John Forbes, master of Forbes, was particularly aggrieved at his brothers in 1591 because of 'the dismembering of his leving and dispositioun of grite portionis thairof to thame'. Some families took action on behalf of an heir, as when the Campbell lairds supported lord Lorne in blocking the seventh earl of Argyll's efforts to have his son by a second marriage infeft in the lordship of Kintyre.[47]

Younger sons, therefore, had few rights to any inheritance and were entirely dependent on the good will of their father and eldest brother, a point James Livingston, a younger son of the first earl of Linlithgow, admitted in 1616. Faced with being 'a g[e]akmane [= fool] to my brother', he decided to seek his fortune elsewhere, knowing 'my estet is lyk to be hard, both at home and abrod'. He became a successful soldier in the continental wars and was created earl of Callendar. More commonly, the failure rate among younger sons who tried to establish their own cadet houses was high. Gordonstoun, a younger son himself, advised the thirteenth earl of Sutherland that while some outlying land might be given to younger children, 'let them hold the most pairt of ther lands of the eldest, wherby they may acknowledge them selfs descended of that house'.[48] The terms of these settlements were designed to ensure land could revert to the feudal superior. In 1573, the fifth earl of Menteith successfully raised a court action to reclaim property alienated by his grandfather, the third earl, who had granted the lands of Gartmore to a younger son, Robert, and the male heirs of his body. Before dying, Robert disponit the land to his younger brother, having no heirs of his own body, but this attempt to circumvent the third earl's intentions was quashed.[49]

The only commonly acceptable reason for breaking the connection between a lineage and the land was biological failure. In some cases this was partial failure in that there were no male heirs of a man's body. There was no problem of fertility in the house of Atholl, where the fifth earl had seven aunts and five sisters, and sired five legitimate daughters. His hopes of a male heir were raised when his wife gave birth to a boy in December 1591.

Sadly, he died shortly after birth. Atholl himself died in August 1595 and a few days later his wife, Mary Ruthven, gave birth to a daughter and so 'for want of an heir that earldom (so much as was not conquest) is at the King's gift'. There was a shortage of males in the wider kindred, and even the succession of fictive heirs married to Atholl's widow and then daughter failed to preserve the Stewart house of Atholl, which died out in 1626.[50]

In fact, the amount of land transferred through females was declining in the late medieval and early modern periods, but the significance of female inheritance should not be dismissed. For example, in Tuscany, female heirs were widely used to maintain the lineage during times of particular pressure created by high male mortality and economic misfortune.[51] In Scotland, female inheritance was preferable to illegitimate male heirs, bastards having no legal rights, even if the community did recognise some degree of responsibility towards them. However, inheritance by heretrixes, or female heirs, was unpopular, being 'always fatall to the surname of the familie'. In the absence of any male heirs, the succession was commonly divided among female heirs, although the eldest daughter might succeed to an entire estate depending upon the nature of the original grant and the willingness of the crown to collude.[52] In the thirty-three cases where heads of houses of the higher nobility had neither a surviving son, grandson, younger brother or nephew as an heir at the time of their death, thirteen of these men did leave surviving daughters. Of these thirteen men, one was an Englishman holding a Scottish peerage, two were younger sons created peers in their own father's lifetime and who predeceased him, three were men raised from the lower ranks of noble society by crown service and whose principal interests were in England, and one was the surviving son of a forfeited traitor who existed on a court pension. All these men, therefore, were barely established in landed society and their line failed. The ambitions of the first earl of Dunbar were destroyed when he died in 1611 leaving two daughters, and within a few years 'none of his posteritie injoyeth a foote broade of land this day of his conqueist in Scotland'. In the remaining cases, a daughter or granddaughter married the heir of tailzie who in all but one instance already shared the same surname, while younger sisters were bought off. Thus in spite of three marriages that left him with six adult daughters, Hugh Campbell, first lord Loudon, failed to replace the loss of his only son, who died in 1612 leaving behind two daughters. The entail provided for the estates to fall to sir John Campbell of Lawers, a distant kinsman, and in 1620 he married Margaret, the eldest of lord Loudon's granddaughters, who succeeded to the title along with her husband on the nobleman's death two years later.[53]

Where there were neither immediate male heirs, or daughters, the entail could still preserve a lineage from extinction. For example, when the eighth earl of Angus died in 1588 'the earldoms of Angus and Morton are fallen into sundry men's hands', the titles and estates being divided between the male representatives of the Douglas houses of Lochleven and Glenbervie.[54] However, it was relatively uncommon for property to have to pass to distant kinsmen without a female heir providing a means of legitimising the process. In rare instances, fictive heirs were the solution to the problem of there being no male heirs, deploying more distant female kinship as a last line of defence. In 1604 the fifth earl of Eglinton married his cousin in a move designed to consolidate land for 'the weill standing and profit of the said hous of Eglintoun and surname of Montgomerie'. Unfortunately, the marriage was a failure and there were no children, so that the entire Montgomery estates passed to a Seton kinsman, a younger son of the fifth earl's aunt, who was required to alter his surname.[55] Only for a very few families did the absence of any close heirs, usually accompanied by financial weakness and political vulnerability, result in extinction.

## Managing Estates

Contemporary Scots praised their country's natural abundance, and there is good evidence to suggest that it possessed the resources to support a growing population while exporting food in substantial quantities.[56] Foreign travellers were usually less generous in diagnosing the agriculture of this 'barren and poor country', and while deteriorating climatic conditions affected all of early modern Europe, Scotland's short growing season made it particularly vulnerable to adverse weather. During the period 1559–1600, there were twenty-four years in which grain prices were unusually high, suggesting poor harvests. In the better conditions of the early seventeenth century, localised famines still occurred – for example, in the Highlands in 1604 – and there was a devastating national famine in 1623.[57] For nobles significantly dependent on the income of their estates, the weather was an all-important topic, extreme conditions having a devastating impact, while even in relatively stable conditions rentals fluctuated.[58] Noble correspondence is peppered with complaints about the effect of the weather on crops, the ability of poor tenants to pay their rents, and labour problems caused by the migration that accompanied local food shortages.[59] Next to acts of God, war and feuding were the most devastating disasters to disrupt the economy of an estate, and the loss of rental was exacerbated by the legal requirement that where lands were laid waste 'be oppen force', tenants need not pay any duties because the landlord had failed to provide adequate protection. Fortunately, after 1573 Scotland suffered no more major warfare, while feuding declined markedly in the 1600s, especially in Lowland regions, and it was the 1640s before large-scale wasting of lands by armies resumed.[60]

In most other respects, nobles held the fate of their estates in their own hands. Many lords took a keen interest in those estates, as is evident in surviving memorials written by nobles like the tenth lord Forbes in August

1620, in business-like account books like that kept by David Carnegie of Colluthie, a dedicated estate improver, and in the daily engagement in estate management by men like sir John Maxwell of Pollok and sir William Douglas of Lochleven. Where landlords were unable to supervise their affairs so closely, sons, wives or mothers might be deployed.[61] There were also specialists in a lord's household or clientage who provided invaluable service. As one of the sixth earl of Morton's creditors told him in 1636, without good chamberlains 'it is impossibill to collect the rentes of the countrie'. These chamberlains and their officers were trusted and skilled men, overseeing the complex business of book-keeping, having a keen knowledge both of the law and of man management. For more technically demanding problems, lords employed expert advisers. In the mid-1560s the newly restored fourth earl of Lennox was provided with a business plan by the sheriff clerk of Dumbarton who had been engaged to help restore the earl's dilapidated estates.[62] There was some irritation among kinsmen and dependants when nobles neglected local counsel in preference for 'your awin men of lawes advyse', but landlords increasingly valued the professional services of men like the third earl of Lothian's agent who 'knowes and hes studied to his tricks of law'. For a court absentee like the first earl of Annandale, the service of a good lawyer was invaluable, and his lands were rescued from mismanagement by sir Thomas Hope of Craighall, who 'knowes more of your estate in this countrie nor yourself does'.[63] From 1603, there is some evidence among the higher nobility of following the fashionable trend among English peers and becoming absentee *rentiers* living in London. The dangers of this were highlighted when Annandale was advised to appoint 'sum man or other to wach over your offisers'. The perils of absenteeism surfaced again when the removal from Scotland of both the young fourth duke of Lennox and the man who headed the commission appointed to administer his neglected estates resulted in 'nouther compt tane of the chalmerlanis, nor yitt of the tennentis'. Absenteeism, however, was uncommon, and as Annandale's adviser suggested, adequate delegation ensured that estates continued to be effectively run.[64]

The estates themselves were either arable, pastoral or a mixture of the two, depending upon local soil, weather and terrain. Much of the rent was in kind, and an English traveller of the 1590s observed that in Scotland 'the Gentlemen reckon their revenewes, not by rents of monie, but by chauldrons of victuals, and keepe many people in their Families'. In the Highlands, cash rentals were being paid in the early sixteenth century, but food remained the dominant form of income into the early seventeenth century because of the social and political uses to which it might be put by clan chiefs.[65] The principal rent a landlord received was the ferme, a payment in grain, stock or cash. On the whole, grain fermes were more common on the arable eastern side of the country – for example, on the Buccleuch estates, or on the first earl of Kellie's lordship of Fenton in

Berwickshire, where in 1631 a total of almost 187 chalders of grain was uplifted.[66] By 1635, the first earl of Melrose's huge estate in the south-east was producing 472 chalders of grain worth £47 200, 69 per cent of his total landed income.[67] Cattle contributed the major part of the ferme in the less accessible Highland regions, where landlords often insisted on pasturage reservations being included in tacks or leases. However, maill or cash fermes increasingly predominated in the pastoral western Lowlands and parts of the Highlands.[68] Additional cash was raised by selling the fermes, often back to the tenants. Placing a cash value on fermes was never easily resolved, and on the Morton estates in 1591, the Glenorchy estates in 1627 and the Mar estates in 1636 the tenants refused to cooperate with lords who wanted the convenience of a cash rental. Landlords also leased rents to a tacksman, or commuted services, and there was additional cash income from feus, casualties and from the lord's mills, fishings, fuel deposits and teinds.[69]

Eastern Europe saw a dramatic increase in the control exercised over the peasantry by nobles demanding greater and greater labour services and demesne farming. In common with most of western Europe, Scottish lords made light demands on their tenants in terms of labour services, or ariage, preferring to lease land and reserving only a few days' service a year on the home farm for labour-intensive services like ploughing, harrowing, harvesting or sheep shearing.[70] Carriage services were unpopular with tenants who commonly engaged in passive resistance of the kind that frustrated the eighth lord Yester's factor in 1627; the latter being informed that 'ass for men thair is neane to be had heir'. In November 1608, the superior of Melrose regality court, the first lord Buccleuch, investigated and set down the carriage due to him, ordering that 'everie officer sall gif in sufficient compt yeirlie of the number under his wand, under the paine of the lose of his office and credit thairefter'. Here was a sure indication that services were being avoided. On the first earl of Nithsdale's estate at Mearns c.1627 the tenants ignored every threat of legal action, refusing to carry out carriage services 'be ressoune it wes the thronge tyme of thair labour'. In the meantime the earl had to pay to have his wine transported from Glasgow to Carlaverock castle.[71]

Over and above leases, landlords had the right to feudal casualties. The trend throughout western and southern Europe was for the relative value of feudal dues to fall, hence the rise in leases. There were exceptions to this pattern, such as in Naples, or in Castile where lords embarked on aggressive 'refeudalisation', but the economic value of lordship was declining.[72] Profits from feudal superiority, especially ward and relief, persuaded Scottish lords to go on exercising such rights as a year's maill on the entry of a vassal or, in the case of a feu ferme, a double payment of the feu duty. Furthermore, Gordonstoun took the view that the feudal superiority of land was essential to the power and authority of the house of Sutherland, counselling his nephew not to alter the terms of any land set for ward and relief.[73] Lords anticipated other forms of subsidy, particularly in the Highlands, where taxes were levied to support military expeditions like the 1594 Glenlivet campaign. Even in peacetime, Highland lords raised voluntary taxes – for example, to help pay a lord's debts, while the paying of calps, or death duties, to Highland chiefs continued after their formal abolition in 1617.[74]

Of the lands owned by a lord, only a small proportion, the mains farm, was directly managed by servants to provision the household. The remainder of the estate was set according to different types of tenancy agreements, such as steelbow by which the lord gave the tenant stock and seed in return for a proportion of the profits, or, in more pastoral regions, agreements with bowmen who reared stock on the lord's land. In each of these cases the lord retained close and flexible control over land use, supplementing the supply of produce for his household. The remainder of the land was granted to vassals by charter, feued, or leased to tenants who had remarkably secure rights. Therefore the extent to which the lord could control the way in which the land was utilised was limited.[75] Leases took many forms, but it was the kindly tenant – that is, a tenant who held his lands by customary agreement, who epitomised much of what was best about lord-man relationships in rural society. In mid-sixteenth-century Glasgow, for example, where the lands immediately around the burgh for up to five miles belonged to the archbishop, 'the rentes hes nocht bene takne frome the heires thir thousand yeiris and mair ... Ilke hes rychteouslie from age to age succeidet till vther, that worthilie thay may be called perpetual heires'. In return for service, men expected a lord's protection. Hence in 1589 James Torvie unilaterally reduced by 20 per cent the entry fine the second earl of Moray was demanding because he was threatened by bandits when the earl lived away from home, neglecting his duties.[76] While lords generally had the upper hand – for example, in negotiating grassums, or entry fines – these tenants held real rights recognised by the courts. However, as was the case with English customary tenants, such rights were coming under pressure in the context of changing lord–tenant relationships. Rack-renting was becoming commonplace, with kindly tenants being displaced by those better able to pay, and the process accelerated in the early seventeenth century when there was less need for strong political affinities, church opposition to increases was reduced, and many tenants were in a position to pay due to an upturn in the rural economy. On the Hamilton estates in lowland Lanarkshire, and on the very different MacLeod estates on the island of Skye, there were similarly sharp increases in rents.[77]

Nobles rarely feued their own heritage lands, the church and crown being the main agents of feuing, but they were beneficiaries of this development. Around one-third of all feu charters were issued to nobles, and the bigger feu charters usually went to magnates like the duke of Châtelherault, who acquired the largest single grant from Kilwinning abbey's barony of Beith. It is unlikely that anyone other than the second earl of Orkney could have paid £2073 6s 8d, around one-eighth of his income, to the king for the feu of Orkney and Shetland. The losers in this transformation were kindly tenants, evicted to make way for feuars who could pay the new, higher rents. However, not all lords were enthusiastic about doing away with kindly tenants, and c.1590 Walter Stewart, commendator of Blantyre, feued the lordship and regality of Glasgow to the existing tenants on terms that were set at the same rate as the old rent. The picture of a proliferation of owner-occupiers must also be modified by the consolidation that took place in the later sixteenth century as greater landlords bought out many of the first generation of bonnet lairds. This occurred on the Coupar Angus abbey estates, where the fourth earl of Atholl had by 1567 acquired and united properties initially feued to seven tenants.[78]

The fixed rental was the key to the growing value of the feu to its holder for, as in the rest of Europe, fixed rents were collapsing in value before the relentless rise in inflation. Some superiors tried to protect themselves from this by having their feus paid in kind, an understandably unpopular policy with feuers like lord Robert Stewart on Orkney. However, many nobles benefited from the erosion of the value of feus. By 1611 John Grant of Freuchie's freehold barony of Freuchie was worth less than one-third in rental than the lands of Glencarnie which he had held in feu from the crown since 1478. For an annual rental of £71 Glencarnie brought in £2024, a substantial income in kind, and the tenants paid him a grassum of £770 every five years. Conversely, inflation created major problems for superiors whose estates had been heavily feued, as was the case with the former commendators and their heirs, the lords of erection. Nevertheless, feuing continued to offer landlords a means of raising large amounts of cash. In 1632, the second earl of Mar desperately resorted to feuing lands in Aberdeenshire, spurning local advice on pricing from his agent. More generally, the stabilisation of prices in the early seventeenth century once again made feuing a good option for landlords. Hence in c.1630 the eleventh earl of Angus feued his third of the lordship of Bothwell to the existing tenants at favourable rates, retaining only Bothwell castle and its mains farm.[79]

The Reformation brought the nobility an entirely new landed income in the form of teinds that were inherited, leased and traded like any other commodity on the land market. These might be collected directly by a titular, or leased to a tacksman, either of whom was obliged to pay the minister his stipend and probably some maintenance for the manse and church fabric. The ingathering of teinds from the share of a standing crop was the cause of bitterness and occasional violence in local society, and a series of parliamentary enactments sought to provide a recognised system that allowed the owner of the land to set aside those corns destined for the teind master. Typical of the complex state of teind ownership was the barony of Yester, where each spring the eighth lord Yester issued letters of inhibition against his tenants to prevent them from interfering in his right to the teindscheaves.[80]

In 1580, a commentator writing about Scottish tenurial relations concluded that the peasantry 'are very poor, and live very hardly', being exploited in a society where 'the lord receives all, but contributes nothing'. This was inaccurate, but the exploitative opportunities available to landlords were there for all to see in the notorious rack-renting. Lethington was scathing about those landlords who pushed up rents: 'We gar our landis doubill pay;/Our tennentis cry "Alace! Alace!/That routh and pittie is away"'.[81] His moral outrage was shared by the church which argued for a moral economy. The 1561 *First Book of Discipline* was bitingly critical of rapacious landlords who now possessed ecclesiastical estates 'so that Papistical tyrannie shall only be changed into the tyrannie of the lord and laird'. Until it was muzzled in the early 1600s, the general assembly continued to condemn the 'cruell oppressioun of the poore tenents, wherby the whole commouns of the countrie are utterlie wracked, by extreme deere setting of their rowmes, and holding out of their cornes by untymous teinding and extreme thraldom in services'. Sensitive and deferential pressure from local clergy who remained on good terms with their patrons might have been more effective, and it was in this spirit that in the spring of 1590 Mr John Knox, minister at Melrose, nudged the fifth earl of Morton towards rethinking his treatment of the kindly tenants on his Teviotdale lands.[82] The crown too drew attention to harsh landlordism, a fault James VI condemned in *Basilikon Doron* (1598), and one he repeatedly intervened to modify throughout his reign when aggrieved tenants appealed to him, condemning as 'ane covert oppressioun' the second earl of Mar's efforts in October 1612 to evict a kindly tenant whose family had held their tack for eighty years. The privy council also warned landlords in 1613 not to pass on taxes to their tenants, highlighting an illegal extortion racket by which some lords raised more from their tenants than they were paying in tax to the crown.[83]

One of the difficulties tenants faced in challenging the economic interests of the nobility was that they lived under the jurisdictional authority of their landlords. Thus in spite of the pity the eighth lord Yester's servant expressed for the 'fatherles bayrnes' of a dead tenant, he knew that 'I must persew to the uttermust of the law'. Scottish lords preserved a tenurial system of estate management in which they retained their economic powers, maximising the financial return from the estate without sacrificing control over the people who worked it. Hence Gordonstoun insisted that the earl of Sutherland keep a strict control over local pricing.[84] Lords used their jurisdictional authority to regulate prices in the interests of the entire community, but the baronial or regality court also adjudicated between the baron and his tenants, and it was the means by which he could introduce new bylaws, or increase levies. Such authority was exploited by the likes of lord

Robert Stewart, who from 1574 established control over udal land on Orkney and Shetland by a combination of intimidation and manipulation of dubious legal technicalities. Lords could restrict the movement of the workforce through the barony court, and in Shetland in 1602 the granting of travel permits was tightened up by the second earl of Orkney. Baronial courts also regulated the economic exchange between the barony and the external world. Repeated complaints between 1621 and 1624 against the tenth lord Forbes, John Gordon of Newton and John Leith of Harthill over the extortionate imposts they were levying at local fairs had little effect, even when the privy council took up the case of the outraged burgesses of Edinburgh, Dundee, Aberdeen, Stirling and Glasgow.[85] Landlords provided services on their estates, such as a mill and a smithy, but these were run as monopolies to which the tenants were thirled, and while it was expected that the system would be exercised fairly, lords operated these services with a view to profit. In 1561, the tenth earl of Sutherland ordered that his tenants should carry their corns to the mill of Forss and pay multures to the factor there instead of using mills scattered throughout his lands. Lords also exercised control over the natural resources of the estate, like fuel. Finally, since most estates retained jurisdictional authority in the form of barony or regality courts, a lord enjoyed an income from the profits of justice.[86]

Yet landlords did not always get their own way in regulating the economy of the locality. In the mid-1570s, John Murray of Blackbarony encountered the determined opposition of George Lawson of Skiprig regarding the multure due by the latter. Skiprig won his case after more than two years of wrangling. William Hay of Urie fought a constant battle with his tenants, imposing repeated fines to enforce the payment of fermes, the rendering of carriage services and the levying of a tax on brewers, or mill service. His court tried to curb widespread pilfering, especially the theft of peats and cutting of wood, and his garden was raided by tenants jumping over the wall. In 1637, the heavily indebted first earl of Nithsdale raised his Renfrewshire rents against the advice of his baillie, but by the autumn of 1638 he confessed that while in the past there had only ever been one tenant who questioned the rent, now 'Lett maisters doe what they can, it is hard to mack al thar tennents content'.[87] Here, perhaps, in Nithsdale's gloomy observation was a dawning that with the Glasgow general assembly then gathering, the world was changing around him.

To some extent landlord paternalism was motivated by self-interest since a poor tenantry led to falling landed incomes, as occurred in later sixteenth-cenury Normandy. Scottish landlords knew that 'puir miserable bodies that knawis na other way to live' would not be good farmers. Gordonstoun told his nephew not to increase his rentals, especially the teinds, and was critical of previous earls of Sutherland for 'raking ther lands to greater dewties then they were able to bear, which makes your tennants poor and miserable'. He sensibly asked, 'How can they pay the dewtie when the ground will not yield it? A poore tennant maks a poore maister, and a rich tennant a rich maister', a sensible maxim that many landlords understood.[88] But landlords also recognised their social responsibilities, and older noble houses were usually the most generous, as was the case in Spain where it was not unknown for communities to petition to become the vassals of a landlord in the belief that he would treat them in a patriarchal, unexploitative manner. Even within noble society there was an appreciation that 'we alwise sie the poore and commoun sorte of people to suffer for great men's follies'. Evidence of nobles operating a moral economy is apparent in the behaviour of men like the sixth lord Lovat, who reputedly gave away fish rather than renting out his salmon grounds, refusing to rent his orchards and leasing property with little consideration of the financial implications, policies that ultimately damaged his house. John Allison in Carnwath must have had some expectation of success when he wrote c.1633 to the countess of Mar excusing his non-payment of eleven hens on account of 'the extrordener bad yeir of the frost'. These 'rests', or outstanding fermes, might be repaid in later years or replaced by labour services, but often the landlord had to write off the loss altogether. Landlords were also expected to respond to crises, and as revolution was breaking out in the late summer and autumn of 1637, the second earl of Buccleuch's officers were trying to combat a severe dearth and plague, distributing food and drink to impoverished households and to homeless 'scavengers'.[89]

## Conclusion

Land remained the greatest source of power, wealth and prestige in early modern Scotland, and by the end of the sixteenth century it was the nobility who possessed in one form or another the greatest share of that land. The crown had declined to the level of a landlord on a par with some of the greater nobles, while the church had been robbed of its landed assets. Some merchant finance was moving into the land market by means of holding rents as collateral for debt, but little ownership was passing into urban hands. Below the nobility, the smaller feuers were emerging as semi-independent farmers, but already by the early seventeenth century many of these were being squeezed out by the bigger estates. The nobility's success in seizing land was spectacular, ensuring their continued economic pre-eminence and allowing the proliferation of cadet houses along with the establishment of new houses among the higher ranks of the nobility. The pattern of the nobility's land ownership was still to endeavour to create a core estate in a particular locality, and land was often bought close to the family seat that had little economic significance. At the same time, the flooding of the market with ecclesiastical estates and teinds resulted in a far more complex portfolio of possessions for the greater landlords whose lands might be scattered across a number of shires. The noble landlord, therefore, varied from the duke of Lennox or the marquis of Hamilton at one end of the scale, with huge landed holdings in almost half of Scotland's shires, through important barons with a major presence in one shire, to relatively insignificant barons clinging on to their meagre estate. In general, there was some correlation between rank and the size or worth of estates, but this was not rigid, and at shire level a baron might easily own more land than a lord of parliament or an earl. The dynamism of the land market, in which land was increasingly traded as a capital asset, allied to royal patronage, good sense and good luck, produced some astonishing success stories in terms of estate accumulation.

Ensuring that landed dominance was maintained from one generation to the next was as important to nobles as enlarging their possessions during their own lifetimes. The noble landlord stood at a fixed point in the history of his lineage, having inherited land from his ancestors, and with a duty to pass the estate on intact to his descendants. To a degree that was more extreme than in much of Europe, Scottish landlords placed their faith in perpetual entails. These restricted succession to the eldest male heir as the best means of ensuring that estates would not be broken up, and that the power, wealth and prestige of the surname would be maintained. Here Scots law was the servant of noble intentions, hence the absence of significant litigation to break entails. There were implications for the management of families in which younger sons and daughters were excluded from the succession, and fathers sought ways to make provision through the temporary alienation of land to the former and ever larger dowries for the latter. Nevertheless, they did not shirk from the accepted practice of passing on their lands to the nearest male heir, even if this meant disinheriting their own daughters.

The extent to which individual nobles managed their lands was a product of inclination and circumstance, but most appear to have had a 'hands-on' attitude. If not actually present to oversee the running of their estates, nobles delegated to their officials or family members; absenteeism was not a feature of this period, except after 1603 among a handful of courtiers. Given the importance of the estate to the economic welfare of a noble house this is unsurprising; neglectful or wasteful management quickly brought financial and often political decline. It is likely that most nobles spent a large amount of time on supervising their estates. As is apparent in the next chapter, some were highly successful entrepreneurs who fully exploited the potential of their lands. However, the bread and butter of the estate was its produce and its tenants. In common with most of western Europe, Scottish landlords only directly farmed a small portion of their lands, leasing the remainder in return for a mix of cash, kind and services. Feudal superiors also had a diversity of incomes from casualties, profits of justice, feus and teinds. While there was a growing emphasis on cash rents, many nobles preferred to market produce directly, and therefore rents in kind were certainly not being replaced universally. However, landlords were increasingly willing to displace kindly tenants, pushing up rents and offering shorter leases. Undoubtedly much of the poverty of the period was a product of natural disasters and of a rising population. Yet the more commercially motivated policies of landlords contributed to that misery, even if self-interested common sense prevented rack-renting rising above what tenants could reasonably afford and a mixture of good lordship and Christian paternalism alleviated some of the effects of impoverishment.

## CHAPTER 2

# Entrepreneurs

Alongside the intense activity in the Scottish land market, the determination to ensure male succession and the personal involvement in estate management, the nobility explored means of increasing their incomes from traditional sources and diversifying their sources of income. In one sense there was nothing new in adopting such strategies, and evidence can be found for medieval nobles doing exactly this, whether it was to extend the land under tillage in the thirteenth century, or to seek rewards for military service in the fourteenth century. Successful nobles had always been required to develop entrepreneurial skills or simply opportunistic reflexes. However, some explanation is required for the growing number of nobles displaying what might broadly be described as entrepreneurial attitudes towards generating income. In part, the explanation lies in those conditions driving economic change in the later sixteenth and early seventeenth centuries. The rise in demand for raw materials in the domestic and international market, a greater awareness of husbandry, the absence of significant involvement in warfare from the early 1570s along with the slow disappearance of the bloodfeud, the gradual adoption by government of mercantilist trade policies, the regal union of 1603; these all offered nobles new and better ways to increase their wealth. However, the opportunites had to be seized, and it was not always the case that noble élites had the energy, aptitude or flexibility to respond to changes of this magnitude. In other words, the explanation also lies inside noble society, in a noble mind that was attuned to economic exploitation without being constrained by too much tradition. It was certainly not the case that all Scottish nobles responded in equal measure but many did respond, seizing the initiative in estate improvements, in promoting new industries and in exploiting the wealth of the crown. In doing so, they made partners of their own tenants, of mercantile interests in the towns and of the king and his officials. For those families with sufficiently aggressive instincts, sound business sense and simple good luck, the rewards were immense, and while there was also an element of risk in all these entrepreneurial activities, not to compete was virtually unthinkable.

## Estate Improvement

On succeeding to his estates in 1569, sir Alexander Fraser of Philorth set about developing Faithlie burgh of barony, founded twenty-three years earlier by his grandfather. A new castle was constructed, the harbour was improved and the burgh was graced with wide streets and fine public buildings. In 1592 its name was altered to Fraserburgh, it was united with Philorth's other lands in a burgh of regality, and authority was granted by the king to found a university in the town. Although the university failed to establish itself, the town and harbour flourished. Unfortunately the cost of Philorth's lofty ambitions was high; creditors pressed in on him and land had to be sold. Philorth died in 1623, his great enterprise having failed, but he made a lasting impression on the economy of the region and was remembered as an energetic innovator and improver.[1] The baron of Philorth was over-ambitious, but he was representative of the confident spirit of the age.

While southern regions of Europe generally sought to maximise profits without altering the agricultural system and some northern regions like south-west Wales were rather backward, parts of northern Europe were adopting a more commercial and improving attitude towards estate management. Fixed rents and feudal dues were of declining importance, making it essential for nobles to exploit the alluring commercial opportunities offered by a rising population and more profitable forms of estate management.[2] While Scottish landowners lagged behind England and Holland, it would be untrue to think they had no interest in improvement, or that the baron of Philorth was unique. Indeed, from as early as the twelfth and thirteenth centuries feudal relationships in Scotland were becoming commercial.[3] Furthermore, sixteenth-century landlords were aware of what needed to be done to improve their estates. In 1595 John Napier of Merchiston wrote *The New Order of Gooding and Manuring All Sorts of Field Land with Common Salt*, in which he discussed enclosures and the rotation of fields for pasture and cropping. A generation later, in 1632, sir Robert Ker of Ancram advised his son to give over marginal arable land to sheep pasture and was particularly keen that waterlogged ground be drained.[4] Philorth's vision for Fraserburgh, Merchiston's pamphlet and Ancram's common-sense advice scarcely amount to a groundswell of opinion advocating change, but neither were they unrepresentative.

One possible drag on improvement was prejudice. Riccarton, writing in *Jus Feudale*, followed Aristotle in expressing the view that 'any condition of service, any manual occupation, any trade, even the hiring of land for a yearly rent or in feu-farm, extinguishes all right to noble rank. Nobility in short cannot stand alongside any common employment'. In some parts of Europe, the idea that nobles should not engage in trade was sustained, especially in France where *dérogeance* – a loss of noble status for as long as a person engaged in activities deemed not to be in keeping with noble rank – became more strictly observed over the course of the seventeenth century. Even in Holland, nobles could face derogation if they engaged in certain kinds of commercial activity. On the other hand, in Italy it was not considered inappropriate for the nobility to be involved in commerce and industry, and in England an interest by nobles in trade or finance directly related to enhancing the productivity and profitability of estates was acceptable, there being no formal process of derogation. Scottish nobles were well aware of this debate. Unlike Riccarton, sir James Balfour of Denmilne noted the permissive attitude of Italians in contrast to parts of Germany where a noble engaged in trade would be despised. His own view was probably close to the European norm, that nobles of modest means could engage in marketing their estate surpluses, and he saw no harm in nobles labouring in their own fields.[5]

Scottish landlords embraced agricultural innovations in piecemeal fashion. While some isolated evidence of enclosure can be traced on a Highland estate like that of Glenorchy by the 1630s, even prosperous Fife had few enclosures in the seventeenth century, and consequently Scotland was spared the social costs associated with this practice.[6] On the other hand, there was enthusiasm for liming which improved the crop yield while also reducing the time needed to rest land. The practice was well established in the largely pastoral estates of Cunninghame in Ayrshire by the early seventeenth century when the cartographer, Timothy Pont, noted that since liming had been adopted land had become 'much more luxuriant then befor'. The uptake was slower in the east, but by the 1620s landlords throughout the Lowlands were employing liming, allowing them to bring new land into cultivation and increasing the rental. Rotations only became common after 1660, but landlords in the early seventeenth century were not ignorant of the practice, and in 1636 the barony court of Monymail in Fife forbade tenants from planting oats in successive years. Other forms of miscellaneous improvement can be found; in 1608, sir Duncan Campbell of Glenorchy spent 10 000 merks on improving the river defences on the Tay to prevent the flooding of his house and garden at Balloch.[7]

One of the greatest difficulties nobles faced in improving their estates was in persuading tenants to cooperate. There is little, if any, evidence in Scotland of estates being surveyed – in spite of the fact that John Napier of Merchiston's logarithms were one of the technical advances that made more accurate surveying possible – as a prelude to developing a coherent leasing policy, as was the case in England from the 1590s. However, from c.1600 there was a steady rise in the number of written leases, an increase in the percentage of long leases (nineteen years or more), and a growing preference among landlords for single tenancies, the most dramatic changes taking place in Lowland localities from the 1620s. Obviously conditions varied greatly from one estate to another, and even within estates. Between 1627 and 1631, the eighth lord Yester set a number of tacks for five, seven and nineteen years, suggesting that there was no clear leasing policy in operation, unless it was one of deliberately spreading the length of leases.[8] In some localities the conditions were not suitable for reform. The lands of the earls of Argyll adopted written leases with more enthusiasm than other Highland localities, but on the island of Jura, lord Lorne's efforts to plant the estate with productive, improving tenants were scuppered by the hostile activities of Hector MacLean of Duart. More commonly, the entrenched conservatism of the tenantry stopped improvement. The difficulty in moving away from proprietary runrig to consolidated farms is demonstrated in the case of Letham in Fife where sir James Melville of Halhill initiated a move in that direction in 1596. Negotiations with the feuars dragged on and various agreements collapsed, leaving the lands still in runrig in the 1680s. Other landlords exploited tenant vulnerability at the time of negotiating a lease to set improving tacks, as did the eighth lord Yester in the 1620s and 1630s when he required tenants to plant trees, build enclosures, repair dwellings or lay down lime in return for concessions on access to peat. By contrast, at Ancram in 1607 it was sir Robert Ker's more adventurous tenants who lobbied for the consolidation of their leases since 'thay war greatlie dampnified ... in thair outfield lands in respect that thay lay rinrig'.[9]

One reason why tenants resisted improvements was that they were usually associated with rent increases. The first and second earls of Orkney forced up their income from £10 747 in 1568 to £44 865 in 1600, arousing enormous resentment among the tenantry. Some of this increase was caused by inflation, by the need to recoup the doubling in 1587 of the feu of the earldom lands, and by increased taxation, but there is no doubt that the earls were rack-renting to finance extravagant lifestyles. The Orkney case stands out at this time because of its severity, although isolated complaints about rack-renting date from the mid-sixteenth century when Lethington was scathing of greedy, oppressive landlords.[10] What is likely, although not yet demonstrable, is that landlords in Scotland, as in Brandenburg, were reacting to a long period of economic decline, the difference being the emphasis on rents rather than services. As in England, sixteenth-century landlords and tenants usually preferred to agree relatively low rents coupled with high entry fines. Landlords placed a greater premium on loyal tenants at a time of political instability, resisting the pressure to increase rents when the market could ill afford it.[11] It was only in the early seventeenth century that landlords began systematic rack-renting in response to inflation. The impact of population growth, the upturn in the economy and the reduced need for other forms of service allowed landlords to find tenants who were willing to pay higher rents and entry fines for their land. In the Hamilton barony of Avondale a stable situation in the sixteenth century was followed by steep rent increases in the decades before 1640. Such changes were closely paralleled by developments in the north-west of England, a region not unlike much of Scotland in geography, climate and social organisation.[12]

However, landlords faced obstacles to imposing change on their tenants, not least the law which could not afford to be too oppressive in a society where one lord might hold land of another lord. Good tenants knew their value and their rights; hence the exasperation of John Murray of Cockpool who exclaimed of his tenants in 1613 that 'thai will do nothinge bot by compultione'. Julia Ker, countess of Haddington, was a tough negotiator, but in 1634 she met with stubborn opposition to her attempts to raise rentals, leaving her enraged at one particularly obstreperous tenant of whom she wrote, 'that foul master cur, that sould not a ben spairit ane day'.[13] Evicting such tenants proved far from easy, and tenants were not unknown to use violence to resist law officers trying to serve eviction letters on them. Between 1598 and 1600 the second earl of Mar raised a whole series of actions against the tenants of the barony of Nisbet for the non-payment of rents, but every decreet was ignored and the last record of the case is of the earl trying to poind the tenants' goods to get his dues. Even if eviction was achieved, the tenants might still have the last word. When in 1629 the eighth lord Yester finally succeeded in getting Andrew Cunningham removed from the barony of Snaid, he discovered that the disgruntled ex-tenant had cut down all the wood on the property and taken it with him.[14]

Just as important as the alterations in agricultural methods was the need to bring the estate into a market system to maximise the cash income. In 1570, the chamberlain of Kelso was setting terms that mixed cash, kind and services, but on many estates a high percentage of a lord's income was in kind, as on the Orkney or Huntly estates, where lords had the inconvenience of having to store, consume or sell their rents. However, in such conditions nobles could control the internal economy of the estate. They were protected from having to buy foodstuffs in large quantities, their income was inflation-proof and, as producers of raw materials, they were free to sell surpluses on the open market. The only major expenditure Orkney or Huntly required to make on food and drink was on imported luxuries such as French wines.[15] This preference for income in kind remained strongest in the grain-producing east where landlords took a more direct interest in marketing produce, but even in these regions there was inconsistency. By the early seventeenth century, the greater part of the eighth lord Yester's income was paid in cash, except on his Dumfriesshire lands, where only a fifth of the value of the rental was money rent; a quarter of the first lord Jedburgh's entire rental of £18 160 was paid in silver; and only 3 per cent of the entire rental of the parish of Monimail in Fife, amounting to 18 557 merks, was in cash in 1639.[16] The pastoral west saw a greater shift to cash rentals; for example, the income from the estates of the earls of Eglinton in Renfrewshire and the earls of Cassillis in Ayrshire were predominantly in cash by the seventeenth century, although both continued to market some produce directly. This region also saw the most severe rack-renting. However, a cash rental was not always to the advantage of landlords, and in the lands of the barony of Urie there was a drop in the real value of rentals between 1604 and 1634 when there was a switch to more money payments.[17]

The late sixteenth and early seventeenth century was a boom time for European grain producers, for whom a rapidly rising population meant cheap labour and a growing demand for food, the price of which rose steadily. In Scotland, there was no switch to regressive demesne farming as occurred in much of eastern Europe, where it was accompanied by landlords insisting on greater estate services by the peasantry.[18] However, rental in kind was crucial to the vitality of grain-producing landlords. Rough estimates produced in the last quarter of the sixteenth century suggest that even during these years of relatively poor grain production, the wealthiest noble houses were drawn from the grain-growing region along the east coast, on estates like that of the laird of Panmure in Angus which was described as 'very fertil, and goud for al kynd of cornes that growes in Scotland'.[19] Regular dearths forced Scotland to import grain in the later sixteenth century, and there were local shortages so that, for example, in 1590 the Campbells of Glenorchy bought one-third of their meal in Lowland markets. Yet even in the mid-sixteenth century, lord Robert Stewart was selling surplus Orcadian grain and butter in Edinburgh. After the dreadful 1590s, imports fell by more than 50 per cent in the subsequent decade, indicating that landowners were producing adequate quantities for the growing population. Of course, food shortages favoured grain producers, while times of plenty drove prices down. Thus Robert Lindsay of Pitscottie wryly commented on the problems of over-production in 1574 that 'mony of the rich men haveand cornis to sell tuik sic displesour that mony of thame deit'. During the 1600s, overseas business continued to expand, allowing nobles to market large surpluses which north-east producers like the ninth earl of Errol and the fifth earl Marischal transported by sea to Leith. Much of this grain was sold on by merchants to the continent, and in 1613 the mercantile interest forced the grain producers to concede greater control over managing the business. Three years later, John Taylor was staggered by the sight of the huge quantities of cereal stacked up on the Leith docks awaiting export to European ports.[20]

The long-term price rise was slow to hit the peripheries of Europe, but from c.1560 there was a sharp upturn in inflation, aggravated by successive debasements of the coinage, before food prices settled down in the 1600s to the more normal pattern of fluctuations caused by variations in the climate and harvest. Typical of this roller-coaster pricing was the experience of the twelfth earl of Sutherland, who in May 1615 was worrying about a local famine yet within four months was giving thanks that 'their wes newir in Sutherland a bettir croipe one the grownd, gif we geit guid weddir to win the sam'. Grain producers, therefore, had to have a finely-tuned ear for victual prices, seeking local advice, hawking their produce around to get the best bargain from merchants, and keeping an eye on the price of grain on the Amsterdam market.[21]

These extreme lurches from times of plenty to times of scarcity, causing wildly fluctuating prices, persuaded nobles to use their lobbying power to seek government assistance. The difficulty was in finding a balance between the interests of the producers, their mercantile partners, and the wider community which wanted prices kept low. The crown could forbid or restrict grain exports in years of shortage, as occurred in 1568, although occasional exemptions were granted. At other times, such as between 1619 and 1623, a duty was imposed on imported grain, ostensibly to prevent the loss of coin from the domestic economy, but the grain lobby was also seeking to hold up their own prices in the face of cheap imports. Furthermore, the government did what it could to support Scottish beer production, thus aiding grain producers against the imports of continental wines and, increasingly, English beer.[22]

Stock breeding was not immune to the pull of commercialisation, and here too there was a steady increase in the price of animals and animal products. The scale of the business is difficult to gauge as testaments consistently underestimated the size of cattle herds and sheep flocks. How much stock was bred for consumption rather than sale is unknown, but cattle prices were relatively high in the early seventeenth century, encouraging Highland landlords like the lairds of Glenorchy to strengthen links with the Lowland economy. Some landlords even set up commercial agents in Edinburgh and Glasgow, and long before 1603 border landlords were engaged in cross-border trade. Thereafter business boomed, and by 1627 the first earl of Annandale was granted a licence to transport cattle from his lands in Ireland to Portpatrick and south to English markets.[23] Cattle ranching had become big business for those nobles with contacts throughout Britain.

From the middle of the sixteenth century, the Scottish wool export trade had been in sustained decline, although as much as £50 000 per annum still was earned through exports in the early seventeenth century, chiefly benefiting border landlords. The size of the flocks listed in the testaments of heads of the house of Buccleuch were 1376 in 1574 at the death of sir Walter Scott of Buccleuch, and 11 000 in 1633 at the death of his grandson, a massive increase indicative of not only the family's land accumulation of the previous half-century, but also of the growing emphasis on sheep farming. In the years 1632 and 1633 the sale of sheep raised £15 777 and £12 841 respectively, while the value of the flocks was conservatively estimated at almost £19 000.[24] Government regulation of the wool trade was confined to restricting exports in times of dearth to depress domestic prices, as occurred in 1616 and again in 1626. Influential noble wool producers lobbied hard to protect their interests, such as in 1622 when the sheep ranchers joined forces with their merchant partners to oppose a court policy of obliging them to sell all their exports in England. More constructively, in 1623 the government responded to pressure from wool producers to increase domestic consumption by setting up a commission to encourage linen production. Individual nobles also investigated innovatory methods, as when David Lindsay of Edzell explored the possibility of employing Dutch weavers, or of sending a woman to be trained by the Dutch 'to lern to handill the woll, quhilk many honest women in this toun has begun to do'.[25]

In seeking to establish a more commercial relationship with the market, landlords developed their own infrastructure. That the economic potential of fairs was highly prized can be ascertained from some of the quarrels that arose over controlling them. Gordonstoun planned to improve the Sutherland estates by encouraging the commercial and residential development of Dornoch as the principal town of the sheriffdom. In addition, he recommended the establishment of a market at Brora 'so you may bring money into your countrey in the summer seasons for your marts, wool and other commodities'. He also wanted to encourage immigration to the area, advising the earl to 'Allure strangers and artificers of all sorts to repair to your countrey, and to inhabit ther'. Gordonstoun's optimistic enthusiasm was typical, and during the 1620s his neighbour, Hugh Fraser, master of Lovat, set about improving his father's estates by setting up malt kilns and creating markets at which he levied tolls. Nevertheless, in spite of the fact that there was from the 1580s a steady rise in the number of new market centres, peaking in the decade 1600–9, many localities remained too distant from a market to be able to enter into commercial trade. Furthermore, a good number of those that were founded failed to have any noticeable effect on the community they were intended to serve.[26]

The problems of communication created by geography and nature in Scotland could not be overcome by the existing technology and low levels of capitalisation. However, landlords were not unaware of the difficulties they faced, or of how they might bring themselves closer to major market centres. In the Highlands, nobles were at the fore in developing the droving routes that took cattle to Lowland markets along with raw materials for processing in Lowland burghs, while importing to the region wine, grain and other luxury items. Sir Duncan Campbell of Glenorchy's many improvements included a bridge at Lochay which he built in 1627 to allow easier access to the south from his estates. Elsewhere, in 1634 sir Patrick McKie of Larg successfully applied for the right to levy a toll on drovers passing to and from England or Ireland, on condition he repaired the decaying causeway and bridge over the Comnenwar Water in Galloway. Within the central Lowlands there was no real interest in a road system, although it is unlikely that those nobles given responsibility for the improvement of the roads in 1616 in preparation for the king's visit did not appreciate the economic significance of what they were doing. But in an age when water transport remained faster and more efficient than land transport, the most important investment was in port facilities. Among those who realised this was the first earl of Winton, who built a new dock at Cockayne for which James VI gave him a free harbour with all the privileges of a royal burgh. His son improved the harbour and also constructed twelve saltpans, although his investment in the harbour proved unlucky when a storm destroyed it in January 1635.[27]

## Diversification and Industry

In addition to the selling of the agricultural produce of the estate, landlords sought to exploit their land by diversification. The fishing resource of an estate was potentially among its most lucrative income earners, fish having for centuries been one of Scotland's top export commodities. Fishing rights, therefore, were jealously protected, and feuds over fishing rights were not uncommon.[28] The largest fishing enterprise was enjoyed by the earls of Argyll, who controlled the fishing grounds on the west coast, particularly the lucrative assize herrings of the 'West Seas' stretching from the Pentland Firth to the Mull of Galloway. Other landlords feued out, or were themselves feuars of relatively small fishing grounds, usually on rivers running through their estates.[29] It was the east coast salmon rivers that were the most profitable, especially those on Speyside, where the earls of Moray struggled to fend off Gordon encroachments in the sixteenth century, and where the first earl of Dunfermline steadily expanded his commercial operations in the early seventeenth century. However, salmon was not confined to the east, and the earls of Mar had salmon fishing rights on the River Clyde.[30] Of course, Scotland contains many freshwater lochs, the biggest being Loch Lomond where the earls of Glencairn had a fishing monopoly close to the important markets at Glasgow and Dumbarton, while Agnes Leslie, lady Lochleven, farmed eels, supplying 1000 to a buyer in St Andrews in 1584.[31]

The fish trade was not an unregulated market. Salmon fishing was subject to the commonly breached restriction that fish caught between the sea mark and the flood mark belonged to the king. Lords were also subject to conservation legislation. In an attempt to maximise their profits, successive lords Oliphant from the 1560s through to the early 1600s built dams and cruives (salmon traps) on the River Earn, ignoring parliamentary legislation regulating the practice because the loss of the salmon fry seriously reduced fish stock.[32] Only royal burghs could engage in the lucrative export of salmon and herring, forcing nobles to engage in partnerships with merchants like that between the second earl of Orkney and Fife fishermen. However, the burghs did not always appreciate this relationship, complaining in 1586 that a number of Highland chiefs were running an extortion racket in the west coast fishing grounds.[33] During the 1620s, the convention of royal burghs campaigned successfully against the first earl of Seaforth's efforts to introduce Dutch fishermen to Lewis in exchange for ground rents and landing dues. The burghs feared superior Dutch fishing technology, and in 1629–30 Seaforth's plan to develop the Hebridean port of Stornoway was blocked. There was similar opposition when in the 1630s a coterie of courtiers sought to exploit Scotland's fishing grounds in a controversial partnership with English fleets.[34]

The English visitor, sir William Brereton, was delighted to arrive at the first earl of Roxburgh's estate with its 'many kinds of wood' after the long journey through the barren landscape of the north of England. One of the most important assets on any estate was its woodland, which was a source of game, fuel and building materials. However, timber was in demand in markets further afield, and landlords in France, England and Scotland saw woods as an investment that could be readily capitalised.[35] It was because woods were so valuable a commodity that they were often targeted during the Marian civil war by punitive raiding parties. Even in peacetime, a wood had to be carefully guarded because of the tensions between lords wanting to exploit their timber assets and tenants who saw green wood as a much-needed local fuel. In the autumn of 1618, the first lord Buccleuch reported that over 450 trees, mostly alders, had been cut down and stolen from his wood at Gorrumberrie.[36] Successive earls of Morton took great care over the management of their timber stocks at Dalkeith, and in 1619 the sixth earl decided to build a wall around the wood in order to protect it from predatory tenants. The crown was equally watchful of its property, warning Henry Stewart, commendator of St Colme, in May 1593 that he must not cut down and sell Doune Wood in Menteith on pain of a fine equal to double the value of the timber. Meanwhile, all the neighbouring burghs were forbidden to purchase wood from him.[37] Furthermore, the capitalisation of wood was hindered by law in an effort to conserve wood stocks and to provide a habitat conducive to deer; hence the pressure put on the burgh of Inverness to cooperate in preventing the sale of wood from the shores of Loch Ness. There were other natural obstacles to commercialisation. In 1618, John Taylor was greatly impressed by the vast forests owned by the second earl of Mar in Braemar, but recognised that 'they doe grow so farre from any passage of water, and withall in such rockie mountaines, that no way to convey them is possible to be passable, either with boate, horse, or cart'.[38] In fact it was easier and cheaper for Lowland merchants to import Norwegian timber.

Nevertheless, in spite of the difficulties and restrictions that faced landlords, woods were managed and harvested. There is clear evidence of forestry management on estates in diverse localities, including the Highlands where Glenorchy constructed parks at Balloch, Finlarg and Glenorchy, planting acorn and fir trees. The Finlarg development was begun in 1627 and completed at a cost of 10 000 merks, a substantial but worthwhile investment.[39] This enthusiasm for tree planting was not only commercially driven. Sir David Lindsay of Edzell, his younger brother,

John Lindsay, lord Menmuir, and their kinsmen all had a passion for tree planting which was as much aesthetic as fiscal in inspiration. The Winton estate in East Lothian was also planted for pleasure with 'apple-trees, walnut-trees, sycamore, and other fruit-trees, and other kinds of wood which prosper well', and a glance at Blaeu's maps quickly indicates how popular an activity tree planting was among the nobility by the early decades of the seventeenth century.[40]

There was a long history of coal mining in Scotland, the most successful operations in the medieval period being run by the abbeys. By the sixteenth century, secular landlords had taken over an industry which was expanding due to a rising population allied to the shortage of wood fuel, along with an insatiable Dutch demand which the Scottish government was keen to supply as a means of earning sound foreign currency. By 1627, there were fifteen collieries exporting 25 000 tons of coal, while the scarcity of surface coal and the introduction of water gins encouraged owners to dig ever deeper. The most profitable and commercial operations were based in the Forth valley, where there was an abundance of high-quality coal, a dense and growing population, and good water communications. Yet even in the far north, Jean Gordon, dowager countess of Sutherland, began boring for coal in the River Brora in 1598.[41] The management of these coal fields varied from the direct control maintained by the sixth earl of Morton in East Lothian, to the kind of leasing arrangements with local merchants that were common in Yorkshire. These might involve single coal masters, as on the fourth lord Ross's Midlothian estates in 1573, or consortiums like that introduced to Carrick in 1625 by the sixth earl of Cassillis.[42]

The scale of coal production by landlords varied enormously. The third marquis of Hamilton not only had coal and salt works on his Scottish estates, but was involved in coal mining in the north of England, making him an important British coal producer. By contrast, sir John Maxwell of Conhaith mined coal for local consumption – 'verie usefull to the countrie people about' – and in the face of a constant struggle to keep the shafts from flooding.[43] The technical difficulties of deep shaft mining were such that any operations below the surface carried a high risk factor; the second earl of Lothian's coal grieve at Cockpen reported on the problems of a collapsing mine in 1620. The most remarkable coal works in Scotland were at Culross, where sir George Bruce of Carnok tunnelled under the Forth estuary. Unfortunately, this sophisticated showpiece of mining engineering was destroyed by a storm in 1625. The other major production cost, that of labour, was more easily dealt with when in 1606 the coal lobby persuaded parliament to pass legislation redefining the status of coal workers as serfs, granting the owners extensive rights over the lives of their workers.[44]

Government had to balance the revenue-earning potential of coal exports to the treasury against the domestic demand for fuel, particularly in severe weather conditions. Hence, for example, in 1563 parliament forbade coal exports, ratifying the legislation episodically as circumstances required it in 1579, 1597 and 1609. The burghs were the principal supporters of controls on exports, succeeding in getting these restrictions imposed. On the other hand, the king was under pressure to help both English buyers and the coal owners, including those nobles and councillors who wanted deregulation to export beyond Britain.[45] That argument became more heated in 1609 when James VI was pressured at court by domestic consumers and worried Newcastle competitors to stop exports on the grounds that the country was being denuded of a necessary fuel. However, the coal lobby mobilised its powerful friends at court and on the privy council to persuade a commission, headed by the sympathetic first earl of Linlithgow, against this policy. The coal masters argued that there was a large surplus of coal for the home market, that exports earned foreign coin, and that the investment made by coal owners, particularly in extracting coal from deeper, waterlogged pits, would be lost if they were unable to sell their coal abroad. Further encouragement came in 1616 in the timely appointment as treasurer of the second earl of Mar, a man whose burgh at Alloa was dependent on coal trafficking.[46] Another Forth valley landlord, the master of Elphinstone, convened a cartel of prominent Forth valley coal producers in 1619 to raise the price from three to four shillings per load as well as coming to an agreement on exports. Opposition from consumers, merchant middle men and the crown tried to outlaw their proceedings, but Elphinstone and his friends accused the merchants of profiteering at their expense. In 1621, a commission under the first viscount Lauderdale agreed a compromise that established the price of coal at three shillings and fourpence per load. Furthermore, in spite of the restrictions that hedged about the freedom of coal-producing landlords, such as another prohibition on exports in 1621–2, they had won the battle with the burghs to export their coal.[47] For the crown, the real issue now was how much money could be squeezed out of the trade, and the privy council progressively tried to tighten up on the widespread evasion of customs duties, while higher and higher tariffs were imposed on exports. The introduction of a new tax on coal by the 1633 parliament enraged coal producers like the first earl of Wemyss who protested that 'this impositioun is so extreame grett that no coillis will be exportit out of this kingdome so it will ruyne my small fortoun', and there was a dramatic fall in the Dutch trade over the succeeding years.[48] Here was one sector of the economy deeply resentful of royal policies by the 1630s.

Salt production was often closely related to coal operations, as on the Sutherland estates, and while landlords were slower to engage in the salt trade, from the 1570s it enjoyed a period of profitable expansion in response to the growing international market, peaking in the 1620s and 1630s. Again it was Dutch demand that fuelled exports, the usual Spanish supply being cut off as a consequence of war. A handful of landowners operated salt pans on their coastal estates, the most profitable being in the Forth Valley and

Lothian coast. At Culross, sir George Bruce erected forty-four salt pans in his integrated coal and salt operations, while on the neighbouring Sinclair and Wemyss estates at Dysart and Wemyss there was large-scale production. In 1628 the future earl of Wemyss expanded his works in expectation of making 4000 merks per annum in profit. At Cockenzie in east Lothian the third earl of Winton invested in new works in the 1630s. However, salt production also took place further afield in Sutherland, and on Orkney where the first earl of Carrick built salt pans in 1633; even a Highland landlord like sir Duncan Campbell of Glenorchy was operating salt pans in the mid-1620s. In this business too nobles entered into partnerships with merchants, as occurred in Aberdeenshire in 1633 when the sixth earl Marischal took up salt production. These noble salt producers and their merchant partners formed an effective pressure group, fighting successfully against export restrictions, getting parliamentary backing to curtail the freedom of their labour force, and campaigning in 1631 against English efforts to prevent the importation of Scottish salt.[49]

Scottish nobles, however, did not become engaged in the production of lead, iron, steel and alum to the extent of some English peers, and while in the early 1570s the fourth earl of Atholl was engaged in exporting lead and ore, this was on an insignificant scale.[50] A more serious interest in mineral extraction was shown when lead mines were discovered in Glenesk on the estate of sir David Lindsay of Edzell. Along with his brother, lord Menmuir, the master of the metals who invented an engine that raised water from coal mines, Edzell brought in Dutch and German experts during the 1590s to develop the site. He entered into a twenty-five-year contract with Hans Ziegler of Nuremberg to mine for a variety of metals.[51] In 1607, sir Thomas Hamilton of Drumcairn was granted all mineral rights within a swathe of baronies in Linlithgowshire that entangled him in the overrated silver mine at Hilderstone. That same mine was leased in 1613 to a consortium of sir William Alexander of Menstrie, Thomas Foulis, an Edinburgh goldsmith, and Paulo Pinto, a Portuguese entrepreneur, who agreed to pay the crown 10 per cent of the profits.[52] Efforts to acquire a monopoly to operate alum mines in Scotland were blocked until 1620 when the first earl of Kellie received a thirty-one-year monopoly with authority to enter into partnerships and to bring in foreign expertise. Unfortunately, he and his business partners ran into difficulties in financing the enterprise and in overcoming local objections.[53] Stone quarrying offered another opportunity for enterprising landlords like John Murray of Tibbermure, who worked a quarry on the outskirts of Perth, the burgh itself being his biggest customer; sir Duncan Campbell of Glenlyon, who leased quarrying rights to his neighbours; and the sixth earl of Cassillis, who worked his own quarry at Maybole.[54]

Access to crown patronage, chiefly by courtiers and crown officials, led to the involvement of nobles in manufacturing enterprises the government hoped to stimulate. In 1610 sir George Hay of Kinfauns was granted a thirty-year monopoly to manufacture glass and iron, and he began operating a glass-making business at Wemyss in Fife as well as building iron works in which he employed foreign expertise. He had to defend that monopoly against competition in 1617, and two years later came close to abandoning the glass industry as the domestic market was too small to cover his production costs. However, Kinfauns received the support of the privy council in making inroads into English markets, and he was a member of a 1621 commission which concluded that the quality of Scottish fine glass was improving markedly, even if it still lagged behind that of England.[55] Lord Erskine was the beneficiary in 1620 of a thirty-one-year tanning patent intended to improve the quality of leather production in the kingdom. He introduced English tanners and bullied Scottish craftsmen into adopting their practices to the extent that his operations were investigated by the committee of grievances in 1624. Erskine survived this attack and subsequent criticisms, and while the king agreed in 1634 that his patent should not be renewed, he continued to operate until the revolution.[56] A different kind of monopoly was the third marquis of Hamilton's sixteen-year grant in 1631 of the imposts on all wine imported to Scotland to offset his costs in raising an army for service in Germany. This 'greatest gift that ever was givine in Scotland', which Hamilton farmed to William Dick of Braid for £74 666 13s 4d per annum, was soon identifed as over-generous. In 1634, the crown negotiated a deal to buy Hamilton out for £480 000 with money from the recently granted tax, this being part of a package to compensate him for other arrears and liabilities under which he stood to gain over £720 000.[57] In a development that was regarded with even greater hostility, the king instructed in 1634 that the first earl of Stirling be permitted to profit from the issue of a new copper coinage for nine years since there was no other way of paying him the £16 000 per annum he was owed in pensions.[58]

While a number of English nobles invested in shipping ventures, the Scots had fewer opportunities, although the fifth earl of Bothwell was engaged in shipping in his capacity as lord admiral, while the first earl of Orkney operated privateering ventures. Others were active in shipping on only a small scale, like sir James Scott of Balweary, a Fife baron, who lost a ship to English pirates in 1599.[59] Union with England introduced Scottish nobles to the colonial trade, and it was courtiers and royal officers who were among the most entrepreneurial figures of the age, taking a direct interest in their commercial activities and often displaying far less conservative business acumen than the jealous merchant sector. In particular, these courtiers were able to take advantage of the joint stock companies established in England in the early seventeenth century. The second duke of Lennox was an investor in a scheme in 1612 to establish a colony on the Amazon, while in 1636 a handful of these courtiers optimistically entered into a contract with a consortium of German and Dutch partners to engage in trade with Africa under a charter issued to the former by the king.[60] Sir

William Alexander of Menstrie developed an interest in a colonisation scheme for Nova Scotia, a sign of his British imperial vision, but this get-rich-quick scheme, which was floated in 1625, flopped.[61] Even Menstrie was upstaged by James Hay, first earl of Carlisle, another London-based courtier whose multifarious business activities included exporting tobacco from his Barbados plantations in the mid-1630s, while the same spirit of aggressive entrepreneurial adventure lay behind the hopeful commission to sir Robert Gordon of Lochinvar in 1627 to establish a colony on Charles Island that would act as a base for privateering against French and Spanish shipping.[62]

No sixteenth- and seventeenth-century Scottish burgh could compare with the financial muscle of London, but these trading communities were dynamic, expanding centres of trade undergoing dramatic transformations from medieval communities to modern towns, offering new opportunities for entrepreneurial nobles. While Scottish nobles never became urbanised in the manner of the Italian or southern French nobilities, the relationship between nobles and merchants in many of the above enterprises was close. As well as seeking merchant capital to develop their estates, the nobility extended their own investments into the towns. Such a development was not new in Scotland, and the earls of Crawford continued to draw modest annual pensions and rents from Aberdeen, Montrose and Dundee that were the fruits of earlier crown grants.[63] However, new landed possessions in and around burghs were often acquired by nobles at the Reformation. The Cistercian and Dominican houses in Aberdeen passed into the hands of the earls Marischal, giving them an interest in land, tenements, houses and annual rents in the burgh.[64] Usually this relationship between royal burghs and a local noble family is unsurprising, being defined by geographic proximity and historic interests. The earls of Eglinton owned at least one tenement in the burgh of Irvine, while the Scrymgeours of Dudhope held the superiorities of land in and around Dundee, the first viscount Lauderdale was involved in property transactions in Edinburgh in 1621, and the first earl of Mar and his wife bought property in Stirling and in Edinburgh.[65] Nobles also took a direct interest in developing their own burghs of barony, and between 1600 and 1650 sixty-four new burghs of barony were founded. In 1607, the fifth earl Marischal moved the judicial proceedings of Kincardineshire to Stonehaven on the grounds that the latter had better facilities for accommodating the magistrates and others with business at law. Five years later, he persuaded the burghs of Edinburgh and Aberdeen to contribute towards the costs of a new harbour in the town, and in 1624 he finally had Stonehaven created a burgh of barony. Highland lords also saw the potential of such developments. New burghs were established at Campbeltown by the seventh earl of Argyll, Gordonsburgh by the first marquis of Huntly, and in 1629 at Stornoway by the first earl of Seaforth.[66] Finally, nobles were often charged by the crown with investigating and reporting on issues affecting urban economic developments.[67]

## Royal Patronage and Pensions

When Patrick Maule of Panmure inherited his estate in 1605 he faced total ruin, and 'Except he had gotten favour in Court, his house had ended'. Royal favour brought Panmure financial security, and 'he began to quit and relieve piece and piece parts of his estate, till at length it pleased God to bless him with great lands'. Nobles like the laird of Panmure had always needed to be close to the centre of political power, and kings had always sought to bind their nobilities to them by bonds of patronage, but by the later sixteenth century the early modern crown offered new opportunities that had a greater and greater impact on the finances of noble houses.[68] James VI had a good understanding of the importance of patronage, arguing that reward and punishment were 'the very ground-stone of good government'. However, the Scottish crown was less able than most to meet the demand for offices and pensions. In 1579, it was reported of the king that 'he is poor, his nobility rich', a situation that had changed little by 1603 as the crown had neither land nor money to make grants. Few offices even had significant fees attached to them. The demanding office of a border warden fell into this category. Only the west warden received a regular payment of £600 per annum up to 1586, leaving wardens to squeeze money out of feudal casualties and the profits of justice, not to mention a share of any illegal traffic in cattle or goods that might be intercepted. Furthermore, in such an irrational spoils system, subject to court faction and the whim of the king, many grants were blocked or challenged at law by rivals. In 1581, when the first earl of Gowrie was given the tenth of all wards, reliefs and non-entries in Perth, the privy council immediately received a protest from the barons of the shire that this should not prejudice their own rights. It has been estimated that the annual pensions bill in 1603 was a mere 500–1000 merks, a significant enough amount to a poor king, but not a substantial infusion of funds into noble coffers.[69]

On the other hand, even a poor king had some patronage. Ratifications of titles cost the crown nothing and were much valued by the nobility, while there was a constant scramble for escheats such that in 1589 one observer noted 'If any escheat or ward fall, the first that bags it hath it'. Former ecclesiastical resources were systematically plundered as a source of patronage with the crown conveying enormous amounts of landed revenue into the pockets of the nobility. Monarchs made all manner of gifts to their servants, like the jewellery given to sir Duncan Campbell of Glenorchy and his family by queen Anne, one jewel alone having twenty-nine diamonds and four great rubies.[70] James VI's necessary generosity repeatedly undermined whatever mechanisms were imposed to control the outflow of royal income into noble pockets, whether this be the revocation of 1578, the stoppage on pension payments in 1587, or the reforms of the Octavian government in 1596–7.[71] Royal favour, therefore, could be rewarding, and even relatively minor offices might supplement landed incomes. James Anstruther, younger of that Ilk, acquired a succession of minor royal household offices in the ten years from when he entered service in 1585. A decade later he had a salary of £222 4s with an additional sum of £111 2s 8d for his 'leveray claithes'. Finally, while the money paid to Scottish nobles by the Tudor government was relatively insignificant, most of the pension paid by Elizabeth I to James VI, amounting to some £60 000 sterling, was commonly disgorged to the king's friends.[72]

Regal union freed up the king's Scottish revenues which could be deployed as patronage, especially as higher taxation enhanced royal revenue. Only a handful of nobles drew a cash income from the king's coffers before 1603, but already there were indications that significant numbers of the higher nobility were prepared to support taxation in exchange for their share of the proceeds. As taxes climbed in the decades after 1603, the rewards grew: £30 000 to the first earl of Abercorn in 1615; £20 000 to treasurer Mar in 1617; £40 000 in 1621 to the second marquis of Hamilton, collector of the taxation. For a notorious debtor like the first earl of Nithsdale, his appointment as collector of the 1625 taxation must have seemed like an answer to a prayer.[73] Nevertheless, the number of nobles drawing a regular cash income continued to be relatively small. In 1625, only forty-nine individuals had the right to draw a pension on the Scottish revenue. Yet the opportunities created by office allowed many high-ranking royal officials to claw their way into the company of the wealthiest men in the kingdom: men like the first lord Thirlestane and the first earls of Dunbar, Dunfermline and Haddington. Haddington was so wealthy that as early as 1617 it is said by some that he had discovered the philosopher's stone. When pressed to reveal his secret, he told the king and his guests that he had acquired his wealth by living according to two simple maxims: never put off to tomorrow what can be done today, and never trust to another's hand what your own can accomplish.[74]

The earl of Clarendon commented that the crown's employment of patronage in Scotland between 1603 and 1637 was injudicious, being squandered on 'obligations cast away upon particular men', a view that was harsh yet not entirely inaccurate. Certainly after 1603 the king had at his disposal the comparatively massive English resources – between £250 000 sterling and £400 000 sterling per annum in fees and gratuities – and he showed no compunction in lavishing gifts on his Scottish friends, much to the irritation of their English hosts. By 1610, the Scots at court had received at least £10 614 sterling in pensions, £88 280 sterling in cash, £133 100 sterling in old debts and £11 093 sterling in annuities.[75] Those members of the Scots-dominated bedchamber were to the fore in managing the privy purse, selling pensions, collecting old debts, exploiting indirect grants and in creaming off revenue from commercial activities in which the crown had a stake. Men like the earls of Dunbar, Somerset, Carlisle and Holdernesse acquired undreamt-of sums of money along with lands, offices and title in England. John Ramsay was created earl of Holdernesse in 1620, and five years later this younger son of a minor Border landowner was able to negotiate an exchange of lands with the crown that gave him an annual landed income of £5000 sterling from scattered English estates in Lancaster, Cambridge and Huntingdonshire.[76]

Office holding in Scotland and England was less venal than in much of Europe, but places in the bedchamber and privy chamber were so lucrative that in 1622 the second earl of Mar was advised to offer between £800 and £900 sterling for a privy chamber position for a younger son that paid £200 sterling per annum. Apart from Sevenhampton in Somerset, Mar sold off his English lands, but received a pension from the chantry rents in the city of London, while his eldest son, lord Erskine, was gifted £300 sterling per annum from the English treasury in 1619. The Erskines were doing very well in England.[77] Both James VI and Charles I deliberately enticed the heads of the grandee houses of Lennox and Hamilton to reside at court, showering them with gifts of every kind. By the 1630s, the third marquis of Hamilton enjoyed, in addition to pensions and cash gifts, control of the large budget that went with his office of master of the horse, he had a share in the wine trade, the right to license hackney cabs in London, salt works in Durham and Northumberland, a partnership in a Derbyshire lead mine, interests in the London coal market, copper mining in Cornwall, the silk trade, Irish plantations and Newfoundland, and he was involved in the establishing of a West India Company.[78] Scots also had access after 1603 to Irish patronage, and the plantation policy adopted by the crown in Ulster opened up opportunities for many land-hungry nobles among whom the first earl of Abercorn, the third lord Ochiltree and the first lord Burleigh were the most successful.[79]

One of the principal reasons why early modern rulers appointed nobles to office was to exploit their private resources, and it was unsurprising, therefore, to find nobles using whatever opportunities came their way to recover such expenditure. Even the regent Morton's friends admitted to the corrupt practices that characterised his rule, while in 1599 the master of Elphinstone exploited his office of treasurer to ensure that almost 25 per cent of the gifts passing under the privy seal were granted to one of his kinsmen. Naturally, political enemies made much of corruption charges; for example, the fifth earl of Bothwell accused his arch-enemy, Thirlestane, of massive corruption in office such that 'of a beggar he has made himself "puisanter" than any two earls.' Scotstarvit's portrait of his colleagues in government suggests universal corruption, villifying the first earl of Traquair as a man who used his position in the treasury to make a fortune, defrauding the king and colluding in other forms of sharp practice.[80] Only occasionally were corrupt officials exposed, as was the first lord Scone in 1608 when it emerged he had struck a deal with the customs farmers to defraud the king, or in 1630 when the first lord Napier reluctantly resigned as treasurer depute, having been accused of underhand dealings in wardships.[81] Not surprisingly, the loss of office suffered by a man like lord Napier could be extremely damaging, and the seventh earl of Menteith's disgrace in 1633 was financially disastrous; his successors were still trying to claw their way out of the mess in the latter half of the century.[82]

Even honourable retirement brought its problems. It was said of the second earl of Mar that while he acquired a vast landed fortune throughout his lifetime, 'yet was his estate nothing bettered therby ... for all that it envanished, and melted like snow off a dyke'. Mar was a royal favourite and councillor for decades before his appointment as treasurer in 1616, an office that carried an annual salary of £4000 and had been described even in 1561 as the most profitable in Scotland. When he finally agreed to resign in 1630, he negotiated with his successor a generous compensation package that provided £4000 per annum and the impost of thirty tuns of wine for the rest of his life. Unfortunately, Mar's accumulated debts in 1631 stood at £83 838, more than twice his income of £35 504, and while he paid off £16 400 of the debt that year, he was forced into mortgaging lands to twice the value of this sum and into feuing on the Aberdeenshire estates. Now that the earl was no longer treasurer, however, his creditors rushed to demand payment. By April 1633, Mar's debts stood at £292 808, while his son, lord Erskine, also owed £225 370, a combined debt of over half a million pounds. In November 1633, the depressed old earl wrote despairingly to his successor as treasurer, the sixth earl of Morton, of 'the greatt streatts that I am into be my sons foleis, a thing of no less consequens than the utter reuine of my houss' and he begged to be paid outstanding pensions. Mar was writing letters about the financial catastrophe in December 1634, the month he died, while his son and grandson were still heavily engaged for the debts in the 1640s. Yet in spite of this apparent shambles, Mar's net testament was worth £75 972 in 1634, ten times more than his father's who had been regent at the time of his death in 1572.[83] The house of Mar was not ruined by the loss of the treasurer's office and was much wealthier in the 1630s than it had been in the 1560s. However, its dependence upon royal favour was also greater, and the loss of the advantages that came with high political office forced a major restructuring of the family's finances that took years to sort out.

Royal office, therefore, was no guarantee of prolonged wealth. Among the *parlementaire* families of Normandy financial success and failure was experienced, evidence that rising officials were just as vulnerable to shifts in economic fortune as older noble houses, and bankruptcy was more common among the newer nobility whose incomes were predominantly dependent on their offices.[84] In Scotland too crown office was not always an automatic route to wealth, and even well-off courtiers like the first earl of Kellie could find themselves unable to pay debts to family and friends when the flow of cash from the court dried up. Richard Cockburn of Clerkington was a privy councillor and officer of state for thirty-six years, yet when he died he owned as much land as he had when he began his career in crown service.[85] It was common for fees and the pensions attached to them to be years in arrears, usually because the crown did not have the capacity to pay. Following the death of treasurer Dunbar in 1611 and the collapse of the Great Contract in England, the extent of the crown's financial weakness became known. Economies were made, new taxes were voted and councillors tried to cut a pensions bill that was consuming an inordinate proportion of the royal income. It also attempted, with little success, to buy back grants and pensions.[86] A lack of cash and 'his Majesteis too greit liberalitie' frustrated the best efforts of James VI's officials, who were in no doubt that the multiplication of pensions 'hath so increased his Majesteis chairges heir as thair is no possibilitie that this estait can subsist'.[87] Under Charles I, the situation worsened as royal income fell, expenditure rose as a consequence of war, and pension arrears mounted. By 1632, the first viscount Stirling was owed £72 000 in pension arrears; hence the scheme to coin copper as compensation and from which it was hoped he would derive sufficient profit to offset the losses from the Nova Scotia scheme. In 1634, a commission of inquiry into the exchequer reported that while the ordinary fees and allowances of royal servants stood at £14 490, the total pensions bill was £169 130 out of an annual expenditure of £302 859, royal debts were £946 487 and the king was paying £78 648 in interest.[88]

Such a dependence on royal pensions threatened the financial and therefore the political independence of the higher nobility, as was the case elsewhere in, for example, Spain and France. That relationship is colourfully invoked by the story of Agnes Gray, countess of Menteith, camping on the chancellor's doorstep in November 1631 in the hope of getting 22 000 merks owed to her husband by the king. A parallel tale can be found in France in 1624 when the duchess de La Tremoille had to wait outside a government minister's door in the hope of securing a pension for her son. Here too nobles sent their womenfolk to beg for royal largesse.[89] This dependency was recognised by the third earl of Lothian who believed that without his father's pension of £2400 sterling per annum, the family finances would collapse. In the autumn of 1637, he warned Ancram 'if your Lordship perswade not my Lord Tresorer to pay the arrearages of your pension, I thinke I shalbe forced this terme to runn away and lett the creditors catch of the estate that catch may'.[90] From the point of view of the nobility, the substantial increase in pensions after 1603 bridged the gap in the finances of many struggling households. Only in the 1630s, when crown officials embarked on the politically dangerous course of cutting pensions, thus damaging patron-client relationships, did the dangers of such clientage to noble finances become apparent.[91]

## Conclusion

The economic circumstances of the later sixteenth century, and especially those of the early seventeenth century, coupled with the fiscal conditions created by the crown after 1603, offered nobles a range of opportunties to enhance their wealth. For those with the entrepreneurial vision and the appropriate openings, the rewards were enormous. On their own estates, noble landlords pursued new methods of farming and farm management, pushing conservative tenants into improvements. In many localities new markets and fairs sprang up, while some efforts were made to enhance the country's poor communication network. For grain producers especially, the sustained rise in population, coupled with improving climatic conditions and the absence of prolonged warfare, all ensured steady demand at favourable prices. Cattle and sheep farming became more profitable, and nobles formed close associations with urban merchants, leading the way in international marketing. The development of the fishing, timber, coal and salt industries all grew out of the desire of noble landowners to maximise the income from their estates, fuelling exports that were increasingly necessary to redress the kingdom's balance of trade deficit. A smaller number of nobles with court connections became involved in manufacturing through royal monopolies, seeking to profit in the creation of a new industrial base. A handful even extended their interests to colonial and trading ventures outside Europe. Inevitably it was that same circle of nobles with access to the court who were most likely to benefit from royal patronage in the form of pensions, gifts and fees, although the trickle-down effect of this should not be underestimated.

It would be unhelpful to anticipate in all of the above the spirit of those eighteenth-century landlords collectively known as 'improvers'. Nevertheless, it is clear that the Scottish nobility of this earlier age were economically dynamic in their approach to managing their own estates, in using their political power to exploit market conditions, and in accessing the crown's finances. Their entrepreneurial activity was not driven by economic desperation, but by the combination of opportunities and confidence. That dynamism often contrasted with the more restrained and cautious approach of the merchant community, or of their own tenants who lacked adequate risk capital. For most nobles, that risk-taking paid off, and the nobility of the 1630s was wealthier than that of the 1560s. The greater part of their wealth was still drawn from landed incomes, but for many there was a growing dependence on the relationship with the market, whether it be the domestic grain market or the Dutch coal market, all subject to sharp fluctuations in profitability. A significant number of nobles, particularly among the higher nobility, were also funding their expensive lifestyles from the fruits of royal patronage, a precarious and often controversial form of income. Therefore the newly gained wealth was far from invulnerable, especially when the extent of borrowing is also taken into account, a topic that is addressed in a subsequent chapter. Yet these reservations about the stability of noble wealth by the 1630s should not detract from the achievements of previous decades. This was an age when men believed they could shape their future for the better, when they caught hold of a vision, whether it be in the laird of Philorth's scheme to build a new town at Fraserburgh or the earl of Stirling's dream of creating a new colony on Nova Scotia. Such dreams were not made reality without great energy, ruthlessness and greed that saw kindly tenants dispossessed, coal workers enslaved, fuel prices held high, craftsmen ensnared by unfair monopolies, lesser landowners squeezed out by richer neighbours, and a vicious, never-ending round of quarrelling over the spoils of office. For a nobility whose status depended to some extent on the ostentatious display of wealth, an entrepreneurial spirit was desirable, even necessary, ensuring their continuing economic dominance of Scottish society.

CHAPTER 3

# Expenditure

Nobles everywhere could be identified by their lifestyle, by patterns of consumption and expenditure. Of course, this was never straightforward, even in medieval society, and the whole point of sumptuary legislation was to prevent non-nobles from living in the style of their social superiors. The poor noble blurred the distinctions that wealth was supposed to make visible, and it was this inability to live nobly that manifestly announced a man could no longer claim to belong in noble society. There was also a great range of expectations, so that the consumption of a high-ranking peer was likely to be much more extravagant than a shire baron. Rank was exposed by how well a man lived, although here too there were incongruities like the lord of parliament who failed to keep pace with neighbouring untitled barons. Expenditure and the lifestyle it facilitated, therefore, provided only a rough guide to rank and status. Nevertheless, it is possible to draw attention to some of the broad patterns, to highlight something of what noble families had to overcome in the course of a generational cycle, as well as indicating the daily round of spending, and the more extravagant or unpredictable outlays. Most expenditure was unavoidable, spending being driven by more than simple necessity. The impetus came from within noble society, from the complex demands of a competitive world in which daughters' dowries were rising in value, households were growing ever more sophisticated, building programmes were becoming more elaborate and ambitious, court life was caught up in an apparent spiral of spending, and taxation was rising. As has been demonstrated already, greater and more diverse incomes were fuelling much of this expenditure, but when income was inadequate, there were loans and the accompanying debt which is the topic of the next chapter. Once the mid-sixteenth-century financial problems had been overcome, there was undoubtedly a period of high living for many noble families, a time of confident, indulgent and even wasteful consumption.

## Family Economics

As a means of consolidating and preserving wealth, the noble family was among the most successful institutions in early modern society, outperforming both the Scottish crown and church from the mid-sixteenth century. However, noble houses were subject to pressures created by their own economic life cycles as one generation succeeded another. Contained within this generational rhythm were the various rites of passage: birth, marriage, the education of children, provision for the heir and for younger sons and daughters, death and inheritance. All of these were predictable, although the timing of each was never known, and a succession of circumstances could create havoc with the financial stability of the lineage. The birth of a large number of daughters, a series of unexpected deaths, the survival of one too many widows, these created pressures on the noble family that could at best provoke financial instability for a generation, at worst set in motion its irrevocable decline.

Compared to most European nobilities, the relatively strong position of wives in Scotland ensured that marriage was particularly important in the economic history of the landed family. That marriage was an institution of enormous economic importance is clear from any cursory examination of a marriage contract, most of which was concerned with financial arrangements. The crucial business in the often tortuous negotiations that preceded agreement on a contract centred on the size of the wife's jointure, the portion of her husband's estate set aside for her maintenance, and the size of the tocher, or dowry, she brought to the marriage. The principles upon which these negotiations were conducted were grounded on Roman law, being preserved in *Regiam Majestatem*. Essentially a prospective husband (or his father) could negotiate to infeft his wife and himself in a conjunct fee of up to one-third of his heritage, one-third being the default required by law if no sum was agreed in the contract. If no contract was agreed, a widow could claim as terce a full third of her husband's estate at the time of his death. Since the size of the estate was likely to be greater at death than at the time of marriage, wives having no right to any lands acquired by their husbands after the marriage, the latter preferred to negotiate a conjunct fee at the outset. Greater landlords were the most determined to reduce the rights of their wives under the law, persuading them to make do with less than the law permitted. There were restrictions on the gifts husbands could make to their wives, these being revocable if there was a marriage contract already defining the wife's rights, although lawyers found ways to circumvent these regulations, and a widow inherited half of her husband's movable property, or one-third if he had children *in familia*.[1]

In law, a husband controlled the conjunct fee in his lifetime, and only at death did his wife assume her rights over it as her widow's terce, in effect claiming an endowment paid for by her tocher. There was some debate over how much freedom husbands had to dispose of all or part of the conjunct fee, and many wives were vulnerable to greedy, stupid or bullying husbands. In 1627, fourteen years after his marriage, sir John Grant of Freuchie's wife, Marie Ogilvy, signed away her conjunct rights because Freuchie's friends had advised that 'for the benefit of his estate, [he] should have in his own person the full right and title of the foresaid lands'. This might have been true, and Freuchie might have been a good husband, but the case illustrates the kinds of pressure wives came under to alter marriage contracts in the interests of their husbands. Ante-nuptial agreements might also have to be hammered out with reluctant or awkward fathers who tried to renege on the terms of the marriage contract. Sir Walter Dundas of that Ilk was reluctantly persuaded to pay his son and daughter-in-law 1000 merks per annum as long as they remained in his household, since the conjunct lands in which they were to be infeft turned out to be burdened with debt. Usually a wife could expect that her life rent would be protected if her husband was forfeited, a form of legal death, and thus in 1581 parliament passed an act ratifying the conjunct fee of Margaret Leslie, wife of the forfeited eighth earl of Angus.[2]

A wife's income was usually calculated as a combination of cash and victual. The 1603 contract between James Hamilton, heir to the first marquis of Hamilton, and lady Ann Cunningham, daughter of the sixth earl of Glencairn, agreed that in return for a tocher of 40 000 merks, she would receive the large annual income of fifty-six chalders of grain and £500 in money rent. Some agreements also provided for income from other forms of estate business such as coal or salt.[3] Because the principals in these marriages were commonly young, and in order to reduce costs, often with a view to allowing mortgaged lands set aside for the conjunct fee to be redeemed, contracts might include provision for room and tabling in the parental home, or arrangements for the appointment of an administrator of the lands.[4] The only occasion on which a tocher was returned to a wife's family was when she died within a year and a day of her marriage, unless she had given birth to a child who had been heard to cry out. The early death of a wife, therefore, could produce a windfall such as the 8000 merks pocketed by the eighth earl of Angus as his first wife's tocher in 1573. Two years later, Mary Erskine was dead and had not even left any children for Angus to maintain.[5]

In an age when the position of women in society was increasingly restricted, widows often held powerful positions in noble families.[6] The ninth earl of Crawford died in 1558, making his wife, Catherine Campbell, the richest widow in the kingdom, and at her death twenty years later she left a large net cash sum of £7807. Another rich noblewoman, the twice-widowed Margaret Ker, dowager lady Yester, was described c.1635 as having 'the greatest conjunct fie that any Lady hes in Scotland'.[7] Not surprisingly, therefore, one of the most damaging burdens inflicted on an estate was the longevity of a widow. By 1571, George Leirmonth of Balcomy was so impoverished by the fact that two-thirds of his estate was held by his mother that the regent Mar granted him leave to stay away from all raids or wappinshaws. The fourth earl of Bothwell divorced Jean Gordon in 1567 after a brief marriage, but she remained in possession of her jointure lands in the earldom until her death in 1629. The Buccleuch estates were burdened with a jointure worth 22 000 merks per annum for maintaining Margaret Douglas from the time she was widowed in 1574 – she had only been married six years – until her death sixty-six years later, having outlived her second husband, her son and her grandson.[8]

The burden placed on an estate by widows was especially heavy where more than one survived. Here the law was unequivocal:

> If the father deceas in the fie, his wyfe getts ane terce of the haill landis quhilk is called ane great terce; therefter the sone dyeing, his wyfe falls a terce of the twa part dureing the great tercer's lyfetyme; and efter her decease falls a tearce of the haill, if the sone wes infeft.

The early deaths of the fifth and sixth earls of Menteith in 1564 and 1579 left expensive widows to be maintained by what was a relatively poor estate. In 1580 the seventeen-year-old second earl of Mar was married while his mother was still alive and in possession of her jointure. She resigned her terce and the third part of all her late husband's lands in return for a modest rental of £254 per annum which Mar continued to pay until her death twenty-four years later. The earl's first wife died in the mid-1580s but in 1592 he married again, and there was only a short period when the estate was not supporting two countesses. A seven-year respite followed his mother's death in 1603, before Mar's eldest son married in 1610; once again there were two women to be maintained. This remained the case after Mar's death in 1634, since his widow survived him by a decade, requiring a settlement that satisfied both the dowager countess and her stepson's wife.[9]

There were, therefore, good reasons for children to oppose a father's remarriage. Not only did a new wife demand a jointure, but there might also be younger brothers and sisters who threatened the share of the inheritance. In 1624, the fifty-four-year-old sixth lord Lovat proposed a third marriage to Katherine Rose, a course his friends and family failed to dissuade him from because of the burden this would place on the estate. Those fears were justified as lady Lovat outlived her husband, who died in 1633, leaving his heirs with a jointure to support for another twenty-five years.[10] Like Mar, therefore, some heirs took steps to buy out the interest in the estate of what were, in effect, unproductive females, be they mothers, stepmothers, aunts, grandmothers or sisters-in-law, thus replacing infeftment with income. In the years following his father's death in 1593, the second earl of Orkney made a succession of agreements with his tough-minded mother who surrendered her terce in return for 8000 merks in arrears, 3600 merks per annum with an undertaking by the earl to collect her remaining mails and duties, and the payment of £4250 as a third share of the value of his father's moveables. In spite of the immediate expense, such agreements were favoured by the male kindred, and when William Fraser of Struy, the tutor of Lovat, succeeded in marrying off the fifth lord Lovat's mother to Donald Gorm Macdonald of Sleat, he was applauded in the family history because he 'did wisely in buying off the jointer'.[11] There was no time limit on when these agreements might be made. Margaret Lyon, countess of Cassillis, had been widowed in 1576 but it was 1623 before her grandson bought out the conjunct infeftment and life rent in return for an annual annuity of only 4000 merks.[12] Where a second family was involved, the pressure to strike a deal was greater. Following his father's death in 1631, sir Colin Campbell of Glenorchy bought out his stepmother's terce for 10 000 merks and his stepbrother's portion for another 7000 merks.[13] Clearly Glenorchy wanted this step-family off his lands as quickly as possible. Many women, therefore, calculated that it was better to arrive at a mutually agreeable settlement rather than enter into a prolonged dispute, and most sons tried to arrive at reasonable and fair arrangements.

For many nobles, the coming of age and marriage of their eldest son often meant a significant loss of revenue. Yet in Scotland, unlike in Normandy or Naples, heirs did not postpone marriage during the life of their fathers in order to reduce the financial burden on the family in the form of separate households or, in the case of their predeceasing fathers, in the form of a widow and her children.[14] Instead, Scottish nobles placed a premium on ensuring the male succession of their houses, encouraging sons to marry relatively young, usually around the age of twenty-one. As in England, the marriage contract was commonly the opportunity for a financial agreement between a father and his eldest son. In the 1628 marriage contract between the master of Angus and a daughter of the third duke of Lennox, his father agreed to resign to his son the entire Angus earldom with reservations that left the earl as a life renter.[15] The creation of a life tenancy allowed Angus to retain economic control of the estate, his son's legal title to the estate was secured, and provision was made for his son's household as a married man with a wife to maintain. Meanwhile, the tocher that the heir's new wife brought to the marriage gave Angus an infusion of cash. Where the heir was married to an heiress who brought with her land rather than money, the short-term financial gain was likely to be sacrificed for the long-term interests of the house. On 1 September 1612, sir John Hume of Coldenknows entered into a formal agreement with his eldest son, sir James Hume of Whitrig, and his wife, lady Anna Hume, daughter and co-heiress of the earl of Dunbar. The two parties agreed to live together in the same house at equal charges for as long as 'they can agrie amongs themselffis according to the bill of household quhilk they sall sett doune and subscryve with their handis', lady Anna being charged to go over the weekly accounts. Coldenknows sacrificed the possibility of a cash windfall in order to acquire the Dunbar estates in Scotland, although he drove a hard bargain, burdening his son with his own debts and the marriages of younger brothers and sisters.[16]

Even for an enormously wealthy French lord like Anne de Montmorency,

Table 3.1 Average birth/maturation/survival rate of peers' daughters, 1560–1637

| | Average no. of daughters | Average no. of adult daughters | Average no. of surviving daughters |
|---|---|---|---|
| 1560–1637 | 2.8 | 2.6 | 2.5 |
| 16th century | 3 | 2.9 | 2.7 |
| 17th century | 2.6 | 2.3 | 2.2 |

provision for his four male and six female children became an overwhelming problem in his later years, and Gaspard de Saulx-Tavannes suggested that his noble readers should 'marry few daughters for that is the ruin of a noble house'. Because of their significant inheritance rights, daughters and sisters placed an enormous burden on an estate, and throughout Europe, from Naples to Ireland, the value of dowries was rising, possibly at the expense of younger sons. Among the Spanish nobility the single biggest item of expenditure was dowries. Even in Venice, where the state tried to regulate the size of dowries, they rose sharply, fed by the growing volume of wealth in female hands, the large donations made by relatives to dowry funds, and by fathers topping up their daughters' dowries above what was expected in order to protect their own honour.[17] On average, Scottish peers produced 2.8 daughters, with a fall from 3.0 in the sixteenth-century sample to 2.6 in the seventeenth-century sample. The average number surviving childhood, and therefore requiring dowries, was 2.6, but this figure conceals enormous variation (see Table 3.1). Some families had no daughters at all, a mixed blessing in that while it removed the financial outlay on tochers, it also reduced their ability to make marital alliances with other houses. Some had to cope with the burden of many daughters; the seventh earl of Argyll and the first marquis of Douglas had ten adult daughters, while the fourth earl Marischal and the fourth lord Gray had eight daughters who survived into adulthood.

Tocher sizes in Scotland varied greatly, although somewhere between one-fifth and one-tenth of the conjunct fee might be a reasonable estimate of the 'going rate', but they were certainly increasing in amount. In 1561, the tocher paid by the rich fourth earl Marischal on the marriage of his eldest daughter to lord James Stewart, the queen's half-brother, was 10 000 merks, a huge sum in a decade when between 3000 and 5000 would be more typical, even among the higher nobility. By the 1580s, sums upwards of 6000 merks were relatively common, and in 1581 the fifth earl of Atholl finally exceeded the Marischal tocher in providing his sister with 15 000 merks for her marriage to the eleventh earl of Crawford. The marriage between the baronial houses of Buccleuch and Cessford in 1586 saw 10 000 merks change hands, clear evidence that over the previous quarter-century inflation had driven up the size of tochers. By the end of the 1590s, a marriage between the baronial families of Tullibardine and Wemyss was accompanied by a tocher of 15 000 merks, while in 1595 the extraordinary sum of 30 000 merks was paid to the sixth lord Lovat on the occasion of his marriage to the only daughter of the first lord Doune. Marriages to barons or younger sons of peers remained within 10 000 and 15 000 merks, but the higher nobility could command more than twice those sums: 40 000 merks for the marriage of a daughter of the sixth earl of Glencairn to the first marquis of Hamilton's heir in 1603, 53 000 merks for the marriage of the only daughter of the first earl of Perth to the thirteenth earl of Sutherland in 1629, 60 000 merks in the same year for the marriage of the youngest daughter of the first lord Carnegie to the fifth earl of Montrose. The proposed tocher in an unfulfilled contract of 1641 between the children of the first marquis of Argyll and the third marquis of Hamilton was a staggering 100 000 merks.[18] The surviving number of marriage contracts is small, but a random selection of sixty-six contracts shows an average tocher of 6000 merks in the period 1560–79, doubling in value to an average of 12 900 merks for the period 1580–99, increasing sharply again to an average of 22 600 merks for the period 1600–19; only then did the rate of increase slow down so that for the years 1620–37 the average tocher was set at 25 500 merks. This evidence suggests that tochers were eroded in value by inflation in the later sixteenth century, and that the first quarter of the seventeenth century represented a catching-up process against a background of relatively steady prices and improved incomes.

By the later sixteenth century, marriage portions for daughters in Scotland were exceeding the value of a mother's tocher, possibly reflecting concerns about rising prices. In 1574, James Leslie, master of Rothes, agreed that any daughters born of his marriage to Margaret Lindsay, only daughter of the sixth lord Lindsay, would be provided with tochers to the sum of 10 000 merks, 25 per cent more than his own wife's dowry. On the other hand, the increasing determination to use male entails to exclude daughters might account for this rise as a form of compensation. Portions were a fixed cash sum, their real worth being less protected than a wife's jointure, much of which represented a share of the landed income that was likely to rise in value with the improvement in estate incomes. The effect, however, was to ensure that while entails concentrated land ownership in the hands of eldest sons, a significant proportion of income was set aside to sustain their sisters, diluting the concentration of wealth.[19] The marriage contracts of parents often explicitly directed that a woman's tocher should be used to finance her daughters' marriages, providing the husband with a fund he could draw on during the marriage but which he must at least restore in preparation for his own daughters' marriages. The system was not unlike that prevailing in France, rather than in southern Italy where women had greater control over their own dowries and where a mother's dowry was not used to fund those of her daughters, this being the sole responsibility of her husband. Some fathers used their testaments to ensure their daughters' rights were protected, such as when in 1608 the tenth earl of Angus bound his eldest son to provide sums of 6000 merks and 2000 merks for his sisters' dowries. It was also possible for mothers to make top-up legacies towards the cost of their daughters' tochers, such as the £4000 the countess of Crawford left her daughter, Margaret, in 1578.[20]

Cash bequests, however, were rarely able to meet the needs of unmarried females and instead the income from portions of the estate had to be set aside, or loans arranged using land as collateral. When the seventh lord Gray succeeded his father in 1612, he had five unmarried sisters, his eldest sister having already been married in 1609 to sir John Wemyss of that Ilk with a tocher of 20 000 merks. In the years that followed, his total outlay was in the region of 50 000 merks, a heavy drain on Gray's finances.[21] If a marriage produced only female heirs who faced disinheritance and demands for high compensation, particular problems ensued. When sir Patrick Murray of Langshaw married his first wife, Margaret Hamilton, it was agreed that he would provide 15 000 merks to be divided among any heirs female of the marriage. Langshaw's wife died, having given birth to one daughter, Christian, and it fell to the girl's maternal kinsmen to ensure that her father made provision for her marriage. He agreed to pay her 20 000 merks on her sixteenth birthday.[22] Marriage contracts usually anticipated such an eventuality. In the 1596 contract of marriage agreed between Alexander Fraser, younger of Philorth, and Margaret Abernethy, sister of the eighth lord Saltoun, it was recognised that in the case of there being no sons, and since the estate was entailed to heirs male, provision would be made for any daughters. Sums for tochers of between 13 000 merks for one daughter and 30 000 merks for more than three daughters were agreed. Until their fourteenth birthdays, when these sums would be made over to their curators, the daughters were to be 'honestlie interteneit and brocht up according to thair birth be the air of tailzie'. If any of the daughters died, however, the sum set aside for her would not pass to her sisters but would revert to the heir of tailzie. The latter, therefore, would inherit an estate and with it an obligation to provide for the disinherited female heirs.[23]

It is possible that these settlements were designed to set a limit on a father's generosity to his daughters, protecting the interests of his heir. In 1615, James Erskine, younger son of the second earl of Mar, agreed a contract with Mary Douglas, countess of Buchan, in which her tocher of 40 000 merks was equalled by the portion set aside for an eldest daughter. However, if there were additional daughters the total sums allocated to portions would rise to at least 60 000 merks, with the eldest daughter and the father standing to be penalised if such a scenario arose. The fifth earl of Montrose's marriage contract similarly bound him to finance portions up to one-third above the tocher of 60 000 merks which his wife brought him in

1629. In addition, he promised 'to educate and aliment them [his daughters] according to their rank'.[24] A family with a large number of daughters faced real problems in funding them, especially if the daughters' interests were protected by their mother's marriage contract. However, on average there was a balancing out of income and expenditure. Between John Grant of Freuchie's own contract of marriage in 1591 and the marriage of the last of his children in 1613, the value of tochers brought in to the family by his wife and daughter-in-law was 23 000 merks. Meanwhile, Freuchie paid out 26 500 merks in tochers for a sister and daughters. That 3500 merks difference was the sum Freuchie paid over and above the terms agreed by him in 1591, suggesting that the equilibrium was upset only by generosity to a favoured younger daughter whose tocher of 9500 merks was nearly as much as that of her eldest sister.[25] Almost certainly the best guarantor of a daughter being provided with a good tocher was not her parent's marriage contract, but a father who was alive at the time of her own marriage.

Scottish fathers, unlike their Italian counterparts who often prevented younger children from marrying, tried to provide for all their children, preferring to take on the financial burden rather than risk biological extinction, a task in which they were aided by the additional resources made available through the secularisation of church lands and crown patronage. The fifth earl of Glencairn granted one younger son, John, the forty shilling lands of Ross in the barony of Kilmaronock in Dumbarton, while another, William, was appointed rector of Inchcailleoch on Loch Lomond.[26] The first lord Doune made good provision for all his children. He arranged the marriage of his eldest son to a wealthy heiress, the countess of Moray, he negotiated a good marriage for his eldest daughter before his death in 1590, and was able to leave substantial cash and goods to his five younger children.[27] In the Glenorchy family history, the listing of sir Duncan Campbell's many children, legitimate and illegitimate, is followed by another list of his extensive landed conquests and their allocation to younger sons. This astonishingly successful Highland baron provided tochers for two sisters and nine daughters amounting to 150 000 merks. These financial settlements were especially complicated when, as in the Glenorchy case, children were born of a second or even a third marriage.[28] These arrangements for younger children could prove to be burdensome indeed. The sixth lord Lovat was married twice, the children of his second marriage proving to be an expensive burden. In 1617, the eldest son of this marriage, sir Simon Fraser of Inverlochy, was married to a daughter of the laird of Moncreiff. Lord Lovat sold the estate at Glenelg, bought lands with an income of 8000 merks a year in which he infeft Inverallochy, and gave him the house at Bunchrive. Unfortunately, sir Simon died in 1622 and his widow continued to enjoy her jointure.[29]

## Ordinary Expenditure

Early modern nobilities had at best a haphazard approach to the accounting of expenditure. However, among the most common and tedious record sources in any noble family's archive are the thousands of discharges that provide overwhelming evidence of their purchasing power.[30] Most bills were paid eventually, and that evidence should be borne in mind when focusing on some of the difficulties that arose when spending outstripped income. This hazard was especially prevalent because of the spending patterns encouraged by the social and cultural trends of the day. Conspicuous consumption was not a new development in the sixteenth century, but greater wealth among more people aspiring to a noble lifestyle meant that extravagance undid more nobles. This was common to most European states, Venice being something of an exception, and was most extreme in the likes of Spain, France and Poland where nobilities were largest.[31]

At the centre of every noble family's lifestyle was the household, that large, porous, constantly changing and often peripatetic body of kin, friends, clients and servants that revolved around the head of the house. Thus the fifth earl of Argyll was praised as 'King of the Gael, the man who maintains the thronged court, prosperous and wealthy'.[32] In size, Scottish households fell within a similar range to those in England. The duke of Châtelherault's household in 1566 numbered thirty-one servants and forty gentlemen who were dependent on him. As a young man in the dangerous political circumstances of 1582, the second earl of Mar had a household of forty-three people; when he became lord treasurer in 1616, almost ninety people are listed; by 1631 the retired earl's household contained a staff of eighty who consumed almost fifty-six chalders of grain and a further £7528 13s 4d worth of purchased foodstuffs. In 1637, even the widowed and elderly first earl of Haddington, a man who had risen through the ranks of nobility as a royal lawyer and councillor, was employing a household of twenty-six male and two female servants, of whom two were cooks, five footmen and one a coachman.[33] The annual cost of Haddington's household was only £792 13s 4d, a small sum to such an enormously rich man, but others were more extravagant. The second earl of Orkney's pompous lifestyle included being escorted everywhere on his domain by a train of gentlemen and guards. Dining was announced by 'thrie trumpetters that soundit still till the meat of the first service was set at table, and siclyke at the second service, and consequentlie efter the grace'. Yet even Orkney's 'princelie and royall revenew' of £56315 by 1600 could not sustain this lifestyle, and he was bankrupt within a few years.[34] The first earl of Buccleuch maintained a large and generous household in the 1620s that included twenty-four pensioners who cost 14000 merks per annum in fees:

> The Barons of Bucleugh they kept at their call
> Four-and-twenty gentlemen in their hall,

All being of his name and kin,
Each had two servants to wait on them.

Buccleuch too found the maintenance costs to be ruinous and was forced to economise. Concern at household costs forced the tenth lord Forbes to scribble a memo in 1620, highlighting the need to 'minut what number of servands I will have in household and what conditione to every ane and to note what is resting [= owing] them and the terme of their entry, and remove all ydill and deboschit men and pay them justly qhat is resting them'.[35]

Gordonstoun urged that a noble should be 'frugall in spending what God sendeth you; but spair no charges when a mater concernes your honour or credit'. Hospitality was central to honour, being a complex exchange of gifts, reflecting closely on reputations. When James VI visited the sixth earl of Glencairn's house at Finlayston in September 1601, the earl's wife refused to greet sir John Ramsay with the customary kiss because he had disparagingly said the earl and his wife 'were misers and grieved to give a good meal'.[36] Entertaining royalty was particularly costly, amounting to a form of voluntary taxation, and the royal progresses of 1617 and 1633 proved so hugely expensive that one English courtier thought the experience 'did very much contribute to the kindling of that fire which shortly after broke out in so terrible a combustion'. Political office might also demand lavish entertainment, as in the summer and autumn of 1607 when the second duke of Lennox, high commissioner to parliament, ran up an expenses account of £1000, including £70 16s 8d on ninety-five gallons of ale 'furneist at the parliament'.[37]

More ordinarily, the ideal of the large household remained, and visitors noted that Scots 'living then in factions, used to keepe many followers, and so consumed their revenew of victuals, living in some want of money'. Robert Bowes poured scorn on this hospitality in 1593, explaining that in Scotland a banquet was merely an occasion at which was served 'provisions of dillicattis havinge spyce meate and wynes' that might take the place of a breakfast and as such was 'of no great matter or value'.[38] This was a typical piece of English misunderstanding of the relaxed tone of Scottish manners. As in France, where contemporaries described noble households as places of *nourriture*, the provision of hospitality was essential to the sustaining of clientages, while feasting was a central ritual of lordship. French magnate houses also developed a formal system of purveyorship to avoid the worst effects of the market on their household costs, a practice that was found in Scotland among the great households like those of the earls of Argyll.[39] More commonly, the direct farming of part of the estate provided the necessary raw produce, while rents in kind allowed nobles to entertain and maintain large households relatively inexpensively. Some nobles, like the earls of Argyll, continued to pursue a peripatetic round of consuming the produce of different estates in their various castles.[40]

Especially in the Highlands, this society hugely enjoyed the wining and dining of guests, feasting having an important political function in focusing attention on the wealth and power of a clan chief. When in 1618 the laird of Grant unexpectedly found himself host to a large company of lords and their servants, he entertained lavishly for four days. At 'every meale foure longe tables [were] furnished with all varieties: Our first and second course being threescore dishes at one board; and after that alwayes a banquet'.[41] By the early seventeenth century, the growing sophistication of tastes was apparent in the cook recommended to sir David Lindsay of Edzell in 1608 because 'thair is nocht the better of him in the schyr'; in the twelfth earl of Sutherland's request in 1615 for his brother to send him some good tobacco which 'is in more estimatione here away then ane better gift'; and in the house of Glenorchy's partiality for exotic spices, Spanish oranges and French wine drunk from imported crystal glasses. Such luxuries were costly. The sixth lord Lovat 'kept a great famely, vast expense, and spending at home and abroad', exporting salmon in order to buy the large quantities of French wine his household enjoyed, all of which contributed to his growing debts.[42] Spiritual writers were not alone in urging moderation. James VI expressed a suspicion of culinary finesse, recommending public dining, plain food and straightforward table manners. Gordonstoun too exorted his nephew to mix generosity with prudence, urging him to 'let your hospitalitie be moderat, equaled to the measure of your estate, rather bountifull then nigardlie, yet not prodigall nor over costlie … I have not hard nor knowen any man growe poore by keiping ane ordinarie, decent and thriftie table'. Most of the time, nobles lived relatively simply, carefully managing their household finances, as is evident in the scrutinised accounts of the tenth earl of Angus in the late 1590s or of the sixth earl of Eglinton in 1616–17.[43]

The most expensive luxury import was wine, which figures prominently in household accounts like those of Eglinton, who drank imported Spanish wine as well as domestically produced *aqua vitae*; French claret formed the single biggest item on the earl of Mar's accounts for 1618–19. The 1605 convention of the estates reiterated the exemption from paying customs on wine imports for nobles and gentlemen who intended to use it in their own houses. Customs officers who tried to enforce the impost were liable to punishment, and nobles were expected to provide testimonials that the wine was intended for domestic consumption, although some were prepared to pay over the odds to get a good vintage before it was snapped up on the quayside.[44] Fynes Moryson related that the Scots deserved their reputation for intemperate drinking, particularly of wine and beer, and an anonymous source indicated that the Scots had taken on the Dutch habit of heavy after-dinner drinking that left guests smashed out of their heads. Certainly the visit of the Danish duke of Holstein in 1598 was an occasion when 'the god Baccus is a great guider among us'. Unfairly perhaps, crown officials targeted the 'extraordinair drinking of strong wynis and acquavitie' in Highland society, where the drinking culture did not necessarily lead to drunkenness.[45] In fact, drunkenness was not approved of in noble society. In spite of his own liking for alcohol, James VI condemned drunkenness as 'a beastlie vice', and Gordonstoun warned against over-drinking which 'impaires health, consumes wealth, and transformes a man into a beast, a sinne of no single ranke, that never walks unattended with a traine of misdemeanours at the heeles'. A similar philosophy guided the sixth lord Lovat, who allowed his household free access to the stocks of beer and ale in his cellar while refusing to have in his retinue any gentleman who was seen drunk, and he immediately paid off servants who were found inebriated.[46]

This was an age in which throughout Europe both sexes in noble society spent large sums on clothing and other forms of personal adornment. Scotland was no different, and sumptuary legislation repeatedly sought to combat wastefulness which contributed to the country's balance of trade deficit, seeking to maintain the visual distinctions of status. Men whose lands were worth less than 2000 merks, or fifty chalders of victual per annum, were prohibited from wearing expensive fabrics, and in 1621 a hypocritical parliament unsuccessfully tried to outlaw expensive feasting and funerals. However, such attempts at regulating dress often had the opposite effect, encouraging nobles to maintain the standards of their rank.[47] James VI made pious pleas for moderation in clothing, aspiring to a dress code that was 'proper, cleanely, comely and honest, wearing your clothes in a carelesse, yet comely forme'. His views on the purpose of clothing were essentially pragmatic, despising effeminate clothing, the use of perfume, long hair and long nails. Gordonstoun's experiences of James's court led him to advise his nephew to be 'not superflous in your rayment lyk a deboshed waster, not yet too baise lyke a miserable wretche'. The trick was never to follow taste too closely, thus avoiding ever being out of fashion, although 'at parliament and hie tymes spare not to be apparreled as your rank and qualetie requireth'.[48]

However, the spread of wealth undermined the half-hearted official efforts at control, and Lethington's 'Satire on the toun ladyes' painted a picture of immoderate and luxurious living by the wives of the nobility and rich merchants even in the mid-sixteenth century. In the early seventeenth century, Denmile noted, 'men are become so luxurious in ther apparrell and clothing that scarce can aney difference be perceaved betuix nobles and the comon rable'. Similar sentiments were expressed by John Wemyss, minister at Brechin, who conceded that clothing was useful 'to distinguish callings, as the noble from the base', but regretted the passing of a simpler age for one in which nobles changed their clothes every day.[49] Indeed, most of the higher-ranking Scottish nobles spent more on clothes than they paid in taxes. In 1610, lord Keith, eldest son and heir of the fifth earl Marischal blew £2448 on clothes, while in 1618–19 the eleventh earl of Angus and his wife purchased £1728 worth of clothes, silks and buttons. Special occasions offered opportunities for even greater extravagance, such as in the spring of 1633, prior to the king's state visit, when the sixth earl of Cassillis went on a spending spree.[50]

The regal union also had an impact on spending. Anna Livingston, countess of Eglinton, had a friend shop in London for her so that in January 1614 she was able to procure items of 'the best fashone', keeping up with the court even at a great distance. This greater level of consumption was reflected in personal jewellery, in the new luxury items on the market, like the watch the third earl of Lothian sent down to his father in London to have repaired, and in household furnishings which grew more elaborate and luxurious over this period.[51] Such richly adorned and decorated people also found a new way to travel as coaches gained in popularity in the early seventeenth century.[52] Even funerals grew increasingly expensive in the early seventeenth century. The tomb of the regent Moray in St Giles cost £134, but the cost of the entertainment provisions alone for the funeral of the first earl of Buccleuch in 1633 amounted to £184. At the second earl of Mar's funeral in 1634, £1737 was laid out for cloth and buttons, while the funeral of a baron like sir Duncan Campbell of Glenorchy cost £4667 in 1631. The funeral expenses of the second lord Melville in 1635 amounted to £946, accounting for one-fifth of the family's expenditure for that year.[53] However, not all nobles succumbed to the fashion for excess, and when the old dowager countess of Sutherland lay dying in July 1628, her niggardly son, sir Alexander Gordon of Navidale, tried to avoid an elaborate funeral which 'wald noche be done without gryt expensis, as also seing it was against the custome off our howss'.[54]

## Extraordinary Expenditure

Gordonstoun expressed the view that ideally a man should hold back 25 per cent of his income for extraordinary expenses, 'otherways you shall leive lyke a rich begger in continuall wants'. What proportion was commonly committed to extraordinary expenses cannot be ascertained, but at least one-quarter of the income seems reasonable for what one English gentleman of the early seventeenth century listed as most damaging to a family's financial health: lawsuits, expenses related to building, serving the prince and the marriage of a daughter (which has already been discussed).[55] Obviously, some control could be exercised over litigation, building costs and royal service, although there was a risk in noble society that a failure to invest in defending the family's interests, in display or in service could damage the reputation and long-term interests of the lineage.

There is no doubt that a good lawyer was a valuable asset to any noble house. In 1574, it was a grateful John Stewart of Minto who wrote to tell John Sharp, then an aggressive young lawyer at the early stage of his career, that 'ane werk man is worth his waige'. More commonly, Scots joined in the clamour throughout Europe against the rising costs of litigation, and as early as the mid-sixteenth century Lethington satirised a legal process that was becoming prohibitively expensive:

> The Barrounis say, that they have far mair spendit
> Upon the law, or thair mater endit,
> Nor it wes wourth: Thairfoir richt fair thay rew
> To found ane plie that ever thay pretendit;
> Bot left it to thair airis to persew.

As a court of session judge, Lethington knew what he was talking about, and over succeeding decades litigation grew ever more expensive, giving credence to the saying that those who went to law 'had gott their mother's malison [= curse]'. Alexander Hume savagely satirised the law courts in his poetry, accusing lawyers and their clerks of every kind of corrupt and immoral practice, among which he listed their preference for wealthy and noble clients regardless of the justice of the cause. It was with good reason, therefore, that sir William Ker advised his father in 1631 to avoid litigation as it 'wilbe tedious and almost desperate', while the countess of Haddington moaned of money worries to her son in 1635 because of 'my mesarable law maters that vexis me to the hairt'. Legal expenses were resented, and while informal justice had never been cheap, gifts, hospitality and maintenance being a drain on resources, the increasing professionalisation of the business of justice within the formal law and the court system gave lawyers and judges greater control over its cost.[56]

Those noble grumbles about paying legal fees were not always justified. At Martinmas 1633 the sixth earl of Cassillis paid out £1500 as interest on his debts, then standing at £88 200, including only £186 13s 4d to the lawyer who handled his complex affairs in Edinburgh.[57] On the other hand, when the eighth lord Forbes drew up a financial statement in 1601, detailing the reasons for wadsetting land with a redemption value of 68 000 merks over the previous thirty years, he highlighted the fact that 28 per cent of the total debt had been raised to cover legal fees 'spendit and debursit ... in craving justice'. As the laird of Glenorchy's lawyer told him in 1616, Edinburgh 'is verray deare in all thingis'. John MacLeod of Dunvegan, a Highland chief with relatively little cash income, spent as much as £3632 9s 4d on pursuing a court case in Edinburgh over a twelve-month period in 1636–7, around one-third of his net annual income. Such an expense explains Gordonstoun's decision in 1617 that 'the house of Southerland wold not weill beir or permitt to enter in sutes of law, being overburdened alreadie with debt'. He therefore went about trying to settle any quarrels by mediation.[58] Of course, that option was not always available and the cost of not fighting a case in the law courts could be even higher.

Building works were the single biggest capital investment a noble household was likely to make, skilled labour and quality materials being expensive. In much of Scotland, it was still necessary to expend money on defence works, and in Orkney during the 1560s, Gilbert Balfour of Westray constructed a massive and austere fortification with sixty-one gun loops at Notland that was solely military in design and function.[59] During the civil war material damage was inflicted on the castle infrastructure of much of the country – for example, at Hamilton where in 1570 the duke of Châtelherault's palace was 'made levell with the ground'. Many other houses were sacked, some never to be repaired, others were only rebuilt at enormous cost over decades.[60] It was precisely because castles and houses represented such a heavy investment of money that the crown chose to punish men by destroying them.[61]

War apart, many nobles faced major rebuilding programmes as castles were modernised; the earls of Angus, for example, possessed a string of what were essentially late medieval castles all in need of improvement and adaptation. Fortunately, the gradual restoration of peace and the availability of credit contributed towards a remarkable building boom, almost paralleling that in England.[62] The takeover of ecclesiastical property also resulted in extensive remodelling of existing buildings to suit the need of their new secular owners, as at Newbattle. Meanwhile, the feuing movement gave many tenants the security necessary for it to be cost-effective to invest in their houses. It was a sign of the growing wealth of sir Robert Melville of Murdocairny that in December 1592 he was able to buy the dilapidated house of Monimail in Fife for 5500 merks and turn it into a pleasing residence.[63] Even without major building projects, maintenance costs were significant, the eighth lord Forbes spending 2000 merks in 1601 on repairs and sir Duncan Campbell of Glenorchy spending over £40 000 on major building projects over a fifty-year period.[64]

Gordonstoun, therefore, gave the thirteenth earl of Sutherland sound advice when he told him to build a new house at Dunrobin, but only after the debts he had inherited from his father were cleared, highlighting the fact that 'None in the kingdome can build cheaper then you, having stone and lyme so near'.[65] If the proximity of good stone could reduce cost, the difficulty of holding on to skilled craftsmen at a time of high demand was driving up wages. In July 1586, sir John Maxwell of Pollok was chagrined to discover that the mason employed to work at Haggs castle had left without completing his contract, having gone off to work for a neighbour to whom Pollok wrote, insisting that the man return and finish the job. Similarly, in the spring of 1592, the laird of Edzell was unable to find someone to cut a piece of marble from his own quarry because skilled men were 'sa skant and sa mekle imployit be gentlemen quha ar bussie in biging houssis'. Such was the shortage of skilled labour that in 1633 the sixth earl of Eglinton had to employ an Englishman to construct a wall around his park.[66]

Kings expected nobles to serve them, and while office did bring rewards, there were high financial costs. By the time of his murder in 1570, the regent Moray had contracted debts of £8526 in connection with his office, and chancellor Thirlestane also found the cost of office high, being described in 1589 as a poor man who 'spends much more than his living'.[67] Ambassadorial office was particularly attractive to nobles because of the prestige and the chance of being rewarded by a foreign prince, but the outlay was enormous. In 1606, Patrick Gray, master of Gray, was still awaiting £19 983 4s 11d from the king for diplomatic services twenty years earlier, and the rich fifth earl Marischal was never compensated for the huge expenses he incurred on the 1589 embassy to Denmark.[68] Nobles were often expected to pay the costs of domestic military expeditions, such as the 1608 expedition to the Western Isles which ruined the third lord Ochiltree, or the 1614–15 campaign on Islay which tipped the seventh earl of Argyll's finances into bankruptcy.[69] The highest risk, as well as the greatest opportunities for profit, lay in financial office. Successive treasurers were left to shoulder the burden of royal debts, and in 1622 a colleague warned treasurer Mar of the high risks of his office, pointing out that even the earl of Dunbar, who could draw on the resources of the English exchequer, had died massively in debt. Mar's successor, the sixth earl of Morton, only surrendered the office in 1635 on getting an assurance from the king to cover his debts.[70] Household accounting was equally risky and Andrew Wood of Largo, who served as comptroller in 1585–7, lost his lands in an apprising action in 1618, being unable to go on servicing debts incurred in office over thirty years before.[71]

Like every other European court, that at Edinburgh necessitated high accommodation and entertainment costs, with those whose estates were furthest from court incurring the greatest expense. Even in the mid-sixteenth century, Lethington was satirising a court in which money was more important than rank or kinship. Successive lords Lovat, for example, found court life far too expensive to risk leaving their distant estates for any length of time. The sixth lord Hume, who lived within easy reach of Edinburgh, brought many of his friends to court in the summer of 1592 to lobby for some of the forfeited Bothwell estates, but he had to dismiss most of them because of the expense of maintaining so many people in the city.[72] Even after 1603, Edinburgh could be a ruinously expensive place in which to live. Highland chiefs were required from 1609 to make an annual appearance in the capital to account for their good behaviour, an experience bards saw as morally corrupting and which led to a huge growth in indebtedness among chiefs like sir Lachlan Mackintosh of Dunnachton. In 1615, the twelfth earl of Sutherland dreaded being confined to Edinburgh on account of his recusancy, as 'I wilbe bot ane wraked man; for my last being in the south hath done me great harme'.[73]

The post-1603 British court, set amidst the sprawl of London, was spectacular in comparison to that James VI left behind in Scotland. Even for the wealthiest English peers, attendance at court could be a financial burden, while for the gentry it was a desperately dangerous gamble, often leading to devastating ruin.[74] Scottish nobles faced an even greater risk for, as lady Binning wrote to her husband in 1613, 'Londin is not at the dor', and as the sixth earl of Morton was warned, 'gentlemen that live at court are at great charge'. Even changing Scottish coin into English gold carried a commission charge for the financial dealers, 2½ per cent being what the second earl of Home paid in 1632. Furthermore, while the official exchange rate was set at 12:1, the real rate of exchange by the 1620s was nearer 16:1 due to the chronic shortage of sound Scottish currency. However, not to go to court was to leave the field open for rivals. Thus the first lord Napier drew Charles I's attention to the fact that the Scots wasted money in London in pursuit of suits, often in efforts to overturn grants made to their enemies.[75]

Those nobles who did journey to London usually maintained a separate account book of their spending, often a testament to their ruin, while the numerous bonds to English merchants provide further evidence of their folly. Hopeful individuals who found their money running out in London were soon writing home asking for more cash from resentful family and friends. In a letter of 1604, sir Robert Murray of Abercairny's sister pleaded with him to return from his spendthrift and dissolute life, to attend to his estate and to get married. She saw the court as the fount of all corruption, asking 'Hes not god callid you bot to pass your tyme and to play at geams and pastymes?'[76] Anne Keith, countess of Morton, bitterly resented her husband's long sojourns at court in pursuit of a pension and office, observing sarcastically, 'I can not mervel aneuche to heir that they that hes no wit nor gret moyen get pensions and pleaces and ye get nothing'. She sensibly suggested that 'ye seik not lettil things and that is the reson that gret things gois by you'. However, the young third marquis of Hamilton avoided the massive debts Morton incurred by refusing to attend court, informing the king in 1628 that he was unable to afford the cost of living in London, his only means of raising money being from the king's generosity or the sale of his own lands.[77] The king gave in, paying Hamilton what he needed. William Lithgow's satire on the effects of court life, therefore, was soundly based:

> Post up, post downe; their states for to undoe:
> Nay, they will morgage all; and to bee breefe,
> Ryde up with gold, and turne againe with greefe:
> Who better far might stay at home, and live,
> And not their meanes to lonelesse labour give.

Closer contact with the rich English peerage also had a damaging effect on nobles who tried to compete in an uneven contest, loaded against them by distance and the unfavourable exchange rate. In April 1622, the first earl of Melrose, a man not given to wasting much time in London, attacked 'ane erronious custume begunne amongs our people to equall their expensis to the maner of England with whom we can not in any degrie compare in wealth, whereof the subjectis have found the harme to the undoing of many of the best sort'. Therefore, when the young eighth lord Yester asked his uncle's advice about launching a court career, chancellor Dunfermline advised him not to risk his estates but to be cautious for 'fortun man be verie hard'.[78]

Whether or not nobles paid direct taxes varied enormously throughout Europe, depending on local political situations.[79] Scottish nobles had no fiscal privileges but they had a role in granting and setting the level of tax in parliament, and the crown permitted some favoured nobles the right to benefit from taxation, either as tax collectors or as tax pensioners. Therefore, while the crown was unable to push taxes up easily because of noble sensitivities, those who benefited from taxation, or hoped to benefit, were likely to give their support in parliament for taxation. The result was an equilibrium of sorts in which the crown never had as much as it needed, while those paying taxes had cause to complain. However, there is no question that the collapse of the crown's traditional means of revenue-raising, land and customs, led to a twenty-fold increase in taxation from the 1560s to the 1590s. Even accounting for hyper-inflation, landlords were being taxed more heavily than had been the case in mid-century, although still irregularly. After 1603, Scottish royal revenues accounted for only 2 per cent of the king's total income, but from 1610 the pressure for money led to further demands for higher taxes. By the 1620s, the crown was collecting around £100 000 per annum in direct taxation, while the rate at which tax was assessed was raised by 50 per cent. There was also a growth in the number of indirect taxes – for example, on coal and on annual rents, sectors of the economy in which nobles were closely involved.[80]

Like most early modern tax systems, that in Scotland was uneven, unfair and subject to exemptions, all of which made it inefficient, although it was an inefficiency most nobles were prepared to collude in preserving, all efforts at reform being resisted. Possibly the chaotic method of tax collection reduced opposition in the localities, and there was a high incidence of successful tax evasion by nobles who had access to good lawyers and who controlled much of the tax-raising apparatus in the localities.[81] Some nobles tried to pass on taxes to their tenants, an abuse parliament repeatedly condemned – for example, in 1597 and 1606 – but which continued to cause widespread resentment. Relief might also be sought from feuars and tacksmen under certain circumstances, but this was always controversial, and the long list of such people who refused to pay the sixth earl of Eglinton's tax relief on the lordship of Kilwinning in 1634 suggests that nobles were being pressurised from below to resist tax rises.[82]

As was the case elsewhere in Europe, Scottish nobles were increasingly discontented with royal taxation policies.[83] Yet even if evasion, legal redress and relief failed, the tax burden was not that great, the rate for nobles being twenty shillings per pound of old extent until 1621 when it was increased to thirty shillings. Under the 1630 taxation, the second earl of Home paid £964 5s 8d per annum on his ecclesiastical lands and £2346 on his other land, a total of £3310 per annum (there was some relief on the lay land), perhaps 5 per cent of his rental. Yet this was still higher than had been paid twenty years earlier. For John Melville of Raith the increase of taxation can be charted from £10 per term in the early 1600s, rising to £15 per term from 1617, to £36 9s per term from 1621, a substantial increase in a relatively short time.[84] Of course, many nobles benefited from pensions generated by tax returns, while others participated in the administration of the tax system.[85] Nor was there a tax strike of the kind so familiar in France, or even in England where the collection of Ship Money proved to be difficult. Sir Patrick Maule of Panmure's correspondence with his local tax officer in the mid-1630s suggests no great concern over his payments. Even as protest was breaking out in July 1637, the eighth lord Yester was obeying a court of session decreet to make two tax payments of £26 9s 1d and £209 13s 4d which he had been withholding.[86]

## Conclusion

All families experience an economic cycle and early modern noble families were no different. In an age in which the overwhelming majority of nobles married, and in which marriage was closely tied to the deployment of economic resources, the business of marrying had a considerable impact upon a family's finances. Setting aside portions of the estate or its income to provide for the male heir, daughters, younger sons and widows required careful management. Circumstances and poor decision-making could place huge burdens on an estate that might not be alleviated for decades. Some nobles were simply unlucky, but the combination of early marriage, relatively large families, a determination to maintain male primogeniture and at the same time make provision for younger children was putting more and more pressure on estates. As long as the secularisation of church land could fuel the growth in the noble population, it was possible to satisfy all these ambitions. However, by the early seventeenth century, the escalating cost of tochers and the growing number of younger sons seeking military service abroad indicate strains on family finances.

Without knowing more about the spending patterns of Scottish nobles over a longer timescale, it is difficult to say much about trends. Nobles always spent conspicuously and the business of being accepted in noble society depended to some extent on visible demonstrations of wealth. The lifestyle to which all nobles aspired was one of self-conscious display, even if there were enormous wealth differentials between the head of the house of Hamilton and some minor shire baron. However, a rise in population alongside greater prosperity, the availability of easier credit and the absence of warfare as an important arena in which noble status might be exhibited all conspired to draw greater numbers of the lesser nobility into competitive display. At the same time, the influence of the richer English nobility was a factor in escalating spending for the higher nobility, although this should not be exaggerated; before 1560 the Scots had long exposure to wealthy French nobles. It is likely, therefore, that the pressure to spend did force more nobles into debt and that some nobles were ruined by their prodigality, but in itself conspicuous consumption was not undermining noble finances. Nor was the average noble necessarily ignorant of his outgoings. Most nobles had some idea of budgeting and many, like the sixth earl of Cassillis, carefully scrutinised their accounts. Cassillis drew up lists of his debts at regular intervals, even querying a 'verie unreasonable' bill in 1634 from his Edinburgh landlady for £54 4s.[87]

Among the extraordinary costs that burdened noble families, litigation, building programmes and royal service were all potentially ruinous. Yet not to defend even the most unreasonable case at law, to go on living in a tumbledown ancient castle or to avoid any form of royal service was to commit a noble house to decline. It was the necessary pressure to engage in these activities that allowed lawyers to increase their fees, stone masons to push up their costs and the price of favour at court to rise. Taxation, however, was an evil that brought no rewards, other than to a relatively small number of pensioners, and the irritation of paying taxes far outweighed the proportionate impact they had on noble finances. On the whole, Scottish nobles could afford to pay their taxes, but it was the one form of expenditure they resented even more than paying their lawyers. Taxes had to be paid, however, just as all the other costs of maintaining a noble house had to be met, from providing for a long-dead brother's widow to the feasting of unwelcome neighbours, from funding a younger son's efforts to get his foot on the ladder of the London court to adding a new wing to the ancestral castle. All were obligations that a noble could only avoid with great public embarrassment, even to the point of calling into question his nobility. Where the estate proved unequal to those demands, and where entrepreneurial activity failed to bridge the gap between income and expenditure, the solution lay in borrowing.

CHAPTER 4

# Debt

One of the common themes surrounding the history of the early modern nobility is that of crisis, particularly financial crisis. Everywhere in Europe nobles appeared to be struggling to pay their debts, mortgaging their lands and selling out to new families from different backgrounds who quickly took on the traditional roles of the nobility. Scotland was no different, and the issue of noble finances has already been linked to the notion of crisis.[1] However, the more evidence that has come to light about the economic history of individual noble houses or from regional studies, the more difficult it is to establish general patterns. Instead, some noble houses were making fortunes, while others faded into provincial obscurity, their fate sealed by political error, religious choices, improvident living, biological misfortune and bad luck. This does not mean there was no pattern at all; it does make a pattern more difficult to identify.

The much greater volume of evidence from the mid-sixteenth century onwards also makes it easier to identify failing families, uncovering in greater detail not only the sensational decline, but also the fairly ordinary, mundane slide into debt. One difficulty in evaluating that evidence lies in the temporal scope of the study. In the life of a noble family, eighty years is a short time, and some of those houses that appeared to be collapsing under the weight of financial obligations in the early seventeenth century are still around today. When in 1612 the third earl of Moray paid a bill incurred by his late father-in-law, who had been dead forty-two years, he was not behaving uncharacteristically for a nobleman.[2] However, there is no question that debt itself became more common for the simple reason that the law restricting lending and the charging of interest was altered, allowing both lending and borrowing to take a leap forward in respectability. Furthermore, mercantile economic success was able to fuel a credit boom. Debt, therefore, became an easy option for those nobles whose incomes were falling short of their expenditure. For some noble houses this contributed towards decay. What remains to be settled is how general was that decay, and whether it added up to something that might reasonably be described as a financial crisis with implications for the perception of the nobility in public life.

## The Credit Environment

As in England, both lending and borrowing money became easier in post-Reformation Scotland, particularly after the 1587 parliament permitted interest to be charged up to a maximum of 10 per cent, and while unofficial rates were often higher, market pressures brought the official interest rate down to 8 per cent in 1633.[3] The steep rise in demand for credit fed a lending boom by the early seventeenth century, and it was against this background that in November 1626 one nobleman's financial adviser told him 'men ar not very desyreous of thair monay at the present as thay have beine in tymes past for thair is monay sufficient to be had upon veray easay conditiounes'. In the mid-sixteenth century, the most common security offered on a debt was silver plate or jewellery, but as the economy improved and the coinage stabilised, lenders increasingly trusted in land as collateral. What attracted the interest of creditors was the reversionary wadset, a disguised loan collateral under which the debtor transferred to the creditor his rights to the income of the land, the annual rent, until the loan was redeemed.[4]

Fortunately, Scottish landlords were less subject to the severe penalties that hampered the development of mortgaging in England, and they were free to wadset entailed land without the need for a royal licence as occurred in Spain in order to circumvent the restrictions of the *mayorazgo* which prevented the sale or mortgage of entailed property.[5] The wadset was crucial to the long-term sustainability of the nobility, allowing flexibility in the use of capital assets while preventing irresponsible heads of houses from permanently alienating land. Occasionally, superiors sold land to a wadetter, but redemption usually took place after relatively short periods. If this proved impossible, the land was not lost forever; thus in 1632–3 the thirteenth earl of Sutherland redeemed land wadset by a previous earl 300 years earlier. In effect the wadset operated in a similar way to the French *retrait lignager*, allowing descendants to repurchase alienated lineage property at the original price plus costs.[6] Wadsetting, therefore, was a valuable tool in the financial management of an estate, and it was one widely employed. By the 1630s, dozens of Aberdeenshire landlords had mortgaged portions of their estate to other members of the local community, from the marquis of Huntly who had wadset 62 502 merks' worth of land down to small sums by lesser landlords.[7]

Unlike the English or Spanish crowns, Scottish kings did not have the resources to be major creditors to the nobility, and it was only with the introduction of a tax on annual rents in 1621 that the crown claimed a stake in the credit market. Foreign credit was limited to money raised while travelling on the continent, and after 1603 to those few courtiers whose English incomes gave them access to the London money market.[8] For the higher nobility, the main source of credit was merchants and lawyers, especially those Edinburgh merchants getting rich on international trade. Business profits fed the nobility's insatiable appetite for funding expensive lifestyles, but it was those self-same merchants who were blamed for demanding repayment. Looking back from the perspective of the 1650s, sir Thomas Urquhart of Cromarty unfairly portrayed merchants as threatening and parasitical, using debt to seize land from nobles. These upstarts 'cast off the vizard of merchant, wherwith they cheated the world, and turning once landed men, they altogether scorn to traffique any longer'.[9] Certainly, apprising actions by creditors against nobles who could not pay their debts grew more common, a trend not peculiar to seventeenth-century Scotland. However, the large influx of merchant capital into land must be kept in perspective as the share of land owned by merchants, or even held in wadset, remained small, except in shires like Lothian and Fife where Edinburgh burgesses were keen to acquire property.[10]

The growth of Edinburgh-based mercantile finance was a factor in enhancing the credit opportunities available, but the lender-borrower relationship was often constructed within the traditional communities of kin and affinity, minimising its commercial nature.[11] Casual borrowing from kinsmen was typical. Sir James Dundas of Arniston had a cash flow crisis in 1626, and he turned to his elder brother, sir Walter Dundas of that Ilk, asking if he had 'sum monyes besyde you to lett out'. This kind of borrowing was preferred, hence the sixth lord Lovat's comment in 1599 that 'he [would] rather take his kinsmens mony than borrow of strangers or sell land', or the eleventh earl of Angus's observation in 1630 that 'I had rather have freinds to be bund unto then strangers'. When forced into extensive wadsetting in the 1620s and 1630s, sir John Grant of Freuchie took care to wadset land only to other members of the Grant kindred so that political control of his territories was not diminished.[12] Merchant lending too often had a kinship relationship undergirding it. The seventh lord Gray's affairs were so bad by 1637 that he mortgaged 250 000 merks' worth of his estates to an Edinburgh merchant financier, but William Gray of Pittendrum was a kinsman. The Seton kindred arranged their borrowing from John Rynd, a wealthy Edinburgh burgess whose wife, Elizabeth Seton, continued the business after Rynd's death as an in-house credit facility for her family. This neighbourliness and fraternity is captured in a bond of February 1602 in which David and Robert Bruce, sadler burgesses of Stirling, struck a financial deal with Archibald Bruce of Wester Kennet 'for the goodwill they have towards the House of Wester Kennet, and the said House towards them'.[13] It was common to spread loans to avoid owing too much to any one creditor, and the nineteen creditors pursuing the fourth lord Ochiltree in 1623 were composed of two peers, five barons, three merchant burgesses, two writers, one advocate, one apothecary, one servant, one minister's son and three others all with a stake in the financial success of this noble house.[14]

Seven of Ochiltree's creditors were nobles, and most nobles did lend money at some time, although collecting debts from other nobles was unpalatable. In spite of the mounting sums owed by the first earl of Nithsdale to the first earl of Buccleuch, the latter was reluctant to take legal action, being 'resolvit to tak up no mens rentis bot my own'; by 1632 the debt stood at 54 940 merks. Nevertheless, some involvement in money lending is unsurprising given that the return from a loan was usually higher than that from investment in land. For a handful of nobles, like that 'heaper and hatcher of wealth', the first earl of Haddington, lending was a money-making business. In addition to the £42 523 owed to him in outstanding rents at his death in 1637, Haddington had lent out £53 333 to friends and associates who were paying him £4267 per annum in interest, a sum equivalent to around 10 per cent of the earl's income from his landed properties.[15] Noblewomen, especially widows, often preferred to lend their surplus income than purchase land. In 1579, it was a grateful sir James Stewart of Doune who acknowledged his debt to the countess of Argyll, admitting that 'I have had mair in borrowing of hir ladyship than of all the rest of Scotland'. Jean Hamilton, the wealthy daughter of the duke of Châtelherault and a divorcee, could even afford to lend to Edinburgh merchants.[16]

However, testaments can suggest a misleading degree of lending by nobles, and most debts owing were usually in the form of unpaid rents, or rests, rather than money advanced in return for annual rents.[17] This kind of debt due to landlords was common, like the two years' outstanding teinds owed to the first earl of Linlithgow by thirty-five tenants in the parish of Coulter in September 1606, or the £11 111 owed by the tenants of Liddesdale in 1633 to the first earl of Buccleuch.[18] The economic conditions of the early seventeenth century generally favoured landlords, allowing them to rack-rent, driving some tenants into accepting leases they could not afford, and hence into arrears. While it suited landlords to charge interest on the debt, most knew there was nothing to be gained in pressing impoverished tenants for payment, and some debts had to be written off entirely. These rests caused real problems for landlords; in November 1617 the fourth lord Elphinstone wrote dejectedly that 'I was never in sick estait for lack of silver: quhair it is restand [= owing] me by my tennentis can nocht get it in'. Elphinstone's troubles were not unique, and landlords had to strike a balance between maximising incomes and setting realistic rents. The knock-on effect of getting this wrong could be disastrous for everyone, as in 1636 when the countess of Haddington fulminated against tenants whose failure to pay their rents had left her unable to meet obligations to creditors.[19]

The greater part of borrowing by nobles took place within a relatively stable financial framework in which credit offered the best means of dealing with an unusual or short-term demand for cash. The most common reasons for borrowing were mundane: the temporary loss of part of the estate's income to support other members of the family, rents being in arrears, the unpredictability of feudal dues or shortages in coin. With seven daughters, a wife and a mother to support, sir William Douglas of Lochleven had reason to be worried when he wrote to his brother in 1568 that 'ye knaw my sonis leving will not be mekle, my Modir [being] payit and my wiffis beand deducit'. Lochleven's financial plight was the product of biology rather than prodigality. Similarly, over a thirty-year period the seventh and eighth lords Forbes raised 20 500 merks by wadsetting in order to meet the costs of tochers and wedding expenses, while a further 2000 merks were raised to pay for the former's funeral. There was nothing remarkable or extravagant about such debts, and borrowing was a useful expedient when faced with the episodes of high spending most families encountered over the course of a generation. Debt might be justified in order to make a suitable investment, as when in February 1615 the twelfth earl of Sutherland advised his younger brother to purchase an estate, pointing out that 'albeit ye wer in debt it is for ane honest caus'. Of course, some of life's misfortunes could never be predicted. Patrick Stewart, master of Orkney, was extremely unlucky in 1590, losing £36 000 worth of jewellery, money and movables to English pirates, forcing him to resort to heavy borrowing in order to make good the losses.[20]

In spite of the changing legal and moral climate in which borrowing was taking place, many nobles remained uncomfortable with debt which appeared to reflect badly on their honour. John Erskine of Dun was deeply worried by his debts c.1570, being determined he would be 'out of all mennis deat' even if he had to endure heavy repayments in the short term. Unfortunately his son did not share this outlook, and 'takis no thocht thairoff bot burdenis me above my awin with his debt'. No doubt the laird of Dun spoke for many fathers from a generation less accustomed to debt. When in 1602 the twelfth earl of Sutherland was charged publicly by a creditor for non-payment, he too was embarrassed and annoyed at his own oversight. Sutherland had been caught out by the unexpected change in victual prices, claiming that 'I nevir braik my day to him befoir'.[21] What such evidence suggests is that over and above the sound financial reasons for disposing of debts quickly, nobles did not easily shed their unease at being in debt, especially to a stranger. In most cases, therefore, it is unsurprising to find debts being cleared within agreed timescales, and even large emergency debts might be serviced quickly. In 1561, the sixth lord Erskine set aside the income of the newly acquired lands of the abbey of Cambuskenneth to pay off the large debt of £10 000 accumulated by himself and his father in the service of James V. Erskine had devised his own sensible repayment plan to deal with an awkward debt.[22]

In spite of the law, which in Scotland offered nobles no legal protection for debt, they did often demonstrate a high-handed attitude towards appeals for payment. In the sixteenth century especially, creditors might face physical danger from nobles refusing to pay their own debts or protecting clients from legal redress. Behind this behaviour was noble irritation with creditors for daring to initiate legal action; hence the indignation of the widowed countess of Moray in March 1570 when her late husband's creditors attempted to arrest her clothing and gear. Faced with the haughty intransigence of such people, angry merchants were often left to collect small amounts from time to time from customers they could not afford to lose. Andrew Fletcher, a Dundee merchant, tried repeatedly in 1620 to get the third earl of Winton to pay money owing to his father, finding 'nathing bot frustrating and to tell you the treuth I have na greate hope of it, or that he sall truble him self meikle in the business'. As late as 1633, William Lithgow felt it necessary to attack such nobles:

> Another great abuse, is that when
> Men runne in Suretyship for other Men;
> Or els morgadged in debt; yet will not pay
> Their Creditors, nor thy just Lawes obey:
> But scorning, horning, Caption Rebells turne;
> And in despight of pow'r, all where sojourne.[23]

As long as these risks attended the lending of money, creditors were bound to be wary, a situation that ultimately was disadvantagous to merchant financiers and potential borrowers.

From the later 1590s, the changing political context, the gradual reduction of feuding, the crown's greater effectiveness in enforcing law and order, and the growing respect for the civil and criminal law, all altered the environment in which lenders and borrowers operated. Inhibitions against insolvent debtors disposing of their lands in order to defraud their creditors were more effectively enforced. In 1607, a privy council dominated by creditors criticised the king's desire to maintain the privilege of legal protection offered to its own members in civil law cases, arguing that the privileges of a councillor should not take precedence over 'the interes of a[n] infinite nomber of creditouris of all rankis'. Meanwhile, more nobles were warded in Edinburgh castle following actions raised against them by creditors. Parliament passed sympathetic legislation, most significantly the 1621 act providing protection for creditors against debtors who tried to defraud them, a measure that eased the passage of a new tax on annual rents. The establishment of a register of apprisings in 1636 underlined the growing number of such actions against debtors and the seriousness with which the crown viewed debt.[24]

The most effective pressure to be applied to debtors was to take action against their sureties, those kinsmen and friends who guaranteed the loans. Formerly, the ineffectiveness of the law made this an obligation with few consequences but by the seventeenth century the risk was higher. Gordonstoun expressed a sensible wariness about offering surety for friends whose financial stability was doubtful 'leist therby you endanger the estate of your successours'. He had good reason to be cautious. In 1616, sir John Maxwell of Pollok was persuaded to become a cautioner for his lord and chief, Robert Maxwell, heir to the forfeited Maxwell estates and titles, thereby tying him up in the disastrous financial affairs of the restored earl of Nithsdale for the rest of his life. The second earl of Lothian became ruinously enmeshed in the financial morass created by Andrew Ker, lord Jedburgh, after agreeing in 1622 that 'I sall do the best offices of a kynd freind' by helping manage his accounts. A similarly misplaced trust in friends and an over-stretched sense of honour led John MacLeod of Dunvegan to run up debts of 80 000 merks in forfeited sureties between 1623 and 1640.[25]

## Indebtedness and Decay

Following the battle of Langside in 1568, the fifth lord Seton fled to Flanders where for a time he 'drove a waggon and four horses for his livelyhood', an episode recorded with the characteristic good humour of the Seton family in a painting in the gallery at Seton house. His son, the first earl of Winton, inherited an indebted estate, but a combination of royal favour, careful management and 'his vertious ladie's good government' all helped to restore the family fortune. That business of financial restoration took the better part of three decades, involving efforts to increase income from entrepreneurial management and royal favour but also retrenchment in the short term. Here was one of a number of strategies noble families devised to deal with the problem of debts that were in danger of becoming unmanageable. A similar calculated prudence guided the second earl of Perth when he succeeded to an indebted estate in 1611. He decided that he had no choice but to adopt a regime of 'honest mannagerie':

> I sold some lands and bought others for commoditie of our house, and lived reasonablie well, according to the times, without debosh or drinking, by diet, ane intolerable fault, and too much approven this unhappie age.

Perth economised and got over his problems. When in 1626 the elderly fourth lord Elphinstone suffered the devastating loss of the barony of Kildrummy in a court of session action, he and his eldest son decided to economise by merging their two households.[26] However, some nobles risked taking a conservative spending regime too far, endangering their social status. When c.1630 Archibald Edmonstone of Duntreath set about re-deeming his estate and restoring the family seat, his mother poked fun at the extent of his economising – 'God forbid ye be sa daft' – dismissing the idea he might have 'to trail a pick a few yeirs'. The loss of prestige, the alienation of servants and the reduction in nobles' ability to serve the king all made savings difficult to identify, especially for those members of the higher nobility with significant public roles. In December 1629, chancellor

Dupplin offered unpalatable advice to the ambitious sixth earl of Morton, to 'frame your self to a moderat expenss suche as monye nobles in this cuntrey live at'. Consequently, 'your house may stand and abyde better tymes as oftymes falls to noble houses'.[27] This was good counsel which sat ill with Morton's political pretensions and the earl plunged further into debt in pursuit of office and pensions.

Voluntary interdicts, which affected the disposal of heritage but not movables, placed the management of a man's affairs in the hands of a family commission and were a common means of curbing expenditure. In 1580, the third lord Drummond placed himself under an interdict preventing him alienating land without the permission of three of his friends, thus restricting his freedom to borrow. The debts incurred by sir Alexander Fraser of Philorth in improving Fraserburgh led in 1608 to much of the estate being placed in commission for over twenty years. In spite of the best efforts of the wife and friends of the seventh earl of Argyll to stave off financial ruin, by 1617 he had no option other than to place his affairs in the hands of a commission. Argyll went abroad 'that my burdenit estait mycht breath in my absence', leaving his son to beg for loans from his vassals.[28] Financial specialists were employed, like John Arnot, the provost of Edinburgh and depute treasurer, who advised the second earl of Orkney on foreign currency dealing. The lawyer, sir Thomas Hope of Craighall, counselled the first earl of Annandale, suggesting in 1627 that 'we must mak the greter expeditioun that your lordschipis money lye not unprofitable in your lordschipis hands'.[29] Wives often played a crucial role in prudent financial management. Hugh Rose of Kilravock was enormously aided by his wife, Katherine Falconer, 'a frugall and good manager, being verie assisting to her husband, particularly in paying the debt and burden upon his fortune'. Anne Keith, countess of Morton, struggled for years with her courtier husband's dangerous financial gambles. She barraged him with letters, demanded he come home and was scathing of his offers to send money, for 'I knaw very weil ye have nothing thair bot as ye borowit'. Furthermore, as has already been established, wives contributed directly to the finances of their house by providing tochers, and marriage contracts often insisted these sums be used to redeem wadsets.[30]

A minority often provided the opportunity for a family to put its affairs in order; for example, the succession of a minor to the Buccleuch estates in 1633 allowed expenditure to fall from a monthly average of £12 611 to £5095. In the case of the Sutherland estates, the business of salvaging something from the young thirteenth earl's inheritance fell to his uncle, who boasted that he 'fred that house from the great debt wherwith it was over-burthened'.[31] There was always some risk that young lords, straining to free themselves from the tutelage of tutors, would endanger their finances. When the sixth lord Lovat skipped off to Ireland in 1587 at the age of sixteen, panicking kinsmen feared he would run up enormous debts and mortgage his lands. Therefore, an interdict was sought to prevent him from personally managing his affairs before his thirtieth birthday. Yet even young lords could be prevailed upon to restrain their expenditure. On 4 January 1582, the already married, twenty-year-old earl of Mar signed a stringent austerity agreement with his mother and other family members, restricting his freedom to spend, prioritising the freeing of mortgages, and authorising his chamberlain to 'put his Lo[rdship's] awin living to the best avale and proffite may be'.[32] Here was a good lesson in economising for James VI's future lord treasurer.

For those nobles who failed to address the problems of rising debts, decay and ruin eventually stared them in the face. By the early 1620s, it was said of the earls of Caithness that their house was 'weill neir ane utter ruyne, liklie to vanish and fall from the familie and surname of Sinckler'. The reasons for Caithness's problems were not only financial, stemming from political miscalculations, but his experience of what was an early modern form of bankruptcy was not uncommon. The countess of Haddington claimed in the mid-1630s that 'I haif so many dets to pay that I protest to god I cannot get spending mony in the menest degre let be to furnes my self in very sober necesars'.[33] Often such crises were temporary, a question of cash flow that in 1632 the thirteenth earl of Sutherland dealt with by offering to pay off the £7000 he owed William Dick in grain and salmon. This was contrary to the advice of his uncle, who took a dim view of making early deals on victual in order to raise money quickly, 'for it undois the tennents and hinders you greatlie, being forced to sell your commoditie for halfe the value'. Instead, Gordonstoun recommended borrowing cash, preferably within the locality rather than in the towns, and holding back his commodities to sell at a more opportune moment.[34]

Indebtedness might have deeper roots. As early as 1583, the estates of the earls of Glencairn were 'of reasonable good lyvinge, if it yt were freed of the mortgages wher[with] some of his auncestors have entangled a good parte therof'. Nothing was done, and the chickens finally came home to roost thirty years later in a spiral of apprisings and damaging litigation between the sixth earl and his eldest son, lord Kilmaurs.[35] One obvious solution for landowners faced with unmanageable debt was to dispose of assets, and the most frantic period of selling on the English land market was between 1585 and 1606, the single biggest reason being an inability to service debts. It made sense to sell rather than accumulate interest, and the income lost in selling land with a value equivalent to the size of the debt was likely to be worth about half the value of the interest saved.[36] The seventh lord Ogilvy inherited debts of £45 698 in 1617, and after years of further wadsetting he belatedly decided in 1634 that the only way to satisfy the creditors was to sell lands to the value of 100 221 merks.[37] Yet this was a last resort. When in 1584 the eighth earl of Angus sold off £12 000 worth of land to pay debts of £14 000, he was roundly criticised by his friends. One nobleman argued that 'gentleman who sels ane acre of land, looseth ane unce of credit, for gentilitie is nothing but ancient riches, so that if the foundation do sink, the building must needs consequentlie fall'.[38]

There was a tension, therefore, between disposing of some free land to clear the estate of debt and tenaciously holding on to everything at the expense of being committed to heavy interest payments. By 1622, the ruined fifth earl of Caithness came to the decision that while 'before I live this [= thus] debarit frome all nobille soseattie throw my deptis, I sall sell the best land I haife'. The first earl of Melrose agreed that Caithness was right to pay off his creditors rather than 'to lye under that servile miserie to be still in their danger, and to permit your estate to be consumed by annuelrentis'. What had to be avoided was the situation prevailing in seventeenth-century Spain, where between one-third and two-thirds of a grandee's income could be committed to the servicing of debts.[39] The temptation to take out ever bigger mortgages to avoid selling was considerable. In August 1625, a desperately worried sir John Maxwell of Pollok warned the first earl of Nithsdale, for whom he was a cautioner, that the lands of both of them were about to be apprised by the earl's creditors. Nithsdale resorted to even more wadsetting, mortgaging his barony of Mearns – 'the most convenient and best haldin barronie in this countrie' – and his financial affairs continued to plummet.[40] The sixth earl of Morton was a prodigous borrower and throughout the 1620s and 1630s more and more land was assigned to Edinburgh financiers. In spite of the warnings of family and friends, Morton went on borrowing and by 1640, with political misfortune now undermining his credit, the earl faced losing control of all his estates.[41]

Debtors were rarely in a position to make advantageous sales. The first lord Blantyre's assurance to an acquaintance that 'the word of ane honest man must be sufficient amonges trewe dealleris', disguises the avaricious nature of the Scottish land market where predators were always on the lookout for easy pickings.[42] The sudden and surprising disgrace of the first lord Balmerino in 1608 exposed him to creditors at a time when he had debts of over £100 000 and no means of relieving them. In the mid-1630s, the seventh earl of Menteith's financial security crashed as a consequence of his loss of office, obliging him to mortgage and sell land 'worth a greate deal more than thrys thos soumes for quhilk they ar ingaged'.[43] Such a buyer's market offered other opportunities too tempting to miss. The securing of loans against estates allowed lord Lorne to assume control over sir Lachlan MacLean of Duart's lands on Mull, Jura and Scarba following the latter's failure to meet the terms of a loan he negotiated with Lorne in 1634. In 1624, the chancellor, sir George Hay of Kinfauns, and his colleague, the first earl of Melrose, used insider knowledge to conspire in exploiting Morton's financial difficulties, purchasing at a favourable price lands the earl was 'so desyrous to sell for keeping credit'. The Lauders of Bass struggled for decades to pay off debts incurred in buying the feu of the Tyninghame estate from their superior in 1568. By 1621 the vultures were closing in, having heard that:

> if they sell als much land as may pay their debt, they will have litle or nothing behind to themselves, and ere ane yeare be at ane end, they will either sell the most part of that estate, or it will be comprised from them.

Melrose passed this information on to his friend, John Murray of Lochmaben, who bought Tyninghame for 200 000 merks, selling it on to Melrose a few years later for the same sum. Here was a land market of ruthless speculators, exploitative estate accumulation and tough bargaining, where men like the second lord Deskford negotiated a wadset with the laird of Glenorchy that imposed 'such strick conditiones as wold uterlie rewin thair estait'.[44]

The dangers of extravagant living were pointed out as early as the mid-sixteenth century by contemporary moralists like Lethington, who criticised spendthrifts who 'care nocht quha the merchand payis,/Quhill pairt of land be put away'. Almost a century later, Cromarty, whose fortune had been wasted by a foolish father, railed against landowners who spent their money on:

> hawks, hounds, wenching, gaming, tipling, swaggering, fidling, rioting, revelling, and other such-like profligate courses of a most effusive and vast expense [who] squander away the money so lent, without casting an eye to any thing tending to the furtherance of the exchange of ware, towards the necessary use of man.

What these commentators had in mind was the likes of the second lord Spynie, described as 'a noble spendthrift and exquisite in all manner of debauchery'.[45] One noble whose roller coaster lifestyle destroyed him utterly was Patrick Stewart, second earl of Orkney. By the mid-1600s, inherited liabilities, an expensive building programme, land purchases, an extravagant lifestyle, fines, further penalties and the interest on the debts left him 'drownit in debt' to the tune of 250 000 merks. Financial vulnerability exposed Orkney to the machinations of his enemies, alienation from the king and coercion from the privy council. He was imprisoned in 1610, unable even to pay for his daily maintenance and being granted an allowance of £4 per day. The estates were turned over to the creditors to manage, and it was his attempt to reverse this loss of fortune in a botched rebellion that brought about forfeiture and execution in 1615.[46] A similar combination of financial incompetence and political misjudgements led to the ruin of the fifth earl of Caithness. Following rebellion in 1622, his estates were placed in the hands of creditors, who paid the earl a modest allowance for his 'honourable intertenyment'.[47] The earls of Crawford, however, had been staving off financial collapse for most of the sixteenth century. The twelfth, or 'prodigal', earl inherited an already decayed estate in 1607, which he further dissipated until his kinsmen had him imprisoned in Edinburgh castle. There he lived until his death in 1620 in conditions of abject poverty, having at times 'not the meanes to sustene and intertene his naturall [lyff], nor to provyde him selff of abuilyeementis and clething'.[48] These were among the most spectacular cases of noble ruin, but heavy mortgaging and selling did cripple nobles of every rank from earls to barons like sir John Bruce of Airth, who had to sell so much land in 1617 that it remained only 'to sie quhat may be gittin to the puire wyff and hir bairnes'.[49]

The poor noble was a familiar figure in the literature of early modern France, Poland or Spain, and while Scotland lacked the legislation of Castile, where impoverished nobles and their children were reduced to commoner status, a de facto derogation took place. For William Park of Glenluce the collapse of his fortune was sudden and dramatic. At midday on 25 June 1635 his house, its contents, his stores and virtually everything he possessed were consumed in fire, reducing this minor noble to seeking charitable aid.[50] The house of Sommerville's decline was less dramatic, but the seventh lord had sold almost all the estate to the second earl of Mar by 1602 after the two had meticulously compiled a book 'whairin wes punctuallie written and sett doun the haill burdeins and distresses lying upon the living of Somervell'. Lord Sommerville ceased using his title altogether, thinking 'his fortune not suitable to that dignity', and he retired to a small property, assuming the status of laird of Drum. Another noble who came close to forfeiting his rank because of his lifestyle was Patrick Gray, master of Gray, who related in a letter of November 1600 that before going into exile he 'levit in Scotland lyk a paysant'. Gray served as a soldier 'wher ever ther is warres in Europe, for I will get a horsmans pay, and be God I will tak it, for that will mak me leive'. Nevertheless, Gray knew he had to find a more worthy means of restoring his fortune, for 'if i should leive longar in that sort, I discredit my self perpetually'.[51] Sommerville's stoicism and Gray's pragmatism in the face of ruin were not shared by all, however. On the morning of 6 March 1624, the second earl of Lothian went into his room to go over his accounts, 'barreth the chamber doore, and cutted his owne throate with a knife, efter he had given himself sundrie wounds with his dagger'. Lothian's suicide was unique, but while few nobles were absolutely poor, such depression over financial difficulties was familiar. Like the third earl of Huntingdon in England, the fourth lord Elphinstone spent his entire life struggling to balance the family accounts. In 1617, he wrote despairingly to his eldest son that debts 'bredis me sick greiff and mis-contentment, as I can nocht declaire, nor abill to indure'. This miserable old lord desperately wished that 'I may be saitlit and puit to sum rest, that giff possible I mycht haeff pace and rest, now in my auld dayis'.[52]

In England it was rare for a noble house to collapse altogether, while in Castile the crown's attachment to a hierarchic society similarly cushioned nobles from the worst consequences of financial mismanagement or bad luck. Noble society was uncomfortable with the idea of financial collapse, and Gordonstoun thought it the responsibility of the earl of Sutherland to prevent the decay of friendly, dependent houses that had fallen under the command of some 'unworthy foolish man'. However, if good advice was spurned then 'make your owne profite by his fall by all good means possible'. In the Orkney, Caithness and Crawford cases the crown cooperated with creditors and local rivals to manipulate these lords for its own political advantage. However, kings too were uncomfortable with the notion of a noble house in decay, this being contrary to their ideal of an unchanging, hierarchic world; hence the appeals to the king for protection against creditors made by leading friends of the house of Hamilton following the unexpected death of the second marquis in 1625.[53] These men rightly anticipated that James VI would not want to see such a great house ruined. The collapse of the house of Atholl is all the more dramatic when one recalls that the fourth earl of Atholl was described in 1577 as 'rich, of great possessions, party and friendship'. Thirty years later its 'imminent decay' was predicted. James VI was 'loath that ony suche house, of that antiquitie and amang the first of the nobilitie of that oure kingdome, for laik of goode gyding in the present possessour sould perishe', but even the king was put off by the scale of debt.[54] Similar paternalism guided James's intervention in the affairs of the daughters of the suicide earl of Lothian. The king recommended a rescue package to the privy council, and the entire mess of the Lothian accounts was dumped on the council table to be sorted out.[55] Royal help for Robert Maxwell, brother and heir to the executed ninth lord Maxwell, led in time to the restoration of his titles and support in regaining the Maxwell estates. James explained that such a course of action was necessary because:

> we ar to prevent that ony other of our subjects (muche less ane ancient noble house) sould, by rigor of law be overthrowne in the persone of one who both by himselff hes done and whois freindis daylie doeth good service.[56]

This determination to prevent the collapse of noble houses extended below the peerage. Sir James Edmonstone of Duntreath had by 1606 'wraikit his house and leveing', prompting the privy council to cooperate with his son and heir in arresting the prodigal knight before he could do any more harm to the estate.[57] Unlike in Spain, the crown in Scotland did not use its authority to override the law, but it did use influence and patronage to protect favoured nobles, creating a form of economic dependence.

## Crisis?

While a period of widespread economic difficulties might have affected European nobilities in the later sixteenth and early seventeenth centuries, relatively few individual noble houses suffered long-term damage by the time fortunes began to recover c.1680. Even in the most economically progressive region of Europe, the Netherlands, the relative decline in the financial power of many nobles did not impact greatly on their political power, or on the superiority of their social status and cultural values.[58] Besides, the argument for a general financial crisis has been dented by individual case studies, demonstrating a complex picture of prosperity in one family existing side by side with decline among their neighbours and of large-scale debts being successfully surmounted. Difficult economic circumstances even provided some more skilful or fortunate families with the opportunities to prosper. The vagaries of fortune were the result of a combination of general economic trends and the individual responses to those circumstances, whether it be the earls of Shrewsbury, Sussex or Derby in sixteenth-century England, the Albret, La Tremoille, Montmorency families and the ducal house of Nevers in sixteenth-century France, or the house of Bejar in seventeenth-century Castile.[59] Tentative suggestions of a financial crisis affecting the Scottish nobility have also been greeted with scepticism, and what looks like part of a trend often turns out on closer inspection to be highly particular.[60] When the twelfth earl of Sutherland died in 1615, his estate was heavily indebted but his brother was able to identify reasons for this state of affairs. Sutherland's Catholicism had cost him in fines, he had been caught up in a number of expensive lawsuits with neighbours, and he invested heavily in new salt pans at Brora that had not yet brought any return. There was no general crisis; Sutherland had simply made poor judgements. Furthermore, in many cases the debts showing in noble testaments were less damaging than they at first appear. Set alongside the first earl of Buccleuch's enormous assets, including the large sums owed to him, debts of £7339 were insignificant, being mostly made up of unpaid obligations rather than borrowings.[61]

Yet there was a perception among many contemporaries that the nobility was becoming impoverished. Impressionistic evidence collected for English intelligence between 1577 and 1583 suggests that as much as half the peerage was in financial trouble as a consequence of defeat in the civil war or of other less tangible economic factors. Unfortunately, it is impossible to reconstruct the effect of financing war to anything like the extent it has been done for the Albret family in France. But it is clear that similar strategies were adopted; for example, in 1570 the fifth earl of Huntly raised £5000 for the war effort by mortgaging land.[62] For the defeated side, war losses were not easily recouped, and when the former governor of Scotland, the duke of Châtelherault, died in 1575, his testament was valued at only £1604, an astonishingly meagre sum for a man widely regarded as the wealthiest in the kingdom throughout the 1540s and 1550s.[63] To take one less prominent example, the fifth lord Hume's castles and lands were occupied by English troops who inflicted such severe damage that his son's income was depressed for decades. As late as 1621, his grandson was still trying to repair the mills

Table 4.1 Average testaments of peers, 1570–1637

| | Value of inventory | Sum owed | Gross estate | Debts | Net estate |
|---|---|---|---|---|---|
| 1570–89 | £5580 | £2505 | £8085 | £997 | £7088 |
| (post-1600 value) | £17 730 | £7837 | £25 567 | £3214 | £22 353 |
| 1590–1609 | £3865 | £4555 | £8420 | £2848 | £5572 |
| (post-1600 value) | £5897 | £7391 | £13 288 | £3524 | £9764 |
| 1610–37 | £10 309 | £19 337 | £29 646 | £5105 | £24 541 |

on the Hirsell estate in Berwickshire. Hume was only one of many 'greate men, now almost ruyned for the part of the late Queene'.[64] Even among those on the winning side, there were substantial losses in the war, the Lennox earldom being 'mortgaged, dismembred, and brought in manner to nothinge'.[65]

But by the 1580s the sense of creeping decay extended beyond war losses. Testaments deliberately created a less healthy financial picture in order to avoid tax, and officials might even be persuaded to take bribes in return for underestimating goods.[66] Nevertheless, evidence from the testaments of fifty-four peers between 1570 and 1637 suggests that in real terms, financial pressures were most serious from around the mid-1580s to the mid-1600s (see Table 4.1).[67] Only three peers whose testaments have been recorded in the commissary courts died leaving net debts, but in some cases the volume of debt and the share it represented of the gross estate was significant. In 1588, the eighth earl of Angus's debts of £5160 ate up 54 per cent of the value of his gross testament.[68] In real terms, therefore, while peers' testaments were worth about 10 per cent more in the period after 1610 than they had been before 1590, between 1590 and 1609 their values were halved. The gross value of the testaments, before outstanding debts were deducted, shows an overall rise of 16 per cent in real terms in spite of a fall in values during the middle period. However, while there was a drop in the real value of inventories by some 40 per cent, the amount of money owed to peers increased by almost 150 per cent, largely due to the inability of tenants to pay rising rents. As for their own debts, these grew by 59 per cent, with most of this increase again taking place before 1590. These changes are expressed a little more clearly in Table 4.2.[69] It appears that in the middle decades, from the 1580s to the 1600s, the nobility were borrowing proportionately more, probably in order to bridge the gap in their finances caused by inflation, static rents and poor harvests. However, there was a recovery in the seventeenth century, due to a fall in inflation, increasing rents, better harvests, an opening up of domestic and foreign markets, and an increase in pensions.

There is no evidence to suggest that financial difficulties particularly affected the higher nobility, although they might have shouldered a greater

**Table 4.2 Changes in average testaments, 1570–1637**

| | Value of inventory | Sum owed | Gross estate | Debts | Net estate |
|---|---|---|---|---|---|
| 1570–89 | £69 | £31 | £100 | £12 | £88 |
| 1590–1609 | £25 | £30 | £55 | £19 | £36 |
| 1610–37 | £41 | £75 | £116 | £20 | £96 |

proportion of war costs, and as was the case elsewhere in Europe, the secular trend was for wealth to concentrate in the hands of a small number of noble families.[70] In late medieval Scotland, the destruction of the great territorial magnates created a peerage that on average was twice as wealthy as the greater baronage. However, by the succeeding century, a few magnate houses, like the earls of Huntly, had already outstripped all their neighbours, including the earls of Errol.[71] Testamentary evidence suggests that normally the earls retained their lead over the lords of parliament who were in turn usually richer than the barons.[72]

There was certainly an expectation in society that there should be a correlation between rank and wealth. When in 1600 it was suggested that sir Thomas Erskine might be created lord Dirleton as a reward for his part in saving the king in the Gowrie Conspiracy, Erskine refused because 'he wants living'. Obviously, it was an issue to which most nobles were sensitive, hence the touchy response in 1586 from the fifth earl of Rothes to his son-in-law, the eighth earl of Angus, when he pointed out that 'although he [Rothes] might not have so great means as he [Angus], yet he was just as much an earl as he'.[73] Where rank and wealth were out of step, political instability often followed. In the mid-1560s the Kennedy lairds of Bargany and Blairquhan were thought to be 'nothing Inferior in Leving to therle of Cassillis, Saving he is there Cheif, and of A surnem'. This was an exaggeration, but Cassillis was embarrassed by the wealth of these powerful cadet houses and in the end he destroyed them in a bloody feud.[74]

This is not to deny that fortunes were made by lesser men pushing their way into the top ranks of nobles. Sir Walter Scott of Buccleuch died in 1574 leaving a gross inventory of £5883 adjusted by debts to a net inventory of £1396. His son, the first lord Buccleuch, was so successful in acquiring much of the Bothwell earldom that he was able to pass on a much enlarged estate to his son in 1611. By the early 1630s, the first earl's aggressive buying provided an income of £88 452, and in 1633 his gross inventory was valued at £188 660.[75] The Scotts of Buccleuch did well out of royal favour, careful estate management, the wool trade and soldiering, but they were not part of a general trend. Baronial families experienced the same range of fortunes that were a product of circumstance, personality and responses to the shifts in society as the older peerage. The contrasting fortunes of the Melville kindred in Fife make this point. The senior branch of the family, the Melvilles of Raith, made little headway in the early seventeenth century, but the junior branch of the family, the Melvilles of Murdocairny, enjoyed decades of royal patronage, acquiring the title of lord Melville. When the second lord Melville died in 1635 he left a net estate of £28 571, dwarfing the £691 of his cousin who died eight years earlier.[76] What made the difference to these two branches of the same family was not the rising fortunes of the lairds or changes in the economy but political success. Even without the wildly unpredictable impact of royal favour, baronial families experienced shifting fortunes from one generation to the next. When John Grant of Freuchie died in 1585, his testament recorded a net value of £47 185, a huge sum for a Highland baron. Unfortunately, mismanagement by his son and grandson resulted in heavy wadsetting and the dismembering of the estate to the extent that the latter was remembered in clan folklore as 'Sir John Sell-the-Land'.[77] The Grants demonstrate Scotstarvit's assertion that 'How the estate will thrive will be known in the third generation,' and the latter repeatedly highlighted the difficulty aspiring noble houses like his own had in sustaining their position, creating a picture of transitory success undermined by indebtedness, the foolishness of heirs, biological misfortunes or political crisis.[78] Such reverses were more easily absorbed by the greater noble houses. Furthermore, lesser nobles were themselves subject to pressures from below, and the privy council recognised in 1597 that on the border shires many non-nobles were 'for the maist parte of bettir rank, substance, moyane and calling nor sindrie of the saidis baronis'.[79]

## Conclusion

In the six decades after the Reformation, Scotland experienced a huge increase in the volume of credit transactions, and especially after 1600 this amounted to a credit boom. This boom was fuelled by the changing legal environment that made lending easier and safer, by the growing number of people with money to lend, especially merchants, and by the need and willingness to borrow. Being among the wealthiest people in society, and with land as a secure form of collateral, nobles borrowed more than most. The need and desire to fund expensive lifestyles contributed something to the rush into credit, although much borrowing was undertaken to cover unavoidable periods of heavy expenditure in the life cycle of the family. However, this was not simply a world in which straitened nobles found themselves in debt to merchant financiers since much lending took place within local and kinship communities. Many nobles also engaged in large-scale lending, or were owed money by their hard-pressed tenants. By the 1630s, there is little doubt that some merchants were over-extended and some nobles were hopelessly in debt; both would be cruelly exposed amidst the chaos of the following decade. For those nobles who faced up to their debts at an early opportunity, financial retrenchment could bring relief, and many nobles took sensible steps to put their affairs in order. Others, even among the highest ranks, were drawn into an escalating spiral of borrowing and land sales that left them personally ruined and their house burdened with servicing debts for decades. Only royal intervention saved these families from complete and utter ruin. However, the poor, indebted noble hiding from his creditors and from increasingly effective officers of the law was already a more common sight by the early 1600s.

But did this amount to a widespread financial malaise among the nobility? While many nobles from every rank were failing to manage their finances for a variety of reasons, some personal, others structural, just as many were doing well, and it is perhaps unhelpful to put too much emphasis on the idea of a financial crisis among the nobility. Certainly there is evidence to suggest that, especially in the later sixteenth century, a significant number of nobles were struggling with the impact of war, poor harvests, static rents and inflation. Borrowing became one way of overcoming some of these problems, leaving a legacy of mortgaged estates that could not easily be redeemed when the economy improved after 1600. Noble society became divided between those who were essentially debtors, unable to maintain their noble lifestyles without heavy borrowing, and those who were essentially creditors whose success as estate managers or whose political fortunes freed them from that necessity. This temptation always to live beyond one's means was created by the pressures within noble society itself, and the individual nobleman was always more likely to choose the risks of indebtedness over those of obscurity. This ensured that even among the richest court grandees, the loss of royal office or favour might bring the creditors running to hammer on the door. Therefore, there is little doubt that borrowing allowed the nobility to fund a range of entrepreneurial activities, to build on a grand scale, and to patronise artists, craftsmen and traders of every description. In the relatively confident economic circumstances of the early seventeenth century, their willingness to take on debt contributed to Scotland's prosperity, and perhaps they should not be blamed for failing to anticipate the disastrous consequences for everyone when the political and economic environment altered so dramatically in 1637.

# Part 2

## Family

CHAPTER 5

# Marrying

Marriage in early modern society was a public institution, not a private relationship. In noble society this was especially true, and noble children were schooled from an early age to serve the interests of the lineage in marriage as in everything else. Marriage was not only about the intimate relationship between two individuals, and in many cases the personal feelings of those individuals were scarcely considered. Instead, it had implications for the political and economic welfare of the entire family and for its dependants. This does not mean that individual choice was unimportant, or that people did not fall in love, but the interests of the individual had to be weighed up against other considerations. Tensions arose between parents and their children, between lords and their kinsmen, between nobles and the king as all sought to bring pressure to bear on those men and women whose marriage was under negotiation. What must be teased out of the often inadequate evidence is the extent to which these competing interests succeeded in getting their way, how much influence each had, and how the process of agreeing a marriage treaty was constrained by these constituencies and determined by their agendas. How much freedom did young noblemen and noblewomen have in choosing their partners? What power did fathers have over their children? Did parents and children listen to the wider body of kinsmen and dependants? There is also the question of what it was people were looking for in a spouse; what were the qualities admired and valued in a potential wife or husband? Here there was a fairly clear consensus within noble society as to what was desirable, even if men and women did not always follow the counsel available to them.

## Parental Influence and Individual Choice

According to James VI, 'the principall blessing that yee can get of good companie, will stand in your marrying of a godly and vertuous wife'. Marriage, he thought, was 'the greatest earthly felicitie or miserie, that can come to a man, according as it pleaseth God to blesse or curse the same'. The king's emphasis on companionship is significant, but early modern marriage was more than a personally gratifying relationship, and the centrality of

Table 5.1 Peers' marriages, 1560–1637

| | No. of peers (total sample = 356) | Percentage of sample |
|---|---|---|
| Never married | 18 | 5% |
| Married once | 202 | 57% |
| Married twice | 115 | 32% |
| Married three times | 21 | 6% |

marriage to the rhythm of noble society is widely recognised by historians interested in both the private lives of a powerful élite, and in its more public activities of economic management and political strategy. Getting married was among the most important events in the life cycle of early modern people, whatever their rank in society, changing entirely the lives of men and women, altering their status in the community and their legal rights, while conferring on them moral obligations and privileges.[1] However, the sixteenth century was also an era of profound religious change, affecting ideas about marriage, women, children, the family's relationship to the state, and competing legal codes. How far religion acted as the catalyst to this transformation is debatable, as is its extent and timing, but there was change and noble society was not impervious to it.[2]

The necessity of begetting heirs to titles and estates made marriage almost obligatory for nobles, particulary for eldest sons. Like the English peerage, few Scottish nobles made a conscious choice not to marry (see Table 5.1). Only 5 per cent of peers in the sample never married, but these eighteen individuals include two who were under the legal age to marry, one who surrendered his title to become a friar, and two others who were killed before they had the opportunity to marry. All but one whose ages are known died before they were forty years of age, suggesting that some at least might have postponed marriage rather than taking an irrevocable decision against it. The single case where not to marry was a conscious decision involved the ninth lord Saltoun, who was so enmeshed in debts and litigation that he could not afford to marry. The popularity of marriage extended to younger sons, many of whom could be resourced by their families from the secularisation of church lands that accompanied the Reformation.[3] Most families were able and willing to fund tochers, or dowries, and only a handful of daughters remained unmarried, most of these being from Catholic families, the Reformation having largely closed off the option enthusiastically adopted by Italian fathers of shutting excess daughters up in a nunnery. Four of the seventh earl of Argyll's daughters from his second marriage to the Catholic Englishwoman, Anne Cornwallis, entered holy orders, and a younger daughter of the first earl of Dunfermline, lady Grissel, was remembered as 'a brave lady, who lived to a good age, but would never marrie though she had nobile suitors'.[4]

**Table 5.2 Spread of ages of peers at first marriage, 1560–1637**

| | No. of peers (total sample = 227) | Percentage of sample |
|---|---|---|
| Under 18 years | 38 | 17% |
| 18–25 years | 137 | 60% |
| 26–35 years | 44 | 19% |
| Over 35 years | 8 | 4% |

The appropriate age of marriage was widely debated by early modern theologians, jurists and doctors. While the orthodox view was that early sexual activity weakened men, reduced female fertility, increased the likelihood of deformed children and invited a lessening of respect between young parents and their offspring, the spiritual and physical effects of sexual repression also caused concern. Early modern society had not entirely given up on the medieval idea that the ideal age for women was between puberty and marriage, but young females especially were thought to suffer from greensickness, a form of chloro-anorexin sometimes called the virgin's disease and thought by many to be curable by copulation, as a consequence of prolonged celibacy.[5] In Scotland, the premium placed on producing heirs meant that marriage took place relatively early in life, unlike in Holland where the nobility married much later, and more like England or France where men first married on average in their early twenties and women a few years younger.[6] Under Scots law, betrothal could take place from the age of seven, and marriage was lawful for males at age fourteen and females at age twelve, with the common assumption that consumation would not take place immediately. Although the evidence for very young marriages can be misleading because the contract usually pre-dates the marriage by some years, 17 per cent of those 227 heads of houses of the higher nobility whose ages are known married or were contracted to marry between the legal minimum of fourteen and seventeen years of age (see Table 5.2).

Patrick Maule of Panmure was married in 1562 at the age of fourteen, while the ninth lord Maxwell was twelve years old in 1597 when he was contracted to marry Margaret Hamilton, daughter of lord Hamilton, his tutor, but it was 1601 before their unhappy marriage was solemnised. Only 4 per cent of Scottish nobles did not enter their first marriage until middle age, a handful being in their later thirties and two in their forties. By far the eldest at his first, and only, marriage was Robert Stewart, bishop of Caithness, who was sixty-two in 1578 when he was created fifth earl of Lennox and thrown into marriage with the vivacious Elizabeth Stewart, dowager lady Lovat, who divorced him three years later on the grounds of impotency.[7]

The average age at first marriage for men was 22.5 years, with the sixteenth-century sample being younger at 21.7, and the seventeenth-

**Table 5.3 Average age of peers at first/second/third marriages, 1560–1637**

| | First marriage | Second marriage | Third marriage |
|---|---|---|---|
| 1560–1637 | 22.5 | 37.3 | 47.3 |
| 16th century | 21.7 | 35.5 | 49.7 |
| 17th century | 23.6 | 39.3 | 45 |

**Table 5.4 Difference in age between peers and wives, 1560–1637**

| Husband's age difference from wife | No. of cases (total sample = 50) | Percentage where both spouses' ages are known |
|---|---|---|
| + 20+ years | 2 | 4% |
| + 15–19 years | 2 | 4% |
| + 10–14 years | 8 | 16% |
| + 5–9 years | 9 | 18% |
| + 1–4 years | 19 | 38% |
| Total husbands older than wives | 40 | 80% |
| Same age (0) | 0 | 0% |
| − 1–4 years | 6 | 12% |
| − 5–9 years | 0 | 0% |
| − 10–14 years | 1 | 2% |
| − 15–19 years | 2 | 4% |
| − 20+ years | 1 | 2% |
| Total husbands younger than wives | 10 | 20% |

century averaging 23.6 years of age, a slight but insignificant increase in the age of first marriage over the period (see Table 5.3). Sixty per cent of these men married for the first time between the ages of eighteen and twenty-five, with a further 19 per cent acquiring a wife by the age of thirty-five.

Generally husbands were a few years older than their wives, but not much older – a factor that might have reduced the authoritarian element in the relationship – and for the fifty-five wives whose ages at the time of their husband's first marriage are known, the average age was eighteen, three years younger than the average age of husbands at their first marriage, with no significant variation between the sixteenth- and seventeenth-century samples. However, comparing the ages in fifty marriages where both partners' ages are known produces a slightly different picture (see Table 5.4). While this sample is small, the general pattern is likely to be accurate. Four out of five husbands were older than their wives, but while 18 per cent were less than five years older than their wives, 38 per cent of these men were between five and nine years older than their wives, and 20 per cent were between ten and nineteen years older. Two husbands, 4 per cent of the sample, were twenty or more years older than their wives; John Maxwell was

Table 5.5 Average duration of peers' marriages, 1560–1637

| | Average (years) of first marriage | Average (years) of second marriage | Average (years) of third marriage |
|---|---|---|---|
| 1560–1637 | 19.4 | 14.2 | 8.9 |
| 16th century | 19.7 | 15.6 | 11.2 |
| 17th century | 19.1 | 12.8 | 6.0 |

thirty-six when he acquired the Herries title in 1548 by marrying the fourteen-year-old heiress to the peerage and estates, and the first earl of Perth was thirty-six when he married his fifteen-year-old bride, Isabella Seton, in 1608. Clearly these were exceptional cases, but there were enough instances of very unequally aged partners around for Lethington to make it the subject of satirical poetry.[8] Nevertheless, ill-matched arrangements, common in parts of Europe, particularly Mediterranean regions where husbands were usually much older, were relatively rare.

In one-fifth of the fifty cases where the ages of both spouses is known, wives were older than their husband at his first marriage. The thirty-six-year-old Gordonstoun was unusual in marrying a fifteen-year-old heiress in 1613, but this did not stop him from sharing in the typical disapproval of young men marrying mature women, threatening to turn upside down the norms of society. In 1567, his father, the eleventh earl of Sutherland, had been forcibly married to Barbara Sinclair, the eldest daughter of the fourth earl of Caithness who seized control of his young neighbour after murdering his parents. Apart from the undesirable political background to the marriage, Gordonstoun could scarcely conceal his disgust at what was 'ane unfitt match indeid, a youth of fyftene mareid to a woman of threttie-two yeiris'![9] The Sutherland case was the most scandalous, being a blatantly political attempt by the wife's father to control the earldom. There was an even greater age difference in the marriage between the twenty-two-year-old fifth earl of Cassillis, who chose in 1597 to marry the wealthy forty-two-year-old Jean Fleming, an heiress and widow of chancellor Thirlestane. These were highly unusual cases, however, and mostly the wives were less than five years older than their husbands.

Early modern marriages endured on average for twenty years. Among the Scottish higher nobility, the average length of those 186 first marriages for which evidence is available was 19.4 years, there being no discernible difference between the sixteenth- and seventeenth-century samples (see Table 5.5). The longest first marriage was that between the fifth lord Boyd and Margaret Colquhoun which endured for perhaps as long as fifty-five years (contract dated 1535) until his death in 1590. Another sixteen peers had marriages of over forty years, one of these being a second marriage between the second earl of Mar and Marie Stewart that lasted from 1592 until the earl's death in 1634. Fifty-seven per cent of the heads of houses of the higher nobility only ever married once (see Table 5.1), but for many early modern people who lost a husband or wife, remarriage was common.

Generally, men opted to find a second wife quickly for companionship, to secure the succession better with more male children, or for financial reasons; for example, a significant minority of second wives after 1603 were English widows with valuable sterling incomes. A little over a quarter of peerage families married a second wife following the death of their first wife, a figure close to that found elsewhere.[10] The average second marriage was for 14.2 years, there being a slight fall in length in the seventeenth century from 15.6 to 12.8 years. Six per cent, some twenty-one individuals, married three times, the average length of these marriages, based on a small sample, being 8.9 years. No nobleman married more than three wives. Often the reason for men remarrying was to provide their children with a mother. Robert Crichton of Cluny remarried in 1572 so that his daughters might benefit from a mother's parenting, but in order not to disadvantage their future marriage prospects he married a fairly humble woman, offering only a small life rent in return for an insignificant tocher. Generally remarriage occurred within a relatively short time of death, but this was not always the case. When sir Robert Melville of Burntisland was widowed in 1594 he waited nineteen years before taking a second wife. Did he miss his first wife so much that he could not consider replacing her, or was the experience of marriage so bad that he dared not repeat it for almost two decades? Certainly there were those who thought remarriage a risky business. The third earl of Lothian, who had a long and happy arranged marriage, observed that 'he that succeeded well in a first marriage should contean himselfe with that good fortune and not putt himself in danger to make a shipwreck in a second'.[11]

Women had slightly different agendas in seeking remarriage. Widowhood was less common in northern European countries like Scotland where spouses were closer in age, and while one noblewoman did not remarry because 'I might wrong my poor children and his memorie that I do and have so much reason to respect', there was less social pressure not to dishonour a dead husband by remarrying. While women were likely to experience some difficulties in finding a second husband after the age of forty, for noblewomen the opportunities for remarriage were higher because of their wealth, and often they had to be wary of potential suitors. Some women who had children from a previous marriage and had financial independence were reluctant to remarry because they might lose the rights to the wardship of their children or control over their income. In 1610, one anonymous lady who had been propositioned replied that 'scho culd not with gud maners hear of mariage for the present tuiching ony man, and wald deall with nain quhill scho had ane provisione for her dochter'. Margaret Hay, daughter of the seventh lord Yester, was only fifteen when in 1607 she was married as his third wife to chancellor Dunfermline, a man thirty-seven years her senior. Thus when her husband died in 1621, she was only twenty-nine years old and rich. However, she chose not to remarry immediately, having financial independence and Dunfermline's six-year-old son and heir in her charge, and it was only when her son married in 1632 that the countess thought it opportune to find another husband. In the following year, aged forty-two, she married the first earl of Callendar, a man closer to her own age who had recently returned from successful mercenary service in Germany. In contrast to her first marriage, when she was treated as a chattel by her father, Margaret Hay drove a hard bargain in the marriage contract.[12]

The age profile in these second and subsequent marriages was different from that in first marriages. The average age of men at their second marriage was thirty-seven, the sixteenth-century sample being younger at thirty-five, while the average age at second marriage in the smaller seventeenth-century sample rose to thirty-nine (see Table 5.3). However, the women they married were much younger, averaging twenty-four years of age in a range from seventeen to forty-four. In this group a large age difference between partners was more common, the biggest being twenty-five years between the forty-four-year-old John Ramsay, viscount Haddington, and his nineteen-year-old English bride. With third marriages the age gap could be even greater, as in the case of chancellor Dunfermline's marriage to Margaret Hay, but there is little data available, and most of this points to marriage between men and women of mature years. For example, the sixth lord Lovat was fifty-eight when he married as his third wife Katherine Rose, a forty-eight-year-old widow. Those older noblemen who married young wives were primarily looking for women with child-bearing potential, although some were also taking advantage of their freedom to choose youth over experience. Of course, some noblemen were still relatively young; the eighth earl of Angus was twenty at the time of his second marriage on Christmas Day 1575 to Margaret Leslie, daughter of the fifth earl of Rothes, five months after the death of his first wife. However, four noblemen were in their sixties, sir Alexander Fraser of Philorth being sixty-nine when he married for a second time in 1606. Twenty-one noblemen, mostly men in their forties and fifties, entered a third marriage, but they ranged from the unlucky ninth earl of Errol who married his third wife in six years in 1590, being only twenty-six at the time, to the eighty-six-year-old first lord Melville who in 1613 married Jean Stewart, lady Lindores, widowed a few years previously. Two of the brides in these twenty-one third marriages were only fifteen.

For nobles, marriage was a long-term ambition, often planned for their children from birth, in some cases even before birth. Rash impetuosity on the part of the young was discouraged, as one would expect in an age grounded in Ciceronian precepts. Hence one uncle advised his young nephew to 'do nothing rashlie therin; for it is in the chose of a wyffe as in a project of warre, wherin to erre but once is to be undone for ever'.[13] Choice was also likely to be dominated by the wishes of parents who would have been behaving neglectfully if they left their sons and daughters to make bad decisions. Undoubtedly, some fathers behaved as though their moral authority and financial power had the sanction of the law. In 1566, the third lord Ruthven and the fourth lord Gray agreed a complicated series of interlocked marriages. At that time the master of Ruthven was married to Gray's eldest daughter, but he was terminally ill. The marriage had been short, no heirs had been produced, and the two lords wanted to continue the alliance between their houses. Therefore, it was decided that if the master of Ruthven died, his brother, William, would marry any one of Gray's five unmarried daughters, the choice being made by Ruthven, but without any additional tocher. Furthermore, Gray's eldest son was to marry Barbara Ruthven in fulfilment of an earlier agreement. Fathers might also impose vetoes, as when in 1575 George Hakett of Pitfirrane found that the father of the woman he wanted to marry had raised objections to his ambitions, leaving him with little to do but write an impassioned plea.[14] Such behaviour was more common in the sixteenth century, although high-handedness on the part of fathers did not die out in the early seventeenth century. In 1623, the second marquis of Hamilton broke off negotiations for the marriage of his daughter to Archibald Campbell, lord Lorne, deciding that he would 'dispose of her another way'. And it was fathers who mattered. The sixth earl of Morton succeeded in marrying his eldest son to one of the duke of Buckingham's kinswomen in 1627 but his wife only found out 'be the coumoun report'. She was worried that her son's views had not been taken into account, warning that 'if it be ane gud match ye sal have al the prais, if it be evil ye wil get uthers to regreat it althoucht it can not [be] mendit'.[15] In the last resort, the degree of latitude allowed to children depended on the relationship between family members and the extent to which fathers or brothers were prepared to use their financial power. In his 1612 testament, the first lord Balmerino made provision for his daughters but left instructions that if any of them either 'abuse thamselfis in harlottrie' or chose a husband other than one selected by his family and friends, then the tocher was to be reduced according to the status of the husband. Balmerino observed that:

> as the law gives tham libertie in thair mariage, whilk I will not haif thair broder to restraine, so I will nocht burding him to give tham any more tocher nor after the custum of the cuntrey may ansuear to the conjunctfie thay ar by thair mariage to resaife.[16]

Early modern parents were unlikely to ignore their children's wishes entirely, and the church's traditional view that restraints should be placed on parental authority was reaffirmed by the Reformation. Besides, in Scotland the legal context was different from somewhere like Italy where fathers had great authority over their children's marriage, or France where new legislation in 1567 required young men up to the age of thirty, or women up to the age of twenty-five, to acquire parental consent before marrying, or England where in 1604 the convocation of Canterbury underlined patriarchal authority. In these countries, marriage without parental consent was seen as a threat to order.[17] The relative freedom to marry that Scottish children enjoyed was based on the enduring influence even after the Reformation of canon law on Scots law which required 'a true consent' by both parties as the basis of marriage, the exchange of vows followed by intercourse being more important in law than religious ritual. While marriage fell under the jurisdiction of the secular commissary courts, the canonical emphasis on consent meant that seeking the permission of the parents was more a question of propriety and a recognition of family power structures than of law.[18]

Fathers like Balmerino could impose their will, even from beyond the grave, but it was uncommon for them to force children into unwanted marriages, and by the seventeenth century it was increasingly likely that sons and daughters would be consulted. Some children did act in defiance of their families, although elopement was rare, being regarded as abduction by the law which sought to prevent young women from being forced into marriage.[19] In 1590, James VI took exception to the secret marriage between the Catholic ninth earl of Errol and Elizabeth Douglas, the youngest daughter of the fifth earl of Morton. The latter, however, shrugged the matter off, claiming 'he could not restrain the affection of his daughter, and was forced to give way unto it'. The earl also had problems in 1592 over a second daughter who married the seventh earl of Argyll against his own and his wife's initial wishes.[20] Perhaps the fifth earl of Morton was an over-indulgent old man, but wise parents did take their children's views into account. The first earl of Kellie advised the second earl of Mar that the marriage plans he had for one of his daughters were all very well but that he should 'follow a lytill of hir owin mynd'. A few years later, Kellie confidently informed Mar that a younger son, Henry, would never marry his mistress, 'nor noe woman else without your approbatione', but in spite of Mar's opposition to the match he was persuaded to agree to it.[21] The countess of Haddington was disappointed by the decision in 1636 of her eldest son, sir Patrick Hume of Polwarth, to marry 'without any gret regaird to my openyon or consent'. She regarded the bride as beneath him and was unsurprised that 'the tocher is very mean'. Margaret Dundas, daughter of sir Walter Dundas of that Ilk, accepted what her male relatives considered to be an unsuitable offer of marriage, and 'uterit in plaine termes that ilk ane of us all stuid [in] awe and feirit uthers, but devill ane schoe stuid [in] awe of, and schoe carit nocht for ane of our consentis'.[22] The subversive behaviour of all these young people was reflected in popular culture. The comedy *Philotus*, fashionable in the first decade of the seventeenth century, was in part about the absurdity of an old man of eighty wishing to marry a young girl of fourteen. It was also about the stupidity of a father who tried to force his daughter to comply, and how the young people in the tale succeeded in circumscribing paternal authority by showing up the foolishness of the older generation.[23]

Medieval and early modern society recognised the aspirations and feelings of those individuals involved in marriage negotiations, and how significant this period was in seeing the emergence of the companionable marriage and of affective relations is debatable. However, the burdens of lineage, status and property meant that nobles were more constrained in their choice of spouse than other ranks in society. Love was not considered a good reason for entering into a marriage, whatever might have emerged afterwards; hence the countess of Haddington reminded one of her sons of the old proverb, 'folow love and it wol fle, fle love and it wol folow ye'.[24] Yet early modern poets had a great deal to say about love. By the mid-sixteenth century, there was in Scotland a long-established tradition of courtly love poetry in which the instructional element emphasised the necessity of always loving God more than man or woman, in which self-control must be exercised, and in which the lover is almost always despairing. Alexander Scott's love poetry is perhaps the best of this genre, he being a poet at queen Mary's court, and his work is in the typical style of courtly love complaint – for example, playing with themes of unrequited love in 'To luv unluvit'. In Alexander Montgomery's poem, 'To his maistress', love is again out of reach. Unattainable love continued to be a theme among early seventeenth-century poets like David Murray, while Robert Aytoun also wrote about the inconstancy of love, poking fun at the extreme expressions of courtly love in which reason was subjected to passion. He counselled moderation, suggesting that 'To think that lovers die as they pretend;/If all that say they die had died indeed,/Sure, long ere now the world had had an end'.[25]

Nevertheless, affection was nurtured by some like Hugh Montgomery, first viscount Airds, who wrote one of the few surviving love letters containing an offer of marriage to Sara Maxwell, countess of Wigton, on 20 April 1625 in which the idea of courtly love was gently expressed with just enough artifice to win her hand. A desire to marry for companionship brought about the marriage in 1638 of Patrick Maule of Panmure, a man of fifty-three, and his third wife, Mary Erskine, a widow. Their marriage contract denied any material motivation in their decision, insisting only on a desire for 'the company and conversation of each other' that sprang from religious compatibility. Significantly, both these cases involved older people able to make their own choices, and both were from the seventeenth century, possibly an indicator of a shift in culture or of the better survival of correspondence. Therefore there does appear to have been a growing sense that marriage should not only be entered into freely, but that it was preferable for it to be preceeded by signs of affection. For, wrote Gordonstoun, 'How many tragedie do wee daylie sie and heir to proceeid from enforced marriage', and he counselled his nephew to seek the advice of kinsmen, 'but seeing the matter concernes you neerest, have the cheifest voice therin your self'.[26] Evidence of such freedom being exercised can be recovered. In the spring of 1591, the seventeen-year-old second duke of Lennox eloped with and married Sophia Ruthven, a sister of the third earl of Gowrie. Lennox wrote to a friend, asking for his help in persuading the king to give his blessing to a marriage he had expressly forbidden:

> And as to the performance of mariages I dowt not bot his Majestie as lykwys all trew christians acknawledgis thame concludit be God In the hevines and cannot be eschewed as I am suir myne hes bene frome the beginning haifing my hairt movit with sick extreme affectione did willinglie be my aithe and faithfull promeis bind my self thairto that nathair with self conscience nor honour culd I schew the same.[27]

The king did forgive Lennox, but sadly Sophie Ruthven was dead within the year, probably a victim of pregnancy.

In general, women were not expected to take the initiative in wooing a husband, although courtship poetry does reveal a distinct female voice. As the fifth earl of Morton wrote in 1593, 'it is a great disgrace for a gentlewoman to woo and then be disappointed'.[28] However, rich and powerful widows did play a more proactive role than previously unmarried girls, having considerable financial independence. A keen awareness of her own self-preservation guided the marriage plans of Margaret Hay, the widowed countess of Dunfermline. In 1633, she insisted that her future husband write a prenuptial marriage contract in his own hand, promising never to meddle in her conjunct fee without her permission, and 'doe by these disclaim all rights, title of right, claims of right whatsoever, I can pretend, therunto as her husband any tyme heirefter'. One of the most sensational marriages of the period occurred in November 1597 when, two years after her husband's death, the forty-three-year-old dame Jean Fleming, lady Thirlestane, married the young fifth earl of Cassillis, a man half her age. The earl, who was not bound by parental constraints and had reached his legal majority, took this step 'without ony off his freindis adwyise', causing outrage among his kinsmen, especially as there was another outstanding marriage contract. Both Cassillis and his new wife had to endure the equivalent of a noble charivari at court which 'mokit the samin mareage, and maid sonattis in thair contempt'. The fact that Cassillis was now unlikely to sire any heirs made his action particularly foolish, and the king regarded it as utterly irresponsible knowingly to marry a barren woman because of other attractions.[29] What gave the new countess of Cassillis the courage to weather this social embarrassment was that as a rich widow she was able to negotiate an attractive marriage contract raising her into the highest ranks of the nobility. Nor would such independently minded women marry any man who came along, whatever his status. When in June 1607, lady Jane Drummond discovered that her name was being touted around as a wife for the recently widowed seventh earl of Argyll who had an heir, five daughters and heavy debts, she wrote that 'I doe not esteem the place of a second wyfe so muche, his estate being as it is'. Another widow, lady Drum, was also approached on Argyll's behalf, and while she was flattered by the earl's status, she was worried about the financial arrangements of a proposed marriage that offered little to her or 'thame that shall come after me, for wee are not borne for our selfis, bot cheifly for our posteritie, wherof if I were cairles I would ne thought and justly, very unadvysed'.[30] Lady Drum had internalised the values of her society to the extent that she did not need a father to instruct her in the value of her marriage to the broader interests of the lineage and her place in the continuum of the kindred's history.

## Kinsmen and Lords

It was this knowledge that an individual only played a part in a greater whole that made it essential to consult widely among kinsmen and friends, who often appeared as signators on marriage contracts. In a preliminary contract in June 1574 it was agreed that before the marriage could take place, a fuller contract would be drawn up 'be advys of freindis and men of judgment'. Where kinsmen were ignored, problems could follow; hence the anger of the Kennedy lairds in 1597. The ninth lord Glamis' marriage in 1595 initiated a lasting rift between the young lord and his uncle and former tutor, sir Thomas Lyon, master of Glamis, who thought the marriage had been brokered against his own advice and wishes. When in 1621 the king negotiated an English marriage on behalf of the second earl of Home, a minor, the Humes were irate, insisting that 'in other matters of importance concerning the earle, the countesse his mother [also an English lady] might make her intentions and courses knowne to them, and heare and respect their faithfull advice therein, which, if scho neglected, they could have no contentment to mell in the bussines'.[31] More commonly, lords did consult kinsmen. In 1630, old sir Duncan Campbell of Glenorchy was warned by a friend against marrying his youngest daughter, Jean, to John Murray, recently created earl of Atholl, for 'quhen ye have gevin them your dochter and greite meins it will be bot a staf to ding your selff with'. It made sense to listen to such advice and, as one noblewoman wrote in 1636, she would never marry without the guidance of family and friends, for she would 'not do rashly that which they might justly blame me for'.[32]

The absence of kinsmen left women in a vulnerable position in the marriage market. Jean Fleming, the only daughter and heiress of the fourth lord Fleming, lost her father in 1558 when she was four years old, while her uncle and tutor died fourteen years later. In 1577, the twenty-three-year-old heiress was still unmarried when she complained to the privy council that her affairs had been mismanaged. In spite of a sympathetic hearing, it was 1583 before she married her first husband, John Maitland of Thirlestane, at the relatively advanced age of twenty-nine. A similar concern exercised Nicolas Murray, who in April 1604 was contemplating an offer of marriage during the absence at court of her brother, sir John Murray of Abercairny. She pleaded for him to pay more attention to the affairs of his house 'sieng ye ar the cheif man that I suld acount of in my fathers place'. Nicolas was worried that her brother's lack of interest in the family's affairs was damaging her prospects, for 'I think I ame lyk one kinles sieng at sic a tyme I have non of my fathiris hous to countinance me'.[33]

For all families, one of the most threatening aspects of a minority was that the marriage of minors – in males a minority ended at twenty-one, while for females a minority ended at fourteen years of age – might pass out of the hands of the kindred. For the feudal superior, the rights of ward and marriage offered an opportunity to strengthen his own clientele, but he also carried a heavy responsibility. As Riccarton observed when discussing female wardship, 'the superior must bear the blame if the marriage turns out ill, and equally if he allows the opportunity of a good marriage to slip'. The marriage of an heir could fall to the king who, as feudal superior, 'hes the powar to dispone his mariage to whome he pleisis, or els to keap it to himself'. In 1574, the regent Morton gave his nephew, the eighth earl of Angus, the marriage of Walter Scott, younger of Branxholm. Marriage, therefore, might be treated as an asset to be traded on the market, such as in 1593 when the king sold the ward and marriage of the third earl of Moray to the fifth earl of Atholl for 'a great pecuniall sowme'. Andrew Wood of Largo was able to sell the ward and marriage of Dorothea Stewart, sister and heiress of the impoverished third lord Methven, to the fifth earl of Rothes in 1585 for 5000 merks, ten times what he had paid by way of composition to the crown a month earlier on his appointment as comptroller.[34] There was a valuable currency in noble marriages that often saw an undignified scramble for wardships. In November 1598, it was reported that the secretary, James Elphinstone, had acquired the wardship of the heir to the dying sixth earl of Menteith even before the latter had passed away. Both the king and his treasurer, sir George Hume of Spott, offended the tenth earl of Angus in 1602 when, on hearing that the earl was dying, James granted Spott a gift of the master of Angus's marriage. Embarrassment followed when Angus made a full recovery.[35] Not surprisingly, fathers and tutors sought to circumvent the pitfalls of their heir's marriage falling into unfriendly and predatory hands, but repurchasing wardship and marriage could be expensive. In 1598, the curators of the third earl of Moray were still paying the second earl of Mar the residue of the 12 000 merks for the wardship and marriage of his long-dead parents. Meanwhile, in 1595, the young earl's own wardship and marriage had exchanged hands for £22 000. As a favour to a noble house the king might refuse to exploit the ward and marriage, as in 1624 when the young fourth duke of Lennox succeeded his father.[36]

All rulers, even popes, interfered in the marriage market, and in England both James VI and I and Charles I increased royal meddling in the marriages of the nobility after Elizabeth's relatively lax approach. In certain cases, James VI offered to pay the dowry of the daughters of favoured nobles, and in 1586 he was so determined that the sixth earl of Huntly should marry Lennox's sister, Henrietta Stewart, that he gave Huntly 5000 merks to cover the expenses of bringing the lady over from France and paid most of the wedding expenses. In 1621, prince Charles helped his bedchamber servant, sir Robert Ker of Ancram, win the hand of Anne Stanley, a well-off widow and the only daughter of the sixth earl of Derby. Charles wrote to the lady's mother 'I desire that you will faver his sute, which I will take to bee a great faver to me'.[37] Where an heir of ward refused to marry according to his superior's wishes, 'his superior haveing offered to him ane marriage without disparage or dishonor', the superior could retain control over the heir's lands until a fine, the double avail, was paid. Only where the superior's choice of wife was inappropriate on account of rank, age or certain medical conditions might the vassal avoid a fine by claiming disparity. The ward and marriage of the sixth lord Hume was in the hands of the first earl of Gowrie when in May 1582 the latter sent his procurator to the young lord's Edinburgh lodgings where he read out an offer of marriage from the earl on behalf of either of his daughters. Hume was too poor to pay the fine and accepted the offer, but as a consequence of Gowrie's fall from power, he never did marry one of the Ruthven sisters.[38] Lords too held the ward and marriage of their vassals. On 12 February 1593, the eleventh earl of Sutherland authorised his two procurators to offer in marriage Margaret Gordon, daughter of John Gordon of Buckie, to Alexander Sutherland of Forse whose ward and marriage was held by the earl. If Buckie refused his lord's choice of a bride, they were to demand the 'doubill availl of his mairriage', failing which all costs and damages. These arrangements appear, on the whole, to have operated effectively and with remarkably little friction. Less formally, ladies also acted as marriage brokers. For example, Jean Stewart, wife of the sixth lord Lovat, married her maidservants to local lairds drawn from similar status to these women with a view to building up her husband's clientele.[39]

Tutors or curators were expected to exercise their authority in order to protect the interests of a minor against the schemes of less scrupulous kinsmen. In 1621, the second earl of Mar and the other curators of Margaret Sommerville, younger daughter and co-heiress of the seventh lord Sommerville, successfully contested a decision by their ward's mother and her second husband to marry her to 'a young man destitute of meanis and nowayes aggrieabill to hir in ony conditioun quhatsumevir', the intention being to defraud her of the greater part of her estate. Sometimes a cautious tutor found himself at odds with a ward who wished to be married. In 1634, the widowed lady Balloch was torn by her daughter's desire to marry a nephew of sir Duncan Campbell of Glenorchy in the face of opposition from her tutor, the seventh lord Ogilvy. The young man wanted to marry without a contract, arguing that he could take Ogilvy to court at a later date to recover his wife's portion, but being a minor he could not infeft the girl in a conjunct fee. Lady Balloch was rightly worried that 'by law he may seik quhat is hirs [her daughter's] but shoe hes nothing to urge ane competent meiting for ane lyfrent'. Here Ogilvy was saving a foolish girl from ruin, but in other cases it was the tutor who exploited his office. In 1636, lawyers acting for the fifteen-year-old lady Elizabeth Scott successfully brought a case against her ten-year-old brother, the second earl of Buccleuch, and his tutor, the greedy secretary Stirling, who had neglected to perform the terms of her father's 1629 testament, providing Elizabeth with an annual rent of £2000 that was to be invested for her marriage portion.[40]

## Marriage Strategies

The surviving literary evidence from early modern society discusses women overwhelmingly in terms of their roles as good or bad wives, as adjuncts of their husbands, and the much fewer Scottish texts betray a similar absence of that autonomous female identity tentatively surfacing elsewhere.[41] Both James VI and Gordonstoun echoed conventional ideas in writing that marriage was 'commanded by God therby to eschew all sinful lust, for procreation of children, and that man should have a wyffe for his helper; these be the cheiffe causes of mariage; as for beautie, riches and allyance, these be but accessorie causes'. Gordonstoun counselled that a bride should be young enough to bear children, there should be no hereditary sickness in her family, she should be a virgin of good character, having the same religion as her husband, be well educated, and her parents should be virtuous. He gave some prominence to physical appearance: 'Make not choise of a dwarf or a foole to be your wyffe, for from the one you may beget a race of pigmeis, and the other will be your daylie greiff and vexation'. Yet while Gordonstoun advised against a wife 'so base and deformed that may breid contempt in others, and bring you to a loathed bed', she should not be too beautiful as 'everie carnell eye shal bespeak you injurie'. In discussing the accessory causes of marriage, beauty, riches and alliances, James VI asked:

> what can all these worldly respects availe, when a man shall finde himselfe coupled with a divel, to be one flesh with him, and the halfe marrow in his bed? Then (though too late) shall he finde that beautie without bountie, wealth without wisdome, and great friendship without grace and honestie; are but fair shewes, and the deceitfull masques of infinite miseries.

The emphasis on looking beyond the superficially beautiful was a common theme of the age, and poets were for ever reminding women in particular 'Be then not proud of that, which at the best/Decrepit age will spoyle, or sicknesse wast'. Patrick Hannay humorously warned of the dangers of breeding dwarfs from a small spouse, and of the likelihood that very tall people might be less intelligent, but counselled women against being fooled by some dandy who spent his time perfecting his appearance – 'Thou must the substance, not the shade esteem'. Zacharie Boyd, minister at Glasgow, was more graphic in his dismissal of youthful beauty. 'Behold her who within these fourtie yeares seemed a perfection of Beautie, a ravisher of eyes; behold her nowin her fourescore with her wrinkled cheekes, and her glassen eyes, and her rotten teeth, and stinking breath'. Of course, there were ways of overcoming physical disadvantages, and in 1596 a generous jointure proved enough to persuade Jean Stewart, one of the queen's ladies in waiting, to marry the ugly sixth lord Lovat.[42]

King James was emphatic that a prospective wife be 'of a whole and cleane race, not subject to the hereditary sicknesses, either of the soule or the body'. Following the Roman satirist, Apuleius, he suggested that 'if a man will be careful to breed horses and dogs of good kinds, how much more careful should he be, for the breed of his owne loines'.[43] One consideration in any breeding scheme had always been kinship. Marriage within the fourth degrees of kinship was forbidden by canon law, and this remained a legal obstacle even after 1560. Ways around the law had always been found, and in March 1565 John Hamilton, archbishop of St Andrews, using those powers devolved to him by the pope, granted a dispensation to the fourth earl of Bothwell and Jean Gordon to be married in spite of the fact that they were 'related in the double fourth degrees of consanguinity'. In 1567, the same grounds of consanguinity were used to justify their divorce. A parliament later that year opened up the marriage market, permitting marriage within the second degree of consanguinity, or affinity, while simultaneously making incest a capital offence. Two years later, the regent Moray sought the kirk's clarification on the interpretation of this sin, and received the reply that a man who slept with a woman who had been his mother's brother's paramour was indeed guilty of incest. Those subsequently executed were never nobles, but the whisperings of incest at the highest levels in society continued to fuel scandalous gossip.[44]

There were other issues to consider. When in 1621 the eighth lord Yester was agonising over a proposed marriage to Jane Seton, daughter of chancellor Dunfermline, he described his proposed wife as 'ane directe puritaine' with a spotless reputation, besides which 'shee is ane very comely wenche, and may be a wyfe to the beste in the kingdome'. Lord Yester's approval of his future wife's religion was a new consideration in the sixteenth century, when discernible Catholic and Protestant communities emerged, seeking suitable alliances within their own ranks, a trend common throughout an increasingly divided Europe.[45] In Scotland, Protestants slowly acquired the upper hand in the marriage market, and when the Catholic fourth earl of Cassillis married the sister of the Protestant eighth lord Glamis in 1566, he took the opportunity to convert. On the other hand, while in 1588 the sixth earl of Huntly was obliged to make a declaration of his Protestant orthodoxy before marrying Henrietta Stewart, both remained stalwart Catholics. However, the church and crown became increasingly intrusive into Catholic marriage arrangements. When in the autumn of 1609 a marriage was proposed between Mar's eldest son and a younger daughter of the ninth earl of Errol, the former thought it wise to seek the king's permission. James approved of the match because he was confident that the Mar household's Protestant orthodoxy would bring the girl around to conforming, as had Mar's own wife a generation earlier. Nevertheless, while such marriages did go ahead, James VI was right to counsel that 'disagreement in Religion bringeth ever with it, disagreement in maners'.[46]

Among a political élite, it was unavoidable that political priorities were significant in planning a family's marriage strategy, although evidence from both France and Italy suggests marriage was not a strong bond on which to found political loyalties.[47] Nevertheless, for families of the first rank and with the greatest national profile, marriage strategies were likely to centre on the court and on national politics. In 1586, the second duke of Lennox responded to an offer from lord Hamilton of his daughter in marriage by thanking Hamilton for his offer 'tending to the unity of our housis'. When in 1622 Kellie heard in London that his cousin Mar's youngest daughter was to marry the first earl of Melrose's eldest son, he instantly realised the ramifications of a match that united the treasurer and the influential secretary, strengthening his own hand against enemies at court.[48] In seeking marriage alliances with English noble families after 1603, the Scots often found social snobbery to be a barrier, although in 1616 viscount Fenton expressed disregard for English exclusiveness, suggesting to Mar that a marriage alliance with the house of Rothes 'maye verrye weill be a matche to onye nobile mans docheter in Ingland'. For others, however, English marriages were attractive, not least for the political advantages. The implications of a marriage in 1620 between the eldest son of the second marquis of Hamilton and a daughter of the English peer, the first lord Feilding, were not lost on one Scottish observer, who commented that as a consequence of the match Hamilton 'will have great frinds heir'.[49]

At a local level these marriage alliances were even more important. The marriage in 1596 of the eldest son of Lauchlan Maclean of Duart and a sister of Kenneth Mackenzie of Kintail was certainly seen by contemporaries as of major political significance in the Western Isles. Women were just as aware of these political implications. In 1607, lady Drum agreed that an alliance to a Highland lord 'is good for my freinds, if the world wer as it had wount to be, bot now since all is peacable, the greatest necessitie of freindship wilbe in the law countrey, if men continew in ther dewtifull obedience'.[50] Marriage was an effective means of estate acquisition, particularly for powerful territorial lords, and even in states like Denmark where primogeniture was weak, the nobility were able to manipulate the marriage of their children in pursuit of consolidating their landed holdings. Because local considerations dominated estate-building strategies, early modern society produced geographically endogamous marriage markets, particularly in more remote regions and, as in Tuscany, in reaction to economic or political pressures. Gordonstoun suggested that when rich heiresses became available in neighbouring shires, his nephew should arrange matches for his sons or friends, and any gentlewoman who married into the country was to be protected to encourage others to look favourably on living in Sutherland. At the same time, the earl should try to prevent Sutherland women from marrying outwith the country 'for that will drawe the riches of your province to your nighbours'.[51] This use of marriage to promote the local and regional interests of a family can be seen at work in the case of the house of Elphinstone, which continued to make its principal marriage alliances in the Stirlingshire locality, while using the marriages of younger sons and daughters to strengthen its precarious hold over the Kildrummy estates in Aberdeenshire.[52] Marriage might be manipulated by families with a history of conflict, hoping thereby to cement a recently concluded peace, although, as was found in Italy, such arrangements were fraught with pitfalls. When on 24 March 1564 the feuding Kers and Scotts signed a peace settlement, it included a marriage alliance between the two kindreds. However, the projected marriage failed to take place, initiating a new quarrel, and the matter was brought before the privy council for judgement in January 1578 when the two families agreed they did not really want to open up old wounds. A marriage in 1588 between Sara Maxwell, sister of the fifth lord Herries, and James Johnstone of that Ilk was arranged in the hope of being 'a spur and a meyne to pacefie all preceiding quarrellis betuix the twa housis, and to burie thayme in tyme cuming'. In this case the bloodfeud was not halted, Johnstone being murdered in the course of it, but the marriage was successful.[53]

All nobilities exuded degrees of social snobbery towards the idea of marriage between people of unequal rank, and the threat of derogation carried by *mésalliance* followed naturally from the idea of nobility as something carried in the blood. On the whole, therefore, an endogamy of rank was practised, although evidence can be found, for example from Normandy, that suggests a more permeable barrier to marriage with people from different ranks.[54] In poetry, if not in real life, the idea that love ignored rank was allowed some expression, thus Alexander Scott's observation that 'luv makis nobill ladeis thrall/To basser men of birth and blud'. Scott's point was that unbridled passion made women behave foolishly, sacrificing their status and their reputations, as well as the interests of their families, for an emotion that ought to be under control. In the mid-sixteenth century, sir David Lindsay of the Mount reflected the concerns among the nobility over marriages between their children and the illegitimate offspring of clerics, and James VI expressed the view that, particularly in the selection of a first wife, a man who married 'basely beneath his ranke ... will ever be the lesse accounted of thereafter'. Denmilne took the view that while canon law had never recognised nobility of descent, children born of lawfully married noble parents, preferably both parents, were themselves noble. There was considerable consensus around his point that 'If a Noble woman marry a plebian, by such a matrimoniall acte sche not only impairs hir dignity bot losses by the law her Nobility as if she had expossed her selve to be a comon strumpet'. Denmilne was reflecting French practice where *mésalliance* had real consequences in the form of derogation and the attendant tax penalties. Riccarton, who was a lawyer, also argued that a noblewoman who married a commoner suffered derogation.[55]

Patrick Hannay's poem, 'A happy husband, or, directions for a maid to choose her mate', raised this problem of rank and concluded that as a general rule people should marry within their own kind:

> In man the fault is more to be excused,
> Who of low birth, for beauty, hath one choosed.
> His lightness therein ever love is deemed,
> Yet as his place, his wife shall be esteemed.
> But when a woman of a noble race
> Doth match with man of far inferior place,
> She cannot him ennoble; he is still
> In place as she first found him, good, or ill.

Even though Hannay believed true nobility to lie in virtue, hence the importance of lineage since such qualities were heritable, yet 'Things different do never well agree,/True liking lodges in equality'. Of course, even within a society so conscious of rank, it was never entirely clear what was meant by equality. When in 1580 James Stewart married Elizabeth Stewart, countess of Moray, thus acquiring an earldom, it was reported that the wedding caused 'the great misliking of the best part of the Earl of Murray's friends [friends of the late regent Moray] to see his daughter so meanly married as to the Abbot of St Combe's son'.[56] But had these friends any cause for such snobbery? The first earl of Moray was only raised to the peerage in 1562 and he was illegitimate, although his father had been James V and his mother the daughter of an earl. The new second earl of Moray, on the other hand, was legitimate and his father was sir James Stewart of Doune, commendator of St Colme, whose own grandfather had been the second lord Avondale and whose mother was a younger daughter of the third lord Lindsay: hardly a mean pedigree.

An analysis of the social status of the women who married peers is

**Table 5.6 Social status of wives of peers (based on wives' fathers), 1560–1637**

| Status of fathers-in-law | Peers | Barons/lairds | Others |
|---|---|---|---|
| **1560–1637** (total sample = 473) | 56.2% | 40.5% | 3.3% |
| **16th century** (total sample = 280) | 52.1% | 42.5% | 5.4% |
| **17th century** (total sample = 193) | 61.7% | 35.7% | 2.6% |

difficult because of the changing status of so many individuals throughout their lifetime. Nevertheless, peers overwhelmingly married within the nobility, 56 per cent of marriages involving peers being to daughters of other peers, and 41 per cent to daughters of barons or lairds (see Table 5.6). There was a significant shift towards favouring daughters of peers in the seventeenth century, but this might reflect the fact that there were many more peers with daughters on the marriage market as a result of new creations. Gordonstoun certainly complained c.1620 that the highest-ranking peerage families were seeking to distance themselves from their social inferiors by refusing to consider marriages with baronial houses. He agreed it was desirable that the earl of Sutherland should marry among his own rank, but 'do not you spair to marie laird or barrone his doughter, of a good stock and well descended, provyding shee lyke you weell, and that shee be wealthie'. He was not concerned that such wives would be of a lower rank, arguing that 'it is not the wyffe that nobilitats the husband, but the husband nobilitats the wyffe'. In fact, many baronial families who sought marital alliances with the peerage were successful. For example, the marriage relationships of successive lairds of Innes in Aberdeenshire between the 1570s and 1630s demonstrates their achievement in penetrating the highest levels of the regional marriage market of the north-east.[57] For those who rose rapidly in rank there were no major obstacles to marriage into the highest circles of the peerage. The children of the first earl of Haddington, perhaps the most obvious outsider in the early seventeenth-century peerage, demonstrate his upward social trajectory. All three of Haddington's own wives were from the lesser nobility, providing him with little social cachet, but between 1610 and 1622 he used his children to form a series of increasingly impressive links with peerage families.[58]

As Gordonstoun suggested, one good reason for negotiating a marriage with families of lesser rank was money. Thus the estate of Robert Stewart of Rosyth was saved in 1577 when his son married the daughter of James McGill of Rankeillor, the clerk register and a man on the make. The acquisition of a rich heiress was attractive whatever her rank within the nobility, but because of entailing these were relatively few, with perhaps 8 per cent of the wives of peers being heiresses or co-heiresses (see Table 5.7). Only daughters were also rare, representing 6 per cent of the wives of peers, and

**Table 5.7 Succession status of peer's wives, 1560–1637**

| | Heiress or co-heiress | Only daughter | Eldest daughter | Younger daughter | Illegitimate daughter | Unknown status |
|---|---|---|---|---|---|---|
| **1560–1637** | 7.6% | 5.9% | 24.7% | 34.7% | 1.5% | 25.4% |
| **16th century** | 7.5% | 5.4% | 23.9% | 33.6% | 2.5% | 27.1% |
| **17th century** | 8.3% | 6.3% | 25.9% | 36.3% | 0% | 20.2% |

25 per cent were eldest daughters of nobles, although these are minimum figures since the data on 38 per cent of the wives is inadequate.

Money, therefore, was one of the chief concerns of Michael Balfour, first lord Balfour, who in 1606 negotiated a deal with Robert Arnot, younger of Newton, to take over all the debts lying on his lands. Arnot altered his own surname as part of a process of adoption prior to marrying Balfour's only daughter and heiress. The curators of the seventeen-year-old fifth earl of Montrose were able to secure for him a lucrative contract when in 1629 he was married to Magdalene Carnegie. In some respects she was a poor match, being the youngest of the first lord Carnegie's six daughters. Carnegie had already secured good husbands for all the other daughters at a cost of 90 000 merks, but his position as the young earl's tutor offered an opportunity for social climbing he could not resist. Montrose's status and the fact that Magdalene was the youngest daughter with no chance of inheriting any of her father's property forced the tocher up to the huge sum of 60 000 merks.[59]

This emphasis on the financial aspects of marriage aroused some criticism. Hannay warned that 'riches dazzle judgement's eye', asserting that 'Who weds for wealth, she only wealth doth wed', and sir Thomas Urquhart of Cromarty asked:

> How can such wedded people lead their lives,
> With a respect unfainedly entire,
> Where husbands are not married to their wives,
> But money to the covetous desire:
> Where men in little estimation hold
> Womens discretion, wit, and chastitie;
> But merely aime at handsomnesse, and gold,
> To serve their avarice, and leacherie:
> Which fashion lately is become so common,
> That first w'espouse the money, then the woman.

Yet while Gordonstoun agreed with these sentiments, he thought there was no point in marrying a poor wife, no matter how virtuous, 'becaus a man can buy nothing in the markett without money'.[60] Certainly marriage contracts, which were growing ever longer and more complex, focused on material matters, and the high survival rate of these documents in family archives points to their financial significance.[61]

A marriage contract was a formal agreement that is likely to have been accompanied by elaborate social rituals. However, not every marriage contract ended up as a marriage. That between lord James Stewart, prior of St Andrews, and Christina Stewart, countess of Buchan, never took place. Instead, in the autumn of 1562, while lord James was campaigning in the north, this wealthy heiress was married to his half-brother, Robert Douglas, a younger son of the laird of Lochleven, an action condemned years later by John Maitland of Thirlestane in a poem. Similarly, in 1565 the ten-year-old eighth earl of Angus was contracted to marry Jane Stewart, a daughter of the fourth earl of Atholl, but changed political circumstances ensured that Angus was married in 1573 to Mary Erskine, a daughter of the late regent Mar. In one tragic case in 1597, Jean Cunningham, eldest daughter of the sixth earl of Glencairn, died, leaving a note to the effect that the reason for her death was that the fifth earl of Cassillis had broken his contract and married instead the much older and wealthier Jean Fleming, widow of chancellor Thirlestane.[62]

For noble society it was particularly important that the culmination of these negotiations, the marriage ritual, should be carried out in public. Like most European societies at this time, Scotland did not have a single form of marriage ceremony, popular custom being observed as often as church marriage, and those rituals were changing under the impact of the Reformation as the kirk sought greater control over them. In 1562, a new marriage service was prescribed by the *Book of Common Order*. Noble marriages, however, involved huge amounts of property and powerful families for whom there must be no risk of misinterpretation. There was even greater need, therefore, for marriages to be approved by the church and the community, and the reading of the marriage banns on three consecutive Sundays, following which a licence was issued by the minister, fulfilled this requirement.[63] As in England, the new Protestant church was disapproving of exuberant marriages, but even its warmest supporters found this attitude difficult to understand. The first earl of Moray and Agnes Keith, daughter of the fourth earl Marischal, were married by John Knox in St Giles church, Edinburgh, on 8 February 1562, when Knox warned them 'to behave thame selves moderatlie in all thingis', but the munificence of the great state banquet at Holyrood palace and the subsequent entertainment, including a masque, still 'offended many godly'.[64] These colourful rituals outlived the exuberance of Mary's reign. The eighth earl of Angus was married to a daughter of the late regent Mar at Stirling on 14 June 1573 'with gret solempnitie', and at his second marriage two years later at Cupar there was another great festival. The marriage of the sixth earl of Huntly to Henrietta Stewart on 21 July 1588 was one of the biggest court extravaganzas of the 1580s, with a convention of the estates being postponed to allow a celebration of 'great triumphe, mirthe and pastyme'. In spite of church disapproval, the weddings of the higher nobility were celebrated by feasting that went on for days and nights, with fireworks, flamboyant decoration and wherever possible the king's presence.[65] Even without a royal court in Scotland, weddings remained important in the social calendar of the nobility. That in 1618 at Perth of William Hay, master of Errol, and Anne Lyon, only daughter of the first earl of Kinghorn, was celebrated at Glamis castle 'with great cheir, and all sorts of pastyme and merrenes'.[66] However, not all nobles could afford to spend on this scale, nor did they wish to celebrate their weddings so publicly. The second marriage of the second duke of Lennox to Jean Campbell, eldest sister of sir Hugh Campbell of Loudon, was a dull, private affair at Sorn in Ayrshire. When the already wealthy sir Thomas Hamilton of Drumcairn's daughter was to be married to the eldest son of sir David Carnegie of Kinnaird in the autumn of 1613, he informed the latter that he could not attend the wedding because of business at court and 'substance must be preferred to circumstances and ceremonies'. Ever the sly lawyer, Drumcairn left his daughter in the care of Kinnaird's wife for 'that now, sche is more youris nor myne'.[67]

## Conclusion

The importance of display in marking marriage highlights its prominent role in a society where it was almost universal, men and women usually marrying young, and where remarriage was common. This enthusiasm for marriage was fuelled by an overwhelming desire to produce heirs, and by an economic environment in which nobles could support large families. In choosing husbands and wives, the weight of family needs and priorities remained significant, impressing on children from infancy the need to do their duty, and fathers did use their moral authority and economic power to get their own way. Yet society and Scots law recognised the undesirability of forced marriages, and the subversive desires of young people, along with some sympathy for feelings of love, led many fathers to approve marriages they might not have chosen for their children. Undoubtedly, there were tough-minded parents prepared to force their children into unsatisfactory relationships, and many of these marriages not only endured but flourished, cemented by children, estates and shared experiences. Circumstances might also place a minor, or a woman, in the hands of a brother, uncle, tutor, feudal superior or the king, giving them control over their marriage. It would be a mistake to suggest that this period saw a hugely profound shift in attitudes or a visible change in trends; power and property remained at the core of most noble marriage contracts. However, in the decades that followed the Reformation, societal attitudes towards the desirability of allowing children to make their own choices, based on some idea of love, were already being transformed, leading to a slow thawing of paternal authority. Gordonstoun's advice to his nephew, like that of James VI to his son, suggests a desire on the part of the older generation to shape the parameters of choice rather than to lay down the law. There was nothing new about the virtuous wife as an ideal type, but a greater emphasis on that ideal was indicative of a need to limit individual choice by other means. That choice continued to be constrained by considerations of religion, politics, wealth and rank, all of which conspired to ensure that duty and not love remained the primary consideration in the choice of a spouse.

## CHAPTER 6

# Spouses

Other people's marriages are a mystery; that is as true of people in the past as it is of people we know. For the historian, there are few subjects so veiled by the absence of evidence or the deliberate obscuring of the truth, and behind the scattered surviving documents exposing the bare bones of the marital experiences of early modern Scottish nobles and their wives lies a range of human feelings, a rich texture of emotions, a barely glimpsed world in which some husbands and wives experienced love, joy, fulfilment and friendship, while others knew only hatred, bitterness, emptiness and loneliness. In between these extremes many put up with the ordinariness of their lives, relishing the moments of happiness and tolerating the instances of disappointment. Few sought to make these feelings known, many concealed them from their spouses, even from themselves, and the nobility were particularly keen to preserve their privacy, a difficult task given the extent to which their lives were lived in public. The historian who seeks to investigate marriage is an intruder, an unwelcome and unwanted presence in the most private corner of human life.[1] Yet it is important to attempt to invade that space, partly because in early modern Scotland almost the only evidence we have about the inner workings of marriages comes from the nobility. Furthermore, these private lives of public figures provide a more holistic view of noble society, redressing the balance created in thinking about them solely, or even principally, as political animals. How much energy goes into making any marriage work – and firstly one has to decide what is meant by 'work' – is difficult to say, but even in a society less obsessed with the bilateral relationship between husbands and wives, noblemen and noblewomen did expend effort in doing something. Within the parameters of male dominance, constrained gender roles, minimal privacy from family, friends and servants, the political and financial significance of the marriage, and the limited understanding of their own emotions, these early modern people tried to make their marriage a success. Measured by the simple statistics of divorce and separation rates or the production of children, the overwhelming majority of marriages were a success. Trying to get behind those bare facts is the purpose of this chapter.

## The Good Marriage

The Reformation probably raised the status of women within marriage, fostering the companionable marriage, even if its effects on women in society at large were more ambiguous, and the debate hinges to a large extent on those differences between theories about women and their roles on the one hand, and daily practice on the other.[2] Certainly Protestant writers did emphasise women's subordinate role, and John Knox's 1558 tract, *The First Blast of the Trumpet Against the Monstrous Regiment of Women*, belongs in that genre. The Scottish parliament's proposal to outlaw a woman from ever again succeeding to the crown, the determination of landed society to adhere to male entails, and the severe persecution of mostly female witches are indicative of a society ill at ease with women as figures wielding authority or power. There is no reason to doubt that the Scots shared the Aristotelian view of women as inferior and subordinate, a view based as much on contemporary ideas about the female body, with the attendant fears over menstruation, as on religious and philosophical texts.[3] Yet there is little evidence of the anxiety articulated in English texts and centring on women's latent power, their voracious sexual appetites, subversive behaviour or wasteful extravagance. Scots law offered women more protection and rights than many contemporary legal systems, and Scottish men appear reasonably self-assured about their dominant role in a society without any tradition of reflective role reversal in its popular culture. The English, whose wives had far fewer legal rights than Scotswomen, liked to tell themselves that their women had greater freedom than any others in the world, and sir Anthony Weldon maliciously compared the wives of the Scottish nobility to slaves. However, another English traveller, sir William Brereton, was struck by the fact that Scottish women were never wholly subsumed into the identity of their husbands, for 'the wives in Scotland never change, but always retain, their own names'.[4]

Marriage law in Scotland was inequitable, being influenced by the restrictive Norman legal code introduced in the twelfth century (in early modern France the crown was seeking to undermine the greater rights wives enjoyed outside Normandy), but it was less severe than English law which treated a wife as the personal property of her husband who had absolute rights over her body, property and children.[5] Nevertheless, a wife could not pursue an action at law without the consent of her husband, he had control over her property, being able to revoke any disposition or infeftment made to her after their marriage, and she could not grant an acquittance of her conjunct fee lands without his consent. However, a husband was not permitted to alter a tack into which his wife had entered without her permission, and he was forbidden from selling her jewellery, often the only secure asset she possessed. While Scots law did not define a wife as the property of her husband, he had rule over her and he could insist on the return of her person if she deserted him, unless she could prove he had mistreated her. For his part, the husband was obliged to provide for his wife according to his means, even after his death, and he was responsible for her debts. However, in criminal law the situation was very different. In September 1570, the court of justiciary refused to accept the argument, advanced by lady Seton, that she should not be prosecuted for hearing mass on the grounds that she could not be tried without the presence of her husband, then in exile. The king's advocate countered that in criminal matters the husband's headship was irrelevant.[6]

This idea that wives were the subordinate partners in a marriage was pervasive. It was utilised by lord Darnley in his campaign to be granted the crown matrimonial; he argued that while queen Mary was of higher status than he by birth, 'yet, now he is her husband, whoe, by the law of God and man, commands above the woman'. If Darnley could say this of a queen, what chance had lesser women? Moralists like John Wemyss insisted that women most pleased God when called 'to live in wedlocke, and to bring up their children in his feare'. Even when they brought greater property to a marriage than their husbands, he thought 'all should be called the husband's'. In an undated letter to 'A Ladey for a friend', Denmilne drew her attention to the fact that 'in nature it is monstrous to see the hands, legs and uther members dominion over the head, lett above', and so he entreated her to learn humility which would guarantee her contentment in this world and in the life to come.[7] Here in this patriarchal sketch of quiet subservience was the pattern for a happy marriage, at least in the eyes of men.

The more common pattern in practice, however, was of marriage as a partnership. In a letter of 1635, James Melville of Halhill exposed his sensitivity to the accusation that 'I have bein oft blamed for following my wyffs counsale', arguing that 'I sall by the lords grace follow the direction of the truth, I hope my wyff sall never preass to persuad me to the contrair'. Halhill did not deny that he discussed important issues with his wife or took her advice; indeed he implied that her counsel was likely to be sound. This role of a wife, or a mother, as a counsellor is often overlooked amidst the emphasis on listening to the advice of kins*men*. While early modern societies restricted women's formal, institutional authority, in a culture where informal ties of patronage were important, noblewomen often exercised considerable power. Some of these women were formidable individuals performing traditionally masculine roles from which they were normally excluded by cultural and social values, but into which they were drawn by their high rank and prepared for by their education. Just like the men of their house, who had been steeped in the ideas of lineage and honour, these wives were the products of a martial society and were not merely conditioned to act as intercessors and pacifiers in their communities. As long as women operated under the ultimate restraint of male authority, knowing when to revert to the feminine type, their exercise of power was not inconsistent with prevailing ideas about their inferior nature.[8]

Noblewomen, therefore, were active in politics. Isobel Hamilton, lady Seton, was exiled in 1570 for continuing a clandestine correspondence with the imprisoned queen Mary; Agnes Keith, countess of Moray, was an intelligent and frightening politician who chillingly told the fifth earl of Huntly on one occasion 'ye haf mad me angary', and her second husband, the sixth earl of Argyll was 'much advised by his wife'; Henrietta Stewart, countess of Huntly, dealt skilfully with her husband's business during his exile in 1595–6 when she 'providentlie governed her husband's affairs, and carefullie solicited his bussines'. At a local level too, noblewomen made their mark, even participating in feuds. Margaret Douglas, countess of Bothwell, was less in control of her life, being convicted of treason in 1592 because of her husband's actions. A decade later, she complained in angry frustration that 'the wicked and unadvised courses my husband runs are so furious and contrary to his own welfare that almost they make me despair either of his "ryssing" or my own and my children's standing, though we live miserably in respect of that we are'.[9] Women were no less aggressive at law. In 1615, chancellor Dunfermline complained of his mother-in-law, the litigious Margaret Ker, lady Yester, that she 'has never used meikill of my advys and hes maed me or makis me al leifull acquent with her adois as onye man'. The countess of Haddington was a tough woman who drove a hard bargain in business, knew the price of everything, and was another bitter opponent in litigation – 'god's curs licht upon him for the truble and vexation he brings to me', she ranted against one poor man with whom she was at law in 1635.[10]

One of the popular male images of early modern women related to their financial irresponsibility. In 'On ladies beauties', the anonymous poet criticised men who married attractive wives who then assumed the upper hand in the marriage, pushing their husbands into greater and greater debt:

> Our lords are so degenerate
> Sen ladies took sic steer [= control],
> They spend their rents upon their weeds [= clothes]
> And baneist has good cheer.

And:

> Sho sall therefore be callit Madame
> Bot and the laird made knicht,
> Grit grit is their grace,
> Howbeit their rents be slicht.

Yet there is considerable evidence to suggest that husbands trusted their wives' financial competence. While James VI thought wives should keep out of political matters, he did suggest they might be entrusted with the management of the household, a major undertaking often combined with administering the estate.[11] The third earl of Eglinton wrote his testament in 1563, a year after his marriage to Agnes Drummond, making his wife his only executrix, placing her in absolute charge of all his affairs; nothing in the twenty-two years of marriage that followed made him change his will. A similar trust moved John Johnstone of that Ilk in 1571 when he granted his wife, Margaret Scott, a life rent over his whole lands and the office of coroner within the bounds of Annandale.[12] Clearly these were competent women, and there is no doubt that some wives were a good deal better at estate management than their husbands. The irresponsible second earl of Moray paid little attention to his estates, and in March 1589 it was to his wife that servants wrote about the mismanagement of affairs at Darnaway castle. Isabel Forbes, the second wife of sir David Lindsay of Edzell, had to put up with a husband more interested in his legal career than estate management, and on 4 March 1600 she wrote him a stinging letter, listing his bungling and warning 'quhen ye will nocht follow counsall I can nocht mend it'.[13] Many women had no choice but to manage their own affairs, being widowed: women like Annabella Murray, dowager countess of Mar, who oversaw the administration of her son's estates throughout his long minority. Annabella Campbell, countess of Lothian, had a detailed understanding of the law and of her late husband's disastrous financial affairs about which she could do little because of her 'womanly waiknes', a description that says more about her frustration than her competency. The thrice-married Jean Gordon, countess of Sutherland, who died in 1629 at the age of eighty-four, managed the minorities of both her son and grandson, and 'by her great care and dilligence brought to a prosperous end many hard and difficult bussines'.[14]

Husbands were often absentees, commonly having to attend court or to deal with business matters elsewhere, while some were away for much longer periods of foreign travel. As in England, it was customary for nobles to marry before going to the continent, allowing time to elapse between the marriage of young partners and the consummation of the marriage, and also to prevent an unsuitable marriage abroad. As to the protestations of a young wife left alone for years, 'their is no guid woman Bot will be miscontent quher hir husband gois fra hir, So no wyss woman Bot will degeist it ffor his gude'. These neglected wives were often left to run their husband's affairs in his absence. Thomas Hamilton of Priestfield's wife managed his estate when he went off to Paris, and in April 1568 he received a letter telling him that 'Your wyff is mair diligent in all your effaris than your self hes bene in tymes bygane'.[15] After 1603, absenteeism became more common, and many courtiers empowered their wives either singly or as one of a commission, to manage their business during what could be long periods in England or on the continent. Often this meant a lonely and burdensome life for the women left behind. Anne Keith, wife of the sixth earl of Morton, was left at home to manage her husband's complex debts, provoking her to remind him in 1629 that 'I and myn childring ar yours and sum tymes men desyrs to sie ther aine'. A few months later, she wrote that 'I am weiriet of living my lone,' telling Morton that 'I am not maried to my childring, I am to you'. In spite of the countess of Morton's loneliness and growing bitterness, this was a strong woman and she got on with the job of looking after her children, running the estate and making it possible for Morton to pursue office at court. Her portrait, like most of those of the period, does not suggest a woman who was weak or subservient, and the visual imagery is suggestive of what were often dynamic working partnerships.[16]

These wives earned their husbands' respect, their skills and advice were valued, and they were in every sense partners. But was there any love? Early modern society could be suspicious of marriages founded on romantic love, seeing this as unhealthy and indulgent. On the other hand, the status, relative freedom and wealth of noblewomen did encourage men to cultivate personal relationships with their wives. Besides, love formed within the confines of many marriages, and much seventeenth-century Protestant literature placed an emphasis on friendship between husbands and wives, encouraging the enjoyment of healthy and exclusive sexual relationships.[17] Yet it is a misconception often held about early modern marriage that it was a brittle, loveless relationship between strangers, bereft of either passion or kindness. Few relationships were as intense as that between Hugh Fraser, seventh lord Lovat, and Isobel Wemyss, who enjoyed twenty-one years of a loving marriage before her death in 1636. Lovat never recovered from this loss, turning the administration of his affairs over to his teenage son, fasting twice a week on which days he refused to see anyone, and setting aside another day for charity work among the poor. Similarly, the death in childbirth of Jane Gordon, wife of George Gray of Cuttill, was 'exceidinglie bewailled and regrated by her husband, who through the love and affection which he did cary unto her, and to the children that he had by her, did not marie agane for seaven yeiris'. Gordonstoun recorded that his own sister, lady Jane Gordon, wife of Hucheon Mackay of Farr, only outlived her husband by six months, dying in February 1615, and 'as they were happie in ther mutuall loves dureing their lyves, so were they not lesse happie that their deaths were so neir one another'. Sir David Lindsay of Edzell was doubly fortunate in being married to two good wives. Shortly before her death in July 1592, his first wife recalled that 'the sun ga'ed never down upon ony wrath that ever was betwixt you and me in this warld'. Not long after Edzell's own death in 1610, his second wife testified that he had been 'most loving, liberal and beneficial to me', attending to her person and interests in spite of her long infirmity and illness. Cromarty urged husbands to cultivate this kindness in their marriages. Instead of domineering over a wife, a husband 'Should towards her behave himselfe, respect her,/Instruct her, love her, and from harme protect her', and it was that element of trust and love that moderated the apparently harsh language of the law or of religious writers.[18]

One of the problems historians of marriage face is that there is a greater likelihood of evidence surviving that relates to marital breakdown than to successful marriage. Separation and divorce create a legal record, fornication and adultery attract the scandalmongering interest of the diarist, while love and fidelity generate little written record. Indeed it is likely that much private correspondence of an intimate kind was deliberately destroyed on the death of one or both parties. Certainly there were practical demonstrations of love. There is the kindness of the dying regent Lennox on 4 September 1571, remembering amidst his pain to ask a friend 'to carry his love to his Meg', Margaret Douglas, countess of Lennox. Or there is the consideration of the third earl of Moray who in 1632 made arrangements to ensure that his wife, Anne Gordon, enjoyed possession of all his silverwork, furniture and other plenishings for the remainder of her life should he predecease this woman he was obliged to marry in settlement of a bloodfeud.[19] In the correspondence of husbands and wives there survive those intimate words and phrases that indicate friendship, fondness and love. Julia Ker, countess of Haddington, wrote to her often absent husband in affectionate tones, urging 'my swet burd, as ye luf me, or desirs to bring any joy to my hairt', to hurry home. She was in many respects a trying wife, having constant money problems and awkward children by a first marriage, and she disapproved of the religious policy her husband enforced. Yet when she died in March 1637, Haddington was dealt a heavy blow, following her to the grave two months later. Their correspondence is not unusual in its tone. The third husband of Sara Maxwell, countess of Wigton, repeatedly addressed her as 'my hart', gently admonishing her for spending so long parted from him. Her own letters were addressed with equal affection, and in one of August 1632 she promised that as soon as she had completed her business, she would join viscount Airds 'iff ye war in the fardest pairt of Irland'.[20]

The greater part of the sexual life of the early modern Scottish nobility, particularly that of wives, is likely to have taken place within the confines of marriage. Unfortunately the evidence is defective; sex only creeps into the record where it is unconventional, and it is too easy for historians to be attracted to salacious tales.[21] The large numbers of children born in noble families indicate a determination on the part of many nobles to go on sleeping with their wives long after the need for an heir had been met. In the eyes of the law and the kirk, women had little choice in submitting to intercourse with their husbands, but those noblewomen described above are unlikely to have been submissive in the bedroom. Furthermore, the choice many women made to marry again and again, often bearing children to a succession of husbands in the early modern equivalent of serial monogamy, suggests a healthy appetite for sex. At the very least, these women chose to have sex with husbands rather than remain lonely. There is little change in emphasis between pre-Reformation and seventeenth-century moralists on the importance of sex in marriage, or on the need for spouses to recognise each other's sexual needs, and it was only in sexual relations that a woman was equal to a man, for 'he is as well subject to his wife, as he is her Lord'.[22] As to sexual practices, there is no Scottish evidence, although it is likely that the Scots shared in the typical medical views of the period relating to the body's humours and fungible fluids. Ancram's English doctor suggested that 'the use of a woman' was best for those men who were by nature hot and moist, while advising against it for those men who were cold and dry. In general, it was believed that procreation and pleasure were best achieved by energetic intercourse, and Ancram was told that sex was beneficial for a man, especially if he was of a melancholy disposition, but that care should be exercised from middle age. Sexual activity was also unwise on a full or empty stomach, and the body should be at a moderate temperature. For women, the optimum time for them to conceive was 'either at the beginning or ending of a woman's evacuation'. Both partners were advised to sleep after sex.[23]

Twelve years after the death in 1624 of Margaret Douglas, lady Skelmorlie, her husband had the following verse engraved on her hugely impressive tomb at Largs:

> Years twenty-four a maiden life
> I lived, and thirty-six a wife.
> Lucina twice gave kindly aid;
> I bore a boy, and then a maid;
> The son reflects his father's face,
> And lives, the hope of all his race;
> My daughter an untimely doom
> Consign before me to the tomb.
> My lineage high, and generous mind,
> With matchless beauty were combined:
> Beloved of God I lived; and He
> In heaven is all things now to me.[24]

Lady Skelmorlie was a good wife and was much missed by her husband, whose remains were later laid to rest beside her. The third earl of Lothian noted the well-known proverb that 'Wives are young men's mistresses, companions for middle age, and old men's nurses', although in his case his loving wife predeceased him. After thirty-seven years of an arranged and highly satisfactory marriage that began in 1630, Lothian wrote his own testimonial to Anne Ker:

> ane woman extraordinary in all the qualifications of goodnes, vertue, modesty, piety; a good wyfe, a good mother, a good woman; excellent in the government of her family and the ordering and provyding for it.

Significantly, those qualities listed by Lothian were not those of a meek, submissive woman but of a valued partner in the management of his estates. Similarly, Robert Douglas, lord Dalkeith, described his wife, Elizabeth Villiers, some years after their marriage in glowing terms, telling his father, the sixth earl of Morton, that 'I doe not think that there is ane better woman living than shee is nor did evere man love ane woman better than I doe hir'.[25] Like his parents, lord Dalkeith and his wife found love in marriage. Others, however, were less fortunate.

## Marital Breakdown

Gordonstoun's orthodox view was that 'Matrimonie is a metter of great importance which you cannot shake of everie day as you list. It cannot be disolved but be one of your deaths', and this was not far removed from that of the pre-Reformation church. After the Reformation, the kinds of marital problem church courts faced were little different in Catholic and Protestant communities, and the strategies adopted by magistrates could also be very similar. However, while most Protestants remained reluctant to consider divorce, the desacramentalisation of marriage and, perhaps, the greater emphasis on the quality of married life led some Protestant states to allow more liberal divorce laws.[26] For the general population of the Swiss city of Neuchâtel divorce was most commonly granted for desertion and adultery; in Nantes the principal reasons for legal separation, the first step of which was separation of property rather than a separation of households, were wife-beating and financial mismanagement; while among the English gentry the most common reasons identified for marital breakdown were financial arguments, usually over the interpretation of the marriage contract, adultery and scolding, or wife-beating. Much the same can be found in Scotland, although there were some idiosyncratic exceptions to this generalisation: the divorce in 1572 that followed from an enforced marriage between the teenage eleventh earl of Sutherland and the much older daughter of the hated house of Caithness, or the insane behaviour of the master of Winton on the night of his wedding in February 1603. These were extraordinary cases, however, and for most married couples, problems were created by the age-old issues of money, sex and violence.[27]

Most marriage contracts worked, evidence of the success of the negotiating process and of the good sense of the marriage partners. There is much evidence of husbands implementing the terms of the agreements, often signing post-nuptial contracts recognising their wives' rights. Less common, perhaps, was the good faith of Robert Swinton of that Ilk who issued a charter in 1619 confirming the rights of his wife to her life rent after the earlier charter granted at her marriage had been lost.[28] But not all husbands were as honest or reasonable; hence the old French proverb that 'Husbands get up three times during the night in order to sell their wives property'. The litigation entered into by early modern families over opposing interpretations of marriage contracts is demonstrable evidence of the failure of premarital negotiations to anticipate every eventuality. Few early modern societies were as generous to wives as that of Brittany where women could seek a separation and legal redress against a husband who was judged to be mismanaging his property, thus endangering her dowry.[29] When in July 1575 lady Garlies discovered that her husband intended mortgaging some of her jointure land, she wrote to a court of session judge that this was 'contrair my will and plesor', warning the latter that if the contract went ahead, 'it will move me and him to gretar waythe nor I will wret'.[30]

In some instances, problems materialised quickly. The marriage contract of the third earl of Eglinton's daughter, Margaret Montgomery, to the master of Seton was made before April 1582 and cost the earl 12 000 merks as tocher, which he soon discovered he could not pay. A further deal had to be negotiated between the two families in which Eglinton was obliged to pay interest on the outstanding sum. Meanwhile Margaret and her husband had their allowance from lord Seton cut proportionately until the earl completed his payments.[31] The marriage in 1592 of Walter Dundas, apparent of that Ilk, to Annas Menteith got off to a bad start because his father failed to provide adequate housing for the young couple. The quarrel was only resolved when, after seventeen frustrating months, Annas moved into her father-in-law's own house, enraging the laird of Dundas who nevertheless signed a new contract with his son, conceding to the demands of his assertive daughter-in-law.[32] A particular set of problems might be created by the death of one of the principals. In January 1587, the ninth earl of Errol married as his second wife Mary Stewart, sister of the fifth earl of Atholl, but she died in the spring of the following year. At the time of her death, the full sum of the £9000 dowry had not been paid, and Atholl claimed that his sister had died because of mistreatment by her husband, thus creating a feud between the two lords.[33] Marriage contracts were even more necessary to protect women against their husband's family after his death. When sir John Maxwell of Pollok was killed in 1595, his wife, Marion Edmonstone, had to go to law against her stepson, a minor at the time, over the possession of Haggs castle. Lady Pollok forced the young laird's curators to reveal the contents of her marriage contract in order to demonstrate the justice of her case. It was because women like Mary Douglas were aware of their vulnerability that she deposited a copy of her marriage contract with the fifth earl of Morton. Many years later, in 1630, when she was under pressure from her husband's family, she retrieved the document so that she could defend herself.[34]

But while the financial terms of a marriage could be negotiated and bound up in a contract, sex was less amenable to regulation. The role of royal courts in setting the tone of sexuality among the nobility was important, and the impression counted almost as much as reality. The sexual laxity of the court, at least until the reign of Charles I, was a constant refrain, and hostile writers accused individual nobles of every vice from the fourth earl of Bothwell's adultery and filthy table-talk to the first earl of Dunbar's alleged sodomy, a sin that was a sure sign of a man's moral corruption rather than sexual orientation.[35] The church's attacks on the culture of immodest behaviour and love-enhancing practices were not especially aimed at nobles, although their social prominence might have brought them under greater scrutiny. Within two years of the 1563 legislation against adultery being enacted, Alexander Drummond of Medhope was charged with carrying on an adulterous liaison with Margaret Drummond, lady Elphinstone. The church also sought to engage the nobility in its moral clean-up of society. In 1574, the general assembly tried to persuade the regent Morton to appoint nobles to commissions charged at a local level with investigating sexual offences and adjudicating in divorce cases.[36] Of course, some nobles agreed with the kirk's teaching, and the king himself argued that a man should come to marriage a virgin, attacking double standards as hypocrisy and arguing that it was wise to marry young since marriage 'is ordeined for quenching the lust of your youth'.[37] Yet many men did not match James VI's ideals, and like Hucheon Mackay of Farr were addicted to 'extraordinarie lust', a vice common in great men who enjoyed wealth and good health unless blessed with 'the speciall grace of God'. The connection between promiscuity and health was not commonly made, although sexually transmitted diseases did disable a number of nobles, the seventh lord Borthwick being one who fatally succumbed to 'the French decease'. Sir Duncan Campbell of Glenorchy was a great womaniser whose rude good health set James VI to wondering how:

> he that hes lived chast from women except his owin quein all his dayis schuld be trubled with the gutt, and you that hes so largly bestowed your talentt amongst them schuld skaipe both gutt and uther diseisses.

Glenorchy long outlived the king and died aged eighty-one in 1631.[38]

To find fornication and adultery rife among rich and powerful men is unsurprising. Jean Gordon, wife of the fourth earl of Bothwell, accused him at her divorce trial of having had intercourse with her near kinswoman before their marriage, thus making the marriage unlawful. To this can be added Bothwell's affair with Janet Beaton, lady Buccleuch, another with his wife's servant, and one with a Danish girl that finally landed him in prison; and these are only the earl's more public infidelities.[39] Bothwell was not alone in his behaviour. Even a sympathetic source admitted to the eighth lord Maxwell's 'abuse of his bodie in wilfull harlatrie aganis the godlie band of wedlok'; a friend told the widowed David Lindsay of Edzell to 'be honorabillie alyait and cast all your bladerrie harlatrie away'; sir Patrick Hume of Polwarth abandoned his newly wed wife for a woman his own mother described as 'ane arant whoor', his wife being 'worth twenty of such a slut as she is'. Equally disgraceful was the behaviour of sir Donald Mackay of Farr who in 1617 installed his mistress, Mary Lindsay, a sister of the twelfth earl of Crawford (who already had a notorious reputation for sleeping with a servant), in his wife's place. Lady Farr, who had only recently given birth and was ejected from her house, accepted that 'thair is mony that, althocht thay abuse thair bodyis in that filthie and detestable vice of whoredome, yit thay interteny thair wyffis with all schawis of love and kyndnes'.[40]

It was not only husbands who committed adultery. Here, of course, was the hidden threat to the agnatic kindred: the adulterous wife who demonstrated the truth of the Roman jurist's maxim that 'maternity is a fact, paternity is a matter of opinion'. Male anxiety about the parentage of children was especially acute because of the widespread belief that, once aroused, females had insatiable sexual appetites. Poets, for example, recognised the at times unrestrained nature of female passion, this being the topic of Alexander Scott's 'Wanton wemen'. This fear of sexually aggressive women was most evident in the case of Elizabeth Stewart, daughter of the fourth earl of Atholl, who divorced her second husband on the grounds of impotency when she was already carrying the child of James Stewart, earl of Arran. Here was a woman who took part in outdoor sport, enjoyed sex, using adultery as a means to express her own power in a highly unsatisfactory marriage, and was a significant player at court. The new countess of Arran was hated by the ministers who described her as a woman consumed by 'inordinat lust' who 'ceasseth not yitt to pervert the king's Majestie's owne youth, by slanderous speeche and countenance'.[41] Elizabeth Stewart was an unconventional woman, hence the unease she aroused in men, but among her neighbours in the north-east in the mid-1570s, when she was happily married to the fifth lord Lovat, were the adulterous wives of the eleventh earl of Sutherland, the laird of Innes and the master of Forbes, all of whom were divorced.[42]

Male reactions to unfaithful wives varied. The divorce in 1587 of the ultra-Protestant eighth earl of Angus and his wife, Margaret Leslie, was due to her alleged affairs, including one with the third earl of Montrose during her husband's exile. Angus tried to catch his wife out, turning up unexpectedly at Dalkeith at midnight in February 1581 when he surprised her awaiting the arrival of her lover. By 1585, Angus had decided on divorce, but for political reasons he did not accuse Montrose and instead Margaret Leslie was said to have had an affair with a stable-boy. When told of his brother-in-law's intentions, the fifth earl of Bothwell opined that 'if the earl of Angus wished to repudiate his wife for this peccadilio that he was minded to treat his own [Angus's sister] in like manner, seeing that she lends herself a little to it'. These tales of noblewomen bedding down with servants were the stuff of the most vicious kind of gossip. Scotstarvit preserved an adulterous story about Annabella Campbell, daughter of the seventh earl of Argyll and wife of the second earl of Lothian. Annabella, who was 'a woman of a masculine spirit, but highland-faced', maintained in her household the young William Douglas of Tofts, 'which was very scandalous, and much talked of in the country'. Rumours grew especially pronounced when her husband committed suicide in 1624.[43] The point of such stories was that ladies who gave themselves to servants were behaving in a particularly shocking manner, dishonouring their own lineage and that of their husband. In the summer of 1607, sir Robert Gordon of Lochinvar killed a servant he suspected of being his wife's lover; Lochinvar escaped punishment and the marriage was dissolved. Here Lochinvar's honour and power had been impugned by his wife's infidelity, exposing his inability to exert authority over her or over his own servant. However, this connection between female infidelity and the honour of a husband was questioned by Cromarty in his 1641 *Epigrams*. There he suggested that a husband was not dishonoured, only the wife, for 'Tis our owne vertu and vice must praise or blame us,/And either make us glorious or infamous'.[44] However, his was not a popular view.

Early modern society could be tolerant of husbands who beat and sexually abused their wives. For example, separations were only granted in France in instances where there was demonstrable evidence of a husband severely abusing his wife over a prolonged period. While the courts took action against the sickeningly debauched Jean de Rohan, whose treatment of his wife, the formerly powerful Diane de Barbacon, led to her death in 1566, in the end he escaped punishment or even censure. Evidence for domestic violence, therefore, is variously interpreted as greater or lesser than today, but the exaggerated picture of a sex war being waged as an allegedly re-invigorated patriarchy was enforced ought to be dismissed.[45] Of course, husbands and wives engaged in violent quarrels, as they always had done. In September 1584, it was reported that William Hay, master of Yester, accidentally stuck a knife into his wife's breast and 'perceiving her to fall as if he had slain her, struck himself immediately with the same knife into the body, and would have slain himself, but they are both, it is thought, past danger'. A more likely explanation of what happened here is that the couple had a vicious argument. Most domestic violence, especially at this level in society, was hidden from public gaze so that in November 1604 all Edinburgh was buzzing with the gossip that the young fifth earl of Cassillis and his fifty-year-old wife had a furious row in front of the privy council that culminated in him striking the countess and dragging her from the chamber.[46] A number of similar incidents were brought to the privy council by women who had suffered serious attacks. In 1583, Jean Cockburn, lady Halton, was fortunate to get privy council help after her husband, sir William Lauder of Halton, locked her up in his castle when she sided with her eldest son against his father. Understandably, wives were reluctant to come forward with such stories. Margaret Crawford, lady Newark, suffered four years of beatings and cruel treatment from her husband, Patrick

Maxwell of Newark, before her experiences were made public in June 1636. The couple had been married forty years and she had borne him sixteen children in what had been a perfectly sound relationship prior to a sudden, unprovoked and public assault. Thereafter a catalogue of mistreatment followed. When summoned to appear before the council, Newark pleaded old age and infirmity, and his violence might have been provoked by advancing senility.[47]

On the whole, the crown took these complaints seriously. In 1626 it imprisoned sir John Stewart of Methven, captain of Dumbarton castle, who beat his wife, chained her to a bed in a cold, ruinous part of the castle with his two mistresses as guards, and threatened to kill her. This maltreatment was sparked off by lady Methven confronting her husband with allegations of his infidelities and was designed to force her to sign papers testifying to his innocence. Sir John was set free after offering his wife 1000 merks a quarter while she sought a divorce, and two years later he was hauled before the justiciary court in Edinburgh on three counts of adultery. On the other hand, in the 1629 case of lady Banff, the privy council was less helpful. She claimed that sir George Ogilvy of Banff attempted to starve her to death, failing which he repeatedly beat her. Lady Banff's dreadful experience has the ring of truth to it, but she was unable to substantiate her testimony and the council cleared her husband of the charges.[48]

There are no known cases of wives beating their husbands at this level in society. However, lord Menmuir was trapped in a miserable marriage with a scold of a wife. Jean Lauder, Menmuir's second wife, made life so intolerable for him that he obtained a royal order confining her north of the Tay. On 15 May 1595, Menmuir entered into a contract with his wife, witnessed by her kinsmen, agreeing to procure her freedom, to accept her back into his household and to provide lady Menmuir with 1000 merks per annum. In return, his wife promised to cease from all 'enormities', and her family gave assurances of 10 000 merks for her good behaviour, including guarantees not to 'spulzie, reif, nor abstract his writs, guids, and gear out of his houses', exploit his tenants or communicate with outlaws. Only in one known instance did a noblewoman take the most extreme course in order to get herself out of a hateful marriage. In 1600 Jean Livingston, daughter of John Livingston of Dunipace, hired a man to murder her abusive husband, John Kincaid of Wariston. Lady Wariston was immediately arrested, tried, convicted and executed. The entire episode was shocking, not only because a man had been done to death in his own house, but because a wife and her servants had conspired to kill a husband and master.[49] No other woman took the law into her own hands in such a drastic manner, unless one considers the murder of Darnley in 1566 to fall into this category. However, when in 1613 friends of the ninth lord Maxwell asked Margaret Maitland, lady Roxburghe, to petition the queen for mercy on his behalf she refused, especially as 'no great proofe hath beene geven of a good housband'.[50]

## Separation and Divorce

The impact of the Reformation on divorce rates in early modern society was modest. Women in counter-Reformation Venice were far from powerless in taking legal action against abusive husbands; in south-west Germany the experiences of Catholics and Protestants before church courts were similar; and in England marriage remained highly stable, there was no demand for legal reform, and only in the higher ranks of society was marital breakdown at all common, with some 10 per cent of peerage marriages ending in bitter quarrelling, separations or annulments.[51] However, Protestant states did have to adjust to a changed relationship with Rome, and a new view of marriage that no longer saw it as less worthy than celibacy or as a sacrament. In the eyes of John Calvin, adultery by a husband or wife was sufficient grounds for divorce, embracing within this desertion, but he ruled out physical disability, including impotence, incompatibility or violence as adequate reasons for ending a marriage. The Scottish church and Scots law drew on Genevan practice and teaching, providing for divorce on the grounds of adultery and desertion, while simultaneously remaining committed to the idea of marriage for life and being determined to regulate both the marriage ritual and sexual behaviour. The parliament of 1560 ended papal authority in Scotland; two years later the general assembly petitioned the crown to transfer those powers necessary for granting a divorce to either the church or a suitable lay body. In 1564, the new secular commissary courts acquired this authority, that based in Edinburgh being responsible for divorce actions. However, the legal principles under which the new courts operated continued to be based in canon law. The church, therefore, stepped back from direct involvement in divorce, but the general assembly lobbied hard to influence society's attitudes to marriage and it succeeded in persuading parliament to introduce the death sentence for adultery in 1563. Four years later, parliament formalised the new framework within which marital law operated. In conjunction with the emphasis on adultery as a reason for divorce, therefore, the sexuality of marriage was given greater emphasis, while the principle of one party being at fault was established. Further legislation in 1573 decreed that after a four-year separation that had not been sanctioned by a judge, a couple could be obliged to appear in court. Should either party fail to obey, they would be excommunicated, thus providing grounds for divorce, the offending party losing the rights to the tocher. Although this act was influenced by Genevan ideas, the more immediate cause was the need for the fifth earl of Argyll to divorce his wife, who had left him but had not committed adultery. Argyll's Highland background might also have been an issue since easy divorce, concubinage and even polygamy was more acceptable in Gaelic society. In 1592, parliament tightened up the law covering divorced women, stating that if a wife guilty of adultery was divorced by her husband, and then married the man with whom she had committed the crime, she could not grant any property to him or to children of that union. However, in allowing divorced people to remarry, a position formerly condemned by the church, the Scots enjoyed greater freedom than most contemporary societies. In effect, legal changes after the Reformation made divorce easier to obtain, allowing both adultery and desertion as just causes, although it remained a difficult and painful process.[52]

Whatever its formal role in law, however, the church retained a moral authority in regulating marriage.[53] The fifth earl of Argyll was married to Jean Stewart, a bastard half-sister of queen Mary, and Knox wrote to this Lord of the Congregation in 1562, telling him that 'Your behaviour toward your wyff is verray offensive unto many godlie,' threatening him with damnation if he continued in his adultery. By 1567 the general assembly had run out of patience with this otherwise godly lord from whom much was expected, and it reprimanded the earl for the 'scandalous offences'. A reluctant submission by Argyll followed, but the marriage was beyond repair and a divorce followed in 1573.[54] In a less celebrated case in December 1593, the presbytery of Glasgow excommunicated the fourth lord Sempill for his persistent adultery with Helen Drummond, who had borne him a child. Sempill had ignored the general assembly and the presbytery, choosing instead to move the woman into his castle. Two years later, the presbytery took an interest in the marriage of sir William Livingston of Kilsyth and his wife 'anent their cohabitatioun togidder', instructing him to 'do the dewtie of ane husband to hir'. But it was extremely difficult for church courts to intrude into the private lives of nobles.[55] When in 1605 the presbytery of Paisley tried to investigate allegations of adultery against sir Neil Montgomery of Langshaw, he protested to the privy council, challenging the church's right to raise a criminal action against him when neither his wife nor the cuckolded husband had levelled accusations. He was also annoyed at being asked to swear an oath and answer a case founded on evidence collected from 'husseis, fellows, and bairnes'. Yet the adultery act could not simply be ignored by nobles. In 1598, the king insisted on putting Alexander Hay of Delgaty on trial for his life in spite of the latter arguing that adultery was not notorious and therefore not subject to the act. Fortunately, he was acquitted, possibly by an assize reluctant to see the law rigorously enforced on a man of baronial rank. It was easier to target noblewomen, at least the lower ranks of noblewomen. In July 1600, Mary Bruce, sister of sir Robert Bruce of Clackmannan, was ordered by Stirling kirk session to make public penance for her fornication, but no penalty was imposed on Henry Stewart, commendator of St Colme, who had fathered her child.[56]

In spite of the easing of the divorce laws, the divorce rate among the nobility remained low, partly because of the church's disapproval but also because of the complications created in matters relating to the marriage contract. Only 3 per cent of the marriages involving the heads of houses of the higher nobility ended in divorce or legal separation, a total of only sixteen marriages.[57] In a society where divorce was difficult, informal separation provided the best solution. The first earl of Orkney and his wife, Jean Kennedy, lived apart after she had provided him with four sons. She never visited Orkney, living instead in a house in the Canongate, where the earl sent her money.[58] Another relatively amicable separation was agreed in 1627 by sir Alexander Falconer of Halkerton and his wife, as the two were 'so farre distractit and alienat in heartie love and affectioun', and a maintenance agreement was brokered by privy councillors.[59] These few cases might hide a world of collusion between spouses who knew they could no longer live together but who were able to work towards some mutually agreeable solution.

Desertion by husbands was likely to arise from a desire to avoid the financial settlements imposed by the commissary courts in formal separations. In 1605, the second duke of Lennox confessed to a friend that after seven years of marriage to his second wife, Jean Campbell, 'ther is no powar in earthe that can make me to use [her] as a wyfe'. Fortunately for the duke, the royal court was a long way away. Jean Campbell was abandoned in Scotland with the children of her first marriage, while Lennox stayed in London, taking with him his own daughter and everything of value, leaving his wife 'in a very sober state'. The duchess died in 1609, and it was left to her grudging brother to arrange and pay for the funeral.[60] But it was not always husbands who left their wives. By the autumn of 1595, lady Hume had had enough of her husband, the sixth lord Hume, leaving him and taking all the best furnishings from his castle. The couple were reconciled but the countess had made her point. The marriage of the fifth earl of Eglinton and his cousin, Margaret Montgomery, was two years old in 1606 when, shortly after the earl made a generous settlement on his wife, she stopped sleeping with him. In June 1608 she ran away, joining her mother, the abandoned duchess of Lennox, in the overcrowded house of lord Loudon. Eglinton had an inhibition issued against his wife, revoked any infeftments he had made, accused her of scheming to defraud him and of neglecting 'the duty and obedience that a wife owes to her husband', but the couple were still separated when he died in 1612.[61]

The more drastic step of a formal divorce was fraught with difficulties because of the division of the assets, and unlike in France, where creditors lobbied for legally enforceable separations because of the threat to their interests when a division of property took place, there was no third party with an interest in a court settlement. Furthermore, one practical consequence of adultery being proved against a husband in Scotland was that over and above her terce or life rent any infeftment made by a husband to his wife could not be revoked, a potentially expensive loss. Difficulties might also arise for mothers in relation to the custody of children, husbands having greater rights to custody. In Scotland, therefore, noblemen were not easily or cheaply quit of their wives. In 1562, the marriage of the third earl of Eglinton to Jane Hamilton, a younger daughter of the duke of Châtelherault, ended in divorce because of the earl's long-standing affair with Agnes Drummond. Eglinton was obliged to make a grant to Jane of heritable lands in Renfrewshire with an annual income of 600 merks and a house at Eastwood, redeemable for 6000 merks. On Eglinton's marriage to Agnes Drummond, she took over the payment of Jane Hamilton's 600 merks until her own tocher of 6000 merks was paid in full. In effect, Eglinton's second wife was obliged to pay his first wife out of her own dowry.[62]

Jane Hamilton had powerful kinsmen who helped get her a fair settlement and she was able to retire to her house in comfort, refusing to remarry. Here was another reason for observing parental wishes in choosing a husband or wife; hence the third earl of Lothian's point that wives were always tolerant of bad husbands they chose themselves against the advice of their families.[63] On the whole, wives had a harder time getting satisfaction and generally they were likely to find themselves much worse off. Even if a settlement was awarded, a wife could face enormous difficulties in making her husband, or ex-husband, pay. If the wife was the guilty party, she would forfeit any right to the tocher or her jointure. Grissel Scott, wife of the dreadful seventh lord Borthwick, endured insults and severe beatings but finally deserted her husband when he moved his two mistresses, one of whom was lady Borthwick's sister, into his castle. In 1578, the commissary court awarded her thirty shillings per day (£547 10s per annum), backdated to when she first initiated legal action, but in spite of privy council intervention supporting lady Borthwick, her husband avoided paying maintenance costs or agreeing to a costly divorce.[64] Similar difficulties faced Elizabeth Beaton, lady Innermeath, after the death of her husband in 1570. Lady Innermeath then married James Gray, 'ane young gentilman unlandit or providit of leaving, in hoip that he sould have mantenit and defendit and done the dewtie of ane faithfull husband to hir in hir aige'. Unfortunately, Gray proved to be an unscrupulous gold-digger and in 1579 lady Innermeath uncovered his adultery with her own niece, now carrying his child. Gray had powerful friends, including his wife's eldest son who joined him in seeking to defraud lady Innermeath of her conjunct fee and living. Her only support came from a younger son who stood by her in the desperate and bloody bid to retain control of Redcastle and its lands. On 10 June 1581, lady Innermeath was finally divorced from her now outlaw husband, whose disreputable career came to an end when he was killed in a brawl in Dundee five years later.[65]

But wives could win at law. Agnes Mure, lady Newark, succeeded in getting a decree of divorce against her husband, Patrick Maxwell of Newark, on 15 February 1591 after pursuing him before Edinburgh commissary court for adultery with two other women. In 1631, the first lord Reay nullified his second marriage to Rachael Winterfield, an Englishwoman, on the spurious grounds that she had already been married in Ireland, so that he could secretly marry his mistress and the mother of his bastard, 'a woman without birth, without meanes, without friendship'. Rachael Winterfield, however, took him to court where she won the right to be acknowledged as his rightful wife, and she followed this by successfully prosecuting him for maintenance. Lilias Graham, lady Luss, found herself abandoned by her husband, John Colquhoun of Luss, in July 1631, when he ran off to London with her younger sister, Katherine. She was left with eight children and no income since the estate was arrested and sequestered. In January 1633, a charge of incest was brought against Luss in the justiciary court, although some effort was made to protect Katherine's reputation by alleging that Luss and his German servant had practised witchcraft against her, luring his sister-in-law into his bed with an enchanted jewel. Of course, it was the diamonds and rubies that did for Katherine's chastity rather than cunning spells but Luss's failure to appear meant that he remained an outlaw on the basis of this ridiculous story. Meanwhile his wife proceeded to get access to the income from her conjunct fee.[66]

## Conclusion

Early modern marriages were never based on equality between husbands and wives, but within the parameters created by the law many husbands and wives formed enduring, loving relationships or negotiated respectful, working partnerships in which strong and talented women seized their opportunities. Some wives were badly treated by husbands who exploited their legal, social, cultural and physical advantages to domineer over a marriage, but many, possibly most, husbands recognised the valuable resource a wife represented. Measuring something as intangible as the marital relationship is difficult even today, and at a distance of 400 years, with only a miscellaneous collection of evidence, it is almost impossible. Documentary sources suggest that, by the early seventeenth century, husbands and wives were expressing their feelings more openly, adopting a gentler, kinder language. This might simply reflect the greater survival of correspondence in comparison to the mid-sixteenth century, although the willingness to give reign to emotional expressions of love is consistent with the growing emphasis on establishing some sense of mutual liking, even love, prior to marriage. It is tempting to make too much of this, and it is always dangerous to underestimate the humanity of medieval society, but early modern noblemen and noblewomen do appear to have become more likely to find love in marriage. The Reformation's emphasis on the benefits of marital love with its more positive view of women, the writings of moralists inspired by a humanist education, and the shift to a more affluent, less martial society, all contributed to this development, creating within marriage the space for people to work out a relationship that still gave due emphasis to the production of heirs, estate accumulation and family alliances, but which also recognised the need for husbands and wives to make emotional commitments to one another.

Sadly, marriage was also an institution that imprisoned people in ill-matched relationships, and the theme of the miserable marriage was certainly taken up in popular poetry.[67] Money, sex and violence were the most common causes of marital breakdown; at least these were the most common causes to reach public notice. Just how many husbands and especially wives endured years of misery in private cannot be known, and it is pointless to guess. In spite of the suggestion that emotional attachments were in general growing between husbands and wives, people did not have a romantic ideal of marriage, and so mere emotional disappointment was unlikely to cause the tension it creates in modern relationships. However, husbands who plundered their wives' assets, putting at risk their welfare in widowhood and possibly the welfare of their younger children, husbands who subjected their wives to public sexual humiliation, or those who engaged in extreme and prolonged forms of physical abuse, did provoke their wives to seek redress. Fortunately, Scots law and the sensible attitude of the kirk allowed for both separation and divorce, although neither was easy and some couples made their own private arrangements for informal separations. Compared to many early modern societies, Scottish noblewomen were treated with some degree of sympathy and fairness, although there is no doubt that the weight of the law and public opinion usually favoured husbands. Ultimately, noble society itself approved of such exit routes in spite of the huge complications of disentangling marriages that not only bound two individuals together, but also created sensitive family relationships and complex property commitments.

CHAPTER 7

# Children

Scottish nobles were remarkably successful at breeding children in the period covered by this book, and they were also able to provide for their children relatively generously. That represents the bare bones of the story of noble family life. A closer examination of the scattering of evidence reveals a complex picture of the role of children in noble families, and of parent–child relationships. In noble households, where kinsmen and servants swelled the numbers living under one roof to scores or hundreds of people, the family might not easily fit into the nuclear unit of parents and children. Furthermore, the noble family throughout Europe still embraced an extended lineage of living and dead kinsmen linked to one another by a web of obligations. However, Scotland had moved with the rest of Europe in shedding many of the characteristics of the extended family in the medieval period. At heart, therefore, early modern Scottish noble families shared some of the characteristics of what was becoming the typical western family: a nuclear centre, relatively old mothers (although on average these were younger than among non-nobles), little age difference between spouses, and the presence in households of other kindred, friends and servants. Of course, no family is static and unchanging; its personnel constantly alters with births and deaths, the forming of bonds and the breaking of them, while relationships warm or cool depending upon circumstance and necessity. For each individual, the family is something distinct, a network of overlapping circles centred on themselves, in which other people move in and out of one's experiences. At the same time, every individual's place in the family alters with differing roles, from younger son to elder brother, from second husband to uncle, and in the case of women from only daughter to elder sister, from wife to mother-in-law, each claiming a place in the hierarchic and patriarchal structure that held it all together.[1]

## The Noble Family

In early modern society children were regarded as desirable and inevitable; thus the pre-Reformation church taught that men and women joined together in marriage 'to beget and religiously educate children'. After 1560,

Scottish Protestants had little to say about children in comparison to English Puritans, an indication perhaps of the more central role children enjoyed in that community.[2] One of the few nobles to comment on children was the third earl of Lothian, who noted in his collected aphorisms that men with wives and children 'hath given hostages to fortune' for they were 'impediments to greate enterpryses either of vertue or much else'. Instead, 'The work of greatest merite for the publike have proceeded from unmarried and childless men whoe have maried and endowed the publike and yett they that have children should rather care for future tymes which they must transmitt their dearest pledges'.[3] For all his grumblings about the burdens of family life, Lothian had both a busy public life, and a happy marriage and fourteen children.

Surprisingly, the world view of the nobility as represented in the visual arts makes little reference to family. Family portraits from this period are rare, an artistic lacuna that is not peculiar to Scotland before the later sixteenth century. The portrait of the fifth lord Seton, his wife and their four sons was exceptional for the sixteenth century, although there are a handful surviving from the early seventeenth century, evidence perhaps of a greater interest in representing the close ties binding together parents and children. It is possible that one of the effects of the concentration on the lineage of a family in early modern society was that there was less emphasis on the living family at any particular moment in time.[4] The most common representation of the nuclear family in England was on tombs where the role of individuals was stylised, their numbers, sex and order of succession being more important than particular features. They were also placed within an armorial display that highlighted their connection to the larger kindred. In Scotland, such representations were attracting patrons by the second quarter of the seventeenth century. The tomb built in 1642 for sir George Bruce at Culross shows reclining figures of him and his wife before which kneel figures of their eight children.[5] There are other evidences in family archives of the significance people attached to their children. The papers of the second earl of Mar and those of the sixth earl of Morton include detailed lists of their children, containing in the former the exact times of their births, an exercise in recording that was unlikely to be only of genealogical value.[6]

The sight of those eight figures on the laird of Culross's tomb is a reminder of the size of these families. The Mar and Morton lists are unusual, and finding the actual numbers of children born, especially daughters who died young, is fraught with difficulties. However, the 356 peers produced 2011 children, an average of 5.6 children each over the course of a lifetime, and of this number 1635, or an average of 4.6 outlived their fathers.[7] Contemporaries believed the normal woman to be fruitful between the ages of eleven and fifty, although the breeding potential of most noblewomen was delayed until after marriage, typically at eighteen, and most women ceased to bear children in their late thirties, providing twenty years for breeding.

**Table 7.1 Peers' marriages without issue, 1560–1637**

| | No. of cases | Percentage |
|---|---|---|
| **1st marriages** (total = 338) | 45 | 13.3% |
| **2nd marriages** (total = 115) | 31 | 27% |
| **3rd marriages** (total = 21) | 8 | 38.1% |
| **All marriages** (total = 474) | 84 | 17.7% |

On average, Scottish noblewomen produced 4.7 recorded children throughout the span of their fertility, but some women recorded remarkable feats of childbearing: Margaret Maxwell, lady Newbattle, allegedly gave birth to thirty-one children, although later sources have only been able to identify twelve.[8] The incidence of children in early modern society was determined above all else by the age of marriage. Since noblewomen married earlier, were better nourished and had the financial resources to employ wet nurses, thus shortening the period when lactation affects ovulation, they generally produced more children. The absence of effective birth control combined with the unwillingness of wives, and society at large, to tolerate concubinage made large families likely, and as has already been demonstrated, the lineage demanded large families in spite of the financial cost.[9]

Among first marriages, the most important category, only 13 per cent produced no children, the figure rising to 27 per cent for second marriages, and 38 per cent for third marriages, producing an overall figure of 18 per cent of all marriages being childless, a figure close to that found in England (see Table 7.1).[10] Indeed few nobles were not fathers, only 12 per cent of the higher nobility failing to produce any legitimate children at all. (Ten per cent were absolutely childless.)

In the early modern world, pregnancy was a constant condition for many women, especially for noblewomen since they did not breast feed, miscarriages were common, infant mortality was high, and many expectant mothers faced considerable risks.[11] The second earl of Perth dismissed his wife's forthcoming labour in January 1621, commenting that she was 'daylie expecting the disease scho likes best, – for other sicknesses brings efter them no contentment, bot this small pane scho is curit be hearing the chyld weepe'.[12] Here was a man's view of childbirth, 'this small pane' that was easily cured. For women, the thought of pain and death was less easily dismissed. The countess of Haddington was indignant when she discovered that one of her daughters was pregnant, her son-in-law having failed to inform her, for 'a gud man lyk him wol sun get ane wyf agane bot hir bairnis wol never get thair mother'. Yet in spite of the risks – the death rate of mothers in childbirth was between 2 and 5 per cent in early modern Europe – women displayed both fortitude and resignation. In November 1618, the countess of Winton, already having borne six children, the latest a daughter in June of that year, wrote about the possibility of being pregnant again, 'let that cum as it pleases God, for I am not very curiouse: if it pleis God they leive with me that I have I am content'.[13] After another three children she died some time in the mid-1620s when still a young woman. Therefore, while wealth might buy them the best medical care available, noblewomen were not much better off than the peasantry in the throes of childbirth. In one family, Elizabeth Stewart, wife of the fifth lord Lovat, suffered a miscarriage in 1567, her eldest son lost his first wife following a miscarriage in 1593, while his second wife bore six children, of whom only three attained adulthood, and she suffered two miscarriages before 'turning gross and too fat'. Meanwhile, among lady Lovat's neighbours, the countess of Moray died giving birth on 18 November 1591. More noblewomen died in childbirth than noblemen died in bloodfeuds, and even for those who did not die the experience of childbirth could cause all sorts of complications.[14]

John Wemyss described the process of a child being formed in the three classic stages. The first of these took place before birth, from birth to the seventh year was the second stage during which the child's hold on life was at best precarious, and in the third stage it steadily rose to its fortieth year when a man 'comes to his perfection and wisdome'. However, while noble children were better fed, clothed and protected from the elements, disease struck just as readily and as suddenly. In October 1637, the five-year-old heir to the earl of Sutherland died of smallpox, preceding his mother by two months. George Seton, third earl of Winton, fathered twenty legitimate children by his two wives, but eight died in childhood and two sons were drowned in later life so that only half his children outlived him. These people experienced real loss when infants died but they often demonstrated considerable resilience to personal tragedy, as when the twelfth earl of Sutherland wrote to his brother after his wife lost a baby, telling him, 'Ye ar boith young aneuch, so if your selffis be in health, I hoip in God yow will have chyldren anew'.[15]

While early modern people liked to emphasise the durability of their lineages, families were subject to repeated change due to this high incidence of death among children and parents. The fragility of life meant that serial monogamy was not uncommon, often creating difficult family relationships. The first earl of Dunfermline was thirty-six before he married in 1591, and the subsequent twenty-two-year quest for a male heir cost the lives of two young women and probably endangered the life of a third wife, the fourteen-year-old Margaret Hay who he married in 1607 and who finally produced a son eight years later. It also created a complex range of kinship relations between his many daughters and his wives that was far from stable. Similarly, when Sara Maxwell, countess of Wigton, married the first viscount Airds in 1626, she became mother of his children by a previous marriage. The countess herself was already mother to James Johnstone of that Ilk and his sister, whose father she had married in 1588, and to two daughters by her second husband, the first earl of Wigton, who also had a large family by his first marriage.[16] Many children were brought up by other relatives as a consequence of the early deaths of their parents. After the death of the fifth lord Fleming in 1572, the fourth earl of Atholl had responsibility for the care of his five children 'whom I haif brocht up hitherto as my awin'. When the first earl of Buccleuch's wife died in 1631 and he went to Holland on mercenary service, the children were placed in the hands of the earl's sister, lady Ross. Buccleuch himself died that year, and while his eldest son became the ward of secretary Stirling, the other children remained in his sister's care.[17]

While the early modern period did see a growing interest in child care, it remained an activity that was primarily the business of women, and one in which there were few changes. Little is known about child care in Scotland, and it is unlikely that there were many developments. Swaddling continued to be recommended in order to straighten the limbs, but by the early seventeenth century the practice of salting new-born babies to toughen the skin was dying out 'in this effeminate and daintie age'. From a young age, children might be deliberately separated from their parents, and most Scottish noblewomen probably put their children out to wet nurses, as was the prevailing case in England and France until fashions began to change in the course of the seventeenth century. Already in the 1630s, the practice had its critics, who pointed out that since children inherited something of their mother's nature from her milk, parents ought to take care in choosing a wet nurse and in looking after her needs, many being poor unmarried mothers of ill repute. After the birth of her daughter Eleanor, Anna Livingston, countess of Eglinton, employed 'ane young milk woman' who was probably of this background. In 1600, lady Garden employed Marion McGrugar as a wet nurse, but soon found herself in trouble with the church which regarded this woman as a notorious fornicator. The kirk session agreed that lady Garden could retain McGrugar's services as long as she kept this 'offensive and sclanderus' woman out of sight and off the streets. A different relationship might have prevailed in the Highlands where, for example, the Fraser kindred had their own arrangement with the Clann an Lighich, the doctor's clan, to whom successive lady Lovats sent their children to be wet-nursed.[18]

Doctors were divided over the timing of weaning, some thinking three years too long, making a child 'dull and unfit for learning'. Even if the child was removed from the care of a wet nurse, it was likely to be entrusted to others besides the mother. The countess of Moray left her daughter in the care of her mother-in-law at Lochleven, from where she received reports on the little girl's development. The children of the sixth earl of Eglinton were split up when very young, being divided between his own household and those of his brother and father-in-law.[19] Among Lowland families, these arrangements often arose as a consequence of educational needs or wardship. In the Highlands, this separation took a formal form in fostering which 'is accompted the strictest poynt of amitie and freindship among all the Hielenders of the kingdome of Scotland, preferring oftentymes their fosters and foster-brethren unto their parents, befor their naturall lords and masters'. These arrangements gave foster children rights to a share of their foster parents' property, and valuable gifts at the end of their period of fostering.[20] The fostering contracts signed between the lairds of Glenorchy and their dependants were specific about the terms of the child care, and in one case even made provision for a replacement if the boy died before reaching his majority. When in 1598 a disagreement between the seventh earl of Argyll and Glenorchy was settled, the earl demonstrated his trust in this kinsman by agreeing to foster his eldest son with him. A contract between the two men stated that 'the same sone and air salbe deliverit to thame immediatlie eftir thair nativitie and to remane with thame and in thair houss ay and quhill thai be reddie and meit to be put to the scholes and lerning'. Lord Lorne warmly recalled his experience in the Glenorchy household when in 1635 he sent his own children to be fostered with sir Colin Campbell of Glenorchy.[21]

Even without the church intoning against fornication and adultery, noble families knew the dangers of siring bastards; as Gordonstoun pointed out, unbridled sexual indulgence could be 'a cursse to your posteritie', haunting the lineage.[22] In law, illegitimate children were unable to inherit any part of the heritage of their fathers, but that did not prevent them from being a nuisance. The eighth lord Sanquhar never married, but during one of his many sojourns in France he set up house with a mistress who bore a son to whom he entailed his lands. After Sanquhar's death in 1612, the rights of this bastard were successfully challenged by a kinsman, but damage was done to the family and the bastard had to be bought off. Financial recompense also concerned Agnes Drummond, who in January 1635 wrote to the tutor of the second earl of Buccleuch, reminding him that she had been the previous earl's mistress, bearing him two children before her own marriage for which service she had been granted a pension of 200 merks per annum for life. Pleading poverty, the now widowed Agnes asked for the sum owing her, or at least that she might have an allowance. A note jotted at the end of her letter ordered that she be paid seven dollars on the condition that she never trouble the family again.[23]

How many nobles fathered illegitimate children before and even after their marriages cannot reliably be calculated. Not all of these children were recognised, many died young, and the parentage of others was hushed up by deferential or frightened vassals. Yet acknowledged bastardy by the nobility remained more common than in England where social attitudes were changing noticeably.[24] One source recorded that the first marquis of Hamilton had so many bastards that 'when any woman brought a child to the gates, he directed them to place them in his kitchen, and call them all Hamilton in the devil's name'. This casual attitude to paternity might conceal an obligation similar to the French law of 1567 that placed the onus on masters to disprove they were the fathers of children born to women in their employ.[25] No doubt the Hamilton story is exaggerated, but hard evidence of a casual attitude to bastardy is not difficult to find. Following in the steps of his father, James V, the illegitimate first earl of Orkney fathered bastards before and after his marriage, and in time he recognised at least ten illegitimate children. The third lord Sempill had eight bastards, and many of the first generation of Protestant lords behaved no differently from their predecessors, although the regent Morton's four illegitimate sons might reasonably be excused on account of his wife's insanity.[26]

In the seventeenth century, some nobles continued to provide for their illegitimate offspring. On 30 April 1616, sir Duncan Campbell of Glenorchy secured legitimisation for two bastard sons, each of whom had a different mother, adding to his tally of eighteen legitimate children. At least one of the first earl of Buccleuch's five known bastards was born before his father's marriage in 1616 at the age of nineteen, the others following later by different mistresses; all were treated generously by their father.[27] However, moral attitudes and social conditions were moving against illegitimacy, and none of the acknowledged bastards born to peers after the Reformation attained great prominence. While 103 illegitimate children of peers have been identified for the period 1560–1637, a little over three-quarters of these were born to peers who inherited their titles before 1600, and the average number of bastards born to peers dropped from 0.4 in the sixteenth-century sample to 0.2 in the seventeenth-century sample. In addition to the legal obstacles they faced over inheritance, illegitimate children had to compete with the high birth rate of legitimate children, and they were now cut off from well-endowed church careers. Among the last of this kind of churchman was George Douglas, an illegitimate son of the sixth earl of Angus, who in 1573 was appointed bishop of Moray by his cousin, the regent Morton, an office he disgraced.[28]

The early deaths of one or both parents, remarriage, wet nursing, fostering and the existence of illegitimate children all contributed to a family life that was unstable. Perhaps it was this very volatility that resulted in such emphasis being placed on an idealised family type in which patriarchal authority was acknowledged by obedient and respectful children. Here was the basis of social order; hence James VI's expression of the conventional view that disrespect for parents was subversive, threatening the political order. The king deployed patriarchal ideas throughout his political ideology, arguing that the natural authority of a father provided a pattern for that of kingship, kings being fathers of their people. Gordonstoun expressed similar orthodoxy in extolling the virtues of good family government: 'Ther is no power on earth more just then that of the father or parent over the sone, nor any service more honest and due then that of the sone to the parent'. Parents, especially fathers, enjoyed real authority over their children, at least until they attained their majority or were married, exercising powers of patronage and influencing the marriages and careers of their children. The relationship between fathers and their married daughters appears to have been superseded by that between these women and their husbands, but since daughters continued to enjoy certain rights to movable property or even, in some cases, to land and titles, it is likely that fathers still exercised a degree of influence over them.[29] Furthermore, while there is no surviving evidence in Scotland of the formalised nature of parental authority that was such a striking characteristic of English and French families, it is unlikely that the ritual greetings, the lowering of eyes when speaking to adults, bowing, doffing of hats, kneeling for blessings, and silence until addressed by an adult were absent from Scottish society. Such deference endured into adulthood. In 1631, sir William Ker was created earl of Lothian at a time when his father remained the laird of Ancram, creating unease in what was a good father-son relationship. The question had to be asked if 'the Sonne should have a tytle before the Father'? It was a difficult dilemma, but Ancram's authority as Lothian's father had not been compromised by his son's elevation to the peerage. Even in adulthood the awareness of a father's displeasure remained a potent means of shaping behaviour. Hence the concern of the eldest son of the first earl of Haddington that his younger brother might 'offend my lord', meaning their father.[30]

Nor should the crucial role of mothers be understated, although it was respect rather than obedience that was stressed in attitudes towards them. When he was on the point of death, the fourth earl of Atholl dictated his will, impressing on his son the need to 'keip lyfe to your mother and offend her not gif my blessing should continow with you, and use her as an housekeeper to you as the word of God commandis, seing what blessing ye shall resaif therby, first of God and sine of men'. Similarly, in July 1583, shortly after his father's death, Duncan Campbell of Glenorchy was advised that if he wished to be honoured by his own children when he came of age, he must honour his mother 'as ane obedient sone to ane honorabill moder'. In 1645, sir Thomas Urquhart of Cromarty dedicated *The Trissotetras* to his mother, extolling her virtues in extravagant terms that nevertheless convey a real respect and fondness for her.[31]

Historians are divided on the question of childhood as a distinct experience in pre-modern society, and over the extent of affective relationships in the family. The weight of the argument is increasingly with those persuaded that medieval and early modern people did not live in families bereft of strong emotional attachments. There might be grounds for thinking that social élites led the way in investing greater emotional energy in their children, and that the early modern era saw a decisive move towards affective relationships as the norm. Even this argument is disputed by medievalists who see greater continuity between their period and the modern world, or who at least identify a different kind of childhood experience for medieval children, rather than none at all. Disapproval of spoiling children often did result in a formal relationship with parents, especially fathers, but evidence that early modern Europeans were suspicious of close and loving family relationships, being discouraged by moralists from forming close emotional attachments, is often contradicted by actual behaviour.[32] The Scottish evidence indicates a range of positive emotions, demonstrating that neither the structures nor the prevailing ideologies of the day precluded affective emotions among parents, children and siblings. Writing in the 1630s, Wemyss recognised that in their desire to endow children with the means of ensuring a degree of immortality, parents were bound to them, this instinct being 'the cause why parents are never wearie of their children more than they are of their health'. The surviving letters between Ancram and his eldest son, Lothian, disclose a considerate, caring and enduring bond between the two men in spite of their later political differences.[33]

Daughters figured no less in the thoughts of their protective fathers. During his time in exile in France in 1585, William Douglas of Lochleven wrote home to his wife, asking anxiously about his pregnant daughter. Even when letters appear stiff and formal, as when the first earl of Linlithgow addressed his daughter, the countess of Eglinton, as 'your ladyship', expressions of paternal love and concern seep through the conventions. When lady Cawdor thought she was dying in March 1606, she wrote to her father, sir Duncan Campbell of Glenorchy, asking that 'your m[astership] willbe ane loving father and overseer of my young bairnes as your m[astership] hes bein to me in tyme past'. Behind the formality of the address is a woman who loved her father, and in entrusting her children to his care, she affirmed his success as a father. In his testament of March 1634, less than a year before his death, the second earl of Mar enjoined his eldest son to care for the children of his second marriage, 'my lytle ones quho can not do for themselffs'.[34] Such affection was reciprocated by children. The young Mary Douglas sent a poem to her father, the sixth earl of Morton, expressing love and devotion to a man who was mostly away from home at the London court. It is an immature but touching little composition, exploring the feelings of a teenage girl yearning to know her remote father. Morton's older sixteen-year-old daughter, Margaret, also wrote, pleading with her father not to go soldiering in Denmark and ending her letter, 'I pray your lo[rdship] let draw your portrait to me as ye promised'.[35]

In the wider family too bonds of affection could be strong. In her will of August 1578, the countess of Crawford enjoined her children 'to stand in mutuall lufe and concord and charitie togidder without ony actionis pleyis querrellis or contraversies amangis thame in tyme cuming'. Gordonstoun was proud of the sibling bonds between his brothers and sisters:

> which mutuall love wes a comfort to themselves, a crose to their enemies, and a great joy to all that favored them; the more notable in that it is extra-

> ordinarie, far exceiding the brotherly love of these our tymes, and without nighbouring example.

In spite of Gordonstoun's claims for exceptionalism, strong fraternal bonds were common. The fifth lord Ogilvy assured his half-brother, David Lindsay of Edzell, that 'I wald to God that we (quhom ar ordinit to be broder) war lyk ane bunsch of hard knout woodis quhilkis war nocht able to [be] lawsit and wald be rycht glaid gif my utter diligence, wit and panis mycht help to perform the sam'. The letters that passed between Anna Livingston, countess of Eglinton, and her kinswomen, sharing news about children, relatives, friends, health and their purchases during the second decade of the seventeenth century suggest a female network of intimate and strong friendships.[36] Relationships with grandparents also had their formal attributes, but this did not mean there was no warmth. Anne Campbell's 1604 letter to her grandfather, the fifth earl of Morton, addressed him as 'My lord and honourable grandfather', and she wrote of being 'movit with that naturall love I am bound to beir to your l[ordship]', yet the underlying tone of the letter is tender. Like any doting grandmother, the countess of Haddington was delighted to receive a lock of the hair of a newly born grandson in January 1635. Resilient family relationships also developed between in-laws. The dowager countess of Lothian approved heartily of her son-in-law, thanking sir Robert Ker of Ancram for the 'sone you have given me … he dayly gains more and more of my afection'.[37] The noble family in early modern Scotland, therefore, was centred on the nuclear unit of husband, wife and their children, but varied greatly in size and composition depending upon the number of children, the presence of older family members or of step-relations, and a wider network of kinsmen. Religious developments questioned the primacy of natural bonds, and greater education fed an awakening self-consciousness, allowing individuals to imagine for themselves a place in the world not necessarily dictated to them by family; nevertheless those family bonds remained powerful.

## Families at War

Of course, not all families remained on good terms. Quarrels could be extremely damaging in what was the most important relationship in any noble family, that between a father and his eldest son and heir. Sons, especially eldest sons, were in the awkward position of knowing that only their father's life stood between them and the wealth and power for which they longed. There was, therefore, a fine balance to be struck between suitably providing for children, especially the eldest son and heir, and impoverishing the father. Sons who were neglected became resentful, while those who pressed too hard for a share of the inheritance aroused suspicion and hurt in fathers who sensed that only their own deaths would satisfy these hungry offspring. As fathers had relatively few legal powers over their adult children, the nature of their relationships with sons especially was a matter of negotiation within the family It therefore required skill and sensitivity in dealing with matters like ill-health. The master of Ross wrote a filial letter to his father, the sixth lord Ross, in July 1630, expressing joy at the latter's recovery from sickness, and assuring his father that 'in conscience the poets saying sall never hold treu one my pairt, "*Filius ante diem patrios inquirit in anno*" [Ovid, *Metamorphosis*, i. 148, 'the son inquires how long his father will live'], for I doubt if ever I sall be aibel to fill your lordships roome'.[38] But sensible families did anticipate the necessary transfer of wealth and power. While the principal reason for infefting a son and heir in his father's possessions before the latter's death was legal, and a life rent guaranteed that fathers continued to control the greater part of the estate, such arrangements also offered the opportunity for a form of early retirement. Old and sick lords could pass on the responsibility for running affairs and draw a pension from the family's income. James Leslie, master of Rothes, might already have been a man of fifty when in 1599 he and his father signed just such an agreement for 'the well standing of the ancient house of Rothes, and for preservation of the honourable estate thereof'. Sadly, some fathers tried to trick their sons. William Stewart of Kinnaird infeft his son, John, in all his lands and heritages in return for a life rent of 2000 merks per annum, and only later did John discover his father had mortgaged some of the lands without his knowledge.[39]

As in noble societies elsewhere, the tension in these relationships expressed itself most keenly in either rancorous fathers maltreating their sons, or in impatient sons seeking to push their fathers aside. Some sons were very badly treated. As a young man, Patrick Stewart, master of Orkney, was 'verray scharplie handillit and extremelie usit' by his father, 'for quhen evir he requiris ather claything or ony uther thing necesser for him my lord boistis him, and saies he sall use him in na uther maner, quhilk the maister can nocht guidlie support'. Arguments over money were an important factor in the appalling relationship between the eleventh earl of Crawford and his son, especially during the latter's miserable time at the university of St Andrews in 1598. James Stewart, master of Atholl, complained in January 1602 that he hated living at home because of his stepmother, who 'careis ane honey toung, bot ane hart of gall', and he was unhappy because he was kept short of money. His maternal uncle took up the matter, telling the earl of Atholl to be 'ane Christiane and kynd father to his hous quairof your lordship was anis also ane sone'. He chided the earl for preventing his son from getting a suitable education, alleging that some men 'will have their bastardis or horse keeparis better arrayit'. Katherine Douglas, wife of sir James Dundas of Arniston, worried over the 'misliking quhilk my husband hes consaviet this lang time towarts his sone, quhilk is maist unnatraill, and daiyly incresis'. She entirely blamed her husband, but Arniston had a different view of his 'foolische sone', who had crossed the Tay and was in the company of rebels, thus placing the interests of the family in jeopardy.[40]

In some regions of France there was criticism of primogeniture and the attendant rules governing the size of portions for other children, chiefly on the grounds that these regulations undermined parental authority, but no one was prepared to reform a system seen as necessary to the survival of the lineage. There was no debate in Scotland but eldest sons still feared they might be set aside in favour of a younger brother. In 1583, sir William Lauder of Halton and his eldest son quarrelled bitterly when Halton sought to 'defraud and dishereis his said sone of that leving quhilk he, of the law of God and man, sould succeid unto'.[41] In a few cases these disputes were vicious. John Sinclair, master of Caithness, was thrown into the dungeons of Girnigo castle in 1571 by his father, who left him there among the rats for seven years until his death, although not before he had killed a younger brother with his chains. One might explain such conflicts as flowing from the denial of their own mortality by psychologically insecure fathers, or as plain greed by miserly old lords. However, because such quarrels could have political repercussions beyond the immediate household, pressure often came from kinsmen or overlords to reach an agreement before the dispute escalated to the level of a damaging family feud. When in 1578 Colin Campbell of Glenorchy tried to redeem his eldest son's lands, the latter enlisted the help of his chief, the sixth earl of Argyll, who gave Duncan a bond of maintenance, promising to protect him until Glenorchy recognised his son's rights.[42]

Although a social and legal system that placed such emphasis on inherited wealth and authority could place enormous power in the hands of young men, the common expectation in early modern society was that the world would be governed by men in their forties and fifties. From the age of fourteen, young men began to exercise some responsibility, but youths still retained much of the imperfection of childhood and it was anticipated that they would engage in disorderly behaviour, drinking, fighting and being sexually promiscuous, at least until the onset of adulthood which came with marriage and the establishment of a household. However, society also viewed the disobedience of parents by their children as so aberrant that it could only be explained as a form of mental illness.[43] In 1591, the fifth lord Ogilvy tried to avoid being dragged into a feud with the eleventh earl of Crawford, promising that if his son did not accept the mediation, 'I sall become as greitt ane unfriend to him as I was and ame ane lufing father'.[44] The most offensive behaviour occurred when sons set themselves against their fathers. In 1591 relations broke down between the old seventh lord Forbes and his eldest son, John, master of Forbes, a man who at forty-nine had run out of patience, seizing and imprisoning his father who he believed was intending to disinherit him at the instigation of his younger brothers. Patrick Gray, master of Gray, believed his father 'hed nevar a caire yet ether of bairne or house', and in 1607 he assumed control of his income and affairs, prompting lord Gray to complain that his son's actions were likely 'to accelerat his faderis gray hairis to the grave with sorow'. Patrick Wood of Bonyton and his wife were terrified of their eldest son, James, whose 'monyfauld insolenceis, shamefull and violent oppressionis' they long endured. Finally, in the spring of 1601, James broke into his father's house and stole his muniments, following which he was captured and executed, his behaviour being anathema in a society where such actions were an affront to the natural order.[45] Highland society saw more extreme behaviour in these disputes, possibly because primogeniture and illegitimacy were less important. In 1575, the eighty-year-old Murdo MacLean of Lochbuy found himself pushed aside by one of his sons who had taken over the administration of his estates and lands against the old man's will, while in October 1612 Rory MacNeill of Barra and his son were captured and placed in irons by two of his illegitimate sons and their followers.[46]

In households where patriarchal authority was great but in which young men strained at the leash to assert themselves, mothers were important figures in resolving conflicts between fathers and sons or between brothers. However, widows also represented a source of division and instability within the family. The growing size of jointures and of the portions assigned to the heir's sisters might have increased the competition for control over the family's financial resources. It was this conflict James VI had in mind when he counselled his son to 'beginne not, like the young lordes and lairdes, your first warres upon your Mother', as many families did indeed engage in bitter quarrels for the control of a widow's assets.[47] Dame Katherine Ker, lady Ferniehirst, took advantage of her son's forfeiture to complain to the privy council in 1571 that he had excluded her from lands and deprived her of her income. Alexander Kirkpatrick of Kirkmichael grew so impatient with his mother that 'he begouth be policie and craft to intyse hir to have renunceit hir haill leving in his favour,' finally locking her up in a chamber in the hope of forcing her to accede to his requests.[48]

But mothers were neither helpless nor harmless. In 1598, the second duke of Lennox was advised by a friend not to press his mother for the family's French lands – she had threatened to divide the assets between the duke and his younger brother if he interfered – for his mother was 'a verie hard woman, yet with good usage ye may be master of all sche hes'. John Kennedy of Blairquhan's grasping mother was so bad that he had the support of his father-in-law when he complained about her to the privy council in 1606.[49] Often these disputes arose at the end of a minority, for while Scottish mothers had no legal rights over their children in the event of their husband's death, only custody of their person until the age of seven, some were nominated as tutors and curators by their husbands on condition they did not remarry until their son was of age. When the eighth lord Yester attained his majority in 1615, he discovered that his finances were heavily in debt and he blamed his mother, initiating an investigation of the previous six years' accounts. Gaps in the paperwork were discovered and large sums of money were unaccounted for, although when challenged over this at a family conference lady Yester 'waxed a litill wilfull and violent in talking of there business'. Friends counselled Yester to be reasonable, but such was the extent of his public financial embarrassment that he had to put his horses out to graze rather than stable them, and he was incensed by his mother's insinuations that he was badly advised 'therby that the world might think him still a bairne'. The affair went to the court of session but a compromise was reached in 1618, following which Yester bought his mother's conjunct fee, life rent and terce for a pension of 1600 merks per annum.[50]

In the majority of cases, the dispute was between an heir and his stepmother. Often these women had to be aggressive to protect the interests of their own children, but some widows were predators; hence the French legislation of 1560 preventing widows transferring their late spouse's wealth to a new husband. Between her husband's death in 1585 and her own thirty-four years later, Agnes Sinclair, dowager countess of Errol, was at the centre of a succession of disputes between herself, her stepsons and her own sons.[51] The quarrel between Sara Maxwell, countess of Wigton, and her stepsons began before her husband's death, necessitating that their affairs were put to arbitration in 1615. Wigton presented a picture of a powerful and scheming woman, seeking 'upoun plane malice' to defraud him and the sons of his first wife to the benefit of herself and her own children by this and a previous marriage.[52] The public row between the old fifth earl Marischal and his eldest son, lord Keith, was created by the former's second wife, Margaret Ogilvy, lobbying on behalf of her own son, James Keith of Benholm, to impose on lord Keith 'fraudfull and onresonable' financial and legal conditions. After Marischal's death on 2 April 1623, his grasping widow wasted no time in marrying sir Alexander Strachan of Thornton, her adviser and lover, plundering the late earl's papers, money, plate and furnishings, and moving everything out of his castle in the middle of the night.[53] Following the death of the second earl of Mar in December 1634, a quarrel over the division of his movables broke out between his eldest son and the latter's stepmother. The dowager countess's lawyer, Craighall, warned her against legal action as the law was 'not the way ather to keip the peax, or to advance the nobill plantis of so nobill a parentage, or to [de]siste the fall and ruyne of that ancient and nobill hous'. However, the dowager countess, whose household expenditure amounted to twenty-four chalders of grain and £11 533 in cash and who had debts of £11 066, was determined to press her case, fearing that any mediation would be undermined by the new earl's wife. The bitterness between these two women grew worse. In 1639, the dowager countess complained to her own son, Charles, about 'that furious ladie' who had been spreading malicious rumours to the effect that 'I nevir loved nor respeakitt my husband … and was presently doing all I could to ruine the hous of Mar'. She also believed her stepson intended 'to defraud mee and my children of our estates to enrich him'; the wrangle between her and her sons on the one part, and the earl on the other, continued until her death in 1644.[54]

The formidable and even aggressive nature of some of these matriarchs was striking. The second earl of Moray was in awe of his mother-in-law, Agnes Keith, countess of Argyll, and on one occasion in 1587 he urged his lawyer to hurry home in order that they could tie up a transaction before her arrival as she 'will work all the hindrance she can'. The third marquis of Hamilton's mother, Ann Cunningham, caused him problems long before the celebrated incident in 1639 when she threatened to shoot him if he opposed the National Covenant. Five years earlier she had publicly defended the disgraced seventh earl of Menteith against the courtiers who destroyed him.[55]

The experience many women gained as partners to their husbands was often continued into the adult lives of their sons. The Scottish evidence, therefore, supports the argument that widowhood did not offer women their only brief opportunity to exercise authority, but was a stage in the experience of powerful and able women. Many widowed mothers worked tirelessly to improve their son's inheritance. Margaret Stewart, widow of the master of Ochiltree, was left with ten children to care for and a feud with the regent Morton that she prosecuted relentlessly.[56] On reaching his legal majority in 1571, the young David Lindsay of Edzell and his curators granted his mother a bond approving her management of his business, commending 'her grete laubouris and travellis tane for the weill releiff and mantenance of my house and heretage in my minoritie'. A few weeks later, Edzell gave her confirmation of her terce. So impressed was the second earl of Abercorn with his mother in acting as executrix to the estate of her deceased husband that even in adulthood he continued to rely on her counsel, entrusting her to run his affairs when he was out of the kingdom.[57] Some mothers were also a good deal more able than their sons. Sir Patrick Hume of Polwarth's mother was highly vexed at her son's poor business sense, praying God 'grant him grace and wisdom to govern both his mynd and his body and estait better nor he hes done'. In 1625, the countess of Lothian, deeply worried about the future of her daughters who had inherited an indebted estate from an incompetent father, vowed 'to look to my childrein whylls they ar myn and indre my corection, since I have no thing to engage for them bot my caire and love to ther well[fare]'.[58]

## Minorities

On 1 September 1584, the king appointed the household of his ten-year-old French cousin, Ludovick Stewart, second duke of Lennox, including a tutor, his personal gentlemen, the master of his stables and an entire establishment. This picture of a king still in his own minority acting in the interests of an even younger cousin is a useful reminder of how commonplace minorities – these ended for males at twenty-one and for females at fourteen – were in this society. The Scotts of Buccleuch were troubled by a series of minorities with no adult male succeeding between 1470 and 1611, and another minority followed in 1633. Similarly, the earls of Menteith suffered one minority after another, and throughout most of the period 1564 to 1610 the earldom was in the hands of a minor. Imbecility also created conditions in which the rights and interests of an individual had to be entrusted to the care of responsible kinsmen or friends.[59]

During these minorities, noble families were vulnerable to a range of predators beginning with the king himself. The justification for the feudal superior's intervention had been the vassal's inability to perform military service, and Scottish kings continued to be protective of wardship. Charles I was particularly aggressive in asserting crown feudal rights; hence his insistence that crown interests be investigated in relation to the minority of the young second earl of Buccleuch, whose wardship was granted to the first earl of Stirling in 1633. In Riccarton's ideal feudal world, a vassal's superior was the best person to exercise guardianship because of the convergence of both parties' interests. There were careful regulations governing how the superior managed the estate but it was common practice for the crown to give or sell these lucrative wards, usually accompanied by the right of marriage, to royal servants.[60] Hence the affairs of the family, and the person of the heir, could fall into the hands of an outsider. The possibility of this occurring was worrying for fathers, who did their best to anticipate such an eventuality. When the sixth earl of Morton contracted what was mistakenly believed to be a fatal disease in Paris in the spring of 1618, he wrote to the king asking that in the event of his death, 'his sones warde and mariage may be bestowed for his well and standing of his house'. Indeed, the crown was usually protective of the interests of minors, and Charles I stated in May 1637 that it has 'being alwayes our princelie care to protect all minors frome oppressioun'. This protection took various forms. For example, king James granted the young James Johnstone of that Ilk blanket legal protection in November 1608 after his father had been murdered. Kings might also be helpful in allowing minors to be served as heirs to their fathers before they attained the legal age. In 1587, the sixth earl of Menteith was served heir to his father in spite of the fact that he was only fifteen, the king having granted a dispensation to secure his titles while under age. The law was solicitous of the rights of minors in principle, securing them from legal pursuit and allowing reductions of actions taken by their tutors. It was also normal for nobles to make a revocation at the end of their minority, as William Douglas of Lochleven did on 28 July 1562. In 1621, parliament strengthened these rights, allowing the redemption of lands comprised from minors up to the age of twenty-five.[61]

Crucial to the interests of the minor was the appointment of a tutor to act in his name, this taking place in a formal ceremony either at the sheriff court or the local burgh court. The tutor might have possession of the ward and marriage of the minor but this was not always the case, and often his first concern was to persuade whoever held the wardship to sell it. By the seventeenth century, the long struggle in the courts between tutors and donators of wardships was leaning in the direction of the former. Tutors had considerable powers during their tenure of office, although these were subject to stringent scrutiny. Thus when tutors demitted office their actions were examined and the tutorial accounts audited, following which they were granted a discharge by their former ward.[62] The business of choosing a tutor was, therefore, of great importance to the well-being of the heir and the family as a whole. Here there was customary and legal pressure to choose the nearest male relative, most commonly an uncle. In 1585, parliament reaffirmed an earlier statute of 1474 that tutors should be the nearest agnate of at least twenty-five years of age, and his obligations and rights were spelled out.[63]

By contrast, mothers had few rights and little influence, and while the situation was less harsh than Italy where they might be sent back to her own family with their dowry, some mothers were severely treated. Following the death of the fifth lord Lovat in 1576, his wife, Elizabeth Stewart, returned to her father but was refused permission to take her son on the grounds that 'the care and conduct of such a great and good father sone, and onely sone, should not be intrusted to any foreigner, being so young, but to his friends alone and his nearest kinsmen'. This insistence on the rights of the agnatic kindred was not untypical. When in August 1578 the eighty-five-year-old sir James Douglas of Drumlanrig contemplated the likelihood of his approaching death, he made a revealing addition to his will, excluding his daughter-in-law, 'ane proud and wilfull woman', from her son's affairs. Another instance in which the mother of the heir was regarded as predatory by the agnatic kinsmen was that of Agnes Elphinstone, countess of Sutherland, mother of the thirteenth earl who was still a child when he succeeded his father in 1615. The boy's uncle, sir Alexander Gordon of Navidale, wrote venomously that 'scho left the howse off Dunrobin sa bair that scho left nocht sa mikill as the cruik thairin, and tuik away the ald kist quhilk keipit the bread in pantrie … I think schoo sall do littill uther guid to hir sone'.[64]

This determination of kinsmen to exclude outsiders from the family's affairs extended beyond mothers. There was 'gritt stryff' in Carrick in 1575 when the eighth lord Glamis was appointed tutor to the fifth earl of Cassillis, he being the boy's maternal uncle, instead of Thomas Kennedy of Culzean, the brother of the deceased fourth earl of Cassillis. Kindreds tried to prepare for such interference with bonds like that signed during the minority of the fifth earl of Atholl by the principal friends of his house, binding themselves to look after his interests.[65] However, the nearest agnatic kinsman was not always a suitable person to take on the responsibility of the tutorial office. When sir James Johnstone of that Ilk was murdered in 1608, he left behind a six-year-old son and tutorial authority was vested in Robert Johnstone of Raecleuch, the nearest male heir but a man of little means. Consequently, the kindred agreed to back Sara Maxwell, lady Johnstone, in buying out the tutor, a remarkable situation in which the agnatic kindred was prepared to back a woman – and even more astonishingly, a Maxwell – because her status, wealth and past record made her the best person to manage her son's minority. Raecleuch turned down the deal, as was his right, but not surprisingly he was ignored when curators were chosen by the young laird in 1617, and disagreements over the tutorial accounts were not settled until 1623. Occasionally the maternal kindred did triumph. The act of curatory of 9 July 1616 for the second earl of Kinghorn granted authority to his mother and any one of the four curators, two of whom were her brothers, allowing power to pass into the hands of the Murrays of Tullibardine.[66]

The majority of tutors did a satisfactory job, handing over the estate to their former wards in what was often a better condition than they received them. Gordonstoun was an effective tutor of Sutherland, telling his nephew that tutors should be honoured as father figures, for 'Ther cannot be a worsse thing on earth then ane ungrate and unthankfull mynd'.[67] Certainly most tutors and curators took their complicated and time-consuming responsibilities seriously. Sir William Douglas of Lochleven found himself lumbered with heavy duties when in 1580 his brother, the earl of Buchan, and his wife both died, leaving behind a son who was less than a year old. Lochleven had to administer the distant estates of his nephew for the better part of two decades, but also had to take on the duties of sheriff wardator of Banff. The second earl of Home and the sixth earl of Morton debated how best to manage the affairs of a minor for whom they were curators, disagreeing over whether to buy land in England or to lay cash aside as security against debt when the sisters of their ward were married. In discussing the affairs of the second earl of Dunfermline in November 1636, one of his wary curators, the sixth earl of Rothes, advised another colleague to be sure to have the account audited before leaving for England. Should any irregularities appear, the chamberlain or tenants could be blamed for the curators 'hav bein clein fingered'.[68]

Yet there were abuses of tutorial powers. The Sutherland family had only to look back to the disaster that befell the young eleventh earl following his father's death in 1567. The fifteen-year-old earl's ward and marriage was sold to the fourth earl of Caithness, the man who had murdered the boy's father. He arranged an unsuitable marriage between Sutherland and his own daughter who was twice the earl's age, burning many of the 'infeftments and evidents pertaining to the house of Sutherland which he could find within the country'.[69] Even more damaging were the misfortunes of the house of Lundie following the death of John Lundie of that Ilk in 1605. His eldest son, James, was declared unfit by the friends of his house, and the government of his affairs passed into the hands of sir James Lundie, the proverbial wicked uncle. He packed the younger boys off to foreign parts as mercenaries and exploited the simpleton nephew's irregular marriage, before finally sending the unfortunate man to Sweden where he died. Thereafter, sir James defrauded each of his surviving nephews in turn, tying them up in a complex web of legal agreements, debts and obligations that had the younger of them, John Lundie of that Ilk, still trying to get control over his estate in 1634.[70] More commonly, accounts were not always in order. Sir John Grant of Freuchie's tutory of William Mackintosh of Torcastell between 1622 and 1634 ended with him having to explain his handling of the Mackintosh chief's affairs and making a £10 000 out-of-court settlement. Sir Hugh Campbell of Loudon was one of the curators of John Maxwell of Pollok in 1597, who he defended against the predatory interest of James Stewart of Ardgowan, accusing him of 'calumnous pley againis a minor'. Twenty-eight years later Pollok expressed dissatisfaction with Loudon's tutorial accounts, demanding that he discuss them 'be sicht of friends' or answer charges in court.[71]

At the age of fourteen, a minor ceased to be subject to a tutor alone and was permitted to choose curators, one of whom was commonly the tutor, who would guide his affairs until the age of twenty-one. The distinction being made was between the government of the minor's person, which remained under the authority of his tutor, and the administration of his property and affairs, which now required the consent of a wider body of friends. The seven curators appointed for the second earl of Mar in 1576 were the regent Morton, a not unexpected choice as it was usual to seek the patronage of a great man, Mar's mother, two of his paternal uncles and three powerful barons who were friends of the house of Mar and clients of the regent.[72] Even at this stage, the potential dangers of a minority might still emerge. James Menteith of Randifurd's father died c.1572, leaving him in the care of his mother, Margaret Colville, but in January 1579 his uncle and heir, William Menteith of West Kerse, abducted the boy from school in order to influence his nephew's choice of curators. The privy council decreed that the boy should return to school and that his curators be chosen with the advice of the earls of Argyll and Mar. Not surprisingly, the legal position of tutors continued to be reviewed. In 1629, the privy council announced a tightening up of procedures governing the appointment of tutors, forbidding powers from being conferred until the prospective tutor dative had given caution to discharge the office 'faithfulie and dewtifullie'.[73]

Great care was taken to secure the charters and other papers of the minor, seeking to prevent these being tampered with during a minority. Throughout the minority of the fifth earl of Bothwell, the security of his papers was ensured by placing them in a locked kist entrusted to one lawyer, while another was given responsibility for looking after the key. The chest containing the papers of the deceased regent Lennox were in the care of John Cunningham of Drumquassil, chamberlain of the earldom. The key to this box was sent to the countess of Lennox in England but eight years later, with Drumquassil in disgrace and the countess dead, the location of the papers was unknown and the key was lost. Eventually the kist was discovered in Stirling castle and the privy council decided to break it open in the presence of a commission. Sir Duncan Campbell of Glenorchy dictated elaborate arrangements in his 1589 testament, ordaining that all his papers be placed in chests in the charterhouse of his castle which would be secured by three locks. The keys to these locks were to be held by his wife and two named friends, all three of whom would have to consent to open it. Furthermore, because his lawyer, Gavin Hamilton, 'knawis the ordour of my evidentis', only he was to remove papers from the chests.[74] Such an obsessive security betrays the real fear men had that during a minority the interests and welfare of their children would be set aside by interfering outsiders.

## Conclusion

Noble society depended on children for its survival, ensuring that the lineage with its history, possessions and dignities carried on for another generation. A failure to produce children represented the end of the line and with it the bitter realisation that the names and honours of the ancestors, and of those yet living, would no longer be remembered. This was more than mere biological reproduction. Of course, excessive reproduction carried its own inherent dangers, but a combination of ruthless male primogeniture and the availability of additional resources allowed noble families to balance out the need to consolidate wealth with that of sustaining all their members. During this period, Scottish nobles were particularly fertile, and fortunately the country and the social system created by its élites was able to cope with the high numbers of sons and daughters these families produced. Beyond that arithmetic, the noble family proved to be an effective nourisher of its offspring. Essentially the family was nuclear, but the members of the nuclear unit changed, often more than once, as parents died and remarried, creating new and different varieties of the model into which a child was born. These children were wanted, and on the whole they were well looked after in families that might have lacked the child-centred idolatry of today but in which affection and discipline complemented one another to mould characters obedient to the greater interests of the lineage without suffocating individuality and initiative. There is certainly little reason for thinking of these children as neglected or ignored, although there might be some grounds for thinking that the more relaxed political, religious and economic conditions of the early seventeenth century allowed parents to indulge in more intimate relationships with their children.

The success of parents in persuading children to accept their values is clear from the extent to which family relations held together. The law and the teachings of the church added enormous weight to the encouragement children received to honour their father and mother, and the older generation's control of patronage acted as a moderating force on the behaviour of the young. Consequently, the extent of familial breakdown was modest. Long-lived fathers were sometimes resented by their middle-aged heirs and mothers, especially stepmothers, could be viewed as unnecessarily expensive by their sons or stepsons and, no doubt, by their jealous wives. It would be astonishing if such tensions did not exist in families; what is remarkable is that so few became public knowledge, and that of these, only a handful reached the point of irretrievable breakdown between family members. Whatever strains there were outside in society, the noble family proved to be resilient and adaptable, riding the changes in religion, in politics and in the economy with the minimum of impact. Even where noble children were deprived of their fathers by death, law and custom operated effectively to best preserve the interests of their house. There were incompetent and bad tutors who did bring hardship to some individuals, and a scattering of families might even have been sabotaged by the effects of a minority or a series of minorities. However, the system was designed to ensure that even with the king's feudal rights of wardship and marriage, the impact of a minority would be minimised. Noble society needed minorities to pass smoothly because such was their frequency and length that the alternative was to risk undermining the basis of a hereditary élite.

# Part 3

## Culture

**Plate 1** Archibald 'the Grim' Campbell, seventh earl of Argyll (1575–1638), portrayed in a style that reflects his martial interests. This great lord, who could field the largest private army in Britain or Ireland, and who as a youth was led weeping from its defeat at the battle of Glenlivet in 1594, was forced in later life to become a mercenary. He entered Spanish military service after going into exile to escape his creditors and in order to practise his new-found Catholic faith. Painted by A. du Chapell c.1625. In a private Scottish collection.

**Plate 2** This remarkable genealogy, unique in Britain for its scale and detail, was painted c.1635 for sir Colin Campbell whose own portrait is second from the top. It is a fantastic visual evocation of lineage. The cherry tree contains nine lairds of Glenorchy on its trunk and 150 discs of genealogical information on its branches, while at its foot is the founder of the family, Duncan Campbell of Lochnaw. Campbell of Glenorchy Family Tree by George Jamesone. Scottish National Portrait Gallery.

**Plate 3** A sombre and dignified painting of the regent Morton (c.1516–81), unusually wearing a hat that might signify his high office. Born outside the ranks of the higher nobility, Morton acquired his wealth and title through marriage to an heiress who proved to be insane. Consequently he left no legitimate heirs. His career demonstrates the mutability of noble houses within even a short timescale. By Arnold Bronckhorst c.1577. Scottish National Portrait Gallery.

**Plate 4** At the very apex of Scottish noble society was the house of Hamilton, represented here by James, third Marquis of Hamilton (1606–49). In spite of the slightly uneasy posture of a man who would rather be on his way, no other picture of the period better captures the wealth, self-conscious authority and courtly elegance of the nobility. Hamilton was one of the greatest art collectors in Caroline Britain and is painted here by Daniel Mytens. Scottish National Portrait Gallery.

**Plate 5** 'Black' sir Duncan Campbell of Glenorchy (1545–1631) was a ruthless Highland baron whose menacing presence is effectively captured in this painting by an unknown artist. The aggressive land acquisition pursued by sir Duncan provided his son, sir Colin Campbell, with the wealth that allowed him to be among George Jamesone's most important patrons of the 1630s. Scottish National Portrait Gallery.

**Plate 6** The Reformation in Scotland was accompanied by a massive secularisation of land as former ecclesiastical estates were plundered by the nobility. This 1791 engraving of Spynie castle shows the ruin of what had been the bishop of Moray's principal residence. In this case the wealth of the bishopric was exploited to create the new secular lordship of Spynie for Alexander Lindsay, a royal favourite and a younger son of the house of Crawford. By James Crawford. Crown copyright: reproduced by permission of Historic Scotland.

**Plate 7** This apparently shy and melancholy man is Mark Ker, commendator of Newbattle abbey (d.1584), a successful opportunist who acquired control of the abbey estates and founded the house of Lothian. Attributed to Willem Key. Scottish National Portrait Gallery.

**Plate 8** Thomas Hamilton, first earl of Haddington (1563–1637), was the son of a lesser noble and judge who ground his way to the top rank of noble society in royal service. His sharp, forensic mind not only made him invaluable to James VI, but was also put to good use in accumulating a fortune and a vast estate to the south of Edinburgh where he mostly lived. By an unknown artist after Adam de Cologne. Scottish National Portrait Gallery.

**Plate 9** Wealth in stone: this stunning frontpiece above the doorway to Huntly castle, rebuilt after the partial demolition of 1594, contains a powerful political and religious message. From the arms of the first marquis of Huntly and his wife above the door, the informed visitor is taken up through panels signifying ascending ideas from the king and queen to the top where Good triumphs over Evil in the Final Judgement. Crown copyright: reproduced by permission of Historic Scotland.

**Plate 10** Quality horses were expensive to buy and maintain, especially in Scotland where there was such a shortage, and they were among the most potent symbols of wealth and rank. This detail from the first marquis of Huntly's funeral procession in 1636 shows one of his many horses. © Copyright of The Trustees of the National Museums of Scotland 2000.

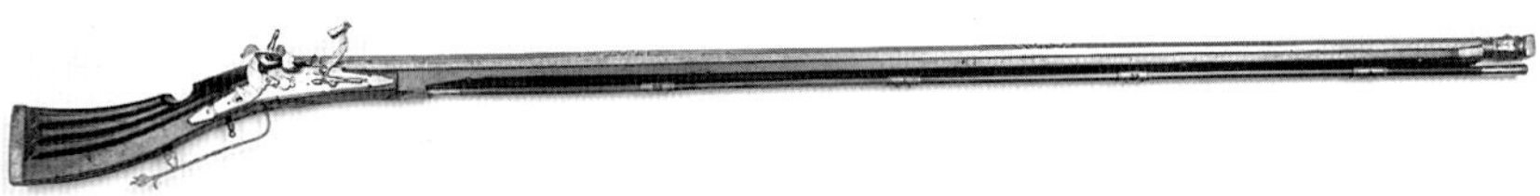

**Plate 11** In addition to their military function, guns were prestige objects. The Breadalbane gun was made in 1599, probably by Patrick Ramsay in Dundee, for sir Duncan Campbell of Glenorchy. © Copyright of The Trustees of the National Museums of Scotland 2000.

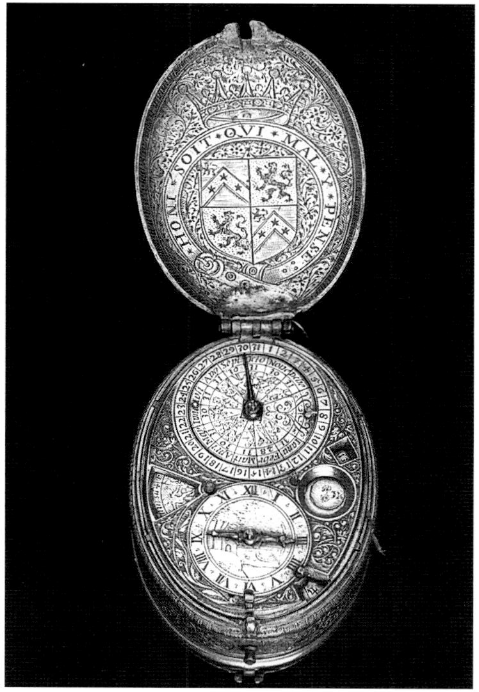


**Plate 12** This beautiful silver pocket watch was a gift from James VI to Robert Ker, first earl of Somerset, and is an example of the kind of high-quality artefact noble consumers enjoyed displaying. © Copyright of The Trustees of the National Museums of Scotland 2000.

**Plate 13** The Cadboll silver cup dates from the later sixteenth century and is French in origin, although it has been locally adapted. It is thought to have come into the hands of the MacLeods of Cadboll, minor Highland nobles, from a Spanish wreck. © Copyright of The Trustees of the National Museums of Scotland 2000.

**Plate 14** Agnes Douglas, Countess of Argyll, c.1574–1607, attributed to Adrian Vanson. The ostentatious, courtly dress and rich jewellery denote the countess's high rank, the wealth of her father and husband, and her own refined tastes. She was married in 1592 and produced seven children before her early death fifteen years later. Scottish National Portrait Gallery.

**Plate 15** The trophy wife: Margaret Graham, sister of the fifth earl of Montrose, was married in 1619 to sir Archibald Napier of Merchiston, whose social climbing paid off in 1627 when he was created lord Napier. This fine painting by Adam de Cologne shows a woman adorned with expensive decoration. Scottish National Portrait Gallery.

**Plate 16** John Erskine, second earl of Mar (1562–1634), grew up in the nursery at Stirling castle alongside James VI, sharing the experience of having George Buchanan as a tutor. Mar and the king remained friends throughout their lives, and James nicknamed him 'Jock o' the Slaits' on account of Mar's arithmetic skills, appointing him treasurer in 1616. However, even Mar's financial abilities were unable to save his house from massive debts following his demission of office in 1630. By an unknown artist, c.1605. In the collection of the earl of Mar and Kellie.

**Plate 17** A marriage proclaimed: Huntly castle showing the ruins of the 1602 rebuilding with the names of George Gordon, first marquis of Huntly (1562–1636), and his wife, Henrietta Stewart (d.1641), clearly visible. Married in 1588, they had a close relationship that endured through many trials for forty-eight years. Crown copyright: reproduced by permission of Historic Scotland.

**Plate 18** The plain young woman staring out from this miniature is Jean Gordon (1544–1629), sister of the fifth earl of Huntly and an important marital pawn in his plans. The portrait was painted as one of a pair to celebrate her marriage in 1566 to the fourth earl of Bothwell, who divorced her in a scandalous case a year later so that he could marry queen Mary. In 1573, she married the eleventh earl of Sutherland, was widowed in 1594, and subsequently oversaw the minority of both her son and her grandson. She was also mother of sir Robert Gordon of Gordonstoun. This remarkable woman, who lived until she was eighty-five, was a powerful matriarchal figure in her family, a staunch Catholic and an astute estate manager. Scottish National Portrait Gallery.

**Plate 19** Agnes Keith, countess of Moray (d.1588), one half of the power couple of the 1560s. Daughter of the richest man in Scotland, the fourth earl Marischal, this clever, acquisitive and steely woman was married in 1562 to lord James Stewart, bastard son of James V, and later the regent Moray. Widowed in 1570, she astutely remarried two years later the younger brother of the childless and about-to-be-divorced fifth earl of Argyll – who died shortly afterwards. Her determination to hold on to queen Mary's jewels fuelled the sixth earl of Argyll's feud with the regent Morton. She was mother of the second earl of Moray and the seventh earl of Argyll. Painted by Hans Eworth as one of a pair with that of her first husband, probably to commemorate their marriage. In a private collection.

**Plate 20** Lady Anne Campbell (d.1638), daughter of the seventh earl of Argyll, was married in 1607 to the son and heir of the first marquis of Huntly as part of the settlement of the bloodfeud between these two powerful houses. The marriage appears to have been a success but the tension between the families remained. The portrait is by George Jamesone and is reproduced with the permission of the Trustees of the Goodwood Collection.

**Plate 21** Margaret Hay, countess of Dunfermline (1593–1659), was painted c.1615 probably following the birth of the son and heir her husband had long sought throughout his three marriages. She was married to the fifty-two-year-old Chancellor Dunfermline in 1607 when aged only fourteen. Following his death in 1622, she waited eleven years before remarrying, first ensuring that her considerable wealth could not be touched by her new husband. By an unknown artist.

**Plate 22** The earliest family portrait in Scotland shows the fifth lord Seton (1531–86), with his daughter and sons, in postures that suggest some degree of emotional bonding, at least between Seton and the two younger boys. His older children, however, appear more detached, looking over his shoulder towards some distant point. Compare this with the following picture of Seton's grandson and family. Scottish National Portrait Gallery.

**Plate 23** George Seton, third earl of Winton (1584–1656), with his sons George and Alexander, is among the most touching and beautiful family compositions of the period. Winton conveys Seton's hierarchic position as a father while his enveloping arms around the boys indicate a warm, protective love. The older boy appears a little stiff, the hat and sword perhaps highlighting his position as the heir, yet his younger brother reaches out to him affectionately, a playful, mischievous smile barely hidden behind the pose he has been forced to adopt. By Adam de Cologne, 1625. Scottish National Portrait Gallery.

**Plate 24** Anne Erskine, countess of Rothes (d.1640), with her daughters is not one of George Jamesone's better paintings, but the all-female subject matter is unusual. The family portraits on the far wall highlight the growing interest in this fashionable medium, and the open jewellery box was among the most prized possessions of any woman since this was one form of property over which her husband had no authority. Scottish National Portrait Gallery.

**Plate 25** A nursing chair belonging to Annabella Murray, countess of Mar, mother of the second earl of Mar. The countess also nursed the infant James VI. National Museums of Scotland.

**Plate 26** One of the infant daughters of the third marquis of Hamilton, painted in the 1630s and attributed to George Jamesone. The fact that young children, especially females, were becoming subjects for artists is an indication of a growing desire by their patrons to recognise their individual identity and might also represent a more public expression of affection. In the Hamilton collection.

**Plate 27** Lady Catherine Hamilton, attributed as a daughter of the third marquis of Hamilton, but if the name is correct she is probably a grand-daughter of the first earl of Abercorn. Like most children of the period, she is dressed in a miniature version of adult fashion; note too the pet dog. Painted c.1620 by an anonymous artist of the English school. In the Hamilton collection.

**Plate 28** Born to command: this cocky youth, dressed almost entirely in red, is William Ker (1605–75), eldest son of sir Robert Ker of Ancram, bedchamber servant to Charles I. His father's connections brought him marriage to an heiress and the title of third earl of Lothian. A devout, studious family man, Lothian became a staunch Covenanter in later life. After George Jamesone and in a private collection.

**Plate 29** Mar's Wark: the remains of the splendid town house built in Stirling in the 1560s by the first earl of Mar. Located on the road leading up to the royal castle of which the earl was keeper, the building would have been the most impressive in the burgh. Crown copyright: reproduced by permission of Historic Scotland.

**Plate 30** This view of the wonderfully three-sided Maxwell fortress of Carlaverock in Dumfriesshire contrasts two architectural visions. The towers, keep and curtain walls of the old castle surround the new Renaissance wing built in the mid-1630s within the courtyard by the first earl of Nithsdale, a man who stretched his creditors to their limits to complete his project. Crown copyright: reproduced by permission of Historic Scotland.

**Plate 31** Painted ceilings were highly fashionable in noble society. This beautifully decorated cupola ceiling is from Pinkie house, chancellor Dunfermline's country residence outside Edinburgh. Crown copyright: reproduced by permission of Historic Scotland.

**Plate 32** A reconstruction of the comfortable and tasteful interior of Argyll's lodgings in Stirling, built in the 1630s for William Alexander, first earl of Stirling. Crown copyright: reproduced by permission of Historic Scotland.

**Plate 33** The elaborately constructed fountain in the garden of Pinkie house, where chancellor Dunfermline deliberately created a neo-Stoic retreat from the cares of business. Crown copyright: reproduced by permission of Historic Scotland.

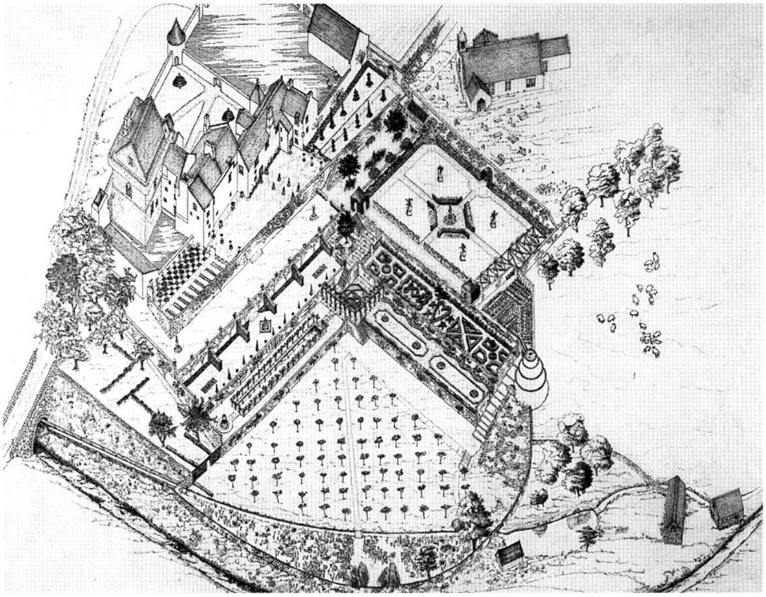

**Plate 34** This artist's reconstruction of the regent Morton's castle at Aberdour provides a good impression of the extensive gardens the earl created on the north side of the Forth estuary. Note the Douglas arms amidst the formal garden. Crown copyright: reproduced by permission of Historic Scotland.

**Plate 35** Artist to the nobility: Aberdeen-born George Jamesone (1589–1644) graduated from decorative painting to portraiture in the 1620s and was soon heavily in demand by a nobility keen to memorialise themselves and their families. The self-portrait demonstrates Jamesone's desire to market himself as an artist with an exclusive clientele. Scottish National Portrait Gallery.

**Plate 36** Detail of a painted ceiling in Crathes castle, Aberdeenshire. This home of the Burnett barons is imaginatively decorated with figures like these female musicians, possibly intended to represent members of the household. Crown copyright: reproduced by permission of Historic Scotland.

**Plate 37** The clarsach was one of the most popular instruments of the day, especially in the households of Highland nobles. This one was made in the west Highlands some time in the latter half of the fifteenth century, and was given to Beatrice Gardyn of Banchory by queen Mary in 1563. © Copyright of The Trustees of the National Museums of Scotland 2000.

**Plate 38** An early seventeenth-century virginal, a relatively expensive instrument that was becoming highly fashionable at this time. This one is thought to have belonged to Marie Stewart, the French-born wife of the second earl of Mar. © Copyright of The Trustees of the National Museums of Scotland 2000.

**Plate 39** Alexander Seton, first earl of Dunfermline, (1555–1622), was one of the foremost scholars of his generation. He turned his brilliant mind to the business of the law and government, rising to become chancellor in 1604 until his death in 1622. Dunfermline had a passion for building and an interest in almost everything. Moderate and humane, his life was guided by neo-Stoic principles and a private devotion to Roman Catholicism. Painted by Marcus Gheeraerts the younger in 1610. National Portrait Gallery of Scotland.

**Plate 40** The sparkling intelligence of sir Robert Gordon of Gordonstoun (1580–1656) is captured in this 1621 portrait by an unknown artist. At this time he was tutor of Sutherland, having retired from England to the family estates where he pursued an interest in the history of his house. Gordonstoun was convinced that the northerly territories over which his family held sway could be 'civilised' by a programme of educational patronage and example. Scottish National Portrait Gallery.

**Plate 41** The most celebrated poet of this age is William Drummond of Hawthornden (1585–1649), head of a minor baronial house in Lothian where he lived out the greater part of his life, cultivating a neo-Stoic philosophy of rural retreat from the politics of Edinburgh and London. However, as a young man he travelled and studied widely on the continent. By an unknown artist. Scottish National Portrait Gallery.

**Plate 42** William Alexander, first earl of Stirling (?1567–1640), a prolific poet, entrepreneur, architectural patron and royal councillor, made his way up from the lower levels of noble society by serving as a tutor to the house of Argyll. Headhunted by the king, he became tutor to prince Henry and prince Charles in succession. Stirling's Nova Scotia scheme reveals the extent of his British vision even if it was coupled with one of his typical money-making scams. Scottish National Portrait Gallery.

**Plate 43** John Napier of Merchiston's (1550–1617) studied pose, the scattered books, the globe and the contemplative gaze into the distance are intended to convey his intellectual nature. Unfortunately, the perspective of the chair is all wrong, being beyond the skills of the anonymous and presumably native artist. Scottish National Portrait Gallery.

**Plate 44** Napier's Bones: this ivory set was cut c.1650, but the rods were devised by John Napier of Merchiston some thirty-five years earlier in order to convert multiplication and division calculations into simple addition and subtraction. © Copyright of The Trustees of the National Museums of Scotland 2000.

**Plate 45** James Stewart, first earl of Moray (c.1531–70), illegitimate son of James V and regent of Scotland from 1567 until his assassination three years later. After his death, this self-assured and well-educated nobleman came to represent for Protestants the archetypical godly magistrate. Painted as one of a pair with that of his wife by Hans Eworth, probably to commemorate their marriage on 8 February 1562. In a private collection.

**Plate 46** Ecclesiastical patronage by the nobility after 1560 was modest and largely self-aggrandising. Burial aisles like the Douglas's at St Bride's church were increasingly common. The clock tower is the oldest in Scotland. Crown copyright: reproduced by permission of Historic Scotland.

**Plate 47** George Gordon, first marquis of Huntly (1562–1636), and his French wife, Henrietta Stewart, were the most powerful Roman Catholic patrons in Scotland. Although married in a Protestant ceremony in 1588, their deep religious convictions were sustained in spite of Huntly's repeated political defeats and, in later life, the prolonged harassment he endured from the Protestant clergy. Sketched after an unknown artist. Scottish National Portrait Gallery.

**Plate 48** Something of the inner demons that drove Robert Ker, second earl of Lothian (d.1624), to suicide within two years of this painting being completed is captured here. The family's long association with the occult was rumoured to be what drove him to cut his own throat, but crushing debts are the more likely cause of Lothian's despair. By an unknown artist in the style of George Jamesone. In a private Scottish collection.

**Plate 49** Detail from the first marquis of Huntly's remarkable funeral procession in 1636. 

**Plate 50** The Skelmorlie aisle, Largs, constructed between 1621 and 1636 by the otherwise unknown sir Robert Montgomery of Skelmorlie as a memorial to his wife, Margaret Douglas, who died in 1624, and himself. The financial investment in this splendid monument must have been enormous for this modestly wealthy baron. Crown copyright: reproduced by permission of Historic Scotland.

CHAPTER 8

# Education

A not uncommon portrait of the sixteenth-century nobleman is as a poorly educated individual, addicted to hunting and warfare, and barely able to control his impulses; no doubt many nobles did fit this description. Yet it is also a construct of humanist propaganda, and of historians who usually have more in common with these bookish critics than with the nobles who were the subject of such disapproval. Like academics today, the educationalists and intellectuals of the early modern era were in the business of convincing the world that they were necessary, that they were the gatekeepers of knowledge and understanding. This is not to say that they were altogether wrong. Nevertheless, this point needs to be made at the outset of a discussion about noble education because nobles themselves had different agendas from those whose world was the narrow precincts of the university. Noble children needed to be taught to serve the long-term interests of the lineage. They had to learn how to ride horses, use weapons, administer their estate, exercise command and win the favour of the king. Many of the skills they needed for life were learned outside the classroom, with kinsmen in the household, observing their fathers in the baronial court, with friends at the hunt, amidst the glittering figures of the royal court, beside companions in the heat of battle. The success of humanist educationalists was in persuading nobles that in addition to all of the skills acquired in such traditional environments, new ones should be added to strengthen their usefulness in a life of public involvement and service. The choice, therefore, was not between horses and swords on the one hand, and Latin and history on the other; nobles had to be comfortable in both these worlds. The extent to which nobles responded to the challenge to retool for a new age would determine to a large extent the cultural values and achievements of Scotland as a whole, but also their own ability to retain a dominant position in those spheres of public activity where other ranks of men might take their place.

## Early Years: the Household and the School

For all nobles, education began and often continued in the family home, the training of women rarely ever stepping outside that environment. Unfortunately, it is difficult to uncover much about the educational experience young children received before attending school, and there is little distinctively Scottish literature of advice on the topic. What is important to realise is that household and family were not poor substitutes for schooling. Among a nobility who believed that birth and breeding were essential, the role of the household and family in socialising noble children for their place in society was crucial. Here was where they began their noble 'apprenticeship', an experience in *nourriture* that introduced the noble child to its responsibilities and privileges. Education, therefore, was not only formal schooling, but also an experience that ideally encouraged those noble merits of selflessness essential in the service of the king and in the interests of the lineage.[1]

The Aristotelian idea that children were imperfect, having to be trained to behave like adults, continued to dominate the thinking of early modern educationalists who possibly held stricter attitudes to education than their medieval predecessors. Children were not innocent: 'the minde is naturally impure even from childhood it doth nothing but imagine wickednesse,' wrote John Abernethy, bishop of Aberdeen. Because of this naturally fallen state, children required to be disciplined: 'Folly is bound in the heart of a child, but the rod of teaching will drive it away from him. Teach a child in the trade of his way, and when he is old, he will not depart from it.'[2] It is likely that, as in England, France and Spain, there was an emphasis on the kind of humanist training that inculcated piety, obedience, respect, self-discipline and manners. Character-building and the cultivation of the mind started as early as possible, so that virtue, especially important in noble families, might be planted successfully, thwarting a child's natural waywardness. The emphasis was on preparing him to serve the interests of the lineage, training him for adulthood when he too would exercise authority. Children learned by stages when to be familiar and when to be formal, and by degree to make the transition from their own 'natural' behaviour to the 'culture' of adult society. They were conditioned to respect authority and hierarchy, initiated in the intricate rules that governed the serving and eating of food, they acquired the etiquette so essential to social interaction in noble society, were instructed in the catechism, and played games central to socialisation.[3]

The responsibility for these early years was likely to be shared by fathers and mothers, as well as private tutors who were given the difficult task of educating and disciplining children and young men who were their social superiors. The most infamous example of this was George Buchanan's instruction of the young James VI. A growing band of graduate teachers, therefore, looked to nobles for employment, a point worth remembering when faced with criticism of the nobility by a profession that had a self-interested need to persuade powerful patrons of the worth of education. That patronage might be exercised in parish schools where the likes of Mr Thomas Buchanan was employed by the first earl of Mar 'for teiching of the scoles'. Or it might be exercised in the private instruction of young nobles, which was the expertise claimed by Mr Patrick Inglis, minister at Kirkwall, who in November 1631 wrote to the dowager lady Freuchie suggesting that her grandson be 'trained up at scholles, and I sall be his pedagog, and salbe as cairfull of him as ever I was of his father'.[4] Catholic families often saw a tutor as an effective means of sustaining their faith within the household, a practice the church sought to eradicate. In 1593, the sixth lord Seton's children were instructed by Steine Ballantyne, a Catholic who had been forbidden to teach in any school and was later excommunicated.[5]

In France, the system of the higher nobility taking pages into their households and becoming responsible for their education survived throughout the seventeenth century. This practice was less common in Lowland Scotland, although instances of something akin to it can be uncovered. The eldest son of the sixth earl of Eglinton was packed off to the household of his Seton kinsmen before he was aged five, and his parents received occasional reports on his progress.[6] In the Highlands, these arrangements were formally entered into through fostering. Young boys were fostered out to kinsmen who were bound by written contracts, making the education of the child the responsibility of the foster parents, a tradition maintained by the Campbell house of Glenorchy well into the seventeenth century.[7] One special household that provided a suitable learning environment for the children of the higher nobility was the royal court. As a child, James VI was educated at Stirling by George Buchanan and Peter Young along with a few boyhood companions like the second earl of Mar and Walter Stewart, commendator of Blantyre. However, following the intimation of the king's majority in 1578 and the creation of an expanded household, Esmé Stewart introduced a bedchamber with offices for young men and boys, chiefly drawn from the higher ranks of the nobility. After 1603, Scottish nobles continued to be employed as bedchamber and privy chamber servants, and as pages in the households of the king, queen and princes where they received a suitable training. In addition, minors were often placed in the care of royal officials like chancellors Thirlestane or Dunfermline, who ensured they were adequately educated for future royal service.[8]

Compared to parts of the south of England, Scottish school provision might have appeared meagre. However, in the 1590s Northumberland had no grammar school, while by 1600 neighbouring Lothian in Scotland had nineteen schools with more being planted every year.[9] Even before the Reformation, school provision in Scotland was high, even if much of it was elementary and coverage throughout the country was uneven. After 1560, the church did remarkably well in providing an educational framework in which the larger towns and more heavily populated Lowland regions like Fife were well provided with schools.[10] However, it was the nobility who held the key to unlocking the financial resources needed to improve schooling, and their greed was the single greatest obstacle to the realisation of the vision of the *First Book of Discipline* to provide at least one school in every parish. On the other hand, household chaplains always had fulfilled some local educational function, and many nobles took seriously their responsibility as leaders of a civil society to raise standards within the community by, for example, acting as patrons of rural 'adventure' schools.[11] One of the consequences of the secularisation of ecclesiastical lands was that in many parishes it was the local noble who paid the schoolteacher's salary. In the constabulary of Haddington it was the eighth lord Yester who paid for 'the educatioun of the youthe at the schooles ... and their godlie exerceis'.[12] That the nobility recognised the public dimension of improving education is evident from the sustained legislative programme of parliament and the interest of the privy council. Education acts were passed by parliament in 1567 and 1579, during a period of royal minority, and the regent Morton's privy council appointed a commission of academics and schoolmasters in 1575 to report on the standardisation of grammar teaching within the kingdom. Further important legislation was passed in 1616 and in 1633, when there was a major commission on parish education.[13] Some nobles took a particular interest in educational issues, the first earl of Dunfermline being a helpful and involved patron of Alexander Hume, rector of Edinburgh High school and author of the 1612 *New Grammar*. Another grammarian and master at Dundee grammar school, Andrew Duncan, dedicated his *First Part of Latin Grammar* (1595) to the young fifth earl of Cassillis who he probably had taught at the university of St Andrews when Duncan was a regent at St Leonard's college, while his *Rudiments of Piety*, an educational aid in religious instruction, was dedicated to the fifth earl of Rothes.[14]

Of course, local schooling did not start from nothing in 1560. Before the Reformation, the fifth lord Lovat was sent to the nearby Cistercian abbey of Beauly in Inverness-shire where the monks 'taught him his catechism, as well as his constructions and grammar'. Twenty years later, in the late 1570s, his son was also sent to Beauly, now in his own family's possession, where some of the old monks continued to live, although the boy's education was in the hands of Mr John Noble, a Protestant tutor from Inverness. The fact that the house of Lovat had a good school on its doorstep was important, and even remote localities might be well served by schools. The twelfth earl of Sutherland's elementary education was at the local Dornoch school under Mr William Pape. Thirty-five years later, in 1616, a heated family debate over the education of the seven-year-old thirteenth earl was resolved by sending him to the local school since 'any learning he mey be capabill off yit, he mey gett the samen in Suthirland'. As this case suggests, the nature and location of a lord's schooling was of interest to more than his immediate family. In 1595, the Maxwell kindred held a conference to discuss the education of the young ninth lord Maxwell and his brothers, recommending to the boys' tutor, lord Hamilton, that the 'youngest twa sones be putt to the schooles in Glasgow quhair it is thocht your lordships kynnisfolks may be freinds to thame'.[15] This confidence among the nobility in local schools was typical, and there was no social pressure to separate young nobles from their inferiors. The most striking difference between the schooling of English and Scottish nobles was the unavailability to the latter of increasingly exclusive schools; in Scotland there was nothing comparable to Westminster or Eton, or the new boarding schools in France or Spain, often run by Jesuits. On the other hand, some schools, especially in the larger royal burghs, were of a higher standard than others. One such was Prestonpans grammar school outside Edinburgh, to which the young sir Patrick Vans of Barnbarroch was sent from Galloway, a region not well provided with schools, Dumfries being the only pre-Reformed school. That decision paid off, for Barnbarroch progressed to the university of Paris where he completed his MA, returning to Scotland to take up a place as a senator of the college of justice.[16]

It was in the Highlands that school provision was most problematic, but even before the 1609 legislation Highland nobles were keen to assimilate themselves to the Lowlands, many chiefs sending their sons to schools there. Others brought civility to their own localities. Sir Duncan Campbell of Glenorchy recognised the damage done to his community by the absence of 'ane qualifeit man to instructe the youth thairof that thay may heireftir be proffitabule instrumentis in the said countrie'. In 1593, therefore, Glenorchy agreed to pay 100 merks per annum to a Mr William Bowie, who had acted as tutor to his eldest son, to build him a house and to provide a croft for pasturing his cattle, in return for teaching his younger children 'in the feir of God and studie of gude lettris'. Furthermore, this Highland baron was concerned that his children 'may be the bettir instructit be the frequent resorting and repairing of utheris countrie bairnis to the sosietie and companie of his saidis bairnis that ane number being togidder may the better prosper in lettris'.[17] Nevertheless, in spite of such individual efforts, the 1609 statutes of Iona highlighted the 'ignorance and incivilitie' of the Western Isles, optimistically requiring landlords to send their children, male and female, to Lowland schools where they would be instructed 'in the knowlege of God and good letters' and 'that thay may be found able sufficientlie to speik, reid, and wryte Inglische'. Gordonstoun too was keen to establish schools throughout the Sutherland region, with a principal school at Dornoch to encourage the speaking of English. He saw advantages to such a policy for the earl of Sutherland, hoping to persuade other local nobles 'to bestowe lairglie upon ther children to make them schollers, for so shall they be fittest for your service'. Here was the same argument that humanist thinkers had applied to nobles as prospective servants of the prince being extended to those who served the nobility. In arguing that Sutherland ought 'to civilize your countrey and the inhabitants therof', Gordonstoun was, like educationalists elsewhere, lobbying for a cultural change that would bring outlying regions into line with civil society anywhere in Europe, 'which you shall observe abrod in your travells among other nations'.[18]

For wealthy nobles, even schooling their sons some distance from home was not expensive. In 1620, Prestonpans was charging the sixth earl of Eglinton 900 merks a year for his son's full board 'and those that sittes at the fuit of the tabill faires als weall as those at the heide'. This was a small sum for an earl, although it was a significant amount for most barons to pay. On the other hand, in 1636 the ten-year-old second earl of Buccleuch was sent to school in St Andrews where he established his own household. During the period of a little over two years for which his account book survives, Buccleuch received £6538 from his chamberlain, almost as much per annum as the entire income of the university of Glasgow. In the first eighteen months alone he bought £1041 worth of clothes, while paying out the relatively small sum of £236 in fees to his schoolmasters and £34 for paper and books that included Wedderburn's *Grammar*, Buchanan's *Psalms*, Ovid's *Works* and other Latin texts. Schooling might even be seen as a form of conspicuous consumption, and young nobles strained against the egalitarian culture of the school environment. Sir Colin Campbell of Glenorchy received a request in the autumn of 1632 for money from his nephew, Alexander, who was at the grammar school in Dundee. The boy wanted Glenorchy to pay his teacher more money because he was embarrassed to discover that the children of meaner families were paying higher fees. A year later, he asked for £20 since such a sum would make him king in a school where none of the other children was the son of a gentleman. However, Alexander suggested that his brother, Duncan, was wasting his own time and the family's money by remaining at school, it being 'bot daffery to had him any longer seing he does not good at it'.[19]

It is difficult to measure the effectiveness of this elementary education, although seventeenth-century Lowland schooling was among the best in Europe, producing relatively high levels of literacy. The curriculum varied greatly from place to place, but for nobles and brighter pupils the aim was to provide a solid grounding in Latin grammar, as Buccleuch's school books suggest, leading on to literary and rhetorical studies, highly important in a still largely oral culture designed to produce men able to make elegant public speeches and to write sharp, incisive papers. Some knowledge of history and mathematics was also essential.[20] Literacy among the nobility was near-universal by c.1600, and while the spread of italic handwriting was irregular and slow, the extent to which it had become the favoured and approved manner of writing among educated gentlemen was little different from England. In an early seventeenth-century commonplace notebook belonging to the young Patrick Hume, eldest son of the laird of Polwarth, italic handwriting exercises largely consisted in copying out the sayings of Greek philosophers, a typical form of humanist learning by which students recorded what they imagined might be useful in their own compositions. The family of sir

Walter Dundas of that Ilk in the 1600s took great pride in their educational attainments. His eldest sons, George who was at St Leonard's college in St Andrews, and William who was at Dunfermline grammar school, both wrote to their father and to one another in Latin about their progress.[21]

Much less is known about the daughters of nobles in a period when the debate about women's education was growing more intense, although there remained a deep suspicion of intellectual women and the principal purpose of any education remained a preparation for marriage. There is little evidence of the Scots engaging in that debate, although there were many educated and cultured women, queen Mary being the most high-profile example. How they acquired this learning is even more illusive. In the spring of 1604, the old fifth earl of Morton received an affectionate letter from one of his granddaughters in which she hoped to impress him with 'my advancing in wreating'. In 1607, the second duke of Lennox recorded that his daughter, who was no older than eight years of age, was 'now come to that aig that scho is capable of instructioun and learning', and that 'cair aucht to be had of hir educatioun and upbringing in that estate and rank quhilk beseamith hir birth.' Perhaps this might be expected of the daughter of a great courtier, but in 1632 a lesser provincial noble like George Gordon of Gight was employing a French governess who had charge of his daughter, bringing her up in 'all verteous exerciseis beseameing a young gentlewoman of hir birthe'.[22] Those exercises are likely to have included music, foreign languages, reading and writing, along with less cerebral skills.

## University

For many sixteenth-century nobles, school was their last experience of formal education. Just how many progressed to university is unknown but it is likely to have been a minority, at least among the lower nobility. This was not unusual in Europe, and only some 5 to 10 per cent of the Spanish nobility had sons enrolled in university, most formal education being undertaken by tutors in the home on account of a deep prejudice against institutionalised learning. A not untypical education was that experienced by Patrick Maule of Panmure in the 1550s, who was sent as a boy to be schooled in Dundee and then Arbroath before being married at fourteen and brought to live in his father's house.[23] Such a truncated period of learning became less common as the sixteenth century wore on, and more fourteen-year-old youths did make their way to universities. Estimating how many nobles attended university is notoriously difficult but the trend was certainly upwards, as was the case in neighbouring England.[24]

Fuelling this shift in attitudes was a desire to acquire knowledge and skills useful to a nobleman throughout his life in government, court and society. Scottish universities never became solely training institutions for government officials, like the Spanish *letrados*, but there is little question that nobles who aimed at state service were advantaged by having some university education. Among the middle-rank Scottish administrators of the later sixteenth century, some 60 per cent (thirty-two individuals) attained the degree of Master of Arts. Nor was it only the lesser barons or the younger sons of peers who attained these levels of education, although eldest sons were more likely to move around different universities without completing their degrees.[25]

The prevalence of St Andrews in the education of nobles was clear. Only Scotland's oldest university drew students from a national pool, while the other universities performed a more regional role, not unlike Oxford and Cambridge colleges. Both the more conservative King's college at Aberdeen (Catholic until 1569) and the Protestant foundation of Marischal college attracted its students largely from the north-east among families like the Frasers or the Gordons. The south-western nobility tended to choose the university of Glasgow. The sons of the fifth earl of Eglinton were sent there where they were taught by Robert Baillie, who was later persuaded to take charge of the family's kirk at Kilwinning.[26] By the early seventeenth century, there was widespread acceptance of the idea that some formal education at university should follow school. The ten-year-old second earl of Buccleuch and his younger brother, David, arrived in St Andrews in 1636, where they were placed in the care of Mr Robert Lermonth, an advocate. They were enrolled in the town school, a tutor was engaged and in 1640, having been prepared by four years of good schooling, they made the transition to university, matriculating at St Leonard's college. The first lord Balcarres sent his eldest son, Alexander, to school at Haddington, where he was taught by Mr David Forret, who reported of the boy that 'in half a day he can do all that either the master or I desires him to do in a whole day.' Later, at the university of St Andrews, this precocious boy's 'delight in learning' impressed all his teachers.[27] This was the model young noble, seriously studying both in school and in university. Of course, intellectual differences within families were recognised. Mr James Lawson recommended to the mother of David Lindsay of Edzell that she bring him home from Cambridge but that his younger brother, John, 'is abill to cum to gryt onderstandynge of letteris'. John Lindsay became a brilliant lawyer and judge, spoke French, Italian and Spanish, composed epigrams and wrote a number of works, collected books and manuscripts; his skill in understanding minerals and metals was widely acknowleged, and he took a keen interest in gardening and architecture. Here was a nobleman who would later grace the office of chancellor of the university of St Andrews.[28]

While Scotland was at the outer rim of Europe, its universities were attuned to what was going on in Italy and France as well as Germany. Particularly from the mid-1570s, when Andrew Melville began his Ramist reforms at Glasgow, until the reaction of the mid-seventeenth century, the university scene in Scotland was vibrant, dynamic and, like Scottish education generally, relatively egalitarian.[29] What did these young men learn at university? While the academic programme retained underlying Aristotelian assumptions, Melville's reforms introduced a broader curriculum, exposing students to a greater range of Greek texts, principally at the expense of metaphysics. Subjects taught included Latin, Greek, rhetoric, logic, theology, arithmetic, Hebrew, science, law and geography. However, much of this was watered down to an elementary level for what were often young, undeveloped minds, and nobles were more interested in acquiring a broad range of knowledge than in mastering a subject.[30]

Following the Reformed church's disappointment at not retaining control of those ecclesiastical revenues that would have allowed it to go on acting as the principal patron of the universities, it was hoped the nobility would fulfill that function. Andrew Melville demanded they redeploy some of the rents they drew from former ecclesiastical lands to establish bursaries, so that 'everie nobleman might have a seminarie of the youth of their owne freinds and servants, within few yeeres, weill instructed in good letters', providing service to themselves and the community.[31] John Wemyss, minister of Lathocker, dedicated his *The Christian Synagogue* (1633) to the first earl of Melrose, a man who fulfilled his ideal of the noble patron:

> If learning bee not sheltered by those who are in eminent places, and if they cast not their shadow over it, it will soone perish, but where they favour it, then it prospers ... where great men are averse to learning, the spirits which otherwise would blossome, will wither, and decay; but where it is upholden by men of higher place, it is like a fountaine of living water.[32]

Few nobles lived up to this ideal. Yet this does not mean they were uninterested, and many nobles involved in government showed a keen awareness of university issues, even if their motives were political. The regent Moray oversaw a thorough purge of King's college in 1569, while Morton carried out a visitation of St Andrews in 1574 which had some influence on the shape of the new foundation four years later. When in 1607 the government decided on a visitation of the university of St Andrews, an eleven-man commission was appointed, more than half of whom were noble graduates.[33] Possibly no noble was as interested in universities as William Keith, fifth earl Marischal, who sat on a number of commissions to reform King's college in the 1580s before founding Marischal college in 1593. At his funeral thirty years later, the oration followed the Italian humanist style of praising his education. The earl was contrasted with those many nobles who neglected the arts, being flatteringly described by one of the college professors as 'the patron and parent of our family and School, the pillar and Maecenas of learning, the famous safeguard of the muses and joint Defender of the Church and common wealth'.[34] No other noble was as generous as Marischal, although the earls of Cassillis were patrons of St Salvator's college at St Andrews; David Carnegy of Colluthie, a member of the Octavian government, endowed a bursary at St Leonard's college in 1592; sir John Scott of Scotstarvit donated a significant quantity of books in 1620 to St Leonard's college, where he endowed a professorship in humanity and Latin; and in 1632 the fourth lord Elphinstone gave the small sum of 100 merks towards the construction and furnishing of a library at the university of Glasgow.[35]

## The Continental Tour

The Scottish universities were able to provide a good grounding in the arts, and for most young nobles who desired a humane education this was satisfactory. For those who wished to pursue academic subjects more thoroughly or who wished to polish off other skills, it was necessary to go elsewhere. Fortunately, within Scotland there was not the prejudice against foreign education and travel that existed in England, where from the early 1570s there was growing suspicion of those who travelled, giving rise to popular images of Machiavellian atheists, Italianate fops and corrupt Catholics. In Denmark too, Christian IV unsuccessfully tried to prevent his nobility from heading off to the new German military academies by founding his own Academy of Chivalry in 1623.[36] By contrast, in 1560 Adam Bothwell, bishop of Orkney, suggested to his brother-in-law, Archibald Napier of Merchiston, that he send his son (the mathematician) to France or Flanders, 'for he can leyr na guid at hame, nor get proffeit in this maist perullous worlde'.[37]

Evidence for nobles travelling abroad to complete their studies is plentiful. The sons of the first earl of Gowrie, a man of sophisticated cultural tastes, were first taught at home by Mr William Rind and then by Mr Robert Rollock, the principal of the university of Edinburgh, before going to France and then Italy, the third earl being elected rector at the university of Padua. He returned to Scotland in 1600 via Geneva, after a seven-year absence and with the reputation of being 'ane gritt schollar'. This was by no means unusual. Following his studies at St Andrews and Edinburgh, Gordonstoun left for France in 1603, where he studied civil law and participated in 'all exercises fitt for a gentleman of his birth and qualitie', he being the son of an earl. The third earl of Winton's children were all carefully educated and a younger son, Alexander Seton, was a precocious Latinist who at twelve years of age impressed Charles I on his 1633 visit to Scotland. Three years later, Alexander was sent to France, where he enrolled with the Jesuits at La Flèshe, studying philosophy and publicly defending his thesis in 1638. Thereafter he travelled to Italy for a year, then Spain, back to France and finally to England, where he arrived in 1640, his education complete and ready to serve his king.[38]

For a number of nobles, foreign travel was a consequence of political exile, particularly in the later sixteenth century.[39] However, the purpose of foreign travel was overwhelmingly educational and travel documents usually made clear the intention 'to learn the languages and fashions abroad', to appreciate 'such virteus, comelie and worthie exercyses as becomeath one of his rank and qualitie' or to travel 'in such places of Chrystendome as he shall thinke moste fitte for his instruction in literature, languages, and customes of divers nations'. As this evidence indicates, any nobleman seeking to leave the country had to acquire a royal licence, specifying where he was going, when he was leaving and how long he would be away. The duration of these licences was usually around five to seven years, and the only condition likely to be imposed was that during his absence a nobleman must not act in a manner prejudicial to the king, the state or religion.[40] It was also necessary to acquire licences from those countries through which one was passing, as in the licence granted in March 1596 by Elizabeth I to the seventh earl of Argyll, and even after 1603 Scots nobles travelling to England required documentation.[41]

When praising the fifth earl Marischal's French education at his funeral in 1623, William Ogston, professor of moral philosophy at Marischal college, stated unequivocally that 'of all countreyes in the World [France] is the Only seal of human knowledge and Courtesie itself', giving a man 'more moderation of mind' than was to be found in northern countries like Scotland.[42] Scots favoured France above all other destinations. Both the third earl of Arran and his younger brother, lord Hamilton, commendator of Arbroath, were in France in the 1550s, being tutored in Paris by Patrick Buchanan, brother of George Buchanan. Three of the keenest minds in James VI's government, the first earls of Dunfermline and Haddington and the first lord Balmerino completed their education in France, following a long-established pattern. All of these men were believed to be *politique* Catholics thoughout their careers but Scottish Protestants also went to France. William Drummond of Hawthornden was educated at Edinburgh High school before taking his MA at the university of Edinburgh in 1605 and going on to study civil law at Bourges for a further three years.[43] Sir Anthony Weldon, that seventeenth-century Scotophobe, was perplexed by the high educational standards of the Scottish nobility he encountered, suggesting that:

> as soon as they fall from the breast of the beast their mother, their careful father posts them away for france, which as they pass, the sea sucks from them that which they have sucked from their rude dams; there they gather new flesh, new blood, new manners; and there they learn to put on their cloaths, and then return into their country to wear them out: there they learn to stand, speak, discourse and congee, to court women, and to compliment with men; then they cume to Englande to gette thair cloathes, and they returne in thair awin countrey to warre them.

Of course this was nonsense, but Weldon was right to be impressed by the persistence of links between France and Scotland. Lowlanders made similar observations about the uncouthness of Highlanders, as when archbishop Spottiswoode recorded that Lachlan Maclean of Duart had been educated on the continent where 'he had learned civility and good manners'.[44]

The attractions of France did not wane in the aftermath of either the Reformation or the regal union. New and expensive academies sprang up first in Paris and then elsewhere, attracting an international clientele including many Scottish nobles. What these institutions offered was an opportunity for young men to polish off their knowledge of ancient Roman civilisation, to learn about the art of war and to acquire those courtly skills and graces that moulded gesture, posture and movement into a distinctively noble style without ever suggesting artifice. Chiefly, instruction was in advanced riding techniques, the *manège*, dancing, fencing and military mathematics, and the Parisian academies also offered an entry to court society.[45] Between 1617 and 1620 the second earl of Mar's younger sons were sent to the continent, spending part of the time under instruction at the Calvinist academy at Saumur, where they studied law and from where their tutor reported favourably on their dancing, fencing and music.[46] The point here was not to allow Mar's sons to acquire university degrees, but to enable them to be ready for entrance into court life or military, diplomatic or administrative service. Herein lay the appeal to kings of young men like James Livingston of Kinnaird who, following a spell at Merton college, Oxford, was sent in 1638 by Charles I to 'be bred in France' as preparation for his recruitment to the bedchamber. Yet it would be inaccurate to give the impression that without a French finish to their education, Scottish nobles were uncultured. When in February 1627 lord Dalkeith's tutor wrote home to the sixth earl of Morton, reporting on how his pupil was performing at the academy in Paris, he was proud to assure the earl that the young man had arrived with as much skill in riding and fencing as many youths who had already spent eighteen months in that establishment.[47]

Nor was France the only port of call. John Ruthven, third earl of Gowrie, attended the university of Padua in the mid-1590s, stopping off at Geneva on the way home to visit Theodore Beza, who was thoroughly impressed by the young earl's earnest religious commitment.[48] The country to which Scotland was moving closest on the continent in the early seventeenth century, particularly in the area of religion and trade, was the United Provinces, described in the mid-1620s by one young Scotsman as 'the fittest academie of youth at this tyme'. However, nobles found republican Holland less attractive than did Scottish clerics.[49] Nor was there much interest in English universities, in spite of efforts by Elizabethan officials to attract Scottish nobles to England, where 'their good affections might be better trained and devoted to our sovereign and realm.' Those few nobles who did end up at Oxford or Cambridge did so either by accident or for little more than a short visit. David Lindsay of Edzell and his younger brother, John, only passed time at Cambridge in 1572 when the massacre of St Bartholomew forced them to flee from France. Their tutor wrote home that 'Letteris ma be lernit heir in Cambrage neir als weill as in Pariss,' but after four months they wanted to return to Scotland, being short of money and having seen 'the faschionis of the cuntrie'. There was a little more contact with English learning after 1603; for example, the anglicised fourth duke of Lennox was briefly sent to the university of Cambridge to fit him for royal service. In 1621, the London-based courtier, sir Robert Ker of Ancram, sent his eldest son, William, to Cambridge, but he wanted to leave and was soon on his way to Paris and other more attractive continental educational centres. The sixth earl of Morton made inquiries at a number of Cambridge colleges in 1626, settling on King's college as it had been the most accommodating because 'noble menis sones had bein their befor.'[50]

Such was the popularity of travel that in 1598 so many of the higher nobility were either out of the country or were planning to leave that concern was expressed about the potential for political instability without their local leadership. Scottish nobles were cosmopolitan Europeans, setting off for the continent to be educated, to soldier or simply to wander, and there was a constant coming and going with young nobles often meeting up on the road. Michael Balfour, first lord Burleigh, engaged in the fashionable trend of collecting the autographs of the people he met on his travels, from royalty and statesmen to Scots he happened to encounter. James Stewart, commendator of Doune, kept a French journal of his journey to Paris in 1560, probably as a language exercise but also suggesting that this experience was one of self-discovery. Similarly, William Ker, later third earl of Lothian, 'had seene the most renowned places of Europe'. In 1624–5, he went to Paris, then journeyed through France, Italy and Switzerland, keeping a journal of his travels in which he enthusiastically described the tourist sights of Florence, Rome and Venice. These generations of nobles were likely to have seen the best that Renaissance Italy and France had to offer, a broadening of the mind that no amount of book learning was likely to equal. Sir Walter Scott of Buccleuch was in France in 1584, he returned in 1593 from another journey to Italy, Flanders and England, he was again absent from Scotland in 1599–1600 when he was in Paris, and he soldiered in Flanders between 1604 and 1609. For those like Buccleuch, the desire to be on the move was never satisfied, and diplomatic service and mercenary work provided ways of prolonging a curiosity sparked into life as youths. Few nobles, however, wandered as far afield as colonel John Forbes, brother of the tenth lord Forbes, who in 1635 carried a letter to the shah of Persia from Charles I. Of course, too much travel was not encouraged, and king James was critical of the eighth lord Sanquhar, a man who was rarely at home on his estates, being 'much given to idle voyages and gadding abroade'.[51]

This experience of travel among European higher nobilities shaped a sense of being a community with continent-wide values. It encouraged young men to separate themselves from their families and homes for what was an extension of their education, and it provided a means of expressing their freedom, creating their own identities. Travel sharpened up modern languages, refined courtly accomplishments like dancing and music, permitted the study of military techniques and fortifications, and encouraged an acquisition of a better understanding of European culture and history.[52] When the eighth earl of Angus was in England as an exile in the early 1580s, he was embarrassed by his own parochial upbringing, using the time to catch up on the academic studies he had neglected at university but also in 'learning to ride great horses, and handling of his armes and weapons, together with using such courtly and manlie exercises as became his age and place'.[53] The youthful sixth earl of Huntly resided in France for some years in the late 1570s and early 1580s, 'the better to inable himselff for the service of his prince and countrey'. His kinsman, Gordonstoun, also travelled widely in his youth, arguing that 'Ther can be no accomplished gentleman without traveling abrod in other kingdomes.' He saw this exposure to European civilisation as an essential experience in ensuring that nobles might 'be bred in all exercises fit for a gentleman'. Not only did he make sure that members of his own family travelled, but as tutor of the fourth duke of Lennox he sent the latter on an extended tour of France, Italy and Spain in preparation for his life as a courtier.[54] The end product of such experiences was a sophisticated, urbane young man, like the much-travelled third earl of Gowrie, who in 1600 was described on his arrival in London as 'one of the best accomplished for his age of that nation, both for learning, travel and good qualities'.[55]

Education and travel were expensive; hence the predominance of higher nobles in the above examples. However, a university education within Scotland was within the reach of most nobles. David Lindsay of Edzell and his younger brothers were boarded at New college, St Andrews, in 1569 at a cost of £96 per annum, while at King's college the annual tuition fee for a peer was £6, for a baron £4 and for others £2. The young fifth earl of Montrose spent £1150 in the period April 1628 to March 1629 during his time as a student at the university of St Andrews. But even noble families had to keep their eye on wasteful students. Archibald Campbell, lord Lorne, complained in July 1627 that he was content to finance his younger half-brother's education in such a manner that 'he sould nather want for his honour nor for his contentment ... bot not for his prodigalitie'. The eleventh earl of Crawford was notoriously mean in providing for his eldest son, making the youth's time at St Andrews both miserable and embarrassing.[56]

For those who went further afield the problems were greater. The cost of living in different parts of Europe varied enormously, it was too risky to carry large sums of cash, and the entire expedition had to be planned with credit facilities arranged well in advance. Sir William Sharp of Houston's son wrote from France complaining of the 'hudge expenses' and making the timeless observation that 'in this countrie the nam of a stranger is able to mak him pay ten schillingis quhair a Frenchman wald have payed bot one.' Letters home were often full of explanations as to why fathers should send more cash. In 1633 three of the sons of the sixth earl of Eglinton were in Paris, where they ran short of money. Alexander, one of the younger boys, wrote a letter in which he buttered up his father with the news that their fencing, dancing and mathematics were all making good progress, but that expensive riding lessons could not be afforded without Eglinton's permission and the guarantee of more money.[57]

Many of those who arrived on the continent found that their money did not last long and resorted to borrowing, usually from Scottish merchants who in the 1630s were charging 10 per cent interest. On his return from the continent in 1599, the sixth lord Hume turned up in London accompanied by only two gentlemen, his party was riding hackneys, he had little in the way of clothes to cut much of a dash at the English court, and he resorted to asking sir Robert Cecil for a loan.[58] But it was not only the financing of the expedition that was costly. The second marquis of Hamilton wrote to his nephew, the sixth earl of Cassillis, in Italy in 1621 (copies were sent to a number of different places in the hope of reaching him), telling him to return home immediately to attend to affairs which were being damaged by his long absence.[59] In some instances, the cost proved too great. Huge debts in the early 1580s prevented lord Robert Stewart from sending his eldest son, Patrick, to France or Geneva to complete his education, even though he knew that such an experience was 'mekle best for his instructioun and upbringing in all kynd of civilitie, as also in learning the languages'. In 1590, the friends of the young eighth lord Sanquhar tried to persuade him 'to abide at home, and rather seek to get a good wife and repair the waste of his inheritance than travel in foreign countries at this season', advice he ignored.[60] Yet in spite of the cost, nobles enthusiastically set out on their adventures and their fathers continued to fund them. As the tutor of the young David Lindsay of Edzell and his brothers explained during their time in France in the early 1570s, there was in places like Paris 'ane goldin marchandreis of letteris quhilkis be na silver nor gold can be bocht'.[61]

Of course, there was an element of risk in allowing young men so much freedom, especially when many were away from home for years. The fifth lord Oliphant left Scotland in 1599 when he was sixteen and did not return until the spring of 1602.[62] This opportunity to refashion themselves did not always please parents. The countess of Haddington believed that the experience of being in France had spoilt one of her sons, altering his good nature and making it impossible to give him advice. It is more likely that he was no longer so willing to do as he was told by an overbearing mother.[63] There is also some indication that the early seventeenth century saw the Scots developing English fears about the moral corruption that lay waiting on the continent. When the second earl of Dunfermline wanted to go on the European tour c.1632, one of his curators advised against it, highlighting the youth's weak moral character and arguing that Dunfermline would use the freedom to 'practise any thing that doeth please him to the ruin of his poor weak body and hurt of his soull'. Nor were such fears always groundless. In 1631 one of the sixth earl of Morton's sons was studying in Paris, where he ended up in prison. His laziness and preference for the gaming table, at which he lost most of his allowance, earned a sharp reprimand from his father, following which his tutor was able to report that the lad was 'bissie at his fencing and dancing and learning to wreitt frenche'.[64] Much of Europe could be extremely dangerous for the traveller. In 1565, the tenth earl of Sutherland was taken prisoner by the English at Berwick while returning from the continent. In 1588, George Dundas of that Ilk urged his eldest son to come home from France, then in the grip of civil war, warning him to take care travelling through England, a country 'full of brigandis', an interesting comment on Scottish perceptions of that country. Tragically, both Laurence Oliphant, master of Oliphant, and Robert Douglas, eldest son of the laird of Lochleven, were killed by Dutch privateers in the spring of 1584. More mundanely, the fussy first marquis of Hamilton sent his eldest son off to France with the warning to be careful in 'provyding aganis the haetis'.[65]

Another objection to allowing young men so much freedom was the fear that these cultural tours would expose them to Catholicism. Hence in 1620 the second duke of Lennox's reservations about his nephew, lord Gordon, going abroad 'without some imployment whitche mycht tye him a lytill the straiter to howld the religione that he now professes'. Certainly Catholic nobles did seek to exploit the opportunities afforded by travel. The eleventh earl of Angus regularly crossed to the continent with only the barest attempt to conceal his determination to escape the attentions of the local clergy. In 1623, he set out on a two-year journey through England and France and on to Rome where he visited St Peter's, arousing the suspicions of the presbytery of Lanark which insisted on investigating the earl on his return home.[66] However, not everyone who went to the continent came back to Scotland an advocate of the counter-Reformation. James Hamilton, third earl of Arran, spent the years immediately before the Reformation in France, but on his arrival back in Scotland he identified himself with the radical wing of the Protestant party. The third earl of Gowrie's time in Italy, where Protestants faced persecution, hardened his contempt for the Catholic religion, and his experience of Rome left him convinced the city was 'that mother of all vyce, and hoorishe synagog of devils'.[67]

## Learning and the Refashioning of the Nobility

From the mid-fifteenth century, humanist academics and intellectuals increasingly succeeded in persuading nobilities to embrace the new learning of the universities and academies if they were to become refined gentlemen and to be of any use in governing states where martial skills alone were no longer adequate. The rapidly expanding university sector in Germany and Spain provided a stream of well-qualified graduates, often drawn from the ranks of the lesser nobility and able to fill royal offices. On the other hand, the absence of an adequately educated population on the European peripheries, in countries like Muscovy, Poland and Sweden, helped the nobilities of these states to maintain a high profile in government.[68] In England, critics like Roger Ascham attacked the unfitness of nobles for office on account of their lack of learning, while in Catalonia, Francesch de Gilabert's 1616 *The Discourse on the Source of Nobility* harangued his fellow nobles for their lack of learning. Similar sentiments were expressed by French writers, and in 1613 a French academic complained that the nobility 'despise letters and sciences'. Yet the early seventeenth century did see a significant shift in the attitudes of many French nobles, whose embracing of the educational programme of their critics allowed them to reinforce their superiority of a social order based on birth, while also equipping themselves to play a dynamic role in a mutating world.[69]

The attack made on the Scottish nobility by their humanist critics, therefore, was part of a Europe-wide onslaught to alter the education of governing élites. As early as the 1520s, John Mair offered a damaging critique of the nobility, seeking to impress on James V the need to ensure that these men acquired an education befitting the rulers of a civil society. The Reformation added further weight to the argument. John Knox and Andrew Melville each demanded a higher level of commitment to learning from the nobility. Melville declared in a paper prepared for the eighth earl of Angus, a man always over-impressed by intellectuals, that 'The Nobilitie and Gentlemen ar unlerned them selffs, and takes na delyt to haiff thair childring and friends brought upe in lettres, to the great reprotche and schame of the Countrey, and thair awin grait hurt and dishonour.' As in the rest of Europe, where Jesuits and Calvinists both advocated the necessity of educating the élite to equip them for government and to instruct them in religion, the church was becoming more didactic. In 1596, the general assembly drew attention to the allegedly scandalous level of learning among the nobility, accusing many civil magistrates of being unfit for their offices, 'ather in respect of the want of knowledge, or of conscience, or both'. As late as the 1620s, one of the professors of Marischal college thought the nobility contemptuous of education, suggesting that 'Idlenes and Sloath' were common among wealthy young men, 'who being descended of a more noble family, do not think it worth their while, on the account of the nobleness of their kindred, to be given to excellent studies'.[70]

But are these opinions anything more than the typically jaundiced views of poorly paid academics looking down their long intellectual noses at men who were richer and more powerful? One can also sense here the expression of a convention from Mair onwards that affected derision for noble dilettantes and backwoodsmen. Undoubtedly, some nobles were unprepared for the more technically demanding offices of government, particularly those judicial roles that required a professional competence in law. When in 1585 Angus returned from exile in England, his supporters urged him to demand the place of lord chancellor, but the earl refused on the grounds that his ignorance of the law disqualified him from exercising that office. One of the reasons that the third earl of Montrose was unsuccessful as chancellor was because he was 'altogether void of learning,' an exaggeration that nevertheless contains an element of truth. But, of course, the level of legal competence required by a chancellor was well beyond what most lawyers ever attained, far less unqualified nobles. Sir John Scott of Scotstarvit, director of chancery, scathingly dismissed the talents of the first earl of Roxburghe because the lord privy seal knew no Latin. Yet James VI himself commented that while this border reiver turned courtier was 'no scollar', nevertheless 'he's neer a kin to learning', an estimation that can be borne out by Roxburghe's interests that included patronage of the arts and his abilities as a poet.[71]

Undoubtedly there are examples in abundance of foolish young nobles and boorish older nobles who cared not a jot for books and learning. A youthful Simon Fraser, sixth lord Lovat, was sent to King's college, Aberdeen, where the principal, Mr William Rait, was employed to instruct him. Lovat was a poor pupil, however, joining with the company of 'loose and debauch young men', and ran away to Ireland. The eighth earl of Angus attended the university of St Andrews in the early 1570s until the age of fifteen, studying under John Douglas, rector of the university. Bored and uninterested by the experience, he wasted his time, being like most young nobles more attracted to 'exercises of the body [which] are esteemed more fit and proper for their place'. His biographer represented the earl's attitude as:

> Letters are thought onely necessary and usefull for mean men, who intend to live by them, and make profession of some Art or Science for their maintenance, but [are] no wayes either suitable or requisite in Noblemen, and such as are of any eminent rank or degree.

Indeed, Godscroft shared the view of most nobles that academic study produced mean-spirited pedants, handicapping their ability to be statesmen or warriors. Another young man who hated being force-fed a diet of classical learning was John Lindsay of Balinscho, who neglected his books and resented being sent on an educational tour of Europe. From Naples he wrote home that 'neither can I speak right Latin, nor make a theme, nor read Greek, and I cannot go to be a mockingstock to the rest.' He sought self-knowledge in other pursuits, becoming a mercenary in Swedish service and being killed in 1631 at the defence of New Brandenburg. Similarly, sir

George Douglas of Mordington's children grew up at the London court and his eldest son, George, was educated at the university of Oxford, acquiring fluency in Latin as well as knowledge of Greek. In spite of this aptitude for learning, he hankered after a military career and so 'thinking the schooles an over soft course of exercise, he left them and betook himselfe to armes, as more suitable both with his complexion and disposition'.[72] George Douglas's choice might well have been right for someone who wanted a military career since the best education available to the would-be soldier was to be found in the army.[73]

This tension between learning and martial qualities should not be exaggerated, and the scholar-knight was one of the great ideals of Renaissance humanism, one that acquired a considerable following within noble society in later sixteenth-century Britain. Besides, stories of young men rebelling against formal education can be uncovered in any century. What is significant is that fathers sent them to university in the first place. The fourth lord Herries turned up at the university of Glasgow in 1578 to reprimand his eldest son publicly for showing a disrespectful attitude towards his tutors. The young master of Herries was forced to make a humiliating apology, recognising his teachers' superiority to him in learning if in nothing else.[74] It is also worth pausing to remember that all the education in the world will not make a man good, virtuous or even merely civil. Francis Stewart, fifth earl of Bothwell, rebel, murderer and seducer of women, had all the advantages of a good education, spending his youth in Italy and France. He was described by the dean of Durham in 1593 as a man 'of wonderfull witt, and as wonderfull a volubilitie of tongue as habilitie and agilitie of bodie on horse and foote; competently learned in the Latine ... Frenche and Italian ... much delighted in poetrie'. He was, in short, the complete Renaissance man. Similarly archbishop Spottiswoode considered the eighth lord Maxwell, another rebel and border gangster who ended his days being slaughtered in a bloodfeud, 'a nobleman of great spirit, humane, courteous, and more learned than nobles commonly are'. The tutor of David Lindsay, twelfth earl of Crawford, reported from the university of St Andrews that his charge was 'above all his equals in learning', but Crawford grew into a bitter and violent man whose spendthrift ways and criminal activities ruined his house.[75]

By the later sixteenth century the level of education among the nobility was high, and the absorption of humanist thinking and values had progressed at much the same pace as elsewhere in northern Europe. As early as 1513, a work like Gavin Douglas's translation of Virgil's *Aeneid* was aimed at a noble audience. Douglas was the son of an earl and clearly the idea of a nobility of virtue, drawing on civic humanism and expressing itself in service to prince and commonweal, had permeated northern European noble circles where it was adapted to local circumstances. In the mid-sixteenth century the courtier-poet, sir David Lindsay of the Mount, exemplified this shift towards Renaissance ideas among Scottish élites. By the time Godscroft came to write his history of the Douglases in the early seventeenth century, the idea of the Renaissance gentleman was common currency, and he projected into the medieval past the values of his own age, constructing for young nobles of the fourteenth and fifteenth centuries an idealised schooling in virtue and letters.[76]

The utility of education was widely understood by a nobility keen to complement martial skills and courtly graces with educated minds. The young thirteenth earl of Sutherland was advised to take care over the education of his children, for 'Learning is the best portion you can give them, for how many meane gentlemen do wee perceave daylie to aryse by learning.'[77] That message was so impressed on the Gordon gentlemen that when the earl went off to university, firstly to Edinburgh and then St Andrews, his kinsmen and dependants agreed to pay for his education and that of his two younger brothers:

> So much did they value and regaird the good breiding and education of him who wes to governe and command them, knowing how much it doth concerne everie state and cuntrey to have weill bred and wyse superiors.

Here was the humanist ideology at work in a frontier locality where the improving value of education on society was perhaps better understood than in more peaceful parts of the kingdom. This Gordon example had its parallels in another European periphery, that of Naples, where clubs, or *monti*, were organised by clans into which money was paid to fund dowries or the education of children.[78] It is no surprise to find that when in 1600 the French duc de Rohan visited Scotland, he discovered a noble society 'full of civility and courtesy', a judgement that was not simply an expression of good French manners. Similarly, that much-travelled poet, William Lithgow, wrote of the Scottish nobility in 1628 that they are 'courteous, discreet, learned scholars weel read in the best histories, delicate linguists, the most part of them being brought up in France or Italy'. A century later, the third earl of Lothian recorded that 'Blood and descent make princes and nobles, valour may make conquerors, but learning and knowledge makes men, and wisdom makes gods,' but this was little more than a conventional aphorism in noble society.[79]

Since the early sixteenth century, the Scots, like most other Europeans, increasingly ascribed to those ideas of a gentleman found in the Italian Baldesar Castiglione's *The Courtier* (1528), the Englishman sir Thomas Elyot's *The Boke Named the Governor* (1531) or the Spaniard Lucas Gracian Dantisco's *The Spanish Galateo* (1593). The purpose of educating a noble was to shape his character such that he could offer leadership, inform him of religion, and equip him with competency in the law, an understanding of military technology, a grasp of classical and contemporary languages, adequate cultural breeding to enliven conversation and sharpen taste, a core of knowledge in the humanities to inform judgement, and a range of courtly skills. Education was not intended to turn him into a pedant.[80] Ludovick Stewart, second duke of Lennox, received the early part of his education in France, and on his arrival in Scotland in 1583 the king's principal physician, Gilbert Moncrieff, 'a man wise and of good learning', was appointed as preceptor to the thirteen-year-old duke with a commission to instruct him in letters, 'guid manneris' and diet. Lennox was no intellectual yet he epitomised the well-rounded, educated courtier of the period and proved to be the perfect companion for James VI for over forty years.[81] By contrast, the fifth earl of Marischal was from childhood educated thoroughly in Latin, Greek, Hebrew and history. In his youth he travelled throughout France, Germany and Italy learning languages alongside courtly skills, and he went to Geneva where he was instructed by Theodore Beza in public speaking, politics and religion; while there he took time to study geography. The man who founded Marischal college in Aberdeen as a Protestant, Ramist alternative to King's college was no dilettante, but a genuine scholar who remained devoted to study for the rest of his life.[82] He too had much to offer James VI. Yet while the gulf in learning and in intelligence between these two magnates was a wide one, Lennox was the better prepared for court life than the studious Marischal, and he had the more successful political career.

## Conclusion

The Scottish nobility was no different from its counterparts elsewhere in Europe in responding to the humanist challenge to re-educate itself with a view to living a life of right moral choices and equipped with the tools needed by the state. The slightly hysterical criticisms of academics and clerics must be viewed in that European context and it must be borne in mind that those levelling such accusations were men who overrated the importance of academic learning. The fifth earl of Montrose did not entirely neglect his studies at the university of St Andrews, even if his greatest passions were sport, recreation and socialising. But it would be wrong to think that he was wasting his time.[83] In adapting themselves to an age in which the martial qualities of the mounted soldier were less crucial to advancement, many nobles were retooling themselves for state service, making themselves useful to kings who needed literate magistrates, administrators and diplomats. Nobles were also ensuring that they had those skills necessary to thrive in a royal Renaissance court. This business of fashioning a young noble for a life of service and of exercising authority began in the home, where from an early age parents and tutors impressed on children the necessity of submitting the individual's will to the needs of God, the king and the family. A locally based school system, complemented by good regional burgh schools for older boys, instilled a sound grounding in Latin and ensured literacy. More and more nobles progressed to a Scottish university, where a broad humanist education was provided and in some cases where a degree was secured. For almost all the higher nobility and some of the lesser nobility their education was rounded off with further studies on the continent and a grand tour, providing an experience that was not new for the Scots but was a continuation of long-established links with the continent. The ideal was a refined gentleman modelled on a Roman magistrate, able to govern his own locality, equipped to enter royal administration or even the law, versed in the latest military technology, fluent in at least French, and at ease in the sophisticated world of the court. Not all met these expectations but more and more nobles did, and in this company the bookish James VI begins to look much less of an anomaly. That educational experience also gave many nobles a taste for learning and high culture that remained with them, guaranteeing that even without a royal court after 1603, Scotland remained locked into the mainstream of European civilisation. Arguably their education became one means by which nobles recognised themselves, and those life-long tastes, fashioned by that process, created a language that allowed them to identify those others who went by the name of gentlemen.[84]

# CHAPTER 9

# Leisure

A noble education was intended to produce men proficient in the necessary skills of war and government but also possessing a good, rounded understanding of the arts, sciences and languages. Those skills and that learning were for life, and it is unsurprising that throughout their careers many nobles continued to participate in activities that honed their military competence, and pursued interests prompted by their education. Others continued to apply a philosophy of self-improvement that brought them into contact with new ideas and offered new challenges. One thinks, for example, of the middle-aged regent Morton learning to play the spinet. Such was the product of an Aristotelian education, there being no artificial distinction between the cultivation of the mind and the exercise of the body. Pursuits like history, music and hunting were bound together in a seamless whole that formed the parameters of noble culture.[1] However, one of the difficulties in discussing the culture of an early modern nobility lies in agreeing what constitutes a distinctively noble culture. Because of their pervasiveness, nobles impacted at every level of cultural life, from the royal court through their own provincial society to involvement in activities that aroused the enthusiasm of the populace such as horse racing. Arguably there were a number of different and overlapping cultures, that of the court and of the country house, that heavily influenced by France and that of the Gaels, a masculine culture and one shaped by the varieties of noblewomen's experiences. It is, perhaps, misleading to try and embrace all under the one heading of noble culture. However, somewhere between a general discussion of Scotland and a differentiated description of complementary cultures, there were the leisure activities of noble society.

## Residences

Evidence for large-scale urban living by Europe's landed nobilities is varied. Much of Italy and southern France were regions with a high proportion of urban patriciate nobilities, while the residential development of cities like London was gathering momentum. Nevertheless, even in parts of Italy, chiefly Naples and Sicily, one must be careful not to exaggerate the extent to which nobles lived in towns.[2] Edinburgh was the principal urban residence of the Scottish nobility, being the second city of Britain and the location of the royal court (until 1603), the law courts, and the best mercantile and medical services, all drawing wealthy families to take up seasonal residence. Foreign travellers were struck by the concentration of castles and tower houses within a short distance of the city. By the 1600s, domestic peace and the advent of coaches made it possible for most Lowland nobles to make frequent trips to Edinburgh.[3] Some nobles owned property in the burgh, like the earls of Eglinton's 'great mansion and dwelling house' located at the head of the Fish Market, or the fifth lord Seton's fine town house with its outer and inner courts and large garden.[4] In spite of the departure of the royal court in 1603, nobles continued to go to Edinburgh to oversee their growing litigation, to attend parliament and to socialise. The city boasted high stone buildings, a long paved High Street and a towering castle, with the fine houses of the nobility tucked away off the narrow wynds, like the 'lofty stone tenement' owned by the first earl of Traquair in the 1630s. In what was an era of significant civic architectural achievement, Moray house was built on the road to Holyrood palace in the mid-1620s for Mary Sutton, the English dowager countess of Home, while chancellor Dunfermline's house at nearby Musselburgh was deliberately designed as a *villa suburba*. Even the jaundiced eye of sir William Brereton conceded the attractions of the 'most complete street in Christendom', thronging with nobles, merchants and fashionable women, although he was disgusted with the stench, unfairly dismissing the houses of earls and lords as 'mean buildings' by comparison to those of mere English gentlemen.[5]

Provincial centres outside Edinburgh were home to notable architectural works like the first earl of Gowrie's spacious town house in Perth. Mar's Wark in Stirling was built in the early 1570s for the first earl of Mar in the self-consciously grand style of the burgh's principal family. In the 1630s, sir Anthony Alexander attractively remodelled the town house of his father, sir William Alexander of Menstrie, a man determined to advertise his new wealth and status. Even in small towns, nobles built comfortable houses, such as at Pittenweem where the London-based first earl of Kellie had a house, or at Maybole where the earls of Cassillis had a tower house alongside a number of other barons. The Boyd family's strong connections with Glasgow were reflected in a portfolio of property in the burgh; the Livingston family possessed a house in Falkirk; the ninth earl of Errol maintained a house in Perth, where in 1630 viscount Dupplin marked his enhanced status by building a summerhouse on the town wall. Inverness remained a regional capital for the Highlands and the north-east, and in 1605 the sixth lord Lovat bought a newly constructed and handsome four-storeyed town house there from a bankrupt merchant. Nobles also contributed to the civic buildings of burghs; for example, in Kirkcudbright a new tolbooth was begun in 1627 with the help of a loan from sir John Gordon of Lochinvar.[6]

Nobles, therefore, did spend part of the year in towns, but the shift towards a preference for urban environments was modest compared to France, where by the early seventeenth century the dominant image of country house culture was of ignorance, vice and impotence, of places where old nobles retired when their usefulness as public servants had ended. Instead, the Scots shared the English preference for rural over urban society, investing in the family's country house and estate rather than urban development, while only taking lodgings in the town when necessary or to take advantage of seasonal attractions. The country seat was not only a building and was not simply intended to impress; it became a living organism, its inhabitants in harmony with their world, living according to timeless traditions.[7] At another level, castles were the most visible symbol of noble authority in the physical landscape, whether this was expressed in functional, unimaginative tower houses or in magnificent palaces, and these constructions were a means of reinforcing the continuity of a lineage and its unique association with a given space. After returning from exile in 1596, the sixth earl of Huntly abandoned subversive politics and 'gave himselff whollie to policie, planting, and building', although his apparent distraction did not signify a retreat from public life. A Highland baron like sir Colin Campbell of Glenorchy was memorialised by the family chronicler as a man who celebrated his lineage in stone, building castles at Balloch and Balquhidder and a lodging at Perth, and making improvements to other castles in his possession. However, the building achievements of the Seton family, both the Winton and Dunfermline branches, outstrip any of their rivals for variety, innovation and sheer style. Chancellor Dunfermline was a skilled amateur architect, and each of his constructions, from the baronial grandeur of Fyvie castle to the Anglo-Flemish domesticity of Pinkie, was a statement of his cosmopolitan taste, sophisticated erudition and political loyalty to the crown. Those in royal service also built in pursuit of public ends. The first lord Thirlestane created at Thirlestane castle a splendid local centre of royal munificence, advertising the king's benevolence to those who served him, providing employment in its construction, and creating a centre of administration and hospitality thereafter. In Scotland, more than in any other northern Renaissance country, a castellated, baronial style was celebrated, emphasising chivalric concepts of display, lineage and hierarchy. Scottish patrons also borrowed from a range of classical and foreign influences, chiefly French, English, Italian and even Spanish designs, although this European humanist tradition was blended carefully with practicality and native taste. The fifth earl of Bothwell's Italianesque interior at Crichton castle did not compromise its defensive capabilities, while for all the baroque appearance of the first earl of Nithsdale's remodelling of the living quarters and courtyard of Carlaverock castle, it retained its external medieval appearance. This rich fusion produced a cluster of unique and remarkable Renaissance tower houses, castles and palaces for noble patrons who spent lavishly and sought out the best craftsmen for working in stone, marble and wood from Scotland and beyond.[8]

The move towards making the castle a comfortable as well as a safe place to live was under way long before the end of the sixteenth century, but this does not mean that defensive features were neglected entirely. It is unsurprising to find that in the north-east the military function of castles still concerned sir George Ogilvy of Dunlugas and William Forbes of Tolquon in the 1580s. Yet even these conservative barons were determined to improve their living space. At nearby castle Fraser, constructed between the mid-1570s and 1636, military considerations were always secondary to those of taste. The end product was a comfortable and pleasing residence, built entirely by local craftsmen yet with a flavour of France and of chivalric culture. The shift in emphasis that gradually saw a decline in the numbers of gun loops, the replacement of open parapets with roofs, the phasing out of angle turrets and the appearance instead of greater embellishment, larger windows and indefensible horizontal extensions was slow but steady. This point is made most effectively on the peripheries of the kingdom, and a building designed primarily for comfort rather than defence was Birsay palace, elaborately constructed on the far-flung Orkney isles between 1569 and 1574 by lord Robert Stewart. Similar evidence of creeping civility can be found on the western islands; for example, on Islay where in 1631 John Campbell of Cawdor received permission to demolish Dunivaig castle and build 'a more commodious house for his own dwelling in a more proper part of the isle'. On the borders, defensive considerations gave way to comfort after 1603, as is clear in sir Robert Ker of Ancram's plans to introduce alterations to the exterior of his house and its surroundings, creating a clean, healthy and attractive environment for his family and guests.[9]

Experimentation, individualism and even eccentricity account for the sheer variety in castle improvements: the lavish courtyard range at Hamilton palace, the horizontal extension of living quarters at Aberdour, the intriguing exteriors at Claypotts in Angus, the neat symmetry of Craigievar, the stunningly elaborate entrance at Huntly castle, the ostentatious anglicisation of the earl of Dunbar's house at Berwick. Interiors were remodelled with broader staircases; family rooms, access stairs and corridors increased privacy; corner towers enhanced the comfort and prospect of bedrooms; heating was improved; and sir David Lindsay of Edzell enjoyed the benefits of a heated garden bathhouse in his remote Angus country house. Oriel windows opened up rooms to light, décor was enhanced with painted ceilings, and plasterwork became more fashionable, as at Balcarres where the plasterworked ceiling was decorated with the Nine Worthies by Nicolaes de Bruyn, while the frieze work begun at Craigievar in 1626 was based on an earlier Flemish engraving by Théodor de Bry. Undoubtedly English décor was mediated by the court, itself heavily influenced by French adaptations of Italian interior design. But the Scots were not merely passive imitators of metropolitan fashions, William Murray's innovations at Ham house in London in the 1630s being an indication of how some Scots were contributing to taste in London. In Scotland, new furnishings were imported; for example, the long, communal table was replaced with a round and more intimate one, and elaborate galleries were designed for exercise, the display of paintings and valuable imported possessions, although there is little evidence for the collection of antiquities outside the court circle. Perhaps the best example of a residence built for comfort was Dunfermline's villa outside Edinburgh where he proclaimed that 'A happy home is preferable to a large home. Often toil and sorrow dwell in palaces, peace and happiness in cottages'. Of course, Pinkie house was neither small nor simple, being an exemplar of the understated wealth and comfort enjoyed by the refined, sophisticated noble families who inhabited these castles.[10]

Among the most idiosyncratic and colourful cultural artefacts of Renaissance Scotland is the painted ceiling, inspired by imported patterns but largely the product of local craftsmen. At Pinkie house, the decorated wooden ceiling in the long gallery displays heraldic devices, moral inscriptions (chiefly from Horace) and symbolic pictures, creating a complex, rhetorical text for an educated and discerning reader. These images drew inspiration from, among others, the 1607 *Theatro Moral de la Vida Humana* of the Dutch artist and poet, Otto van Veen, and from the 1596 Frankfurt edition of Denis Lebey de Batilly's *Emblemata*. Sir George Bruce decorated Culross palace in a similar style, the European influences being mediated through the Englishman George Whitney's 1586 *Emblèmes*. Decorative painting found its way into funerary monuments like the Skelmorlie aisle at Largs, where the early seventeenth-century patron and his artist drew inspiration from Etienne Délaumea, a French designer of ornament, who died in 1583. Such creativity points to a refined clientele that knew what it wanted from architects, craftsmen and skilled decorative artists like John Anderson, who was employed by the first marquis of Huntly and other north-eastern nobles.[11]

The Reformation in Scotland inspired a remarkably self-confident iconoclasm that destroyed much of the medieval artistic legacy. However, art did not disappear, and nobles sought pictures to place in new galleries like that installed by the first earl of Gowrie at his Perth house in 1584, or the two large galleries at Seton palace. The patronage of continental artists can be traced back at least to the mid-sixteenth century. In 1561, Hans Eworth visited the country, painting excellent pictures of lord James Stewart and his wife, Agnes Keith, while the fine miniatures of the fifth earl of Bothwell and his wife were also painted in the 1560s. Perhaps the most beautifully and richly textured portrait of the period is that of the Catholic fifth lord Seton by an anonymous artist a decade later, and the Seton family continued to commission individual and family portraits, as well as the colourful, if fanciful, Seton armorial of 1591. The later sixteenth-century Stewart court was influenced by the mimetic style of painting, popular in the Netherlands, and noble patrons like the fourth earl of Morton and lord Seton sat for Arnold Bronckhorst and Adrian Vanson. Foreign artists continued to be employed after 1603, and prolonged absences at the London court might have enhanced the memorial value of the portrait. Adam de Cologne was popular with noble patrons in the 1620s, and among his work is the sensitive grouping of the Winton family. Most Scottish artists, however, were armorial painters, like James Workman the elder who probably painted the first marquis of Huntly's funeral procession. It was from this tradition that the Aberdeen-based George Jamesone emerged, producing portraiture in which carefully observed characterisation overcomes the often mediocre composition. Yet even when his popularity resulted in over-hurried work in the 1630s, Jamesone produced portraits of real quality like that of the first earl of Southesk. In 1634, he also completed a major commission for sir Colin Campbell of Glenorchy, who in the previous year paid a German painter £1000 to paint twenty-four pictures of the kings and queens of Scotland alongside thirty-four portraits of the house of Glenorchy and its kinsmen. At sir John Grant of Freuchie's castle in Strathspey, the laird had an Aberdeen painter decorate his newly panelled gallery with portraits, and he imported fabulously sculptured beasts, including a rhinoceros and a gorgon. Like other early modern European nobilities, the Scots took up the collection of paintings. In the reign of Charles I, collecting came to indicate an involvement in the competitive aspects of court life, the third marquis of Hamilton being a major collector of paintings, exceeded only by the earl of Arundel and the king with whom he exchanged gifts. In 1636, Charles gave Hamilton two works by the Dutch painter, Geertgen tot Sint Jans, after they had been presented by an embassy from the States General, and the marquis had his own portrait painted by Daniel Mytens. Access to an international art market allowed the first earl of Buccleuch to purchase a number of tapestries from Jan Russelhaer at the Hague, including six hangings depicting the life of Caesar, a subject that appealed to Buccleuch's military imagination, and another set entitled 'The History of Susanna'.[12]

Surprisingly, landscape art attracted little interest before 1639–40 when Alexander Kierinex produced views of the Scottish royal palaces for Charles I. Yet the palaces, castles and tower houses of the nobility were located in rural vistas, reflecting a mental landscape in which their owners sought some bond with the natural world. In describing Fife as it appeared to him in 1598, the English traveller, Fynes Moryson, thought it a prosperous shire 'full of Noblemens and gentlemens dwellings commonly compassed with little groves, though trees are so rare in those parts, as I remember not to have seene one wood'. A similar enthusiasm for altering the landscape with tree planting was observed by Timothy Pont in Ayrshire in the 1600s; for example, he enthused over Blair house, 'ane ancient castell and strong dominioun, weill beutified with gardens, orchards and partiers'. In designing his house, Ancram advised that any inconveniently placed tenants' houses should be removed (with compensation) and new parks be laid out for recreational sports and the pasture of horses; the approach to the house was to be made noble and grand, trees felled to facilitate riding, new tree-lined walkways devised, the roads linking different parts of the estate widened, bridges constructed, walls erected around the park in the English style and a new enclosed orchard planted. A planned garden should face the sun, 'which in Scotland is a mayne consideration', while fish ponds were to be established and stocked with the likes of perch.[13]

These people were engaged in something more than estate management, their planting being a form of landscape sculpture, aesthetic as much as functional. Thirty years before he retired from court, sir James Melville of Halhill affected the fashionable idea of a neo-Stoic rusticity, relating that 'As armytis [= eremite] wer wont to retire them in solitary places, even so am I drawen to a quyet maner of lyving, content with the portion which God has geven me'. Sir David Lindsay of Edzell corresponded with a legal colleague who addressed himself as 'The Wood President', writing lyrically about the Angus countryside in February 1588 from his home in Edinburgh, where the sound of chirping birds brought to mind the northern mountains, 'albeit presentlie environit with thair quhyte winter robbes, yit befoir I visie thame sall be deckit with thair grene fragrant May garmentis'. By the seventeenth century, this theme had become even more popular. Denmilne glorified 'the pleasur of the feildis', delighting 'in my retired quietness from out of the City', while Gordonstoun was sensitive of the natural environment, taking great pleasure in describing the geography of Sutherland along with its produce and wildlife. This yearning for nature influenced the building of castles, which were constructed with rooms having views not only of gardens, but also of mountain scenery or the sea, as in the spacious guest apartments overlooking the bowling green at Dunottar castle perched high on its craggy isthmus above the crashing waves of the North Sea.[14] Here was a contemplative nobility, with a Plinian awareness of the natural surroundings of the Scottish landscape, keen to articulate a desire to rest from the court, from government and the cares of the world.

Gardens adjoining castles and houses were more than mere horticultural decorations, their construction and upkeep requiring skills like mathematics and hydraulic engineering. A garden united science and art in a mimetic form, embracing sculpture and classical literature on a stage that represented the world. In Scotland, the crown led the way in adopting the Italian- and French-inspired continental enthusiasm for garden construction, particularly at Holyrood palace, and nobles were not slow to follow.[15] It is not surprising that the regent Morton, a man who placed much emphasis on law and order, was fascinated by the relatively new science of creating formal gardens. He laid out a terraced Renaissance garden at Aberdour castle, and following his demission of the regency in the spring of 1578, retired to Lochleven castle where he passed his time 'devysing the situation of a fayre gardene with allyis'.[16] It is tempting to see in Morton's action an exemplar of neo-Stoicism in which gardening provided a consoling retreat from the troubles of a violent and unstable world. Certainly poets liked to reflect on natural themes; for example, John Stewart of Baldynneis's 'Of a fountain' or Alexander Hume's 'Of the day estivall', a glorious celebration of summer. Hawthornden self-consciously cultivated this idea of the garden as a retreat, celebrating its natural beauties in verse and cutting himself off from the harsher environment beyond his idyllic creation. Other neo-Stoicists who were gardening enthusiasts included the first earls of Dunfermline, Stirling and Ancram, all active politicians. In the wall of his fountained garden at Pinkie house, Dunfermline intimated his Stoic philosophy, rejecting the need for martial features to the buildings and offering 'the kind welcome and hospitable entertainment of guests, a fountain of pure water, lawns, ponds and aviaries'. Dunfermline's nephew, the third earl of Winton, set about planting a herb garden at Seton house in 1620; Gordonstoun was proud of the earl of Sutherland's castle at Dunrobin, surrounded with 'fair orchards, wher ther be pleasant gardens, planted with all kynds of froots, hearbs, and floors, used in this kingdome, and abundance of good saphron, tobacco, and rosemarie'; and Glenorchy was employing a gardener on his Highland estate in 1606.[17] However, the best surviving garden of the period is that at Edzell, where between 1604 and 1610, sir David Lindsay created a playful Renaissance puzzle using planetary deities, the liberal arts and the virtues, all drawn from continental prints. Unfortunately the project brought on his own bankruptcy.[18]

## Hospitality, Sports and Pastimes

Throughout Britain, nobles adhered to a self-fashioned image of themselves as a rural élite of honourable, rustic gentlemen with simple, uncluttered tastes, living in castles or country houses where they practised hospitality as a public duty. It was this world of hierarchic obligations, set amidst the rural estate, that was idealised in those country-house poems fashionable in early seventeenth-century England. This was in contrast to the selfish and private lifestyle of nobles who took to living in the city, a lifestyle criticised by James VI and I and by Charles I.[19] However, while English poetry reflects some anxiety about sustaining that ideal in the face of the city's attractions, and a shift towards a more private lifestyle, Scottish noble society remained more committed to a form of hospitality that often bordered on prodigality, ignoring the Aristotelian strictures about balancing generosity with prudence. Gaelic society especially was sensitive to the obligations of hospitality, so that among the Highland clans of the Western Isles 'when one is invited to another's hous, they never depairt so long as any provision doth last', following which the company moved on to the next host. The generosity of the earls of Argyll was legendary, it being said by one poet that whoever visted the house of MacCailein Mor would never want to leave. Hospitality was also an obligation men owed their lords; hence the fifth earl of Argyll's anger when in the spring of 1570 he was confronted by a dependant's castle 'halden as ane fortres, nocht preparit as we wald have belevit to our honour'.[20] But hospitality was not only a Gaelic custom. John Leslie drew attention to the emphasis placed on hospitality, relating that the nobility 'With glade wil and frilie thay use to ludge kin, freind and acquaintance, ye and strangers that turnes in to thame. A sclandirous thing they esteime it to be, to deny this, and a poynt of smal or na liberalitie'.[21] Foreign travellers were struck by the generosity they experienced. John Taylor was hugely impressed in 1618 when confronted by modest lairds, the backswoodsmen of landed society, whose 'chiefe delight being only to give strangers entertainment *gratis*'. In contrast to England, where traditions of open hospitality were in decline, Taylor painted an evocative, bucolic picture of these minor nobles in their unsophisticated homes, plainly dressed and yet maintaining large households of between thirty and fifty people, daily providing charity at their gates to three or four score unfortunates and offering generous hospitality to astonishing numbers of guests of every rank in their homes.[22]

Prior to 1603, a peripatetic Scottish court ensured that at its highest levels, noble society remained rooted in cultural rituals associated with the countryside. In August 1562, queen Mary went on progress to Perthshire, where she and her court were entertained for fourteen days by the fourth earl of Atholl, culminating in a great hunt when as many as five hundred deer were slaughtered and gourmet banquets of 'all kynd of delicattis that culd be gottin'. James VI also practised peripatetic kingship, hunting with noble friends, dining in their homes, taking part in family occasions and touring their localities.[23] Obviously this form of socialising, with its political purpose and focusing on the king, ended for all but a select few in 1603, but thereafter a lively country-house culture kept the rituals of hospitality alive. Family letters repeatedly refer to a round of visiting and the expectation of visits, suggesting a spirited and friendly social life. The social activity of the sixth earl of Eglinton and his wife was framed by their ordinary residence in Ayrshire, her family home in Callander, the Seton houses in Lothian and business in Edinburgh. Evidence such as the fourth lord Elphinstone's household book indicates that lords spent a good deal of time calling on friends and relatives or being visited by them. In Elphinstone's case it was not uncommon to find him making long trips north from his Stirlingshire base to see his daughter, the countess of Sutherland. Living in relatively isolated communities, with few educated or well-born companions, nobles and their families sought out sociable company, and the most remote localities could be the centres of a busy round of gregarious activities. In 1615, the twelfth earl of Sutherland's intimation that he intended to winter in Dornoch was a signal for the 'haill gentilmen of the contrey' to join him and 'so be tyme we think to mak the toun better'. Often these gatherings arose because there was a christening, a marriage or even a funeral, as in December 1589 when there was a large gathering at the Kincardine home of the third earl of Montrose for the christening of his grandchild. More peaceful times in the early seventeenth century probably stimulated travel, and the greater use of coaches eased the discomfort for older people and less skilled horsewomen.[24]

The Arcadian ideal of a simple country life was particularly attractive to those members of the lesser nobility who could expect no better and so claimed to despise the court, thus making a noble virtue out of their limitations. A man like William Rose of Kilravock, who died in 1611, was remembered by a later generation as a plainly garbed man who was 'provident and frugall, given to hospitalitie, friends and strangers being kindlie entertained in his house'. Such rude simplicity was criticised by some, as when sir William Brereton disparaged the hospitality he received at the hands of sir Alexander Kennedy of Culzean in 1636. He found the dining room 'very sluttishly kept, unswept, dishes, trenchers and wooden cups thrown up and down, and the room very nasty and unsavoury'. Here the visitor was reflecting a shift in English decorum rather than poor taste on the part of his hosts.[25] However, there was some awareness of the differences between urban and rural, between court and country. In the summer of 1635, Julian Ker, countess of Haddington, was embarrassed when her eldest son, sir Patrick Hume of Polwarth, rode into Edinburgh on 'unworthy nags', with no company other than a badly dressed servant who looked like 'a naiket hog'. The countess was humiliated but Polwarth 'cairs not quhat he wair', expressing himself freely and giving the impression that this was how 'daft folks spek'. Polwarth was a commissioner of the peace for Berwickshire, but in spite of his rank and standing in the local community, he did not live up to his mother's elevated position in Edinburgh society, and she wished him home on the Merse.[26] While there is little Scottish evidence of the metropolitan disdain for the parish nobility as boorish and unsophisticated yokels that was becoming common among English or French nobles, both parliament and moralists commented on the drift to the towns and the vice of private living. Even in the middle of the sixteenth century, Lethington's 'Satire on the age' expressed an old man's disappointment and puzzlement at living in a time when 'All houshalding is worne away'. In 1581, parliament was sufficiently concerned to condemn the fashion of living in burghs or in ale houses, requiring nobles to reside at home where they might encourage the good maintenance of their dwellings, support the poor with alms and entertain their neighbours. By 1633, when Lithgow was expressing regret at the passing of traditional lordship, this criticism had become an established refrain, and he too looked back to an ideal past when 'Nobles keept good houses', before London drew men away from their localities. However, this harking back to a past that never existed can to some extent be dismissed as the sentimental ramblings of the old and the wistful longings of the romantic, and the second marquis of Huntly's inability to set the right tone of friendly familiarity with his dependants in the late 1630s was noted precisely because it was unusual.[27]

When c.1621–2 the second marquis of Hamilton commissioned Rubens to paint *The Munich Lion Hunt*, he was associating himself with an activity intimately identified with both the countryside and with noble society. Hunting was more than a sport, being a means of defining nobility, its complex rituals reinforcing hierarchy and rank, while the eating of game, as opposed to butcher's meat, was in itself a denotation of status. Hunting was also an essential part of young noblemen's education and was central to their socialisation. Surprisingly, there was no equivalent of the fifteenth-century *Book of St Alban's*, the most popular English hunting text of the period, and the Scots produced no literature of their own on hunting.[28] However, hunting was enormously popular. King James set the tone for the rest of his family, most of whom were painted in hunting poses, and he enormously enjoyed the chase with hounds, regarding the use of guns and bows as 'a theevish forme of hunting'. He was less keen on hawking since it required little energetic activity; it also lacked the legitimacy of antiquity. Gordonstoun recommended hunting as 'a martiall sport, and resembleth the warres much', while Denmilne qualified his enthusiasm for this noble pursuit with the warning that men 'doe not profussly waste ther estait idly on the same'.[29] Denmilne may have had in mind men like Thomas Maule of Panmure, a skilled and fanatical hunter who favoured goshawks for hawking and greyhounds for hunting, and whose expertise was eagerly sought by the king and the first marquis of Hamilton. A more exotic form of hunting was practised by David Lindsay of Edzell, who hunted wolves on his estate in the 1580s. One friend informed him in 1588 that he looked forward to being in Angus in the spring to hunt at 'Willie wolffis taill', assuming 'we be not interruptit be the Spainzie Navie', an interesting comment on parochial priorities.[30] It was in the Highlands that hunting was seen at its most dramatic, especially the great Braemar hunt organised in August by the second earl of Mar, who used the occasion to enhance his claims to Gaelic lordship. At the 1618 hunt, John Taylor witnessed the cream of the nobility dressed and armed in plain, Highland fashion amidst a huge mobile camp of some 1500 men who were set to make massive sweeps of the countryside, driving scores of deer into a killing zone where dogs and men indulged in an orgy of blood lust. Most hunts were far less sensational, but all these events were social occasions serving wider purposes, as in August 1595 when the seventh earl of Argyll organised a hunt with Lauchlan Maclean of Duart to discuss selling mercenaries to the English government in Ireland.[31] The currency in hunting dogs and birds of prey also promoted a gift culture, transcending international borders and allowing engagement in a friendly banter that eased social relations. Correspondence is full of references to exchanging and borrowing dogs or hawks, and the king often pressurised his nobles for the best of their kennels or hunting birds in what could be a keen test of their loyalty. Some nobles explored breeding programmes, like that managed c.1610 by sir George Buchanan of that Ilk who raised fallow deer, and in the mid-1630s the third marquis of Hamilton created a deer park on his estates, bringing young deer down from the Highlands.[32]

Scottish nobles never resorted to the savagery of the forest laws in England where local poaching wars were common, but parliament was worried about game management. In 1563, it expressed concern that over-zealous hunting by the gun-toting commons was so reducing the stock of game that 'the Nobil men of the realme can get na pastyme of halking and hunting'. Parliament, therefore, repeated earlier legislation against the shooting of game, but four years later the topic was again discussed, and it continued to be a trying issue in succeeding decades.[33] The crown too tried to restrict hunting privileges, ostensibly in the name of conservation. For example, in January 1613 royal letters were issued to the commissioners of the peace in Linlithgowshire, instructing them to restrict hunting because the ownership of greyhounds had become so common that 'no sporte is lefte for such of the better sorte who keepe kennellis of houndis'.[34] Lords also allowed limited hunting by tenants on their estates as a means of herd management. In 1612, sir Duncan Campbell of Glenorchy set the tack to Patrick Dow, keeper of the forest of Mamlorne, specifying that neither he nor his men would shoot deer with a gun. The second earl of Mar set tacks in 1632 to Donald Farquarson of Camusnakist whose principal responsibility was to prevent poaching, charging him to attend the earl with his men and dogs when he hunted and to oversee the organisation of the hunt. Yet in spite of all the efforts of government and nobles, illicit hunting for food and profit did go on, as is clear from the complaints of the first marquis of Huntly in 1622 against rapacious poacher gangs.[35]

Hunting encouraged good horsemanship and the horse was a potent symbol of royal and noble authority, riding being praised as a noble art by antiquity, and the mastery of the horse being a visual demonstration of rulership: hence the equestrian pose in so many of the royal portraits of the early seventeenth century. For James VI and his family that enthusiasm for horse riding went beyond the exploitation of a powerful icon – strangely James, who was a superb horseman, was never painted on a horse – and prince Henry began building a new riding school in London in 1607. This was against a background of a perceived decline in horsemanship in Britain, highlighted two years later by Nicholas Morgan in his *The Perfection of Horsemanship*, and there is no doubt that the best training was at the expensive academies of Italy and France. Scottish nobles, like their king, spent an enormous amount of time in the saddle, but they experienced great difficulty in maintaining an adequate number of horses, largely because of the absence of adequate meadows and the high cost of winter feeding. Often they resorted to importing horses from England.[36] Nevertheless, horse racing was pursued enthusiastically, and after 1603 it was James VI's patronage of the sport that increased its popularity in England. The second earl of Home had his best horses – including his favourite, Sweepstakes, that was looked after by its own attendant – sent to London to take part in races and hunting in the south. The sociability and the competitive edge of racing, usually accompanied by betting, generated keen rivalry in a theatrical setting. In 1575, an international race was held on Solway sands between the Scots and English at which the best horse proved to be one owned by lord Hamilton, a keen horseman. But there were also dangers in such gatherings when fights broke out between rival supporters, or when youths used the occasion to pursue family feuds.[37] These events created a point of cultural contact between nobles and popular society since horse racing attracted large social gatherings, like that on the first earl of Roxburgh's estates in 1622. Nobles acted as race patrons; for example, the first marquis of Huntly donated a silver cup and spur as the prize for an annual race by the sea at Inverness among the young nobles of the north. In April 1608, the burgh of Paisley intimated that a four-ounce silver bell would be offered by the first earl of Abercorn as a prize for an annual horse race within the burgh. The race did not run regularly, and in May 1620 a more complete set of rules was produced along with prize money contributed by the burgh magistrates and the local nobility. In the following year, a parliament full of horse-daft nobles expressed concern at the growth in the passion for racing and gambling, seeking to limit the size of wagers to 100 merks on pain of the winnings being forfeited and distributed to the poor of the parish. Away from the disapproving eye of the anti-gambling lobby, enthusiasts like Abercorn continued to organise races with rich purses at stake.[38]

There were many other sports suitable for a gentleman. Exercise and games were integral components of a child's education, providing important life skills, and were encouraged by a philosophy owing as much to the rediscovery of the ancient world's respect for the body as to the martial traditions of chivalric culture.[39] Noble culture was permeated with sporting activities and even vocabulary. When in 1616 Gordonstoun was told by a client of his family that 'your worschipe hes gottin the ball at your fuit', the allusion would have been well understood. Like James VI, Gordonstoun largely followed the English educationalist, Roger Ascham, in listing those sports appropriate for a nobility still conscious of its military function, sports like running, jumping, fencing, wrestling, dancing, tennis, archery, riding, tilting, the ring (= a game on horseback), hawking and hunting which 'maketh a man hardie and skilfull in all grounds'. Account books, like those of the young fifth earl of Montrose, indicate that sport in the form of golf and archery was part of his common recreation.[40] Almost all these sports and games were played with the purpose of training for war, as exercise and as a means of passing the time. Queen Mary's courtiers took part in the popular pastime of running at the ring, and in December 1561 there was the added exoticism of three nobles dressing as women and another three as foreigners. When the sheriff court met in Inverness in the 1570s, the fifth lord Lovat brought his followers to join in the archery, football, putting of the stone and throwing of the caber in an early version of the Highland games.[41] Others pursued private disciplines, like chancellor Dunfermline, still practising archery in the last year of his life with 'the same bowis that served me at 40'.[42] Golf was popular with many nobles, and tennis, which was played in Edinburgh and on the royal tennis court in Falkland, was an exclusive game, although one associated with gambling and rowdy behaviour.[43] Football was a slightly subversive sport enjoyed by nobles and commoners alike. James VI disliked it, being a sport 'meeter for laming, then making able the users thereof', a comment inspired perhaps by his memory of an occasion in 1583 when the master of Marischal hacked the fifth earl of Bothwell during a game, leading to a punch-up and demands for a duel. An enthusiasm for football cost the fifth earl of Huntly his life when he had a fatal stroke during a game in 1576, having earlier sent one of his servants to buy a new ball. However, in spite of the king's distaste, treasurer Mar was instructed in 1617 to ensure that 'the football and the rowbowles and sutche manlye exercisses maye be pracysed and exercised befor his Majesties cumming to Scotland, that their pepill heir [in England] maye see the owld exerceisses if that cuntrye'.[44] The significance given to sport is reflected in the design of parks around castles and houses. At the first earl of Orkney's palace at Birsay there were facilities for archery, bowling and golf. Ancram suggested his son create a park within which men might participate in riding games like running at the ring, even though 'you care not for it nor no horsemanship', and a green for playing football.[45]

The most common indoor game was playing at cards, often with gambling, although noble society was suspicious of games that relied heavily on chance, where rank had no advantage. Lethington, James VI and Gordonstoun did not share the clergy's disapproval of cards and dice, but the king thought the latter required little skill, and both Lethington and Gordonstoun only allowed playing for limited sums on the understanding that the game would always be played in a spirit of fairness. Certainly the amounts charged to the fourth lord Elphinstone's household accounts for card playing in 1603 were modest.[46] Another indoor pursuit was chess. In spite of his cerebral nature, James VI followed Castiglione in being suspicious of chess, which required too much study to be worthy of a nobleman. Instead of providing relaxation, 'it by the contrarie filleth and troubleth mens heades, with as many fashious toyes of the play, as before it was filled with thoughts on his affaires'. Italy remained the home of chess in Europe, there being no English manual until 1614, and in June 1622 signor Leonardo Crema, a hard-up Italian noble, tried to worm his way into Scottish noble society by offering his travelling companion to play all comers, 'knowing that the Scotch nobility in particular delight in this ingenious game'.[47] Less common was billiards, which the sixth earl of Morton played at Dalkeith palace.[48]

Musical entertainment was rich and varied in Scotland after the Reformation, in spite of a gradual retreat from religious music other than the 'plain and dulce' Scots psalms favoured by Protestant clergy and nobles. However, the decline was noted. In 1579, parliament expressed its concern at the fall in musical standards, and a year later the king established a new song school in Edinburgh.[49] Outside the context of worship, fiddling and dancing provided the common entertainment at Mary's court, where her mother's innovations were continued, David Rizzio being a beneficiary of the queen's musical patronage. Instrumental music for the cittern, virginals, spinet and viol was popular, although John Bellenden thought viols inappropriate for a martial nobility since the soft airs 'spouts sweet venom in their ears/And makes their minds effeminate'. Dances like the pavane and the galliard, which aroused the ire of John Knox, were also encouraged by the court. James VI was keen on music, his snobbery against nobles themselves ever playing being counteracted by Aristotle's recommendation, and he reinvigorated royal patronage of music in the 1580s and 1590s only for it to be cut off in 1603. Yet, while church disapproval against certain kinds of popular music was sustained, when Mr Alexander Hume, minister of Logie Wallach, published a collection of *Hymns or Sacred Songs* in 1599, he noted that lay attitudes towards music often did not accord with those of the church:

> In Prince's courts, in the houssis of great menn, and at the asembleis of young gentlemen and young damsels, the chief pastime is to sing prophaine sonnets and vain ballattis of love, or to rehers some fabulos faites of Palmerine, Amadis, or uther such like reveries.[50]

In the absence of church patronage and with the withdrawal of the crown's support for native musicianship after 1603, it fell increasingly to the nobility to sustain a musical tradition.

Yet so many people peddled their musical skills that in 1579 parliament legislated against itinerant beggars and entertainers, including 'all menstrallis, sangstars, and tailtellaris' not in the employment of nobles or burghs.[51] Nobles liked their music, as is evident in the depiction of the Muses on the ceilings painted in 1599 in Crathes castle, and individual lords maintained musicians in their service, men like 'Stewart the fidlair' employed by the second earl of Mar in 1584, or 'the blind violer' who was one of his household in 1617, and James Harvie who played the lute for the third earl of Moray, a service for which he was paid twenty shillings per annum. Within noble chambers, entertainment was commonly provided by lute players but more exotic instruments were growing in popularity. The twelfth earl of Sutherland tried to purchase a pair of virginals from London in 1615, 'seing my bearnis ar learning to play and sing'. In 1620, the children of sir Duncan Campbell of Glenorchy were being taught to play this instrument at a cost of 100 merks per annum, while this musical family owned harpsichords and appreciated a pair of organs that were installed at Finlarg chapel. The teaching of music to the Glenorchy children was a normal constituent of a noble education, even among lesser nobles like John Lennox of Cally, who paid James Lauder, 'musiciner', £82 10s in June 1599 for his son's board. Not surprisingly, women figure prominently in musical activities. The first earl of Gowrie had music sent from London for his daughters in the early 1580s; Anne Ker, countess of Lothian, possessed a song book of sacred and secular music compiled between 1600 and 1610; and lady Anne Campbell, daughter of the first earl of Loudon, was taught music by Duncan Burnett, master of the song school in Glasgow, beginning what would become a lifetime's commitment to the collection of music.[52] Among the earliest collections of Scottish music was that assembled during the second decade of the early seventeenth century by sir John Skene of Curriehill and his eldest son. Sir William Mure of Rowallan made a small collection of ballads and dances, including his own arrangements for the lute which he published in 1629 as *The True Crucifixe for True Catholickes*. Nobles were also the subject of popular ballads, from the scandalous 'Ladye Rothemayis lilt' or 'Ladie Cassilles lilt', to the tragic 'The laird of Waristoun' and 'The bonnie earle of Murray'.[53]

Robert Maule, the commissary of St Andrews, related that the harp and clarsach were the favoured instrument of the ancient Scots, 'and noble men usit to heave them in thear bedchalmers, quhar thay usit to play until the maister wes falline a sleipe; and this forme, I heir, is zit observit in the Hielandis'. When the young Simon Fraser, master of Lovat, was dying, he was surrounded by musicians who played and sang until he passed out of this mortal life, carried into eternity on the airs of his bards. The position of musicians was especially regarded in the Highlands, where there was a professional hierarchy of fili, bard and druth, the fili being much more than mere entertainers, having responsibility for the clan's history and genealogy, as well as for providing counsel in the form of prophecy. Highland nobles took pride in the achievements of harpists or pipers, whose task was to praise lords and their ancestors, particularly their martial achievements – for example, in the 'Battle of Carinish' – and clarsachs were employed by all the leading families, from island chiefs like the MacLeans of Duart and the MacLeods of Dunvegan to the earls of Argyll and Sutherland. Donnchadh MacRaoridh was bard to the MacDonalds of Sleat but he also enjoyed the favour of the powerful Mackenzie chiefs of Kintail, and it was following the death in 1630 of the first lord Kintail that he wrote '*Fada ata mise an deidh chaich*' ('Too long I live after these'), lamenting the passing of the last of a generation of men he had served. However, even in the Lowlands, Gaelic musicians were prized, a point made by George Buchanan, and it was a blind Irish musician, Rory Dall O'Cahan, who wrote 'Give me your hand' for the countess of Eglinton.[54]

## Learning

While the classical world reinforced an attraction for country living and traditional values, a humanist education also inspired enquiry about a world extending beyond the country estate. Like other Renaissance thinkers, James VI believed education was a lifetime experience, fed by a delight in reading morally uplifting texts. Denmilne similarly believed that the liberal sciences enhanced nobility, recommending to a friend that he read for at least an hour each morning. He highlighted religious texts along with history, enthusiastically advising lord Elcho to read everything three times, 'first to see ther Method, next ther matter and lastly to gather instructions'. Gordonstoun recommended history, cosmography and geography, seeing reading as a discipline: 'Reid choysed and approved authours, not confusedlie a piece of one then a piece of ane other, for the turning over of dyvers volumes togidder breids confusion'. Nor should knowledge be kept to oneself, and the young earl of Sutherland was exhorted to create an outpost of learning in his library at Dornoch, filling it with 'sufficient store of books, boith for your credit and the weel of this countrey, to amend ther ignorance which increases through laik of bookes'. This pursuit of private learning was vigorously upheld by the first lord Balcarres, an enthusiastic devourer of natural philosophy who believed 'that day misspent on which he knew not a new thing'.[55]

When Napier of Merchiston was painted in 1616, he was portrayed as a scholar seated in his study, his hand resting on one of a number of books scattered on a table where there is also a globe, his expression one of serious contemplation. Not all nobles were as studious as Merchiston, but increasingly the construction of libraries in castles provided private, physical places where educated men drew apart not only to relax, but also to enter the world of the intellect, cultivating their learning. Ancram advised his son that a small study with book cabinets was 'so necessary that it can not be found wanting for a man that understands these things'. The serious collection of books did not become common until the seventeenth century, but even in the mid-sixteenth century significant private libraries had been accumulated by some individuals.[56] Most works were imported, but domestic printers met a steady demand for volumes like *The Seven Sages*, adapted in Scots by John Rolland, a client of the regent Morton, and sufficiently popular to be printed six times between 1578 and 1631. John Barbour's metrical poem, the *Buik of the Most Valzeand Conquerour Alexander the Great*, was first printed in Edinburgh by Alexander Arbuthnot in 1582 and was stocked throughout the 1590s by the king's printer, Henry Charteris. He found a ready market for a range of patriotic, chivalric literature by Barbour, Blind Harry, Robert Henryson, Gavin Douglas and sir David Lindsay.[57] These popular books appealed to a noble readership but many nobles developed more sophisticated tastes. The first earl of Moray's library reflected the interests of a man 'weill learnit in humayne sciences', while his wife, Agnes Keith, continued to buy books regularly after his death. John Lyon, eighth lord Glamis, a bibliophile who made presents of books to the young king, was an excellent Latinist and informed theologian who read Theodore Beza's works 'with the utmost pleasure and admiration'. By the early seventeenth century, noble bibliophiles were more common. Some, like the second lord Melville, left evidence of catalogued libraries, while others like Gordonstoun, whose library extended to 2000 books, including both religious works and French romances, not only collected but read their books. At his death in 1633, the first earl of Buccleuch had a library of 1200 volumes, valued at £2666 13s 4d, predominantly in Latin, Italian and French with a smaller number in English and fourteen volumes in Spanish. Not surprisingly, for a man who was a professional soldier, the most common theme was warfare and military science, including mathematics, horsemanship and history. Ancram was a collector of French titles and was followed in this enthusiasm by his son. In the Highlands, sir Duncan Campbell of Glenorchy read popular histories, while his mother, Catherine Ruthven, shared the enthusiasm of the house of Gowrie for reading. His son, sir Colin, was fluent in Latin and read works in French and Italian, often scribbling Latin and Italian apophthegms in the margins of his volumes.[58] Books were relatively inexpensive items and buyers varied in their purchasing habits, from an occasional buyer like the fourth lord Elphinstone, who spent modestly on books when he made his visits to Edinburgh, to Ancram, who used continental contacts to scour foreign book markets; for example, in 1617 he asked a friend with the embassy in Spain to get a book praised by Cervantes. Travel brought opportunities for purchasing less easily obtained books. Patrick Gray, master of Gray, supplied lord Hamilton with gifts of books during his exile in Paris at the end of the 1580s. Forty years later, Hawthornden used his prolonged continental tour to stock a library that amounted to some 1600 books, an impressive and eclectic collection gathered from Europe's great publishing centres at Frankfurt, Paris, Lyon and Venice.[59]

Scotland's sixteenth-century nobles were surprisingly slow to patronise writers. The first book published in the Gaelic language was the Protestant *Book of Common Order*, translated by John Carswell, superintendant of Argyll, with the support of the fifth earl of Argyll. The earls of Argyll were the most important patrons of Gaelic poets, and in the MacEwan family they had household poets, bards and sennachies, or genealogists, who ran a bardic school and whose principal function was to praise the Clan Campbell.[60] Outside this Highland tradition, the civil war of the 1560s and

1570s brought to the fore a new generation of writers, men like Robert Sempill and George Buchanan, but thereafter there was a slow development of literary patronage. Scattered instances of dedications and poetry can be identified in the later sixteenth century but the sum total is unimpressive.[61] After 1603, even the most accomplished of English poets, like Samuel Daniel and John Donne, sought the approval of Scottish courtiers like Ancram, who placed himself at the centre of a circle of diverse British writers on medical, religious and political topics, but these were isolated examples.[62]

While Scottish nobles never approached the literary achievements of the Venetian nobility, as in England there was a growing body of nobles who were respected writers and scholars in their own right.[63] Lethington was a collector and composer of poems, an enthusiasm he passed on to his son, chancellor Thirlestane, who wrote 'The earl of Northumberland', while William Fowler dedicated his translation of 'The triumphs of Petrarke' to lady Thirlestane in 1587. James VI was a decent enough poet and gathered around himself the Castalian band of poets in the 1590s, among whom were John Stewart of Baldynneis, a minor Perthshire nobleman. After 1603, royal patronage moved to London from where minor nobles like sir William Alexander of Menstrie, who wrote voluminously in the Senecan tradition, sir David Murray of Gothrie, and Ancram, all continued to exert a significant literary influence.[64] These courtier intellectuals were not divorced from a native country-house culture of amateur noble poets. In 1625, Ancram's fellow borderer, sir Patrick Hume of Polwarth, with whom he exchanged books and views on poetry, complained that his own writing was getting nowhere since he was too busy with the 'combersome office of shereffchep'. Ancram's eldest son, the third earl of Lothian, jotted down hundreds of maxims over the course of his life and built up his own considerable library. The old feuding rivals of the Kers, the Scotts, gave financial backing in 1634 to Mr Alexander Gibson, younger of Durie, 'for putting of the Scottis poeteis to the press, and that in respect thair is ane speciall peis thairin upoune this Erle of Buccleuch'.[65] This literary society of border nobles, to which one should add David Hume of Godscroft, was not unique. Sir John Scott of Scotstarvit stirred up local enthusiasm in Fife in 1615 for a project to collect and publish 'our Scottish poets, in the imitation of the French and Italians'. This was finally published in Amsterdam in 1637 under the title *Delitiae Poetarum Scotorum*. In Ayrshire, Rowallan produced a good translation of 'Dido and Aeneas' as well as a range of love and religious poetry.[66] But the most accomplished of these gentlemen poets was Hawthornden, a man with a European reputation, in spite of his determination to remain in Lothian from where he kept up a wide range of contacts at court and locally.[67] Perhaps the most unusual mind of the period was that of sir Thomas Urquhart of Cromarty, whose anodyne *Epigrams* were published in London in 1641 with a dedicatory epistle to the third marquis of Hamilton, concealing the more flamboyant and bizarre outpourings that would appear over the next two decades.[68]

History, especially Roman history, offered the key for the private man seeking moral exemplars, and it encouraged nobles to seek out a life of public service, equipping them with the rules of government and patriotic inspiration. It was praised by James VI and by Denmilne, who conventionally described history as 'the eyie of humane knowledge and the mirror quherin you may cleirly behold the passages of all ages'. Lothian too approved the idea that history should be read, so that 'one may as by looking in a glasse order his life, words, actions and thoughts'.[69] Scottish élites were exposed to the classical legacy common to most of Europe, but they also knew their own history, public debate being littered with references to history, much of which was drawn from the hugely popular Hector Boece.[70] Of course, history was a dangerous subject. When in October 1560 an ailing Lethington compiled a short *Table of the Kingis of Scotland*, he had no intention of attracting attention, 'becaus in thir dayes I think parell to mell with materis of grit importance'. Hawthornden's *History of Scotland*, dedicated to the second earl of Perth, also stopped well short of his own times. By contrast, George Buchanan's noble patrons wanted a contemporary history to justify their version of queen Mary's reign, his 1582 *Historia Scotorum* being outlawed by her son. The fifth lord Herries was also determined to explain recent events. He began an account of Mary's reign, collecting source material that was used by his great-grandson to complete the work. The first earl of Haddington was another avid collector of documents, mostly government records from the fifteenth century to his own times, although he never shaped these into a narrative. Only in sir James Melville of Halhill's *Memoirs* is there a glimpse of the inner, reflective self awakened by the Renaissance.[71]

Between national histories and Halhill's biography was the family history, and when sir Anthony Weldon observed that the Scots 'all know their pedigrees well enough' he was highlighting one of the great enthusiasms of the age.[72] Early modern society was intensely interested in genealogy, particularly from the early seventeenth century when scholarly research was extended by enthusiasts like sir Gilbert Dugdale in England and Denmilne in Scotland. It was an age when noble families demonstrated a new level of historical consciousness, placing the lineage and its individual members in a context that advertised their noble worthiness, drawing attention to those exemplars of blood, virtue, longevity and martial exploits that legitimised their nobility. However, one should not underestimate the recreational aspect of family history for intellectuals like Rowallan, who wrote a history of the Mures.[73] A baronial family like the Maules of Panmure demonstrated a voracious appetite for antiquarian research that embraced national and family history. Robert Maule of Panmure was an 'expert in countine of genealogies'; his grandson, Henry Maule of Melgum, was the author of a history of the Picts; another grandson, Robert Maule, commissary of St Andrews, wrote a family history as well as a Latin treatise *De Antiquitate Gentis Scotorum*; and a great-grandson, sir Patrick Maule of Panmure, compiled a history of William Wallace. Even the women of the family were steeped in history, and Margaret Haliburton, wife of Thomas Maule of Panmure, 'delytit mikil to talk of auld histories, [and] knewe the heale genealogie of hir father's hous, as also of her mothers'.[74] Noble families, like the Maules, set great store by compiling genealogies that served as a record of their ancestry. The 'Genealogy of the illustrious family of the Hamiltons' was compiled in the mid-1640s at a time when patriotic credentials were particularly necessary; this unpublished work claimed that the family arrived in Scotland in 1307. Such material might be represented architecturally or in other visual forms, as when in 1635 sir Colin Campbell of Glenorchy employed George Jamesone to devise and paint a genealogy modelled on the *Tree of Jesse* in a style that combines the iconic with the decorative. Some of this enthusiasm was fed merely by a fashion for the archaic, and in one infamous case genealogical research led to disgrace when the seventh earl of Menteith joked that his claim to the crown might be better than that of Charles I.[75]

The most sophisticated family histories were produced for the Gordons and the Douglases. The house of Huntly found its first historian in John Ferrerius, an Italian who dedicated a short, sketchy history of the Gordons to the fourth earl of Huntly in 1545. From the 1590s there was a stream of histories, collections and geneaologies centred around the Gordon kindred and the life of the first marquis of Huntly, while many cadet houses spawned their own accounts. Gordonstoun's focus was the related house of Sutherland. He began to research the family history while residing in Salisbury, writing home to his brothers for documentation and putting together genealogical tables of the principal Gordon families. His history is written in the tradition of neo-Stoic philosophy and he claimed an empirical rigour in his research, deploying documentary evidence and first-hand oral accounts but ignoring 'all forged auntient traditions and whatsoever els bairds and rymers (delyting in decayed antiquitie) doo religiouslie father upon tymes out of mynd'. Nevertheless, while his methodology was relatively sound, Gordonstoun was not above seeing magical portents in nature.[76] The principal Douglas historian was Godscroft, secretary to the eighth earl of Angus, who cut his teeth on a 1611 Latin history of his own Hume kindred. Although Godscroft was commissioned by the tenth earl of Angus, his *History of the House of Douglas and Angus* was not in circulation until 1633–4. He drew on historians like Boece, Buchanan and Holinshed, and also utilised record sources, bemoaning the vandalism of Edward I who destroyed so many Scottish records. Nevertheless, this exercise in encouraging moral improvement by way of history's 'bright mirror' required some embellishment of the truth. Godscroft, therefore, glorified the Douglases, his narrative being 'illustrat everie where, with manie precepts of moral vertues'. The eleventh earl of Angus revised the work, removing politically sensitive material prior to publication in 1644. Meanwhile, the earl's own historical interests led in the 1620s to correspondence with a number of Italian nobles claiming Douglas ancestry, one of whom, count Marc Antonio Scoto d'Agazano, claimed that his own house, the Scoti of Piacenza, was decended from a Douglas ancestor who entered Italy with Charlemagne.[77]

Closely related to history and genealogy was the science of heraldry, which aroused great passions among the nobilities of the late medieval and early modern period. Heraldry offered a means of regulating honour under the jurisdiction of the lord lyon king of arms and his officers, and sir David Lindsay's 1542 *Register* remained influential as an armorial guide, being given privy council approval in 1630. New works included the *Hamilton Armorial*, produced for the third earl of Arran in the early 1560s; the *Dunvegan Memorial*, which was probably the work of James VI's multi-talented master-mason, William Shaw; the *Seton Armorial*, made in 1591 for the fifth lord Seton; and the *Armorial Register*, created between 1598 and 1600 by sir David Lindsay of the Mount. Denmilne also collected and preserved manuscripts of arms during his tenure as lord lyon. These badges provided a shorthand insight into a family's history. Thus Lethington boasted that the Gordon house of Huntly was decended from his patrons, the Setons, pointing out that 'to verifie the samin, they [the Gordons] weir the armes of the hous of Seytoun in ane quarter of thair schield'. This interest was far from parochial. Sir Robert Melville of Murdocairny possessed an attractive manuscript book of English heraldry with genealogical notes on the English peerage, acquired on a visit to Elizabeth I's court. A similar international interest was often displayed on painted ceilings, where heraldic devices from around Europe were placed alongside those of native families advertising their noble credentials.[78]

While heraldry was the most popular science, it was by no means the only form of scientific enquiry. A fascination with alchemical sciences grew over the course of the sixteenth century, and the early seventeenth-century court was much influenced by neo-Platonic ideas about forms of intellectual magic, often expressed in emblematics.[79] The fifth earl of Bothwell had an abiding interest in hermeticism gleaned from his travels in Italy as a young man, and his alleged interest in witchcraft might have grown out of those experiences. The Ruthven family too had a persistent association with the occult sciences over three generations, and the third earl of Gowrie's astrological enquiries were possibly stimulated during his time as a student at Padua where he studied the cabbala, being able to read Hebrew. It was said he explored methods of devining the future and other esoteric sciences. The painted ceiling at Prestongrange house, completed in 1581 for Mark Ker, commendator of Newbattle, contained obscene figures and symbols, some of the former being based on *Songes Drolatiques de Pantagruel*, published in

Paris in 1565. His son, the first earl of Lothian, who also studied in Italy and Paris, was rumoured to have an interest in the occult. The family hobby continued in the person of the suicide second earl of Lothian, yet another product of the suspect Italian schools. He was a student of astrology and was joined in his investigations by William Douglas of Tofts, 'a gentleman of a good spirit, generous, and learned *in omni scibili*, especially in the mathematicks, wherein he had attained to so great a perfection that he had no equal in his own countrey, perhaps few in Christendome'. However, esoteric and dangerous interests were shunned by the great majority of the nobility, who were more likely to be found stamping out witchcraft.[80]

Many sixteenth-century nobles shared the magical world view of a writer like Pitscottie, who believed in the significance of comets or strange happenings, like the birth of deformed children, as signs of the times.[81] However, a more rational enquiry was espoused by some nobles. James VI wrote a book about witchcraft, *Daemonologie* (1597), but was disparaging of those who interpreted dreams, and the third earl of Lothian despised astrologers, noting that they were intolerably arrogant. Cromarty was particularly sceptical of magic, maddening the local clergy during the 1630s with his rational interventions and dismissing all superstition as 'the trivial tattle of idly imployed and shallow braind humorists'.[82] The point of contact between Pitscottie's mid-sixteenth-century world of magic and Cromarty's more recognisably scientific method of thought two generations later was blurred. John Napier of Merchiston was one of a number of Scottish intellectuals, including Robert Pont and James Maxwell, who shared an interest in an arcane world of magic, astrology, prophecy and mathematics. These men had close contacts with the court and their science attracted the interest of other nobles, informing a wider vernacular audience that was drawn to freemasonry. Undoubtedly Merchiston was the most profound scientific scholar Scotland produced at this time, his most enduring work being the 1612 *Minifici Logarithmorum Canonis Descriptio*. Merchiston's scientific circle included chancellor Dunfermline, whose architectural interests inspired a shared enthusiasm for geometry. He kept Dunfermline informed of his discoveries which were designed to facilitate numeric calculations ('Napier's Bones'): hence his groundbreaking book on logarithms, as well as the less successful numerating rods, or rhabdologia, the promtuary of multiplication, his local arithmetic, a form of calculating on a chess board, and inventions like a hydraulic screw for removing water from mines and a burning mirror for destroying ships from land. Sir John Skene of Curriehill was also acquainted with the nature of Merchiston's studies, seeking his advice on questions of measurement. Cromarty's curiously obscure *The Trissotetras*, published in London in 1645, demonstrated that he too was versed in mathematical sciences. This northerly nobleman was scornful of the local hunting fraternity, preferring to spend his time investigating:

> optical secrets, mysteries of natural philosophie, reasons for the variety of colours, the finding of the longitude, the squaring of a circle, and wayes to accomplish all trigometrical calculations by sines, without tangents, with the same compendiousness of computation.

Here was a different mind from the historian Denmilne who, when faced with the mathematical challenges of astronomy, 'lay prostrat at the Almighties power', admiring 'his wisdoome in the motione, and adore his goodnesse in the present apparitione'.[83]

## Conclusion

For a martial nobility there had always been powerful reasons for encouraging a culture that enhanced its military image. Living in castles was in part a legacy of that tradition, and Scottish architecture continued to draw attention to the war-like purpose of residences, even in the early seventeenth century when that purpose was no longer essential. Hunting and sporting activities also continued to reflect something of that martial ethos. Much of the nobility's sense of its own identity was about being a landed élite who lived in castles, obsessed with their horses and weapons, chasing deer and searching for lost golf balls. However, the impact of the Renaissance on education, and on élite society in general, meant that the cultural values of the nobility had become more complex and more refined. Like nobles everywhere, the Scots were persuaded to refashion themselves to take account of the rediscovered learning, cultivating the attributes of Roman gentlemen. That process had been going on for most of the sixteenth century, and within that context the regal union of 1603 was relatively insignificant, bringing little in the way of anglicisation and making no great difference to contacts between Scottish nobles and European culture. Although the evidence is less impressive for Gaelic society, it is clear that Renaissance ideas had permeated the world of the Highland nobility, who also continued to be patrons of their own distinctive brand of culture. Increasingly, nobles were expected to be familiar with a broad range of learning, to have cultivated tastes, to be patrons of artists, and to be at ease in the richly textured world of Renaissance thought. Of course, just because nobles were expected to be gentlemen with all these characteristics it did not mean that Scotland was dominated by an élite of philosopher magistrates. Some individuals, like chancellor Dunfermline, did attain a remarkable level of philosophical enlightenment; many others no doubt conformed to fashion with no reflection on what it all meant. One should be careful, therefore, of assuming that these rich men were embracing an artist's vision simply because they bought the artistic product.

Nevertheless, in spite of this caveat, the nobility came to accept a range of ideas that shaped their culture. Country living was underpinned by a glorification of the natural world and by a profound commitment to open hospitality, allowing the castle to be either a place of retreat or a centre of activity. The desire to make these places comfortable and attractive led to a remarkable architectural flowering, while both external and internal décor was manipulated to display not just power but also refinement and learning. Furthermore, the allocation of space for reading, music and paintings was functional, not merely fashionable, since it is clear that nobles did read their growing collections of books, or listen to and even play music. The idea of the noble scholar was taken seriously, and while there was only one Merchiston and only one Hawthornden, there were many who dabbled in science or poetry and devoured history. Noble society in Scotland had its own cultural idiosyncrasies, like the painted ceiling or the patronage of the clarsach-playing bards, indications of a self-confident and relaxed national identity, while being simultaneously tuned into the main currents of European culture.

CHAPTER 10

# Religion

It has become fashionable in recent years to underplay the radical nature and impact of the Scottish Reformation.[1] Yet the events of 1559–60 were sudden, dramatic and epoch-making, unleashing ideas and forces that did not begin to wain until the mid-eighteenth century. One key to unlocking the successful progress of that revolution in religious ideas lies in an understanding of the faith of the nobility, those godly magistrates in whom Protestant reformers placed so much hope. Hence the emphasis by John Knox and others on targetting nobles in the evangelistic missions of the 1550s, or the general assembly's pronouncement in October 1572 that 'in the reformatioun of the Nobilitie consistis the chieff exampill of the haill cuntrie'.[2] It was an example that later Jesuit missions tried to emulate, channelling their energies into converting prominent nobles. However, those political struggles between Protestants and Catholics, or between church and crown, in which the nobility played such a decisive part, are not the subject of this chapter. Its focus is not the Reformation, the counter-Reformation or the origins of the Covenanters, but the religion of the nobility. Making such a distinction is not easy when the religion of the nobility was so intimately tied up with the course of Scotland's religious history at this time. In broad terms, the issue here is the personal faith and pious works of noblemen and their families, although faith was not a private matter in early modern society, especially for people of this rank, and public acts flowed from it. It would, however, be mistaken to imagine that all educated lay people left thinking about religion to the clergy, accepting new orthodoxies as they came along and implementing whatever policies were agreed between the king and the church without reflecting on what they were doing and why they were doing it. What has to be asked is how successful was the clergy in persuading the nobility to share its vision of a godly, reformed kirk and society? Clearly, in the case of Catholic nobles, the answer is not at all. Others responded with varying degrees of enthusiasm from the evangelical to the bored and uninterested. In seeking answers to such questions, one is faced with problematic evidence. Looking into men's souls is never easy, especially in an age when societal expectations required individuals to express conformity with the religion of their community. For nobles there was a particular responsibility to maintain religious order in their role as magistrates and to avoid making political miscalculations, both of which tended to discourage the translation of private religious views into public commitments. Such calculations contribute to an understanding of the religious orthodoxy of sixteenth-century French *parlementaires*, or of the lower nobility of Germany, wary of sacrificing the emperor's patronage. It also helps to explain how James VI could appoint the Catholic Alexander Seton, first earl of Dunfermline, as his chancellor in 1604.[3] There is also the problem that those who did leave evidence of their genuine religious enthusiasm were likely to have been atypical.

## Faith and Works

It is not difficult to point to nobles who in their lifetime were important leaders in their religious communities because of the force of their personalities and the immense territorial power of their house. Archibald Campbell, fifth earl of Argyll, was a crucial figure in securing the Protestant Reformation; Archibald Douglas, eighth earl of Angus, was a powerful friend of the Presbyterians in the 1580s; George Gordon, first marquis of Huntly, led the most dangerous Catholic rebellions of the 1590s; John Leslie, sixth earl of Rothes, consistently opposed the crown's ecclesiastical policies throughout the 1620s and 1630s. All these men were active politicians at the head of great magnate houses, whose politics were inspired to a greater or lesser extent by their religion. But while the outward actions are easily visible – Argyll was one of the Lords of the Congregation in 1559–60, Angus supported the Ruthven Raid in 1582, Huntly rebelled in 1594, Rothes voted against the Five Articles of Perth in 1621 – their private religious beliefs are less clear.[4] Political involvement necessarily muddies the waters, and motives become less pure or more complex when examined closely. When Henri IV of France again converted to Catholicism in 1593, it is unlikely that many people believed in the sincerity of his experience, even if they chose to recognise it as genuine, and it is not altogether clear what lay people, even among the nobility, thought they were doing in changing their faith. After all, apologetics was essentially a matter for the clergy. The fourth earl Marischal's announcement of his conversion to Protestantism at the Reformation parliament in 1560 was prompted by the failure of the bishops to defend Roman Catholicism, leading him to conclude that the Protestants must be right.[5]

Like Henri IV, many nobles formed their religious allegiances for reasons that were not in themselves wholly religious, although these need not have been as blatantly political as to gain a throne. For a nobility, the emphasis on spiritual élitism that is characteristic of most evangelical Protestantism could heighten their own sense of hierarchy. It is certainly unlikely that more than a handful of sixteenth-century nobles were theologically literate, and while the eighth lord Glamis could correspond about doctrinal issues with Theodore Beza, such expertise was rare.[6] Marischal's no-nonsense pragmatism is likely to have been more common than Glamis's intellectual sophistication. Even a generation later, David Calderwood was astonished at the condemned second earl of Orkney's lack of awareness of religious fundamentals, he being 'so ignorant, that he could scarce rehearse the Lord's Prayer'. A delay in the execution of this condemned traitor followed while the ministers ensured Orkney went to the block adequately informed. However, given the growing grip of Calvinist ideas among the Scottish clergy, for whom even the early fathers were suspect, it is likely that by the early seventeenth century at the latest, the informed Protestant laity were uniting around a Calvinist consensus.[7]

Unpacking what early modern people believed from conventional expressions of religious conformity is difficult. Following his return from Europe in 1582, the fifth earl of Bothwell appeared before the general assembly to declare 'he would live and dee in the reformed religion professed within this realme'. Of course, Bothwell was unlikely to say anything else, and all such formal public statements of belief are suspect. There is room for scepticism in reading the pre-execution confession of the fourth earl of Morton, a man who demonstrated a keen desire to be assured of salvation at a moment when he was about to be confronted with the source of his beliefs.[8] Those thoughts of the dying preserved in testaments reveal relatively little since such documents were overwhelmingly secular in content, the religious element often being formulaic; they were concerned with the disposal of movable assets and were often drawn up years in advance. Nevertheless, wills are not entirely useless and something of the religious views of the élite society of Ayrshire and Angus has been gleaned from meagre testamentary evidence.[9] One of the earliest Protestant lords, the fourth earl of Argyll, died in 1558 'most constant in the trew faith of Jesus Christ, with a plane renunciatioun of all impietie, superstitioun, and idolatrie'. He urged his son to 'study to set fordwarte the publict and trew preaching of the Evangell of Jesus Christ, and to suppress all superstitioun and idolatrie, to the uttermost of his power'. Unfortunately, statements of what became the new orthodoxy might indicate very little. The testament of the fourth earl of Atholl, who died in 1578, 'recommends my sauld to the mercie of God and Jesus Christ his Son, who sched His blude upon the Croce for me and all mankind', but one has to be careful not to read too much into this religious fence-sitter's apparent understanding of the redemptive power of the cross. A generation later, lord Menmuir's will ran the whole gamut of Protestant theology from confession through redemption to assurance.[10] Catholic testaments were often little different, probably because they had no desire to draw attention to any theological dissent in a legal document. The first lord Balmerino, who died in 1612, made a simple and uncontroversial statement, committing 'my saull to Goddis eternell mercy, to enjoy that immortell inheritance conquesit to me by the merit and pretious blood of my blesed redeimer, Christ Jesus'.[11]

When Lethington encouraged the Catholic fifth lord Seton in his walk with God 'as becummis the dewtie of ane gude and faythfull cristin man', it is unlikely he had a precise view of how that walk should be conducted.[12] Besides, Lethington's mid-sixteenth-century Christian humanism was being replaced by a more rigorous Protestantism, soon to be paralleled by post-Tridentine Catholicism, both of which required greater self-discipline, study and contemplation. In addition to communal observances, the evangelical eighth earl of Angus was 'Giffen to reiding, and privat prayer and meditation', favouring the recent Latin translations of the Bible by John Immanuel Tremellius and Franciscus Junius that were fashionable in Calvinist circles. The 'Good Earl', as he was to be remembered, admitted 'I wald be hartlie content to spend all my lyff in this esteat and forme,' a pious wish his rank and power denied him.[13] Such enthusiasm for the printed word was present from the beginning of the Reformation in Scotland. As early as the 1540s the fourth earl of Glencairn allowed his name to be used as author of the satirical 'Epistle directit fra the holye armite of Allarit to his brethern the Grey Freiris', while the regent Moray collected religious books, creating a substantial working library.[14] That commitment to the religious book as an aid to personal devotion increased in the seventeenth century. Lilias Murray, the dowager lady Freuchie, made a list c.1630 of twenty-eight religious books which she owned, a sizeable little library for the wife of a lesser baron living out most of her life on Speyside. The sixth earl of Rothes exchanged books by authors like John White with Ancram at court and with the Presbyterian historian, William Scott, minister at Cupar.[15] Godly nobles and their families were singled out by authors of religious works for dedications. Robert Norvell's *The Merroure of an Christiane* (1561), among the earliest Protestant books published in Scotland, was dedicated to the fifth earl of Argyll. In the 1625 *Godly Man's Journey to Heaven*, David Lindsay, minister at Leith, dedicated his work to a number of patrons he regarded as friends of the kirk, including Anna Ker, lady Balmerino, and her husband, the young second lord Balmerino, a future Covenanter leader and already regarded as 'shining as a most bright light above so many'.[16] Here was a book-buying élite for whom works of a devotional and theological nature were becoming the staple diet of their reading.

Emphasis was placed on memorising responses and biblical texts. Alexander Lindsay, younger of Balcarres, wrote home from the university of St Andrews to his father in February 1628, enthusiastically relating that his tutor had promised him a box of books as a reward for being able to answer 'the little book of questions on the Byble perqueir [= by heart]'. Such study had as its purpose the instruction of the mind, providing a guide to moral actions, but it had to be undertaken in a disciplined manner. Gordonstoun advised his nephew to follow a course of daily bible reading and of informed self-examination 'of all your last dayes actions, what you have committed that you should not, or omitted that yee should do, either in your Christian or worldlie calling'.[17] Unfortunately, the laity wrote little about religion, this properly being the domain of the clergy, and many must have shared the view of the third earl of Lothian that 'Evangelical learning came not into the world by human discovery or observation ... but by divine revelation'. While significant numbers of nobles pursued spiritual understanding in reading and in private study, the only insights one has to more profound thinking by laymen on the nature of their belief is among a handful of intellectuals, like Alexander Montgomery, Ancram or Rowallan, who wrote religious poetry and translated the Psalms.[18]

More commonly, perhaps, religious instruction was acquired at public worship, in which the preaching of the word was central. Mr Patrick Galloway, minister at Perth, vainly speculated that one reason for the first earl of Gowrie's unpopularity at court in the early months of 1584 arose from the fact that 'his Lordship resortit daylie to my sermons'. Perth remained a centre for good preaching, and in 1635 the second viscount Stormont negotiated the lease of the laird of Glenorchy's town house so that he and his wife might be 'neir the kirk quhar wie heire gud sermonis'. But the enthusiasm of Gowrie and Stormont for sermon-going might not have been typical. In 1585, an English observer noted the contrast between the eighth earl of Angus and lord Hamilton, both regular church-goers, with the behaviour of the king and most of his young courtiers who preferred to go hunting. Kirk session records are unhelpful in building up a more informed picture than these anecdotes permit. Only occasionally do they make mention of the attendance of the patron or other powerful individuals, as when on 14 September 1628 the first earl of Haddington was present in Tyninghame parish church with all his family, the event possibly being so rare as to require that it be recorded.[19]

Patrick Galloway also recounted how in June 1582 his sermon was repeatedly interrupted by the first duke of Lennox, a French Catholic who did not appreciate his style of straight talking. The duke 'did plainlie minasse me in the pulpit, and called me pultron, villane, mischant, with manie other injurious words, and threatened to thrust me through with a rapper, till his Majestie himself was compelled to lay his hand on his mouth and stay his furie and malicious language'. Others, no doubt, shared Lennox's irritation at ministers whose sermons appeared subversive. But the crucial role of nobles as community leaders explains the church's determination to encourage their attendance at services. Hence in 1593, the presbytery of Tranent's condemnation of the Catholic sixth lord Seton as 'ane ill frequenter of the kirk'. Three years later, the presbytery of Glasgow took the view that the reason many people in the parish of Lenzie did 'byd away fra the kirk to heir

Godis word preichit on the Sondaye' was due to the absence of the sixth lord Fleming.[20]

The kirk was even more concerned to influence the next generation of nobles. In the mid-sixteenth century, Lethington exhorted his patron, the Catholic fifth lord Seton, to 'bring up thy bairnis in vertu, science, and knawledge of God'. Although medieval nobles commonly employed chaplains, the origins of household worship lay in the days of the underground privy kirks. When during his 1556 evangelistic tour of Scotland, John Knox visited the home of the fourth earl of Glencairn, he officiated at a clandestine communion for the earl, his wife, two of their sons and a number of friends of the family. Furthermore, the 1561 *First Book of Discipline* followed Martin Bucer in recognising that due to the deficiencies in the post-Reformation organisation of religious instruction, the masters of households would have an essential role in instructing children in 'the principalls of the Christian Religion'. At its most elementary level, these household activities involved chaplains in the instruction of children, who Protestants believed had a degree of responsibility for their own faith. When the first earl of Wigton was a child in the 1570s, his tutor was the fiery radical, Mr Archibald Simpson, who threatened to whip the boy when he addressed a bishop as 'my lord'.[21]

Unfortunately, there is no distinct Scottish literature of advice on the topic of household worship, and it is not known whether books like *A Godly Form of Household Government*, published in London in 1598 by the English puritan Robert Cleaver, were in circulation. Certainly Protestant households operated along the informal lines typical in England rather than like the formal household consistories found among French Huguenots. Calvinist households provided instruction and facilitated sanctification for all their members, acting as agents of change in a locality and providing a point of contact between national and local issues and individuals. The impact of this godly instruction as an instrument of mass indoctrination has been questioned, but something of its fruits can be gauged from the generational conformity that characterised militant Protestant or steadfastly Catholic families over decades. Certainly in the case of the one Protestant household that has been studied, that of the fifth earl of Argyll, its effectiveness as an evangelistic tool throughout Campbell territories was impressive.[22] According to George Buchanan, the regent Moray's household was like 'a holy temple ... free from impiety ... [and] from improper conversation', a description repeated by other writers. Political flattery created an exaggerated picture of Moray's piety but the clergy's expectations of a model household were high, as is apparent in the formal arrangements made for the 'godly' eighth earl of Angus during his Newcastle exile in 1584–5. This strict 'Ordor and Maner of Exercise of the Word for Instruction and Discipline for Correction of Maners' was drawn up by clerical refugees, including Andrew Melville, then serving as Angus's chaplain. More mundane evidence comes from the early 1570s, from John Davidson, regent of St Salvator's college at the university of St Andrews, who enthused over the 'good exemple of pietie and holie exercise' in the household of a minor Ayrshire baron, Robert Campbell of Kinzeancleuch and his wife, who inspired him to write a 'Memorial of the Life and Death of two worthye Christians'.[23]

From its beginnings, women were involved in the Scottish Reformation, in the underground church before 1560 and thereafter in consolidating its work. As wives and mothers, as well as powerful landlords, noblewomen had important roles to play in the spiritual lives of their families, households and estates. The Protestant convictions of the house of Edzell were shaped by the dominant role of Catherine Campbell, dowager countess of Crawford, who took an active interest in her sons' education. In a book modelled on a work of sir Philip Sidney and dedicated to the countess of Pembroke, James Caldwell's 1625 volume, *The Countess of Mar's Arcadia*, celebrated a woman who was 'a true Paterne of modest Pietie, a perfect mirror of feminine gravitie, and a liberall supplier of the necessities of the poore'. Similarly, in the dedication of his 1632 book, *An Exposition of the Ceremoniall Lawes of Moses*, Mr John Wemyss, minister at Kinnaird, commended Ancram's mother, Margaret Dundas, who had supervised his godly upbringing, commenting 'Good cause have you to keepe that methode, as yee have begun it in your eldest Sonne'. However, in the 1599 edition of *Hymnes or Sacred Songs*, dedicated to Elizabeth Melville, lady Cumrie, the author of the inspirational 'Ane godlie dreame', Alexander Hume was critical of noblewomen in general. Hume bemoaned the fact that few of them shared lady Cumrie's pious devotion, but instead 'delite mair in covetousnes and in oppression of the puire for the intertainement of their pride, or else to spend their dayes in chambering, wantones, decking of their bodies in delicat feeding, and in satisfying their lustes'.[24]

The church intended that the godly households in which these women had their greatest influence would enhance hierarchic and paternal authority, but the social dynamic of the household could be unsettled. Protestant family worship often amplified the role of women, and as in French Huguenot or English Puritan communities, wives and mothers played prominent roles in organising and supervising religious observances, often acquiring a moral influence beyond that expected of them.[25] A dying Marion Guthrie, the pious wife of lord Menmuir, told her husband to beware the influence on their children of his rich and godless friends, a strong indication that she thought him easily led. In 1629, Anna Livingston, countess of Eglinton, was converted to an evangelical faith by the underground presbyterian preacher, Robert Bruce. Her days as a 'formall Christian' now being ended, the countess became an active supporter of dissidents in Ayrshire and Ulster, using her household to promote their religious views. However, she was anxious about the fate of her husband, illiciting from

Bruce the unsympathetic observation that 'Suppose ye be unequallie yoked, it is for your guid and for your humiliation'; he therefore urged her to pray. Such tension in a marriage raised questions about a husband's authority; hence Bruce's reinforcement of patriarchal values. Another of Bruce's dissident colleagues, John Livingston, was supported by Catherine Erskine, lady Binning, whose husband could only bring himself to accept her behaviour as an involuntary reaction to the workings of the spirit rather than to independent thought.[26]

Nobles also had a responsibility to their servants, and from his death-bed in 1634 the first viscount Kenmure reminded those who served him that they could not claim ignorance of the Gospel, since 'I discharged myself in that point toward you, and appointed a man to teach you'. Kenmure interviewed each of his servants, begging their forgiveness if he had ever treated them harshly. It would be premature to suggest that godly households eroded hierarchy, but there was something remotely egalitarian in the observance of common religious exercises before God. An absence of deference is apparent in the general assembly's observation in March 1596 that bible reading and prayer were not widely practised in households because servants were so resistant that 'the maister of the famileis [were] ashamed to use thir exercises of godlinesse in their owne persons, and no conference at their tables, but of profane and wordlie maters'. It is possible that nobles used their servants' behaviour as an excuse to deflect the criticism of the clergy, but the church was not easily fooled and there might have been popular discontent at attempts by nobles to impose Protestant religious instruction on their more conservative servants. On the other hand, many nobles were dismissive of church strictures, James VI's household being attacked for the absence of religious exercises and the tolerance of ungodly cursing and dancing.[27]

For early modern people, religion was not a private matter, and for nobles especially their religious commitment had public significance. They were expected to cooperate as godly magistrates in promoting the kirk's doctrinal and moral teaching among a populace generally unenthusiastic about either. Indeed, the kirk's promotion of the idea of a territorial nobility taking on the responsibilities of a godly magistracy was for the former one of the attractions of Protestantism. At the same time, the church's desire to impose a national programme of confessionalisation often ran up against the local power of the nobility and their families. Therefore, the nature of religious change in a locality was much determined by the attitude of its nobles, a pattern repeated elsewhere; for example, in Elizabethan Suffolk. This harnessing of noble energy is evident in Carrick, where in April 1568 the recently converted fourth earl of Cassillis was instructed by the regent Moray to investigate recusancy. In 1638, Cassillis's grandson was appointed by the presbytery of Ayr as one of its ruling elders to attend the Glasgow assembly that would overthrow the episcopalian order in the church.[28] The continuity of the involvement of the earls of Cassillis in local church affairs was important in shaping the religion of that locality, and it was here that the nobility performed their most valuable role in creating God's kingdom on earth.

Crucial to this local involvement was the nobility's jurisdictional authority. On 30 January 1586, the barony court of Calder sentenced George Tennent to:

> cum and stand at the pillar of repentance one Sonday nixt in the kirk of Calder and the nixt two Soundays thairefter the time of the haill sermondis without clok or wapin and ask forgivenes of God and the kirk for the offence committit be him one Sounday last in speking to the minister in pulpet.

Here the secular lord was working with the kirk session to enhance the authority of the church, as was the first lord Melville when in 1612 he decreed in his regality court of Monimail that the sale of ale would be forbidden during the time of church services. The crown often reinforced that partnership, as when in May 1624 the seventh earl of Menteith and three other landlords were empowered to arrest people making pilgrimages to Christ's well in the locality and if necessary to scourge them.[29] However, the cause of godliness often made slow progress, dependent on the attitude of the local lord, his kinsmen and friends, and their relations with the church courts. In February 1604, that old Reformer, the fifth earl of Morton, received a letter from the presbytery of Linlithgow thanking him for his offer to punish anyone within his regality of Caldercleir who was guilty of breaches of church discipline, an offer that made the presbytery wishful that 'we might have the lyk experience of all the nobilitie of this land'. In Stirling presbytery only one baron had bothered to write its rules concerning excommunication into his own court by the end of the sixteenth century.[30] In some localities, Catholic nobles were deliberately obstructive. At Tranent in 1588–9, the presbytery of Haddington had difficulty enforcing Sabbatarian principles because of the obstinacy of the sixth lord Seton, who was threatened with 'the hard measures of the kirk' if he did not move his market from a Sunday. Seton was a powerful lord, but lesser landlords increasingly had to take account of the church's views. In 1613, David Kennedy of Kirkhill was forced by Carrick presbytery to move his quarterly fair from a Sunday as it 'gaif verie grite occasioun of scandaill'. Even a peer like the young sixth earl of Rothes was obliged in 1611 to give assurances that he would remove obstacles to the attendance of his tenants at church services.[31]

For the church, the noble sinner presented a particularly intractable problem, especially as the rich and powerful were thought more vulnerable to sin. Surprisingly, perhaps, when the *First Book of Discipline* had taken the view that 'To discipline must all the estates within this Realm be subject, as well the Rulers, as they that are ruled,' the nobility offered no objection.[32] Working this out in practice, however, was controversial, and the church's teaching on the moral depravity of all men – David Lindsay told his socially mixed congregation that they were 'loathsomely stinking in the eyes of God' – cannot have been easily digestible by nobles. John Davidson specifically attacked the nobility for 'their blood[shed], their rease [= extreme bad temper or frenzy], their oppressioun of their owne tennants, and others weaker than themselves, sacriledge, whooredome, blasphemie, witchcraft, and all kinds of vice'. Even the milder James Melville told the eighth earl of Angus in 1584 that many nobles were 'defiled with sacriledge, swearing, blasphemie, blood, adultereis, reafe, and oppressioun'.[33]

Because the church was not satisfied with 'a general reformation', it targeted individuals and their vices in its courts, and the most common sins in noble society were sexual, or some form of religious or political dissent. Parish and presbytery records indicate a great deal of successful obstruction by nobles, and in many localities bitter power struggles developed between clergy and nobility. In Stirlingshire, the presbytery criticised the eighth earl of Errol and the third earl of Montrose, warning the latter in 1583 to co-operate in disciplining his servants or face discipline himself. During the 1590s, the presbytery of Glasgow made an unsuccessful effort to bring the fourth lord Semple to book for adultery, and the sixth lord Fleming was castigated for non-attendance at church.[34] The precociousness of these presbyteries is all the more startling when the social background of the clergy is taken into account. Hence the incredulity of an English agent in 1563 that 'the Lord treasurer of Scotland, for getting a woman with child, must on Sunday next, do open penance before the whole congregation' in Edinburgh. A decade later, sir Mathew Campbell of Loudon, sheriff of Ayr, was sentenced to do penance on three Sundays for his adultery. Prior to the fourth earl of Morton's execution in 1581, he publicly admitted to having been 'a filthy abuser of my bodie in the pleasing of the fleshe, given over much to the world and pleasures therof'. What the crowd saw and heard was a magnate stripped bare of his rank and confessing his sins to the world. This apparent inversion of the social order was again on display in 1589 at the public humiliation of the fifth earl of Bothwell, an event occasioned by his political vulnerability, exposing this great lord to the kirk's discipline and a hard-hitting sermon from Robert Bruce that was deeply critical of noble behaviour and the bonds of lordship.[35]

Not surprisingly, therefore, nobles found such censures an affront to their own honour and dignity and to that of their lineage. Attacks by nobles on ministers were not uncommon. In October 1595, the sixth lord Sommerville vented his displeasure on the minister of Libberton by throwing a knife at him in the churchyard.[36] What specifically provoked these assaults is unknown, but possibly anticlericalism was stimulated by the growing financial and jurisdictional confidence of the ministers. In some localities the problem was disguised by malleable bishops like James Paton, bishop of Dunblane, reprimanded by the general assembly in 1574 because he had failed to excommunicate the fourth earl of Atholl and his wife for their persistent Catholicism. Patrick Adamson, archbishop of St Andrews, voiced concerns ten years later in his 'Exhortation to the nobilitie of Scotland', pointing out that 'it is intollerable that your subjects and inferiours sould have place to controll your maners'. The threat to hierarchic relationships contained in such clerical admonitions was recognised in February 1587 when the privy council issued a proclamation forbidding ministers from slandering 'be worde or writt, privatlie or publiclie' the king, his nobility, councillors or laws, and during the 1590s nobles lost patience with outspoken clergy, withdrawing their support for the Presbyterian-inclined wing of the church.[37]

The restoration of bishops in the following decade helped to silence public criticism of nobles and their families. In October 1610, the presbytery of Glasgow heard a complaint from the sixth lord Boyd against Mr John Bell, minister of Cader, 'becaus of the ill will that he careis to him, abusis his tennentis baithe be worde and deid, and walde not gif thaim justice'. Boyd's evidence was sufficiently convincing for the archbishop of Glasgow to order a visitation of the parish. Another nobleman to feel aggrieved was sir David Lindsay of Edzell, who in July 1617 accused a minister of abusing the pulpit, taking into it 'your awn wardlie businesses, and if ye think ye be tuitchett in anie thing, incontinent it sall be proclaimet out of that place that sould be the chyr of veritie'. The nobility's growing control of church patronage after 1587 was also helpful in acting as a brake on clerical outbursts. Walter Tully, minister at Dalmeny, wrote to dame Annas Menteith, lady Dundas, c.1600 apologising for 'sum purposis haldin be me in pulpit'. He sought to excuse his comments, distancing himself from the congregation's interpretation of his sermon – 'we haif na lawis for thochts' – and assuring lady Dundas that he would never do anything to land her before a church court. The apologetic minister then reminded her to pay his stipend.[38]

## God and Mammon

In 1624, the bishop of Lismore lectured sir Duncan Campbell of Glenorchy on his refusal to provide a church located on a small island, or inch:

> Remember sir that seing God hes givin to you many myllis of landis and kepit one insche to him self, it is not gud to depryve him of that, least he depryve you of more; bot howevir, it is gud sir, that we all rememberit that sex or sevin foot will serve ilk one of us er it be long.[39]

The bishop's attempt to shame the baron of Glenorchy represented one small episode in a running battle between kirk and nobility that had its origins in 1560–1, when the financial proposals of the *First Book of Discipline* were rejected by the government. Even before the Reformation, noble houses like the Hamiltons had acquired many of the resources of the church, especially abbatial lands. After 1560, the process of secularisation accelerated, and John Knox could not hide his bitter disappointment at the nobles' refusal to surrender to the church the patrimony of the old benefice system, alleging that 'Thair was none within the Realme more unmercyfull to the poore Ministeris then war thei whiche had greatest rentis of the Churches'. John Davidson's 1573 tract, *A Dialogue Betwixt a Clerk and a Courteour. Concerning the State of the Parish Kirks in Scotland*, attacked the government's failure to address the problem with such ferocity that he had to flee into exile. His was a view echoed throughout succeeding decades by James Melville, David Calderwood and others.[40]

Here was the point at which enthusiasm for godly reform ran against the instinctive impetus in noble families to expand their landed possessions. And it was not only clerics who levelled such charges; lay Catholics and Protestants were also critical.[41] While the Reformation left the crown as the major ecclesiastical patron, over the succeeding decades that patronage was frittered away into the hands of the nobility, leaving ministers to despair at the likes of the regent Morton who presided over the 'destructione of the kirke'. In what amounted to a massive transfer of land into lay hands, the abbeys and the temporalities of the bishoprics were acquired by new owners employing a range of tactics from outright bullying to underhand dealings. By 1585, most of the higher ecclesiastical benefices were held either by nobles, or 'hirelings to noblemen' like Andrew Graham, bishop of Dunblane, who set in feu to the third earl of Montrose the entire lands of his bishopric, so angering Stirling presbytery it complained that 'ane thousand of our soverane Lordis commonis and pure people wilbe put to uter heirschip and extreme beggartie'.[42] Gordonstoun privately conceded that 'Few noble men in Scotland can frie themselfs from robbing of the church in some degrie', his own family having plundered the bishopric of Caithness. This Protestant noble slyly admitted that teinds and vicarages were the rightful property of the church, while arguing that these should be retained as long as the law allowed it and should only be returned to the kirk when a national policy was agreed. However, in the mean time, he advised the earl of Sutherland to finance the parish ministry and maintain church buildings.[43]

By the last quarter of the sixteenth century, most of the great ecclesiastical estates were in noble hands, and the grand vision of the early reformers gave way to a pragmatic desire to press nobles for the payment of stipends and the maintenance of church buildings. It was not uncommon for churches on former abbatial lands to have no ministers. There were complaints in the general assembly in 1583 that stipends had not been paid out of the fruits of the once enormously rich Arbroath abbey, then in the hands of the second duke of Lennox. Noble patrons used every excuse to wriggle out of their responsibilities, and many ministers were never adequately funded. Mr

Peter Hamilton, the exasperated minister at Livingston, wrote c.1600 to sir Walter Dundas of that Ilk to remind the laird to supply the elements for communion and to pay his stipend, writing that 'it is ane greit syan to you to pay it to another seing that I serve the cure of the kirk'.[44] Catholic nobles had additional cause to make life difficult for Protestant clergy. The ninth earl of Errol blocked the appointment of a minister at Cruden in Aberdeenshire in 1597 by refusing to pay the stipend. At Paisley, the Hamiltons of Abercorn played havoc with a succession of clergy, and as late as 1626, Claud Hamilton, brother of the second earl of Abercorn, incited a Catholic mob to eject Mr Robert Boyd from his manse. Two years later, his servant beat up a burgh officer attempting to carry out the presbytery's instructions.[45] Ministers also faced intimidatory tactics from lords determined to keep them out of the parish. By 1634, Mr Archibald Cameron, the unfortunate minister of Inchcallioch, had laboured in his parish for twenty years against the opposition of sir John Buchanan of that Ilk. In spite of court of session decisions in his favour, Cameron had no stipend, he was afraid to work his glebe, his manse was a ruin, he was forced to live seven miles away in Dumbarton, and even his efforts to make the journey to the parish were regularly interrupted.[46] However, the growing authority of the bishops did have an impact, and in the decades after 1600 the incomes of ministers rose. Archbishop Spottiswoode grew frustrated at the lack of cooperation from teindmasters like John Grant of Freuchie, warning him in 1616 that unless his kirks in Strathspey were better funded, he would be forced to 'keip a more strict and rigorous dealinge with you, and cal you quhair you must bothe answer and mak redresse'.[47] Unfortunately, Charles I's attempt to restore church finances, separating teinds from the lay superiors, only succeeded in angering landlords, who argued that any help for the clergy should not be bought at the expense of the nobility, and that any investigation of teinds should come out in favour of those 'housis and families that sustains the burding'.[48] Since there was no way of making the teind commission work effectively without hurting those noble houses who had exploited ecclesiastical lands, such attitudes made its achievements predictably limited.

Yet it would be mistaken to imagine that nobles provided the clergy with no financial support. When in 1569 the fourth earl of Glencairn made a gift of the thirds of the bishopric of Glasgow to the church, he was behaving relatively generously; the archives of many noble houses contain evidence of payments to ministers, like those made by the second earl of Mar from the 1570s to the 1630s, including in 1630 300 merks to a minister's widow.[49] Patrons took a helpful interest in parish life that often went beyond paying the stipend. The seventh earl of Menteith's worries about Aberfoyle parish in 1618 were genuine, there being no resident minister 'quhairthrow the maist pairt of the paroschinneris thairof remanes in great blindnes and ignorance'. In 1621, the kirk session at Tyninghame intimated its gratitude to the first viscount Annan when he presented it with a copy of Christopher

Barker's translation of the bible and a new bell.[50] The church often turned to local nobles for fabric repair, as in 1604 when the presbytery of Linlithgow petitioned the fifth earl of Morton for money to establish a new kirk, or when in 1618 a peeved first lord Binning agreed to part-fund the enlargement of Melrose parish kirk in spite of the fact that the parishioners had rejected his plans for the building. Involvement in church building appealed to noble vanity, and the kirks at Scone, Dalgety Bay and Portpatrick bear the stamp of their enthusiastic patrons.[51] Nobles might have coughed up money grudgingly, but the painstaking business of rebuilding the church from parish to parish continued with their help. At Kirkintilloch in 1607 a new church was completed with the reluctant aid of the first earl of Wigton, while in the mid-1630s lord Lorne and Colin Campbell of Glenorchy co-operated in the planning of an entirely new church for the parish of Kildachrenan. Of course, the plans and ambitions of noble families did not always coincide with those of the congregation or presbytery. When in 1633 James Maxwell of Innerwick acquired the patronage of the kirk of Gullane he moved the church to Dirleton.[52]

Prior to the Reformation, a handful of younger sons of nobles pursued clerical careers, but after 1560 the church was no longer an option for nobles since 'the childrein of the great and riche are not desirous of divinitie'. Even among the lesser nobility, clerical incomes were regarded with such disdain that it was considered 'unthrift to bestow their children's barne's part of the geare in susteaning them at the studie of theologie'. A few families continued to impose unsuitable younger sons on local churches. At Yester the minister from 1576 was William Hay, a bastard son of the fifth lord Yester and a man constantly in trouble with the ecclesiastical authorities. Few nobles had a real religious vocation, and even the likes of Robert Bruce, a younger son of sir Alexander Bruce of Airth, found his family opposed to his decision to study theology at St Andrews.[53] However, nobles did value ecclesiastical patronage as a means of rewarding their servants and clients, although initially patronage of the bulk of the kirk's former patrimony remained under crown control. In March 1560, the fourth earl of Morton, one of the Lords of the Congregation, issued a charter to Mr John Douglas, rector of Kirkbride, granting him the chaplaincy of the rude altar within his collegiate church of Dalkeith whenever it was vacated. Here was Douglas family business carrying on in the midst of the Protestant revolution, and a generation later Morton's nephew, the evangelical eighth earl of Angus, held on to his ecclesiastical patronage.[54] After the 1587 act of annexation which alienated the temporalities of former abbatial lands, the nobility enjoyed greater rights of patronage. The fifth earl of Bothwell acquired the patronage of thirty-seven churches along with Kelso abbey in 1588, bringing his total ecclesiastical patronage up to fifty-nine churches, 5 per cent of the total in Scotland; by 1592 lord Claud Hamilton had the patronage of the twenty-nine churches annexed to Paisley abbey; in 1608, Arbroath abbey returned to the first marquis of Hamilton along with the patronage of thirty-seven churches. As might be expected, much of this patronage was used to reward kinsmen and clients, such as when in 1575 the sixth lord Livingston gifted a chaplaincy in Falkirk parish church to a younger son who had no clerical ambitions. In 1630, when the kirk at Longforgan fell vacant, the first earl of Kinghorn, who owned the entire parish, lobbied to get his client nominated, arguing that 'it concerns me much not to suffer that plaice to be fillit with ane stranger bot with ane of my awne'.[5]

Some nobles saw beyond exploiting former church resources, seizing the opportunity to exercise ecclesiastical patronage, and the kirk encouraged them to take an interest in the establishment of a preaching ministry throughout their possessions. A few, like the eighth lord Glamis, understood the European-wide scale of the task facing Protestant churches. In the years before the Reformation, lord James Stewart exploited his position as commendator of the Augustinian priory in St Andrews to promote Protestant clergy in the burgh. The regent Morton used his authority to impose a Protestant ministry on Aberdeen in 1574. Other Protestant nobles exercised a similarly crucial role in staffing local churches with ministers of whom they approved. The fifth earl of Argyll played a hands-on role in establishing a Protestant ministry throughout his extensive territories, working closely with John Carswell, the earl's servant and superintendant of Argyll. That policy and partnership was actively continued by his brother after Argyll's death in 1573. In Angus and in Ayrshire the local nobility was equally crucial in negotiating with the church a policy of successful church planting.[56]

This interest in the qualities of ministers continued into the seventeenth century, holding off the interference of the bishops, and it was to lay patrons that prospective ministers often had to direct their attentions. When in the spring of 1632 the minister at Aberdour was dying, the first lord Wemyss recommended to the patron one of his own kinsmen, Mr Mathew Wemyss, 'quha I houp in his doctrine and in his lyf and conversatione he sall give your L[ordship] full contentment'. The first earl of Haddington took seriously his rights of presentation, expecting to be consulted by bishops and congregations when vacancies arose. He intervened at Haddington in 1629, causing embarrassment to archbishop Spottiswoode, who informed the earl that his first choice, Mr Harry Rollock, did not want to leave Edinburgh, while the earl's next choice, Mr John Wemyss, had refused to subscribe the five articles of Perth which Haddington was busy enforcing.[57] To Gordonstoun, it seemed only reasonable that nobles retain some ecclesiastical patronage through the funding of chaplaincies, 'Not that you should reape any commoditie therby, but becaus it is a seemlie thing to have some benefices at a noble man's gift, that he may therby pleasour such of the churchmen as he thinks worthie'. When in 1605 the first lord Spynie resigned the temporalities of the bishopric of Moray to the king in order that the latter might restore the bishopric, he reserved the patronage of more than fifty church livings. Here it was local influence that mattered, not monetary gain, and it is quite possible that when in 1632 the second earl of Buccleuch swore he derived no financial income from kirk patronage, he was telling the truth.[58]

Along with ecclesiastical patronage came enhanced social obligations. When the Burnet barons of Leys in Aberdeenshire acquired properties formerly belonging to Arbroath abbey, they became responsible not only for the repair and decoration of the kirk at Banchory, but also for the maintenance of nine paupers of the parish.[59] Unfortunately, the avaricious swallowing up of ecclesiastical resources meant that the kirk's social programme of widely available schooling, poor relief, hospitals and hospices was strangled at birth. In common with most other early modern élites, the Scottish nobility showed little sympathy for what a convention of the estates described in 1574 as 'strang and idle beggaris', and the harsh legislation of parliament in 1579 indicated a nervousness about the able-bodied poor whose movements had to be controlled.[60] On the other hand, the nobility recognised a social responsibility towards those poor who were legitimately unable to fend for themselves. Offering hospitality to the poor, distributing alms at the doors of houses and other forms of casual generosity were a feature of noble lifestyles. Great men like the regent Moray and the duke of Châtelherault cultivated the image of themselves as generous lords, their propagandists making sure the world heard of their munificence. This was an aspect of noble society that the church endeavoured to encourage. In spite of Alexander Hume's attack on the vanity and greed of noblewomen, rich noblewomen like lady Binning and lady Panmure were generous, while some saw charity as a means of exercising power. In Aberdeen, Marian Douglas, lady Drum, a younger daughter of the fourth earl of Buchan, was instrumental in funding educational and charitable ventures in the burgh from the 1630s. Nobles received letters like that from a widowed mother to the sixth earl of Morton, pleading him 'to saiff me and my sone from the overthrow of my present estaitt', and household accounts indicate that small but frequent disbursements were made to the poor. When the second duke of Lennox was in Edinburgh as high commissioner at parliament in 1607, his servants distributed forty shillings at the abbey window of Holyrood palace, fifty-four shillings and four pennies were handed out at the head of the Canongate, and thirty-three shillings and four pennies to the poor at Stirling. But in an account that totalled £1000 this was charity on a small scale, particularly when compared to the sixty shillings the duke spent on 300 cherries. During 1628–9 when the fifth earl of Montrose was a student at St Andrews, he disbursed 1½ per cent of his total expenditure in charity to the poor. A six shilling haircut cost almost as much as his weekly charitable disbursement.[61]

It was typically human that noble generosity was all too often inspired by the imminent threat of death and impending judgement.[62] Nevertheless, the composition of testaments was one occasion when rich people did consider the poor. Catherine Campbell, dowager countess of Crawford, wrote her will in the summer of 1578, leaving 300 merks to 'the puir folkis being in the hospitall of Dundie'. In a similar spirit, the eighth lord Yester paid for the lodgings of four 'auld faillit pepill' in Peebles and provided 500 merks for the hospital in the town. In his will, drawn up in 1629, the immensely rich first earl of Haddington requested that he be buried simply, 'in decent and modest maner, without pompe or superfluitie', and his executor was instructed instead to provide the poor with 'a bountifull distributioun'.[63] Yet such charity was all relatively mean, and a justified sinner had less cause to leave great sums of money to good works – and certainly nothing to the welfare of his own soul – than previous generations. When John Grant of Freuchie died in 1585, he left assets valued at £47 592, including a remarkable £20 000 in cash, and yet his only charitable legacy was forty merks to a pauper. Lady Jean Hamilton, a sister of lord John Hamilton and a wealthy divorcee, left a total of £210 to various charitable causes and £1405 to her children and servants, but the largest single sum was the £900 set aside to pay for her own funeral expenses. On the evidence of their testaments, the nobility were not generous in giving to good causes, being little drawn to philanthropic deeds; their benefactions were small and small-minded, lacking any vision of what might be accomplished by an outpouring of good works.[64]

## The Catholic Nobility

The question of the continuity of Scotland's Catholic community has not been fully explored, but certainly in the first two decades after 1560 it offered little threat to Protestantism. It was only after 1579 that Jesuit activity began to claim conversions like the eighth lord Maxwell, and until 1594 a Catholic counter-Reformation was pursued by a minority of activists. Although there was some geographic concentration of Catholic support in the north-east and the south-west of the country, Catholics could be found among the families of the higher nobility in most regions. Often this was skin-deep, the result of a youthful flirtation, and it was easily abandoned in the face of pressure from the crown, the church or the family itself. However, in many instances a devotion to Catholicism was the result of deeply held religious beliefs or of a family tradition that had become entangled with the identity and honour of the lineage. Therefore, the regular formulaic submissions of Catholic nobles to Protestant orthodoxy might mean little. Some nobles demonstrated a remarkable ability in spinning out theologically technical talks about their faith with irritated Protestant ministers. When in 1586 Maxwell agreed to disavow the mass and to accept a Protestant chaplain in his company with whom 'he may confer for his bettir resolutioun in the heid of religioun', he was simultaneously planning rebellion. Yet, apart from the desperate rebellions of the late 1580s and early 1590s, the activities of Catholic nobles were often more of an embarrassment than a threat to the Protestant church, as the Jesuits and their noble patrons conceded.[65]

As was the case in other Calvinist states like England and Holland, the persecution of Catholics often depended on local circumstances, and in the latter a *de facto* local toleration only ceased after c.1600. Elsewhere in Europe, it was Protestants who suffered as confessionalisation was adapted by state authorities; for example, in Lower Austria where Protestants were squeezed into conformity. In Scotland too, the pressure to ensure conformity grew in the early seventeenth century once the crown's authority was thrown behind those bishops who were keen to emphasise their Calvinist orthodoxy, and it became relentless after the death of James VI in 1625.[66] The purpose of persecution, however, was not to drive the recusant community to desperation. When in 1608–9 the earls of Huntly and Errol were again imprisoned and excommunicated, the king wanted his servants to be sensitive in ensuring that 'neither they be too much trusted upon there too easie yealding, nor yett driven to dispaire by ressaveing no comfort in there conforming'. Their crime was the civil one of non-conformity, not the religious offence of heresy.[67]

At a local level, this resulted in persistent harassment. The synod of Fife pestered the young seventh lord Gray for four years until in 1614 he signed a full recantation of his Catholicism, a confession of Protestant orthodoxy and recognition of the royal supremacy.[68] Royal favour protected the eleventh earl of Angus from similar treatment when he returned from Rome in 1627 displaying religious ambivalence, but the presbytery of Lanark turned on his servants, bullying them either into conformity or out of the earl's employment.[69] Noblewomen in particular were targeted, being more vulnerable than their husbands. Both lady Livingston and lady Seton were harassed into submission in the later 1590s, while in the 1620s similar tactics were used against the countess of Nithsdale and lady Herries, both excommunicated by the presbytery of Dumfries. The countess of Abercorn's ongoing refusal to respond to excommunication resulted in banishment. The conversion of the countess of Linlithgow was considered such a coup by the church that an account of her experience was published in 1629, shortly after her death, as part of the anti-Catholic campaign that year.[70]

There is little doubt that such tactics by the church took their toll. The twelfth earl of Sutherland had no record of political disloyalty, but in 1612, after ten years of ignoring the church's admonitions, he was ordered to present himself before the high commission at St Andrews where he was confined in a state of agitated bewilderment, complaining that 'I think me not weill used ... My haill affaires at home ar lost'.[71] Perhaps what is most significant about this kind of evidence is not so much the kirk's dogged determination to grind away at men's consciences, as the fact that these nobles risked so much in maintaining their religious integrity. Unfortunately for them, the concentration of patronage in the hands of the crown prior to 1587 made it difficult for Catholic nobles to promote their own candidates when the Protestant kirk was weakest. Pockets of territorial seigneurial Catholicism survived, and even in the 1620s the Maxwell family was seen by Rome and by the Scottish crown as important in preserving Catholicism in the south-west.[72] But these were irritations that only stemmed the advance of Protestantism, and Catholics like the sixth lord Hume found themselves forced to give financial support to the local Protestant clergy.[73] Nevertheless, the faith of these lords was sustained by a steady supply of Catholic literature and Jesuit teaching. In Aberdeenshire and Buchan the first marquis of Huntly shielded his Catholic friends until 1633, when Charles I finally forced him to surrender his shrieval authority. Such protection allowed the likes of John Gordon of Gight, who proclaimed his faith on the external decoration of his castle, to maintain a chapel on his estate for years. Even in the 1620s, sir John Campbell of Cawdor and John MacDonald of Moidart were claimed for Rome by missionaries active on the western seaboard. [74]

Without any schools of their own, the households of the Catholic nobility were important nurturing grounds for their confessional community. In Ayrshire, a largely Protestant locality from an early date, the third earl of Eglinton's household acted as a screen behind which Catholicism was protected even after his conversion in 1566. Therefore, one means of preventing a new generation of Catholics emerging was to separate the children from their families, ensuring they received a Protestant education and upbringing. In 1602, the general assembly issued 'Instructions for the brethern', commissioning a number of ministers to live with the families of the Catholic earls of Huntly, Errol and Angus for three months, during which time they were to instil in them 'the haillgrounds of true religioun and godlinesse'. This was neither the first nor the last time this policy had been adopted with these lords, but the effectiveness of such practices was minimal. The efforts of the kirk to get its hands on the first earl of Nithsdale's eldest son in the 1620s were frustrated by this wily noble, who was expected to 'infect and poysoun' his son. In 1629, similar care was taken to ensure that the eleventh earl of Angus's daughters received Protestant instruction, while a younger son was removed to supervised lodgings in Edinburgh. Yet seven years later the local presbytery was still trying to enforce conformity on the earl's wife, children and servants.[75]

Many Catholic families saw a foreign education as the best route to reinforce their children's religion, and there is some evidence that Jesuits deliberately set out to convert travellers. Examples of young nobles being 'corrupted' were not uncommon. A youthful tenth earl of Angus went to

Paris in 1577, and during his three years in the city his nascent Catholic leanings were irrevocably confirmed by attending sermons and lectures at the Sorbonne.[76] The general assembly viewed the matter seriously, complaining in 1601 of the 'negligent educatioun of the childrein of noblemen' who were allowed to go to Catholic countries in the company of suspect tutors. When Robert, master of Seton, and his younger brother, George, returned from France in 1602, they were obliged to give Haddington presbytery an assurance that they 'studied other arts nor theologie'.[77] The crown too showed an episodic interest in using its authority to license travel as a means of controlling the flow of young men to Catholic states. In 1609, James VI expressed fears that 'the vessell will ordinarlie ather a lang tyme or for ever reteyne the taist of the liquour first putt thairunto'. Successive legislation over the next twenty years placed restrictions on unaccompanied travel, and in 1629 the privy council threatened property confiscation for those who allowed their children to be educated in Catholic schools or seminaries on the continent. Protestant parents and guardians were equally concerned, especially about the dangers of Italy where their sons might learn bad habits, all sorts of vice being associated with Catholic culture.[78]

For those young men who strayed into Catholicism, remedial action was taken. In the course of 1601, the twenty-three-year-old Alexander Elphinstone, the eldest son of the lord treasurer, was sufficiently frightened by a privy council investigation and five months' instruction under Andrew Melville to put him off attending the mass for ever.[79] However, some strong-minded individuals retained the faith they learned as children and youths. The tenth earl of Angus survived being beaten up in the streets of St Andrews by Protestant students in the 1570s, and refused to give up his religion when faced with disinheritance in the 1580s. He was subsequently forfeited for identifying with the Catholic rebellions of the 1590s, enduring harassment, imprisonment and final exile in the 1600s. Angus was denied permission to return to 'give my last gudnicht to my contrey, familie, and friendes', living out his remaining days at the abbey of St Germain-des-Prés, impressing the religious community with his intense prayer and devotion, and encouraging Jesuit missions to Scotland. His funeral in 1611 attracted a great crowd as well as inspiring a hagiographic pamphlet.[80] Like many of his contemporaries, Angus fixed on his religious loyalties early in life and stuck by them.

As the treatment meted out to Angus suggests, among the more obvious beliefs that characterised the Protestant mind was a fear of Roman Catholicism. In sir Anthony Weldon's heavy-handed satire on Scotland, he was uncommonly accurate in his comment that as far as Scottish Protestants were concerned, 'To be opposite the pope, is to be presently with God'. Among the nobility there were individuals who encapsulated such attitudes, men like the fifth earl of Glencairn who went around Edinburgh smashing up Catholic images in the 1560s.[81] Yet by the standards of the day, religious persecution was mild in Scotland. The nobility showed little enthusiasm for it, and even the unswervingly Protestant eighth earl of Angus was accused of being soft on Catholics, a charge that left him 'half benumbed of his senses'. One explanation for this reluctance to initiate persecution was suggested by John Leslie, who thought it was due to 'a certane benignitie of nature, quhen in na manis bluid sie tha neid to dip thair hand'. This gentle image of the Scottish nobility must be greeted with a wry scepticism, but the desire to avoid being dragged into an unwanted bloodfeud with Catholic neighbours did dampen religious antagonisms. Even the rebellion by the Catholic earls in 1594 did not move the nobility of the north-east from a view that 'bloodshed [was] ane unfitting mean to work any man's conversion'.[82]

This was especially true because of the existence of so many strong bonds and obligations that cut across religious divisions. Agnes Leslie, countess of Morton, had impeccable Protestant credentials, yet two of her daughters were married to Catholic lords, the sixth lord Hume and the ninth earl of Errol. In 1593, her friendship towards her sons-in-law and the notoriously Catholic tenth earl of Angus was such that she was accused of having 'allured her husband to help them so far beyond his profession in religion that her husband and herself have covertly been noted and checked in pulpits for the same'. Familial and other loyalties, therefore, created complex relationships that served to dilute religious enmities, an experience found elsewhere; for example, in Tudor Lancashire. Arthur Forbes, master of Forbes, was unequivocally a Protestant, but he explained in 1600 that he was 'more careful to confirm my awin conscience than curious to knaw controversies and more desirous to preuve myself of that Kirk than willing to judge of others whether they be of it or no'. Forbes' irenicism was shaped by having two elder brothers enter a Capuchin order at Ghent and Antwerp, where they lived saintly lives, particularly John Forbes, brother Archangel, who became the subject of a number of hagiographies after his death in 1606.[83] These contacts with Catholic kinsmen reached into the heart of the political establishment. George Elphinstone, brother of the fourth lord Elphinstone who served as James VI's treasurer, became a Jesuit and was at various times rector of the Scots college at Rome and at Douai. Another of Elphinstone's brothers, the Catholic first lord Balmerino, was secretary of state. Sir Thomas Hamilton of Drumcairn, the lord advocate, was a suspected Catholic and his uncle, John Hamilton, was a priest who became rector at the university of Paris in 1584 until his expulsion from France for supporting the extreme Catholic League. From 1604 to 1622 the chancellorship was even in the hands of a known Catholic.[84]

It is too easy to underestimate the extent to which rival confessional communities found ways of living with one another in early modern Europe, creating a form of *de facto* toleration. Nevertheless, the idea of liberty of conscience was not popular in early modern society. When in 1593 the king raised the topic in a suspiciously staged dinner conversation with lord Hamilton, suggesting it might be appropriate to allow freedom to the Catholic earls, Hamilton's reply was hysterical: 'Sir, then we are all gone, then we are all gone, then we are all gone! If there were no more to withstand, I will withstand'.[85] The king could not allow public toleration, telling the sixth earl of Huntly after his return from exile in 1597 that if his conscience remained troubled by the prospect of conforming, James would protect his family and living, 'but for yourself look never to be a Scottishman again … think not that I will suffer any professing a contrary religion to dwell in this land'. The tenth earl of Angus received a similar rebuff, but he continued to argue that there was no relationship between Protestantism and loyalty, protesting that he had given his oath of allegiance 'quhilk I vnderstand to be skarslie allowit of sum of the preceiser sort and urgeris of this hard cours aganis me', an illusion to the earl's Presbyterian critics that would have struck a sympathetic chord with the king. While James could never allow the logic of this position to be publicly accepted, he was more indulgent when people complained about the cross Angus wore in his hat, scorning the 'people's daftness'. Nevertheless, it was rare for the crown to concede toleration explicitly, as it did in 1614 when Jean Gordon, countess of Sutherland, was permitted to practise her religion in private after an agreement was reached that she would not receive Jesuits.[86]

## Conclusion

At his funeral in 1623, the godliness of the recently deceased fifth earl Marischal was contrasted with nobles in general who 'becomes so proud with the title of nobilitie, that they think not God worthy of honour and reverence'. Here, in this exemplary dead lord, was a man with a lifetime of devotion to studying the scriptures, which he could read in the original languages, daily prayer and care for the poor.[87] Marischal was a pious and learned man, but how easy was it for men born to such wealth and power to meet the spiritual expectations of an ever more demanding church? The above evidence suggests that noble society was gripped by religion, that many Protestants and Catholics took seriously the working out of their own salvation. Of course, there were exceptions: those indifferent and wicked men and women who sought refuge in formal religion and in their own sins. There was also much insincerity and ruthless exploitation of religion for political interests. But for many of those who lived in Scotland in the decades between the Reformation of 1560 and what would be known as the Second Reformation of the 1640s, religion was a compelling business. Within two decades of 1560, Calvinist doctrine was widely accepted and notionally understood by most nobles, few Protestants deviating from that ideology. By the 1580s, Catholic nobles were nurturing in their households post-Tridentine ideas, a system of belief every bit as evangelical as that inspired by Geneva. In family worship, in private reading, in church attendance and in the patterns of their thought and speech, the Scottish nobility was transformed into a publicly devout and even a privately pious élite. In spite of the confessional divide between Protestants and Catholics, however, they avoided the excesses of France, keeping persecution low-key and bloodless. The nobles were never as godly as the radical clergy wanted them to be; hence the elevation to near-secular sainthood of the exemplary lives of men like the first earl of Moray, the eighth earl of Angus and the fifth earl Marischal. It is, however, the purpose of clergy to demand from all what is attainable for only a few.

The church's recognition that it needed noble cooperation was a pragmatic one, and it flattered their pretensions in order to get it. At a national and at a local level there was considerable input from the nobility in the creation of the godly commonweal, from supporting parliamentary legislation on witchcraft or adultery, to enforcing the kirk's regulations through their own local courts. Nobles also acted as partners in church planting. To some extent they were even prepared to recognise the kirk's authority in matters of moral behaviour. However, the church's disappointment and disillusionment with nobles centred on two issues: discipline and money. Conceding the former in principle was one thing; submitting to an interfering, high-minded but low-born clergy was quite another. The nobility too became disillusioned, distancing themselves from kirk discipline and taking refuge behind the screen of the king's preference for less inquisitive bishops. For Catholics, however, the church became increasingly intrusive in the early seventeenth century as the crown backed its bishops in a policy designed to make life as uncomfortable as possible for those who denied its teachings. If the experience of the Protestant kirk's discipline was a long, slow learning process for the nobility, there was never any question of making concessions on finance. The opportunity to expand a family's landed possessions at the expense of the church and the community was too great to be passed up. Even those nobles who were attracted to the reformers' vision of a godly people, educated and cared for by a well-resourced kirk, could not divest themselves of their own riches. Noble paternalism ensured the poor and unfortunate in this society were not entirely abandoned to the church's meagre means, but charity was the least practised of the Christian virtues among them. Of course, Christ himself had predicted as much when discussing wealth and spirituality. It would have required more than the usual share of faith for an entire nobility to agree to turning their own world upside down.

CHAPTER 11

# Death

Remarkably little is known about death in medieval and early modern Scotland. How Scots anticipated death, the rituals that accompanied it, and the memorialisation of the dead are not subjects that have attracted the interest of historians. Therefore, in investigating death and the nobility in a time of considerable changes in public culture, largely brought about by the Reformation, one faces two significant problems. Firstly, without some sense of specifically Scottish medieval attitudes to dying and to death it is difficult to avoid making assumptions based on European trends that might not always be entirely appropriate. Secondly, it is not possible to say with any confidence to what extent the developments in élite culture in Scotland were accompanied by a more general transformation in society's understanding of death and of those rituals that accompanied it. Nevertheless, from the scattered evidence assembled here, it does appear that there were changes in how Scottish nobles engaged with the business of dying, and that those changes had resonances with experiences elsewhere in Europe. Principally these amounted to an adoption of a Christian attitude towards dying that reflected the renewal of religious ideas throughout the confessional divide but that had a broadly Protestant tone to it. In a sense this was the business of the individual noble whose privileged rank brought no advantages when facing death. At the same time, the memorialisation of the dead was the business of the living lineage, a corporate body that did not die. Here there was a distinct process of secularisation as a consequence of the Protestant church's retreat from funerals and its exclusion of the dead from the community of the living. Into this vacuum the nobility poured greater and greater resources and emotional energy, creating a cult of the dead that was intended to provide moral exemplars to the lineage, promoting its welfare and fame throughout society.

## Confronting Death

The fear of death that was so characteristic of late medieval society resulted in enormous effort being put into reconciling people to it: for example, in the Italian confraternities, institutions unknown in Scotland where the collegiate church and mortuary masses fulfilled a similar psychological need

Table 12.1 Spread of ages at death of peers, 1560–1637

| Age group (years) | No. of peers of known death age | Percentage of total |
|---|---|---|
| 0–20 | 3 | 1% |
| 21–35 | 42 | 16% |
| 36–50 | 68 | 26% |
| 51–65 | 77 | 29% |
| 66–80 | 65 | 24% |
| Over 81 | 10 | 4% |
| Total | 265 | 100% |

before the Reformation.[1] But, of course, death was an experience that none could avoid, whatever their rank. On average Scottish peers lived 52.4 years, with those inheriting their titles in the sixteenth century living eighteen months longer (see Table 11.1).

Looking at the spread of ages, just over 1 per cent of peers died before attaining their legal majority at twenty-one – for example, the thirteen-year-old second earl of Gowrie – and another 16 per cent were dead by the age of thirty-five. Thereafter, the rate of dying increased sharply; 26 per cent died between the ages of thirty-six and fifty, while 29 per cent died between the ages of fifty-one and sixty-five. Nevertheless, more than a quarter of the higher nobility lived beyond the age of sixty-five, a high life expectancy even by modern standards. Another quarter died between the ages of sixty-six and eighty, but 4 per cent lived even longer. These ancient nobles included the eighty-three-year-old first earl of Southesk, the ninety-year-old tenth lord Saltoun, and the amazing Robert Melville, first lord Melville, who was born in 1527 when James V was a young man, and died ninety-four years later in 1621.

Yet however long anyone lived, all must die. As the first earl of Buccleuch's melancholy will recorded, 'there is nothing more certain to all men then death and nothing more uncertain then the sure manner and place therof'. Cromarty gave expression to the same idea in a more poetic form when he wrote that 'though old age stand/A great way off, death alwaies is at hand;/Who, without taking heed to time or yeares,/No living creature spares when she appeares'. It was commonplace to regard death fatalistically, as an ever-present possibility timed within a divine plan that nurtured a holier and a better life. Poems such as Alexander Gardyne's eulogy on the death of sir John Wishart of Pittarow expressed these widely held notions that somehow balanced human uncertainty with the assurance that was derived from providence. People were encouraged to confront death, 'to looke upon the ugly shape therof', remembering that 'by death the slumberer is cut off from the world, his pompe cannot follow him'.[2]

Yet death was not seen as an ending. It was a part of the whole experience of any individual, a stage in a process of life that had birth at one end, death at the other and dying in the phase between these two points. It was important, therefore, to find ways of making sense of what was a daunting ordeal that had never been part of God's original plan for mankind but was a punishment for sin. It was equally necessary to impose order on death, making the business of dying a life-long preparation for the inevitable. Typical of such thinking was *The Godly Man's Journey to Heaven* (1625) by David Lindsay, minister at Leith, or William Murray's *A Short Treatise of Death* (1631), dedicated to Elizabeth Beaton, lady Stormont, or Zacharie Boyd's 1628 *The Last Batell of the Soule in Death* (1628). These works were written in the same tradition as the English Puritan, Thomas Becon's, *The Rich Man's Salve* (1561), in which he recommended meditating upon death as a necessary preparation for its unavoidable but unpredictable eventuality. Such thoughts, it was hoped, would discourage sin, and while it was natural to fear dying, it was a great wrong to fear what followed death. For the Calvinist elect, death was a natural state that followed old age, a safe haven into which the ship of life entered for rest.[3]

In confronting death, élite society encouraged a cultivation of the mental composure necessary to overcome fear and a self-discipline that upheld the social order, even to the extent of enacting a piece of domestic theatre in which family, friends and servants each had a familiar role in a ritual as public as marriage. This 'tame death', in which there was no futile struggle, no undignified clinging to the last few breaths of life, was commonplace.[4] It is there, for example, in a letter from the dying first duke of Lennox in June 1583 bidding a friend 'an honest guid nicht'. Of course, for some individuals, death brought relief from life's pains and the prospect of a better existence. On hearing of the death in February 1616 of his sister after a long illness, chancellor Dunfermline found the news easier to bear because of 'hir continuall wisches to be fred be Goddis will of that miserie, be passage to a better lyffe'. Boyd advanced the familiar analogy of a tenant living in a clay cottage who is offered lodgings in his lord's palace as a guest. The possibility of the tenant refusing the offer was absurd – 'What Lord in the Land was ever troubled with such an answere?'[5]

Dwelling on death and resignation to it had a profound psychological and potentially depressing impact on the mind, but people did strain against this obsession. Sir Patrick Hume of Polwarth chided sir Robert Ker of Ancram, then a man in his mid-fifties, for dwelling overmuch on his age and mortality, and he proved to be right as Ancram lived for another twenty-two years. An octogenarian sir Duncan Campbell of Glenorchy must have grown weary of people anticipating his death. In October 1629, the morose seventh earl of Argyll informed Glenorchy that he wanted to return to Scotland after a twelve-year absence to see old friends, 'especialy souch as you ar who ar neer the winning of thair days, that befoir we go to rest we mycht bid on ane uther fairwaile'. Right up until his death in 1631, Glenorchy continued to receive letters from well-wishers urging resolution in the face of imminent death and 'praying God for patience and ane happie end to him'. Such brooding invited the typically black humour of Cromarty, who warned a man newly recovered from a serious illness not to rejoice too much since his dying day was now even closer than it had been when he was sick. Cromarty ended this depressing correspondence with the words, 'Let this thought then your gladnesse mortifie,/That once againe you must fall sicke and dye', not the most encouraging get-well note to send anyone.[6]

Zacharie Boyd recognised that, for some individuals, preparing for death was a source of enormous anxiety, since it was thought to hasten it, a view he roundly rejected. While melancholia could be an affected style favoured by artists, it is possible that people did die earlier than they might have done because of such fatalism. Certainly it was widely believed that the will to live affected one's health, and early modern society's deep interest in melancholy is obvious from the success in England of Robert Burton's *The Anatomy of Melancholy* (1621).[7] Such psychosomatic illnesses were ascribed to a number of nobles of this period whose political fortunes, like those of James V who died in a fit of depression in 1542, declined sharply. The dysentery that killed the first duke of Lennox in Paris on 26 May 1583 was put down to melancholy arising from his exile, although in typically acerbic fashion Calderwood added that the duke suffered from gonorrhoea. Depression was also thought to have killed sir Gideon Murray of Elibank in 1621. Having been charged with various corruption offences in his capacity as treasurer-depute, Elibank went home, refused to eat and died. Denmilne was of the view that the unfortunate first lord Balmerino, sentenced to death for treason in 1609 but allowed to live on in disgraced retirement, died of a broken spirit three years later. However, there is only one known case of suicide. On 6 March 1624, the heavily indebted and depressive second earl of Lothian shut himself up in his study and 'cutted his owne throate with a knife, efter he had given himself sundrie wounds with the dagger'.[8]

For those who knew they were dying, there were practical matters to settle, most obviously their financial affairs, although the greater part of a family's provision was settled long before death in contracts between its members. Nevertheless, to a greater extent than ordinary people, the nobility were concerned about the long-term prospects of their houses. When the first marquis of Hamilton knew he was close to death in the spring of 1604, he recommended his son to the king, asking James VI to become the boy's principal curator, ensuring the continuing pre-eminence of the Hamilton family. In a similar vein is a letter of 15 December 1636 to the third marquis of Hamilton from the tenth earl of Errol, 'being now at the poynt of death', commending his family to Hamilton's protection that its fortune might be repaired and 'the hous being raisit up and maid habill to subsist with honor'.[9] Here were dying lords whose thoughts were burdened by the secular matter of the durability of the lineage. It was for such men, clinging to life in order to lay up treasures for their children, that Boyd cited the old proverb, 'Well is the Heire whose fathers soule is in Hell,' adding the gloss that 'Hardlie can the father inrich his children, but by lossing his own Soule. What a woefull bargaine is this?' Such worldly concerns were to be laid aside, and Boyd was scathing of those rich men who, like spiders, 'spend their verie bowels in weeving a web wherewith thay may catch a flee'.[10]

The frequent observation of death within the rhythms of life, and the schooling for its eventuality, allowed people to step easily into those roles prepared for them. In some cases the theatrical elements involved in the ritual of the 'good death', the *ars moriendi*, had the semblance of artifice, but society took this play-acting seriously, developing the parts in a ritual from which the church was retreating. As the English writer, Robert Hill, observed in *The Pattern to Prayer and Pietie* (1610), dying is 'the art of all arts, the science of all sciences'.[11] This drama of death was most obvious on the scaffold. When the fourth earl of Morton faced execution in 1581, he enacted a performance of studied stoicism, as befitted his rank, alongside pious submission to providence. In bowing to the crown's demands for his life, Morton had the luxury of being able to control his mental preparation to the instant of death, being neither surprised by the unexpected or distracted by pain. The old earl forgave his enemies, expressed loyalty to the king who had condemned him, said farewell to his friends, studied the scriptures and other religious books, prayed for long hours and 'shew[ed] most violent tokins of the inward motioun of the Spirit of God', repeating the words 'Lord Jesus, receave my soule' even as the blade struck, and thus 'he died constantly the servant of God'.[12] This role of the martyred magnate was similarly performed in 1584 by the first earl of Gowrie, who went to his death 'most constant in God', a 'devot christien, and a resoluit Romane, mekle regretted with many that wer present, and hard his grave harangue, and saw his constant end'.[13]

But while these set-pieces offered the greatest opportunity for stage management, the theatricality was pervasive, shaping a role crafted to the prevailing artistic view that death should be serene. Most accounts of dying nobles record a scene of peaceful leave-taking and pious resignation to God's will. The regent Lennox had little to say as he lay dying from a painful gunshot wound in 1571, struggling for dignity as he prayed for mercy and forgiveness, making 'a very godly end'. The *ars moriendi* tradition also opened up to women a means of expressing their stoic heroicism in a way that did not challenge male authority, although there is no specifically Scottish evidence.[14] However, chancellor's Thirlestane's efforts to prolong his life by offering God future good works in compensation for his earlier neglect of them was considered both distasteful and futile. Boyd was scornful of such death-bed repentances, warning his readers that daily preparation for death was far better than awaiting illness and then seeking to bargain with God.[15]

These social rituals engaged people at every age. Sir Claud Hamilton of Shawfield was a young man with a successful court career when death ambushed him in Dublin in 1614. Yet he made peace with God, calmly instructing his friends in what to do with his papers, and asking them to take turns in sitting with him through the height of the fever that slowly took its hold. For the old, death came as less of a surprise, and perhaps it was easier to be reconciled to its timing. Thomas Maule of Panmure was in his seventy-ninth year when he sensed death's cold touch in the first week of March 1600. He had his favourite greyhounds removed from the chamber and, as patriarch of his family, said farewell to each member in turn. He blessed his sons, said the catechism and the Lord's Prayer, sent his family off to dine and quietly died. In a scene of unreal serenity, the saintly sir Robert Arbuthnott of that Ilk was lying on his death-bed in September 1631 when a little bird sat at his chamber window and:

> sang there with such a melodious and unheard of voice as ravished the ears of all in the room, and struck them into a kind of admiration and consternation of spirit, and continued in this delightful harmony till he breathed his last, and immediately away it flew and was never seen or heard of afterwards.[16]

Here is family hagiography, recounting a scene that might not have been real but which people wanted to be real, a death that was painless, tranquil and morally instructive.

Although most of the surviving evidence is suggestive of the idea that men faced death with courage and equanimity, it was not always the case. Shortly before his execution, Morton confessed to that 'natural fear of death which sticks and remains in men, even though they have assurance of the forgiveness of their sins'.[17] The suspicion among some Renaissance intellectuals that there was nothing after death but annihilation surfaced in the poetry of John Donne, and Hawthornden too raised some of the common fears of those facing death in 'A cypress grove'.[18] Furthermore, while Protestant teaching offered men assurance, and Calvinist predestination even encouraged fatalistic attitudes, it also impressed on people a deep sense of their own depravity which, as death drew near, could create an enormous tension as hope struggled against an anxiety that could no longer be removed by any sacramental palliative.[19] The powerful belief that the eternal welfare of the soul might be determined by one's mental and spiritual condition at the point of death – a survival from medieval Catholicism which portrayed the death-bed as a scene of cosmic struggle between the forces of heaven and hell – was also influential in shaping how death was managed. This was true even in Calvinist communities, where in the seventeenth century such ideas were increasingly in conflict with the doctrine of an elect whose salvation was assured; hence the need for books like Murray's *Short Treatise on Death*.[20]

In a rare insight into a nobleman's mind as he faced up to a terminal illness, the thirty-five-year-old John Gordon, first viscount Kenmure, confessed to a minister in the late summer of 1634, a fortnight before he died, 'I never dreamed that death had such a sour and austere gloom, and such a terrible and grim-like countenance'. Kenmure was terrified of damnation, 'because I find my sins so grievous and so many, that I fear my accompts be ragged and out of order, and not so as becometh a dying man'. In the days that followed, the clergy ministering to Kenmure reduced him to a quivering wreck as they confronted him with the prospect of divine judgement and eternal punishment. Only then was he fit to face death, and only then could the counselling dwell on the joys of communion with God and of the life to come. Kenmure's dying now became a witness and exemplar to the living as he pleaded with the succession of kinsmen, friends, neighbours and servants who visited him to live a godly life while they had the opportunity. Such was the impression he made that one clergyman, probably Samuel Rutherford, wrote down and later published an account of Kenmure's final days in the hope it would have a similar inspirational impact as the death of another Calvinist noble, the English third earl of Huntingdon, who died in 1595. When Kenmure's time came, on Friday, 12 September, he died in the Lord, 'the expiring of his breath, the ceasing of the motion of his pulse, (which the physician was still gripping,) trysted all precisely with the "Amen" of his prayer: and so died he sweetly and holily, and his end was peace'.[21] Of course, one would not expect writers to recall the painful screams, the nauseating stench of decay, sickness and excrement, or the wild-eyed terror of those for whom death had come too soon. This does not mean there was collusion in hiding the physical realities of death; indeed, religious writers like Murray dwelt longingly on the grotesque effects of the body's decay, stressing its reduction to an empty, putrefying husk after the soul had taken its flight to paradise.[22]

What did disturb contemporaries was unexpected death, those sudden reminders of humanity's impermanence that denied an individual the opportunity to direct his mind to God at the point of death, imperilling his soul, preventing him from putting his earthly affairs in order or from taking leave of the living.[23] Even the greatest of men might be taken without warning. On the morning of 16 February 1624, Ludovick Stewart, second duke of Lennox, the grandee of James VI's court, felt drowsy and complained of a headache. He asked his servant to close the curtain of his bed and waken him when it was time to get ready for attending the king at the riding of the English parliament. When his servant returned a short time later, Lennox was dead, taken suddenly by apoplexy in his fiftieth year.[24] Again and again the whisperings of poison surrounded the death-beds of magnates and courtiers like Lennox or the fifth earl of Argyll in 1573, chancellor Thirlestane in 1595, the earl of Dunbar in 1611, the second marquis of Hamilton in 1625 and even the king himself a few weeks later.[25] When the fourth earl of Atholl died in 1579, after dining at Stirling, it was widely believed that he had been poisoned by his host, the fourth earl of Morton. In spite of a grisly autopsy that proved nothing, the allegations against Morton continued to circulate, and two men were executed for composing rhymes on the subject.[26] Such explanations, though seductive in their dramatic appeal, are all unlikely. John Gordon, tenth earl of Sutherland, and his countess are the only verifiable victims of poison, administered to them by a trusted kinswoman in June 1567.[27] When the grim reaper came in such an unannounced manner for the great men of the kingdom, contemporaries found it hard to resist making a moral tale of the drama, seeking explanations that were as much metaphysical as medical. Hence the shock occasioned by the death of the fifth earl of Huntly in 1576 in the midst of a vigorous after-lunch football match. Almost immediately, this incident was turned into a tale of sorcery and of God's visitation on a lord too much concerned with the size of his barns, like that rich man in one of Christ's parables.[28] Similarly, the death of the stout Protestant eighth earl of Angus in the summer of 1588 became the focus for a titanic struggle between light and darkness set against the backdrop of the threatened Spanish invasion. The 'godly' Angus's early death at the age of thirty-three was explicable only in terms of an apocalyptic tale in which 'the witches were turning his picture in waxe before a fire'.[29] As the witch craze gained a hold in the imagination of élite society over the succeeding decade, more stories surfaced of demonic possession being directed at these godly magistrates, each untimely struck down at an early age or with a suddenness that defied natural explanations.[30]

## The Living, the Dead and the Social Order

Whatever the circumstances of death, the living continued to have a relationship with those who were now dead, even if it was a more tenuous one in post-Reformation Scotland. Excessive grieving was regarded with distaste in many of the Protestant communities of northern Europe. Yet at the same time, the Renaissance recognition of the need for consolation and sorrow was slowly permeating early modern society.[31] In his last will and testament, lord Menmuir asked 'my friends and bairns rather to be merry nor to make lamentation for my deceasse, and to think that their lamentation will do me na guid, nor can not be foundit upon any guid reason, gif they hope that I will be in a guid estate'. Menmuir's sentiments were entirely correct for a good Protestant, but it was difficult to tell the living not to grieve for the loss of those they loved, far less to expect them to rejoice at the departed person's good fortune in entering the Kingdom of Heaven. A more common attitude was resignation to the will of God. Following a loss in the countess of Eglinton's family in the spring of 1620, her mother-in-law reminded her that 'As for thes quhaim it hath pleasit God to tak, praise God for the samyn, and tak in goode patience: the Lord geveth and the Lord taketh'.[32]

Nevertheless, it is a misconception to imagine that the people of this period were little touched by death due to its great intimacy with their lives. Contemporaries knew that what was recognised as the second stage of life, from birth until the seventh year, was one of great vulnerability, and that only thereafter was there 'hope that he shall be lively'. Yet in spite of the high mortality, parents suffered a great sense of loss at the death of children, possibly further evidence of the growing affection in parent-child relationships.[33] In the chapel of St Mirren in Paisley abbey, the first lord Paisley and his wife erected a mural tablet to the memory of three infant children who had died between 1577 and 1587, recording each child's name and exact age in months and days. These sorrowful parents had cherished every moment of their children's lives. In 1572 the countess of Moray's daughter, Annabel, died while in the care of her grandmother, Margaret Erskine, lady Lochleven, who wrote this was 'the greittest greif that ever came to my hertt'.[34] Arguably the early seventeenth century saw a growing willingness to express feelings of grief, and there is more evidence from people like Ann Cunningham, marchioness of Hamilton, who sadly recalled the death of 'my youngest soune ane windorous fayne boye'. When on 17 April 1630, sir David Lindsay of Balcarres's fifteen-year-old daughter died, he was devastated. On that same day he wrote to his brother-in-law, the first earl of Lauderdale, telling him that God had called Margaret 'to the joys of heaven'. Lauderdale received this 'woeful news' with great sadness, yet he was able to encourage his friend that 'God knoweth best what is best for us all'. A year later, Lauderdale buried his own nineteen-year-old daughter, Jane, and Hawthornden composed an elegy for this 'most choice, holy, comely, and gentle virgin, to whose divine wit and industry nothing ever appeared difficult which did become a noble and chaste maid'.[35] Such tragic losses were not easily borne by parents in any age.

Medieval society used corpses to reaffirm social order, understanding the necessity of recognising the spiritual obligations of the living towards the dead which the Reformation sundered. Yet after 1560, responsibilities to lords and kinsmen did not end entirely with death. There remained the question of what to do with the corpse in an age which retained some residual belief that a soul was not fully at rest until burial, and in which the church required that dead bodies be accorded respect since they would be needed at the resurrection.[36] The importance of honourably disposing of the dead can be best appreciated in extreme examples. The fourth earl of Huntly died a traitor at the battle of Corrichie in 1562, following which his body was carried south to face treason charges and forfeiture. Three years later, the forfeiture was overturned. What remained of his corpse was exhumed from the Blackfriars graveyard in Edinburgh, and carried in procession to the port of Leith from where it was sent home by sea for honourable burial. It was important to Huntly's family and followers that this macabre ritual be performed, just as it was necessary to the Ruthven family to have the head of the executed first earl of Gowrie sewn back on by a servant prior to his burial.[37] Even in more normal circumstances the body might not be buried for weeks after death, and it was common for the corpses of dead nobles to be disembowelled and embalmed. The body of the murdered second earl of Moray was embalmed in 1592 for £100, although here the motive was tied up with the need to extract revenge before he could be laid to rest, there being a popular belief that the corpse itself cried out for vengeance.[38] In the case of the second lord Kinloss, killed in a duel at Bergen-op-Zoom in 1613, the body was interred there, but his heart was removed, placed in a silver casket and sent home to Culross church for burial.[39] However, while there was a growing fascination with the body and its internal workings, the early modern period saw a decline in the medieval fashion for dissecting the body and burying it in multiple sites. In his 1624 testament, sir Duncan Campbell of Glenorchy asked that after death no incision be made on his corpse in order to preserve any part of it, and that it be accompanied without ceremony by his neighbours to Finlarg chapel for a quiet and simple burial.[40] Such thinking was more in tune with church teaching that the body was 'a stable for wormes' or 'an heape of earth made up like a piece of mud-wall', so corrupted by sin it was 'a living death, a sensible carrion, a portable sepulcher'.[41]

Protestant thinking in England and Scotland was that rites for the dead should be minimalist, cutting down on the funeral services and removing the element of intercession for the dead from the church's activities. This topic was debated during the course of 1560, when the problem arose of what to do with the corpse of Mary of Guise before deciding that no 'superstitious rytes' should be employed. In contrast to Catholic Spain, where people continued to invest huge sums of money and emotional energy in helping their dead relatives and friends, there was nothing that Protestant Scots could do for the souls of the departed. The *First Book of Discipline* stated emphatically the new church's determination to follow a Calvinist line in drawing as little attention as possible to the dead.[42] Of course, Catholic rites did not disappear entirely, and nobles were better able than most to ignore clerical disapproval. At the funeral of William Gordon of Gight in 1605, one of his tenants carried a crucifix on top of a spear at the head of the procession in what was a defiantly Catholic ceremony. When the fifth lord Ogilvy was buried in 1606, his funeral caused raised eyebrows since he was laid to rest amidst 'some superstitious ceremonies and rittes as gif the professioun of papistrie had been specialie licensed and tolerated'.[43]

Death was a disturbingly egalitarian experience for a hierarchic society, and as one noble poet observed:

'Mongst all the rites that Nature can pretend
In justice, this is chiefest, and a sequell
Which doth on mortall principles depend,
That drawing neare to death we are all equall;
Therefore we otherwise then by the sense,
Should betwixt man and man make difference.

This message that all men were equal in death was a favourite theme of the clergy. Zacharie Boyd told his noble readers in the 1620s:

Your State is great, your place is high: What then?
God calls you gods, but ye shall die like men.

For ministers like William Birnie extravagant burial ceremonies designed to glorify dead nobles were little more than an imitation of non-Christian rituals among which he listed mourning for the dead, addressing the corpse, the use of trumpets and mourning clothes, and especially conveying the corpse to the place of burial. The funeral procession in particular outraged him:

> For althogh the death of all men should be thoght to be a kynde of defeat from God, yet our Heroik burials are oft led lyke a martiall triumphe ... as if by an undantoned courage they would quarrelously demand the combate in revenge of the dead.[44]

Birnie's outrage was not merely a product of Protestantism since it drew heavily on medieval piety for inspiration, and among both Catholics and Protestants there were nobles who did respond to the church's teaching, even if there is often an ambiguity in the evidence. Instructions in wills to be buried without pomp did not mean the same as an insistence on plain simplicity. In a spirit close to what the reformers intended, Catherine Campbell, dowager countess of Crawford, wrote in her will in 1578 that her body should be buried 'in the kirk of Dundie or the isle in Edzell kirk, whichever is nearest at the time'. In 1618, the first earl of Abercorn instructed that his corpse be buried by his family and friends in the Hamilton vault in Paisley abbey, and 'I desyre that thair be no vaine nor glorious seremonie usit at my buriell, rayring [= making ready] honouris'.[45] In the case of the Catholic ninth earl of Errol, who was buried at Slains on Saturday, 16 July 1631, the same day as his death, other factors might have had a bearing on the funeral arrangements. Errol was:

> convoyit quyetlie with his awin domestiks and countrie freindis, and with torche licht. It wes his will to have no gorgeous buriall, nor to convocat his noble freindis with making greyte charges and expenssis, bot to be bureit quyetlie, and sic expenssis as sould be wairit [= spent] prodigallie upone his buriall to give the samen to the poore.

Both his Catholic religion and his financial problems might have encouraged the earl's kinsmen to put his remains to rest quickly and simply. While financial considerations played a part in discouraging some nobles from spending heavily on funerals, there was strong pressure from clergy not to make funerals an occasion for vainglorious pomp.[46]

Yet it was unrealistic to expect great lords and their houses to deny themselves the opportunity for extravagant display that funerals offered, especially as these had a broader cultural and political function. The move towards more flamboyant funeral rites in fifteenth-century Florence was closely associated with the rise in Medici fortunes and the triumph of noble over republican values. In sixteenth-century Madrid, there was no question that the cult of the dead was stimulated by greater and greater amounts of disposable income which was deployed to preserve hierarchies in the afterlife.[47] Funerals engendered communal beliefs about the relationship between the dead and the living that were expressed in the ritual of mourning, fostering the idea of the permanency of the lineage in the face of the passing of an individual. Such occasions drew attention to the greatness of that individual, allowing the still-living kinsmen, friends and dependants to display their own particular place in the order of the community that was a noble household. Among the late Tudor nobility and gentry these funerals were increasingly secular in nature, drawing inspiration from classical Rome, and the emphasis in the ceremonial was transformed into something chivalric rather than mystically religious.[48] In Scotland, there was an equivalent tension between Christian teaching and a secular, chivalric ideology that filled a gap created by the church's distancing of itself from the occasion. Yet that impetus towards display, so characteristic of noble society, could not be reined in, especially if it had the backing of the crown. When the regent Moray was buried in February 1570, the affair was solemn and subdued, but his body was carried in stately procession from Holyrood palace to St Giles where John Knox preached the funeral oration on the theme *Beati mortui qui in domino moriuntur*. Similarly, great staged state events were held for chancellor Thirlestane in 1595 and chancellor Kinnoul in 1634.[49]

For noble society, these funerals were significant events that allowed there to be a demonstration of the community's hierarchy and of its bonds. The death of the fifth lord Lovat in January 1576 was followed by a gathering of his kinsmen and friends that culminated in over 2000 men taking part in the final convoy of his corpse to Beauly. Often the pious wishes of the dying were not observed by their families, and it is possible that kinsmen were not expected to observe them. The Catholic first earl of Winton asked for a burial at Seton collegiate kirk 'in maist humbell quyet modest and Cristiane maner, without all extraordinarie pomp or unlawful serimonie'. Nevertheless, this nobleman's funeral procession in April 1603 was sufficiently long to cause James VI and his courtiers to move off the road on the way south to take possession of the English throne.[50] This funerary extravagance increased in the seventeenth century, partly due to the greater disposable income available, but also as a means of affirming the values of a buoyant and self-confident noble society in which display could be manipulated to emphasise distinctions of rank. By the second quarter of the seventeenth century, possibly even earlier, corpses were being drawn in procession in elaborate and expensive hearses.[51] This extravagance did not only concern the church. In England, the college of heralds regulated funeral arrangements, and the crown intervened to demonstrate its power, often at the expense of the lineage. There was no equivalent body in Scotland, although in 1621 parliament tried to halt the move towards flamboyant funerals, restricting the size of processions and outlawing elaborate feasts. However, the nobility paid no attention, as is clear from the records of the lord lyon, sir James Balfour of Denmilne, who collected details of the increasingly more lavish funerals of the 1620s and 1630s.[52]

As cultural events, these funerals focused on establishing the deceased person's 'social body' rather than on the disposal of their natural body.[53] The sheer effort and energy that was invested in them was astonishing. Following the decease of the second marquis of Hamilton in March 1625, his body was conveyed from Whitehall in the company of 400 coaches, including most of the English privy council and the court, providing a suitable escort for Hamilton's corpse as it began its long journey home to Scotland.[54] The embalmed corpse of the first earl of Buccleuch, who died in London of apoplexy on 20 November 1633, was sent home to Scotland by ship, arriving fifteen weeks late after encountering a storm and crossing to Norway. The cadaver then lay in the kirk at Leith for another twenty days while the Scott kindred put the finishing touches to the postponed funeral arrangements. It was carried in a great procession from Edinburgh to Branxholm through the towns of Dalkeith, Lauder and Melrose, in each of which alms were distributed. A further period of waiting followed before, on 11 June 1634, Buccleuch's remains were brought in solemn procession to St Mary's church at Hawick. There, after a funeral sermon, the burial took place, some seven months after the earl's death. This long, complex and largely secular ritual proclaimed to the world that the late earl was descended of a great and noble lineage, was the feudal lord of a vast domain, and that he was a mighty warrior with a renowned military reputation who stood high in the eyes of the state.[55] The old first marquis of Huntly died on 13 June 1636, in Dundee, from where his friends, wearing mourning clothes, collected his corpse twelve days later, placing it in a coffin covered in black taffeta, and transported it north in great solemnity, ending ten weeks later in a remarkable torchlight procession – increasingly fashionable in Britain in the seventeenth century – to the family aisle at Bellie kirk in which over 300 nobles took part. The funeral procession was painted on a roll of paper of almost seventeen feet by eight inches, a testimony both to the scale of the proceedings and of the family's determination to record the great marquis's funeral.[56] Nor should one imagine that these displays of noble power were confined to the male members of the family. In March 1636, the funeral of Sara Maxwell, countess of Wigton, took place at Holyrood, setting new standards in excessive funerary arrangements as befitted a woman who was a daughter of the fourth lord Herries and had been married successively to sir James Johnstone of that Ilk, the first earl of Wigton and the first viscount Ards.[57] For the citizens of Edinburgh, as for those tenant farmers who watched Buccleuch's or Huntly's procession, there could be few more impressive visual reminders that they lived in a world where the nobility remained dominant even in death. By the seventeenth century, nobles might no longer desire to ride at the head of long columns of armed retainers, but in death they still commanded impressive followings and their funerals allowed them to exercise aspects of lordship that ensured a continuity between an earlier age and the more civil culture of the 1630s.[58]

Another issue that exercised ministers was the funeral sermon, a form of Christian oration revived along classical lines in the Middle Ages. On the one hand, the Protestant clergy disapproved of the glorification of mortal men, but their efforts to keep funeral sermons short and to the point made little impression on nobles, who wished to see their family praised. At the same time, the clergy's own humanist education encouraged them to see an opportunity to exemplify virtue. The kind of clash between Christian and chivalric culture that was probably commonplace is apparent in a case from June 1594, when the sixth lord Seton ignored the presbytery of Haddington's warning against a Sunday funeral for his brother, employing the local schoolmaster, Mr Thomas Seggat, almost certainly a Catholic, to preach the funeral sermon.[59] Yet, by the seventeenth century, the question of a funeral sermon had become less controversial, the revived episcopate being more tolerant. James Law, the archbishop of Glasgow, preached at the funeral of the second marquis of Hamilton in 1625, while at the funeral of chancellor Kinnoul a decade later, Mr James Foster, minister at Kinfauns, preached on Proverbs 16:20, 'Whoever gives heed to instruction prospers, and blessed is he who trusts in the Lord'. The sermon delivered on 30 June 1623 by William Ogston at Marischal college, on the occasion of the funeral of the college's founder, the fifth earl Marischal, took the form of a classical oration, glorifying his family's history over the previous 1600 years, but concentrating on the earl's role as a patron of the arts and as a man of godliness. At lady Jane Maitland's funeral in 1633, the preacher used the fact of her youth to highlight the transitory nature of life, the mourners being told that 'death is a change, and our preparation a waiting for this change'. Such had been the transformation in fashion that this sermon, along with a selection of poems and epitaphs, was printed shortly afterwards.[60]

## Memorialisation

Godly modesty led Margaret Ker, lady Yester, to have a simple plaque erected after her death in 1647 in the Edinburgh church she founded, stating that 'Its needless to erect a marble tomb'.[61] By contrast, in Catholic and Protestant countries throughout Europe, the clergy struggled to halt the gradual filling of space in church buildings with monuments to the ancestors of assertive patrons. In Scotland the church faced similar problems as it tried to oppose burial within its buildings, endeavouring to expel the dead to the kirkyard. The general assembly forbade the practice in 1588, and in 1597 it persuaded the king to agree that parliament should be petitioned to legislate that 'every Nobleman sould bigge a sepulture for himself and his awin familie'. However, no act followed, and the practice of burying in kirks remained contentious. In 1606, William Birnie, minister at Lanark, published a sermon, *The Blame of Kirk Burial*, attacking those who made the kirk 'a cairne of dead men['s] skulls'. He argued that the burial in churches of nobles or other privileged people, was little more than a profane expression of pride that drew its inspiration from ancient paganism. Their monuments, he believed, were 'Pyramides of pomp, others pillers of pride, some mousolies of marvel'. Instead, Birnie argued that the well-off should build their tombs in specially constructed aisles or outside the church altogether.[62] Sir James Melville of Halhill shared these sentiments, and on his own tomb in Colessie kirkyard he had engraved the inscription:

> Defyle not christ's kirk with your carion,
> A solemn sait for God's service prepar'd,
> For praier, preaching, and communion,
> Your byrial should be in the kirk yard.[63]

Humble proclamations of this nature, however, did not come easily to great lords even in death, and lesser nobles were disciplined by presbyteries for burying members of their family within the church building. In March 1626, James Lindsay of Belstrane appeared before the presbytery of Lanark, where he admitted he had buried his child within the kirk of Carluke, promising instead to build 'ane yle for his awin buryall'.[64]

Early modern people, especially Protestants, had to find new ways of memorialising the dead that were consistent with their beliefs about the afterlife and the fate of the body. They also wanted to make statements about the individual and his place in the social hierarchy and the lineage. The dying too wanted to be remembered, knowing this was their last opportunity to impress on the living a defiant statement of their own worth. Preserving the memory of the ancestors from the ravages of time, therefore, was a sacred duty, and in spite of the intentions of the early reformers, the absence of places associated with religious cultic figures by dint of their relics was filled by secular alternatives: that is, by the tombs of the nobility. Funerary representations of the dead became a means to fill the void in human relations created by death and by the banishment of Purgatory from the Protestant mind. The entire thrust of Renaissance funerary architecture was to glorify temporal status, representing the triumph of fame over death rather than the medieval notion of death overcoming all men.[65]

The king too had an interest in publicly glorifying his servants. In this spirit, the young James VI wrote to the heir of the dead chancellor Atholl in April 1579, suggesting that prominent friends and kinsmen of the king should be buried 'in sic honorable and publict places as we mycht the rather be moved to remember thame, and thair gude service, in thair lyvetymes, and thair posterities for thair sakes'. Another of that king's more prominent servants was chancellor Thirlestane, in memory of whom James VI wrote a laudatory poem that was inscribed on a back panel of his English-style tomb at Haddington. These tombs often drew attention to royal service. The first lord Belhaven's tomb in Holyrood abbey, where many royal councillors and servants were buried, praised his 'loyalty towards his Prince, love of his country, kindness to his relations, and charity to the poor'. Even Francis Irvine, provost of Dumfries, proclaimed from beyond the grave that 'for king and country have I served'.[66] Not surprisingly, prominent royal servants often had the most elaborate tombs. Treasurer Dunbar, who died in 1611, was commemorated at the east end of the chancel of Dunbar parish church, where there was erected a massive and extremely expensive tomb, supported by armoured knights and surrounded by the female figures of wisdom, justice, fame and peace. Made in England by the Flemish artist, Maximilian Colt, who was employed by other Scottish nobles like the first viscount Scone, it was the first in Scotland to display a distinctly Italian influence.[67] Chancellor Kinnoul's tomb contained a near-life-size and realistic figure of the earl in the unusual pose of a living figure actively engaged in the interests of his life, a style that was at the edge of European innovative funerary sculpture. The realism is combined with carefully balanced symbolism, drawing inspiration from the complex frontispiece of sir Walter Raleigh's *History of the World*. Kinnoul himself personifies history, being surrounded by a display of nature, manufacture and religion, and the size of the monument, some twenty feet high, was intended to inspire awe.[68] For those buried in England, tombs might be even more ostentatious. That of the second duke of Lennox and his third wife, Frances Howard, in Westminster abbey was the grandest of any Scottish noble of this period, once again demonstrating Italian influences.[69] The internationalism of Scottish funerary architecture extended to France, where the tenth earl of Angus died in 1611, following which his family erected a magnificent black and white marble monument in the abbey at St Germain-des-Prés.[70]

It was not only important royal officials and court grandees who aspired to greatness in funerary architecture, and there was no obvious demarcation in the cultural aspirations of the peerage and the lesser nobility. As in England, the tombs of the baronage proclaim that these were men to be reckoned with in their localities, inhabiting a seemless noble culture. Sir John Stewart of Minto, provost of Glasgow, who died in 1583, was commemorated on a brass plaque in Glasgow cathedral as the lineal descendant of the barons and knights of the house of Minto. Following his death on 1 July 1591, the ninth earl of Angus was buried in the Douglas aisle of Glenbervie kirk, where his wife erected a monument and mural tablet containing a genealogical table tracing the lairds of Glenbervie back to the year 730, a clear statement that this man did not need his recently inherited title to claim noble descent.[71] Perhaps the most beautiful and impressive surviving piece of didactic funerary sculpture is the Skelmorlie aisle, completed in 1636 by sir Robert Montgomery of Skelmorlie, some fifteen years before his death. Skelmorlie's pharaonic construction expressed the conviction that life was a long process of dying, a Latin inscription referring to the fact that 'I was dead before myself; I anticipated my proper funeral: alone, of all mortals, following the example of Caesar,' a reference to the emperor Charles V. Skelmorlie possessed a modest-sized estate in north Ayrshire, yet this aisle surpasses in grandeur, complexity and sheer style anything built by most of the great magnate houses. The aisle is twenty feet high, above which is the imaginatively painted ceiling, the work of James Stalker, with its forty-one panels depicting biblical, moral, emblematic, fanciful and heraldic themes, much of it influenced by Dutch landscape; in the centre are the arms of the Montgomery and Douglas families. The tomb itself is in the fashionable and costly Italian style of the day, impressing on the visitor the affluent, self-confident assurance of the man who commissioned it and of the landed society he represented.[72] Women too engaged in self-fashioning through the medium of their tombs. Janet Erskine, countess of Stirling, revealed much about herself in the expensive burial vault her husband purchased in Stirling east church in 1632. She drew attention to her parents who were now dead, but 'in hope of the resurrection', took pride in her father's status as a knight, her mother's godly virtues, her husband's achievements as a royal servant, and the quality of their long and fruitful marriage.[73]

While tombs placed great emphasis on worldly status and lineage, the personal aspect of memorialisation was not overlooked. When the young first earl of Perth died in December 1611, he was buried in Seton church, the resting place of his wife's kindred. Some eleven years later, his widow, Isabel Seton, who had since remarried, erected in his memory a grand mural monument, topped by an escutcheon bearing the impaled coats of arms of the two houses. Hawthornden, who had been a kinsman and friend of the dead earl, composed the epitaph that is carved at the base, reflecting how much she still missed him, ending 'no tyme her love can bound'.[74] The fashion for representing children in the funerary architecture of their parents was slow to appear in Scotland. It grew more popular in the early seventeenth century, with a good example at the Abbey church of Culross erected by sir George Bruce. At Kilmaurs parish kirk, the tomb of the eighth earl of Glencairn and his wife unusually shows the earl and his wife facing the onlooker surrounded by figures of their eight children. An inscription standing over the silent family reminds the observer that 'Nothing surer then death/Be terfor sobor and watch in prayer'.[75] Jean Stewart, lady Lovat, did not erect any monument to her much-loved son who died in 1620, but when she lay dying two years later, she settled all her affairs, requesting that she be buried in the Rood church in Inverness next to his remains.[76] Quite different sentiments were carved on the tombstone of sir James Johnstone of that Ilk. This monument was erected in 1608 following Johnstone's murder, the inscription preserving for ever the fact that the dead chief 'was maist tresonabillie murtherit, by the eighth lord Maxwell'.[77] Yet in spite of all the efforts to preserve the names and memory of dead kinsmen, contemporaries were aware that the march of time would overtake the best exertions of the stonemason. As Hawthornden wrote, 'Tombes and adopted pillars lye buried with those which were in them buried'.[78] Yet that did not stop men trying to ensure that the names of the dead remained among the living.

It was in the aisles or small transepts added on to the side of church buildings, in effect secular shrines, that noble families took greatest pride. Many wills specified where nobles wished to be buried; the fifth lord Ogilvy requested that he be interred 'in my sepultrie in the Isle of the Kirk of Kynnell', while sir Alexander Fraser of Philorth left instructions on the dimensions of the new aisle he wanted built at Fraserburgh.[79] Against all the injunctions of the kirk, the nobility used their enhanced role as owners of ecclesiastical patrimony to colonise church buildings as family memorials. Like the Radcliffe earls of Sussex who had the remains of their ancestors relocated, the first earl of Mar not only had himself buried in the newly acquired Cambuskenneth abbey, but he decreed that the remains of all his predecessors should also be moved there. The choir of Terregles kirk was appropriated by the Maxwell lords of Herries, the aisle in the parish church of North Berwick by the earls of Angus, Seton collegiate kirk by the lords of Seton and Haddington kirk by the Maitlands of Thirlestane; St Mirren's chapel in Paisley abbey became the burial place of the Hamilton house of Abercorn, and Kilmarnock parish kirk that of the lords Boyd.[80]

Baronial families followed this fashion. Sir Colin Campbell of Glenorchy enclosed the churchyard at Finlarg, where his father was buried in 1631, with a stone wall and gates decorated with a morthead and the anatomy of death as well as the family arms, all at a cost of 1000 merks. Other families opted for the more cost-effective lair, a mausoleum erected in the churchyard, the earliest known example being built in 1594 for Thomas Crawford of Jordanhill and his wife at Kilbirnie, while sir Thomas Hope of Craighall built one in Greyfriars kirkyard in Edinburgh.[81] These baronial houses were less able to defy ecclesiastical authority but more often than not the church was prepared to compromise. Sir James Dundas of Arniston marked his rising social status in 1606 by persuading the minister and elders of the kirk at Borthwick to allow him to have a burial place for his family in the church in return for contributing towards the repair costs of the building. In 1635, Malcolm Crawford of Cartsburn admitted before the court of high commission that he had broken into the kirk of Greenock at night and buried his mother, Margaret Blair, lady Kilbirnie. Punishment was avoided when Cartsburn and his kinsmen agreed to pay for the enlargement of the south aisle of the kirk.[82] Clearly expense was an issue here, and as in much of the rest of Protestant north Europe where the religious significance of burial declined, secular burial clubs developed to help defray the cost. The principal Fraser families clubbed together in 1634, agreeing jointly to fund the building of a new chapel and tomb at Kirkhill church which they would all use. Similarly, Gordonstoun hoped that his nephew, the thirteenth earl of Sutherland, would add to the family vault at Dornoch, 'and cause paint about the inner walls of that isle, or upon the silerine theroff, the portratours and pictours of all the Earles of Southerland, with the somme of ther lyfs from the beginning'.[83] On occasion, this responsibility to the dead kin led to conflict in the locality, especially among the lesser nobility who might not have exclusive rights to a burial place in the local church. The gothic story of the missing corpse from Durisdeer parish kirk arose over the winter of 1606–7 because of a clash between Adam Menzies of Enoch and sir James Douglas of Drumlanrig over who had burial rights within the church building.[84]

Less obviously permanent than stone monuments with their inscriptions were written memorials composed to honour departed nobles. One popular form of this was the heroic ballad. The dramatic assassination in January 1570 of the regent Moray was the occasion for a number of ballads lamenting his murder and attacking his enemies, while the murdered second earl of Moray was also commemorated in ballad form. Gaelic society expressed its regard for the dead in song. Following the execution of her husband, Gregor MacGregor of Glenstrae, in 1570, his grieving wife composed a beautiful Gaelic lament, *Cumhn Ghriogair MhicGhriogair Ghlian Sreith*.[85] More commonly, funeral elegies were growing in popularity, there being a great range in the quality of these mementos of the dead. Lady Jane Maitland, daughter of the first earl of Lauderdale, was fortunate in being eulogised in 1633 by Hawthornden. Most had to make do with more amateur productions. In 1622, John Lyon of Auldbar, having dissipated his father's fortune, published *Teares for the Death of Alexander Earle of Dunfermling*, in which he expressed the usual sentiments that 'Thy Pride, thy State, thine Honour, Blood and Gold,/Can not Death's stroak one minuts space with-hold'. The first earl of Buccleuch had to wait a few years before John Lauder, a captain in his regimen, had printed in Middelburg a laudatory poem entitled 'Aretophel or, a funeral elegy on the Death of the Right Honourable Walter Earle of Buccleuche' with apologies for having taken so long to produce the work.[86] Like the stone tombs these writings were attempts to defy time, to claim immortality based on earthly fame rather than on spiritual salvation.

## Conclusion

Like other early modern societies, that in Scotland engaged in a complex dialogue over the meaning of death, how to die, what to do with dead bodies and the most appropriate way to remember the dead. For the nobility, that debate was important because the lineage expected more from them in dying and in death. Noble power, and the values that undergirded that power, had to be able to survive those threats and the uncertainties death raised up, impressing on the rest of the community that whatever lay on the other side of the grave, everything on this side of it, down to the memorialisation of the dead, bespoke the authority, the wealth and the moral superiority of this privileged order. Death also brought nobles into competition with one another, so that each individual knew he, or she, was required to aspire to die better, be buried with greater piety or greater pomp, and be remembered with more funereal flamboyance than his or her neighbour. Of course, there were those who genuinely accepted the church's advice and instruction to go quietly from this world, but most succumbed to their hereditary obligations and to a lifetime of conspicuous behaviour and consumption. This was particularly the case in the seventeenth century as the critical voice of the clergy was quietened, the Reformation generation of nobles passed away, disposable incomes increased and fashions changed. As the church retreated from ritual, the nobility created their own elaborate and secular death rituals. In death, as in life, nobles proclaimed they were not as other men, and even today the architecture and inscriptions of their tombs defy the passing of the centuries, as was their intent.

# Conclusion

Noble society is not easily identified. The separation of the more obviously political roles and activities of early modern nobles, the public domain of their lives, from the more private spheres discussed in this book is to some extent artificial. Nevertheless, the world of the estate, of the immediate family, of learning, living, believing and dying embraces something close to a recognisable community. None of these themes was without public profile or political impact, but the focus of this study has been the inner life of the noble house and its lineage. Here lie the values and the strategies that kept these families on top, that energised their public actions.

In recognising that the nobility was much more than a handful of peers, that it was not even restricted to the heads of baronial houses but encompassed their wives and children too, the very extensive nature of this community gives it a wholly different dimension. Spurious arguments over the rise of supposedly 'new' nobles or the eclipse of allegedly 'traditional' nobles can be laid aside. The fact that one small cadre of families is overtaken momentarily, or even permanently, by another cadre of families in the course of a relatively short period – and in the life of a noble lineage eighty years is a short time – has no significance outside the realm of a narrow version of baronial politics. As long as the socio-economic foundations and the ideological self-consciousness of noble society were not challenged, far less overturned, it is only of limited interest to learn that one noble house has fallen to make way for another. As early modern commentators themselves recognised, that is always how it had been. Therefore, a nobility that has at its apex fifty or even one hundred titular peers, and at its base an unknown number of barons, lairds, chiefs and younger sons of peers and their families is not altered by social mobility within that society. This is particularly true when those at the base ascribe to the same values as those at the apex, desiring only to pull themselves to the top or to displace those whose ancestors had given their rival's lineage a temporary advantage.

The nobility, therefore, was never merely a handful of lords of parliament, an error that arises from concentrating overmuch on the political role of its most individually powerful members. Rather, it was a large, organic body, composed of interrelated lineages, expanding on one branch while contracting at another, its tentacle-like arms reaching out into every area of economic and cultural activity. So entwined were these families that their common roots required the same soil, the same sun and the same rain; hence the refusal of any to connive in the undermining of the whole society. A branch here or there might be lopped off as the head of a house was forfeited or when there was an absence of male heirs, but the whole remained, re-growing itself through some cadet house or exploiting its female members. This was noble society, a community so deeply entrenched in the structures of power, so much a part of the fabric of early modern Scotland that it is sometimes difficult to disentangle it from the broader picture of Scottish history.

The potent energy of the nobility has been one of the themes of this book. Here is a nobility that was not tottering towards the fag-end of a medieval world, nervously holding on to power and wealth in the face of vigorous new challenges from kings or from commoners. In economic, biological and ideological terms, noble society was aggressive and imaginative, consolidating the old and seeking out the new in order to increase its wealth, numbers and intellectual resources. The impact of significant economic, political and intellectual developments on the nobility has not been minimised in the above discussion, but what is most striking is how successfully noble society adapted and changed in order to retain its dominance. In spite of the huge population rise of the sixteenth century, the massive price inflation of the period, the opportunities offered to tenants by feuing, the many repercussions of the Protestant Reformation, the gradual absorption of Renaissance ideas, and the shock of the removal of the royal court to London, noble society proved remarkably resilient. There were changes, for example, in estate exploitation, in family relationships, in attitudes to education, but the world nobles inhabited in the 1560s was not unrecognisable from that of the 1640s. Continuity is a more persistent theme than change.

Understanding the economic health of the nobility is made particularly difficult by the nature of the sources, and in this topic, more than any other, the temporal length of study can enormously alter the picture. The range of experiences of different noble houses was also considerable, and previous suggestions about financial crisis perhaps suffered from looking too closely at those families struggling to pay their creditors while paying too little attention to the more sucessful and entrepreneurial cases. What has emerged here is a nobility ferociously gobbling up former ecclesiastical lands, operating skilfully in a dynamic land market, exploiting perpetual male entails to hold on to their lands, seizing every opportunity to diversify incomes from their estates and elsewhere, spending heavily in support of a lifestyle that was consistent with their status and demonstrating considerable ability in manipulating credit. Furthermore, most noble houses appear to have been wealthier on the eve of the Covenanting revolution than their forebears had been in the mid-sixteenth century when warfare severely dented economic resources. In terms of the broad, secular economic history of the nobility, this period was one of growth and self-confidence. The greatest families expanded their activities further afield than ever before, both geographically and in terms of the kinds of enterprise in which they were engaged; at the same time, many more baronial houses raised their standards of living and the opportunities for younger sons were exceptionally good. There were also financial problems of a general kind and some houses were overwhelmed by them. Indications of land saturation were evident by the second quarter of the early seventeenth century, and there are signs that fathers were finding it difficult to balance the logic of entails with the needs of their children. Above all, credit was becoming a necessity in sustaining standards of living for too many families that could not really afford to live as they did, paying ever higher tochers, embarking on ruinous building projects, engaging in expensive litigation and living at the royal court. In such a context, it was all too easy to blame strains on the family budget on taxation that was rising steadily. More particularly, over-ambitious land acquisition, entrepreneurial speculation, unrestrained extravagance and dangerous levels of mortgaging all generated examples of individuals who brought ruin on their lineage, sometimes for a generation. In only a few instances was the damage permanent. Perhaps this never amounted to a crisis, but it exposed a vulnerability to economic circumstances, and to the management of these circumstances, that was a new experience for a nobility being drawn into a more complex and more commercial market than ever before.

If the landed estate was the foundation on which noble houses rested, at the heart of the lineage were its members, dead, living and as yet unborn. The obligation that the individual members of the family owed both to ancestors and to descendants, reinforced by the powerful bonds of duty, loyalty and affection among those living, created a remarkably resilient institution. Here marriage was hugely important to the family, having an enormous impact on its biological success and on its economic, as well as political, fortune. Marriage was a necessary obligation individuals owed to the family, and it could not be left to the mere whims of individual choice. While Scottish law upheld the canonical view of marriage as a state entered into freely by two individuals, considerable restraints were placed in the way of exercising free choice. If this period did see fathers becoming a little gentler in the disposal of their children in marriage, and a greater degree of emotional involvement in people deciding on a spouse, marriage nevertheless remained an institution shaped primarily by the needs of the lineage. Within marriage, many noblemen and noblewomen found varying degrees of contentment, love even, and the extent to which that relationship was a partnership between two highly trained people deployed in the service of the family cannot be underestimated. No less than their husbands, wives served their own parental family in entering into marriage. Thereafter they served the interests of their husbands' and children's lineages. The church's obstacles to dissolving that marriage bond served the nobility well, reinforcing the durability of the alliances it created and stabilising the accompanying property transactions. Where marriages broke down completely, ways were found to minimise any impact on the family, and divorce was a last and rare resort. The children that were the product of these marriages were plentiful, the high fertility rate being a consequence of universal and relatively young marriages. That in turn was due to the emphasis placed on children as an asset, and to economic conditions that allowed fathers to provide for them adequately. However, while most noble families, as distinct from the wider household, had a nuclear appearance, they were, like early modern families in general, more fluid in their membership than a father, mother and children model suggests. The constant change of personnel, occasioned by early death, remarriage and a high birth rate, suggests an unstable environment in which a need to hold on to ancestors as fixed points becomes understandable. The noble family also generated its own internal tensions, creating competition between generations and between siblings, but on the whole the disciplined structure provided by male primogeniture and the educative process to which all were exposed ensured that few families were torn apart by those tensions. And while duty and responsibility shaped behaviour with astonishing success, the very real bonds of friendship, affection and love between parents and children should not be overlooked.

The early modern noble *mentalité* was shaped by land and family above all else. Education was designed to ensure that young nobles were prepared for the world so that they could best serve the long-term interests of the lineage, represented at any one moment in time by those landed possessions and its living members. Social and intellectual changes meant that increasingly the educational assumptions of an earlier age, in which martial abilities and estate management figured most prominently, were being replaced by a more diverse agenda requiring the acquisition of new skills. In this, as in their economic adaptations, the nobility proved to be enthusiastic learners, striking the right balance between educationalists who over-emphasised the importance of books and the backwoods tendency to despise men of letters. A scholarly nobleman was admirable, but a nobleman who was merely a scholar was of little use to anyone. Noble society continued to pursue sporting activities designed as training for war, while also putting to use the new learning to cultivate roles as courtiers or as patrons of the arts which were deployed in the glorification of that society. Scotland's late Renaissance was the product of noble society, proclaiming its worth in an artistic environment from which the kirk and the crown had largely withdrawn. Furthermore, if the nobles were in the process of becoming more like privileged members of civil society than the prominent figures in martial society, they were also experiencing a religious re-awakening. This is not to deny that the late medieval Scottish nobility had its religious enthusiasts or to suggest that early modern nobles were all deeply religious men and women, but the personal and communal religion of nobles in general was much more important than it had been since the twelfth century. Their role as lay religious leaders had never been more important, being promoted by both ministers of the kirk and by Jesuit missionaries who each looked to godly magistrates to drive forward their own versions of the Kingdom of Heaven. It was a partnership that in the mid-seventeenth century took the nobility to the edge of their own destruction. Yet even in the decades between Reformation and Covenant, there was a tension between church and nobility, between the aspirations of a Christian commonwealth and the realities of a privileged élite determined to uphold its wealth and power. That tension was apparent over death, not so much in the dying in which noble ideas about stoic restraint chimed with the church's message of resignation to God's will, as in the business of disposing of the dead. Here noble society was insistent on the responsibilities of the living to honour the dead, to ensure that the honour, reputation and status of the lineage was upheld. As in so much else in this society of privileged people, death was yet another opportunity to proclaim their self-assurance, wealth and power.

The origins of this book lay in a question about the nature of the Scottish nobility at the outbreak of the Covenanting revolution of 1637. That revolution shattered noble society far more fundamentally than the previous civil war, or wars, of the mid-sixteenth century. Both conflicts profoundly unsettled the crown and the church, but while the former left noble power intact and even strengthened it, the conflict of the 1640s saw the higher nobility nearly eclipsed. During the following decade their power was broken by an army of English republican sectarians. For much of the remainder of the seventeenth century, noble families had to work hard to recover ground lost in these twenty-odd years. For many historians, however, that decline in the 1640s was only the culmination of a long process, beginning in the mid-sixteenth century, that saw the nobility edged aside by crown, kirk, merchants, lawyers and lairds. In other words, the nobility did not just lose control of events in 1648, they had been losing their grip for decades. This analysis has never been convincing given the longevity of nobles as a powerful élite in Scottish history. It has become increasingly less persuasive as studies of nobilities elsewhere in Europe point to the durability of their hold over early modern society. Yet, before engaging with the more immediately obvious topics of politics and government, it has been necessary to understand this noble world better, to provide a more rounded picture of an élite too often seen only as political leaders without financial worries, marital problems or private interests. One of the absurdities of seeing nobles as nothing more than political animals is that other important aspects of their lives are neglected. On this basis, one historian reached the naive conclusion that Charles I's exclusion of the nobility from government resulted in a situation in which 'the Scottish nobles had too little to do,' as though nobles never did anything but plot the next rebellion.[1] This examination demonstrates that they had a great many other interests and preoccupations, and that political issues often had little direct impact on wealth, family and culture. Whatever the more overtly political context of events in 1567, 1603 or 1637, noble society was barely affected; its disillusionment with Mary, its reaction to the departure of James VI and its outrage at Charles I did not spring out of a community bewildered by change or fearful of its own future.

The pursuit of noble society is interesting for much more than whatever contribution it makes to the debate on the origins of revolution or relations between crown and nobles. Hopefully, it shines some light on the Scotland of the late sixteenth and early seventeenth centuries, a Scotland in which the dynamic and energetic leadership of its nobility ensured it was fully locked into the main developments and fashions of continental Europe. Scotland's noble society was certainly no backwater waiting to be rescued by a closer relationship with England. What is most significant about England is how little it impacted upon the Scottish nobility before and after the union of 1603. This book also offers another example to be set alongside similar investigations elsewhere in Europe, adding a little to the weight of argument in favour of the sustained vigour of nobilities from Poland in the east to Portugal in the west, from Naples in the south to Scotland in the north.

# Notes

*(ch. = chapter; Ch. = Charter; n = note; no. = number; prt. = part; ser. = series)*

## Introduction

1. Stone, *Crisis of the Aristocracy*, 747; Wrightson, 'Estates, degrees, and sorts', 30–52; Burke, 'Language of orders'; Arriaza, 'Mousnier and Barber'; Beik, *Absolutism and Society*, 8; Bush, 'Anatomy of nobility'; John Ferne, *The Blazon of Gentrie* (London, 1586), 26, quoted in Howard, 'Kinnoull aisle'; Clark, *State and Status*, 15–18. For a recent restatement of a class-based understanding, Heller, *Iron and Blood*.
2. Price, 'The Dutch nobility', 84; Bisson, 'Nobility and family'; Lansing, *Florentine Magnates*; Dewald, *European Nobility*, 19–22.
3. Mettam, 'Definitions of nobility'; Mettam, 'French nobility', 114–15; Bitton, *French Nobility in Crisis*, 92–117; van Winter, 'Knighthood and nobility'.
4. Mason, 'Chivalry and citizenship'; Brown, *Bloodfeud*, ch. 7.
5. Keen, *Chivalry*, 243, 247; Schalk, *Valor to Pedigree*, 3–20; Bitton, *French Nobility in Crisis*, 27–41; Smith, *Culture of Merit*, 37–9, 42–9.
6. *Historie*, 146; Calderwood, *History*, ii. 414–16; Spottiswoode, *History*, ii. 88; Wormald, *Lords and Men*; Macinnes, *Clanship, Commerce and the House of Stuart*, 57–9.
7. Brown, *Bloodfeud*. For France, Dewald, *Aristocratic Experience*, 45; Bitton, *French Nobility in Crisis*, 27–41; Wood, *Nobility of Bayeux*, 81–95. For England, Stone, *Crisis of the Aristocracy*, 266; Bernard, 'The Tudor nobility in perspective', 8–9.
8. *APS*, iii. 91–2; iv. 188; *Ancram and Lothian*, i. 482; *RPC*, first ser., vii. 407; viii. 78, 676–7; second ser., i. 191–2; ii. 559–60, 571.
9. Stone, *Crisis of the Aristocracy*, 201–17; Dewald, *Aristocratic Experience*, 62; *Melrose Papers*, i. 55; *RPC*, first ser., x. 746–7; second ser., ii. 37–9. There is a good deal more about Morton's military preparations in NLS MS 82.
10. Motley, *Becoming a French Aristocrat*, 48–50; James, 'English politics and the concept of honour', 311–12; Hume, *House of Douglas*, i. 68–127, 209–36; Kellie, *Pallas Armata*.
11. *CSP Scotland*, v. 504; Urquhart, *Jewel*, 98. For Buccleuch and Lindsay, Fraser, *Buccleuch*, i. 235, 253–9; NAS GD 224/889/3; Lindsay, *Lives of the Lindsays*, ii. 53–7; *House of Forbes*, 168–9, 178; *HMC Second Report*, i. 195.
12. Fraser, *Sutherland*, ii. 358, and see too *Chronicles of the Frasers*, 150, 184, 257.
13. Zulager, 'Middle-rank administrators', 51–3; Jespersen, 'Danish nobility', 41–70; Bush, *Noble Privilege*, 4–5; Wood, *Nobility of Bayeux*, 12–15.
14. Craig, *Jus Feudale*, i. 155–8, 213–15, 219–21.
15. Fraser, *Haddington*, ii. 151.
16. Dalrymple, *Institutions*, 331–2, 372–3; he cites an act of 1503, *APS*, ii. 252. The case for a territorial basis to nobility is also argued in the nineteenth century by Riddell, *Scottish Peerages*, i.
17. Fraser, *Chiefs of Grant*, iii. 10.
18. *Family of Kilravock*, 80.
19. *RPC*, first ser., x. 334; Brown, 'Scottish aristocracy', 566–7.
20. Knox, *Works*, i. 272. In Russia titles were increasingly a reflection of office, Banac and Bushkovitch, 'Nobility in the history of Russia and eastern Europe', 8–9.

21. James, 'English politics and the concept of honour', 381.
22. Maitland, *Funerall Sermon*, 2–3; McCordick, *Scottish Literature*, i. 772; *Political Writings*, 29, 35; NLS Adv. MS 15.2.14/83–4. On France, Schalk, *Valor to Pedigree*, 37–144; Major, *Renaissance Monarchy to Absolute Monarchy*, 105; Smith, *Culture of Merit*, 61–4; Wood, *Nobility of Bayeux*, 29; Motley, *Becoming a French Aristocrat*, 11–12; Bitton, *French Nobility in Crisis*, 77–91; Dewald, *Aristocratic Experience*, 7. Much of the evidence for this debate is literary. For an interesting case in which Franco-Scottish mutual understanding of nobility is apparent, *Melrose Papers*, ii. 384–5.
23. Macinnes, *Clanship, Commerce and the House of Stuart*, 3; *CSP Scotland*, v. 46; Craig, *Jus Feudale*, i. 210; Hume, *House of Douglas*, 20–1. Scottish noble houses were content to have their own individual origin myths, and there was no uniform belief in a Frankish, Gothic or Sarmatian ancestry as was the case in France and Germany, Spain and Sweden, and Poland, Bonney, *European Dynastic States*, 378.
24. Innes, *Scots Heraldry*, 101–10; Meikle, 'Invisible divide', 72; Leslie, *Historie*, ii. 469; and on bastards, Craig, *Jus Feudale*, i. 220.
25. *Ancram and Lothian*, p. xxviii; Craig, *Jus Feudale*, i. 220.
26. *Miscellany of the Scottish History Society*, ii. 133–228; *House of Seytoun*, pp. ix–xi, 20–3; Smith, *Culture of Merit*, ch. 2; Ranun, *Artisans of Glory*, 3–12.
27. Dawson, 'Fifth earl of Argyle', 22–3; Sellar, 'The earliest Campbells'; Sellar, 'Family origins'.
28. Fraser, *Sutherland*, ii. 115, 365–6; Gordon, *Sutherland*, 24–30; *House of Gordon*, i. p. xxxv; ii. 111–52; *House of Forbes*, i. p. xxxiii.
29. Leslie, *Historie*, ii. 10; Pont, *Topographical Account*, 14; Gordon, *Sutherland*, 13–15; NRA(S) 5/3/6; Fraser, *Buccleuch*, i. pp. xx–xxiii. Both the rival Crawford and Edzell branches of the Lindsays compiled genealogies in the early seventeenth century, NRA(S) 237/A.
30. Fraser, *Buccleuch*, i. p. xxiv.
31. van Nierop, *Nobility of Holland*, 22–3, 35–8; Schalk, *Valor to Pedigree*, 145–73; Clark, *State and Status*, 158–61.
32. NLS Adv. MS 15.2.14/57–9.
33. Bush, *Noble Privilege*, 2–3; Dewald, *European Nobility*, 28–32; Scott and Storrs, 'Introduction', 10–13; Stone, *Crisis of the Aristocracy*, 54–5; Stone and Stone, *An Open Elite?*, 407.
34. Wormald, 'Lords and lairds', 186; NLS Adv. MS 15.2.14/15.
35. Bush, *Rich Noble, Poor Noble*, 1–6; Scott and Storrs, 'Introduction', 9–11, 21–2.
36. Kamen, *European Society*, 140, 178–80; de Win, 'Lesser nobility', 97; Thompson, 'Nobility in Spain', 185–7; Major, *Renaissance Monarchy to Absolute Monarchy*, 58; Stone and Stone, *An Open Elite?*, 6–7, 184, 239–55; Heal and Holmes, *Gentry in England and Wales*, 6–19; Morgan, 'Individual style', 18.
37. NLS Adv MS 15.2.14/22–3.
38. NLS MS 20001/126.
39. *Historie*, 12; Calderwood, *History*, ii. 362; *RPC*, v. 446–7; vi. 169; vii. 167–77, 214.
40. *Maitland Miscellany*, i. prt. 2, 396. Balfour saw the work of this commission and the king's imposition of a dress code at parliament as part of a general desire to enhance the dignity of the peerage, *Works*, ii. 8.
41. Nisbet, *System of Heraldry*; Innes, *Scots Heraldry*, 20, 29, 31–2, 38, 44. Innes goes on to quote Bishop Leslie, who commented that pride in ancestry was shared 'by the haill people, nocht only the nobilitie', ibid., 4.
42. Howard, 'Thrie estates'.
43. *RPC*, first ser., xiii. 616–17, 633–4, 649–51; second ser., i. 122–4, 173, 355–6; Balfour, *Works*, ii. 136. Urquhart, *Jewel*, 168–70; *HMC Laing*, i. 168. Twenty-eight sales took place before the end of 1626, and in spite of the initially slow uptake a total of 113 baronetcies had been sold by 1638, Macinnes, *Making of the Covenanting Movement*, 49, 72 n. 2. For England, Stone, *Crisis of the Aristocracy*, 71–97.
44. *House of Seytoun*, 57.

45. Dewald, *European Nobility*, 26–7; Bonney, *European Dynastic States*, 336, 377; Miller, *Henry VIII and the English Nobility*, 6–37; Stone, *Crisis of the Aristocracy*, 97–128; Stone and Stone, *An Open Elite?*, 261–2; Major, *Renaissance Monarchy to Absolute Monarchy*, 311–13; Harding, *Anatomy of a Power Elite*, 80–4; Wood, *Nobility of Bayeux*, 45–6; Atienza Hernández, '"Refeudalisation" in Castile', 253–6.
46. Figures do not include extinctions. Fraser, *Melvilles*, i. 82–124.
47. *Abbotsford Miscellany*, 213; Lindsay, *Lives of the Lindsays*, i. 323; Macinnes, *Making of the Covenanting Movement*, 4; and see NAS GD 40/2/12/22.
48. In Spain 250 of the 272 patents of nobility issued between 1552 and 1700 were bought, Bonney, *European Dynastic States*, 340; Stone, *Crisis of the Aristocracy*, 103, 107, 109, 119–28; Rubinstein, *Captain Luckless*, 16.
49. NLS MS 83/50; NAS GD 112/39/48/16, 112/39/48/18, 112/39/48/21, 112/39/49/1; Fraser, *Annandale*, ii. 31, 290; Fraser, *Menteith*, ii. 25.
50. Upton, 'Swedish nobility', 17–18.
51. NLS Adv. MS 15.2.14/12–19, 15.2.14/29. For a discussion of noble virtue in a Dutch context, van Nierop, *Nobility of Holland*, 29–31.
52. *APS*, iv. 292.
53. Moysie, *Memoirs*, 34; *CSP Scotland*, xiii. prt. 1, 451; Balfour, *Works*, ii. 8; Calderwood, *History*, v. 95–8; *RPC*, first ser., vi. 36.
54. For a post-1603 creation, *RPC*, first ser., xii. 671; xiii. 383; *HMC Fourteenth Report*, 7; Fraser, *Buccleuch*, i. 238; ii. 261–2; Balfour, *Works*, ii. 8–9, 202–4. For the oath taken by the new marquis of Douglas, Fraser, *Douglas*, iii. 328–9. One side effect of this economy in ceremony was that the lyon king of arms and his officers lost money, ibid., first ser., ix. 485–6; xii. 41–2, 392–5.
55. As occurred with the Angus earldom in 1565 and again after 1588, Calderwood, *History*, iii. 244; Lee, *Maitland of Thirlestane*, 176; NRA(S) 237/F/482–3; *APS*, iii. 588–9. For some general discussion, Clark, *State and Status*, 155–89.
56. Spottiswoode, *History*, iii. 217. For Eglinton, *Melrose Papers*, i. 113–17, 170–3, 182–3, 185–7, 189–90, 195–7; *RPC*, first ser., ix. 474; x. 32–3, 310–11. For Lothian, *Ancram and Lothian*, ii. 488; Fraser, *Carlaverock*, ii. 77–8; *RPC*, second ser., iv. 418, 441–3. See too the Oliphant and Melville cases in the 1630s, *RPC*, second ser., iv. 119; vi. 17, 26; Paul, *Scots Peerage*, vi. 552; Fraser, *Melvilles*, i. 190–1; ii. 21, 83. The best discussion of jurisdiction is in Riddell, *Scottish Peerages*, i. 1–40.
57. Goodare, 'Nobility and the absolutist state', 164 n. 11, and more confusingly in Macinnes, *Making of the Covenanting Movement*, 2–23. For England, Heal and Holmes, *Gentry in England and Wales*, 380; Coward, 'A "crisis of the aristocracy" in the sixteenth and seventeenth centuries?'; Cooper, 'Ideas of gentility'; Bernard, *Power of the Early Tudor Nobility*, 176; Mertes, *English Noble Household*, 4–5; Stone, *Crisis of the Aristocracy*, 1–2, 50–3; Stone and Stone, *An Open Elite?*, 3; Cannon, 'British nobility', 54–7.
58. Bush, *Noble Privilege*, 130–43.
59. Barrow, *Anglo-Norman Era*; Grant, 'Development of the Scottish peerage'.
60. *Chronicle of the Kings of Scotland*, 158; Craig, *Jus Feudale*, i. 209–15; Spottiswoode, *History*, i. 62; Gordon, *Sutherland*, 23–4; Hume, *General History*, 205; *Registrum de Panmure*, i. p. xcvi; Melville, *Memoirs*, 372; Leslie, *Historie*, ii. 38.
61. Macinnes, *Making of the Covenanting Movement*, 7. For a variety of sources that appear to distinguish between nobles and barons see *HMC Eleventh Report*, 8; Moysie, *Memoirs*, 86; Melville, *Memoirs*, 226, 237; *Historie*, 14, 20, 23; Knox, *Works*, i. 410–11; Bannatyne, *Memorials*, 15, 17; Calderwood, *History*, ii. 380, 419; v. 185; *Maitland Miscellany*, i. prt. 1, 63–4; *RPC*, first ser., ix. 26.
62. *RPC*, first ser., vii. 465–6; Macinnes, *Making of the Covenanting Movement*, 7.
63. *APS*, iii. 91–2; *RPC*, first ser., ii. 525, 548, 569; iv. 787; *RPC*, second ser., i. 272. Spottiswoode projected back into the 1580s the political agenda of the 1620s and 1630s, 'to free the barons of their dependence upon noblemen' which echoes the official language of the day, Spottiswoode, *History*, ii. 377; *RPC*, 2nd ser., i. 228; Macinnes, *Making of the Covenanting Movement*, 60–1. Melrose also referred in 1627 to the gentry in the context

of thinking about parliamentary representation, NLS MS 80/64 and 80/58.

64. Thompson, '*Hidalgo* and *pechero*', 53–78; de Win, 'Lesser nobility'; du Boulay 'Was there a German "gentry"?'; Contamine, 'France at the end of the Middle Ages'; Bush, *Rich Noble, Poor Noble*, 30–58; Jones, 'Introduction', *Gentry and Lesser Nobility*, 8–9; Major, *Renaissance Monarchy to Absolute Monarchy*, 106.
65. *CSP Scotland*, xiii. prt. 1, 106; *APS*, iii. 40; *RPC*, first ser., iv. 198, 227–8; Craig, *Jus Feudale*, i. 155–8; *Political Writings*, 29; Balfour, *Works*, i. 344; NLS Adv. MS 15.2.14/22–3. Denmilne placed knights above other untitled nobles, in contrast to Holland where they were not regarded as noble, van Nierop, *Nobility of Holland*, 23. This broad understanding of nobility has received some recognition, Meikle, 'Invisible divide'; Zulager, 'Middle-rank administrators'.
66. MacKay, 'Lesser nobility'; Thompson, 'Nobility in Spain', 174; Amelang, *Honoured Citizens*, 86.
67. *CSP Scotland*, iv. 2; Wormald, 'Lords and lairds', 186–7; *RPC*, first ser., ix. 51; Lindsay, *Lives of the Lindsays*, ii. 2–3; *Honorum de Morton*, i. 121; *HMC Various*, 117; Hope, *Diary*, 39.
68. Fraser, *Douglas*, ii. 376. See too the tombs of the laird of Airdrie in Crail kirkyard dated 1598, or sir Thomas MaClellan of Bombie erected in Kirkcudbright in 1597, MacGibbon and Ross, *Ecclesiastical Architecture*, ii. 155; v. 209–10; Beveridge, *Churchyard Memorials of Crail*, 132–50.
69. NAS GD 112/20/5/5; *RPC*, first ser., vi. 134–5; Knox, *Works*, ii. 560–1; Calderwood, *History*, ii. 363–4; *Registrum de Panmure*, i. pp. v–xl, xcix–c.
70. Melville, *Memoirs*, 383–4; Craig, *Jus Feudale*, i. 213; *HMC Mar and Kellie*, i. 68.
71. Leslie, *Historie*, i. 10, 13–14, 31; *CSP Scotland*, v. 252–64; vii. 577; ix. 257, 666–9; x. 29–34; xi. 256–8; xiii. prt. 2, 1115, 1117–18; *Estimate*; Meikle, 'Invisible divide', 73.
72. Bonney, *European Dynastic States*, 376–7; Dewald, *European Nobility*, 22–6; Bush, *Rich Noble, Poor Noble*, 7–29; Mettam, 'French nobility', 114; Schimert, 'Hungarian nobility', 149; Frost, 'Nobility of Poland-Lithuania', 191–3; Jespersen, 'Danish nobility', 44 5; Upton, 'Swedish nobility', 17; van Nierop, *Nobility of Holland*, 38–45; Stone, *Crisis of the Aristocracy*, 1–2, 50–3; Thompson, 'Nobility in Spain', 175, 188.
73. NLS Adv. MS 34.4.16/2, NLS MS 3717, NLS MS 6402; NAS GD 158/2983; Monipenny, *Certeine Matters Concerning the Realme of Scotland*; and NLS MS 20 774/44 for a 'who's who' compiled c.1620 for the second earl of Wigton that was added to over the succeeding twenty years.
74. *RPC*, first ser., ii. 398–401, 548–9; iii. 634.
75. Ibid., first ser., iv. p. liii, p. lvi, 783–7, 803. Also useful on numbers is Meikle, 'Lairds and gentlemen', 24–40.
76. Grant, 'Scottish peerage', 11–12.
77. Bush, *Rich Noble, Poor Noble*, 59–102; Bisson, 'Nobility and family', 605; Frost, 'Nobility of Poland-Lithuania', 187, 193–5; Kaminski, 'The *szlachta* of the Polish-Lithuanian Commonwealth and their government', 23–6; Thompson, 'Nobility in Spain, 178–80; Stone and Stone, *An Open Elite?*, 16–29; Stone, *Crisis of the Aristocracy*, 190–7. See Bacon's warnings on the dangers of a large nobility, many of whom were certain to be relatively poor, *Essayes*, 42.
78. *House of Seytoun*, pp. xii–xiii where Lethington also placed his faith in the moral order to bring about decay to those houses that rose on the back of oppression.
79. Hume, *General History*, 390–1.
80. *CSP Scotland*, iv. 432.
81. Hume, *General History*, 278–9, 357; *CSP Scotland*, iv. 540.
82. Wormald, *Court, Kirk and Community*, 31–2; Wormald, 'Lairds and lords', 182–95.
83. *Chronicle of the Kings of Scotland*, 174; Scott and Storrs, 'Introduction', 23–4; Meikle, 'Invisible divide'.
84. Wormald, *Lords and Men*, appendix A, 333–41, Maxwell.
85. Stone and Stone, *An Open Elite?*, 279–80; Wood, *Nobility of Bayeux*, 58–68.
86. *Chronicle of the Kings of Scotland*, 170.

87. Sanderson, *Scottish Rural Society*, 115, 139–40; *House of Gordon*, 27–54.
88. Bush, *Rich Noble, Poor Noble*, 43–58; Wood, *Nobility of Bayeux*, 20–42; Smith, *Culture of Merit*, 49–57; Bonney, *European Dynastic States*, 344, 377; Dewald, *European Nobility*, 21–2; Clark, *State and Status*, 169–74, 200–3; Stone, *Crisis of the Aristocracy*, 66–9; Cooper, 'Ideas of gentility', 73–7.
89. *APS*, iii. 554–5; Wood, *Nobility of Bayeux*, 20–42; *RPC*, second ser., ii. 164–5; iii. 594–6; GD 45/1/26.
90. NLS Adv. MS 33.2.28/39–40. This also occurred in England, Stone, *Crisis of the Aristocracy*, 65.
91. *RPC*, first ser., x. 124–5, 127–9, 180–2.
92. *CSP Scotland*, xi. 666.
93. Zulager, 'Middle-rank administrators', 39–42.
94. *CSP Scotland*, vi. 106; viii. 141; Hume, *General History*, 365; *Historie*, 188; Zulager, 'Middle-rank administrators', 146–8. Denmilne described Arran and his wife, both of whom were children of peers, as 'two such mussrooms that had arrisen bot yesterday almost from the earth', Balfour, *Works*, i. 383.
95. Mettam, 'Definitions of nobility'; Lindsay, *Historie*, ii. 196; Zulager, 'Middle-rank administrators', 38; Calderwood, *History*, iii. 90–1, 106–11; Bannatyne, *Memorials*, 141–58; Neuschel, *Word of Honor*, 65–8, 103–31.
96. *Memorials of Montrose*, i. 33; NLS MS 5787/20; NLS Adv. MS 15.2.14/25–8; *Works of Sir Thomas Urquhart*, 49. Sir Francis Bacon usefully observed that 'new *Nobility* is but the Act of Power; but Ancient *Nobility* is the Act of Time,' Bacon, *Essayes*, 42.
97. Dewald, *European Nobility*, 17. For a useful cautionary discussion see Bush, *Rich Noble, Poor Noble*, 100–2. For apparently high rates of extinction in the Netherlands and England, Price, 'Dutch nobility', 84–8; van Nierop, *Nobility of Holland*, 46–53; Stone, *Crisis of the Aristocracy*, 169; Stone and Stone, *An Open Elite?*, 86; Heal and Holmes, *Gentry in England and Wales*, 40–1; Grant, 'Extinction of direct male lines'.
98. Dawson, 'Fifth earl of Argyle', 26. Elder sons were also set aside in cases of idiocy. In 1585, parliament recognised Francis Hay as ninth earl of Errol in succession to his elder brother who was insane, *APS*, iii. 420–1.
99. *House of Seytoun*, pp. xii–xiii; Fraser, *Sutherland*, ii. 337; Gordon, *Sutherland*, 13, 179; Hume, *House of Douglas*, i. pp. lxiii–lxiv, 27–8, 31; ii. 300–1; Hume, *General History*, 215; *Philotus*; *Works of Sir William Alexander*, ii. 546; *Poems of William Drummond*, 230; Heal and Holmes, *Gentry in England and Wales*, 20–30; Dewald, *European Nobility*, 7–9.

## Chapter 1: Landlords

1. Craig, *Jus Feudale*; *HMC Various V*, 17. Although in Denmark most of the crown's land was administered by the nobility, who owned 44 per cent of the country's cultivated land, Jespersen, 'Danish nobility', 45.
2. Fraser, *Buccleuch*, i. 173–6; *HMC Fourth Report*, iv. 474–5, nos 20, 23, 26; *HMC Sixth Report*, 615; *HMC Laing*, i. 105.
3. Zulager, 'Middle-rank administrators', 146. Gogar's grant of part of the Gowrie estates in Berwickshire became the basis of the lordship of Fenton, NAS GD 6/222, 297, 301, 309, 321–5, 457, 458.
4. *Political Writings*, 74; Burns, 'George Buchanan and the anti-monarchomachs', 144; introduction to *Inquisitionum*; Craig, *Jus Feudale*, ii. 715–829. For examples of a new erection, the service of heirs, general retours, dispensations and parliamentary ratifications, Fraser, *Haddington*, i. 21; ii. 282; Fraser, *Sutherland*, iii. 141–50, 168; *House of Gordon*, i. 314–18; NAS GD 124/3/8; Fraser, *Elphinstone*, i. 158–9; *HMC Third Report*, ii. 398, no. 30; *RPC*, first ser., viii. 417, 423; x. 276; *APS*, iii. 587–656. For the earl of Argyll's feudal dependence on the king, Macinnes, *Clanship, Commerce and the House of Stuart*, 5–7; Dawson, 'The fifth earl of Argyle', 8.

5. Fraser, *Douglas*, ii. 370–4; iii. 247–51, 255–62, 292–4, 298; iv. 32–3.
6. Burgess, *Perpetuities*, 58–62. For such negotiations see the fourth lord Herries in 1567 and the tenth earl of Angus in 1602, *APS*, ii. 558–9; iv. 311–12; Fraser, *Douglas*, ii. 396, 398. For concerns about the activities of corrupt officials, *APS*, iv. 287–8.
7. Lee, *Road to Revolution*, 152–3; Stevenson, 'Scottish revenues', 22–3; Macinnes, *Making of the Covenanting Movement*, 56, 68–9; Hope, *Diary*, 29; *HMC Mar and Kellie*, i. 164–8.
8. For example, a convention of estates had authorised such an inquiry in 1574, *APS*, iii. 89–90; *RPC*, second ser., iii. 307; Balfour, *Works*, ii. 128, 134; Macinnes, *Making of the Covenanting Movement*, 45–72, 77–97; Lee, *Road to Revolution*, chs 1 and 2; Goodare, 'The nobility and the absolutist state', 162, 168–9.
9. Sanderson, *Scottish Rural Society*, 64–77, 111–12; van Nierop, *Nobility of Holland*, 113–25; Leslie, *Historie*, i. 11, 13, 37.
10. Herries, *Memoirs*, 38, 55. For the rise of the lairds, Makey, *Church of the Covenant*, ch. 1 and 165–78; Makey, 'Presbyterian and Canterburian; Wormald, '"Princes" and the regions', 72.
11. It was formally erected in 1606, NAS GD 124/1/965–7, 124/1/969–76, 124/1/978, 124/1/980–3, 124/1/992, 124/1/1001, 124/1/1005, 124/1/1008. See the example of Kelso, *HMC Fourteenth Report*, 40–1.
12. Fraser, *Sutherland*, i. 112–13, 142–3; iii. 116–24; Kirk, 'Royal and lay patronage', 138.
13. Goodare, 'Parliamentary taxation', 31. With the teinds came some responsibility to maintain the church building in a reasonable state of repair and to provide for the communion, NAS GD 137/55. For Fife teind valuations c.1628, GD 45/1/8.
14. Goodare, 'Parliamentary taxation', 28–30; Sanderson, *Scottish Rural Society*, 189; *APS*, iv. 38; Spottiswoode, *History*, i. 327; NAS GD 150/3438/3, Traquair to Morton, undated letter.
15. Zulager, 'Middle-rank administrators', 143; Lee, *Maitland of Thirlestane*, 142–3 and appendix.
16. NAS GD 25/9/32 bundle dated 1600–88 contains many court of session decreets of the 1620s and 1630s on these cases; *HMC Eleventh Report*, i. 67; ii. 30–1.
17. Lee, *Government by Pen*, 62–4; Kirk, 'Royal and lay patronage', 139–40; *HMC Third Report*, iii. 394, no. 185; *APS*, iv. 321–63; for example, see the erection of the lordship of Cardross GD 15/3, 15/5–7. For the success story of the Kers of Newbattle see Sanderson, *Mary Stewart's People*, 166–78. Nevertheless, the crown never gave up trying to increase its share of these estates. For example, see Kilwinning abbey in 1612, Fraser, *Eglinton*, i. 55.
18. Macinnes, *Making of the Covenanting Movement*, ch. 3, 69; Makey, 'Presbyterian and Canterburian', 161; Lee, *Road to Revolution*, 48–62; Foster, 'A constant platt achieved'; the first lord Napier provides a useful summary of the objections in *Memorials of Montrose*, i. 65–9. Litigation often followed, NAS GD 137/72, 137/291–4.
19. Craig, *Jus Feudale*; Hope, *Major Practicks*, i. 147–284; Fraser, *Haddington*, i. pp. xxix–xxxiv; ii. 265, 277; *Melrose Papers*, ii. 399.
20. NAS GD 65/29–30, 65/34, 65/37–8, all were held of the marquis of Hamilton; Fraser, *Haddington*, ii. 143–5; NAS GD 124/15/30/6, 124/15/92/1.
21. Fraser, *Sutherland*, ii. 117; Dodgshon, *Chiefs to Landlords*, 31–54; *Ancram and Lothian*, i. 90–2; NRA(S) 3246/261. For a study of one minor French noble house over the long term, Mentzer, *Blood and Belief*.
22. *HMC Fifteenth Report*, i. 5; Fraser, *Buccleuch*, i. 251–3; *Black Book of Taymouth*, 30–71; de Folco, 'The Hopes of Craighall'.
23. NLS MS 14 542/9; Cliffe, *Yorkshire Gentry*, 110, 380–3. This, however, primarily reflects the unfavourable exchange rate. For some comparative perspectives, Greengrass, 'Property and politics in sixteenth-century France; Dewald, *European Nobility*, 60.
24. Melville, *Memoirs*, 383; Connacher, 'Land tenure in the seventeenth century', 24–9; Habakkuk, 'Long-term rate of interest'; Stone and Stone, *An Open Elite?*, 11–12.
25. Price, 'Dutch nobility', 89; van Nierop, *Nobility of Holland*, 22; Stone, *Crisis of the Aristocracy*, 156–7, 162, 264, 273; Bernard, *Power of the Early Tudor Nobility*, 177–9;

Wood, *Nobility of Bayeux*, 141–55; Dewald, *Aristocratic Experience*, 158–63; Woolf, 'Economic problems of the nobility in the early modern period'; Benadusi, *A Provincial Elite*, 138–62; Thompson, 'Nobility in Spain', 215–17. Atienza Hernández, '"Refeudalisation" in Castile during the seventeenth century'; Dewald, *European Nobility*, 62–5, 76–82; Gates-Coon, *Landed Estates of the Esterhazy Princes*.

26. *Early Travellers*, 156–7.
27. Fraser, *Sutherland*, i. 145–6; iii. 135–9, 346, 352.
28. Grant, 'Development of the Scottish peerage'; Wormald, 'Lords and lairds', 187; NAS GD 39/1/82, 39/1/85, 39/1/87, 39/5/65.
29. *Inquisitionum*, i–ii. Some important noble houses do not appear in this source. For example, in addition to a still-expanding territoral heartland in the western Highlands, the earls of Argyll owned estates in Perthshire, Fife, Edinburgh, Clackmannanshire and Renfrewshire, Dawson, 'Fifth earl of Argyle', 8–9; NAS GD 124/1/11–12, 124/1/15.
30. Callender, *Pattern of Landownership*, chs 2–3; NRA(S) 237/C/166–7. For a discussion of the technical problems that exist in England where archival resources are better, see Cooper, 'The social distribution of land and men in England'; Stone, *Crisis of the Aristocracy*, 144–52.
31. Shaw, 'Landownership in the Western Isles', 34–9; *Inquisitionum*, i. Clackmannan nos 1–26, i. Ayr, nos 10–449; ii. 'Inquisitiones Speciales, Renfrew', nos 8–101; *CSP Scotland*, v. 254; vii. 577; *RPC* first ser., iv. 787; *Sheriffdoms of Lanark and Renfrew*, 1–68, 141. The usefulness of land valuations is discussed in McKechnie, 'Early land valuations'.
32. NAS GD 26/5/236; Fraser, *Sutherland*, i. 145; ii. 345, 352; iii. 135–9. At the death of the fourth earl Marischal in 1581 he had an estimated income of £15 000 sterling per annum and a testament valued at £44 664, four times the average for that decade, Paul, *Scots Peerage*, vi. 48; *Estimate*, 8, 31; NAS CC 8/8/11/53–9, 8/8/12/330b. The income seems unbelievably high, being seven times that of the average English peer, Williams, *Tudor Regime*, 98. Yet in 1608 the fifth earl Marischal's chamberlain was operating on a budget of around £27 000, about £2300 sterling, NLS MS 21 176/5–11.
33. *CSP Scotland*, v. 564; ix. 664; Anderson, *Black Patie*, 34; NAS GD 28/1389; Scott, *Staggering State*, 58; Fraser, *Haddington*, ii. 160–6; the Buccleuch figure is based on a range of rentals from the 1630s, NLS MS 14 542/32; NAS GD 224/935/6–7. A wealthy English noble like the sixth earl of Derby had an income from his estates of some £5000 sterling c.1600, Coward, *The Stanleys*, 186.
34. See the pride with which the Setons preserved the acquisition of their Lothian lands in return for service to Robert I, *House of Seytoun*, 21.
35. NAS GD 112/5/3–4; *Black Book of Taymouth*, 12, 15–16; NAS GD 124/1/8 and see GD 124/1/10; *RPC*, v. 46–7; *APS*, iv. 80, 543–4; Fraser, *Annandale*, i. p. xcv, cxiii; *HMC Fifteenth Report*, 32. In 1617 the earl of Sutherland's charter chest was misplaced causing panic among his curators, NLS MS 175/33.
36. NAS GD 124/5, especially no. 7 and no. 14/4. It might have been Marischal who started the tradition that there were links between the Erskines and the Norse god, Odin, on the basis of evidence found in a volume of the Danish 'Chancellours Bibliotheck', information he could have picked up in Denmark three decades earlier, item no. 13.
37. McQueen, *Common Law*; Craig, *Jus Feudale*, ii. 633–779, quotation p. 634. On this see Stone and Stone, *An Open Elite?*, 78–9; Squib, 'The end of the name of arms clause?', 219–25.
38. Fraser, *Sutherland*, ii. 344; *Poems of Sir Richard Maitland*, 101–4, quotation from 102–3; *Poems of William Drummond*, 219; Wemyss, *Workes*, i. 113.
39. Thirsk, 'The European debate on customs of inheritance'; Cooper, 'Inheritance and settlement', 198–204, 252–93; Nicholls, 'Irishwomen and property in the sixteenth century', 26–7; Bonney, *European Dynastic States*, 378; Macfarlane, *Nobility of Later Medieval England*, 61–82; Spring, *Land, Law and Family*, 27–35; Stone, *Crisis of the Aristocracy*, 178–83; Simpson, 'Entails and perpetuities', 7–9; Burgess, *Perpetuities*, 24–48; Thompson, 'Nobility in Spain', 195; Major, *Renaissance Monarchy to Absolute Monarchy*, 86–90; Mentzer, *Blood and Belief*, 104–19.

40. Burgess, *Perpetuities*, 49; Dalrymple, *Essay*, 161–70; Simpson, 'Entails and perpetuities', 7–18; *Regiam Majestatem*, i. 133–4; Craig, *Jus Feudale*, ii. 633–750, quotation on pp. 655–6; and compare with Cooper, 'Inheritance and settlement', 192–6. Riccarton was less certain of the nature of English entails, Burgess, *Perpetuities*, 66–9; Bonfield, *Marriage Settlements*, 11–54.
41. Bonfield, *Marriage Settlements*, 69–73; NRA(S) 885/Box 10/209, and for another example from the earls of Crawford, NRA(S) 237/C/168–9. Parliamentary records contain many ratifications of such charters – for example, in 1594, *APS*, iv. 87–90. For Yester, *RPC*, first ser., iii. 688–9; and Sutherland, Fraser, *Sutherland*, i. 143–4, 175; iii. 153–4.
42. Craig, *Jus Feudale*, ii. 697–713. In England the Common Law made it more difficult to prejudice female succession, Spring, *Land, Law and Family*.
43. Fraser, *Melvilles*, i. 82–194; Scott, *Staggering State*, 64.
44. Burgess, *Perpetuities*, 15–23; Stone and Stone, *An Open Elite?*, 72–82; Giesey, 'Rules of inheritance and strategies of mobility'; *House of Forbes*, 160–2, 167; Fraser, *Elphinstone*, i. 103, 109–10, 114–15, 178, 181–2.
45. *House of Gordon*, ii. 26–44.
46. Stone and Stone, *An Open Elite?*, 69–70; Cooper, 'Inheritance and settlement', 212–22; Spring, *Land, Law and Family*, 66–91; NAS GD 4/61–90, 4/93–4, 4/96–100, 4/123, 4/128, 4/132–4, 4/137–46, 4/155, 4/169, 4/173.
47. *RPC*, first ser., iv. 617; xiii. 626–7.
48. Fraser, *Eglinton*, i. 200–1. Fraser, *Sutherland*, i. 145; ii. 346, 352; iii. 135–9.
49. *HMC Third Report*, iii. 399.
50. Paul, *Scots Peerage*, i. 444–72; *CSP Scotland*, x. 594; xii. 5–6, 13, 21–2, 174.
51. Goody, 'Inheritance, property and women'; Spring, *Land, Law and Family*, 9–38; Benadusi, *A Provincial Elite in Early Modern Tuscany*, 125–33. In England only about 7 per cent of estates were transferred through female inheritance, Stone and Stone, *An Open Elite?*, 118.
52. Craig, *Jus Feudale*, ii. 667–80. See the succession dispute following the death of the eighth lord Sanquhar when the king opposed public opinion and made it clear he would never prefer 'a base borne, a stranger, to the righteous heir male of so ancient a house', *Abbotsford Miscellany*, i. 197–209; *Melrose Papers*, i. 132–3, 264–5; *RPC*, first ser., x. 542–3, 624, 638–9; xi. 44–5, 269–70, 273; *Family of Kilravock*, 88.
53. Calderwood, *History*, vii. 153; NAS GD 59/27–34; Paul, *Scots Peerage*, v. 498–9.
54. Fraser, *Douglas*, iii. 256, 311–14; *CSP Scotland*, ix. 653; Sanderson, *Mary Stewart's People*, 61.
55. Fraser, *Eglinton*, i. 55–6. For a similar arrangement in the Ker house of Lothian in the 1620s see *Ancram and Lothian*, i. pp. xlviii–li. Spring's observations on this in England are of interest, *Land, Law and Family*, 94–5.
56. For examples of various localities over different periods, Leslie, *Historie* i. 12, 18–19, 35, 43–4; Pont, *Topographical Account*, 5–7; Gordon, *Sutherland*, 11. Whyte, *Scotland before the Industrial Revolution*, chs 8–9 provides a useful introduction to the rural economy.
57. *Early Travellers*, 154; Lythe, *Economy of Scotland*; Devine and Lythe, 'The economy of Scotland under James VI'; Lythe, 'The union of the crowns in 1603 and the debate on economic integration'; Mathew, *Scotland under Charles l*, 92–104; Donaldson, *Scotland. James V to James VII*, 238–55; Dodgshon, *Land and Society*, chs 4–6; Sanderson, *Rural Society*; Whyte, *Agriculture and Society*, 10–12; Macinnes, *Making of the Covenanting Movement*, 102–27; Lee, *Government by Pen* is also useful on government economic policies.
58. The first earl of Buccleuch's rental from the Forest of Ettrick was £13 053 in 1630, £12 742 in 1631 and £13 991 in 1632, NLS MS 14 542/49.
59. Fraser, *Elphinstone*, ii. 166; *Melrose Papers*, i. 137; *House of Forbes*, i. 176; Fraser, *Haddington*, ii. 123; *Ancram and Lothian*, i. 97–8; *Early Travellers*, 154–5; NAS GD 150/3438/3.
60. For the impact of the Marian civil war see *CSP Scotland*, iii. 403, 407, 426; and for a comparison with the French religious wars, Eurich, *The Economics of Power*, 1–29. For the

destructive capacity of a number of prominent bloodfeuds see Fraser, *Annandale*, i. p. xcv, cxiii; *HMC Fifteenth Report*, 32; NRA(S) 217/2/4/80; Fraser, *Sutherland*, i. 163–4; Gregory, *History of the Western Highlands and Islands*, 269; *Black Book of Taymouth*, 37–8; Brown, *Bloodfeud*; Hope, *Major Practicks*, i. 230.

61. *House of Forbes*, 162–3; NLS MS 14480/38, MS 14480/60, 14480/62; NAS GD 224/906/40/4–5; NLS MS 20777/13, 20777/15; NLS MS 16760/10; NLS MS 16760/33; Zulager, 'Middle-rank administrators', 163-4; NRA(S) 2312/107/8/4–8; Sanderson, *Mary Stewart's People*, 63; *Chronicles of the Frasers*, 249; *Ancram and Lothian*, i. 82; NAS GD 52/327.
62. NLS MS 83/34. Morton's grandfather employed a chamberlain on each of his seven baronies, Sanderson, *Mary Stewart's People*, 62–3. For Lennox, *HMC Third Report*, iii. 394. For an example of the contrast between an effective factor and a bullying chamberlain on the Yester estates, NAS GD 28/1314, 28/1318, and for another problem case, NAS GD 52/326.
63. Fraser, *Douglas*, iv. 246; *Ancram and Lothian* i. 59. The Lothian estates were run by the competent Mark Cass who reported to Ancram, NAS GD 40/2/13/50–71. See the kind of business conducted by Mr James Donaldson for sir David Lindsay of Edzell in Edinburgh, NRA(S) 237/F/472–6. For Hope's dealings, Fraser, *Haddington*, i. 178; *Miscellany of the Scottish History Society*, i. 99.
64. *Melrose*, ii. 543, 592–3; Sanderson, *Scottish Rural Society*, 25–8; Whyte, *Agriculture and Society*, 31, 42–51; Macinnes, *Clanship, Commerce and the House of Stuart*, 14–23 for Highland estates; Stone, *Crisis of the Aristocracy*, 303.
65. For a survey of farming in the seventeenth century see Whyte, *Agriculture and Society*, 57–91; *Early Travellers*, 88; Dodgshon, *Chiefs to Landlords*, 55–101.
66. Cash rents amounted to only £833 6s 8d with another £168 17s 6d being uplifted in feu duties, NAS GD 6/1677, 1678/1–2. In 1640, the Buccleuch rental was 110 chalders and 12 bolls of ferme grain, 75.5 chalders of teind grain, 24 540 merks in silver mails and 8700 teind silver, NAS GD 224/906/40/18. This excludes wool income.
67. Fraser, *Haddington*, i. 160–6; *Melrose Papers*, i. 163.
68. For a pasturage reservation from 1627, NAS GD 28/1324.
69. *Honoris de Morton*, i. 176–7; for the negotiations of the Glenorchy tacksman with his tenants over the price of marts, NAS GD 112/39/37/8. For Mar, NLS MS 5070/32. In some cases the cash value of the ferme was agreed in advance and written into the lease, see an example on the Yester estates in 1626, NAS GD 28/1312. Sanderson, *Scottish Rural Society*, 28–34; Whyte, *Agriculture and Society*, 33, 35–6.
70. Banac and Bushkovitch, 'The nobility in the history of Russia and eastern Europe', 3–4; Bush, *Noble Privilege*, 146–50; Sanderson, *Scottish Rural Society*, 30; Whyte, *Agriculture and Society*, 35–6; for an example of 'dayworkis of scheiring', NAS GD 86/240.
71. NAS GD 28/1318; *Melrose Regality Records*, 75–6; Fraser, *Carlaverock*, ii. 107–8.
72. Dewald, *European Nobility*, 70–6; for Naples, Astarita, *Continuity of Feudal Power*, 37–46; Atienza Hernández, '"Refeudalisation" in Castile during the seventeenth century', 263–5; Jago, 'The "crisis of the aristocracy" in seventeenth-century Castile'; van Nierop, *Nobility of Holland*, 96–108.
73. Craig, *Jus Feudale*, ii. 801–29; Hope, *Major Practicks*, i. 176; Fraser, *Sutherland*, ii. 347, 351–3.
74. *CSP Scotland*, xi. 381, 385, 496; Gordon, *Sutherland*, 259–60; *Black Book of Taymouth*, 77; Macinnes, 'Crown, clans and fine', 32, 44–5; Wormald, *Lords and Men*, 190, appendix A, Argyll no. 54.
75. Sanderson, *Scottish Rural Society*, 21–4; Whyte, *Agriculture and Society*, 137–72; Gordonstoun makes these points, Fraser, *Sutherland*, ii. 346.
76. Leslie, *Historie*, i. 17; NRA(S) 217/3/229.
77. Sanderson, *Scottish Rural Society*, 46–54, 58, 61–3; Waus, *Correspondence*, i. 232–3; Makey, *Church of the Covenant*, 167–74; *Book of Dunvegan*, i. 145–7, 263–4, 268–70, 273. For similar conditions in northern England, Appleby, 'Agrarian capitalism or seigneurial reaction?'; Hoyle, 'An ancient and laudable custom'.

78. Sanderson, *Scottish Rural Society*, 77–8, 104, 127, chs 7 and 11; Connacher, 'Land tenure in the seventeenth century'; Whyte, *Agriculture and Society*, 30–1; Anderson, *Black Patie*, 34; *Sheriffdoms of Lanark and Renfrew*, 28; and for the customary view, *Historie*, 266.
79. Dewald, *European Nobility*, 73; Heal and Holmes, *Gentry in England and Wales*, 99; Anderson, *Earl of Orkney*, 67–9; Fraser, *Chiefs of Grant*, i. p. xxxix, lvi; iii. 305–13; Makey, 'Presbyterian and Canterburian', 159; NAS GD 124/15/91/1, 124/15/91/2–5; *Sheriffdoms of Lanark and Renfrew*, 38; and for parliament's attempt in 1606 to protect the interests of feudal superiors from feuing, *APS*, iv. 287. Habakkuk, 'Rise and fall of English landed families' raises questions about the impact of inflation on rents and landed incomes.
80. For an example of teind management see the house of Mar, NAS GD 124/8, and for the sale of teinds by the first lord Scone in 1608 and the second earl of Abercorn in 1619, NAS GD 42/141–2; NAS GD 6/1190. On the legal context, Hope, *Major Practicks*, i. 119–26; and for the Yester case, NAS GD 28/1317, 28/1370–6, 28/1405, 28/1408. Complex legal settlements of these disputes were not unusual, see that reached over the teinds of the parish of Crail between 1598 and 1611, GD 20/1/362–73.
81. *CSP Scotland*, v. 564; *Poems of Sir Richard Maitland*, 24; Edington, *Court and Culture*, 136–7; Heal and Holmes, *Gentry in England and Wales*, 102–4.
82. *First Book of Discipline*, 156–7; Knox, *Works*, ii. 340–1; Calderwood, *History*, ii. 282, 288–9, 397–9, 470; v. 276, 410, 437; *Honoris de Morton*, i. 167.
83. *Political Writings*, 24; Fraser, *Douglas*, iv. 43; *HMC Mar and Kellie*, i. 68–9; *Honoris de Morton*, i. 129–30, 133–4; NAS GD 24/5/57/3, 24/5/57/17; *RPC*, first ser., x. 78–9. Neighbouring landlords can also be found interceding on behalf of impoverished tenants, NAS GD 40/9/2.
84. NAS GD 28/1427; Fraser, *Sutherland*, ii. 362.
85. Dalrymple, *Institutions*, 387; *Barony of Urie*, pp. xliii–xlix; Anderson, *Earl of Orkney*, 72–3; Whyte, *Agriculture and Society*, 12–13; *RPC*, first ser., xii. 437–8; xiii. 653–4.
86. Whyte, *Agriculture and Society*, 32–3; Fraser, *Sutherland*, i. 127; *Melrose Regality Records*, i. p. xii; NAS GD 96/122.
87. *HMC Various V*, 26–7; *Barony of Urie*, 13–14, 16–17, 22, 25, 35–6, 50–84; NRA(S) 2312/113/951–2.
88. Dewald, *Formation of a Provincial Nobility*, 201–20; NLS MS 16501/72–3; Fraser, *Sutherland*, ii. 354. Gordonstoun opposed altering teinds from a silver duty to victual as it principally benefited the teind masters.
89. Thompson, 'Nobility in Spain', 201; Stone, *Crisis of the Aristocracy*, 303–7; Gordon, *Sutherland*, 196; *Chronicles of the Frasers*, 250; NAS GD 124/17/629; Whyte, *Agriculture and Society*, 36; Sanderson, *Scottish Rural Society*, 50–1; NAS GD 224/903/26/50, 224/903/25/17.

## Chapter 2: Entrepreneurs

1. Fraser, *Philorth*, i. 152–5, 159–63; ii. 254–69.
2. Dewald, 'The ruling class in the marketplace'; Dewald, *European Nobility*; for Naples, Astarita, *Continuity of Feudal Power*, 68–107; for Wales, Lloyd, *Gentry of South-West Wales*; and for England, Stone, *Crisis of the Aristocracy*, 329; Stone and Stone, *An Open Elite?*, 282–3; Bernard, 'The Tudor nobility in perspective', 7; Heal and Holmes, *Gentry in England and Wales*, 102–16; Overton, *Agricultural Revolution in England.*
3. Stringer, 'Early lords', 44–61; Grant, *Independence and Nationhood*, 65–8; Wormald, *Lords and Men*, 23.
4. NLS MS 963/25–8. Enclosure was widely believed to increase the value of land by half on both pastoral and arable estates. Ancram criticises his countrymen 'for not ordering our springs and not encloseing our grounds, wheroff an inche is worth an yard exposed to all weathers and common pasture', *Ancram and Lothian*, i. 71–2.

5. Craig, *Jus Feudale*, i. 220–1; NLS Adv. MS 15.2.14/64–70; Kamen, *European Society*, 98–103; Brunelle, 'Narrowing horizons', 63–79; Mettam, 'French nobility', 118; Bitton, *French Nobility in Crisis*, 64–76; van Nierop, *Nobility of Holland*, 33–5; Donati, 'Italian nobilities', 250–1; Stone, *Crisis of the Aristocracy*, 335–84; Heal and Holmes, *Gentry in England and Wales*, 127; Cooper, 'Ideas of gentility', 49.
6. Whyte, *Agriculture and Society*, 126, 129–30 argues that evidence of convertible husbandry is limited; *Early Travellers*, 86; Dodgshon, *Land and Society*, 174–204; NAS GD 112/20/1/8/1.
7. Whyte, *Agriculture and Society*, 201–18; Pont, *Topographical Account*, 6; Macinnes, 'Crown, clans and fine', 42–3; *Black Book of Taymouth*, 36.
8. Stone, *Crisis of the Aristocracy*, 211–12; Whyte, *Agriculture and Society*, 140, 155–60; NAS GD 28/1324, 1366, 1404.
9. *RPC*, first ser., xii. 340–1; Macinnes, 'Crown, clans and fine', 41–2; Whyte, *Agriculture and Society*, 149–52; NAS GD 28/1327, 28/1325, 28/1407, 28/1417, 28/1452; NAS GD 40/2/12/68.
10. *Oppressions of Orkney*, 117–23; *Poems of Sir Richard Maitland*, 42–4; Dodgshon, *Land and Society*, 136–40.
11. Kershaw, 'Power and duty'; Stone, *Crisis of the Aristocracy*, 307–10, 313–22; Kerridge, 'The movement of rent', 208–26; Hagen, 'How mighty the Junkers?'
12. Makey, 'Presbyterian and Canterburian', 157–8; Makey, *Church of the Covenants*, 6, 168–74; Appleby, 'Agrarian capitalism or seigneurial reaction?', 574–94. Pressure on Highland lords to push up rents was encouraged by the loss of income from mercenary service and from greater contact with wealthier cultures in the south, Macinnes, 'Crown, clans and fine', 41–2.
13. Hope, *Major Practicks*, i. 226–36. Although lords tried to prevent the leasing of their land to noble subtenants, Fraser, *Chiefs of Grant*, iii. 431. Fraser, *Haddington*, ii. 126; NAS GD 158/2697/10–11, 158/2697/31.
14. For example, see *RPC*, first ser., v. 219–20, 276–7; NAS GD 28/1341–2, 28/1402–3. For a useful explanation of eviction, Sanderson, *Scottish Rural Society*, 23, chs 4 and 5. Lethington believed that a lord should only evict a tenant in extreme circumstances, *House of Seytoun*, p. x. NAS GD 124/6/44–7; and in 1590 at Inverie, GD 124/6/31; in 1617–21 at Ellem in Berwickshire, GD 124/6/56, 124/6/59–60; in 1618 at Inchemaho GD 124/6/57; in 1620 at Kellie in Aberdeenshire, GD 124/6/58; in 1631 in the earldom of Mar, GD 124/6/70.
15. NAS GD 86/227; *Oppressions of Orkney*, 117, 119; *Spalding Miscellany*, iv. 261–319.
16. NLS MS 14745/2; NAS GD 28/1313; NAS GD 28/1389; NAS GD 26/5/236.
17. Fraser, *Eglinton*, ii. 260–83; NAS GD 25/9/48; *Barony of Urie*, pp. lii–liii; Whyte, *Agriculture and Society*, 179; Sanderson, *Scottish Rural Society*, 28; Makey, *Church of the Covenant*, 167.
18. Gibson and Smout, *Prices, Food and Wages*, 19–184; English landlords commonly avoided direct involvement in grain production and distribution, Stone, *Crisis of the Aristocracy*, 299–302. For eastern Europe, Hagen, 'How mighty the Junkers?'; Subtelny, *Domination of Eastern Europe*.
19. *Registrum de Panmure*, i. p. xciii; Whyte, *Agriculture and Society*, 64, 78; *Estimate*, 7–8, 13–14, 17–19, 22, 24–6, 30–2, 34–6, 38–9.
20. Dawson, 'Origin of the "Road to the Isles"', 102 n. 78; Anderson, *Earl of Orkney*, 71; and for his son, Anderson, *Black Patie*, 36–40; Lythe, *Economy of Scotland*, 32, 64; Devine and Lythe, 'Economy of Scotland'; Gibson and Smout, *Prices, Food and Wages*, 162–4, 167–71; Whyte, *Agriculture and Society*, 179; *CSP Scotland*, v. 181; Lindsay, *Historie*, ii. 316, 319–20; *RPC*, first ser., x. 118–19; second ser., iv. 248–51; *Early Travellers*, 112.
21. Gibson and Smout, *Prices, Food and Wages*; Lythe, *Economy of Scotland*; Wormald, *Court, Kirk and Community*, 166–7; Mitchison, 'Movement of Scottish corn prices', 293; Dodgshon, *Land and Society*, 134–6; Fraser, *Sutherland*, ii. 118, 123, 128; *HMC Sixth Report*, 650; NAS GD 124/15/99, GD 124/19/1.
22. *Historie*, 21–2; *RPC*, first ser., ix. 551–3; x. 207–8; xii. 94–5, 455–6, 702–4; xiv. 579;

second ser., v. 241.

23. See what are almost certainly underestimates for John Grant of Freuchie in 1584 and sir Colin Campbell of Glenorchy in 1640, Fraser, *Chiefs of Grant*, iii. 286–8; NAS GD 112/20/5/5. Gibson and Smout, *Prices, Food and Wages*, 185–224; Macinnes, 'Crown, clans and fine', 42–3; Whyte, *Agriculture and Society*, 235–7; *RPC*, second ser., i. 591, 626–7. There were occasional government attempts to prevent exports, ibid., second ser., i. 138–9.
24. Guy, 'Scottish export trade', 63–4; Blanchard, 'Northern wools and Netherlands markets'; Lee, *Government by Pen*, 87; NAS GD 224/930/38/9; 224/935/11; 224/393/6/2–3, 224/393/6/15; NLS MS 14543/48; Fraser, *Buccleuch*, ii. 269–70.
25. *RPC*, first ser., x. 592–3; xiii. 70, 106, 141, 773–7; second ser., i. 75–6, 93–4, 199–200, 278, 383–4, 670–5; *Melrose Papers*, ii. 490–3, 500–2, 520–1; Lee, *Government by Pen*, 214; NRA(S) 237/F/482–3.
26. For a quarrel from August 1569, *RPC*, first ser., ii. 13. Fraser, *Sutherland*, ii. 361–2; Gordon, *Sutherland*, 243; *Chronicles of the Frasers*, 249; Whyte, *Agriculture and Society*, 181–92.
27. Dawson, 'Origin of the "Road to the Isles"', 80–91; *Black Book of Taymouth*, 67; *RPC*, second ser., v. 339. For 1616, ibid., first ser., x. 529–30, 543–4, 548–9, 570–2; and Winton's harbour, *House of Seytoun*, 59, 75.
28. *RPC*, first ser., vi. 111; second ser., iv. 393–5.
29. *HMC*, iv. 481, nos 145–52; NAS GD 86/203; *Charters of Ayr*, 116–28; *HMC Fourth Report*, 503, no. 90.
30. *HMC Sixth Report*, 650; Brown, *Bloodfeud*, 147; *RPC*, first ser., iv. 86–7; NLS MS 16501/5–9, 16501/11–13; NAS GD 94/59, 94/67, 94/70, 94/72, 94/76, 94/79, 94/85, 94/151; NAS GD 124/1/11.
31. NAS GD 39/5/68; NAS GD 150/3441/3.
32. Hope, *Major Practicks*, i. 213; *APS*, ii. 537–8; *RPC*, ix. 37, 228, 235, 241–2, 244, 336; *Chronicle of Perth*, 13.
33. Anderson, *Black Patie*, 40; Donaldson, *Scotland. James V to James VII*, 247; *RPC*, first ser., iv. 121–3.
34. Macinnes, *Making of the Covenanting Movement*, 108–9; *RPC*, second ser., iii. 94–6, 420–1, 495–6; NLS MS 82/18.
35. *Early Travellers*, 135; Eurich, *Economics of Power*, 36–42; Dewald, *Pont-St-Pierre*, 198–205; Stone, *Crisis of the Aristocracy*, 295; Donaldson, *James V to James VII*, 243.
36. Sir Thomas Ker of Ferniehirst estimated his total losses in the civil war at 200 000 crowns, *CSP Scotland*, v. 162, 164. For Buccleuch, *RPC*, first ser., xi. 437, and for similar complaints from John Stewart of Traquair and the first earl of Melrose, ibid., first ser., xii. 23, 172; second ser., iv. 222–3.
37. NAS GD 150/646–52, 150/661; *RPC*, first ser., v. 73. See too NAS GD 112/17/1/3, 112/17/1/4/11 and 112/17/1/4/14 for examples of tenants convicted of cutting the laird of Glenorchy's woods in 1634–5.
38. *Melrose Papers*, ii. 528–9; Fraser, *Chiefs of Grant*, iii. 128–9, and also *RPC*, first ser. ii. 500–1; *Early Travellers*, 123.
39. *Black Book of Taymouth*, 45, 67; NAS GD 112/16/11/2. For the estates of Rose of Kilravock, Panmure and Burnet of Leyis, *Family of Kilravock*, 294–5; Whyte, *Agriculture and Society*, 120; NRA(S) 2847/1/32.
40. Lindsay, *Lives of the Lindsays*, i. 345–6; ii. 408; NRA(S) 237/F/472–5; *Early Travellers*, 136; Stone, *Illustrated Maps*.
41. Hatcher, *British Coal Industry*, 40–5, 96–111; Macinnes, *Making of the Covenanting Movement*, 29–30; Donaldson, *James V to James VII*, 246; Gordon, *Sutherland*, 237; Fraser, *Sutherland*, i. 168–9; ii. 116. As with other important assets, coal fields were often the cause of feuding, *RPC*, first ser., x. 6, 27. A similar interest in coal production was found among the English nobility, Stone, *Crisis of the Aristocracy*, 340–2.
42. NAS GD 150/661; Fraser, *Melvilles*, i. p. xlii; NAS GD 25/9/46 bundle 'coal'; Heal and Holmes, *Gentry in England and Wales*, 121.

43. Macinnes, *Making of the Covenanting Movement*, 118; NRA(S) 3438/622/33; *RPC*, second ser., iii. 563.
44. GD 15/243, 15/245, 15/345–6, 15/896–8; GD 40/8/149–50; Bowman, 'Culross colliery'; *Early Travellers*, 115–17; Lee, *Government by Pen*, 89.
45. *APS*, ii. 543; iii. 147; iv. 136, 408; Hope, *Major Practicks*, i. 6–7; Lee, *Government by Pen*, 86–7, 199–200; Armstrong, 'Two papers relating to the export of coals from Scotland'. For export licences to Bruces of Airth, NAS GD 37/312–13, 37/317.
46. *RPC*, first ser., viii. 568–9, 575–6; x. 277, 372, 382–3; NAS GD 124/17/510–12.
47. Fraser, *Elphinstone*, i. pp. xxi–xxiii; ii. 156; *RPC*, first ser., xii. 387–8, 418–19, 433–5, 467, 474, 605–6; *APS*, iv. 630–1. For exemptions, *RPC*, first ser., xii. 752–3; xiii. 207–9.
48. *RPC*, first ser., xi. 306–8; second ser., ii. 72–3; v. 190; NLS MS 81/48; NAS GD 150/3438/4; NAS GD 406/1/11138–9; Macinnes, *Making of the Covenanting Movement*, 118.
49. Whatley, *Scottish Salt Industry*, 33, 37, 39–40, 78–80; NAS GD 86/271; NAS GD 112/10/65; NLS MS 21 178/30; *RPC*, second ser., iv. 255–7.
50. Stone, *Crisis of the Aristocracy*, 342–55; Hewitt, *Scotland under Morton*, 153.
51. NRA(S) 237/F/454–5, 237/F/489–90, 237/F/493–4; Lindsay, *Lives of the Lindsays*, i. 342–5, 376.
52. Fraser, *Haddington*, i. 94–9; *Melrose Papers*, i. 35–8, 41–2; *RPC*, first ser., ix. 703; x. 15–17; Hope, *Diary*, 20–2.
53. *HMC Mar and Kellie*, ii. 96–7; *RPC*, first ser., viii. 593, 596; xii. 231–2; second ser., ii. 333–4, 337; NLS MS 16501/109–12, 16501/16, 16501/119, 16501/122–3, 16501/126–8. In 1628 the second earl of Linlithgow acquired a patent for the manufacture of saltpetre throughout Scotland.
54. *RPC*, first ser., v. 531–2; NAS GD 112/18/1/1/1; NAS GD 25/9/46 bundle 'quarries'; also the Panmure estate in Angus, GD 45/18/645.
55. *Melrose Papers*, i. 337–8; *RPC*, first ser., xi. 138–9; xii. 428–9, 439–41, 451–2; xiv. 567; Lythe, *Economy of Scotland*, 44–5.
56. *RPC*, first ser., xii. 189–93, 304–7, 398–400; xiii. 240, 242–8, 635–46; second ser., i. 237–8; iii. 107–9, 611–12; iv. 241, 281; vi. 20–1 for 1635. Lythe, *Economy of Scotland*, 93–4; Lee, *Government by Pen*, 196–8, 215; Macinnes, *Making of the Covenanting Movement*, 106–7. See too the bundle of documents in GD 124/10/134 that are concerned with Erskine's business dealings.
57. NAS GD 112/39/42/1; *RPC*, second ser., v. 305–15; Macinnes, *Making of the Covenanting Movement*, 85, 115–16; Lee, *Government by Pen*, 209–10.
58. *RPC*, second ser., v. 437–8.
59. Stone, *Crisis of the Aristocracy*, 363–7; Macpherson, 'Earl of Bothwell'; for Orkney see Anderson, *Earl of Orkney*, 88–9; and Balweary, *CSP Scotland*, xiii. prt. 1, 453, 519, 657, 947, 950.
60. Stone, *Crisis of the Aristocracy*, 368–75, 381–4; BL Hl 1583/25; Law, 'Scottish Guinea Company'; NAS GD 6/1247.
61. *RPC*, first ser., xii. 774–5; Paul, *Scots Peerage*, viii. 172–4; Lythe, *Economy of Scotland*, 71–4.
62. Schreiber, *First Carlisle*, chs 1–2, 5–6. In 1635 he was able to raise capital by mortgaging his monopoly to license taverns in Ireland, NAS GD 34/889, 34/920, 34/922–3. For Lochinvar, *RPC*, second ser., ii. 13.
63. Lynch, *Early Modern Town*, especially the editor's 'Introduction'; Ashton, *City and Court*, for London; NRA(S) 237/C/166–7, 237/C/176–7, 237/E/377–8.
64. NAS GD 67/133.
65. *Ayr and Wigton* (AWAA), viii. 183; ix. 195; NAS GD 137/13, 137/26, 137/375–6, 137/378, 137/380–1, 137/384–5; NAS GD 6/883; NAS GD 124/1/610, 124/1/615, 124/1/639, 124/1/641, 124/1/1144. Other nobles with a stake in Stirling in the later sixteenth century were sir William Murray of Tullibardine and sir Archibald Stirling of Keir, NAS GD 7/1/21; GD 124/17/198. In 1597 sir Michael Balfour of Balgarvie acquired property in Cupar which he sold to lord Lindsay eight years later, GD

20/1/357. Sir John Maxwell of Pollok collected rental from property he owned at the Trongate in Glasgow, NRA(S) 2312/112/2.

66. Whyte, *Scotland before the Industrial Revolution*, 179–85; Howard, *Architectural History*, 115, 139; *Barony of Urie*, 3–4 n. 6. Marischal had founded a new burgh at Peterhead in 1593 where he made harbour improvements with help from parliamentary subsidies, *APS*, iv. 35. For the Highlands, Macinnes, 'Crown, clans and fine', 42–3. For Stornoway, *RPC*, second ser., iii. 42.
67. See the privy council's involvement in constructing a new bridge at Perth in 1608, and again after the 1621 flood, *RPC*, first ser., viii. 41; xii. 599, 748–9, and in the repair of the bridge at Dumfries in 1620, ibid., first ser., xii. 251, 261–2.
68. *Registrum de Panmure*, i. pp. xxxvii–xxxix; Aylmer, *King's Servants*, 160–225; Eurich, *Economics of Power*, 44–77; Mentzer, *Blood and Belief*, 48–80.
69. *Political Writings*, 38; Peck, '"For a king not to be bountifull were a fault"'; *CSP Scotland*, v. 370; Rae, *Administration of the Scottish Frontier*, 29–33, appendix 3; *RPC*, first ser., iii. 427–8; Goodare, 'Nobility and the absolutist state', 171.
70. See, for example, the parliamentary ratification of the earldom of Mar in 1567, *APS*, ii. 549; *CSP Scotland*, x. 19; Kirk, 'Royal and lay patronage', 134–6; NAS GD 112/3/57. For the patronage of the crown generally see still largely unanalysed records of the great seal and the privy seal, *RMSRS*, v–viii; *RSSRS*, iv–ix.
71. *RPC*, first ser., iii. 48–9, 285, 384–6, 522–3, 609–10; iv. 185; for the Octavians, ibid., v. 254–9.
72. NAS GD 63/53, 63/55, 63/62, 63/65; Zulager, 'Middle–rank administrators', 132–70; Brown, 'Price of friendship'.
73. Goodare, 'Nobility and the absolutist state', 169–70; Stone, *Crisis of the Aristocracy*, 494–7. For Abercorn, *RPC*, first ser., x. 380–1; for Mar, ibid., xi. 586; *HMC Mar and Kellie*, i. 84, and another £10 000 in 1629, Fraser, *Chiefs of Grant*, 53; for Hamilton, Lee, *Government by Pen*, 209–10 and for other tax gifts to that house, *RPC*, first ser., iv. 437; *HMC Mar and Kellie*, i. 115; Balfour, *Works*, ii. 200; for Nithsdale, *RPC*, second ser., i. 233–4. Good service might also be rewarded with tax relief, NAS GD 406/1/10473.
74. *RPC*, second ser., i. 200–5; Fraser, *Haddington*, i. 129–30. Thirlestane built up a sizeable estate and left £14 864 in his testament when he died in 1595, Zulager, 'Middle-rank administrators', 139–40; NAS CC 8/8/33 (no page number). When Dunbar died in 1610 his testament recorded a net estate of £24 392, NAS GD 59/89; NAS CC 8/8/47/27–9. Dunfermline left no debts at all and was worth a staggering £70 151 at his death in 1622, *House of Seytoun*, 64; NAS CC 8/8/54/147–51, 8/8/54/352–55b; Seton, *Family of Seton*, ii. 654–5; NAS GD 94/41. Haddington accumulated a large estate in the south-east and in 1637 his testament was valued at £43 079 after debts of a little over £7000 had been deducted, NAS CC 8/8/47/1516–5.
75. Hyde, *History*, i. 108; Stone, *Crisis of the Aristocracy*, 403–49, 475–6; Peck, 'Court patronage and government policy'; Peck, *Court Patronage and Corruption*; Wormald, 'Two kings or one?'; Brown, 'Scottish aristocracy, anglicization and the court'; Cuddy, 'Revival of the entourage'.
76. For an example of old debts being assigned to Dunbar in 1606, BL Add MSS 12 497/153; Seddon, 'Robert Carr, earl of Somerset'; Schreiber, *Carlisle*, chs 1–2, 5–6; Brown, 'Aristocracy, anglicization and the court', 557–64; for Ramsay's land settlement of 1625, BL Add MSS 5755/60.
77. *HMC Mar and Kellie*, ii. 127; NAS GD 124/1/1195–9, 124/1/1200–5, 124/1/1208–9, 124/1/1212, 124/6/49, 124/7/31. The Scots in the privy chamber were highly successful in the patronage stakes, Seddon, 'Patronage and officers', 155–72, appendix 3.
78. For Lennox, Brown, 'Aristocracy, anglicization and the court', 20; BL Add MSS 36 767/236, 36 767/240, Add MSS 38 170/87b, 38 170/142, 38 170/258; Gordon, *Sutherland*, 127–8, 209. On Hamilton, see Scally, 'Hamilton'; Macinnes, *Making of the Covenanting Movement*, ii. 35–6 note 34; Rubinstein, *Captain Luckless*, 46; Aylmer, *King's Servants*, 350.

79. Gillespie, *Colonial Ulster*; Perceval-Maxwell, *Scottish Migration to Ulster*; Hill, *Historical Account of the Plantation*.
80. This point is also made by Harding in a French context, *Anatomy of a Power Elite*, 167; Hewitt, *Scotland under Morton*, 143–62; Hume, *General History*, 335; Zulager, 'Middle-rank administrators', 135–6; *CSP Scotland*, x. 827; Scott, *Staggering State*, 61–3. On the corruption of the London court see Peck, *Court Patronage and Corruption*.
81. *Melrose Papers*, i. 690–70; *RPC*, first ser., viii. 593–4; Lee, *Road to Revolution*, 85–6.
82. Fraser, *Menteith*, i. 341–2, 345–8; ii. 12, 36–7, 39, 40; *HMC Third Report*, 400, no. 157; Lee, *Road to Revolution*, 125.
83. Scott, *Staggering State*, 59; *HMC Mar and Kellie*, ii. 71; *CSP Scotland*, i. 560; NAS GD 150/2198; NAS GD 124/2/28–9, 124/2/33/1–5, 124/2/34, 124/2/62, 124/3/11, 124/5/91; NLS MS 80/49–50; NAS GD 21/5/4/296; Paul, *Scots Peerage*, v. 621.
84. Wood, *Nobility of Bayeux*, 128–31; Dewald, *Formation of a Provincial Nobility*, 221–45; Mentzer, *Blood and Belief*, 60–72.
85. Kellie excused himself from paying off the countess of Mar in 1625 and 1627, NLS MS 5070/6, 5070/8; Scott, *Staggering State*, 94; Zulager, 'Middle-rank administrators', 163. Sir James Fullerton failed to use his position in Charles's bedchamber to make his fortune, Aylmer, *King's Servants*, 317–18.
86. Lee, *Government by Pen*, 130–2; *Melrose Papers*, i. 93–4, 101–2, 135–6; *RPC*, first ser., xiii. 121–2.
87. *HMC Mar and Kellie*, i. 84, 94, 99–103, 106–10; *Melrose Papers*, ii. 441–2; Lee, *Government by Pen*, 209–10; Lee, 'Unpublished letter', 177; NLS MS 14480/4.
88. Lee, *Road to Revolution*, ch. 5; Macinnes, *Making of the Covenanting Movement*, 105–6, 120–1; Goodare, 'Nobility and the absolutist state', 171; NLS MS 14480/14.
89. Fraser, *Menteith*, ii. 125–8; Dewald, *Aristocratic Experience*, 160. Almost half the income of a great French magnate like Henry d'Albret in the mid-sixteenth century was derived from royal pensions and gifts, Major, *Renaissance Monarchy to Absolute Monarchy*, 78.
90. *Ancram and Lothian*, i. 90–3, 97–8, and for earlier warnings, ibid., i. 79–80.
91. *RPC*, second ser., i. 187–8; Brown, 'Aristocratic finances'; Lee, *Road to Revolution*, chs 5 and 6, 87, 187–90; Stevenson, 'Scottish revenues', 20–6. For English comparisons, Stone, *Crisis of the Aristocracy*, 475; Peck, '"For a king not to be bountifull were a fault"'.

## Chapter 3: Expenditure

1. Craig, *Jus Feudale*, ii. 853–88; Dalrymple, *Institutions*, 118–21; Hope, *Major Practicks*, i. 106–7, 199; *Regiam Majestatem*, 118–32; Marshall, *Virgins and Viragos*, 75–6; Forte, 'Aspects of the law of marriage', 109–12. For some comparisons, Stone, *Crisis of the Aristocracy*, 642–5; Macfarlane, *Marriage and Love*, 263–90; Dewald, *Formation of a Provincial Nobility*, 248–85; Erickson, *Women and Property*; Spring, *Land, Law and Family*, 39–65 discusses the declining negotiating position of women, particularly in marriages among the greater landowners.
2. Fraser, *Chiefs of Grant*, iii. 437–40; NAS GD 75/12; *APS*, iii. 267–8.
3. *HMC Eleventh Report*, 55; Fraser, *Elphinstone*, i. 169–75; NAS GD 11/83.
4. *HMC Buccleuch*, i. 25; NRA(S) 217/1/28, 217/1/53, 217/1/79; Fraser, *Eglinton*, ii. 214–16; *Ayr and Wigton* (AWAA), iii. 199; NLS Ch. 10723. For shared households in England and Normandy where there was a decline in such arrangements in the seventeenth century see Heal and Holmes, *Gentry in England and Wales*, 68–9; Dewald, *Formation of a Provincial Nobility*, 276.
5. Craig, *Jus Feudale*, 867–9; Dalrymple, *Institutions*, 120. If the husband died then the wife had to surrender her conjunct fee; NAS GD 124/3/10.
6. Mirrer, *Upon My Husband's Death*, 12–15; Rosenthal, *Patriarchy and Families of Privilege*, 175–256; Houlbrooke, *The English Family*, 207–15.
7. Lindsay, *Lives of the Lindsays*, i. 329; NRA(S) 237/E/401–2; NAS GD 28/1451; Seton,

*Family of Seton*, ii. 901.

8. Hope, *Major Practicks*, i. 199, 203; Honoris de Morton, i. 73–4; Gordon, *Sutherland*, 169; Fraser, *Buccleuch*, i. 159–61; Paul, *Scots Peerage*, i. 171; NAS GD 224/906/40/10, 224/906/40/18. For comment on this in England see Stone, *Crisis of the Aristocracy*, 172; Heal and Holmes, *Gentry in England and Wales*, 141–5.
9. Hope, *Major Practicks*, i. 199, 203; Fraser, *Menteith*, i. 329, 332–3; NAS GD 124/1/6–7, 124/1/732. On a few rare occasions, a divorce settlement left two women drawing an income from the estate, NAS GD 224/906/37/7.
10. *Chronicles of the Frasers*, 248; Heal and Holmes, *Gentry in England and Wales*, 83–4.
11. Anderson, *Black Patie*, 47–8; *Chronicles of the Frasers*, 145–6, 148; and also Fraser, *Douglas*, ii. 325–6.
12. *HMC Eleventh Report*, 55. The elderly Margaret Lyon was by then also the widow of the second marquis of Hamilton. For another example, *HMC Third Report*, iii. 399, no. 37.
13. *Black Book of Taymouth*, 73, 81–2. For a case in which an elder brother's widow had to be bought off, NAS GD 49/95.
14. Dewald, *Formation of a Provincial Nobility*, 260ff; Astarita, *Continuity of Feudal Power*, 171; Harding, *Anatomy of a Power Elite*, 112.
15. The tocher was £40 000, Fraser, *Douglas*, ii. 433–4; and see Fraser, *Chiefs of Grant*, iii. 144. For England, Stone, *Crisis of the Aristocracy*, 635; Macfarlane, *Marriage and Love*, 263–90.
16. *HMC Twelfth Report*, 120; *RPC*, first ser., ix. 613–14, 617–18; for comparison, Stone, *Crisis of the Aristocracy*, 176–7.
17. Chojnacki, 'Nobility, women and the state'; Queller and Madden, 'Fathers of the bride'; Greengrass, 'Property and politics', 397; Harding, *Anatomy of a Power Elite*, 160; Major, *Renaissance Monarchy to Absolute Monarchy*, 86; Thompson, 'The nobility in Spain', 211; Astarita, *Continuity of Feudal Power*, 171; Stone, *Crisis of the Aristocracy*, 173–8; Heal and Homes, *Gentry in England and Wales*, 142; Cooper, 'Inheritance and settlement', 221–3, 249; Nicholls, 'Irishwomen and property in the sixteenth century', 21–6; Morgan, 'Dowries for daughters in west Wales'.
18. *HMC Sixth Report*, 647; NRA(S) 237/C/175–6; Fraser, *Buccleuch*, ii. 242–6; *Chronicle of the Frasers*, 224; NRA(S) 234/523/100; *HMC Eleventh Report*, 55.
19. *HMC Fourth Report*, iv. 502, no. 82. For a useful discussion of the tensions in settlement arrangements in England see Bonfield, 'Affective families'. Also see Spring, *Land, Law and Family*, 105–7; Stone, *Crisis of the Aristocracy*, 636–49 where he calculates the going rate for portions as being at one year of the father's income.
20. Astarita, *Continuity of Feudal Power*, 191–203; Mettam, 'French nobility', 137; Fraser, *Douglas*, iii. 321–2; NRA(S) 237/E/397–9. Mothers often provided younger children with windfalls of cash and jewels in their wills; for example, see the bequests made by Anne Murray, countess of Kinghorn, who died in 1618, NRA(S) 885/178.
21. NRA(S) 217/1/15–16, 217/1/19–20. The seventh lord Yester and his eldest son had to find 32 000 merks for the marriages of the daughters of his late elder brother, NLS Ch. 10 727–8, Ch. 10 730–2.
22. NAS GD 32/2/9, 32/2/14.
23. Fraser, *Philorth*, ii. 246–54; see also NRA(S) 3246/I Miscl. Docs 1538–1713/44.
24. NRA(S) 885/12/244; *HMC Second Report*, i. 168; also illustrative is Fraser, *Buccleuch*, i. 248, 269–70.
25. Fraser, *Chiefs of Grant*, iii. 401–5, 410–12, 418–19. The financial arrangements of the Dundas family's are equally illuminating on the profit and loss of marriage, NAS GD 75/7–8, 75/12–13, 75/15, 75/18, 75/20, 75/30, 75/33, 75/35, 75/42–4, 75/76–7, 75/79, 75/83, 75/89–90, 75/95, 75/119, 75/134–5, 75/139, 75/142, 75/144, 75/568.
26. Donati, 'Italian nobilities', 255–7; Astarita, *Continuity of Feudal Power*, 166–82; NAS GD 47/32; NAS GD 39/5/61; Paul, *Scots Peerage*, iv. 242–3.
27. NRA(S) 217/1/52. English younger sons commonly got a portion equivalent to their father's annual income, Cooper, 'Inheritance and settlement', 232.
28. *Black Book of Taymouth*, 23–71.
29. *Chronicles of the Frasers*, 244, 246, and for another example, Fraser, *Melvilles*, iii. 128–31.

30. Mertes, *English Noble Household*, 76–91; Dewald, *Formation of a Provincial Nobility*, 194. For a good example of discharges, see the 207 discharges in the Yester papers for the period 1486–1599 and the 141 items for the years 1600–10, indicating that purchasing power and record keeping improved dramatically in the early seventeenth century, NLS MS 14402, 14403.
31. Dewald, *European Nobility*, 98–105; Burke, *Venice and Amsterdam*, 71–7, 111–15; Stone, *Crisis of the Aristocracy*, 184–8, 555–81; Heal and Homes, *Gentry in England and Wales*, 137–40.
32. Neuschel, 'Noble households'; Mertes, *English Noble Household*, 183–93; Stone and Stone, *An Open Elite?*, 344; Heal, 'The idea of hospitality'; Dawson, 'The fifth earl of Argyle', 21.
33. *HMC Eleventh Report*, 43; NAS GD 124/7/20, 124/17/4–5, 124/17/6–7; *HMC Mar and Kellie*, i. 159–60; Fraser, *Haddington*, i. 130. For an English household, Coward, *The Stanleys*, 84–93.
34. *Historie*, 386; *Oppressions of Orkney*, 123. Stone estimated that an English noble of the seventeenth century would have required to spend £5000 sterling per annum to meet the ordinary costs of his household, a figure that seems astonishingly high, Stone, *Crisis of the Aristocracy*, 548. For a good introduction to household finances, Woolgar, *Household Accounts*, 3–65.
35. Fraser, *Buccleuch*, i. 249; *House of Forbes*, 163.
36. Fraser, *Sutherland*, ii. 345; *CSP Scotland*, xiii. prt. 2, 872.
37. For various progresses and entertainments of the king, *CSP Scotland*, xiii. 2, 748; *House of Seytoun*, 59, 74–5; McNeill and McNeill, 'Scottish progress of James VI, 1617'; Fraser, *Elphinstone*, i. 151; *RPC*, xi. 52–3; Hyde, *History*, i. 108; *Maitland Miscellany*, i. 161–91.
38. *Early Travellers*, 88–9; *CSP Scotland*, xi. 162.
39. Eurich, *The Economics of Power*, 124–63; Dawson, 'Fifth earl of Argyle', 9. For a useful and colourful introduction to sixteenth-century eating habits, Sim, *Food and Feast*; Mertes, *English Noble Household*, 95–102. The larger and more mobile a noble household, the bigger the proportion of its income spent on food, and hence its greater vulnerability to market prices, Major, *Renaissance Monarchy to Absolute Monarchy*, 78–81.
40. Dawson, 'Fifth earl of Argyle', 9. For a list of provisions consumed by the house of Glenorchy in 1590, *Black Book of Taymouth*, p. xxiv.
41. Dodgshon, 'West Highland chiefdoms, 1500–1745'; Dodgshon, *Chiefs to Landlords*, 84–101; *Early Travellers*, 123–4. The scale of entertaining often necessitated the purchase of local produce, Sanderson, *Mary Stewart's People*, 69–70.
42. NRA(S) 237/F/313–14; Fraser, *Sutherland*, i. 116; NAS GD 112/16/7/1, 112/39/51/16; *Chronicles of the Frasers*, 218–19, 245, 267. For references to tobbaco, NRA(S) 237/F/511–12; *Memorials of Montrose*, i. 85–6; *HMC Eighth Report*, 303; *RPC*, first ser., xiii. 92, 102–4. James VI, of course, detested it, issuing in 1604 his 'Counterblaste to tobbaco'. Robert Aytoun, however, confessed to its relaxing and uplifting qualities, at least for a while, in 'Upon tobacco', McCordick, *Scottish Literature*, i. 722.
43. Abernethy, *A Christian and Heavenly Treatise*, 50–1, 417–25; Fraser, *Sutherland*, ii. 345; NLS MS 2200/1–58; Fraser, *Eglinton*, ii. 276–83; Curle, 'Angus' household'.
44. Fraser, *Eglinton*, ii. 278–9; NAS GD 124/17/4–5; NRA(S) 237/F/512–13; NAS GD 112/39/48/1; *RPC*, first ser., vii. 56, 177–8; x. 510–11.
45. *Early Travellers*, 89–90; *CSP Scotland*, xii. 499; xiii. prt. 1, 206–7, 209. The great cost of the 1598 celebrations, for which taxes were re-routed, caused a boycott by many nobles, ibid., xiii. prt. 1, 214–17. On the Highlands, *RPC*, first ser., ix. 28; Macinnes, 'Crown, clans and fine', 39–40. The chief effect of the 1610 anti-drink legislation was to alter Highland tastes from wine to local ale and spirits.
46. *Political Writings*, 51; Fraser, *Sutherland*, ii. 338, 345, 365; and Abernethy was also critical, *A Christian and Heavenly Treatise*, 426–35; *Chronicle of the Frasers*, 219.
47. Eurich, *The Economics of Power*, 166–78; Stone, *Crisis of the Aristocracy*, 562–6; Roche, *Culture of Clothing*; Harte, 'State control of dress and social change'; *APS*, iii. 220–1; iv. 625–6; and *HMC Fourth Report*, 527 for a humorous incident.

48. *Political Writings*, 52–3; Fraser, *Sutherland*, ii. 365; Schreiber, *The First Carlisle*, 8–11.
49. *Poems of Sir Richard Maitland*, 27–31; NLS Adv. MS 15.2.14/56–7; Wemyss, *Workes*, i. 214–15.
50. NLS MS 21 176/21–5; NLS MS 973/9–16, 973/21–36; NAS GD 25/9/3 Fergus Kennedy bundle. For clothing accounts among the papers of the houses of Glenorchy and Buccleuch see NAS GD 112/23/7/12–14; NAS GD 224/393/7, 224/906/25/20.
51. Fraser, *Eglinton*, i. 194; Fraser, *Sutherland*, i. 278; *Ancram and Lothian*, i. 93. Compare, for example, the inventory of the households of lord James Stewart in 1562 or the regent Mar a decade later with those of the first earl of Melrose in 1624 or the first earl of Buccleuch in 1633, *HMC Sixth Report*, 646–9; *HMC Mar and Kellie*, ii. 30–2; Fraser, *Haddington*, i. 179–80, ii, 288–92, 294, 97–304; NLS MS 14 542/43, MS 14 543/37.
52. In December 1603 the fourth lord Elphinstone bought his wife a hackney carriage at the cost of £186, Fraser, *Elphinstone*, i. 153.
53. *HMC Sixth Report*, 646; NAS GD 224/295/50/10; NAS GD 26/5/516; NLS MS 5100/17–18; *Black Book of Taymouth*, 72. This was a feature of noble society elsewhere, Stone, *Crisis of the Aristocracy*, 572–81; Cressy, 'Death and the social order', 108–10.
54. Fraser, *Sutherland*, ii. 151.
55. Ibid., ii. 345; Heal and Homes, *Gentry in England and Wales*, 141.
56. NAS GD 30/1613; *Poems of Sir Richard Maitland*, 49–52; *Family of Kilravock*, 91; McCordick, *Scottish Literature*, i. 660–8; *Ancram and Lothian*, i. 55; NAS GD 158/2697/ 15; Donaldson, 'Legal profession'; Wormald, 'Bloodfeud, kindred and government', 91–3; Wormald, *Lords and Men*, 161–3; Brown, *Bloodfeud*, 239–65.
57. NAS GD 25/9/13/ Corrie bundle; in 1626 the debts had stood at £53 060, GD 25/9/27/3. Also see the small payments for legal fees in the account book of Peter Algeo for the second earl of Abercorn between 1632 and 1636, NLS MS 976/82–95.
58. *House of Forbes*, 124–7; NAS GD 52/1091; NAS GD 112/39/26/7; *Book of Dunvegan*, i. 200–1; Macinnes, 'Crown, clans and fine', 45; also see Fraser, *Chiefs of Grant*, iii. 321–34; Gordon, *Sutherland*, 344.
59. Anderson, *Earl of Orkney*, 33–41.
60. *CSP Scotland*, iii. 192–3; Spottiswoode, *History*, ii. 133; Bannatyne, *Memorials*, 51; Herries, *Memoirs*, 128; Lindsay, *Historie*, ii. 230–1, 237; Calderwood, *History*, ii. 562, 564; *Historie*, 29, 56, 58, 60; *CSP Scotland*, iii. 196–8.
61. *RPC*, first ser., ii. 31–2; *Bannatyne Miscellany*, i. 23–9; Herries, *Memoirs*, 105–6; *Historie*, 342–3; *CSP Scotland*, xi. 470, 474.
62. Howard, *Scottish Architecture*, 48–107; Cruden, *Scottish Castle*; Fenwick, *Scottish Baronial Houses*; Leslie, *Historie*, i. 22, 36; Fraser, *Douglas*, ii. 594–617; Stone, *Crisis of the Aristocracy*, 549–55; Stone and Stone, *An Open Elite?*, 349, 354–5.
63. Sanderson, *Scottish Rural Society*, 147–50; Meikle, 'Invisible divide', 77–8; Fraser, *Melvilles*, i. 115–16; iii. 133–6.
64. *House of Forbes*, 127; *Black Book of Taymouth*, 35–71.
65. Fraser, *Sutherland*, ii. 363. On labour costs, Gibson and Smout, *Prices, Food and Wages*, 273–7, 305–15.
66. NRA(S) 2312/113/13, 2312/113/746; NRA(S) 237/F/489–90.
67. *HMC Sixth Report*, 647, 654, 655–7; *CSP Scotland*, x. 19.
68. *RPC*, first ser., vii. 745; Paul, *Scots Peerage*, vi. 52.
69. The three sets of muddled accounts Ochiltree presented to the privy council claimed expenses varying from £19 000 to £40 000, but the king agreed to pay him only £10 000, *RPC*, first ser., viii. 281. For Argyll, *RPC*, first ser., x. 346–7, 350, 435, 439, 744–53, 757–66; xi. 224, 641–2.
70. For the financial misfortunes of treasurer Gowrie, Fraser, *Elphinstone*, ii. 163; Glamis, *CSP Scotland*, xi. 604, 609, 637; Cassillis, Brown, 'A house divided', 181–2; Dunbar, Lee, 'Unpublished letter', 178 and *RPC*, first ser., ix. 613, 642–3, 743–4; Morton, NLS MS 78/25.
71. Zulager, 'Middle-rank administrators', 167–9. Similarly, the first lord Scone, who was comptroller from 1599 to 1608, was pursued for royal debts, *RPC*, vii. 416.

72. 'Sum tyme to court I did repair', in Watson, *Poetry of Scotland*, 156–7; 'Na kindness at court without siller', in McCordick, *Scottish Literature*, i. 90–1; *CSP Scotland*, x. 765. However, the crown did provide some compensation for favoured servants, *Chronicles of the Frasers*, 149, 235–6.
73. Shaw, 'Landownership in the Western Isles', 43–8; Macinnes, 'Crown, clans and fine', 45; Macinnes, 'Scottish Gaeldom'; Fraser, *Sutherland*, ii. 118.
74. Peck, *Court Patronage and Corruption*; Stone, *Crisis of the Aristocracy*, 449–63; Heal and Holmes, *Gentry in England and Wales*, 128–33.
75. Fraser, *Haddington*, 124; NLS MS 84/57; *HMC*, xii. 8, 109, no. 59; Macinnes, *Making of the Covenanting Movement*, 34–7; *Memorials of Montrose*, i. 27.
76. For an account book see that for 1633 kept by Fergus Kennedy, factor to the sixth earl of Cassillis, NAS GD 25/9/13 Fergus Kennedy bundle. Lord Dalkeith's bond to a London tailor in 1633 was for the sum of £1652 9s, NAS GD 29/1251; for the laird of Panmure, GD 45/18/830–2, 45/22/10; NAS GD 24/1/353/2–3, 24/1/354; Hope, *Diary*, 6.
77. NLS MS 78/27, 78/31, 78/34. The £300 sterling per annum the sixth earl of Morton was finally awarded in 1631 was worth £3600 Scots, NAS GD 150/2295. For Hamilton, NAS GD 406/1/97.
78. Lithgow, 'Scotland's Welcome to Her Native Son' in Maidment, *Poetical Remains*; Lee, 'Unpublished letter', 177; Lee, *Road to Revolution*, 237; NLS MS 14401/3.
79. Henneman, 'Nobility, privilege and fiscal politics' is a good example of how conditions might change; Bush, *Noble Privilege*, 27–64.
80. Goodare, 'Parliamentary taxation', 23, 27; *APS*, iii. 108, 189–90, 328–30, 424–6, 523–4; iv. 50–2, 142–3, 289–92, 475–80, 581–5, 597–605; v. 13–20, 167–74, 209–17; Donaldson, *James V to James VII*, 300–3; Stevenson, 'Scottish revenues', 18–20.
81. Goodare, 'Parliamentary taxation', 28–42; Macinnes, *Making of the Covenanting Movement*, 8–9; *RPC*, first ser., vii. 311–12, x. 55–7. For unpaid taxes, ibid., first ser.,viii. 19; ibid., second ser., vi. 31; *HMC Laing*, i. 182–3; NAS GD 406/1/99. On legal advice see NLS MS 14401/8; NAS GD 11/104, and for appeals against assessment, *RPC*, first ser., iv. 628–9; vi. 333–4; vii. 284–5; *Melrose Papers*, i. 25–6; NAS GD 39/1/234. The English experience was little different, Heal and Holmes, *Gentry in England and Wales*, 156–60.
82. *APS*, iv. 290–1 for 1606; Goodare, 'Parliamentary taxation', 27; Balfour, *Works*, ii. 43; *RPC*, second ser., v. 587–90. Feuars would only pay if compelled.
83. Bonney, *European Dynastic States*, 219. On opposition to taxes in parliament, see examples in 1604, 1612, 1617, 1621 and 1633, Goodare, 'Parliamentary taxation', 40–5; Lee, *Government by Pen*, 19, 119–20, 206–7; Donaldson, *James V to James VII*, 302, 307; Stevenson, *Scottish Revolution*, 41–2, 51; Stevenson, 'Scottish revenues', 23–4; Macinnes, *Making of the Covenanting Movement*, 132–5; *APS*, iv. 597–605; *CSP Scotland*, xiii. prt. 1, 181–2, 584–5; *Melrose Papers*, ii. 271–2, 275, 381, 392–3; Fraser, *Douglas*, iv. 190–1; *HMC Mar and Kellie*, ii. 43–4; Balfour, *Works*, ii. 180. For private complaints see Fraser, *Buccleuch*, ii. 352; NAS GD 112/39/50/31; *Poems of William Drummond*, 274. That the nobility was resentful of the growing fiscal demands of the state is denied by Lee, *Road to Revolution*, 241–2; Lee, 'Scotland and the "General Crisis"'.
84. *HMC Twelfth Report*, 109; NAS GD 26/5/511/1; and also NRA(S) 217/4/734.
85. For example, *RPC*, first ser., vii. 327, 331–2; viii. 14.
86. NAS GD 45/14/8/7; NLS MS 14479. The July 1637 receipts are nos 66 and 70.
87. NAS GD 25/9/27/3 and 25/9/13 Corrie bundle. It is not true that the Scottish nobility knew little about arithmetic, Mitchison, *Lordship to Patronage*, 36.

## Chapter 4: Debt

1. Brown, 'Aristocratic finances'; Brown, 'Noble indebtedness'.
2. NRA(S) 217/4/476.
3. Although the market rate continued to be higher, Hope, *Major Practicks*, i. 120; *RPC*, vi.

20–2; ix. 424–6; *APS*, v. 39–40; *Regiam Majestatem*, 189–243; also see Guth, 'Age of debt'; Stone, *Crisis of the Aristocracy*, 505–46.

4. NAS GD 150/3442/7; *HMC Sixth Report*, 644, and for worries about the reliability of Scottish coinage, NAS GD 60/27. In some instances, any difference between the income from the land and the interest due was made up by the debtor, Paton, *Introduction*, 183–93; Hope, *Major Practicks*, i. 119–20, 185–93; *Formulary*, 86–7.
5. Stone, *Crisis of the Aristocracy*, 524–8; Heal and Holmes, *Gentry in England and Wales*, 160–3; Jago, 'Influence of debt', 26, 219; Jago, 'The "crisis of the aristocracy" in 17th-century Castile'; Bonney, *European Dynastic States*, 379–80.
6. Land held by a vassal in ward was subject to restrictions as to its use without the permission of the superior, Hope, *Major Practicks*, i. 159. For various redemption agreements, NRA(S) 237/C/171–2; Gordon, *Sutherland*, 460–1; Fraser, *Menteith*, i. 334; NAS GD 11/98–9; Major, *Renaissance Monarchy to Absolute Monarchy*, 89.
7. *Spalding Miscellany*, iii. 71–139.
8. See the efforts in the 1580s of the Italian banker, Timothy Cagnioli, to recover money lent to Scottish nobles, *RPC*, iv. 66–7; Paul, *Scots Peerage*, ii. 475; NRA(S) 217/2/67. For the second earl of Mar's loans in London as early as 1604, NAS GD 124/2/4–8. Interest rates in England were around 12 per cent until 1572 when they were set at 10 per cent, at which level they remained until 1624 when they fell to 8 per cent.
9. Brown, 'Edinburgh merchant elite', especially chs v and vii; Sanderson, 'Edinburgh merchants in society', 187–8; Sanderson, *Mary Stewart's People*, 91–102; *Works of Sir Thomas Urquhart*, 300–1, 326–7; and for the source of his bitterness, NRA(S) 2570/190.
10. Craig, *Jus Feudale*, ii. 921–46; Zagorin, *Rebels and Rulers, 1500–1660*, i. 131; and for an example, *RPC*, first ser., x. 18; *RMSRS 1620–33*, no. 1403. The picture is exaggerated in Brown, 'Edinburgh merchant elite', ch. vii.
11. The twelfth earl of Sutherland borrowed heavily from Aberdeen merchants, the lairds of Perthshire were able to find credit among Perth merchant burgesses, and the second earl of Mar raised cash from Walter Cowan, merchant burgess of Stirling, who lent him £1000 in 1595, Fraser, *Sutherland*, ii. 360–1; NAS GD 38/1/98 and 120; NAS GD 124/1/658 and 124/1/694.
12. NAS GD 75/588; *Chronicles of the Frasers*, 235, 253; NLS MS 79/3; Fraser, *Chiefs of Grant*, i. 211; and see *House of Gordon*, i. 13.
13. Seton, *Family of Seton*, ii. 902; NAS GD 11/87; NRA(S) 217/1/22.
14. This was the advice offered in 1634 to the first marquis of Douglas, NLS MS 973/41; *RPC*, first ser., xiii. 818–19.
15. Dewald, *European Nobility*, 93; NAS GD 224/61/1/11, 224/61/2/1, 224/61/9–10; Fraser, *Haddington*, ii. 305–9; Paul, *Scots Peerage*, vi. 471.
16. NRA(S) 217/43/176; Fraser, *Eglinton*, ii. 233–4.
17. For example, the sums owed at death were the first earl of Mar in 1572 (£6820), the fourth earl Marischal in 1582 (£14 440), the fourth lord Boyd in 1590 (£12 194), the fifth lord Herries in 1603 (£10 262), the first earl of Dunbar in 1609 (£20 407), the first earl of Home in 1619 (£36 274) and the first earl of Haddington in 1637 (£44 657), NAS CC 8/8/3/388–9b, 8/8/11/53–9, 8/8/21/238–244b, 8/8/40/79–81, 8/8/47/27–9, 8/8/51/46b–9, 8/8/58/151b–5. In real terms the sums owed to Marischal were equivalent to those owed to Haddington over half a century later. The percentage of cash loans for these sums is well below the 30–40 per cent which Brown found in the testaments of Edinburgh merchants, Brown 'Edinburgh merchant elite', 270.
18. *RPC*, first ser., vii. 254–5; NAS GD 224/38/9; Fraser, *Buccleuch*, ii. 270–1. The total sum owed to Buccleuch was £167 900, but there were relatively few personal bonds, the largest being for £2000 owed by the sixth earl of Morton.
19. Fraser, *Elphinstone*, ii. 187; NAS GD 158/2697/33; *Ancram and Lothian*, i. 97–8.
20. Stone, *Crisis of the Aristocracy*, 505–7; Sanderson, *Mary Stewart's People*, 72; *House of Forbes*, 124–7; Fraser, *Buccleuch*, i. 264–6; Fraser, *Sutherland*, ii. 117; Anderson, *Black Patie*, 22–3.
21. NRA(S) 237/E/392–4; Fraser, *Elphinstone*, ii. 165–6. The dead were also concerned that

their reputation should not be sullied by kinsmen failing to pay off their debts, NLS MS 175/34.

22. NAS GD 124/1/969. See the regular discharges in the Yester accounts for 1614–37, NLS MS 14477–8 and also MS 14618–19 and NAS GD 28/1319–20, 28/1369 for further records of that family's financial management. For a good example of a large debt being paid quickly, Fraser, *Eglinton*, ii. 259. Gordonstoun advised his nephew to be cautious in repaying debts, Fraser, *Sutherland*, ii. 36.
23. *Honoris de Morton*, i. 51–2, 79; Sanderson, *Mary Stewart's People*, 72; NLS MS 16501/76–9; 'Scotland's Welcome to Her Native Sone' in *Poetical Remains of William Lithgow*. For a complaint to the privy council in 1602 against the first lord Spynie who was sitting at the council table, *RPC*, first ser., vi. 508. Clients lobbied their lords for protection, NLS MS 14401/25, 14401/27–9; and got it, *RPC*, first ser, iv. 83; vi. 488.
24. Brown, *Bloodfeud*, prt. iii 'Uprooting the feud'; Craig, *Jus Feudale*, i. 226–8; *RPC*, first ser., vii. 415; *APS*, iv. 597–600, 609–12, 627; v. 39–40, 185; *Melrose Papers*, i. 30–1; Paton, *Introduction*, 222–38; *RPC*, second ser., vi. 184; Hope, *Major Practicks*, i. 118–19.
25. Fraser, *Sutherland*, ii. 356; NRA(S) 2312/113/14; NLS MS 976/76, and for the long-term effects on the Lothian estate, NAS GD 40/2/13/68, 40/2/13/79, 40/2/13/85; *Book of Dunvegan*, i. 264. In 1698 Duncan Forbes of Culloden wrote that the Innes kindred enjoyed three blessings, 'First, that their inheritance never went to a woman; next that none of them ever married an ill wife; and thirdly, that no friend ever suffered for their debt', *Familie of Innes*, 44. For the nervous comments of one of the sixth earl of Morton's cautioners on the subject of surety see NLS MS 81/1.
26. *House of Seytoun*, 56, 60; *Spalding Miscellany*, ii. 395, 398, 400; Fraser, *Elphinstone*, i. 196.
27. *HMC Various V*, 138; NLS MS 82/37.
28. Dalrymple, *Institutions*, 147–9. Similar arrangements were made by Spanish nobles, Jago, 'Influence of debt', 229; NAS GD 137/1600; Fraser, *Philorth*, i. 162–3, 169–70. For the Argyll case, NAS GD 112/39/24/6, 112/39/25/2–3, 112/39/25/14, 112/39/26/3, 112/39/26/5, 112/39/27/3, 112/39/27/5, 112/39/28/19, 112/39/30/2. For the 1617 commission, 112/14/6/1, and later repercussions 112/39/25/5, 112/39/31/3, 112/39/35/15, 112/39/47/5; *RPC*, first ser., x. 439.
29. Anderson, *Black Patie*, 79; *Miscellany of the Scottish History Society*, i. 95–6.
30. *Family of Kilravock*, 74; NLS MS 78/32, 78/34, 78/49; Fraser, *Eglinton*, ii. 221–3. For European trends, Bonney, *European Dynastic States*, 380.
31. NAS GD 224/935/6–7; Gordon, *Sutherland*, 364; and also *House of Seytoun*, 65–6.
32. *Chronicles of the Frasers*, 192–6; NAS GD 124/7/20.
33. Gordon, *Sutherland*, 149; NAS GD 158/2697/2, 158/2697/39.
34. Fraser, *Sutherland*, ii. 157–8, 362.
35. *Estimate*, 33; NAS CC 8/8/3/156–8b; NAS GD 39/1/83, 39/1/89, 39/1/92–3, 39/1/95, 39/1/100–1, 39/1/104, 39/1/107, 39/1/142, 39/1/153, 39/1/156, 39/1/161–2, 39/1/167, 39/1/169, 39/1/179, 39/1/183–4, 39/1/187, 39/1/191–2, 39/1/197, 39/1/213, 39/1/222, 39/5/48, 39/5/59–60.
36. Habakkuk, 'Rise and fall'; Stone, *Crisis of the Aristocracy*, 157–8, 539–40. The English figure of a 5 per cent return on land is roughly applicable to Scotland, Habakkuk, 'Long-term rate of interest'.
37. NAS CC 8/8/43/109–11b; NAS GD 16/2/88–94, 16/42/188, 16/43/4.
38. *CSP Scotland*, vii. 426–7; Fraser, *Sutherland*, ii. 345.
39. Fraser, *Haddington*, ii. 140–1, 143; Thompson, 'Nobility in Spain', 211.
40. Fraser, *Carlaverock*, ii. 71–2; NRA(S) 2312/107/4/23–49, 2312/113/170, 2312/113/174, 2312/113/175, 2312/113/195, 2312/113/726, 2312/113/739, 2312/113/855, 2312/113/857.
41. NAS GD 150/3438/3 Traquair to Morton, 5 June 1636, 150/512, 150/2127–8, 150/3442/8, 150/3442/18; NAS GD 224/318/1, 224/318/3; NAS GD 124/1/1163; NAS GD 29/1023; NLS MS 83/37, 84/54, 84/56.
42. NRA(S) 237/E/513–15. Nobles were among the most likely to initiate bankruptcy against one another in seventeenth-century France, Wood, *Nobility of Bayeux*, 131–7.

43. Fraser, *Elphinstone*, ii. 184–5; Fraser, *Menteith*, ii. 155.
44. Fraser, *Haddington*, ii. 143; *Melrose Papers*, ii. 404–5; NAS GD 112/27/2/23; and see Macinnes, 'Crown, clans and fine', 46.
45. *Poems of Sir Richard Maitland*, 25; *Works of Sir Thomas Urquhart*, 393. Scotstarvit preserved the story of the second earl of Dunfermline in which he gambled away much of his father's fortune, Scott, *Staggering State*, 47–9. For the law on prodigality, Craig, *Jus Feudale*, i. 223–4.
46. *RPC*, first ser., vii. 140, 337, 617; ix. 586; x. 90; *Historie*, 385; Spottiswoode, *History*, iii. 219–22; Anderson, *Black Patie*, 80.
47. Fraser, *Sutherland*, ii. 133; Fraser, *Haddington*, ii. 84–5, 134–8, 140–1; *RPC*, first ser., x. 583; xi. 68, 209; xii. 368; xiii. 124, 138–9, 253–4, 280–4, 394–5, 523, 617–19, 628, 631, 646, 667–8, 686–7, 708, 801; second ser., i. 38, 74, 100–1, 125, 207, 241, 257, 316–17, 368–70, 372; *HMC Laing*, i. 154; *HMC Mar and Kellie*, i. 117; Gordon, *Sutherland*, 339, 363–4, 371–3, 377; *Historie*, 390–1.
48. On the eleventh earl, *Estimate*, 32; *CSP Scotland*, x. 69; NRA(S) 237/C/116–18, 237/C/177–80; *RPC*, first ser., vii. 274–5. For the twelfth earl, *RPC*, first ser., viii. 66, 154, 282–3, 352, 368, 392, 411, 438, 482; ix. 3, 68, 74–5, 82, 97; x. 171–2, 335, 440, 457; NRA(S) 237/C/121–4, 237/C/126, 237/C/186–91, 237/C/193–4; NAS GD 45/16/6; Lindsay, *Lives of the Lindsays*, ii. 51–2. For the subsequent bad fortune of the house of Crawford, Paul, *Scots Peerage*, iii. 32, 34; *RPC*, first ser., ix. 82; xii. 331–2, 341–2, 360; xiii. 71, 275, 282; second ser., i. 405–6; ii. 122, 176–7, 524, 580–1; NRA(S) 237/C/126–9, 237/C/132–3.
49. Among the peerage see the house of Saltoun, Fraser, *Philorth*, ii. 65–6: Borthwick, Paul, *Scots Peerage*, ii. 111, 113; *RPC*, first ser., xii. 122; xiii. 66, 71, 74: Oliphant, Paul, *Scots Peerage*, vi. 551; *RPC*, first ser., xi. 171, 178, 219, 405, 451; xii. 104; xiii. 283; Ochiltree, Paul, *Scots Peerage*, vi. 516; *RPC*, first ser., ix. 420, 438–9, 456, 478, 499, 818–19; Ross's testament is at NAS CC 8/8/57/273–6: Marischal, Paul, *Scots Peerage*, vi. 48; *RPC*, first ser., vii. 395, 436–7; viii. 49, 333, 411; Herries, *RPC*, first ser., viii. 412, 479; xi. 57, 63, 173, 229, 400; xii. 500; and others, *RPC*, first ser., viii. 310; x. 87, 566; xi. 35, 173, 434–5; second ser., ii. 158–9. For Airth, Fraser, *Elphinstone*, 187.
50. Jago, 'Influence of debt', 227; Dewald, *European Nobility*, 40–1; Bush, *Rich Noble, Poor Noble*, 111–31; Kamen, *European Society*, 140; *RPC*, second ser., vi. 50–1.
51. *RPC*, second ser., iii. 141–2; Paul, *Scots Peerage*, viii. 23–7. Mar acted as a receiver and paid £44 466 13s 4d. Mar was again called in as a financial adviser in the affairs of the laird of Balnagown in 1622, *Family of Kilravock*, 310–14, 317; GD 124/7/25. For Gray, *HMC Sixth Report*, 661.
52. NAS GD 124/15/41; *RPC*, first ser., xiii. 453 n. 1; Fraser, *Elphinstone*, ii. 187–8; Cross, *Puritan Earl*, 61–111.
53. Cooper, 'Inheritance and settlement', 250–1; Stone and Stone, *An Open Elite?*, 157–60; Jago, 'The "crisis of the aristocracy" in seventeenth-century Castile', 90; Fraser, *Sutherland*, ii. 368; NLS MS 80/64.
54. Paul, *Scots Peerage*, i. 446; *CSP Scotland*, v. 254; xii. 6, 13, 21, 174; NRA(S) 237/ii/214–15, 237/ii/F/ii/226–7; *RPC*, first ser., vii. 338, 357, 511, 527, 530–1, 566; viii. 7, 220–1, 243–4, 429, 432, 545–6, 557, 563, 566–7, 790, 796; ix. 109–10, 113, 130, 610, 668; Scott, *Staggering State*, 40; *Chronicles of the Frasers*, 243.
55. *RPC*, first ser., xiii. 488–9, 546–8.
56. MacDowall, *Burgh of Dumfries*, 293–4; Fraser, *Maxwells of Pollok*, ii. 193–4; *HMC Mar and Kellie*, i. 82, 126; Fraser, *Carlaverock*, ii. 4–5, 9–13; *RPC*, first ser., xiii. 574–5, 593, 606–7.
57. *RPC*, first ser., vii. 281–2. For other barons of this rank, *RPC*, first ser., x. 606–7, 646, 678–81; *HMC Mar and Kellie*, i. 95, 113, 119.
58. Scott and Storrs, 'Introduction', 25–7; Price, 'Dutch nobility', 88–9; van Nierop, *Nobility of Holland*, 126–34.
59. Bernard, 'Tudor nobility in perspective', 6–7; Doran, 'Finances of an Elizabethan nobleman'; Pollard, 'Estate management'; Kershaw, 'Power and duty', 267; Coward,

'A "crisis of the aristocracy"'; Coward, *The Stanleys*, 28–40; Major, *Renaissance Monarchy to Absolute Monarchy*, 75–86; Eurich, *Economics of Power*; Wood, *Nobility of Bayeux*, 140; Jago, 'The "crisis of the aristocracy" in seventeenth-century Castile'.

60. Bernard, 'Tudor nobility in perspective', 8; Macinnes, *Making of the Covenanting Movement*, 6.
61. Gordon, *Sutherland*, 313; NAS GD 224/930/38/9; Fraser, *Buccleuch*, ii. 271–4, but see the debts in NLS MS 14 542/35.
62. *Estimate*, 7–39; Eurich, *Economics of Power*, 30–1, 194–218; *CSP Scotland*, iii. 257.
63. NAS CC 8/8/4/190–1b, and for an estimate of losses in 1570, *CSP Scotland*, iii. 454.
64. *HMC Twelfth Report*, 100–1, 107; *Historie*, 55–6; *CSP Scotland*, iii. 304; iv. 288. For others see *Estimate*, 16–17, 20, 22, 37, 39.
65. *Estimate*, 29–30; *CSP Scotland*, iii. 242; *HMC Mar and Kellie*, i. 27.
66. NAS GD 112/39/42/30.
67. NAS CC 8/8/3–44; NAS CC 20/4/5–6, 20/4/9; NAS CC 9/7/17, 9/7/19, 9/7/22, 9/7/25; CC 21/5/4–5. Post-1600 prices have been calculated by multiplying by factors of 3.5 for the 1570s, 3 for the 1580s, and 2 for the 1590s.
68. NAS CC 8/8/21/44b–49b. The debts of the fourth earl of Glencairn amounted to £3904, leaving his heir with a net deficit of £513 in 1575, CC 8/8/3/256–8b; the fifth lord Ogilvy's debts of £2350 exceeded the gross value of his testament in 1606 by £580, CC 8/8/43/109–11b; and the first marquis of Hamilton had a net deficit of £4445, having debts of £21 313 when he died in 1604, CC 8/8/44/77–9.
69. NAS CC 8/8/3–44; NAS CC 20/4/5–6, 20/4/9; NAS CC 9/7/17, 9/7/19, 9/7/22, 9/7/25; CC 21/5/4–5.
70. As in Normandy and Denmark, Wood, *Nobility of Bayeux*, 122–6; Jespersen, 'The rise and fall of the Danish nobility, 47–8.
71. Grant, 'Scottish peerage', 15; Wormald, *Lords and Men*, 100. When the seventh earl of Errol died in 1574 the net value of his testament was a mere £151, NAS CC 8/8/3/96–7b.
72. Between 1570 and 1589 the average earl's testament had a gross value six times that of a lord of parliament, £12 006 compared to £2547; by the period 1590 to 1640 this had fallen to only two and a half times greater, £22 497 compared to £9381, NAS CC 8/8/3–44; NAS CC 20/4/5–6, 20/4/9; NAS CC 9/7/17, 9/7/19, 9/7/22, 9/7/25; CC 21/5/4–5. For a comparison of peers and barons on the eastern march, Meikle, 'Invisible divide', 77.
73. Clark, *State and Status*, 227–30; Stone, *Crisis of the Aristocracy*, 56–7; Thompson, 'Nobility in Spain', 190–3; *CSP Scotland*, viii. 637; xiii. prt. 2, 731; for Angus's testament, Fraser, *Douglas*, ii. 363–4, n. 3.
74. *Ayr and Wigton* (AWAA), iv. 18; Brown, 'A house divided'.
75. Fraser, *Buccleuch*, i. 158, 235, 249–53; ii. 454–9; NAS GD 224/930/38/9, 224/935/6, 224/935/11.
76. Fraser, *Melvilles*, i. 131; iii. 149–51, 161–2.
77. Fraser, *Chiefs of Grant*, i. xxiii–xci, 128, 151, 204, 208–9; iii. 286–91. For the declining fortunes of the house of Kilravock, *Family of Kilravock*, 281–4, 300–2. The best study of the economic fortunes of the lairds is Meikle, 'Lairds and gentlemen', 207–72.
78. Scott, *Staggering State*, 66, 77, 94, 99–100, 105.
79. *RPC*, first ser., v. 366, 373. Further down the scale, Sanderson suggested that a comfortably off farmer on an estate in the south-east might be worth £500–£600 at his death, Sanderson, *Mary Stewart's People*, 176.

## Chapter 5: Marrying

1. *Political Writings*, 38; for a recent discussion of noble marriage, van Nierop, *Nobility of Holland*, 67–92; Cressy, *Birth, Marriage and Death*, 285–92.
2. Hay, *Lectures*; Marshall, *Virgins and Viragos*; Scanlan, 'Husband and wife'; Ireland, 'Husband and wife', 82–9; Ozment, *When Fathers Ruled*, 3–49.

3. As few as 2 per cent of the English peerage, most of whom were eldest sons, remained unmarried in the sixteenth century, Stone and Stone, *An Open Elite?*, 259; Emigh, 'Land tenure, household structure and age of marriage'.
4. *House of Seytoun*, 65; Paul, *Scots Peerage*, i. 350; iii. 373; ix. 22; Ago, 'Young nobles', 283–7.
5. Hay, *Lectures*, 155–9; Phillips, 'Maidenhood as the perfect age'; Macfarlane, *Marriage and Love*, 211–17; Fletcher, *Gender, Sex and Subordination*, 48–52.
6. Major, *Renaissance Monarchy to Absolute Monarchy*, 310; Cressy, *Birth, Marriage and Death*, 285; Stone and Stone, *An Open Elite?*, 96; Stone, *Crisis of the Aristocracy*, 652–4; van Nierop, *Nobility of Holland*, 55–7; Ozment, *When Fathers Ruled*, 37–8.
7. *Registrum de Panmure*, i. p. xxxvii; Fraser, *Carlaverock*, i. 301; for other examples, Fraser, *Menteith*, i. 329; Fraser, *Douglas*, ii. 413; *CSP Scotland*, vi. 43; *Chronicle of Perth*, 19.
8. *Poems of Sir Richard Maitland*, 40–1, for his 'On the folye of ane auld manis maryand ane young woman'. In England, the legal age of marriage was the same as in Scotland, Stone and Stone, *An Open Elite?*, 259–60; Houlbrooke, *The English Family*, 63–8; Cressy, *Birth, Marriage and Death*, 311; Ingram, *Church Courts*, 128–31.
9. Gordon, *Sutherland*, 151, 289.
10. Dupaquier et al., *Marriage and Remarriage*. In England some 25 per cent of peers remarried, but the rate of remarriage slowed down in the seventeenth century, Stone and Stone, *An Open Elite?*, 91; Stone, *Crisis of the Aristocracy*, 619–23; Heal and Holmes, *Gentry in England and Wales*, 86.
11. *HMC Sixth Report*, 697; Fraser, *Melvilles*, i. 132; Paul, *Scots Peerage*, vi. 101; NLS MS 5787/1.
12. Dupaquier et al., *Marriage and Remarriage*; Hufton, *Prospect Before Her*, 217–50; Calvi, 'Reconstructing the family'; NLS MS 5070/34; NRA(S) 2847/2/20, 2 September 1610; Paul, *Scots Peerage*, ii. 362, iii. 372–3.
13. Fraser, *Sutherland*, ii. 342; and on strategies generally, Hufton, *Prospect Before Her*, 59–98.
14. Following the master of Ruthven's death, Mary Gray spurned William Ruthven's offer of marriage and instead married David Seton of Parbroath. However, her father had his revenge and granted a tocher of a mere £100, NRA(S) 217/1/5–7; Paul, *Scots Peerage*, iv. 261–3, 282–4. For Pitfirrane, NLS MS 6406/3–4.
15. NAS GD 112/39/33/26; NLS MS 78/27–8.
16. Craig, *Jus Feudale*, ii. 831–3; Fraser, *Elphinstone*, ii. 266.
17. Watt, *The Making of Modern Marriage*, 70–87; Ozment, *When Fathers Ruled*, 25–44; Hufton, *Prospect Before Her*, 99–133; Pollock, *Forgotten Children*; Ago, 'Young nobles'; Dean, 'Fathers and daughters'; Major, *Renaissance Monarchy to Absolute Monarchy*, 89–90; for a depressingly bleak view of marital negotiations, Gilbert, *Women in Seventeenth-Century France*, 41–58; for contrasting views of English marriage, Ingram, *Church Courts*, 135–40, Stone, *Crisis of the Aristocracy*, 594–9, and an intriguing case study is presented in Wall, 'For love, money, or politics?'
18. Hay, *Lectures*, 5–35, 177–83; Sellar, 'Marriage, divorce and the forbidden degrees', 61–2; Smout, 'Scottish marriage'; Forte, 'Some aspects of the law of marriage', 105–6.
19. For unsuccessful cases, *RPC*, first ser., v. 55, 86; viii. 552–3; Paul, *Scots Peerage*, iv. 284; Calderwood, *History*, v. 252. For some Dutch comparisons, van Nierop, *Nobility of Holland*, 85–92.
20. *RPC*, first ser., iv. 506–7; Spottiswoode, *History*, ii. 408–9; *CSP Scotland*, x. 281, 285, 335, 347, 351–2; *Honoris de Morton*, i. 187.
21. *HMC Mar and Kellie*, ii. 56–7, 154, 157–8, 200; Paul, *Scots Peerage*, ii. 365.
22. NAS GD 158/2697/32; NAS GD 75/581.
23. This was a common theme of playwrights; for example, the 1607 *The Miseries of Enforced Marriages* by George Wilkins.
24. Watt, *The Making of Modern Marriage*; Dean and Lowe, 'Introduction: issues in the history of marriage', 7–11. The debate in England typifies the range of views, from Macfarlane's world of negotiation and compromise to Stone's softening patriarchy, Macfarlane, *Marriage and Love*, 119–47; Stone, *Crisis of the Aristocracy*, 596–9; also

Dockray, 'Why did fifteenth-century English gentry marry?', 61–80; Ingram, *Church Courts*, 141–2; Houlbrooke, *The English Family*, 68–78; Cressy, *Birth, Marriage and Death*, 233–66. For Scotland, Marshall, *Virgins and Viragos*, ch. 3; NAS GD 158/2697/4.

25. Hughes and Ramson, *Poetry of the Stewart Court*, 134–48, 413–82; Watson, *Poetry of Scotland*, 170–1; Scott, *Scotch Passion*; McCordick, *Scottish Literature*, i. 613–14, 718–23.
26. Fraser, *Annandale*, ii. 278–9; *Registrum de Panmure*, i. pp. xlii–xliii; Fraser, *Sutherland*, ii. 342.
27. *Honoris de Morton*, i. 173–4;; Paul, *Scots Peerage*, v. 357; *CSP Scotland*, x. 410, 502.
28. Bell, *Elizabethan Women and the Poetry of Courtship*; Marshall, *Virgins and Viragos*, 69.
29. NLS MS 14480/82–4. For Cassillis, *Kennedy*, 18, 24–5, 111; *CSP Scotland*, xiii, prt. 1, 125, 150–1, 168, 230, 327–8; *Chronicle of the Kings of Scotland*, 156; Spottiswoode, *History*. vi 1847–51; iii. 78; *RPC*, v. 314; *Political Writings*, 40.
30. NAS GD 112/39/20/2–3, 112/39/20/6, 112/39/20/10.
31. Fraser, *Elphinstone*, i. 109; *CSP Scotland*, xi. 594–5, 597, 599; *Melrose Papers*, ii. 403–4; also NAS GD 150/3441/18.
32. NAS GD 112/39/40/3; NLS MS 5070/34.
33. *RPC*, first ser., iii. 253–4; Paul, *Scots Peerage*, viii. 542–3; NAS GD 24/1/353/2.
34. *Historie*, 281; Fraser, *Douglas*, ii. 328; Zulager, 'Middle-rank administrators', 159; Paul, *Scots Peerage*, v. 168–9; NRA(S) 234/523/97; see also *CSP Scotland*, viii. 365.
35. *CSP Scotland*, xiii. prt. 1, 344; Fraser, *Douglas*, ii. 398.
36. *RPC*, first ser., ii. 312–13, 318. For Moray, NRA(S) 217/3/140, 217/3/271, 217/4/84; and see the payment to treasurer Gowrie for the ward, relief and non-entry of the fifth earl of Caithness in 1583, NAS GD 96/206. For Lennox, *HMC Mar and Kellie*, ii. 211, and see *RPC*, first ser., xiv. 410–11.
37. Fosi and Visceglin, 'Marriage and politics at the papal court', 197–224; Stone, *Crisis of the Aristocracy*, 605–9; *RPC*, first ser., iv. 103; *Ancram and Lothian*, i. 27–8. See James's brokering of the marriage between the first lord Spynie and the widowed countess of Angus in 1589–90, Fraser, *Douglas*, iv. 34–5; Lindsay, *Lives of the Lindsays*, i. 322; Paul, *Scots Peerage*, viii. 97. Her lands in Kinross-shire alone were worth 11 000 merks per annum, Zulager, 'Middle-rank administrators', 161.
38. Craig, *Jus Feudale*, ii. 842–51; Hope, *Major Practicks*, i. 255; *HMC Twelfth Report*, 103.
39. Fraser, *Sutherland*, iii. 175–7; *Chronicles of the Frasers*, 234–5; for wardship in England, Stone, *Crisis of the Aristocracy*, 600–5.
40. *RPC*, first ser., xii. 614; Paul, *Scots Peerage*, viii. 26; NAS GD 112/39/53/19; NAS GD 124/6/72.
41. Henderson and McManus, *Half Humankind*, 72; Cox, 'The single self'; Fletcher, *Gender, Sex and Subordination*, 376–83; Ozment, *When Fathers Ruled*, 58–72; Houlbrooke identifies four criteria men prioritised in the choice of a marriage partner: the advancement of the individual or family, the ideal of parity, the general character of the prospective partner and love, *The English Family*, 73.
42. Fraser, *Sutherland*, ii. 342–4; *Political Writings*, 40; McCordick, *Scottish Literature*, i. 773–4; *Works of Sir Thomas Urquhart*, 25; Boyd, *Last Batell*, 508; *Chronicles of the Frasers*, 223–4.
43. *Political Writings*, 41.
44. Fraser, *Sutherland*, iii. 131–2; *APS*, iii. 26; Hope, *Major Practicks*, i. 137; Hay, *Lectures*, 185–257; Sellar, 'Marriage, divorce and the forbidden degrees'. Some cases did reach the courts, see Pitcairn, *Criminal Trials*, i. prt. 2, 167, and for a tale of noble incest and its consequences, Scott, *Staggering State*, 111.
45. *Ancram and Lothian*, 18; Stone, *Crisis of the Aristocracy*, 614–15; Mentzer, *Blood and Belief*, 81–103.
46. Knox, *Works*, ii. 533; *CSP Scotland*, ix. 587; x. 773, 778, 780; *HMC Mar and Kellie*, i. 65; *Political Writings*, 41.
47. Davies, 'Politics of the marriage bed'; Queller and Madden, 'Father of the bride', 700–4; Molho, *Marriage Alliances*, 25–6.
48. NAS GD 406/1/33; *HMC Mar and Kellie*, ii. 115–16.

49. *HMC Mar and Kellie*, ii. 56–7, 121; see Brown, 'Scottish aristocracy, anglicization and the court'.
50. *CSP Scotland*, xii. 149, 151; NAS GD 112/39/20/5.
51. Stone, *Crisis of the Aristocracy*, 170–1; Heal and Holmes, *Gentry in England and Wales*, 61–2; Jespersen, 'The rise and fall of the Danish nobility', 48–9; Benadusi, *A Provincial Elite in Early Modern Tuscany*, 113–25; Stone, *Crisis of the Aristocracy*, 623–6; and for a closely monitored endogamous marriage market, Molho, *Marriage Alliances*; Fraser, *Sutherland*, ii. 368.
52. Fraser, *Elphinstone*, i. 3–4; Paul, *Scots Peerage*, iii. 534–41. See too Meikle's study of the eastern march, 'Lairds and gentlemen', 46–50.
53. Brown, *Bloodfeud*, 58; Delille, 'Marriage, faction and conflict'; *RPC*, first ser., ii. 665, 671; Fraser, *Buccleuch*, i. 136–41; ii. 445–53; *Historie*, 296.
54. Stone, *Crisis of the Aristocracy*, 627–8; Macfarlane, *Marriage and Love*, 245–62; van Nierop, *Nobility of Holland*, 67–76; Wood, 'Endogamy and *mésalliance*'; Wood, *Nobility of Bayeux*, 99–119.
55. 'Luv preyis but comparesone', Watson, *Poetry of Scotland*, 171; Edington, *Court and Culture in Renaissance Scotland*, 31; *Political Writings*, 41; NLS Adv. MS 15/2/14/35, 15/2/14/42–9, 15/2/14/54–5, 15/2/14/71; Craig, *Jus Feudale*, i. 220.
56. McCordick, *Scottish Literature*, i. 771–2; *CSP Scotland*, v. 611.
57. Fraser, *Sutherland*, ii. 343; *Familie of Innes*, 29, 41–2; Paul, *Scots Peerage*, iii. 536.
58. Fraser, *Haddington*, i. 189; ii. 292–3; Paul, *Scots Peerage*, iv. 314–15; v. 401. It was of the Melrose-Mar marriage alliance between two of his most important officials that James VI allegedly commented 'The Lord haud a grup o' me! If Tam o' the Cowgate's son marry Jock o'Sklates' dochter, what's to come o' me.'
59. Habakkuk, 'The rise and fall of English landed families', 187–95; Stone, *Crisis of the Aristocracy*, 617–19; NAS GD 11/65; Paul, *Scots Peerage*, i. 542; viii. 68; *HMC Second Report*, i. pp. 168–77; also see the Lothian case, *Ancram and Lothian*, i. 81.
60. McCordick, *Scottish Literature*, i. 774; *Works of Sir Thomas Urquhart*, 19; Fraser, *Sutherland*, ii. 343.
61. For a long contract see that between the second lord Buccleuch and Marie Hay, daughter of the ninth earl of Errol, in 1616, NAS GD 224/903/33/1. Correspondence relating to marriage dwelt on financial issues, *HMC Various V*, 117–18, 125.
62. Cressy, *Birth, Marriage and Death*, 267–76; *Honoris de Morton*, i. 9–10; Fraser, *Douglas*, iii. 259; *HMC Mar and Kellie*, i. 30–1; *CSP Scotland*, xiii. prt. 1, 150–1; Paul, *Scots Peerage*, iv. 245; McCordick, *Scottish Literature*, i. 608; Brown, 'A house divided', 179–80.
63. Marshall, *Virgins and Viragos*, 31–3, 81–6. For English wedding festivities, Cressy, *Birth, Marriage and Death*, 350–76; Stone, *Road to Divorce*, 51ff; NLS MS 82/2–3.
64. Similar festivities took place at the marriage of the fourth earl of Bothwell and Jean Gordon in 1566, Cressy, *Birth, Marriage and Death*, 350–5; Knox, *Works*, ii. 314; Lindsay, *Historie*, i. 173, 186; Calderwood, *History*, ii. 173–4; *CSP Scotland*, i. 590.
65. Lindsay, *Historie*, ii. 305, 322–3; Moysie, *Memoirs*, 69; NAS GD 75/563. For extravagant festivities in 1581, 1597 and 1600, *CSP Scotland*, v. 611; xiii. prt. 1, 78, 87; xiii. prt. 2, 621; Moysie, *Memoirs*, 34.
66. *Chronicle of Perth*, 20. It is highly likely that Scottish nobles, like those elsewhere, rented and borrowed in order to mount these festivities, Allerston, 'Wedding finery in sixteenth-century Venice'.
67. *CSP Scotland*, xiii. prt. 1, 276–7; *HMC Seventh Report*, 723; and also NAS GD 112/39/32/17.

## Chapter 6: Spouses

1. Pollock, 'Living on the stage of the world'.
2. Ozment, *When Fathers Ruled* and Fletcher, *Gender, Sex and Subordination* argue that Protestantism was beneficial to women. Others have taken the view that little changed

at the Reformation, Harrington, *Reordering Marriage and Society*, or that women were the victims of an enhanced 'patriarchy', Roper, *Holy Household*. For a range of studies, Brooke, *Medieval Idea of Marriage*; Stone, *Family, Sex and Marriage*; Eales, *Women in Early Modern England*; Watt, *Making of Modern Marriage*, 11–14; Safley, *Let No Man Put Asunder*; Shorter, *Making of the Modern Family*; Hufton, *Prospect Before Her*, 134–72; Anderson and Zinsser, *History of Their Own*, i. 228–350.

3. *John Knox. On Rebellion*, 3–47; *APS*, iii. 38; Larner, *Enemies of God*; for entails see ch. 1, pp. 34–9; Hay, *Lectures*, 147–9; see Atkinson and Atkinson, 'Subordinating women'; Crawford, 'Attitudes to menstruation'.
4. *Early Travellers*, 102, 152; Fletcher, *Gender, Sex and Subordination*, 1–29, 105–25, 401–2; Fletcher, 'Men's dilemma'; Foyster, 'A laughing matter?'; for the use of ballads as a commentary on husband-wife relations, Brown, 'The laird, his daughter, her husband and the minister'.
5. Dewald, *Formation of a Provincial Nobility*, 248–51; Hanley, 'Family and state'; Stone, *Road to Divorce*, 12–13; Houlbrooke, *The English Family*, 96–102.
6. Hope, *Major Practicks*, i. 135–7; Dalrymple, *Institutions*, 112–18. Women were free to dispose of their jewellery as they wished, see *HMC Third Report*, iii. 404; Pitcairn, *Criminal Trials*, i. prt. 2, 14.
7. Herries, *Memoirs*, 74; Wemyss, *Workes*, i. 268, 282; NLS Adv. MS 33.7.26.
8. NAS GD 26/13/319; Kettering, 'The patronage power of early modern French noblewomen'; Pollock, 'Teach her to live under obedience'; Bennett, 'Public power and authority'; Hanawalt, 'Lady Honor Lisle's networks of influence'; Coss, *The Lady in Medieval England*, 182–3; Houlbrooke, *The English Family*, 106–10; Ward, 'English noblewomen and the local community'; Mendelson, *Mental World of Stuart Women*.
9. For lady Seton, Lindsay, *Historie*, ii. 237; the countess of Moray, *HMC Sixth Report*, 649; *CSP Scotland*, v. 37, 42–3, 49, 53–4, 56–7, 253; the countess of Huntly, Gordon, *Sutherland*, 208; *CSP Scotland*, xi. and xii. *infra*; the countess of Bothwell, Pitcairn, *Criminal Trials*, i. prt. 2, 268–74; *CSP Scotland*, xiii. prt. 2, 1050–1. The countess of Lennox tried to hold her husband's clientage together after his assassination in 1571, NLS Adv. MS 22/3/14/4. For feuds, see the activities of lady Ogilvy in 1575, *RPC*, first ser., ii. 479–80; and the countess of Atholl in 1598, ibid., first ser., v. 440.
10. NLS MS 14401/3; NAS GD 158/2697/14.
11. McCordick, *Scottish Literature*, i. 544–5; *Political Writings*, 42.
12. Fraser, *Eglinton*, ii. 195–7; Fraser, *Annandale*, i. p. lxxi; for another example, Seton, *Family of Seton*, ii. 897–8.
13. NRA(S) 217/3/226–7; NRA(S) 237/F/498–500.
14. NAS GD 124/7/20; NAS GD 40/9/10; Sanderson, *Mary Stewart's People*, 34–54; Fraser, *Sutherland*, i. 167–8; Gordon, *Sutherland*, 168–9.
15. Stone, *Crisis of the Aristocracy*, 658–9; NAS GD 112/39/58/12; Fraser, *Haddington*, ii. 116; for another example, NAS GD 40/11/68.
16. For the countess of Morton, NAS GD 150/2286–7; NLS MS 78/29, 78/31–2, 78/34. When Morton died in 1648, she was heart-broken and died later that year having told her son that 'the lose of your father is mor than I can beir,' NLS MS 78/35–6. For the wives of the second earl of Mar, NLS MS 80/51–3; the first earl of Buccleuch, NAS GD 224/906/87/3; the second marquis of Hamilton, NLS Ch. 10776; the first marquis of Huntly, NLS MS 175/98. On portraits, Marshall, *Virgins and Viragos*, 87–8.
17. The view that marriage was cold and loveless, especially among the higher ranks in society, is argued in Dewald, *Aristocratic Experience*, 120–4; Stone, *Family, Sex and Marriage*; Harding, *Anatomy of a Power Elite*, 115; Gilbert, *Women in Seventeenth-Century France*, 59–69. More ambivalent evidence is presented in Houlbrooke, *The English Family*, 102–5; Ingram, *Church Courts*, 143–4; Fletcher, *Gender, Sex and Subordination*, 173–91; Chojnacki, 'Power of love'. Advice literature can also be read both ways, Davies, 'Continuity and change', 65–6; Leites, *Puritan Conscience*.
18. *Chronicles of the Frasers*, 260; Gordon, *Sutherland*, 278, 311; Lindsay, *Lives of the Lindsays*, i. 379, 392–3; *Works of Sir Thomas Urquhart*, 19; Fletcher, 'Men's dilemma'; Davies,

'Continuity and change'.

19. Calderwood, *History*, iii. 141; NRA(S) 217/4/730.
20. Fraser, *Haddington*, ii. 122–6; Fraser, *Annandale*, ii. 284–7. See also the letters of the Eglinton family, Fraser, *Eglinton*, i. 182, 197–9, 207, 209–10.
21. For the sensational, see Quaife, *Wanton Wenches*, and for a more measured view, Ingram, *Church Courts*, 159–61.
22. Hay, *Lectures*, 135–9; Wemyss, *Workes*, i. 264–5.
23. NLS MS 5775, pp. 98ff on 'Carnall Copulation'; Fletcher, *Gender, Sex and Subordination*, 44–59.
24. Wilson, 'The Skelmorlie aisle', 69.
25. NLS MS 5787/19b; *Ancram and Lothian*, i. pp. cvii–cvii; NLS MS 78/44.
26. Fraser, *Sutherland*, ii. 342; Hay, *Lectures*. For a summary of Catholic and Protestant ideas see Phillips, *Untying the Knot*, 1–27; Phillips, *Putting Asunder*, 1–133; Safley, *Let No Man Put Asunder*.
27. Watt, *The Making of Modern Marriage*, 121–62; Hardwick, 'Seeking separations'; Heal and Holmes, *Gentry in England and Wales*, 72–6; Paul, *Scots Peerage*, v. 301; viii. 593.
28. For example, the eighth lord Maxwell, Fraser, *Carlaverock*, i. 228; and the second earl of Mar's two wives, NAS GD 124/3/14, 124/3/18. For Swinton, NAS GD 12/175.
29. Giesey, 'Rules of inheritance', 274; Heal and Holmes, *Gentry in England and Wales*, 68; Watt, *The Making of Modern Marriage*, 57–70; Hardwick, 'Seeking separations', 161.
30. Waus, *Correspondence*, 95; for a later case from the 1630s, NLS MS 14 549/1–79.
31. Fraser, *Eglinton*, ii. 221–3; Paul, *Scots Peerage*, iii. 442; viii. 591.
32. NAS GD 75/568.
33. *CSP Scotland*, x. 276; Paul, *Scots Peerage*, iii. 576.
34. NAS GD 150/3442/16–17; NRA(S) 2312/107/1/120–1, 2312/107/1/124, 2312/107/1/126–31, 2312/113/146–50.
35. Dewald, *Aristocratic Experience*, 124–9, 662–8; Melville, *Memoirs*, 178; Calderwood, *History*, iii. 775–6; vii. 163; Stone, *Crisis of the Aristocracy*, 662–8; Bray, 'Homosexuality and the signs of male friendship'.
36. *BUK*, i. 305; Pitcairn, *Criminal Trials*, i. prt. 1, 465; for polemics on behaviour, Abernethy, *Christian and Heavenly Treatise*, 435ff.
37. *Political Writings*, 38–40; Fraser, *Sutherland*, ii. 343.
38. Gordon, *Sutherland*, 302; Paul, *Scots Peerage*, ii. 111; NAS GD 112/39/32/10.
39. Calderwood, *History*, ii. 355; Spottiswoode, *History*, ii. 52; Lady Buccleuch was described as Bothwell's 'olde frende and lover' in 1560, *CSP Scotland*, i. 482.
40. NRA(S) 237/F/484–5; NAS GD 158/2697/13/36; NLS MS 175/26, 175/43; *Historie*, 300, 395–6; Fraser, *Sutherland*, ii. 122, 128; Paul, *Scots Peerage*, iii. 31; vii. 168; *RPC*, first ser., xi. 2–3, 23–4.
41. Stone, *Road to Divorce*, 7; Fletcher, *Gender, Sex and Subordination*, 4–12, 29–57; Scott, *Scotch Passion*, 143–5; Calderwood, *History*, iii. 593, 595–6, 658; iv. 29; *Chronicles of the Frasers*, 178, 180–3; *Historie*, 185.
42. Murray, 'The marriage of the earl of Sutherland, 1567', 237–41; Fraser, *Sutherland*, i. 133; Gordon, *Sutherland*, 150–1, 163; Calderwood, *History*, iii. 350; *House of Forbes*, 112–13.
43. Paul, *Scots Peerage*, i. 196–7; vii. 294; Hume, *General History*, 360; *CSP Scotland*, v. 645–6; vi. 537, 552, 562; viii. 637; Moysie, *Memoirs*, 30; Fraser, *Douglas*, iv. 238; Scott, *Staggering State*, 91–2.
44. *RPC*, first ser., vii. 435, 540–1; Pitcairn, *Criminal Trials*, ii. 558; Balfour, *Works*, ii. 26–7; Paul, *Scots Peerage*, v. 113–16; *Works of Sir Thomas Urquhart*, 33; Fletcher, *Gender, Sex and Subordination*, 101–5. For French examples of similar violence, Gilbert, *Women in Seventeenth-Century France*, 64–5. There was no equivalent in Scotland of the English practice of financial compensation for husbands, Stone, *Road to Divorce*, 231–73.
45. Hardwick, 'Seeking separations', 160, 164–5; Potter, 'Marriage and cruelty'; Sharpe, 'Domestic homicide in early modern England'; Stone, *The Family, Sex and Marriage*, 98–100, 116–18; Underdown, 'The taming of the scold', offer different perspectives on this issue.

46. *CSP Scotland*, vii. 334; *RPC*, first ser., vii. 16; *Melrose Papers*, i. 4.
47. *RPC*, first ser., iii. 108, 206, 351, 402, 597–8, 601, 637. For the most harrowing account of lady Bargany's flight from abuse, ibid., first ser., xii. 144–5, 147–8, 228–9. For Newark, ibid., second ser., vi. 264–6.
48. For lady Methven, ibid., second ser., i. 416–18; *Selected Justiciary Cases*, i. 92–4; and lady Banff, *RPC*, second ser., iii. 263–4.
49. Lindsay, *Lives of the Lindsays*, i. 378; Brown, 'The laird, his daughter, her husband and the minister'. In 1579, Helen Colquoun, lady Aiket, was charged with administering poison to her husband, Pitcairn, *Criminal Trials*, i. prt. 2, 80.
50. Fraser, *Haddington*, ii. 119; Fraser, *Carlaverock*, i. 313–14; *HMC Eleventh Report*, 68.
51. Ferraro, 'The power to decide'; Safley, *Let No Man Put Asunder*; Carlson, *Marriage and the English Reformation*; Ingram, *Church Courts*, 145–50, 177–88; Stone, *Road to Divorce*, 67–71; Stone, *Crisis of the Aristocracy*, 661–4; Macfarlane, *Marriage and Love*, 218–44; also Ireland, 'Husband and wife: Post-Reformation canon law'; Gilbert, *Women in Seventeenth-Century France*, 84–96; on the general context see Phillips, *Putting Asunder*, 1–94.
52. Ozment, *When Fathers Ruled*, 80–99; Guthrie, 'The history of divorce in Scotland'; Smith, 'The reformers and divorce'; Ireland, 'Husband and wife: divorce, nullity of marriage and separation', 90–8; Sellar, 'Marriage, divorce and concubinage in Gaelic Scotland', 464; Sellar, 'Marriage, divorce and the forbidden degrees'; Forte, 'Aspects of the law of marriage', 112–14; Dawson, 'Protestant earl and godly Gael', 358–62; Hay, *Lectures*, 57–75, 99–103; Knox, *Works*, ii. 339–40; *APS*, ii. 548; iii. 539, 543–4; iv. 233; Calderwood, *History*, ii. 193; Hope, *Major Practicks*, i. 137; Dalrymple, *Institutions*, 109–10.
53. For the kirk's regulatory practices see Parker, '"The kirk by law established" and "the taming of Scotland"'; Graham, *Uses of Reform*.
54. Dawson, 'Protestant earl and godly Gael'; Knox, *Works*, ii. 375–8; Calderwood, *History*, ii. 397; *Historie*, 86; *APS*, iii. 81; Paul, *Scots Peerage*, i. 342–3; *CSP Scotland*, iv. 550–1, 553, 570, 583, 592.
55. *Maitland Miscellany*, i. 62–3, 65, 71, 74, 76, 82.
56. *RPC*, first ser., vii. 130; and for a successful prosecution by Ayr presbytery in 1598, ibid., first ser., viii. 66, 92. For Delgaty, Pitcairn, *Criminal Trials*, ii. 46–52, 64–7, 104, 111–12, 130; and for Mary Bruce, *Maitland Miscellany*, i. 133.
57. The second lord Torthorwald was unique in that he was twice divorced, in 1615 and again in 1622, on each occasion for his own adultery, Paul, *Scots Peerage*, ii. 394.
58. Anderson, *Earl of Orkney*, 131; NLS Adv. MS 22/3/14/19, 22/3/14/22, 22/3/14/24, 22/3/14/28, 22/3/14/31, 22/3/14/36, 22/3/14/38, 22/3/14/43. But she was suing him for divorce at the time of his death in 1593, Anderson, *Black Patie*, 47.
59. *RPC*, second ser., i. 540–2, 548–50, 568.
60. *HMC Various V*, 111, 114–7.
61. *CSP Scotland*, xii. 41, 74; Paul, *Scots Peerage*, iv. 465–6; vi. 373–4, 550; Fraser, *Eglinton*, i. 57–8; *RPC*, first ser., viii. 820–1; ix. 391.
62. Hardwick, 'Seeking separations', 160; Hope, *Major Practicks*, i. 107; Fraser, *Eglinton*, i. 44–6; ii. 163–90; *CSP Scotland*, i. 637; *RPC*, first ser., ii. 303–4. In 1582 the countess was charged with carrying on a ten-year adulterous relationship with David Dundas of Preistinch, Pitcairn, *Criminal Trials*, i. prt. 2, 100.
63. NLS MS 5787/19b.
64. Paton, 'Husband and wife'; *RPC*, first ser., iii. 34–5, 54–5, 108–9, 204–5, 251, 328, 402, 467; *Estimate*, 39; Paul, *Scots Peerage*, ii. 230–1. Both of lady Borthwick's sisters were charged with adultery and incest, one being acquitted while the case against the other was deserted, Pitcairn, *Criminal Trials*, i. prt. 2, 83–4.
65. *RPC*, first ser., iii. 125–6, 154–6, 171–2, 188–9, 211, 218–19, 230, 276, 278, 361; Paul, *Scots Peerage*, iv. 282.
66. NRA(S) 2312/107/1/104; Gordon, *Sutherland*, 458–9, 485; *RPC*, second ser., v. 18, 42–3, 105–6; *Selected Justiciary Cases*, i. 213–18.
67. Anon., 'God gif I were widow now', in McCordick, *Scottish Literature*, i. 543.

## Chapter 7: Children

1. Watt, *The Making of Modern Marriage*, 1–3; Laslett, 'Characteristics of the Western family', 13; Kent, *Household and Lineage in Renaissance Florence*; Rosenthal, *Patriarchy and Families of Privilege*, 1–19; for a case study see Slater, *Family Life in the Seventeenth Century*. For the alternative view, Shorter, *Making of the Modern Family*, and Stone, *Family, Sex and Marriage*.
2. Hay, *Lectures*, 35; Sommerville, *The Discovery of Childhood in Puritan England*.
3. NLS MS 5787/19.
4. Children do appear elsewhere in Seton portraits, see Seton, *Family of Seton*, i. facing 198, and 207; Strong, *English Icon*, 110, 112, 277, 291; Heal and Holmes, *Gentry in England and Wales*, 58.
5. Heal and Holmes, *Gentry in England and Wales*, 56; MacGibbon and Ross, *Ecclesiastical Architecture*, v. 206–7.
6. NAS GD 124/5/9; NLS MS 78/37.
7. English peerage families also produced on average five recorded children each, Stone and Stone, *An Open Elite?*, 260; Stone, *Crisis of the Aristocracy*, 168; Houlbrooke, *The English Family*, 127–201. A combination of no new recruits and increasing levels of infant mortality were the principal reasons for the decline in the numbers of the nobility of Holland, van Nierop, *Nobility of Holland*, 46–66.
8. Wemyss, *Workes*, i. 56–7; Scott, *Staggering State*, 91; Paul, *Scots Peerage*, v. 457–8.
9. McLaren, 'Marital fertility and lactation'; Crawford, 'The sucking child', 29–37; Debrisay, 'City limits'.
10. Stone, *Crisis of the Aristocracy*, 167–8.
11. Cressy, *Birth, Marriage and Death*, 15–94; Hufton, *Prospect Before Her*, 173–216; Ozment, *When Fathers Ruled*, 101–21.
12. Lindsays, *Lives of the Lindsays*, ii. 407–8. Perth regarded the matter of childbirth as a 'small danger … albeit sumquhat apprehensive to that sexe'.
13. NAS GD 158/2697/24; Fraser, *Eglinton*, i. 208.
14. Stone and Stone, *An Open Elite?*, 94–5; *Chronicles of the Frasers*, 156, 219, 225, 237, 242; Paul, *Scots Peerage*, vi. 318; *CSP Scotland*, x. 594; NAS GD 158/2697/12 and 158/2697/14–15.
15. Wemyss, *Workes*, i. 42; Fraser, *Sutherland*, i. 278; ii. 113; *House of Seytoun*, 77–9.
16. NLS MS 14466/1 contains lists of all the marriages and children of the Dunfermline family and appears to have been compiled in the mid-1640s; Fraser, *Annandale*, ii. 286.
17. NAS GD 38/2/1/69; Fraser, *Buccleuch*, i. 274–5; NAS GD 224/295/50/8, 224/295/50/11. Lady Ross received an allowance from her brother to cover the costs, £2616 13s 4d being paid to her in 1633.
18. Marwick, 'Nature versus nurture'; Wemyss, *Workes*, i. 69–75; Marshall, 'Wetnursing in Scotland'; Debrisay, 'City limits'; McLaren, 'Marital fertility and lactation'; Crawford, 'The sucking child'; Gilbert, *Women in Seventeenth-Century France*, 3–5; Stone, *Crisis of the Aristocracy*, 592–3; Cressey, *Birth, Marriage and Death*, 87–94; Motley, *Becoming a French Aristocrat*, 24–7; Fraser, *Eglinton*, i. 207; *Maitland Miscellany*, i. 133–4; *Chronicles of the Frasers*, 236.
19. Wemyss, *Workes*, i. 75; *HMC Sixth Report*, 651, 652, 654; Fraser, *Eglinton*, i. 211.
20. Macinnes, *Clanship, Commerce and the House of Stuart*, 13–14; Gordon, *Sutherland*, 374; Fraser, *Sutherland*, i. 131.
21. Dawson, 'The fifth earl of Argyle', 24; *Black Book of Taymouth*, 223–4, 228–30; *HMC Fourth Report*, iv. 511; NAS GD 112/3/64, 112/24/5/6, 112/39/42/4, 112/39/47/14, 112/39/48/12.
22. Fraser, *Sutherland*, ii. 342; and for similar observations, *Political Writings*, 41.
23. Hope, *Major Practicks*, i. 319; Anton, 'Parent and child', 123–4; Spottiswoode, *History*, iii. 215; NAS GD 224/903/26/49.
24. Stone, *Crisis of the Aristocracy*, 663. See also, Stone, *The Family, Sex and Marriage*, 502–3,

612–15; Laslett, 'Long-term trends in bastardy in England'; Wrightson, 'The nadir of English illegitimacy'; Adair, *Courtship, Illegitimacy and Marriage*, 48–91.

25. Scott, *Staggering State*, 86; Watt, *The Making of Modern Marriage*, 95.
26. Anderson, *Earl of Orkney*, 43; Fraser, *Douglas*, ii. 321–2; Hume, *General History*, 278.
27. NAS GD 122/3/49–50; Fraser, *Buccleuch*, i. 270–2; Paul, *Scots Peerage*, ii. 234–5.
28. Fraser, *Douglas*, ii. 293–4.
29. *Political Writings*, 23–4; Fraser, *Sutherland*, ii. 341–2; Dalrymple, *Institutions*, 123–30; Kuehn, 'Women, marriage and *patria potestas*'.
30. Stone, *Crisis of the Aristocracy*, 591–2; Motley, *Becoming a French Aristocrat*, 36; *Ancram and Lothian*, i. 56; Fraser, *Haddington*, ii. 170.
31. NAS GD 38/2/1/69; NAS GD 112/39/15/9; *Works of Sir Thomas Urquhart*, 55–8.
32. Aries, *Centuries of Childhood*; Flandrin, *Families in Former Times*; de Mause, 'The evolution of childhood'; Shorter, *Making of the Modern Family*, 11, 170, 192–6; Macfarlane, *Marriage and Love*, 51–78; Stone, *Family, Sex and Marriage*; Pollock, *Forgotten Children*; Watt, *The Making of Modern Marriage*, 3–10; Heal and Holmes, *Gentry in England and Wales*, 48–96, 77–80; Dewald, *European Nobility*, 168–74; Houlbrooke, *The English Family*, 140–5. For the medieval perspective, Schultz, *Knowledge of Childhood*; Shahar, *Childhood in the Middle Ages*; Wilson, 'The myth of motherhood a myth'.
33. Wemyss, *Workes*, i. 113; *Ancram and Lothian*, i. and ii.; also *Familie of Innes*, 208ff.
34. *Honoris de Morton*, i. 143–4; Fraser, *Eglinton*, i. 211; NAS GD 112/39/19/16; NAS GD 124/3/35.
35. NLS MS 78/60, 78/61. Mary's poem is as follows:

    Sweeter than pleasur is thy love
    Ther is no comfort so devin
    Underneath the stars that move
    As those kind armes of thin
    Thy circling charmes al formes of joy
    Wish in themselves combined.

    Others their love may praise as high
    But you allone are deer to mee
    And yours I must live and die
    My fortune so decreed
    If I have all my harts desir
    Who can not happie bee.

36. NRA(S) 237/E/399–402, 237/F/472–5; Gordon, *Sutherland*, 169; Fraser, *Eglinton*, i. 190–5, 199–218.
37. NLS MS 3138/1; NAS GD 158/2697/13; *Ancram and Lothian*, i. 59–60.
38. Rosenthal, *Patriarchy and Families of Privilege*, 23–101; Dewald, *Aristocratic Experience*, 71–5; Kuehn, 'Honor and conflict'; Anton, 'Parent and child', 119–20; Fraser, *Eglinton*, i. 229. I am grateful to Roger Mason for identifying this quotation.
39. The master of Rothes died in 1607, four years before the earl who was therefore succeeded by his grandson, a minor, *HMC Fourth Report*, iv. 508–9, no. 135; for the Kinnaird case, NAS GD 38/1/91; and for another case, NAS GD 49/87.
40. Anderson, *Earl of Orkney*, 130. For Crawford, NRA(S) 237/F/496–7; *Familie of Innes*, 207. For Atholl, NRA(S) 237/F/500–3, 237/F/503–4. For Dundas, NAS GD 75/578–9. Money and inheritance were the most common causes of dispute among the English gentry, Heal and Holmes, *Gentry in England and Wales*, 81–4.
41. Harding, *Anatomy of a Power Elite*, 165–6; *RPC*, first ser., ii. 207–8; iii. 108, 206, 351, 402, 597–8, 601, 637.
42. Gordon, *Sutherland*, 163–4, 168; *Black Book of Taymouth*, 221–2; and for another example, *RPC*, first ser., iii. 568–9, 600.
43. Schindler, 'Guardians of disorder'; Fletcher, *Gender, Sex and Subordination*, 88–94, 207–8; Thomas, 'Age and authority'; Ben-Amos, 'Service and the coming of age of young

men'. The temptation to exaggerate the tension in father-son relations should be avoided, Pollock, *Forgotten Children*.

44. NRA 237/i/C letter dated 3 November 1591, Ogilvie to Crawford, and the reply is undated. For another feud escalated by sons against the wishes of their fathers, *RPC*, xi. 439; xiii. 769; Pitcairn, *Criminal Trials*, iii. 443, 479–81, 542; *Melrose Papers*, ii. 449–50.
45. For Forbes, *RPC*, first ser., iv. 497, 617–18; *House of Forbes*, 120–1. For Gray, *CSP Scotland*, xiii. prt. 2, 619; *RPC*, first ser., vii. 346; *Letters and State Papers*, 111–13; *HMC Sixth Report*, 661. For Bonyton, *RPC*, first ser., v. 278–9; vi. 233, 235; Pitcairn, *Criminal Trials*, ii. 340–7; Calderwood, *History*, vi. 102–5.
46. *RPC*, first ser., ii. 483–4; x. 6–7.
47. Motley, *Becoming a French Aristocrat*, 51–2; *Political Writings*, 47; and for Gordonstoun's similar counsel, Fraser, *Sutherland*, ii. 341–2. James VI intervened in a number of such cases, *Honoris de Morton*, i. 130–1; *HMC Mar and Kellie*, i. 118. For background literature see Mirrer, *Upon My Husband's Death*; Rosenthal, 'Fifteenth-century widows and widowhood'; Hufton, *Prospect Before Her*, 217–50.
48. *RPC*, first ser. ii. 104–5, 320–1; iv. 621–2; and for another bitter dispute, ibid., first ser., iv. 392–3, 405, 433–4.
49. *HMC Sixth Report*, 659; *RPC*, first ser., xiv. 425–7.
50. Anton, 'Parent and child', 119; NLS MS 14401/3, 14401/5–6, 14401/18, 14404/7–13, 14404/16, 14404/18–19, 14404/27, 14404/43–4, 14404/112, 14404/114; NLS Ch. 10757–7; NAS GD 28/1311; there is a useful narrative in MS 14475/17. In 1618 the seventh lord Boyd made a similar deal with his mother, NAS GD 8/598.
51. *Letters and State Papers*, 80–1; *RPC*, first ser., viii. 76–7; x. 75–6; xii. 146–7. For other interesting cases see *RPC*, first ser., vii. 8; *Melrose Papers*, i. 8–10 for the house of Atholl; *RPC*, first ser., ii. 287–8, 294–6, and Paul, *Scots Peerage*, viii. 584 for the house of Seton; Fraser, *Carlaverock*, ii. 66 and *RPC*, second ser., i. 189–90 for the house of Ogilvy.
52. NLS MS 20779/11–12, 20779/55–9, 20795/44.
53. NLS MS 21174/55, 21174/57–8, 21174/66–7; *RPC*, first ser., xiii. 591, 764–5. For a similar case that entangled the house of Ogilvy in litigation, NAS GD 16/186.
54. NLS MS 5070/17, 5070/27, 5070/34, 5070/47, 5103, 5127/4–8, 5127/11, 5155/12–13, 5158/1; NAS GD 124/3/37; *Miscellany of the Scottish History Society. Volume I*, 106–8.
55. NRA(S) 217/3/135; early on in his marriage, Moray had been dependent on the countess of Argyll for money, 217/3/361–3. NLS MS 78/21.
56. Kalas, 'A noble widow's place in the patriarchal household'; *RPC*, first ser., ii. 531; iii. 89–90, 119–20, 141–2, 206, 275, 292, 765; Paul, *Scots Peerage*, vi. 514–16.
57. NRA(S) 237/E/377–81, 237/E/396–9; *RPC*, second ser., iv. 82–3, 170; for another discharge following a minority, Fraser, *Melvilles*, i. 132.
58. NAS GD 158/2697/16; NAS GD 40/9/10.
59. NLS MS 5127/1; Fraser, *Buccleuch*, i. 242; Fraser, *Menteith*, i. 323–32. For examples of imbecility, *RPC*, first ser., xii. 629–30; Fraser, *Carlaverock*, i. 252.
60. Montgomery, 'Guardian and ward'; Craig, *Jus Feudale*, ii. 801–29; NLS MS 14480/12; Hope, *Major Practicks*, i. 250–5.
61. *HMC Mar and Kellie*, i. 83; *RPC*, second ser., vi. 441; Fraser, *Annandale*, ii. 13–16; also see NAS GD 38/1/77; Fraser, *Menteith*, i. 329; NAS GD 150/333; *APS*, iv. 609–10; Hope, *Major Practicks*, i. 321–8.
62. Dalrymple, *Institutions*, 137, 145–7; for examples, Fraser, *Buccleuch*, ii. 225–6; *Chronicles of the Frasers*, 156.
63. Hope, *Major Practicks*, i. 328–35; Dalrymple, *Institutions*, 131–6.
64. Hufton, *Prospect Before Her*, 224–6; *Chronicles of the Frasers*, 181; *HMC Buccleuch*, i. 27–9; Fraser, *Sutherland*, i. 210, 211–12.
65. *Chronicle of the Kings of Scotland*, 131; *Black Book of Taymouth*, 227. Maternal uncles had greater rights in some circumstances, Craig, *Jus Feudale*, ii. 805–6.
66. Fraser, *Annandale*, i. pp. clxviii, clxx–clxxiii; NRA(S) 885/163. On occasion these disputes led to dangerous feuds, Cowan, 'Clanship, kinship and the Campbell acquisition of

Islay'. Less dramatically, see the differences among the Hamiltons in 1604, *HMC Eleventh Report. Hamilton*, 46; *RPC*, first ser., vii. 31.

67. Fraser, *Sutherland*, i. 214; ii. 342; Gordon, *Sutherland*, 321 ff. For the papers relating to his time as tutor, NRA(S) 239/47/1804–12, 239/55/1971–8, 239/100/1–8.
68. *Honoris de Morton*, i. 124; NAS GD 150/1606–35; NLS MS 80/2; NLS MS 14401/48, MS 14539–41, Chs 11032–255; see also lord Lorne's letter regarding the Kenmure minority, NLS MS 13500/13.
69. Fraser, *Sutherland*, i. 132–7.
70. *RPC*, second ser., v. 628–32, 639–40, 644–5, 647–8.
71. Fraser, *Chiefs of Grant*, i. 217–18; NRA(S) 2312/113/154, 2312/113/178.
72. Dalrymple, *Institutions*, 143–7; NAS GD 124/3/12; for other examples, NRA(S) 885/1/23, 885/11/228; *HMC Various V*, 20.
73. *RPC*, first ser., iii. 92–3; second ser., iii. 53; Dalrymple, *Institutions*, 136–43.
74. *RPC*, first ser., ii. 580; iii. 162–3, 182, 253, 256–9; NAS GD 112/3/36; and see the interesting example in NRA(S) 217/4/402.

## Chapter 8: Education

1. Ago, 'Young nobles in the age of absolutism', 296–8; Neuschel, *Word of Honor*, 85–7; Neuschel, 'Noble households in the sixteenth century'; Motley, *Becoming a French Aristocrat*, 18–19; Smith, *Culture of Merit*, 11–17, 65–9; Mertes, *English Noble Household*, 172–5.
2. Shahar, *Childhood in the Middle Ages*, 162–253; Schultz, *Knowledge of Childhood*; Abernethy, *Christian and Heavenly Treatise*, 59, 63.
3. Bushnell, *A Culture of Teaching*, 73–116; Cunningham, *Children and Childhood*, 42–61; Heal and Holmes, *Gentry in England and Wales*, 247–54; Houlbrooke, *The English Family*, 146–53; Motley, *Becoming a French Aristocrat*, 18–67; Bitton, *French Nobility in Crisis*, 80–2; Ozment, *When Fathers Ruled*, 132–77.
4. Bushnell, *Culture of Teaching*, 23–72 discusses James VI's education; Motley, *Becoming a French Aristocrat*, 82–6; GD 124/3/11; Fraser, *Chiefs of Grant*, ii. 56.
5. Seton, *Family of Seton*, i. 212.
6. Motley, *Becoming a French Aristocrat*, 20–2; Fraser, *Eglinton*, i. 208–9. Naturally, some mothers were anxious about such arrangements, NRA(S) 2312/113/11.
7. NAS GD 112/3/64; 112/24/1/10.
8. Melville, *Memoirs*, 261–2; *RPC*, iii. 322–3; Cuddy, 'Revival of the entourage'; Brown, 'Scottish aristocracy, anglicization and the court'; Simon, *Education and Society*, 343–5.
9. Stone, *Crisis of the Aristocracy*, 683–4; Stone and Stone, *An Open Elite?*, 47–9; James, 'English politics and the concept of honour', 358; Simon, *Education and Society*, 333–68; McNeill and McQueen, *Atlas of Scottish History*, 437–9.
10. Scotland, *History of Scottish Education*, i; Durkan, 'Education in the century of the Reformation'; O'Day, *Education and Society*, 223–30; McNeill and McQueen, *Atlas of Scottish History*, 437–9.
11. Durkan, 'Education: the laying of fresh foundations', 124, 129; Donaldson, *James V to James VII*, 262–5; Wormald, *Court, Kirk and Community*, 171; Cowan, *Scottish Reformation*, 199–204; Scotland, *History of Scottish Education*, i. 44–8; Durkan, 'Education in the century of the Reformation'; Durkan, 'Cultural background'.
12. NLS Ch. 10780; NAS GD 150/2212.
13. Scotland, *History of Scottish Education*, i. 51–2; *RPC*, first ser., ii. 478.
14. Durkan, 'Education: the laying of fresh foundations', 138–44.
15. *Chronicles of the Frasers*, 147, 183; Fraser, *Sutherland*, i. 171, 211; ii. 123; GD 406/1/58.
16. Stone, *Crisis of the Aristocracy*, 683–4; James, 'English politics and the concept of honour', 358; Motley, *Becoming a French Aristocrat*, 98–9, 108–18; Amelang, *Honoured Citizens*,

159–70; Scotland, *History of Scottish Education*, i. 71–89; Zulager, 'Middle-rank administrators', appendix V. no. 54; McNeill and McQueen, *Atlas of Scottish History*, 437–9. In 1595 the young third earl of Moray was granted a passport for schooling in England, but there is no evidence that he did attend school there, *CSP Scotland*, xi. 530, 582–3, 586, 590, 604, 625.

17. Macinnes, 'Crown, clans and fine', 47; *CSP Scotland*, xiii. prt. 1, 262; GD 112/23/12/3.
18. *RPC*, first ser., ix. 28–9; Goodare, 'The statutes of Iona in context'; Macinnes, *Clanship, Commerce and the House of Stuart*, 56–87; Fraser, *Sutherland*, ii. 359; O'Day, *Education and Society*, 25–76; Alexander, *Growth of English Education*, 185–207.
19. Fraser, *Eglinton*, i. 214; NAS GD 224/940/7, 224/940/16; Couts, *History of the University of Glasgow*, 97; NAS GD 112/39/45/21, 112/39/46/2, 112/39/46/8–9, 112/39/46/22, 112/39/46/25, 112/39/47/3, 112/39/50/34.
20. Houston, *Scottish Literacy and the Scottish Identity*; Durkan, 'Education: the laying of fresh foundations', 130–50; Scotland, *History of Scottish Education*, i. 80–6; Bushnell, *Culture of Teaching*, 117–43; Motley, *Becoming a French Aristocrat*, 11–13; Neuschel, *Word of Honor*, 103–31.
21. Simpson, *Scottish Handwriting*; Dawson and Kennedy-Skipton, *Elizabethan Handwriting*; Hay, 'Scotland and the Italian Renaissance', 123; NAS GD 150/2983; NAS GD 75/573–5.
22. Kelso, *Doctrine for the Lady*; Gilbert, *Women in Seventeenth-Century France*, 17–40; Fletcher, *Gender, Sex and Subordination*, 366–72; NLS MS 3138/1; *RPC*, first ser., vii. 440, 696; *House of Gordon*, i. 260–1; *RPC*, first ser., xiii. 365–6. For a more negative view from Ireland, McCurtain, 'Women, education and learning'.
23. Kagan, *Students and Society*; Thompson, 'The nobility in Spain', 205; Stuart, *Registrum de Panmure*, i. p. xxxvii.
24. The share of English nobles attending university never exceeded 40 per cent, Stone and Stone, *An Open Elite?*, 262–6; Stone, *Crisis of the Aristocracy*, 687–92; Alexander, *Growth of English Education*, 157–84.
25. Kagan, *Students and Society*, 77–105; Zulager, 'Middle-rank administrators', 58, 67–70, 77, appendix V; Calderwood, *History*, v. 267.
26. Cant, *University of St Andrews*, 45–66; Morgan, 'Cambridge university and "the country" 1560–1640'; Stevenson, *King's College*; *Chronicles of the Frasers*, 237–8, 242, 257–8, 260; *House of Gordon*, i. appendix III for a list of Gordon graduates; Durkan and Kirk, *University of Glasgow*, 380–4; Fraser, *Eglinton*, i. 76–9; Baillie, *Letters and Journals*, i. p. xxvii.
27. Fraser, *Buccleuch*, i. 277–8; Lindsay, *Lives of the Lindsays*, ii. 13–14.
28. NRA(S) 237/E/394–6; Lindsay, *Lives of the Lindsays*, i. 351–80.
29. de Ridder-Symoens, *History of the University in Europe*; Scotland, *History of Scottish Education*, i. 134–73; Hay, 'Scotland and the Italian Renaissance', 115–18; Wormald, *Court, Kirk and Community*, 183–5; Donaldson, *James V to James VII*, 265–8; Durkan, Education: the laying of 'fresh foundations', 150–9; MacDonald, *Library of Drummond*, 15; Durkan and Kirk, *University of Glasgow*, 347–92; Mackie, *University of Glasgow*, 57–98; Couts, *History of the University of Glasgow*, 49–99; Cant, *University of St Andrews*, 45–57; Cant, *College of St Salvator*, 167–76; Stevenson, *King's College.*
30. Kirk, '"Melvillian" reform in the Scottish universities'; Mackie, *University of Glasgow*, 63; Scotland, *History of Scottish Education*, i. 143–4; Macdonald, *Library of Drummond*, 15–17. For the curriculum at Oxford and Cambridge, O'Day, *Education and Society*, 106–31.
31. Melville, *Diary*, 129–30; Durkan and Kirk, *University of Glasgow*, 262–92.
32. Wemyss, *Workes*, i.
33. Stevenson, *King's College*, 20–7; Cant, *University of St Andrews*, 49–51; *RPC*, first ser., vii. 335.
34. McManamon, *Funeral Oratory*, 51–61; Stevenson, *King's College*, 30–7; NLS MS 21 187A/3, 21 187A/16–18, 21 187A/23.
35. Cant, *College of St Salvator*, 22–3; Zulager, 'Middle-rank administrators', appendix v. no.

7; Scott, *Staggering State*, 3; Fraser, *Elphinstone*, i. 152–3, 160; Pringle, 'An early humanity class library'.

36. Warkneke, *Images of the Educational Traveller*, 105–37; Heal and Holmes, *Gentry in England and Wales*, 274; Jespersen, 'Danish nobility', 51.
37. Napier, *Arte Logistica*, p. liii.
38. Calderwood, *History*, iv. 21; vi. 27, 59, 67; *Chronicle of the Kings of Scotland*, 160; *CSP Scotland*, xiii. prt. 2, 700; *Chronicle of Perth*, 7; for Gordonstoun, Gordon, *Sutherland*, 239, 249, 255; for Winton, *House of Seytoun*, 81–2.
39. Gordon, *Sutherland*, 144; NRA(S) 237/F/468–9; *CSP Scotland*, vii. 14; xii. 145–6.
40. For these and other licences, *CSP Scotland*, xii. 78, 285–6; *RPC*, first ser., vii. 441; viii. 363; ix. 261–2; x. 5; xii. 650; Fraser, *Haddington*, ii. 81–2; *HMC Sixth Report*, 659–66; NRA(S) 217/3/148; *Honoris de Morton*, i. 150.
41. *HMC Sixth Report*, 611 and for the corresponding Scottish licence, ibid., 614–15. These were required even after 1603, ibid., first ser., vi. 602–3.
42. NLS MS 21 187A/16–17. Marischal's eldest son, William, travelled in France in 1601 and 1619, MS 21 174/9, 21 174/40.
43. Durkan, 'James, third earl of Arran'; Durkan, 'French connection'. Dunfermline studied in France, possibly at the law school in Bourges, and previously at Rome and Salamanca, *Tears for the Death*, 4; *House of Seytoun*, 63; Haddington at Paris, Fraser, *Haddington*, 34–6; Balmerino at Angers and Poitiers, Zulager, 'Middle-rank administrators', 65, appendix v. no. 31; for Hawthornden, *Poems of William Drummond*, iii; Brockliss, *French Higher Education*, 277–334 for the curriculum. In France, Huguenot nobles used education to hoist them into royal service, just like Scottish Catholics, Mentzer, *Blood and Belief*, 121.
44. *Early Travellers*, 102; Spottiswoode, *History*, ii. 344.
45. Stoye, *English Travellers*, 15–46; Vale, *Gentleman's Recreations*, 73–82; Schalk, *From Valor to Pedigree*, 174–201; Motley, *Becoming a French Aristocrat*, 123–68, 199–208; Brockliss, *French Higher Education*, 111–81; Bryson, 'Rhetoric of status'; Leidtke, *Royal Horse*, 87–90. Four-fifths of French nobles could not afford to send their sons to the Paris academies.
46. *HMC Mar and Kellie*, ii. 82–4ff; NAS GD 124/15/32, 124/15/34–6.
47. NLS MS 83/4–5, MS 78/43; Hyde, *History*, iii. 396.
48. *Bannatyne Miscellany*, i. 352–5; Calderwood, *History*, vi. 67.
49. Cameron, 'Scottish students and teachers'; Macinnes, *Making of the Covenanting Movement*, 27–30; Forbes, *Familie of Innes*, 214.
50. O'Day, *Education and Society*, 81–99; *CSP Scotland*, i. 644; xi. 177; NRA(S) 237/W/394–6; Gordon, *Sutherland*, 390; *Ancram and Lothian*, p. xlv, 16; NAS GD 150/3442/5; NLS MS 83/16, 83/20; NLS MS 78/38.
51. *CSP Scotland*, x. 521; xiii. prt. 1, 362–3; NRA(S) 217/43/46; *Ancram and Lothian*, i. pp. xlv–xlvii; NLS MS 5785; NLS MS 16000; Nevinson, 'Illustrations of costume in the *Alba Amicorum*'; Johnstone, *Alba Amicorum*; Paul, *Scots Peerage*, ii. 232–4; Fraser, *Buccleuch*, 171–3; ii. 345; Fraser, *Haddington*, i. 81; ii. 248, 250, 340–1, 343–4; *House of Forbes*, 168, facing 200 for the letter; *Abbotsford Miscellany*, 207; *HMC Mar and Kellie*, ii. 79; *RPC*, first ser., xi. 10; NLS MS 973/41; Gordon, *Sutherland*, 374–5;
52. Maczak, *Travel in Early Modern Europe*; Stoye, *English Travellers Abroad*; Dewald, *Aristocratic Experience*, 86–94; Motley, *Becoming a French Aristocrat*, 187–92; Stone, *Crisis of the Aristocracy*, 692–702; Simon, *Education and Society*, 346; Moryson, *Itinerary Written*.
53. Hume, *General History*, 362.
54. Fraser, *Sutherland*, ii. 365; Gordon, *Sutherland*, 128, 207, 298.
55. *CSP Scotland*, xiii. prt. 2, 630.
56. NRA(S) 237/E/362–4, 237/E/376–7, 237/F/496–7; Stevenson, *King's College*, 57; *Memorials of Montrose* i. 156–80; NLS 79/15–16, 79/33–4.
57. Maczak, *Travel in Early Modern Europe*, ch. 3; NAS GD 30/1696; Fraser, *Eglinton*, i. 230; for others, *HMC Mar and Kellie*, 78–84, 86–90, 92–4, 97, 99; NLS MS 175/25; NLS MS

21 176/3–4, 21 176/40–54.

58. *CSP Scotland*, xiii. prt. 1, 462; and for another example see MS 20 795/50–1, NLS MS 20 795/52–4.
59. NAS GD 25/9/38.
60. Waus, *Correspondence*, i. 238–9; *CSP Scotland*, x. 403.
61. NRA(S) 237/E/393–4.
62. *CSP Scotland*, xiii. prt. 2, 961. Nobles going abroad established commissions of kinsmen and friends to manage their affairs, NAS GD 124/7/32.
63. NAS GD 158/2697/1/1.
64. Warkneke, *Images of the Educational Traveller*, 191–216; NLS MS 14 401/42; NLS MS 84/8–10; NLS MS 78/39.
65. *RPC*, first ser., xiv. 237; NAS GD 75/561, 75/563, 75/564; and also NAS GD 40/12/38. For Lochleven, Calderwood, *History*, iv. 46–7; *CSP Scotland*, xiii. prt. 1, 555; Paul, *Scots Peerage*, vi. 550; and Hamilton, NAS GD 406/1/14. On the dangers of travel, Maczak, *Travel in Early Modern Europe*, ch. 8.
66. Stone, *Crisis of the Aristocracy*, 692–702; Warneke, *Images of the Educational Traveller*, 160–90; *HMC Mar and Kellie*, ii. 104; Fraser, *Douglas*, iii. 322–4; iv. 44–5, 196, 291–310; *RPC*, first ser., xiii. 205; Fraser, *Carlaverock*, ii. 68–9.
67. Durkan, 'James, third earl of Arran', 154–66; *Bannatyne Miscellany*, i. 352–5; Calderwood, *History*, vi. 67.
68. Orme, *Education and Society*, 153–75; Hexter, 'Education of the aristocracy'; Bonney, *European Dynastic States*, 334–40; Dewald, *European Nobility*, 151–7.
69. Stone, *Crisis of the Aristocracy*, 672–83; Heal and Holmes, *Gentry in England and Wales*, 243–75; Simon, *Education and Society*, 340–1; Bernard, *Power of the Early Tudor Nobility*, 194; Bushnell, *Culture of Teaching*, 48–9; Cooper, 'Ideas of gentility'. For Catalonia, Amelang, *Honored Citizens of Barcelona*, 102–26. The French context is discussed in Schalk, *Valor to Pedigree*, 59–61, 72; Dewald, *Aristocratic Experience*, 79–86; Mentzer, Blood *and Belief*, 120–41; Motley, *Becoming a French Aristocrat*, 6–7, 68; Major, *Renaissance Monarchy to Absolute Monarchy*, 100–2.
70. Mair was exaggerating, Durkan, 'Education: the laying of fresh foundations', 124; Williamson, 'Patriot nobility'; Knox, *Works*, iv. 491; Melville, *Diary*, 129–30; and see *Historie*, 182; Calderwood, *History*, v. 411; NLS MS 21 187A/16–18, 21 187A/23.
71. Hume, *General History*, 429–30; Scott, *Staggering State*, 45, 48, 95; *Bannatyne Miscellany*, i. 194–6; and see the comments on Mar, *CSP Scotland*, xiii. prt. 1, 181, 189.
72. *Chronicles of the Frasers*, 192–3; Hume, *General History*, 360–1 where he observed that the French nobility especially 'deeme it honourable to be illiterate and ignorant'; Lindsay, *Lives of the Lindsays*, ii. 52–3; *Ancram and Lothian*, i. p. xxviii.
73. Hale, 'Military education of the officer class'; Supple, *Arms Versus Letters*; Supple, 'Education of the "*noblesse d'épée*"'.
74. Ferguson, *Chivalrie Tradition*, 89–92; Cooper, 'Ideas of gentility', 48–51; Melville, *Diary*, 50–1.
75. *CSP Scotland*, vi. 53; Moysie, *Memoirs*, 37; Gavin, 'Two letters of Tobias Mathew', 111; Spottiswoode, *History*, ii. 446; Lindsay, *Lives of the Lindsays*, ii. 49–51; Macpherson, 'Francis Stewart', 120–37.
76. James, 'English politics and the concept of honour', 324, 377–8; Edington, *Court and Culture*, 87–8, 208–9; Hume, *House of Douglas*, i. 68.
77. He particularly recommended music, Fraser, *Sutherland*, ii. 344; see the comment by an English herald in James, 'English politics and the concept of honour', 83.
78. Gordon, *Sutherland*, 314–15, 389; Fraser, *Sutherland*, i. 214–15; ii. 149; Astarita, *Continuity of Feudal Power*, 182–91.
79. *Early Travellers*, 95; Howard, *Architectural History of Scotland*, 8; NLS MS 5787/36b.
80. Kearney, *Scholars and Gentlemen*; Motley, *Becoming a French Aristocrat*, 78–123; Burke, *Venice and Amsterdam*, 84–93.
81. NLS MS 5127/1; Paul, *Scots Peerage*, v. 616; Spottiswoode, *History*, ii. 306; *CSP Scotland*, x. 17.

82. NLS MS 21 187A/16–18; Carter and McLaren, *Crown and Gown*, 20–5.
83. *Memorials of Montrose*, i. 108–26.
84. For evidence that this emphasis on education and learning extended down into the lesser nobility, Meikle, 'Lairds and gentry', 273–318.

## Chapter 9: Leisure

1. Melville, *Diary*, 23; Koenigsberger, *Renaissance Man*.
2. Stone, 'Residential development'; Astarita, *Continuity of Feudal Power*, 119–31.
3. *Early Travellers*, 83, 93; *CSP Scotland*, x. 23; NAS GD 158/2697/16.
4. Fraser, *Eglinton*, ii. 197–8; NAS GD 6/868–9, 873; Seton, *House of Seton*, i. 196–8.
5. MacGibbon and Ross, *Castellated and Domestic Architecture*, ii. 529ff; Howard, 'Thrie estates', 35; NAS GD 6/1186; Balfour, *Works*, ii. 179; *Early Travellers*, 110, 138–41, 145; Glendinning et al., *History of Scottish Architecture*, 59–70.
6. Howard, *Scottish Architecture*, 144, 146, 152–6; NAS GD 8/389, 8/440, 8/453; *HMC Seventh Report*, 733; *Chronicle of Perth*, 17, 33; *Chronicles of the Frasers*, 238, 247; *Tolbooths and Town Houses*, 122–6; for the receipts for the payment of the tenth earl of Angus's rent between 1592 and 1606, NLS MS 973/1–4.
7. Dewald, *European Nobility*, 48–50, 89–92; Bush, *Rich Noble, Poor Noble*, 153–71; Dewald, *Aristocratic Experience*, 20–1; Stone, *Crisis of the Aristocracy*, 357–63; Stone and Stone, *An Open Elite?*, 16–17; McClung, 'The country house Arcadia'; Hibbard, 'Country house poem'.
8. Gordon, *Sutherland*, 231; *Black Book of Taymouth*, 22; *House of Seytoun*, 37, 39–40, 44–5, 59, 74–5, 100; Seton, *Family of Seton*, ii. 788–822; *Familie of Innes*, 206; Hay, 'Scotland and the Italian Renaissance', 114; Howard, *Scottish Architecture*, 48–107; Kemp and Farrow, 'Humanism in the visual arts', 32–47; Howard, 'Thrie estates', 53–6; Dunbar, *Historic Architecture*; Glendinning et al., *History of Scottish Architecture*, 40–59; Lubbock, *Tyranny of Taste*, 55–69; *Registrum de Panmure*, i. pp. cxliii–cxlvi. Some styles were never popular in Scotland, Stone and Stone, *An Open Elite?*, 301, 330–1, 341. For craftsmen, *CSP Scotland*, x. 598; Fraser, *Sutherland*, ii. 363; *RPC*, second ser., v. 29.
9. Dunbar, *Historic Architecture*, 36–81; Nicolson, *Great Houses*, 80–5; Anderson, *Earl of Orkney*, 74–5; *Chronicles of the Frasers*, 225, 241, 245; *RPC*, second ser., iv. 186; *Ancram and Lothian*, i. 62–76; Scott, *Staggering State*, 90–1.
10. Glendinning et al., *History of Scottish Architecture*, 50–9; Howard, *Scottish Architecture*, 48–94, 106; *French Connection*, 29–54; Wells-Cole, *Art and Decoration*, 167–8; Vale, *Gentlemen's Recreations*, 83–8; Hill and Cornforth, *English Country Houses*, 65–74; *Ancram and Lothian*, i. 63–5; Fraser, *Haddington*, ii. 303–4; Mathew, *Scotland under Charles I*, 103–26. Even island chiefs had access to good English furniture, *Dunvegan Castle, Isle of Skye, Scotland*, castle guide book 1995. For some ideas on the control of consumption, Lubbock, *Tyranny of Taste*, 70–86.
11. Bath, 'Painted ceilings'; Bath, 'Alexander Seton's painted gallery'; Apted, *Painted Ceilings*; Kemp and Farrow, 'Humanism in the visual arts', 42–4; MacMillan, *Scottish Art*, 37–68; Howard, *Scottish Architecture*, 86–90; Wells-Cole, *Art and Decoration*, 40–1; Seton, *House of Seton*, ii. 812–20.
12. Kemp and Farrow, 'Humanism in the visual arts', 39–41; MacMillan, *Scottish Art*, 37–68; Thomson, *Painting in Scotland*, 11–16, 22–31, 58–67; Cursiter, *Scottish Art*, 17–24; Caw, *Scottish Painting*, 7–12; *Great Scots*, 7–13; Hume, *General History*, 377; Calderwood, *History*, iv. 21; Seton, *House of Seton*, ii. 789, 837–8; *Ancram and Lothian*, i. 2; *Black Book of Taymouth*, 75, 77–8; NAS GD 112/20/5/5, 112/39/53/12; Fraser, *Chiefs of Grant*, i. 211–12; Dewald, *European Nobility*, 158–60; Stone, *Crisis of the Aristocracy*, 712–15; Wendorf, *Elements of Life*; Jackson-Stops, *Treasure Houses of Britain*, 125–43; Thornton, *Seventeenth-Century Interior Decoration*, 7–51; Strong, *English Icon*, 43–50; Howarth, *Images of Rule*, 228–9, 259–60; Howarth, 'Charles I, sculptor and sculptors', 102; Haskell, 'Charles I's collection of pictures', 217–18; Rubinstein, *Captain Luckless*, 46–7; Marshall,

*Duchess Anne*, 44–5; NAS GD 124/461. The third earl of Lothian continued to collect pictures into the troubled 1640s, MacMillan, *Scottish Art*, 50.

13. Harris, *Artist and Country House*, 26–7; *Early Travellers*, 85; Pont, *Topographical Account*, 12, 17; NAS GD 112/39/44/4, 112/39/51/20, 112/39/62/3; *Ancram and Lothian*, i. 62–76. Women especially were associated with the idea of tranquillity in a rural setting, Lewnlski, 'The lady in the country-house poem'.
14. Fraser, *Melvilles*, i. 147–8; NLS Adv. MS 33.7.26/8b–9a; Gordon, *Sutherland*, 1–12; NRA(S) 237/F/477–8, 237/F/480–2; Howard, 'Thrie Estates', 57–8.
15. Kaufman, *Mastery of Nature*; Lazzaro, *Italian Renaissance Garden*; Adams, *French Garden*; Mosser and Teyssot, *History of Garden Design*; Brown, *Art and Architecture of English Gardens*, 19–39; Fleming and Gore, *English Garden*, 9–46; Charlesworth, *English Garden*; Hunt, *Garden and Grove*, 103–26; Hunt, 'The British garden'; Allan, 'The private countrey life'; Stone and Stone, *An Open Elite?*, 334–5; Howard, *Scottish Architecture*, 100–4; Jamieson, 'The royal gardens of Holyroodhouse'.
16. *Historie*, 165; Hume, *General History*, 332, 342; Melville, *Memoirs*, 264; Howard, *Scottish Architecture*, 103.
17. Howard, *Scottish Architecture*, 102; Allan, 'The private countrey life'; McCordick, *Scottish Literature*, i. 604, 647–52; Morford, 'Stoic garden'; Fraser, *Eglinton*, i. 214; Fraser, *Sutherland*, ii. 363; Gordon, *Sutherland*, 8; NAS GD 112/20/5/3/1.
18. Howard, *Scottish Architecture*, 100–1; Wells-Cole, *Art and Decoration*, 153–7.
19. For England see Heal, 'Idea of hospitality'; Heal, *Hospitality*; Heal and Holmes, *Gentry in England and Wales*, 282–9; Lubbock, *Tyranny of Taste*, 43–55; Fowler, *Country House Poem*.
20. Heal, *Hospitality*, 26–8; Gordon, *Sutherland*, 189; Dogshon, 'West Highland chiefdoms'; Dawson, 'The fifth earl of Argyle', 21; NAS GD 112/39/7/5.
21. Leslie, *Historie*, i. 103; also Fraser, *Douglas*, 246.
22. *Early Travellers*, 88, 92, 127–8; and for England, Heal, 'Idea of hospitality', 79–89.
23. Lindsay, *Historie*, ii. 181. For some examples of James's progresses see *CSP Scotland*, xiii. prt. 1, 276, prt. 2, 967; and for their impressive impact, Cameron, 'Continental visitors', 49.
24. *Early Travellers*, 113ff; Fraser, *Eglinton*, i. 181ff, 210, 213; Fraser, *Elphinstone*, i. 142; Fraser, *Sutherland*, ii. 120; *CSP Scotland*, x. 218.
25. *Family of Kilravock*, 91; *Early Travellers*, 127–8, 157.
26. NAS GD 158/2697/17; 158/2697/24.
27. *Poems of Sir Richard Maitland*, 23; *APS*, iii. 222–3; Lithgow, 'Scotland's Welcome to Her Native Sone' in Maidment, *Poetical Remains*; Heal, 'Idea of hospitality'; Gordon, *Short Abridgement of Britane's Distemper*, 76–7; Stevenson, 'English devil'.
28. Howarth, *Images of Rule*, 259–60; Salvadori, *La Chasse*; Heal and Holmes, *Gentry in England and Wales*, 289–93; Vale, *Gentlemen's Recreations*, 27–57; Hands, *English Hawking and Hunting*; Gransby, 'Decline of falconry'. For a hunting song, see John Stewart of Baldynneis, 'The hunter', in McCordick, *Scottish Literature*, i. 605.
29. Fraser, *Sutherland*, ii. 363; NLS Adv. MS 15.2.14/78; *Political Writings*, 56; Leidtke, *Royal Horse*, 254–8; Gilbert, *Hunting*.
30. *Registrum de Panmure*, i. pp. xxxv; NRA(S) 237/F/475–8.
31. *Early Travellers*, 120–3, and see Leslie, *Historie*, i. 19–20; *Chronicles of the Frasers*, 219, 221–2; *CSP Scotland*, xi. 685; but see Gordon, *Sutherland*, 301–2.
32. Fraser, *Douglas*, iv. 224–5; Fraser, *Chiefs of Grant*, ii. 46; Fraser, *Sutherland*, ii. 132; NAS GD 38/2/1/11; NAS GD 112/39/43/17; *HMC Sixth Report*, 611; NAS GD 406/1/10433; *CSP Scotland*, xii. 480; *HMC Eleventh Report*, 67; *Letters and State Papers*, 76–8; Fraser, *Menteith*, i. 335; *HMC Mar and Kellie*, i. 80–1; ii. 2–7–18; *Family of Kilravock*, 235; NRA(S) 237/F/476–7, 237/F/478–80, 237/F/485–6; *HMC Various V*, 117; NAS GD 112/39/52/9.
33. *APS*, ii. 541; iii. 26, 225–6, 453; iv. 629. Landlords too were prosecuted for shooting deer, Pitcairn, *Criminal Trials*, i. prt. 2, 48; Manning, *Hunters and Poachers*; Beaver, 'The great deer massacre'.

34. NAS GD 75/606; Fraser, *Elphinstone*, i. 139, 143–4.
35. NAS GD 112/10/29; *HMC Fourth Report*, iv. 533; *RPC*, first ser., xii. 691–2. As in England, it is possible that recusants were seen as soft targets by poachers, Manning, *Hunters and Poachers*, 220–5.
36. Leidtke, *Royal Horse*, 223, 255–8, 260–3; Vale, *Gentlemen's Recreations*, 19–24; *CSP Scotland*, iv. 502, 519; xii. 350; Fraser, *Douglas*, iv. 233; Gladitz, *Horse Breeding*, 141–92.
37. *HMC Twelfth Report*, 109; *Historie*, 158. For examples of races at Ayr, Teviotdale and Annandale, *Kennedy*, 12; *CSP Scotland*, xiii. prt. 2, 825, 834; *RPC*, first ser., vii. 352; ix. 152–3.
38. Lindsay, *Lives of the Lindsays*, ii. appendix xxxiii/iii; *Chronicles of the Frasers*, 247; *Maitland Miscellany*, i. 197–201; *APS*, iv. 613–14.
39. Motley, *Becoming a French Aristocrat*, 55–9; Vale, *Gentleman's recreations*, 58–72.
40. Fraser, *Sutherland*, ii. 122, 363; *Political Writings*, 56; *Memorials of Montrose*, i. 85–6; Carter, *Medieval Games*; Armitage, *Men at Play*, 46–9; McLean, *English at Play*; Vale, *Gentlemen's Recreations*.
41. *CSP Scotland*, i. 576; v. 611; *Chronicles of the Frasers*, 165.
42. *Ancram and Lothian*, i. 23.
43. For golf, *CSP Scotland*, x. 578; NAS GD 112/35/1/4; and tennis, *CSP Scotland*, ix. 98; Heal and Holmes, *Gentry in England and Wales*, 293–4.
44. *Political Writings*, 56; *CSP Scotland*, vi. 475; Bannatyne, *Memorials*, 333–4; *HMC Mar and Kellie*, ii. 72.
45. Anderson, *Earl of Orkney*, 134; *Ancram and Lothian*, i. 68–9.
46. Walker, 'Gambling and the Venetian noblemen'; *Poems of Sir Richard Maitland*, 20; *Political Writings*, 56–7; Fraser, *Sutherland*, ii. 363; Fraser, *Elphinstone*, i. 152.
47. *Political Writings*, 57; Eales, *Chess*, 71–93; Fraser, *Douglas*, iv. 295.
48. Sanderson, *Mary Stewart's People*, 71.
49. Purser, *Scotland's Music*, 93–100; Donaldson, *James V to James VII*, 269–70; Wormald, *Court, Kirk and Community*, 187–9; *APS*, iii. 174.
50. Purser, *Scotland's Music*, 101–24; Knox, *Works*, ii. 415–16; Farmer, *History of Music*, 80; *Ancient Scottish Melodies*, 34, 58–132; Vale, *Gentleman's Recreations*, 94–9; Hume, *Hymns*.
51. *Ancient Scottish Melodies*, 79–80; *APS*, iii. 140.
52. Purser, *Scotland's Music*, 123; NAS GD 124/17/4, 124/17/192; NRA(S) 217/4/743; Fraser, *Sutherland*, ii. 121; Fraser, *Eglinton*, ii. 277; NAS GD 112/20/5/5, 112/29/10/15, 112/39/23/8; NAS GD 10/661; *CSP Scotland*, vii. 24; NLS MS 5448; NLS MS 9449.
53. *Ancient Scottish Melodies*, 12–13, 138, 255–6, 268–70, 290–94; Henderson, *Minstrelsy*, ii. 177–80; Brown, 'The laird, his daughter, her husband and the minister'.
54. *Registrum de Panmure*, i. p. cxlvi and for music in the Panmure household, GD 45/26/94–5; *Chronicles of the Frasers*, 265; Purser, *Scotland's Music*, 71–80, 125–33; Watson, *Poetry of Scotland*, 212–15.
55. Bushnell, *A Culture of Teaching*, 117–43; *Political Writings*, 44; NLS Adv. MS 15.2.14/75; MS 33.7.26/12b–13b; Fraser, *Sutherland*, ii. 364–5; Lindsay, *Lives of the Lindsays*, ii. 3–4.
56. MacMillan, *Scottish Art*, 60; Durkan and Ross, *Early Scottish Libraries*; *Ancram and Lothian*, i. 64; Mann, 'Book trade'; Shaw, 'Adam Bothwell'; Macdonald, *Library of Drummond*, 43–4; Hay, 'Scotland and the Italian Renaissance', 120; Heal and Holmes, *Gentry in England and Wales*, 277–82.
57. Rolland, *Seven Sages*; *Buik of the Conquerour*; *Adversaria*; *Bannatyne Miscellany*, ii. 157–60; *Moral Fables*; *Palice of Honour*.
58. For Moray, Melville, *Memoirs*, 222; *Historie*, 47; Doughty, 'Library of Moray'; *HMC Sixth Report*, 657–8. For Glamis, *Miscellany of the Scottish History Society*, pp. xxiv, xlix; Donaldson, 'Glamis and Beza', 121–2, 128. For Gordonstoun, NAS GD 26/6/124; Fraser, *Sutherland*, i. 203; Gordon, *Sutherland*; *Library of Sir Robert Gordon*; Birrell, 'Reading as pastime', 121–3. Buccleuch's significant library was accumulated in his lifetime for no books were listed in the inventories of his father in 1611 or his grandfather in 1574, NAS GD 224/930/38/9, 224/935/11, 224/935/22. It was catalogued by Sir

John Scott of Scotstarvit. Lothian had a library of 1361 volumes at his death in 1666, *Ancram and Lothian*, i. 3. For Glenorchy, NAS GD 112/5/4; *Black Book of Taymouth*, pp. v–vii.

59. Fraser, *Elphinstone*, i. 152–3; *HMC Ninth Report*, ii. 194; NAS GD 406/1/8390; *HMC Mar and Kellie*, ii. 97; *Poems of William Drummond*, p. vi; Macdonald, *Library of Drummond*, 1–3, 37–51; NLS MS 5786, 5818, 5828/1–2, 5829, 5830.
60. Dawson, 'Protestant earl and godly Gael', 351–3. Why Esther Inglis should have dedicated her elegant calligraphic copy of 'Le livres de l'ecclesiaste ensemble les Lamentations de Jeremie' to the seventh earl of Argyll is, however, puzzling, NLS MS 20498.
61. Lyall, 'Complaint, satire and invective', 57–61; Hume, *General History*, 360–2; Phillips, 'George Buchanan and the Sidney circle'; Donaldson, 'Scottish Presbyterian exiles', 186; Lee, *Maitland of Thirlestane*, 245; NRA(S) 217/3/339; *Works of William Fowler*, i. 259.
62. *Ancram and Lothian*, i. pp. xxviii–xxxiv; i. 24–5; ii. 513; NLS MS 5775; BL Ro. 17c, xxxiv, BL Ro. 10b, xiii.
63. Burke, *Venice and Amsterdam*, 94, and for England, Stone, *Crisis of the Aristocracy*, 703–10. This was not a new departure for the Scottish nobility, Lyall, 'Two of Dunbar's Makars'.
64. *Poems of Sir Richard Maitland*, 121–43; *Maitland Quarto*; *Bannatyne Miscellany*, i. 301–24; *Poems of Alexander Montgomerie*; *Works of William Fowler*, i. 15–17; *Works of Sir William Alexander*; *Poems of James VI*; *New Poems by James I*; *Ancram and Lothian*, i. 24–5, ii. 487–522; McCordick, *Scottish Literature*, i. 603–782; Spiller, 'Poetry after the union'; Reid, 'Prose after Knox'; Wormald, *Court, Kirk and Community*, 185–7; Lynch, *Scotland. A New History*, 257; Donaldson, *James V to James VII*, 259–60.
65. *Ancram and Lothian*, ii. 77, 481–3; NLS MS 5787; NAS GD 224/479/1.
66. Lindsay, *Lives of the Lindsays*, ii. 5–6; Scott, *Staggering State*, 4; *Works of Sir William Mure of Rowallan*.
67. *William Drummond of Hawthornden*; *Poetical Works of William Drummond*; Macdonald, *Library of Drummond*, 23–31; Patterson, *Johnson's Conversation with Drummond*; Fogle, *Critical Study*; Smart, 'Monarchy and toleration'; Cummings, 'Drummond's *Forth Feasting*; Atkinson, 'The religious views of Drummond'; Atkinson, 'Drummond as baroque poet'; Reid, 'Royalty and self-absorption'; *HMC Ninth Report*, ii. 199.
68. *Works of Thomas Urquhart*, 3–5; Napier, *Plaine Discovery*.
69. *Political Writings*, 46; NLS Adv. MS 15.2.14/75; MS 33.7.26/12b–13b; NLS MS 5787/52; Styles, 'Politics and historical research'; Morford, 'Tacitean *prudentia*'; McCrea, *Constant Minds*.
70. For examples, *CSP Scotland*, viii. 440; Calderwood, *History*, v. 155, 160. Lindsay, *Historie*, i. 'Introduction', 12; NLS Adv. MS 33/7/21.
71. *House of Seytoun*, p. vii; Rae, 'The historical writing of Drummond', 22–6; *Kennedy*; Fraser, *Haddington*, i. pp. xlvi–xlviii, pp. liii–lv; Melville, *Memoirs*; Dewald, *Aristocratic Experience*, 16–17.
72. *Early Travellers*, 99; Sellar, 'Highland family origins'; Stone, *Crisis of the Aristocracy*, 25–6; Adamson, 'The baronial context of the English civil war', 94–5; Kidd, *Subverting Scotland's Past*, 165.
73. Maclagan, 'Genealogy and heraldry'; Ellis, 'Genealogy, history and aristocratic reaction'; for Denmilne, see the four volumes in NLS Adv. MS 33.2.38–41; *Works of Sir William Mure of Rowallan*, ii. 233–56; and see how the imprisoned fourth lord Ochiltree passed his time during the 1630s, NLS Adv. MS 34.3.18.
74. *Registrum de Panmure*, i. pp. xxx–xxxi, xxxvi–xxxviii; GD 45/26/52, 45/26/59.
75. NLS MS 7114; NAS GD 112/20/5/5; NAS GD 150/3438/3, 16 March 1631; *Black Book of Taymouth*, p. vii n. 4; *RPC*, second ser., iv. 316–17 for the patent; Ferguson, *Chivalric Tradition*, 126–38.
76. Allan, 'Ane ornament'; *House of Gordon*, i. pp. xxxii–xxxv; ii. 1–75, 111–52; NLS Adv. , MS 34/1/6, MS 34/6/18, MS 34/6/23, MS 35/5/5A; Fraser, *Sutherland*, ii. 115, 365–6; Gordon, *Sutherland*, p. xi, 21–30, 394, 422–3; *House of Gordon*, i. p. xxxv; ii. 111–52. The genealogies were completed by his son in 1659; *House of Forbes*, i. p. xxxiii.

77. *Familia Humia Wedderburnensi*; Hume, *House of Douglas*, i. pp. x–xiv, xxx–xxxiii, lvi–lx, lxxi–lxxii, 2, 4, 8–9, 13–17, 45; Fraser, *Douglas*, iv. 291–310. For other Italian and one Polish connection, Leslie, *Historie*, ii. 101–2; *CSP Scotland*, x. 730.
78. It was the eighteenth century before a fully developed heraldic system was published in Scotland, Nisbet, *System of Heraldry*; Innes, *Scots Heraldry*, 75–6; *House of Seytoun*, 28; NAS GD 26/14/1. For the broader cultural importance of heraldry, Day, 'Primers of honour'.
79. Debus, *Man and Nature*; Debus, *Chemistry, Alchemy and the New Philosophy*; Schuler, *Alchemical Poetry*; Yates, 'The hermetic tradition'; Hart, *Art and Magic*.
80. Cowan, 'The darker vision of the Scottish Renaissance', 138–40; Calderwood, *History*, ii. 213, 505; vi. 47–8, 59–60, 78; vii. 595; *CSP Scotland*, i. 687; *Bannatyne Miscellany*, i. 99–100, 143, 155; Spottiswoode, *History*, ii. 314; *Historie*, 375; *Ancram and Lothian*, i. pp. xlvii–xlviii; Larner, *Enemies of God*.
81. For example, Lindsay, *Historie*, ii. 193.
82. *Political Writings*, 51; NLS MS 5787/24b; *Works of Sir Thomas Urquhart*, 363–5.
83. Williamson, 'Number and national consciousness'; Stevenson, *Origins of Freemasonry*; Stevenson, *The First Masons*; Napier, *Arte Logistica*, pp. xii, xxviii–xxx, xli–xlii; *Works of Sir Thomas Urquhart*, 59–147, 331; Balfour, *Works*, ii. 72–3.

## Chapter 10: Religion

1. McRoberts, *Essays on the Scottish Reformation*; Cowan, *Scottish Reformation*; Lynch, *Edinburgh and the Reformation*; Mason, 'Covenant and commonweal'. A similar trend can be discerned elsewhere, Haigh, *English Reformation Revised*.
2. *BUK*, i. 252–3.
3. Powis, 'Order, religion and the magistrates'; Roelker, *One King, One Faith*; Press, 'Adel, Reich und Reformation'; Lee, 'King James's popish chancellor'.
4. Brown, 'Godly magistrate'; Dawson, 'Protestant earl and godly Gael' for Argyll.
5. Wolfe, *Conversion of Henri IV*; Calderwood, *History*, ii. 37–8; Spottiswoode, *History*, i. 327.
6. Waite, 'Dutch nobility and anabaptism'; Donaldson, 'Glamis and Beza'.
7. Calderwood, *History*, vi. 195; Mullan, 'Theology in the Church of Scotland'.
8. Calderwood, *History*, iii. 559–60, 565, 689.
9. Sanderson, *Ayrshire and the Reformation*, 139–40; Bardgett, *Scotland Reformed*, 148–50; Houlbrook, 'Death, church and the family', 31–2; Altred, 'Preparation for death'; Beaver, 'Sown in dishonour, raised in glory'; Alsop, 'Religious preambles'; Zell, 'The use of religious preambles'.
10. Knox, *Works*, i. 290; NAS GD 38/2/1/69; Lindsay, *Lives of the Lindsays*, i. 373, 378–9; for others, NRA(S) 885/178, and NAS GD 224/930/38/9.
11. Fraser, *Elphinstone*, ii. 265; also Fraser, *Douglas*, iii. 321–2, and *Sheriffdoms of Lanark and Renfrew*, 75 for equally innocuous Catholic testaments.
12. *House of Seytoun*, p. ix.
13. Hudson, 'Catholic challenge to Puritan piety'; Melville, *Diary*, 124–7; Calderwood, *History*, iv. 149; Hume, *General History*, 362–3.
14. Knox, *Works*, i. 72; Doughty, 'Library of Moray'.
15. Fraser, *Chiefs of Grant*, ii. 54; and for other examples, Fraser, *Elphinstone*, i. 160; *House of Forbes*, 166; *Ancram and Lothian*, i. 35–6. In 1625 Rothes was reading White's *Workes Together with a Defence of the Way to the True Church* (London, 1624) and sir Nicholas Brent's 1620 translation of *The History of the Council of Trent* by Paoli Sarpi.
16. Dawson, 'Protestant earl and godly Gael', 350; Lindsay, *Godly Man's Journey*.
17. Lindsay, *Lives of the Lindsays*, ii. p. xxxiii; Fraser, *Sutherland*, ii. 337.
18. NLS MS 5785/3; *Poems of Alexander Montgomerie*, i. 225–72; *Works of Sir William Mure*, i. 29–30, 197–300; ii. 55–232; Atkinson, 'Religious views of Drummond'.

19. *Bannatyne Miscellany*, i/I. 120; NAS GD 112/39/54/9, 112/39/54/13, 112/39/55/3, 112/39/55/15; Calderwood, *History*, iv. 117; *CSP Scotland*, viii. 157; Fraser, *Haddington*, i. p. xxvii.
20. Calderwood, *History*, iv. 113; Seton, *House of Seton*, i. 212–13; *Maitland Miscellany*, i/2. 77, 82.
21. *House of Seytoun*, p. x; Knox, *Works*, i. 250; *First Book of Discipline*, 185; Calderwood, *History*, vii. 347, 436, 446.
22. Dawson, 'Campbells and the Scottish Reformation'. There was nothing new in the household functioning as a religious community, Mertes, *English Noble Household*, 139–60. For France, Harding, *Anatomy of a Power Elite*, 86; Mentzer, *Blood and Belief*, especially chs 2 and 8. On England, Morgan, *Godly Learning*; Cross, *Puritan Earl*, 22–60; Cliffe, *Puritan Gentry*, 9; Hill, 'The spiritualization of the household'; Cliffe, *Yorkshire Gentry*, 12; Tudor, 'Religious instruction for children and adolescents'; Cunningham, *Children and Childhood in Western Society*, 46–57; Cust and Lake, 'Sir Richard Grosvenor', 40–3; Larminie, *Godly Magistrate*. Strauss, *Luther's House of Learning* raises doubts.
23. Lee, *Moray*, 283; Spottiswoode, *History*, ii. 121; Calderwood, *History*, ii. 312, 511; iv. 149; Hume, *General History*, 360–3, 391–2; Melville, *Diary*, 124–7; *Wodrow Miscellany*, i. 284; Dawson, 'Campbells and the Scottish Reformation', 221–8. For comparisons, Heal and Holmes, *Gentry in England and Wales*, 359–74.
24. Frankforter, 'Elizabeth Bowes and John Knox'; Bardgett, *Scotland Reformed*, 150–4; Caldwell, *Countess of Mar's Arcadia*; *Ancram and Lothian*, i. p. xxix; NAS GD 40/2/13/81; *Poems of Alexander Hume*, 3–5, and 184–97 for the 'Dreame'; see also Dawson, 'Campbells and the Scottish Reformation', 225–8.
25. Wells, 'Origins of Covenanting Thought and Resistance', 99–133; Roelker, 'Noblewomen in the French Reformation'; Roelker, 'Appeal of Calvinism to French noblewomen'; Willen, 'Godly women'; Houlbrooke, *The English Family*, 111–14; Fletcher, *Gender, Sex and Subordination*, 347–63; Hufton, *Prospect Before Her*, 359–418; Crawford, *Women and Religion*, 73–97.
26. Fraser, *Eglinton*, i. 218, 223–5; Lindsay, *Lives of the Lindsays*, i. 374; Wells, 'Origins of Covenanting Thought and Resistance', 107–8.
27. *Select Biographies*, i. 401, 405; Calderwood, *History*, v. 408–10; Stone, *Crisis of the Aristocracy*, 743–5; Row, *History*, 171–2; and see Hume's critical comment on the regent Morton, Hume, *General History*, 335.
28. Bast, 'From two kingdoms to two tables'; Hsia, *Social Discipline*; Bardgett, *Scotland Reformed*; Graham, *Uses of Reform*; Lenman, 'The limits of godly discipline'; Parker, 'The "Kirk by law established"'; Foster, *Church before the Covenants*; MacCulloch, 'Catholic and Puritan'; NAS GD 25/9/2.
29. NLS MS 3724/54; NAS GD 26/2/2. The court book is not paginated; *RPC*, first ser., xiii. 506.
30. *Honoris de Morton*, i. 192; *Stirling Presbytery*, 119–20.
31. Seton, *House of Seton*, i. 212; *RPC*, first ser., x. 167; *Synod of Fife*, 31.
32. Cliffe, *Yorkshire Gentry*, 10; *First Book of Discipline*, 173; *Second Book of Discipline*, 233; Graham, 'Equality before the kirk?'
33. Lindsay, *Godly Man's Journey*, 53; Calderwood, *History*, v. 338; Brown, *Bloodfeud*, 184–207.
34. Graham, 'Equality before the kirk?'; *BUK*, i. 252–3; Stirling Presbytery, 115–16, 207–8, 211–12; *Maitland Miscellany*, i. prt. 2, 62, 65, 82.
35. *CSP Scotland*, ii. 31–4; iv. 590; vi. 18; *Maitland Miscellany* i/I. 126; for Bothwell, *CSP Scotland*, x. 192; Calderwood, *History*, v. 68–9; Melville, *Diary*, 186; Bruce, *Sermons*, 345–66.
36. *RPC*, first ser., v. 245; vi. 586; *Presbytery of Lanark*, 5; *Maitland Miscellany*, i. prt. 2, 411.
37. Calderwood, *History*, iii. 303; iv. 726–8; *BUK*, i. 317; *RPC*, first ser., iv. 143; Brown, 'Godly magistrate'; Graham, *Uses of Reform*, 147–62.
38. *Maitland Miscellany*, i. prt. 2, 417–18; NRA(S) 237/I/563–4; NAS GD 75/572.
39. NAS GD 112/39/34/6.

40. *First Book of Discipline*, 70–5; Finnie, 'House of Hamilton'; Knox, *Works*, ii. 128–9, and also 92, 310, 418; Davidson, *Dialogue*; Calderwood, *History*, ii. 42; iv. 152; Melville, *Diary*, 129–30.
41. Herries, *Memoirs*, 55; Bannatyne, *Memorials*, 197–204.
42. Kirk, 'Exercise of ecclesiastical patronage by the crown'; Hewitt, *Scotland under Morton*, 83–102; Bannatyne, *Memorials*, 206–7; Calderwood, *History*, iii. 144–6; Kirk, 'Royal and lay patronage', 134–6; *CSP Scotland*, vii. 577; NRA(S) 217/2/111–12, 217/2/126. For a case of violent possession, *RPC*, first ser., iii. 88–91.
43. Fraser, *Sutherland*, ii. 338–9.
44. Kirk, 'Royal and lay patronage', 138; *RPC*, first ser., iv. 102–3; NAS GD 150/3441/12; NAS GD 75/571; *Synod of Fife*, 29; Calderwood, *History*, vii. 303; *Maitland Miscellany*, i. prt. 2, 415–16.
45. Sanderson, 'Catholic recusancy', 98–9; *RPC*, second ser., i. 421–2; ii. 327–9, 343–4, 358–9, 392, 433, 596–7; Balfour, *Works*, ii. 146.
46. *RPC*, second ser., v. 213–16; and see ibid., first ser., ii. 313–14; viii. 361–2.
47. Foster, 'A constant platt achieved'; Fraser, *Chiefs of Grant*, ii. 41. Ministers also complained to the privy council, *RPC*, first ser., viii. 27.
48. NAS GD 28/1451. In spite of the teind commission, nobles continued to acquire new tacks, ibid., 28/1464.
49. Calderwood, *History*, ii. 470; NAS GD 124/17/197, 124/17/201–2, 124/17/623; NAS GD 16/34/8; for lords Yester and Elphinstone see NLS MS 14761, 14762; NAS GD 124/8/8.
50. Fraser, *Menteith*, i. 336–7; ii. 320–3; *HMC Third Report*, iii. 399, nos 39 and 41; Fraser, *Haddington*, i. p. xxvi.
51. *Honoris de Morton*, i. 192; Fraser, *Haddington*, ii. 139–40; Yule, 'James VI and I'; Glendinning, *History of Scottish Architecture*, 30–5; and see Gordon, *Sutherland*, 361.
52. *Maitland Miscellany*, i. prt. 2, 407–8; NAS GD 112/39/44/13; NAS GD, 6/1147.
53. Bardgett, *Scotland Reformed*, 93–4; Scott, *Fasti*, i. 398–9; Calderwood, *History*, iv. 18–19, 153, 634–8. In France the number of church offices that were coveted by nobles was relatively few, Major, *Renaissance Monarchy to Absolute Monarchy*, 98.
54. Kirk, 'Exercise of ecclesiastical patronage by the crown'; Kirk, 'Royal and lay patronage'; NAS GD 86/185; *RMSRS, 1546–1580*, 557 no. 1125, 747 no. 2737; *RSSRS*, vii. 421 no. 2368, 267–8 no. 1669; viii. 538 no 2085; Cowan and Easson, *Medieval Religious Houses*, 213, 215–16, 218. For Angus's other ecclesiastical patronage see *RSSRS*, viii. 55–6 no. 336, 55 no. 335, 60 no. 538, 91 no. 549, 104 no. 620.
55. Kirk, 'Royal and lay patronage', 141, 146; Macpherson, 'Francis Stewart', 312–70; *HMC Seventh Report*, 733; NLS MS 80/7.
56. Donaldson, 'Glamis and Beza'; White, 'Morton's visitation'; Kirk, 'Royal and lay patronage', 141–2; *CSP Scotland*, v. 34; Dawson, 'Protestant earl and godly Gael'; Dawson, 'Campbells and the Scottish Reformation', 231–4; Bardgett, *Scotland Reformed*, 104–7; Sanderson, *Ayrshire and the Reformation*, 108–9. For England, Stone, *Crisis of the Aristocracy*, 733–9; Healey, 'The preaching ministry'; Cross, 'Noble patronage in the Elizabethan church'; Heal and Homes, *Gentry in England and Wales*, 319–45; O'Day, 'Law of patronage'.
57. NLS MS 78/34, 81/112; Fraser, *Haddington*, ii. 158–62. Haddington finally succeeded in getting Mr Robert Balcanquhal; for another case, NRA(S) 2312/113/202, 2312/113/228.
58. Fraser, *Sutherland*, ii. 340; Lindsay, *Lives of the Lindsays*, i. 324; *RPC*, second ser., iv. 519–21.
59. NRA(S)2847/1/10/23–4, 2847/1/21/3, 2847/2/12.
60. *APS*, iii. 86–9, 139–42.
61. Calderwood, *History*, ii. 511; Spottiswoode, *History*, ii. 121; *Historie*, 151; NLS MS 83/86; Fraser, *Elphinstone*, i. 153; NLS MS 20 781A/7–8; *Maitland Miscellany*, i. 183–4; *Memorials of Montrose*, i. 156–80; also NRA(S) 217/4/823; Heal, 'Idea of hospitality'; Stone, *Crisis of the Aristocracy*, 44–9. For women, Fraser, *Haddington*, i. p. xxviii; *Registrum de Panmure*, i. p. xxxvi; Debrisay, 'City limits', 44–5.

62. *CSP Scotland*, vi. 14; xii. 18, 28; Melville, *Memoirs*, 267; Calderwood, *History*, v. 382.
63. NRA(S) 237/E/399–401, 237/F/450–5, 237/F/469–70, 237/F/478–9; NLS Ch. 10 780; Lindsay, *Lives of the Lindsays*, i. 379; Fraser, *Haddington*, ii. 311.
64. Fraser, *Chiefs of Grant*, iii. 292; Fraser, *Eglinton*, ii. 234–6. By way of contrast, Jordan, *Philanthropy in England*, 142–365.
65. Brown, 'The making of a *politique*'; *RPC*, first ser., iv. 62. For other examples, see the earls of Atholl, Caithness and Eglinton in the 1570s, Calderwood, *History*, iii. 341, 347, 401–2, or the sixth lord Hume in the 1590s, ibid., v. 263, 316–21; *CSP Scotland*, xi. 341–2, 376, 613–15; xiii. prt. 1, 362. For the debate on continuity in England, Bossy, *English Catholic Community*; McGrath, 'Elizabethan Catholicism'; Haigh, 'Continuity of Catholicism'.
66. Kooi, 'Popish impudence'; Smith, 'Persecution of Staffordshire Roman Catholic recusants'; Gordon, 'Patronage and parish'; Calderwood, *History*, vii. 224.
67. *HMC Mar and Kellie*, i. 60–3.
68. *Synod of Fife*, 36, 45–6, 48, 52–3, 56, 58–9, 72, 80–2; for others, ibid., 6, 45–6, 60–1.
69. Fraser, *Douglas*, ii. 418; iv. 196–7; *Presbytery of Lanark*, 5–6, 8, 10; *RPC*, second ser., iv. 184–5, 418; NLS MS 973/39.
70. *Maitland Miscellany*, i. 66–7, 86; Seton, *House of Seton*, i. 214; *RPC*, second ser., iii. 96–7, 109–10, 246, 417; iv. 285; *Confession and Conversion*.
71. Fraser, *Sutherland*, i. 186–8; ii. 114, 118–19; iii. 188; Gordon, *Sutherland*, 298.
72. Kirk, 'Royal and lay patronage', 145–6; Wormald, '"Princes" and the regions', 69; Sanderson, 'Catholic recusancy', 98–9; Calderwood, *History*, iv. 658–66; Brown, 'The making of a *politique*'; Fraser, *Carlaverock*, ii. 67–8, 76–7.
73. *CSP Scotland*, x. 816; xi. 181, 184; *BUK*, iii. 835–6, 839–42; *Historie*, 288–9; for the success of Catholic patrons in England, MacCulloch, *Later Reformation in England*, 96–7.
74. Calderwood, *History*, vi. 767; *House of Gordon*, i. 72–4; Roberts, 'Popery in Buchan and Strathbogie'; Macinnes, 'Crown, clans and fine', 48. Huntly castle also had Catholic imagery carved on the astonishing armorial panels that adorned the doorway, Howard, *Scottish Architecture*, 65–6.
75. Sanderson, *Ayrshire and the Reformation*, 124; *BUK*, iii. 983–6; for Nithsdale, *RPC*, second ser., iv. 363, 396; for Angus, ibid., second ser., iii. 45, 69–70, 88–9, 100, 119, 125, 145, 156, 159, 166, 190, 220, 232–3; for England and France, Stone, *Crisis of the Aristocracy*, 739–41; Hudson, 'The Protestant struggle for survival'.
76. *CSP Scotland*, xi. 616; xiii. prt. 1, 507; Melville, *Diary*, 58; Fraser, *Douglas*, ii. 380; Calderwood, *History*, iv. 253.
77. Calderwood, *History*, vi. 115; Seton, *Family of Seton*, i. 215.
78. *RPC*, first ser., viii. 550–2; x. 337–9; second ser., i. 157–8; iii. 20–1; *APS*, iv. 406, 428; Calderwood, *History*, vi. 115, 180–1; Fraser, *Menteith*, ii. 1–2; Fraser, *Sutherland*, ii. 345.
79. *CSP Scotland*, xiii. prt. 2, 794; Fraser, *Elphinstone*, i. 179–81; ii. 143; and for the young lord Seton in 1629, *RPC*, second ser., iii. 99–100.
80. *RPC*, second ser., iv. 521, 548, 619, 624; vi. 380; *CSP Scotland*, x. 419, 425, 531; Calderwood, *History*, v. 129; *BUK*, 494, 507–10; Fraser, *Douglas*, ii. 295–6, 298–300, 381–2, 386–95, 398–404, 408; iv. 35–6, 191–6; *Maitland Miscellany*, i. prt. 2, 412–13; *Letters and State Papers*, 144–5.
81. *Early Travellers*, 101; Knox, *Works*, ii. 167, 562, 565, 566.
82. Wormald, '"Princes" and the regions', 78; *CSP Scotland*, vii. 426–7; Leslie, *Historie*, ii. 464; *Spottiswoode Miscellany*, i. 261.
83. *CSP Scotland*, xi. 179, 182; Coward, 'A "crisis of the aristocracy"', 66–70; *House of Forbes*, i. 114–16, 138–45, 148–9.
84. Fraser, *Elphinstone*, 104; *HMC Ninth Report*, ii. 199; Fraser, *Haddington*, i. 15–17; Lee, 'Popish chancellor'.
85. Hanlon, *Confession and Community*; Calderwood, *History*, v. 268–9.
86. Spottiswoode, *History*, iii. 47–8; *CSP Scotland*, xiii. prt. 1, 355, 371, 374; Fraser, *Douglas*, iv. 192; Gordon, *Sutherland*, 320–1.
87. NLS MS 21 187A/24–6.

## Chapter 11: Death

1. Banker, *Death in the Community*.
2. NAS GD 224/930/38/9; *Works of Sir Thomas Urquhart*, 11, 13, 28; *Garden of Grave and Godlie Flowers*; Abernethy, *Christian and Heavenly Treatise*, 96–7.
3. Llewellyn, *The Art of Death*, 9–12; Engel, *Mapping Mortality*; Murray, *Short Treatise*; Lindsay, *Godly Man's Journey*; Boyd, *Last Batell*; also in the same vein is Campbell, *Treatise upon Death*.
4. Aries, *Western Attitudes to Death*; Aries, *Hour of Our Death*; see also Gittings, *Death, Burial and the Individual*; Muir, *Ritual in Early Modern Europe*, 44–52.
5. *HMC Sixth Report*, 637; for other examples, Fraser, *Douglas*, iv. 187; NLS MS 81/64; Fraser, *Haddington*, ii. 133; Boyd, *Last Batell*, 22–3. The allegory of the tenant was a common one of the period, Cressy, *Birth, Marriage and Death*, 381.
6. *Ancram and Lothian*, i. 77; NAS GD 112/39/39/9, 112/39/40/27, 112/39/42/3; *Works of Sir Thomas Urquhart*, 41.
7. Boyd, *Last Batell*, 7–9; Abernethy, *Christian and Heavenly Treatise*, 343–66; Engel, *Mapping Mortality*; Babb, *Elizabethan Malady*; Strong, *English Icon*.
8. For Lennox, Calderwood, *History*, iii. 714–15; *CSP Scotland*, vi. 446–7, 466, 475, 481. For Elibank, Scott, *Staggering State*, 66; Calderwood, *History*, vii. 462. For Balmerino, Paul, *Scots Peerage*, i. 561 and Lothian, Calderwood, *History*, vii. 595–6.
9. NAS GD 406/1/62, 406/1/346.
10. Boyd, *Last Batell*, 52, 502.
11. Binski, *Medieval Death*, 33–47; Greenblatt, *Renaissance Self-Fashioning*; Cressy, *Birth, Marriage and Death*, 389–95; Houlbrooke, 'Death, church and the family', 26–7; Beier, 'The good death in seventeenth-century England', 43–61.
12. Melville, *Diary*, 83–4; Calderwood, *History*, iii. 559–75; Hume, *General History*, 351–6; Bannatyne, *Memorials*, 317–32; Moysie, *Memoirs*, 50; *CSP Scotland*, vi. 20–3; Smith, 'English treason trials'; Sharpe, 'Last dying speeches'; Wunderlie and Broce, 'Final moment before death', 270–4.
13. Melville, *Memoirs*, 326–7; Calderwood, *History*, iv. 35–7, 41–2; Nicholls, 'The theatre of martyrdom'.
14. *Historie*, 94; Melville, *Memoirs*, 242; Spottiswoode, *History*, ii. 166; Llewellyn, *Art of Death*, 28–34; Aries, *Images of Man and Death*; Lamb, 'The countess of Pembroke and the art of dying'.
15. Knox, *History*, ii. 392–3; Calderwood, *History*, ii. 179, 199, 229–30, 463–4; v. 382; NAS CC 8/8/20/49; *Melrose Papers*, ii. 456; *CSP Scotland*, xii. 18–19; Boyd, *Last Batell*, 7–9.
16. *HMC Laing*, i. 132–5; *Registrum de Panmure*, i. p. xxxvi; Paul, *Scots Peerage*, i. 300–1.
17. Hume, *General History*, 355.
18. Watson, *The Rest is Silence*, 3–11, 35–6; McCordick, *Scottish Literature*, i. 756–70.
19. Stannard, *Puritan Way of Death*, 72–95.
20. Wunderlie and Broce, 'Final moment before death'.
21. *Select Biographies*, i. 383–409; Cross, 'The third earl of Huntingdon's death-bed'.
22. Murray, *Short Treatise*.
23. Wanderlie and Broce, 'The final moment before death', 259–75.
24. Calderwood, *History*, vii. 595; *HMC Mar and Kellie*, ii. 192; Scott, *Staggering State*, 118 suggested he was poisoned.
25. Lindsay, *Historie*, ii. 310; *CSP Scotland*, xii. 23–4, 39, 43; Calderwood, *History*, vii. 153, 630–1; Scott, *Staggering State*, 57, 86–7; *HMC Mar and Kellie*, ii. 222.
26. *APS*, iii. 175–7; Calderwood, *History*, iii. 442–3; Moysie, *Memoirs*, 21, 23; NRA(S) 234/523/90 for the autopsy report.
27. Paul, *Scots Peerage*, viii. 342.
28. Bannatyne, *Memorials*, 334. Huntly's father also died of a stroke in 1562 and in June 1586 his son, the sixth earl, was suffering from 'ane frensy', *CSP Scotland*, viii. 427.
29. *CSP Scotland*, ix. 586; Hume, *History*, 431–2; Calderwood, *History*, iv. 680; Spottisoode,

*History*, ii. 389–90; *Honoris de Morton*, i. 171; NAS CC 8/8/20/49.

30. Paul, *Scots Peerage*, ii. 70, 113; *CSP Scotland*, xi. 639–40, 642; xii. 317, 476, 485, 500, 505–6; xiii. prt. 1, 73; *RPC*, second ser., ii. 442, 624.
31. McClure, *Sorrow and Consolation*, especially ch. 5; Cressy, *Birth, Marriage and Death*, 393–5; Houlbrooke, *The English Family*, 202–7. For some interesting observations by Cromarty, *Works of Sir Thomas Urquhart*, 43.
32. Lindsay, *Lives of the Lindsays*, i. 374; Fraser, *Eglinton*, i. 211.
33. Wemyss, *Workes*, i. 42. For the French and English experiences see Dewald, *Aristocratic Experience*, 97–9; Houlbrooke, *The English Family*, 134–40.
34. Seton, *Family of Seton*, i. 202; *HMC Sixth Report*, 652.
35. NAS GD 112/39/33/4; Lindsay, *Lives of the Lindsays*, ii. 9–12.
36. Geary, *Living with the Dead*; Watson, *The Rest is Silence*, 4–5; Finucane, 'Sacred corpse, profane carrion'; Cressy, *Birth, Marriage and Death*, 384–8.
37. Lindsay, *Historie*, ii. 189; Balfour, *Works*, i. 378.
38. Brown, *Bloodfeud*, 30; *Archaelogia Scotica*, iii. 80–1; NRA(S) MS 217/1/202; Stone, *Crisis of the Aristocracy*, 572.
39. *Archaelogia Scotica*, ii. 116–27. It was discovered in 1808 by workmen.
40. Binski, *Mediaeval Death*, 63–9; Sawday, 'The fate of Marsayas'; NAS GD 112/3/57, 112/39/38/4.
41. Wemyss, *Workes*, i. 12; Abernethy, *Christian and Heavenly Treatise*, 31.
42. Kay, *Melodious Tears*, 1–8; *First Book of Discipline*, 199–201; Knox, *Works*, ii. 160. For contrasting ideas on the impact of Protestantism, Stannard, *Puritan Way of Death*, 96–134; Cressy, *Birth, Marriage and Death*, 396–420; for Spain see Eire, *From Madrid to Purgatory*.
43. For Gight, *House of Gordon*, i. 212; *RPC*, vii. 345. For Ogilvy, Spottiswoode, *History*, iii. 187–8 and Paul, *Scots Peerage*, i. 119.
44. *Works of Sir Thomas Urquhart*, 27; from the dedication to Charles I in Boyd, *Last Batell*; Birnie, *Blame of Kirk Burial*, ch 7. English clerics made similar observations, Cressy, 'Death and the social order', 99; Cressy, *Birth, Marriage and Death*, 412–16.
45. Cressy, *Birth, Marriage and Death*, 105–6, 403–9, 412–16; NRA(S) 237/E/397–9; *Sheriffdoms of Lanark and Renfrew*, 75; and another, Balfour, *Works*, ii. 223.
46. Spalding, *Memorial*, i. 25; Stone, *Crisis of the Aristocracy*, 575–8; Heal and Holmes, *Gentry in England and Wales*, 140; Clarkson, *Death, Disease and Famine*, 160–1; Llewellyn, *Art of Death*, 60–4.
47. Strocchia, *Death and Ritual*, 226–35, 237; Eire, *From Madrid to Purgatory*, 19–251.
48. McManamon, *Funeral Oratory*, 37, 45–53; Huntington and Metcalf, *Celebrations of Death*, 23–43; James, 'Two Tudor funerals'; Clarkson, *Death, Disease and Famine*, 150–74; Cressy, 'Death and the social order'; Altred, 'Preparation for death'; Spence, 'A noble funeral in the great civil war'.
49. *CSP Scotland*, iii. 84; xii. 55; Balfour, *Works*, ii. 222; NLS Adv. MS 33/2/11.
50. *Chronicles of the Frasers*, 174–5; Seton, *Family of Seton*, i. 215–17; ii. 786–7.
51. For some drawings see NLS Adv. MS 34/4/16/4, and for the instructions at the second earl of Mar's funeral in 1635, NAS GD 124/15/115.
52. *APS*, iv. 626; NLS Adv. MS 33/2/11; on England, Llewellyn, *Art of Death*, 60–1; Broce and Wunderlie, 'Funeral of Henry Percy, sixth earl of Northumberland'.
53. Finucane, 'Sacred corpse, profane carrion', 41; Llewellyn, *Art of Death*, 46–9.
54. *HMC Mar and Kellie*, ii. 223; NLS Adv. MS 33/2/11.
55. Fraser, *Buccleuch*, i. 262–6; Hope, *Diary*, 9; NLS Adv. MS 33/2/11; Llewellyn, *Art of Death*, 65–72; Houlbrooke, 'Death, church and the family', 34–5. James, 'Two Tudor funerals', 176–87 argues that in Tudor England older families had funerals that were more locally rooted and more obviously linked to the idea of the lord as a war leader.
56. *House of Gordon*, i. p. xxxiv; Spalding, *Memorial*, i. 74. Torchlight processions were considered by some to be more honourable, Clarkson, *Death, Disease and Famine*, 162.
57. Fraser, *Annandale*, i. p. clxv.
58. For invitations and summonses to attend noble funerals see, NRA(S) 217/3/241; *Familie*

*of Innes*, 231. Lords might also be asked to honour their men by attending a family funeral, NAS GD 16/34/9.

59. *First Book of Discipline*, 201; D'Avray, *Death and the Prince*; McManamon, *Funeral Oratory*, 5–35, 63–87; Seton, *Family of Seton*, i. 213.
60. NLS Adv. MS 33/2/11; NLS MS 21 187A; Maitland, *Funerall Sermon*, 2–3; McManamon, *Funeral Oratory*, 5–35. Even bishops were privileged with a funeral sermon, *Funeral of a Right Reverend Father in God Patrick Forbes*.
61. Rogers, *Monuments and Monumental Inscriptions*, i. 80.
62. Cressy, *Birth, Marriage and Death*, 460–5; Binski, *Medieval Death*, 70–7; Colvin, *Architecture and the After-Life*, 220–1; Curl, *A Celebration of Death*, 119–20; *BUK*, ii. 733, and Appendix 1597–1603, 949; Birnie, *Blame of Kirk Burial*, chs 1–2, 9–10.
63. Rogers, *Monuments and Monumental Inscriptions*, i. 33; ii. 80; for that of James Lumsden of Airdrie at Crail, Beveridge, *Churchyard Memorials*, 132–50.
64. *Presbytery of Lanark*, 3–4, 8.
65. Binski, *Medieval Death*, 92–122; Boase, *Death in the Middle Ages*; Duffy, *Stripping of the Altars*, 299–376; Colvin, *Architecture and the After-Life*, 217–18; Llewellyn, *Art of Death*, 102–4, 106–21; Clarkson, *Death, Disease and Famine*, 163–5; Llewellyn, 'Honour in life, death and in the memory'; Cressy, 'Death and the social order', 112.
66. *HMC Twelfth Report*, 9; Moysie, *Memoirs*, 23; MacGibbon and Ross, *Ecclesiastical Architecture*, v. 203–5; *Archaelogia Scotica*, i. 102–5; Howard, *Scottish Architecture*, 206; Rogers, *Monuments and Monumental Inscriptions*, i. 99–116, 289. Typically the king neglected to pay the expenses of chancellor Montrose's funeral in 1608, Calderwood, *History*, vii. 38.
67. Donaldson, 'Dunbar monument'; MacGibbon and Ross, *Ecclesiastical Architecture*, v. 202–3; Hay, 'Scotland and the Italian Renaissance', 115; Colvin, *Architecture and the After-Life*, 298–9; Esdaile, *English Church Monuments*, 48–9; Howard, *Scottish Architecture*, 202–3.
68. Howard, *Scottish Architecture*, 206; Howard, 'The Kinnoull aisle and monument', 36–53.
69. Curl, *A Celebration of Death*, 119–20; and for others buried in England, Paul, *Scots Peerage*, i. 228, and Llewellyn, 'Honour in life, death and in the memory', 185–6.
70. Fraser, *Douglas*, ii. 406.
71. Paul, *Scots Peerage*, ii. 80; Fraser, *Douglas*, ii. 376, 622–8; and for sir William Bruce of Earlshall who lies in the chancel of Leuchars church, Rogers, *Monuments and Monumental Inscriptions*, ii. 113–14; Heal and Holmes, *Gentry in England and Wales*, 1.
72. Wilson, 'The Skelmorlie Aisle'; Bath, 'Painted ceilings, 1550–1650', 296–8; MacGibbon and Ross, *Ecclesiastical Architecture*, v. 193–200; Apted, *Painted Ceilings*, 21–3; Howard, *Scottish Architecture*, 203.
73. Rogers, *Monuments and Monumental Inscriptions*, ii. 43.
74. *House of Seytoun*, 209; for another example, Rogers, *Monuments and Monumental Architecture*, i. 103.
75. MacGibbon and Ross, *Ecclesiastical Architecture*, v. 206–7; Howard, *Scottish Architecture*, 205. Sir Duncan Campbell of Glenorchy placed a memorial plaque in the chapel erected above the grave of his chief's son who died in his foster care in 1618, NAS GD 112/39/28/5, 112/39/29/10.
76. *Chronicles of the Frasers*, 246; Paul, *Scots Peerage*, v. 530–1.
77. Fraser, *Annandale*, i. p. clxvii.
78. *Poems of William Drummond*, 230.
79. Colvin, *Architecture and the After-Life*, 253–82; Paul, *Scots Peerage*, i. 119; Fraser, *Philorth*, i. 165.
80. NAS GD 124/3/9; Cressy, 'Death and the social order', 111; Fraser, *Carlaverock*, i. 569; Fraser, *Douglas*, ii. 404, n. 3; *House of Seytoun*, 42; Spottiswoode, *History*, ii. 464–5; Paul, *Scots Peerage*, i. 47; Rogers, *Monuments and Monumental Inscriptions*, i. 384–5, 422–4; Fraser, *Elphinstone*, 146.
81. *Black Book of Taymouth*, 74; Dobie, 'The parish church of Kilbirnie'; MacGibbon and Ross, *Ecclesiastical Architecture*, v. 200–1; Rogers, *Monuments and Monumental Inscriptions*,

i. 22; Colvin, *Architecture and the After-Life*, 301. Colvin points out that the first mausoleum built in England was erected in 1656 by Thomas Bruce, first earl of Elgin, a Scot, ibid., 312–13. Craighall also built an aisle on to Cramond parish kirk, Hope, *Diary*, 27.

82. NRA(S) 3246/I Miscl. Docs 1538–1713/14; *RPC*, v. 658–9.
83. Colvin, *Architecture and the After-Life*, 283–326; *Chronicles of the Frasers*, 266–7; Fraser, *Sutherland*, ii. 339.
84. *RPC*, first ser., vii. 315–17; 337–8.
85. *CSP Scotland*, iii. 65–6; Ives, 'The bonny earl of Murray'; Olsen, 'The dreadful death of the earl of Murray', 281–310; Thomson, *Gaelic Poetry*, 107–9.
86. Kay, *Melodious Tears*; *Poems of William Drummond*, 295. Much of the poetry at Lady Jane Maitland's death dwelt on her youth and virginity, Maitland, *Funerall Sermon*. Rowallan also wrote epitaphs for noble ladies, *Works of Sir William Mure of Rowallan*, i. 33–4, 36–7; *Teares for the Death of Alexander Earle of Dunfermling*; NAS GD 224/903/12.

## Conclusion

1. Donaldson, *James V to James VII*, 300.

# Bibliography

## (i) Manuscript Sources


**National Archive of Scotland (NAS)**

| | | |
|---|---|---|
| CC | 8 | Edinburgh Commissary Court Records |
| CC | 9 | Glasgow Commissary Court Records |
| CC | 20 | St Andrews Commissary Court Records |
| CC | 21 | Stirling Commissary Court Records |
| GD | 4 | Benholm and Hedderwick Writs |
| GD | 6 | Biel Muniments |
| GD | 7 | Blebo Writs |
| GD | 8 | Boyd Papers |
| GD | 10 | Broughton and Cally Muniments |
| GD | 11 | Bruce of Kennet Charters |
| GD | 12 | Swinton Charters |
| GD | 15 | Cardross Writs |
| GD | 16 | Airlie Muniments |
| GD | 17 | Carnock and Plean Writs |
| GD | 19 | Closeburn Writs |
| GD | 20 | Crawford Priory Collection |
| GD | 21 | Cunninghame of Thorntoun Collection |
| GD | 24 | Abercairny Muniments |
| GD | 25 | Ailsa Muniments |
| GD | 26 | Leven and Melville Muniments |
| GD | 28 | Calendar of Yester Writs |
| GD | 29 | Kinross House Papers |
| GD | 30 | Shairp of Houstoun Muniments |
| GD | 32 | Elibank Muniments |
| GD | 34 | Hay of Haystoun Muniments |
| GD | 37 | Airth Writs |
| GD | 38 | Dalguise Muniments |
| GD | 39 | Glencairn Muniments |
| GD | 40 | Lothian Muniments |
| GD | 42 | Dunecht Writs |
| GD | 45 | Dalhousie Muniments |
| GD | 47 | Ross Estate Muniments |
| GD | 49 | Barclay Allardice Papers |
| GD | 52 | Lord Forbes Collection |
| GD | 59 | Inventory of Wilkie of Foulden Muniments |
| GD | 60 | Inventory of Fergusson Kennedy, Bennan and Finnart Muniments |
| GD | 63 | Inventory of Bell-Brandel Muniments |
| GD | 65 | Inventory of Carlops and Abbotskerse Muniments |
| GD | 66 | Inventory of Boswell of Balmuto Muniments |

| | | |
|---|---|---|
| GD | 67 | Gordon of Cairness Muniments |
| GD | 75 | Inventory of Dundas of Dundas Papers |
| GD | 77 | Fergusson of Craigdarroch MSS |
| GD | 84 | Reay Muniments |
| GD | 86 | Fraser Charters |
| GD | 94 | Writs of Lordship of Urquhart |
| GD | 96 | Inventory of Mey Papers |
| GD | 112 | Breadalbane Muniments |
| GD | 122 | Little Gilmour of Craigmillar and Liberton |
| GD | 124 | Mar and Kellie Muniments |
| GD | 137 | Scrymgeour Wedderburn of Wedderburn Earl of Dundee |
| GD | 150 | Morton Papers |
| GD | 158 | Hume of Marchmont |
| GD | 224 | Buccleuch Muniments |
| GD | 406 | Hamilton Muniments (Correspondence) |

**National Register of Archives (Scotland) (NRA(S))**

| | |
|---|---|
| 5 | Arbuthnott Muniments |
| 217 | Moray MSS |
| 217 | Lord Gray's Papers |
| 234 | Atholl, Duke of |
| 237 | Inventory of the Scottish Muniments at Haigh |
| 239 | Catalogue of Dunrobin Muniments |
| 581 | Earl of Annandale |
| 885 | Charters and Documents From Glamis Dated 1329–1668 |
| 2177 | Duke of Hamilton |
| 2312 | Stirling-Maxwell of Pollok |
| 2570 | Craigstoun Castle Muniments |
| 2847 | Burnett of Leys Muniments |
| 3246 | Dundas of Arniston |
| 3438 | Duke of Hamilton |

**National Library of Scotland (NLS)**

| | |
|---|---|
| MS 75, 78–84 | Morton Chartulary and Papers. Vols 3, 6–12 |
| MS 175 | Gordon Cumming of Altyre |
| MS 963 | Commonplace Book of the Earl of Buchan, c.1778–91 |
| MS 973 | Douglas Papers |
| MS 976 | Campbell Papers |
| MS 2200/1–58 | Household Accounts of the Tenth Earl of Angus |
| MS 3138 | Argyll Papers |
| MS 3416 | Mure of Rowallan |
| MS 3717 | Seton Armorial |
| MS 3724 | Court Book of the Barony of Calder |
| MS 5070, 5100, 5103, 5127, 5155, 5158 | Erskine Murray Papers |
| MS 5448 | Nisbet Papers |
| MS 5775, 5785–7, 5818, 5828–30 | Newbattle Collection |
| MS 6402 | Scottish Armorial |
| MS 6406 | Pitfarrane Papers |
| MS 7102 | Yester Papers |
| MS 7114 | Genealogy of the Illustrious Hamiltons |
| MS 9449 | Lady Jean Campbell's Music Book |
| MS 13 500/13 | c.1637, Lord Lorne to Goodman of Erlestone |

| | |
|---|---|
| MS 14 401–4, 14 466, 14 475–8, 14 539–41, 14 479–80, 14 539–43, 14 549, 14 618–19, 14 745, 14 761–2 | Yester Papers |
| MS 16 000 | Album Amicorum of Sir Michael Balfour |
| MS 16 501, 16 760–1 | Saltoun Papers |
| MS 20 001 | Lennox Charters (copies) |
| MS 20 498 | Esther Inglis 'Livres' |
| MS 20 772, 20 774, 20 777–9, 20 781A, 20 793–5 | Fleming of Wigton |
| MS 21 174, 21 176, 21 178, 21 183, 21 187A | Murray of Auchertyre |
| Ch. 10 723–35, 10 747–77, 10 778, 10 780, 11 032–55 | Yester Charters |
| MS 15/2/14, 15/2/18, 15/2/31, 17/2/4, 22/3/14, 25/2/2, 33/2/11, 33/2/28, 33/2/38–41, 33/7/5, 33/7/21, 33/7/26, 34/1/6, 34/3/16, 34/3/18, 34/4/16, 34/6/18, 34/6/23, 35/5/5A | Advocates Library |

**British Library (BL)**

Add MSS 5755/60, 12 496/41, 12 497/153, 36 767/236, 36 767/240, 38 170/87b, 38 170/142, 38 170/258

Eg. 2597/32

Ro. 10b, xiii

Ro. 17c, xxxiv

Hl 1583/25

Hl 7623/9


## (ii) Printed Sources

**Abbreviations for Historical Associations, Clubs and Societies (publication)**

| | |
|---|---|
| AC | Abbotsford Club (Edinburgh) |
| AWAA | Ayrshire and Wigtonshire Archaeological Association (Edinburgh) |
| BC | Bannatyne Club (Edinburgh) |
| GC | Grampian Club (London) |
| MC | Maitland Club (Glasgow) |
| SC | Spalding Club (Aberdeen) |
| SHS | Scottish History Society (Edinburgh) |
| SpS | Spottiswoode Society (Edinburgh) |
| StS | Stair Society (Edinburgh) |

STS Scottish Text Society (Edinburgh)
WS Wodrow Society (Edinburgh)

[*Abbotsford Miscellany*] *Miscellany of the Abbotsford Club*, ed. J. Maidment (AC 11, 1837).

[Abernethy, *Christian and Heavenly Treatise*] *A Christian and Heavenly Treatise Containing Physicke for the Soule*, M. I. Abernethy (London, 1630).

*Adversaria. Notices Illustrative of the Earlier Works Printed for the Bannatyne Club*, ed. D. Laing (BC 115, 1867).

*Ancient Scottish Melodies, from a Manuscript of the Reign of James VI*, ed. W. Dauney (MC 43, 1838).

[*Ancram and Lothian*] *Correspondence of Sir Robert Kerr, first Earl of Ancram, and his son, William, third Earl of Lothian*, ed. D. Laing (2 vols, BC 125, 1875).

[*APS*] *Acts of the Parliaments of Scotland*, ed. T. Thomson and C. Innes (12 vols, Edinburgh, 1844–75).

[Bacon, *Essayes*] *Sir Francis Bacon. The Essayes or Counsel, Civill and Morall*, F. Bacon, ed. M. Kiernan (Oxford, 1985).

[Baillie, *Letters and Journals*] *Letters and Journals of Robert Baillie*, R. Baillie, ed. D. Laing (3 vols, BC 73, 1841–2).

[Balfour, *Works*] *Historical Works of Sir James Balfour*, J. Balfour, ed. J. Haig (4 vols, Edinburgh, 1825).

[Bannatyne, *Memorials*] *Memorials of Transactions in Scotland. AD MDLXIX–MDLXXIII*, R. Bannatyne, ed. R. Pitcairn (BC 51, 1836).

*Bannatyne Miscellany* (3 vols, BC 19, 1827, 1836, 1855).

[*Barony of Urie*] *Court Book of the Barony of Urie in Kincardineshire 1604–1747*, ed. D. G. Barron (SHS, first ser., 12, 1892).

[Birnie, *Blame of Kirk Burial*] *Blame of Kirk Burial, Tending to Perswade Cemeteriall Civilitie*, W. Birnie (Edinburgh, 1606).

*Black Book of Taymouth*, ed. C. Innes (Edinburgh, 1855).

*Book of Dunvegan*, ed. R. C. MacLeod (2 vols, Third SC, 1938–9).

[Boyd, *Last Batell*] *The Last Batell of the Soule in Death*, Z. Boyd (Edinburgh, 1628).

[Bruce, *Sermons*] *Sermons by the Rev Robert Bruce*, R. Bruce, ed. W. Cunningham (WS 6, 1843).

*Buik of the Most Noble and Vailzeand Conquerour Alexander the Great*, ed. D. Laing (BC 46, 1831).

[*BUK*] *Booke of the Universall Kirk of Scotland: Acts and Proceedings of the General Assemblies of the Kirk of Scotland from the Year MDLX*, ed. T. Thomson (4 vols, BC 81 and MC 49, 1894–6).

[Calderwood, *History*] *History of the Kirk of Scotland*, D. Calderwood (8 vols, WS 7, 1842–9).

[Caldwell, *Countess of Mar's Arcadia*] *Countess of Mar's Arcadia*, J. Caldwell (Edinburgh, 1625).

[Campbell, *Treatise upon Death*] *Treatise upon Death*, N. Campbell (Glasgow, 1630).

[*Charters of Ayr*] *Charters of the Royal Burgh of Ayr*, ed. W. S. Cooper (AWAA, 1883).

*Chronicle of Perth. A Register of Remarkable Occurrences, Chiefly Connected with that City, from the Year 1210 to 1668* (MC 10, 1831).

*Chronicle of the Kings of Scotland, from Fergus the First to James the Sixth* (MC 8, 1830).

*Chronicles of the Frasers*, J. Fraser (SHS, first ser., 47, 1905).

*Confession and Conversion of My Lady, C of L* (Edinburgh, 1924).

[Craig, *Jus Feudale*] *Jus Feudale*, T. Craig, translated by J. A. Clyde (2 vols, Edinburgh, 1934).

[*CSP Scotland*] *Calendar of State Papers Relating to Scotland and Mary, Queen of Scots, 1547–1603*, ed. J. Bain, W. K. Boyd and A. I. Cameron (13 vols, Edinburgh, 1898–1969).

[Dalrymple, *Institutions*] *Institutions of the Law of Scotland*, J. Dalrymple, viscount Stair, ed. D. M. Walker (Edinburgh and Glasgow, 1981).

[Davidson, *Dialogue*] *Dialogue Betwixt a Clerk and a Courteour. Concerning the State of the Parish Kirks in Scotland*, J. Davidson (Edinburgh, 1829).

[*Early Travellers*] *Early Travellers in Scotland*, ed. P. H. Brown (Edinburgh, reprinted, 1973).

*Estimate of the Scottish Nobility during the Minority of James VI*, ed. C. Rogers (GC 6, 1873).

[*Familia Humia Wedderburnensi*] *Davidis Humii de Familia Humia Wedderburnensi liber*, D. Hume, presented by J. Miller (AC 15, 1839).

[*Familie of Innes*] *Account of the Familie of Innes, compiled by Duncan Forbes of Culloden, 1698*, ed. C. Innes (SC 34, 1864).

[*Family of Kilravock*] *Genealogical Deduction of the Family of Rose of Kilravock*, ed. C. Innes (SC, 1848).

*First Book of Discipline*, ed. J. K. Cameron (Edinburgh, 1972).

*Formulary of Old Scots Legal Documents*, ed. P. Gouldesbrough (StS 36, 1985).

[Fraser, *Annandale*] *Annandale Family Book of Johnstones*, W. Fraser (2 vols, Edinburgh, 1894).

[Fraser, *Buccleuch*] *Scotts of Buccleuch*, W. Fraser (2 vols, Edinburgh, 1878).

[Fraser, *Carlaverock*] *Book of Carlaverock*, W. Fraser (2 vols, Edinburgh, 1873).

[Fraser, *Chiefs of Grant*] *Chiefs of Grant*, W. Fraser (3 vols, Edinburgh, 1883).

[Fraser, *Douglas*] *Douglas Book. Memoirs of the House of Douglas and Angus*, W. Fraser (4 vols, Edinburgh, 1885).

[Fraser, *Eglinton*] *Memorials of the Montgomeries of Eglinton*, W. Fraser (2 vols, Edinburgh, 1859).

[Fraser, *Elphinstone*] *Elphinstone Family Book*, W. Fraser (2 vols, Edinburgh, 1897).

[Fraser, *Haddington*] *Memorials of the Earls of Haddington*, W. Fraser (2 vols, Edinburgh, 1883).

[Fraser, *Maxwells of Pollok*] *Memoirs of the Maxwells of Pollok*, W. Fraser (2 vols, Edinburgh, 1863).

[Fraser, *Melvilles*] *Melvilles Earls of Melville and the Leslies Earls of Leven*, W. Fraser (3 vols, Edinburgh, 1890).

[Fraser, *Menteith*] *Red Book of Menteith*, W. Fraser (2 vols, Edinburgh, 1880).

[Fraser, *Philorth*] *Frasers of Philorth*, W. Fraser (3 vols, Edinburgh, 1879).

[Fraser, *Sutherland*] *Sutherland Book*, W. Fraser (3 vols, Edinburgh, 1892).

*Funeral of a Right Reverend Father in God Patrick Forbes* (Aberdeen, 1635).

*Funeral Sermons*, ed. C. F. Shand (SpS 5, 1845).

*Garden of Grave and Godlie Flowers, by Alexander Gardyne*, ed. W. B. D. D. Turnbull (AC 36, 1845).

[Gordon, *Short Abridgement of Britane's Distemper*] *Short Abridgement of Britane's Distemper from the Year of God MDCXXXIX to MDXLIX*, P. Gordon (SC 10, 1844).

[Gordon, *Sutherland*] *Genealogical History of the Earldom of Sutherland*, R. Gordon (Edinburgh, 1813).

[Hay, *Lectures*] *William Hay's Lectures on Marriage*, W. Hay, ed. J. C. Barry (StS 24, 1967).

[Herries, *Memoirs*] *Historical Memoirs of the Reign of Mary Queen of Scots and a Portion of the Reign of King James the Sixth*, J. Maxwell, ed. R. Pitcairn (AC 6, 1836).

*Historical Account of the Principal Families of Kennedy*, ed. R. Pitcairn (Edinburgh, 1830).

[*Historie*] *Historie and Life of King James the Sext*, ed. T. Thomson (BC 14, 1825).

[*HMC*] *Historical Manuscripts Commission* (15 vols, London, 1871–97).

[*HMC Buccleuch*] *Historical Manuscripts Commission: Buccleuch* (3 vols, London, 1899, 1903, 1926).

[*HMC Laing*] *Historical Manuscripts Commission. Report on the Laing Manuscripts*, i. (London, 1914).

[*HMC Mar and Kellie*] *Historical Manuscripts Commission: Mar and Kellie* (2 vols, London, 1904, 1930).

[HMC Various] *Historical Manuscripts Commission. Various Collections V* (London, 1909).

[*Honoris de Morton*] *Registrum Honoris de Morton*, ed. T. Thomson (2 vols, BC 94, 1853).

[Hope, *Diary*] *Diary of the Public Correspondence of Sir Thomas Hope of Craighall, bart., 1633–1645*, T. Hope, ed. T. Thomson (BC 76, 1843).

[Hope, *Major Practicks*] *Hope's Major Practicks, 1608–33*, T. Hope, ed. J. A. Clyde (2 vols, StS 3–4, 1937–8).

*House of Forbes*, eds A. Tayler and H. Tayler (Third SC 8, 1937).

*House of Gordon*, ed. J. M. Bulloch (2 vols, New SC, 1903, 1907).

[*House of Seytoun*] *History of the House of Seytoun to the Year MDLIX. By Sir Richard Maitland of Lethington, Knight. With the Continuation, by Alexander Viscount Kingston, to MDCLXXXVII*, R. Maitland, ed. J. Fullarton (MC 1, 1829).

[Hume, *General History*] *General History of Scotland from the Year 767 to the Death of King James*, D. Hume (London, 1657).

[Hume, *House of Douglas*] *David Hume of Godscroft's The History of the House of Douglas*, D. Hume, ed. D. Reid (2 vols, STS fourth ser., 25–6, Edinburgh, 1996).

[Hume, *Hymns*] *Hymns and Sacred Songs*, A. Hume, presented by J. G. Kinnear (BC 41, 1832).

[Hyde, *History*] *History of the Rebellion*, E. Hyde (6 vols, Oxford, 1888).

*Inquisitionum ad Capellam Domini Regis Retornatarum Quae in Publicis Archivis Scotiae Adhuc Servantur Abbreviato* (3 vols, Edinburgh, 1811).

*John Knox. On Rebellion*, ed. R. Mason (Cambridge, 1994).

[Kellie, *Pallas Armata*] *Pallas Armata or Military Instructions for the Learned*, T. Kellie (Edinburgh, 1627).

[*Kennedy*] *Historical and Genealogical Account of the Principal Families of the Name of Kennedy*, ed. R. Pitcairn (Edinburgh, 1830).

[Knox, *Works*] *Works of John Knox*, J. Knox, ed. D. Laing (6 vols, WS 12, 1846–52).

[Leslie, *Historie*] *Historie of Scotland*, J. Leslie, ed. E. J. Cody (2 vols, STS, 1888–95).

*Letters and State Papers during the Reign of King James the Sixth*, ed. J. Maidment (AC 13, 1838).

[*Library of Sir Robert Gordon*] *Catalogue of the Singular and Curious Library of Sir Robert Gordon of Gordonstoun* (London, 1816).

[Lindsay, *Godly Man's Journey*] *Godly Man's Journey to Heaven*, D. Lindsay (London, 1625).

[Lindsay, *Historie*] *Historie and Cronicles of Scotland*, R. Lindsay, ed. A. J. G. Mackay (3 vols, STS, 1899–1911).

[Maitland, *Funeral Sermon*] *Funeral Sermon Preached at the Buriall of the Lady Jane Maitland*, J. Maitland (Edinburgh, 1633).

[*Maitland Miscellany*] *Miscellany of the Maitland Club*, eds J. Dennistoun and A. Macdonald (4 vols, vol. i in two parts, MC 25–6, 53, 59, 69, 1840–7).

*Maitland Quarto Manuscript*, ed. W. A. Craigie (STS, new ser., 3, 1920).

[*Melrose Papers*] *State Papers and Miscellaneous Correspondence of Thomas, Earl of Melrose*, ed. J. Maidment (2 vols, AC 9, 1837).

[*Melrose Regality Records*] *Selections from the Records of the Regality of Melrose, 1605–1661*, ed. C. S. Romanes (3 vols, SHS, second ser., 6–7, 13, 1914–15, 1917).

[Melville, *Diary*] *Diary of Mr James Melvill, 1556–1601*, J. Melville, ed. J. R. Kinloch (BC 34, 1829).

[Melville, *Memoirs*] *Memoirs of His Own Life, 1549–93*, J. Melville, ed. T. Thomson (BC 18, 1827).

*Memorials of Montrose and his Times*, ed. M. Napier (2 vols, MC 66, 1848–50)

*Miscellany of the Scottish History Society. Volume I* (SHS, first ser., 15, 1893).

*Miscellany of the Scottish History Society. Volume II* (SHS, first ser., 44, 1904).

*Miseries of Enforced Marriages*, G. Wilkins (Malone Society Reprints, 1963).

[Monipenny, *Certeine Matters Concerning the Realm of Scotland*] *Certeine Matters Concerning the Realme of Scotland*, J. Monipenny (London, 1603).

*Moral Fables of Robert Henryson. Reprinted from the Edition of Andrew Hart*, R. Henryson (MC 15, 1832).

[Moryson, *Itinerary Written*] *An Itinerary Written*, F. Moryson (London, 1617).

[Moysie, *Memoirs*] *Memoirs of the Affairs of Scotland from 1577 to 1603*, D. Moysie, ed. J. Dennistoun (BC 39, 1830).

[Murray, *Short Treatise*] *Short Treatise of Death*, W. Murray (Edinburgh, 1631).

[Napier, *Arte Logistica*] *De Arte Logistica Joannis Naperi Merchistonii Baronis, Libri Qui Supersunt*, J. Napier, ed. M. Napier (BC 62, 1839).

[Napier, *Plaine Discovery*] *Plaine Discovery of the Whole Revelation*, J. Napier (Edinburgh, 1593).

*New Poems by James I of England*, J. Stewart, ed. A. F. Westcott (New York, 1911).

[Nisbet, *System of Heraldry*] *System of Heraldry, Speculative and Practical*, A. Nisbet (2 vols, Edinburgh, 1984 [1722]).

*Oppressions of the Sixteenth Century in the Islands of Orkney and Zetland*, ed. D. Balfour (AC 31, 1859).

*Palice of Honour. By Gawyn Douglas, Bishop of Dunkeld*, G. Douglas, ed. J. G. Kinnear (BC 17, 1827).

*Philotus: a Comedy. Reprinted from the Edition of Robert Charteris*, presented by J. W. Mackenzie (BC 50, 1835).

[Pitcairn, *Criminal Trials*] *Criminal Trials in Scotland from 1488 to 1624*, ed. R. Pitcairn (3 vols, Edinburgh, 1833).

*Poems of Alexander Hume (?1577–1609)*, A. Hume (STS, old ser., 48, 1902).

*Poems of Alexander Montgomerie*, A. Montgomery, ed. J. Cranstoun (2 vols, STS 9, 59, 1887, 1910).

*Poems of James VI of Scotland*, J. Stewart, ed. J. Craigie (STS, new ser., 22, 26, 1955, 1958)

*Poems of Sir David Murray of Gothry*, D. Murray, presented by T. Kinnear (BC 22, 1823).

*Poems of Sir Richard Maitland*, R. Maitland, ed. J. Bain (MC 4, 1830).

*Poems of William Drummond of Hawthornden*, W. Drummond, ed. T. Maitland (MC 18, 1832).

*Poetical Remains of William Lithgow*, W. Lithgow, ed. J. Maidment (Edinburgh, 1863).

*Poetical Works of William Drummond of Hawthornden*, W. Drummond (2 vols, STS, new ser., 3–4, 1913).

*Political Works of James I*, J. Stewart, ed. C. H. McIlwaine (New York, 1965).

[*Political Writings*] *King James VI and I Political Writings*, J. Stewart, ed. J. P. Sommerville (Cambridge, 1994).

[Pont, *Topographical Account*] *Topographical Account of the District of Cunningham, Ayrshire. Compiled about the Year 1600, by Mr Timothy Pont*, T. Pont (MC 76, 1858).

[*Presbytery of Lanark*] *Ecclesiastical Records. Selections from the Registers of the Presbytery of Lanark, MDCXXIII–MDCCIX*, presented by J. Robertson (AC 16, 1839).

*Regiam Majestatem and Quoniam Attachiamenta*, ed. T. M. Cooper (StS 11, 1947).

*Registrum de Panmure*, J. Stuart (2 vols, Edinburgh, 1874).

[*RMSRS*] *Registrum Magni Sigilli Regum Scotorum*, eds J. M. Thomson, J. B. Paul, J. H. Stevenson and W. K. Dickson (8 vols, Edinburgh, 1882–1914).

[Rolland, *Seven Sages*] *Seven Sages, in Scottish Metre*, R. Rolland, ed. D. Laing (BC 57, 1837).

[Row, *History*] *History of the Kirk of Scotland*, J. Row, ed. D. Laing (WS 4, 1842).

[*RPC*] *Register of the Privy Council of Scotland*, first ser., eds J. H. Burton and D. Masson (14 vols, Edinburgh, 1877–98).

[*RPC*] *Register of the Privy Council of Scotland*, second ser., ed. P. H. Brown (8 vols, Edinburgh, 1899–1908).

[*RSSRS*] *Registrum Secreti Sigilli Regum Scotorum*, eds M. Livingstone, D. H. Fleming and J. Beveridge (Edinburgh, 1908– )

[Scott, *Staggering State*] *Staggering State of Scottish Statesmen from 1550–1650*, J. Scott, ed. C. Rogers (Edinburgh, 1872).

*Second Book of Discipline*, ed. J. Kirk (Edinburgh, 1980).

*Select Biographies*, ed. W. K. Tweedie (2 vols, WS 9, 1845–7).

*Selected Justiciary Cases, 1624–1650*, eds A. Gillon and J. I. Brown (3 vols, StS, 16, 27–8, 1953, 1972, 1974).

[*Sheriffdoms of Lanark and Renfrew*] *Descriptions of the Sheriffdoms of Lanark and Renfrew Compiled about MDCCX*, ed. J. Maidment (MC 12, 1831).

[Spalding, *Memorial*] *Memorial of the Troubles in Scotland and in England. AD 1624–AD 1645. By John Spalding*, J. Spalding, ed. J. Stuart (2 vols, SC 21, 23, 1850–1).

[*Spalding Miscellany*] *Miscellany of the Spalding Club*, ed. J. Stuart (5 vols, SC 3, 6, 16, 20, 24, 1841–52).

[Spottiswoode, *History*] *History of the Church of Scotland*, J. Spottiswoode, eds M. Napier and M. Russell (3 vols, SpS 6, 1847–51).

*Spottiswoode Miscellany*, ed. J. Maidment (2 vols, SpS 3–4, 1844–5).

*Stirling Presbytery Records, 1581–1587*, ed. J. Kirk (Edinburgh, 1981).

[*Synod of Fife*] *Ecclesiastical Records. Selections from the Minutes of the Synod of Fife, MDCXI–MDCLXXXVII*, ed. G. R. Kinloch (AC 8, 1837).

*Teares for the Death of Alexander Earle of Dunfermling*, presented by J. Maidment (BC 4, 1823).

[Urquhart, *Jewel*] *The Jewel*, T. Urquhart, eds R. D. S. Jack and R.J. Lyall (Edinburgh, 1983).

[Waus, *Correspondence*] *Correspondence of Sir Patrick Waus*, ed. R. Vans Agnew (2 vols, Edinburgh, 1887).

[Wemyss, *Workes*] *Workes of Mr John Weemse*, J. Wemyss (3 vols, London, 1633).

*William Drummond of Hawthornden. Poems and Prose*, W. Drummond, ed. R. H. MacDonald (Edinburgh, 1976).

[Wodrow, *Miscellany*] *Miscellany of the Wodrow Society*, ed. D. Laing (WS 11, 1844).

*Works of Sir Thomas Urquhart of Cromarty*, T. Urquhart, ed. T. Maitland (MC 30, 1834).

[*Works of Sir William Alexander*] *Poetical Works of Sir William Alexander Earl of Stirling*, W. Alexander, eds L. E. Kastner and H. B. Charlton (STS, new ser., 11 and 21, 1921, 1929).

*Works of Sir William Mure of Rowallan*, W. Mure, ed. W. Tough (2 vols, STS 40–1, 1897–8).

*Works of William Fowler*, W. Fowler, ed. H. W. Meikle (3 vols, STS, new ser., 6–7, 13, 1914, 1936, 1940).

## (iii) Secondary Works: Books

Adair, R., *Courtship, Illegitimacy and Marriage in Early Modern England* (Manchester, 1996).

Adams, W. H., *The French Garden 1500–1800* (London, 1979).

Alexander, M. C, *The Growth of English Education 1348–1648. A Social and Cultural History* (Pennsylvania, 1990).

Amelang, J. S., *Honored Citizens of Barcelona. Patrician Culture and Class Relations 1490–1714* (Princeton, 1986).

Anderson, B. S. and J. P. Zinsser, *A History of Their Own. Women in Europe from Prehistory to the Present. Volume I* (New York, 1988).

Anderson, P. D., *Robert Stewart Earl of Orkney Lord of Shetland 1533–1593* (Edinburgh, 1983).

Anderson, P. D., *Black Patie. The Life and Times of Patrick Stewart Earl of Orkney, Lord of Shetland* (Edinburgh, 1992).

Apted, M. R., *The Painted Ceilings of Scotland 1550–1650* (Edinburgh, 1966).

*Archaelogia Scotica: or Transactions of the Society of Antiquaries of Scotland* (5 vols, Edinburgh, 1792–1890).

Aries, P., *Centuries of Childhood. A Social History of Family Life* (London, 1962).

Aries, P., *Western Attitudes to Death from the Middle Ages to the Present* (Baltimore and London, 1983).

Aries, P., *The Hour of Our Death* (Harmondsworth, 1983).

Aries, P., *Images of Man and Death* (Cambridge, MA and London, 1985).

Armitage, J., *Men at Play. Nine Centuries of Pleasure Making* (London, 1977).

Ashton, R., *The City and the Court 1603–1643* (Cambridge, 1979).

Astarita, T., *The Continuity of Feudal Power: the Caracciolo di Brienza in Spanish Naples* (Cambridge, 1992).

Aylmer, G. E., *The King's Servants. The Civil Service of Charles I, 1625–1642* (London, 1974).

Aylmer, G. E. and J. Morrill eds, *Land, Men and Beliefs. Studies in Early-Modern History* (London, 1983).

Babb, L., *The Elizabethan Malady. A Study of Melancholia in English Literature from 1580 to 1642* (East Lansing, 1965).

Banac, I. and P. Bushkovitch eds, *The Nobility in Russia and Eastern Europe* (Columbus, 1983).

Banker, J. R., *Death in the Community. Memorialisation and Confraternities in the Italian Commune in the Late Medieval Ages* (Athens and London, 1988).

Bardgett, F., *Scotland Reformed. The Reformation in Angus and the Mearns* (Edinburgh, 1989).

Barrow, G. W. S., *Anglo-Norman Era in Scottish History* (Oxford, 1980).

Beik, W., *Absolutism and Society in Seventeenth-Century France: State Power and Provincial Aristocracy in Languedoc* (Cambridge, 1988).

Bell, I., *Elizabethan Women and the Poetry of Courtship* (Cambridge, 1998).

Benadusi, G., *A Provincial Elite in Early Modern Tuscany. Family and Power in the Creation of the State* (Baltimore and London, 1996).

Bernard, G. W., *The Power of the Early Tudor Nobility. A Study of the Fourth and Fifth Earls of Shrewsbury* (Brighton, 1985).

Bernard, G. W., *The Tudor Nobility* (Manchester and New York, 1992).

Beveridge, E., *The Churchyard Memorials of Crail* (Edinburgh, 1893).

Binski, P., *Medieval Death. Ritual and Representation* (London, 1996).

Bitton, D., *The French Nobility in Crisis 1560–1640* (Stanford, 1969).

Boase, T. S. R., *Death in the Middle Ages. Mortality, Judgement and Remembrance* (London, 1972).

Bohanan, D., *Old and New Nobility in Aix-en-Provence 1600–1675* (Baton Rouge, LA, 1992).

Bonfield, L., *Marriage Settlements, 1601–1740* (Cambridge, 1983).

Bonney, R., *The European Dynastic States 1494–1660* (Oxford, 1992).

Bossy, J., *The English Catholic Community, 1570–1850* (London, 1975).

Brockliss, L. W. B., *French Higher Education in the Seventeenth and Eighteenth Centuries* (Oxford, 1987).

Brooke, C., *The Medieval Idea of Marriage* (Oxford, 1989).

Brown, J., *The Art and Architecture of English Gardens* (London, 1989).

Brown, K. M., *Bloodfeud in Scotland, 1573–1625: Violence, Justice and Politics in an Early Modern Society* (Edinburgh, 1986).

Burgess, R., *Perpetuities in Scots Law* (Stair Society 31, 1979).

Burke, P., *Venice and Amsterdam. A Study of Seventeenth-Century Elites* (Cambridge, 1994).

Bush, M. L., *The European Nobility Vol. 1. Noble Privilege* (Manchester, 1983).

Bush, M. L., *Rich Noble, Poor Noble* (Manchester, 1988).

Bush, M. L. ed., *Social Orders and Social Classes in Europe since 1500: Studies in Social Stratification* (Harlow, 1992).

Bushnell, R. W., *A Culture of Teaching. Early Modern Humanism in Theory and Practice* (Ithaca and London, 1996).

Callender, F., *A Pattern of Landownership in Scotland* (Finzean, 1987).

Cant, R. G., *The University of St Andrews* (Edinburgh, 1946).

Cant, R. G., *The College of St Salvator* (Edinburgh, 1950).

Carlson, E. J., *Marriage and the English Reformation* (Oxford, 1994).

Carter, J. J. and C. A. McLaren, *Crown and Gown 1495–1995* (Aberdeen, 1994).

Carter, J. M., *Medieval Games. Sport and Recreation in Feudal Society* (New York, 1992).

Caw, J. L., *Scottish painting. Past and Present, 1620–1908* (Chippenham, 1908, reprinted 1990).

Charlesworth, M. ed., *The English Garden. Volume 1 Chronological Overview: 1550–1730* (Mountfield, 1993).

Clark, S., *State and Status. The Rise of the State and Aristocratic Power in Western Europe* (McGill, 1995).

Clarkson, L., *Death, Disease and Famine in Pre-Industrial England* (Dublin, 1975).

Cliffe, J. T., *The Yorkshire Gentry from the Reformation to the Civil War* (London, 1969).

Cliffe, J. T., *The Puritan Gentry: the Great Puritan Families of Early Stuart England* (London, 1984).

Colvin, H., *Architecture and the After-Life* (New Haven and London, 1991).

Corfield, P. J. ed., *Language, History and Class* (Oxford, 1991).

Coss, P., *The Lady in Medieval England 1000–1500* (Stroud, 1998).

Couts, J., *A History of the University of Glasgow from the Foundation in 1451 to 1909* (Glasgow, 1909).

Cowan, I. B., *The Scottish Reformation. Church and Society in Sixteenth-Century Scotland* (London, 1982).

Cowan, I. B. and D. E. Easson eds, *Medieval Religious Houses, Scotland* (London, 1976).

Cowan, I. B. and D. Shaw eds, *The Renaissance and Reformation in Scotland* (Edinburgh, 1983).

Coward, B., *The Stanleys Lords Stanley and Earls of Derby 1385–1672. The Origins, Wealth and Power of a Landowning Family* (Chetham Society, third ser., xxx. Manchester, 1983).

Crawford, P., *Women and Religion in England 1500–1720* (London, 1993).

Cressy, D., *Birth, Marriage and Death. Ritual, Religion, and the Life-Cycle in Tudor and Stuart England* (Oxford, 1997).

Cross, C., *The Puritan Earl. The Life of Henry Hastings, Third Earl of Huntingdon, 1536–1595* (London, 1966).

Cruden, S., *The Scottish Castle* (Edinburgh, 1960).

Cunningham, H., *Children and Childhood in Western Society since 1500* (London, 1995).

Curl, J. S., *A Celebration of Death* (London, 1980).

Cursiter, S., *Scottish Art to the Close of the Nineteenth Century* (London, 1948).

D'Avray, D. L., *Death and the Prince. Memorial Preaching before 1350* (Oxford, 1994).

Dalrymple, J., *An Essay Towards a General History of Feudal Property in Great Britain* (London, 1757).

Dawson, G. E. and L. Kennedy-Skipton, *Elizabethan Handwriting, 1500–1650* (Chichester, 1968).

De Mause, L. ed., *The History of Childhood* (London, 1976).

De Ridder-Symoens, H. ed., *A History of the University in Europe. Volume II. Universities in Early Modern Europe* (Edinburgh, 1996).

Dean, T. and K. Lowe eds, *Marriage in Italy, 1300–1650* (London, 1998).

Debus, A. G., *Man and Nature in the Renaissance* (Cambridge, 1978).

Debus, A. G., *Chemistry, Alchemy and the New Philosophy* (New York, 1995).

Dewald, J., *The Formation of a Provincial Nobility: the Magistrates of the Parlement of Rouen, 1499–1610* (Princeton, 1980).

Dewald, J., *Pont-St-Pierre, 1398–1789: Lordship, Community and Capitalism in Early Modern France* (Berkeley, 1987).

Dewald, J., *Aristocratic Experience and the Origins of Modern Culture. France, 1570–1715* (Berkeley, 1993).

Dewald, J., *The European Nobility 1400–1800* (Cambridge, 1996).

Dodgshon, R. A., *Land and Society in Early Scotland* (Oxford, 1981).

Dodgshon, R. A., *From Chiefs to Landlords. Social and Economic Change in the Western Highlands and Islands, c.1493–1820* (Edinburgh, 1998).

Donaldson, G., *Scotland. James V to James VII* (Edinburgh, 1965).

Duffy, S., *The Stripping of the Altars. Traditional Religion in England c.1400–c.1580* (Yale, 1992).

Dunbar, J. G., *The Historic Architecture of Scotland* (London, 1966).

Dupâquier, J., E. Hélin and P. Laslett eds, *Marriage and Remarriage in Populations of the Past* (London, 1981).

Durkan, J. and J. Kirk, *The University of Glasgow, 1451–1577* (Glasgow, 1977).

Durkan, J. and A. Ross, *Early Scottish Libraries* (Glasgow, 1961).

Eales, J., *Women in Early Modern England 1500–1700* (London, 1998).

Eales, R., *Chess. The History of a Game* (London, 1985).

Edington, C., *Court and Culture in Renaissance Scotland. Sir David Lindsay of the Mount* (Amerherst USA and East Linton, 1994).

Eire, C. M. N., *From Madrid to Purgatory. The Art and Craft of Dying in Sixteenth-Century Spain* (Cambridge, 1995).

Engel, W. E., *Mapping Mortality. The Persistence of Memory and Melancholy in Early Modern England* (University of Massachusetts, 1995).

Erickson, A. L., *Women and Property in Early Modern England* (London, 1993).

Esdaile, K. A., *English Church Monuments 1510–1840* (London, 1946).

Esler, M. and M. Kowalski eds, *Women and Power in the Middle Ages* (Athens and London, 1988).

Eurich, S. A., *The Economics of Power: the Private finances of the House of Foix-Navarre-Albret during the Religious Wars* (Kirksville, Missouri, 1994).

Farmer, G., *A History of Music in Scotland* (London, 1947).

Fenwick, H., *Scottish Baronial Houses* (London, 1896).

Ferguson, A. B., *The Chivalric Tradition in Renaissance England* (Cranbury, 1986).

Flandrin, J. L., *Families in Former Times: Kinship, Household and Sexuality* (Cambridge, 1979).

Fleming, L. and A. Gore, *The English Garden* (London, 1979).

Fletcher, A., *Gender, Sex and Subordination in England 1500–1800* (New Haven and London, 1995).

Fogle, F. R., *A Critical Study of William Drummond of Hawthornden* (New York, 1952).

Foster, W. R., *The Church of the Covenanters. The Church of Scotland 1596–1638* (Edinburgh, 1975).

Fowler, A., *The Country House Poem. A Cabinet of Seventeenth-Century Estate Poems and Related Items* (Edinburgh, 1994).

Fox, L. ed., *English Historical Scholarship in the 16th and 17th Centuries* (Oxford, 1956).

*French Connection. Scotland and the Arts of France* (Edinburgh, 1985).

Gates-Coon, R., *The Landed Estates of the Esterhazy Princes. Hungary during the Reforms of Maria Theresia and Joseph II* (Baltimore and London, 1994).

Geary, P. J., *Living with the Dead in the Middle Ages* (New York, 1994).

Gent, L. ed., *Albion's Classicism: the Visual Arts in Britain 1550–1660* (New Haven, 1993).

Gibson, A. J. S. and T. C. Smout, *Prices, Food and Wages in Scotland 1550–1780* (Cambridge, 1995).

Gilbert, J. M., *Hunting and Hunting Reserves in Medieval Scotland* (Edinburgh, 1979).

Gilbert, W., *Women in Seventeenth-Century France* (Basingstoke, 1989).

Gillespie, R., *Colonial Ulster. The Settlement of East Ulster 1600–1641* (Cork, 1985).

Gittings, C., *Death, Burial and the Individual in Early Modern England* (London, 1984).

Gladitz, C., *Horse Breeding in the Medieval World* (Dublin, 1997).

Glendinning, M., R. MacInnes and A. MacKechnie eds, *A History of Scottish Architecture. From the Renaissance to the Present Day* (Edinburgh, 1996).

Goody, J., J. Thirsk and E. P. Thompson eds, *Family and Inheritance. Rural Society in Western Europe 1200–1800* (Cambridge, 1976).

Graham, M. F., *The Uses of Reform. 'Godly Discipline' and Popular Behaviour in Scotland and Beyond, 1560–1610* (Leiden, 1996).

Grant, A., *Independence and Nationhood. Scotland 1306–1469* (London, 1984).

*Great Scots. Scottish National Portrait Gallery* (Edinburgh, 1983).

Greenblatt, S., *Renaissance Self-Fashioning. From More to Shakespeare* (Chicago, 1980).

Gregory, D., *History of the Western Highlands and Islands* (Edinburgh, 1975).

Haigh, C. ed., *The English Reformation Revised* (Cambridge, 1987).

Hale, J. R., *War and Society in Renaissance Europe, 1450–1620* (London and Baltimore, 1985).

Hands, R. ed., *English Hawking and Hunting in the Boke of St Albans* (Oxford, 1975).

Hanlon, G., *Confession and Community in Seventeenth-Century France. Catholic and Protestant Co-existence in Aquitaine* (Philadelphia, 1993).

Harding, R. H., *Anatomy of a Power Elite. The Provincial Governors of Early Modern France* (London and Yale, 1978).

Harrington, J. F., *Reordering Marriage and Society in Reformation Germany* (Cambridge, 1995).

Harris, J., *The Artist and the Country House. A History of Country House and Garden View Painting in Britain, 1540–1870* (London, 1979).

Hart, V., *Art and Magic in the Court of the Stuarts* (London, 1994).

Hatcher, J., *The History of the British Coal Industry. Volume 1. Before 1700: Towards the Age of Coal* (Oxford, 1993).

Heal, F., *Hospitality in Early Modern England* (Oxford, 1990).

Heal, F. and C. Holmes, *The Gentry in England and Wales 1500–1700* (Basingstoke, 1994).

Heller, H., *Iron and Blood. Civil Wars in Sixteenth-Century France* (Montreal, 1991).

Henderson, T. F. ed., *Minstrelsy of the Scottish Border* (4 vols, Edinburgh, 1932).

Henderson, K. U. and B. F. McManus, *Half Humankind. Contexts and Texts of the Controversy about Women in England, 1540–1640* (Urbana, 1985).

Hewitt, G., *Scotland under Morton, 1572–80* (Edinburgh, 1982).

Hill, G., *An Historical Account of the Plantation in Ulster at the Commencement of the Seventeenth Century* (Shannon, 1970).

Hill, O. and J. Cornforth, *English Country Houses. Caroline, 1625–1685* (London, 1966).

Houlbrooke, R. ed., *Death, Ritual and Bereavement* (London and New York, 1989).

Houlbrooke, R. A., *The English Family, 1450–1700* (London, 1984).

Houston, R. A., *Scottish Literacy and the Scottish Identity. Illiteracy and Society in Scotland and Northern England, 1600–1800* (Cambridge, 1985).

Howard, D., *The Architectural History of Scotland. Scottish Architecture from the Reformation to the Restoration, 1560–1666* (Edinburgh, 1995).

Howarth, D., *Images of Rule. Art and Politics in the English Renaissance, 1485–1649* (Basingstoke, 1997).

Hufton, O., *The Prospect Before Her. A History of Women in Western Europe. Volume I, 1500–1800* (London, 1995).

Hughes, J. and W. S. Ramson eds, *Poetry of the Stewart Court* (Canberra, 1982).

Hunt, J. D., *Garden and Grove. The Italian Renaissance Garden in the English Imagination: 1600–1750* (London, 1986).

Huntington, R. and P. Metcalf, *Celebrations of Death. The Anthropology of Mortuary Ritual* (Cambridge, 1979).

Ingram, M., *Church Courts, Sex and Marriage in England, 1570–1640* (Cambridge, 1987).

Innes, T., *Scots Heraldry* (Edinburgh, 1956).

Jack, R. D. S. ed., *The History of Scottish Literature. Vol I. Origins to 1660* (4 vols, Aberdeen, 1988).

Jackson-Stops, G. ed., *Treasure Houses of Britain. 500 Years of Private Patronage and Art Collecting* (London, 1985).

James, M. E., *Society, Politics and Culture. Studies in Early Modern England* (Cambridge, 1988).

Johnstone, J. F. K., *The Alba Amicorum of George Strachan, George Craig, Thomas Cuming* (Aberdeen University Studies 95, 1925).

Jones, M. ed., *Gentry and Lesser Nobility in Late Medieval Europe* (Gloucester, 1986).

Jordan, W. K., *Philanthropy in England, 1480–1660. A Study of the Changing Pattern of English Social Aspirations* (London, 1959).

Kagan, R. L., *Students and Society in Early Modern Spain* (Baltimore, 1974).

Kamen, H., *European Society, 1500–1700* (London, 1984).

Kaufman, T. D., *The Mastery of Nature. Aspects of Art, Science and Humanism in the Renaissance* (Princeton, 1993).

Kay, D., *Melodious Tears. The English Funeral Elegy from Spenser to Milton* (Oxford, 1990).

Kearney, H., *Scholars and Gentlemen. Universities and Society in Pre-Industrial Britain, 1500–1700* (London, 1970).

Keen, M., *Chivalry* (New Haven and London, 1984).

Kelso, R., *Doctrine for the Lady of the Renaissance* (Urbana, 1978).

Kent, F. W., *Household and Lineage in Renaissance Florence. The Life of the Capponi, Ginori, and Rucellai* (Princeton, 1977).

Kidd, C., *Subverting Scotland's Past. Scottish Whig Historians and the Creation of an Anglo-British Identity, 1689–c.1830* (Cambridge, 1993).

Kirk, J., *The University of Glasgow, 1451–1577* (Glasgow, 1977).

Koenigsberger, D., *Renaissance Man and Creative Thinking. A History of Concepts of Harmony* (Hassocks, 1979).

Kuehn, T., *Law, Family and Women. Towards a Legal Anthropology of Renaissance Italy* (Chicago, 1994).

Lansing, J. B., *The Florentine Magnates. Lineage and Faction in a Medieval Commune* (Princeton, 1991).

Larminie, V. M., *The Godly Magistrate. The Private Philosophy and Public Life of Sir John Newdigate, 1571–1610* (Stratford-upon-Avon, 1982).

Larner, C., *Enemies of God. The Witchhunt in Scotland* (Oxford, 1981).

Lazzaro, C., *The Italian Renaissance Garden from the Conventions of Planetary Design and Ornament to the Grand Gardens of Sixteenth-Century Central Italy* (London, 1990).

Lee, M., James Stewart, Earl of Moray. *A. Political Study of the Reformation in Scotland* (Westport, CT, 1953).

Lee, M., *John Maitland of Thirlestane and the Foundation of the Stewart Despotism* (Princeton, 1959).

Lee, M., *Government by Pen. Scotland under James VI and I* (Urbana, 1980).

Lee, M., *The Road to Revolution. Scotland under Charles I* (Urbana, 1985).

Leites, E., *The Puritan Conscience and Modern Sexuality* (Yale, 1986).

Leneman, L. ed., *Perspectives in Scottish Social History* (Aberdeen, 1988).

Levi, G. and J. C. Schmitt eds, *A History of Young People in the West. Volume One. Ancient and*

*Medieval Rites of Passage* (Cambridge, MA, 1997).

Liedtke, W., *The Royal Horse and Rider. Painting, Sculpture and Horsemanship 1500–1800* (New York, 1989).

Lindsay, A., *Lives of the Lindsays* (2nd edn, 3 vols, London, 1849).

Llewellyn, N., *The Art of Death. Visual Culture in the English Death Ritual c.1500–c.1800* (London, 1991).

Lloyd, H. A., *The Gentry of South-West Wales, 1540–1640* (Cardiff, 1968).

Lubbock, J., *The Tyranny of Taste. The Politics of Architecture and Design in Britain 1550–1960* (New Haven, 1995).

Lynch, M., *Edinburgh and the Reformation* (Edinburgh, 1981).

Lynch, M. ed., *The Early Modern Town in Scotland* (London, 1987).

Lynch, M., *Scotland. A New History* (London, 1991).

Lythe, S. G. E., *The Economy of Scotland, 1550–1625* (Edinburgh, 1960).

MacCulloch, D., *The Later Reformation in England 1547–1603* (Basingstoke, 1990).

MacCurtain, M. and M. O'Dowd eds, *Women in Early Modern Ireland* (Edinburgh, 1991).

MacDonald, A. A., M. Lynch and I. B. Cowan eds, *The Renaissance in Scotland* (Leiden, 1994).

MacDonald, A. R., *The Jacobean Kirk, 1567–1625. Sovereignty, Polity and Liturgy* (Aldershot, 1998).

MacDonald, R. M., *The Library of Drummond of Hawthornden* (Edinburgh, 1971).

Macdougall, N. ed., *Church, Politics and Society in Scotland 1408–1929* (Edinburgh, 1983).

Macfarlane, A., *Marriage and Love in England. Modes of Reproduction, 1300–1840* (Oxford, 1986).

Macfarlane, K. B., *The Nobility of Later Medieval England* (Oxford, 1973).

Macgibbon, D. and T. Ross, *The Castellated and Domestic Architecture of Scotland from the Twelfth to the Eighteenth Centuries* (5 vols, Edinburgh, 1887–92).

Macgibbon, D. and T. Ross, *The Ecclesiastical Architecture of Scotland: from the Earliest Times to the Seventeenth Century* (3 vols, Edinburgh, 1896–7).

Macgregor, A. ed., *The Late King's Goods. Collections, Possessions and Patronage of Charles I in the Light of the Commonwealth Sale Inventories* (London, 1989).

Macinnes, A. I., *Charles I and the Making of the Covenanting Movement 1625–1641* (Edinburgh, 1991).

Macinnes, A. I., *Clanship, Commerce and the House of Stuart, 1603–1788* (East Linton, 1996).

Mackie, J. D., *The University of Glasgow 1451–1951* (Glasgow, 1954).

MacLean, L. ed., *The Middle Ages in the Highlands* (Inverness, 1981).

MacMillan, D., *Scottish Art 1460–1990* (Edinburgh, 1990).

MacQueen, J. ed., *Humanism in Renaissance Scotland* (Edinburgh, 1990).

Maczak, A., *Travel in Early Modern Europe* (Cambridge, 1995).

Maidment, J. ed., *The Poetical Remains of William Lithgow* (Edinburgh, 1863).

Major, J. R., *From Renaissance Monarchy to Absolute Monarchy. French Kings, Nobles and Estates* (Baltimore and London, 1994).

Makey, W. H., *The Church of the Covenant, 1637–51. Revolution and Social Change in Scotland* (Edinburgh, 1979).

Manning, R. B., *Hunters and Poachers. A Social and Cultural History of Unlawful Hunting in England 1485–1640* (Oxford, 1993).

Marshall, R., *Virgins and Viragos. A History of Women in Scotland from 1080–1980* (London, 1983).

Marshall, R. K., *The Days of Duchess Anne. Life in the Household of the Duchess of Hamilton* (London, 1973).

Mason, R. A. and N. A. T. Macdougall eds, *People and Power in Scotland. Essays in Honour of T. C. Smout* (Edinburgh, 1990).

Mathew, D., *Scotland under Charles I* (London, 1955).

McClure, G. W., *Sorrow and Consolation in Italian Humanism* (Princeton, 1991).

McCordick, D. ed., *Scottish Literature. An Anthology. Volume One* (New York, 1996).

McCrea, A., *Constant Minds. Political Virtue and the Lipsian Paradigm in England* (Toronto, 1997).

McDowall, W., *History of the Burgh of Dumfries* (Dumfries, 1972).

McLean, T., *The English at Play in the Middle Ages* (Windsor Forest, 1983).

McManamon, J. M., *Funeral Oratory and the Cultural Ideals of Italian Humanism* (Chapel Hill and London, 1989).

McNeill, P. and H. L. McQueen eds, *Atlas of Scottish History to 1707* (Edinburgh, 1996).

McQueen, H. L., *Common Law and Feudal Society in Medieval Scotland* (Edinburgh, 1993).

McRoberts, D. ed., *Essays on the Scottish Reformation* (Glasgow, 1962).

Mendelson, S. H., *The Mental World of Stuart Women* (Brighton, 1987).

Mentzer, R. A., *Blood and Belief. Family Survival and Confessional Identity among the Provincial Huguenot Nobility* (West Lafayette, 1994).

Mertes, K., *The English Noble Household 1250–1600* (Oxford, 1988).

Miller, H., *Henry VIII and the English Nobility* (Oxford, 1989).

Mirrer, L. ed., *Upon My Husband's Death: Widows in the Literature and Histories of Medieval Europe* (Ann Arbor, 1992).

Mitchison, R., *Lordship to Patronage. Scotland 1603–1745* (London, 1983).

Molho, A., *Marriage Alliances in Late Medieval Florence* (Cambridge, 1994).

Morgan, J., *Godly Learning. Puritan Attitudes to Learning and Education, 1560–1640* (Edinburgh, 1979).

Mosser, M. and G. Teyssot eds, *The History of Garden Design. The Western Tradition from the Renaissance to the Present Day* (London, 1991).

Motley, M., *Becoming a French Aristocrat: the Education of the Court Nobility, 1580–1715* (Princeton, 1990).

Mousnier, R., *Social Hierarchies, 1450 to the Present*, translated by P. Evans (New York, 1973).

Muir, E., *Ritual in Early Modern Europe* (Cambridge, 1997).

Neuschel, K. B., *Word of Honor: Interpreting Noble Culture in Sixteenth-Century France* (New York, 1989).

Nicolson, N., *Great Houses of Britain* (London, 1979).

Nisbet, A., *A System of Heraldry … of the most considerable Surnames and Families in Scotland* (2 vols, Edinburgh, 1722).

O'Day, R., *Education and Society 1500–1800. The Social Foundations of Education in Early Modern Britain* (Harlow, 1982).

Orme, N., *Education and Society in Mediaeval and Renaissance England* (London, 1989).

Orso, S. N., *Art and Death in the Spanish Habsburg Court. The Royal Exequies for Philip IV* (Columbia, 1989).

Outhwaite, R. B. ed., *Marriage and Society. Studies in the Social History of Marriage* (London, 1981).

Overton, M., *Agricultural Revolution in England. The Transformation of the Agrarian Economy, 1500–1850* (Cambridge, 1996).

Ozment, S., *When Fathers Ruled. Family Life in Reformation Europe* (Cambridge, MA, 1983).

Paton, G. C. ed., *An Introduction to Scottish Legal History* (Stair Society 20, Edinburgh, 1958).

Patterson, R. F., *Ben Johnson's Conversation with Drummond of Hawthornden* (London, 1923).

Paul, J. B. ed., *Scots Peerage* (9 vols, Edinburgh, 1904–14).

Peck, L. L., *Court Patronage and Corruption in Early Stuart England* (London, 1990).

Perceval-Maxwell, M., *The Scottish Migration to Ulster in the Reign of James I* (London, 1973).

Phillips, R., *Putting Asunder: A History of Divorce in Western Society* (Cambridge, 1988).

Phillips, R., *Untying the Knot: a Short History of Divorce* (Cambridge, 1991).

Po-chia Hsia, R., *Social Discipline in the Reformation: Central Europe 1550–1750* (New York, 1989).

Pollock, L., *Forgotten Children. Parent-Child Relations from 1500–1900* (Cambridge, 1983).

Purser, J., *Scotland's Music. A History of the Traditional and Classical Music of Scotland from Earliest Times to Today* (Edinburgh, 1992).

Quaife, G. R., *Wanton Wenches and Wayward Wives. Peasants and Illicit Wives in Early Seventeenth-Century England* (London, 1979).

Rae, T. I., *The Administration of the Scottish Frontier 1513–1603* (Edinburgh, 1966).

Ranun, O., *Artisans of Glory. Writers and Historical Thought in Seventeenth-Century France* (Chapel Hill, 1980).

Riddell, J., *Inquiry into the Law and Practise in Scottish Peerages* (2 vols, Edinburgh, 1842).

Roche, D., *The Culture of Clothing* (Cambridge, 1994).

Roelker, N. L., *One King, One Faith. The Parlement of Paris and the Religious Reformation of the Sixteenth Century* (Berkeley, 1996).

Rogers, C., *Monuments and Monumental Inscriptions in Scotland* (2 vols, London, 1871).

Roper, L., *The Holy Household: Women and Households in Reformation Augsburg* (Oxford, 1989).

Rosenthal, J. T., *Patriarchy and Families of Privilege in Fifteenth-Century England* (Philadelphia, 1991).

Rubinstein, H. L., *Captain Luckless: James, First Duke of Hamilton, 1606–1649* (Edinburgh, 1975).

Safley, J. R., *Let No Man Put Asunder. The Control of Marriage in the German Southwest. A Comparative Study, 1550–1600* (Kirksville, 1984).

Salvadori, P., *La Chasse sous l'Ancien Régime* (Paris, 1996).

Sanderson, M. B. H., *Scottish Rural Society in the 16th Century* (Edinburgh, 1982).

Sanderson, M. B. H., *Mary Stewart's People. Life in Mary Stewart's Scotland* (Edinburgh, 1987).

Sanderson, M. B. H., *Ayrshire and the Reformation. People and Change 1490–1600* (East Linton, 1997).

Schalk, E., *From Valor to Pedigree: Ideas of Nobility in France in the Sixteenth and Seventeenth Centuries* (Princeton, 1986).

Schreiber, R. E., *The First Carlisle. Sir James Hay, First Earl of Carlisle as Courtier, Diplomat and Entrepreneur, 1580–1636* (Philadelphia, 1984).

Schuler, R. M. ed., *Alchemical Poetry 1575–1700* (New York, 1995).

Schultz, J. A., *The Knowledge of Childhood in the German Middle Ages 1100–1350* (Philadelphia, 1995).

Scotland, J., *The History of Scottish Education. Volume One. From the Beginning to 1872* (London, 1969).

Scott, A. ed., *Scotch Passion. An Anthology of Scottish Erotic Poetry* (London, 1982).

Scott, H. ed., *Fasti Ecclesiae Scoticanae* (8 vols, Edinburgh, 1915–50).

Scott, H. M. ed., *The European Nobilities in the Seventeenth and Eighteenth Centuries* (2 vols, Harlow, 1995).

Seton, G., *A History of the Family of Seton* (2 vols, Edinburgh, 1896).

Shahar, S., *Childhood in the Middle Ages* (London, 1990).

Shorter, E., *The Making of the Modern Family* (New York, 1975).

Sim, A., *Food and Feast in Tudor England* (Stroud, 1997).

Simon, J., *Education and Society in Tudor England* (Cambridge, 1966).

Simpson, A., *The Wealth of the Gentry, 1540–1660* (Cambridge, 1960).

Simpson, G., *Scottish Handwriting 1150–1650* (Aberdeen, 1986).

Simpson, G. ed., *Scotland and the Low Countries 1124–1994* (East Linton, 1996).

Slater, M., *Family Life in the Seventeenth Century. The Verneys of Claydon House* (London, 1984).

Smith, J. M., *The Culture of Merit. Nobility, Royal Service and the Making of Absolute Monarchy in France, 1600–1789* (Ann Arbor, 1996).

Smout, T. C. ed., *Scotland and Europe 1200–1850* (Edinburgh, 1986).

Sommerville, J., *The Discovery of Childhood in Puritan England* (Athens and London, 1992).

Spring, E., *Land, Law and Family: Aristocratic Inheritance in England 1300–1800* (Chapel Hill and London, 1994).

Stannard, D. E., *The Puritan Way of Death. A Study in Religion, Culture and Social Change* (Oxford, 1977).

Stevenson, D., *The Scottish Revolution, 1637–44* (Newton Abbot, 1975).

Stevenson, D., *The Origins of Freemasonry. Scotland's Century 1590–1710* (Cambridge, 1988).

Stevenson, D., *The First Masons. Scotland's Early Lodges and Their Members* (Aberdeen, 1988).

Stevenson, D., *King's College, Aberdeen, 1560–1641. From Protestant Reformation to Covenanting Revolution* (Aberdeen, 1990).

Stone, L., *The Crisis of the Aristocracy, 1558–1641* (Oxford, 1965).

Stone, L., *The Family, Sex and Marriage in England 1500–1800* (London, 1977).

Stone, L., *Road to Divorce. England 1530–1987* (Oxford, 1990).

Stone, L. and J. C. F. Stone, *An Open Elite? England 1540–1880* (Oxford, 1984).

Stone, T., *Illustrated Maps of Scotland. From Blaeu's Atlas Novus of the 17th Century* (Aberdeen, 1990).

Stoye, J., *English Travellers Abroad 1604–1667* (New Haven and London, 1989).

Strauss, G., *Luther's House of Learning* (Baltimore, 1978).

Stringer, K. ed., *Essays on the Nobility of Medieval Scotland* (Edinburgh, 1985).

Strocchia, S. T., *Death and Ritual in Renaissance Florence* (Baltimore, 1992).

Strong, R., *The English Icon: Elizabethan and Jacobean Portraiture* (New York, 1969).

Subtelny, O., *Domination of Eastern Europe: Native Nobilities and Foreign Absolutism, 1500–1715* (Gloucester, 1986).

Supple, J. J., *Arms Versus Letters* (Oxford, 1984).

Thomson, D., *A Virtuous and Noble Education* (Edinburgh, 1971).

Thomson, D., *An Introduction to Gaelic Poetry* (London, 1974).

Thomson, D., *Painting in Scotland 1570–1650* (Edinburgh, 1975).

Thornton, P., *Seventeenth-Century Interior Decoration in England, France and Holland* (New Haven, 1981).

*Tolbooths and Town Houses. Civic Architecture in Scotland to 1833* (Royal Commission on the Ancient Historical Monuments of Scotland, Edinburgh, 1996).

Trevor-Roper, H. R., *The Gentry, 1540–1640* (Cambridge, 1953).

Twigg, J., *The University of Cambridge and the English Revolution 1635–1688* (Cambridge, 1990).

Vale, M., *The Gentleman's Recreations. Accomplishments and Pastimes of the English Gentleman 1580–1630* (Cambridge, 1977).

Van Nierop, H. F. K., *The Nobility of Holland. From Knights to Regents, 1500–1650* (Cambridge, 1984).

Walker, S. S. ed., *Wife and Widow in Medieval England* (Ann Arbor, 1993).

Warkneke, S., *Images of the Educational Traveller in Early Modern England* (Leiden, 1995).

Watson, R. ed., *The Poetry of Scotland. Gaelic, Scots and English* (Edinburgh, 1995).

Watson, R. N., *The Rest is Silence. Death as Annhilation in the English Renaissance* (Berkeley, 1994).

Watt, J. R., *The Making of Modern Marriage. Matrimonial Control and the Rise of Sentiment in Neuchâtel, 1550–1800* (Ithaca and London, 1992).

Wells-Cole, A., *Art and Decoration in Elizabethan and Jacobean England. The Influence of Continental Prints* (New Haven, 1997).

Wendorf, R., *The Elements of Life. Biography and Portrait-Painting in Stuart and Georgian England* (Oxford, 1990).

Whatley, C., *The Scottish Salt Industry 1570–1870* (Aberdeen, 1987).

Whyte, I. D., *Agriculture and Society in Seventeenth-Century Scotland* (Edinburgh, 1979).

Whyte, I. D., *Scotland before the Industrial Revolution. An Economic and Social History c.1060–c.1750* (London, 1995).

Williams, P., *The Tudor Regime* (Oxford, 1979).

Wolfe, M., *The Conversion of Henri IV. Politics, Power and Religious Belief in Early Modern France* (Cambridge, MA, 1993).

Wood, J. B, *The Nobility of the Election of Bayeux, 1463–1666* (Princeton, 1980).

Woolgar, G. M. ed., *Household Accounts from Mediaeval England. Part 1* (Oxford, new ser., 17, 1992).

Wormald, J., *Court, Kirk and Community. Scotland 1470–1625* (London, 1981).

Wormald, J., *Lords and Men: Bonds of Manrent 1442–1603* (Edinburgh, 1985).

Zagorin, P., *Rebels and Rulers, 1500–1660* (2 vols, Cambridge, 1982).

## (iv) Secondary Works: Articles and Essays

**Abbreviations**

| | |
|---|---|
| *AHCAW* | *Archaeological and Historical Collections Relating to the Counties of Ayr and Wigton* |
| *AHR* | *American Historical Review* |
| *ARH* | *Archive for Reformation History* |

| | |
|---|---|
| *BIHR* | *Bulletin of the Institute of Historical Research* |
| *CC* | *Continuity and Change* |
| *CH* | *Church History* |
| *CJH* | *Canadian Journal of History* |
| *CSSH* | *Comparative Studies in Society and History* |
| *EcHR* | *Economic History Review* |
| *EHQ* | *European History Quarterly* |
| *EHR* | *English Historical Review* |
| *Emblematica* | *Emblematica: an Interdisciplinary Journal for Emblem Studies* |
| *FHS* | *French Historical Studies* |
| *HJ* | *Historical Journal* |
| *HR* | *Historical Research* |
| *IR* | *Innes Review* |
| *JBS* | *Journal of British Studies* |
| *JEH* | *Journal of Ecclesiastical History* |
| *JFH* | *Journal of Family History* |
| *JGH* | *Journal of Garden History* |
| *JHI* | *Journal of the History of Ideas* |
| *JIH* | *Journal of Interdisciplinary History* |
| *JMH* | *Journal of Modern History* |
| *JR* | *Juridical Review* |
| *JSH* | *Journal of Social History* |
| *LQR* | *Law Quarterly Review* |
| *NS* | *Northern Scotland* |
| *PP* | *Past and Present* |
| *PSAS* | *Proceedings of the Society of Antiquaries of Scotland* |
| *RQ* | *Renaissance Quarterly* |
| *RSCHS* | *Records of the Scottish Church History Society* |
| *SCH* | *Sixteenth-Century Studies* |
| *SH* | *Social History* |
| *SHR* | *Scottish Historical Review* |
| *SLJ* | *Scottish Literary Journal* |
| *SS* | *Scottish Studies* |
| *SCJ* | *Sixteenth Century Journal* |
| *SSL* | *Studies in Scottish Literature* |
| *ST* | *Scottish Tradition* |
| *TGSI* | *Transactions of the Gaelic Society of Inverness* |
| *TRHS* | *Transactions of the Royal Historical Society* |

Adamson, J. S. A., 'The baronial context of the English civil war', *TRHS*, 5th ser., 40 (1990), 93–120.

Ago, R., 'Young nobles in the age of absolutism: paternal authority and freedom of choice in seventeenth-century Italy', in Levi and Schmitt eds, *Young People in the West*, 283–324.

Allan, D., '"A commendation of the private countrey life": philosophy and the garden in seventeenth-century Scotland', *JGH* 25 (1997), 59–80.

Allan, D., 'Ane ornament to you and your famelie: Sir Robert Gordon of Gordonstoun and the *Genealogical History of the Earldom of Sutherland*', forthcoming.

Allerston, P., 'Wedding finery in sixteenth-century Venice', in Dean and Lowe eds, *Marriage in Italy*, 25–40.

Alsop, J. D., 'Religious preambles in early modern English wills as formulae', *JEH* 40 (1989), 19–27.

Altred, L. C., 'Preparation for death in sixteenth-century northern England', *SCJ* 13 (1982), 37–66.

Anton, A. E., 'Parent and child', in Paton ed., *Introduction to Scottish Legal History*, 116–24.

Appleby, A. B., 'Agrarian capitalism or seigneurial reaction? The northwest of England, 1500–1700', *AHR* 80 (1975), 574–94.

Armstrong, W. B., 'Two papers relating to the export of coals from Scotland, 1596–1614', *PSAS*, new ser., 12 (1889–90), 474–7.

Arriaza, A., 'Mousnier and Barber: the theoretical underpinning of the "society of orders" in early modern Europe', *PP* 89 (1980), 39–57.

Atienza Hernández, I., '"Refeudalisation" in Castile during the seventeenth century: a cliché?', in I. A. A. Thompson and B. Y. Casalilla eds, *The Castilian Crisis of the Seventeenth Century* (London, 1994), 249–76.

Atkinson, C. and J. B. Atkinson, 'Subordinating women: Thomas Bentley's use of biblical women in "The monument of matrones" (1582)', *CH* 60 (1991), 289–300.

Atkinson, D. W., 'The religious views of Drummond of Hawthornden', *SSL* 21 (1986), 197–209.

Atkinson, D. W., 'William Drummond as a baroque poet', *SSL* 26 (1991), 394–409.

Banac, I. and P. Bushkovitch, 'The nobility in the history of Russia and eastern Europe', in Banac and Bushkovitch eds, *Nobility in Russia*, 1–16.

Bast, R. J., 'From two kingdoms to two tables: the Ten Commandments and the Christian magistrate', *ARH* 89 (1998), 79–95.

Bath, M., 'Painted ceilings, 1550–1650: applied emblematics in Scotland', *Emblematica* 7 (1993), 259–305.

Bath, M., 'Alexander Seton's painted gallery', in Gent ed., *Albion's Classicism*, 79–108.

Beaver, D., '"Sown in dishonour, raised in glory": death, ritual and social organisation in northern Gloucestershire, 1590–1690', *SH* 17 (1992), 389–419.

Beaver, D., 'The great deer massacre: animals, honor and communication in early modern England', *JBS* 38 (1999), 187–216.

Beier, L. M., 'The good death in seventeenth-century England', in Houlbrooke ed., *Death, Ritual and Bereavement*, 43–61.

Ben-Amos, I. K., 'Service and the coming of age of young men in seventeenth-century England', *CC* 3 (1988), 41–64.

Bennett, J. M., 'Public power and authority in the medieval English countryside', in Esler and Kowalski eds, *Women and Power*, 18–36.

Bernard, G. W., 'The Tudor nobility in perspective', in Bernard ed., *Tudor Nobility*, 1–48.

Birrel, T. A., 'Reading as pastime: the place of light literature in some gentlemen's libraries of the 17th century', in R. Myers and M. Harriss eds, *Property of a Gentleman. The Formation, Organisation and Dispersal of the Private Library 1620–1920* (Winchester, 1991), 113–32.

Bisson, T. N., 'Nobility and family in medieval France', *FHS* 16 (1990), 597–613.

Blanchard, I., 'Northern wools and Netherlands markets at the close of the Middle Ages', in Simpson ed., *Scotland and the Low Countries*, 76–88.

Bonfield, L., 'Affective families, open elites and strict family settlements in early modern England', *EcHR*, second ser., 41 (1988), 341–54.

Bowman, A. J., 'Culross colliery: a sixteenth-century mine', *Industrial Archaeology* 7 (1970), 353–72.

Bray, A., 'Homosexuality and the signs of male friendship in Elizabethan England', in *History Workshop Journal* 29 (1990), 1–19.

Broce, G. and R. M. Wunderlie, 'The funeral of Henry Percy, sixth earl of Northumberland', *Albion* 22 (1990), 199–215.

Brown, J. J., 'Merchant princes and mercantile investment in early seventeenth-century Scotland', in Lynch ed., *Early Modern Town*, 125–46.

Brown, K. M., 'Burghs, lords and feuds in Jacobean Scotland', in Lynch ed., *Early Modern Town*, 102–24.

Brown, K. M., 'The price of friendship: the "well affected" and English economic clientage in Scotland before 1603', in R. A. Mason ed., *Scotland and England 1286–1815* (Edinburgh, 1987), 139–62.

Brown, K. M., 'The making of a *politique*: the Counter Reformation and the regional politics of John Eighth Lord Maxwell', *SHR* 66 (1987), 152–75.

Brown, K. M., 'Aristocratic finances and the origins of the Scottish revolution', *EHR* 104 (1989), 46–87.

Brown, K. M., 'Noble indebtedness in Scotland between the Reformation and the revolution', *HR* 62 (1989), 260–75.

Brown, K. M., 'In search of the Godly magistrate in Reformation Scotland', *JEH* 40 (1989), 553–81.

Brown, K. M., 'The laird, his daughter, her husband and the minister: unravelling a popular ballad', in Mason and Macdougall eds, *People and Power*, 104–25.

Brown, K. M., 'The Scottish aristocracy, anglicization and the court, 1603–38', *HJ* 36 (1993), 543–76.

Brown, K. M., 'A house divided: family and feud in Carrick under John Kennedy, fifth earl of Cassillis', *SHR* 75 (1996), 168–96.

Brunelle, G. K., 'Dangerous liaisons: mésalliance and early modern French noblewomen', *FHS* 19 (1995), 75–103.

Brunelle, G. K., 'Narrowing horizons: commerce and derogation in Normandy', in M. P. Holt ed., *Society and Institutions in Early Modern France* (Athens and London, 1991), 63–79.

Bryson, A., 'The rhetoric of status: gesture, demeanour and the image of the gentleman in sixteenth and seventeeth-century England', in L. Gent and N. Llewellyn eds, *Renaissance Bodies: the Human Figure in English Culture c.1540–1660* (London, 1990), 136–53.

Burke, P., 'The language of orders in early modern Europe', in Bush ed., *Social Orders and Social Classes*, 1–12.

Burns, J. H., 'George Buchanan and the anti-monarchomachs', in R. A. Mason ed., *Scots and Britons. Scottish Political Thought and the Union of 1603* (Cambridge, 1994), 138–60.

Bush, M. L., 'An anatomy of nobility', in Bush ed., *Social Orders and Social Classes*, 26–46.

Calvi, G., 'Reconstructing the family: widowhood and marriage in Tuscany in the early modern period', in Dean and Lowe eds, *Marriage in Italy*, 275–96.

Cameron, J. K., 'Some continental visitors to Scotland in the late sixteenth and early seventeenth centuries', in Smout ed., *Scotland and Europe*, 45–61.

Cameron, J. K., 'Some Scottish students and teachers at the University of Leiden in the late sixteenth and early seventeenth centuries', in Simpson ed., *Scotland and the Low Countries* (1996), 122–35.

Cannon, J., 'The British nobility, 1660–1800', in Scott ed., *European Nobilities*, i. 53–81.

Chojnacki, S., 'The power of love: wives and husbands in late medieval Venice', in Esler and Kowalski eds, *Women and Power*, 126–48.

Chojnacki, S., 'Nobility, women and the state: marriage negotiations in Venice, 1420–1535', in Dean and Lowe eds, *Marriage in Italy*, 128–51.

Connacher, H., 'Land tenure in the seventeenth century', *JR* 50 (1938), 18–50.

Contamine, P., 'France at the end of the Middle Ages: who was then a gentleman?', in Jones ed., *Gentry and Lesser Nobility*, 201–16.

Cooper, J. P., 'The social distribution of land and men in England, 1436–1700', in G. E. Aylmer and J. S. Morrill eds, *Land, Men and Beliefs: Studies in Early Modern History* (London, 1983), 17–42.

Cooper, J. P., 'Ideas of gentility in early modern England', in G. E. Aylmer and J. S. Morrill eds, *Land, Men and Beliefs: Studies in Early Modern History* (London, 1983), 43–77.

Cooper, J. P., 'Patterns of inheritance and settlement by great landowners from the fifteenth to the eighteenth centuries', in Goody, Thirsk and Thompson eds, *Family and Inheritance*, 192–327.

Cooper, T. M., 'Freehold in Scots Law', *JR* 57 (1945), 1–5.

Cowan, E. J., 'Clanship, kinship and the Campbell acquisition of Argyll', *SHR* 58 (1979), 132–57.

Cowan, E. J., 'The darker vision of the Scottish Renaissance: the devil and Francis Stewart', in Cowan and Shaw eds, *Renaissance and Reformation*, 125–40.

Coward, B., 'A "crisis of the aristocracy" in the sixteenth and seventeenth centuries? The case of the Stanleys, earls of Derby, 1504–1642', *Northern History* 18 (1982), 54–77.

Cox, V., 'The single self: feminist thought and the marriage market in early modern Venice', *RQ* 48 (1995), 513–81.

Crawford, P., 'Attitudes to menstruation in seventeenth-century England', *PP* 91 (1981), 47–73.

Crawford, P., 'The sucking child: adult attitudes to child care in the first year of life in seventeenth-century England', *CC* 1 (1986), 23–51.

Cressy, D., 'Death and the social order: the funerary preferences of Elizabethan gentlemen', *CC* 5 (1989), 99–119.

Cross, C., 'Noble patronage in the Elizabethan church', *HJ* 3 (1960), 1–16.

Cross, C., 'The third earl of Huntingdon's death-bed – a Calvinist example of the *ars moriendi*', *Northern History* 21 (1985), 80–107.

Cuddy, N., 'The revival of the entourage: the bedchamber of James I', in D. Starkey ed., *The English Court from the Wars of the Roses to the Civil War* (Harlow, 1987), 173–225.

Cummings, R., 'Drummond's *Forth Feasting*: a panegyric for King James in Scotland, *The Seventeenth Century* 2 (1987), 1–18.

Curle, A. O., 'The kitchen and buttery accounts of the earl of Angus's household in Glasgow and the Cannongate from June to November 1608', *PSAS*, fourth ser., 42 (Edinburgh, 1907–8), 191–207.

Cust, R. and P. Lake, 'Sir Richard Grosvenor and the rhetoric of magistracy', *BIHR* 54 (1981), 40–53.

Davies, J., 'Family service and family strategies: the household of Henri duc de Montmorency, ca. 1590–1610', *Bulletin of the Society for Renaissance Studies* 3 (1985), 27–43.

Davies, J. M., 'The politics of the marriage bed: matrimony and the Montmorency family, 1527–1612', *FHS* 6 (1992), 63–95.

Davies, K. M., 'Continuity and change in literary advice on marriage', in Outhwaite ed., *Marriage and Society*, 58–80.

Dawson, J. E. A., 'The fifth earl of Argyle, Gaelic lordship and political power in sixteenth-century Scotland', *SHR* 183 (1988), 1–27.

Dawson, J. E. A., 'The origin of the "road to the isles": trade, communications and Campbell power in early modern Scotland', in Mason and Macdougall eds, *People and Power*, 74–103.

Dawson, J. E. A., 'Clan, kin and kirk: the Campbells and the Scottish Reformation', in N. S. Amos, A. Pettegree and H. van Nierop eds, *The Education of a Christian Society. Humanism and the Reformation in Britain and the Netherlands* (Aldershot, 1999), 211–42.

Dawson, J. E. A., 'The Protestant earl and godly Gael: the fifth earl of Argyll [c.1538–73] and the Scottish Reformation', in D. Wood ed., *Life and Thought in the Northern Church c.1100–1700* (Studies in Church History 12, 1999).

Day, J. E. R., 'Primers of honor: heraldry, heraldry books, and English Renaissance literature', *SCJ* 21 (1990), 93–103.

De Folco, J., 'The Hopes of Craighall and land investment in the seventeenth century', in T. M. Devine ed., *Lairds and Improvement in the Scotland of the Enlightenment* (Glasgow, 1978), 1–10.

De Mause, L., 'The evolution of childhood', in de Mause ed., *History of Childhood*, 1–74.

De Win, P., 'The lesser nobility of the Burgundian Netherlands', in Jones ed., *Gentry and Lesser Nobility*, 95–118.

Dean, T., 'Fathers and daughters: marriage laws and marriage disputes in Bologna and Italy, 1200–1500', in Dean and Lowe eds, *Marriage in Italy*, 85–106.

Dean, T. and K. Lowe, 'Introduction: issues in the history of marriage', in Dean and Lowe eds, *Marriage in Italy*, 1–21.

Debrisay, G., 'City limits: female philanthopists and wet nurses in seventeenth-century Scottish towns', *Journal of the Canadian Historical Association*, new ser., 8 (1997), 39–60.

Delille, G., 'Marriage, faction and conflict in sixteenth-century Italy: an example and a few questions', in Dean and Lowe eds, *Marriage in Italy*, 155–73.

Devine, T. M. and S. G. E. Lythe, 'The economy of Scotland under James VI: a revision article', *SHR* 50 (1971), 91–106.

Dewald, J., 'The ruling class in the marketplace: nobles and money in early modern France', in T. L. Haskell and R. F. Teichgraeber eds, *The Culture of the Market. Historical Essays* (Cambridge, 1993), 43–65.

Dickinson, W. C., 'Freehold in Scots Law', *JR* 57 (1945), 135–51.

Dobie, J. S., 'The parish church of Kilbirnie', *AHCAW*, ii. 111–35.

Dockray, K., 'Why did fifteenth-century English gentry marry? The Pastons, Plumptons and Stonors reconsidered', in Jones ed., *Gentry and Lesser Nobility*, 61–80.

Dodgshon, R. A., 'West Highland chiefdoms, 1500–1745: a study in redistributive exchange', in R. Mitchison and P. Roebuck eds, *Economy and Society in Scotland and Ireland 1500–1939* (Edinburgh, 1988), 27–37.

Donaldson, G., 'Lord chancellor Glamis and Theodore Beza', in G. Donaldson, *Scottish Church History* (Edinburgh, 1985), 120–36.

Donaldson, G., 'Scottish presbyterian exiles in England 1584–8', in G. Donaldson, *Scottish Church History* (Edinburgh, 1985), 178–90.

Donaldson, G., 'The legal profession in Scottish society in the sixteenth and seventeenth centuries', *JR* 31 (1976), 1–19.

Donaldson, G., 'The Dunbar monument in its historical setting', *East Lothian Field and Naturalists Society* (1987), 1–16.

Donati, C., 'The Italian nobilities in the seventeenth and eighteenth centuries', in Scott ed., *European Nobilities*, i. 237–68.

Doran, S., 'The finances of an Elizabethan nobleman and royal servant: a case study of Thomas Radcliffe, third earl of Sussex', *BIHR* 61 (1988), 286–300.

Doughty, J., 'The library of James Stewart, earl of Moray, 1531–1570', *Innes Review* 21 (1970), 17–29.

Du Boulay, F. R. H., 'Was there a German "gentry"?, in Jones ed., *Gentry and Lesser Nobility*, 119–32.

Durkan, J., 'Education in the century of the Reformation', in McRoberts ed., *Essays on the*

*Scottish Reformation*, 145–68.

Durkan, J., 'The cultural background', in McRoberts ed., *Essays on the Scottish Reformation*, 274–331.

Durkan, J., 'James, third earl of Arran: the hidden years', *SHR* 65 (1986), 154–66.

Durkan, J., 'The French connection in the sixteenth and early seventeenth century', in Smout ed., *Scotland and Europe*, 19–44.

Durkan, J., 'Education: the laying of fresh foundations', in McQueen ed., *Humanism in Renaissance Scotland*, 123–60.

Ellis, H. A., 'Genealogy, history and aristocratic reaction in early eighteenth-century France: the case of Henri de Boulainvilliers', *JMH* 58 (1986), 414–51.

Emigh, R. J., 'Land tenure, household structure and age of marriage in fifteenth-century Tuscany', *JIH* 27 (1997), 613–35.

Ferrano, J. M., 'The power to decide: battered wives in early modern Venice', *RQ* 48 (1995), 492–515.

Finch, J., 'According to the qualitie of the person deceased', *Scottish Architecture* 8 (1991), 105–14.

Finnie, A., 'The house of Hamilton: patronage, politics and the church in the Reformation period', *Innes Review* 36 (1985), 3–28.

Finucane, R. C., 'Sacred corpse, profane carrion: social ideals and death rituals in the later Middle Ages', in J. Whaley ed., *Mirrors of Mortality. Studies in the Social History of Death* (London, 1981), 40–60.

Fletcher, A., 'Men's dilemma: the future of patriarchy in England 1560–1660', *TRHS*, sixth ser., 4 (1994), 61–81.

Forte, A. D. M., 'Some aspects of the law of marriage in Scotland: 1500–1800', in E. M. McCraik ed., *Marriage and Property* (Aberdeen, 1984), 104–18.

Fosi, I. and M. A. Visceglin, 'Marriage and politics at the papal court in the sixteenth and seventeenth centuries', in Dean and Lowe eds, *Marriage in Italy*, 197–224.

Foster, W. R., 'A constant platt achieved: provision for the ministry, 1600–38', in Cowan and Shaw eds, *Reformation and Revolution*, 124–40.

Foyster, E. A., 'A laughing matter? Marital discord and gender control in seventeenth-century England', *Rural History: Economy, Society, Culture* 4 (1993), 5–21.

Frankforter, A. D., 'Elizabeth Bowes and John Knox: a woman and Reformation theology', *CH* 56 (1987), 333–47.

Frost, R. I., 'The nobility of Poland-Lithuania, 1569–1795', in Scott ed., *European Nobilities*, ii. 183–222.

Gavin, J. B., 'Two letters of Tobias Mathew to lord Burghley, August 1593, concerning the fifth earl of Bothwell', *SHR* 54 (1975), 107–14.

Gibson, A. and T. C. Smout, 'Food and hierarchy in Scotland, 1550–1650', in Leneman ed., *Perspectives in Scottish Social History – Essays in Honour of Rosalind Mitchison*, 33–52.

Giesey, R., 'Rules of inheritance and strategies of mobility in pre-revolutionary France', *AHR* 82 (1977), 271–89.

Goodare, J., 'Parliamentary taxation in Scotland, 1560–1603', *SHR* 68 (1989), 23–52.

Goodare, J., 'The nobility and the absolutist state in Scotland, 1584–1638', *History* 78 (1993), 161–82.

Goodare, J., 'The statutes of Iona in context', *SHR* 77 (1998), 31–57.

Goody, J., 'Inheritance, property and women: some comparative considerations', in Goody, Thirsk and Thomson eds, *Family and Inheritance*, 10–36.

Gordon, R. J., 'Patronage and parish: the nobility and the recatholicization of Lower Austria', in K. Maag ed., *The Reformation in Eastern and Central Europe* (Aldershot, 1997), 211–27.

Graham, M. F., 'Equality before the kirk? Church discipline and the élite in Reformation-era Scotland', *ARH* 84 (1993), 289–310.

Gransby, R., 'The decline of falconry in early modern England', *PP* 157 (1997), 37–62.

Grant, A., 'The development of the Scottish peerage', *SHR* 57 (1978), 1–27.

Grant, A., 'Extinction of direct male lines among Scottish noble families in the fourteenth and fifteenth centuries', in Stringer ed., *Nobility of Medieval Scotland*, 210–31.

Greengrass, M., 'Property and politics in sixteenth-century France: the landed fortune of Constable Anne de Montmorency', *FHS* 2 (1988), 371–98.

Guth, D. J., 'The age of debt, the Reformation and English law', in D. J. Guth and J. W. McKenna eds, *Tudor Rule and Revolution* (Cambridge, 1982).

Guthrie, C. J., 'The history of divorce in Scotland', *SHR* 8 (1910), 44–52.

Guy, I., 'The Scottish export trade, 1460–1599', in Smout ed., *Scotland and Europe*, 62–81.

Habakkuk, H. J., 'The long-term rate of interest and the price rise of land in the 17th century', *EcHR*, second ser., v (1952), 26–45.

Habakkuk, H. J., 'The rise and fall of English landed families 1600–1800', *TRHS*, fifth ser., 29 (1979), 187–208.

Hagen, W. W., 'How mighty the Junkers? Peasant rents and seigneurial profits in sixteenth-century Brandenburg', *PP* 108 (1985), 80–116.

Haigh, C., 'The continuity of Catholicism in Elizabethan England', in Haigh ed., *The English Reformation Revised*, 176–208.

Hale, J. R., 'The military education of the officer class in early modern Europe', in C. H. Cough ed., *Cultural Aspects of the Italian Renaissance* (Manchester, 1976), 440–61.

Hanawalt, B., 'Lady Honor Lisle's networks of influence', in Esler and Kowalski eds, *Women and Power*, 188–212.

Hanley, S., 'Family and state in early modern France: the marriage pact', in M. J. Boxer and J. H. Quintaert eds, *Connecting Spheres. Women in the Western World 1500 to the Present* (Oxford, 1987), 53–63.

Hardwick, J., 'Seeking separations: gender, marriages and household economies in early modern France', *FHS* 21 (1998), 157–80.

Harte, N. B., 'State control of dress and social change in pre-industrial England', in D. C. Coleman and A. H. John eds, *Trade, Government and Economy in Pre-Industrial England. Essays Presented to F. J. Fisher* (London, 1976), 132–65.

Haskell, F., 'Charles I's collection of pictures', in Macgregor ed., *Late King's Goods*, 203–31.

Hay, D., 'Scotland and the Italian Renaissance', in Cowan and Shaw eds, *Renaissance and Reformation*, 114–24.

Heal, F., 'The idea of hospitality in early modern England', *PP* 102 (1984), 66–93.

Healey, R. M., 'The preaching ministry in Scotland's First Book of Discipline', *CH* 58 (1989), 339–53.

Henneman, J. B., 'Nobility, pivilege and fiscal politics in late medieval France', *FHS* 13 (1983), 1–17.

Henneman, J. B., 'The military class and the French monarchy in the late Middle Ages', *AHR* 83 (1978), 946–65.

Hexter, J. H., 'The education of the aristocracy in the Renaissance', in J. H. Hexter, *Reappraisals in History* (London, 1961), 45–70.

Hibbard, C., 'The country house poem of the seventeenth century', *Journal of the Warburg and Courtauld Institutes* 19 (1956), 159–74.

Hill, C., 'The spiritualization of the household', in C. Hill ed., *Society and Puritanism in Pre-Revolutionary England* (London, 1964), 443–81.

Houlbrooke, R., 'Death, church and the family in England between the late fifteenth and the early eighteenth centuries', in Houlbrook ed., *Death, Ritual and Bereavement*, 26–7.

Howarth, D., 'Charles I, sculpture and sculptors', in Macgregor ed., *Late King's Goods*, 73–113.

Howard, D., 'Scotland's "Thrie Estates"', in Gent ed., *Albion's Classicism*, 51–78.

Howard, D., 'The Kinnoull aisle and monument', *Architectural History* 39 (1996), 36–53.

Hoyle, R. W., 'An ancient and laudable custom: the definition and development of tenant-right in north-western England in the sixteenth century', *PP* 116 (1987), 24–55.

Hudson, E. K., 'The Protestant struggle for survival in early Bourbon France: the case of the Huguenot schools', *ARH* 76 (1985), 271–95.

Hudson, E. K., 'The Catholic challenge to Puritan piety, 1580–1620', *Catholic Historical Review* 77 (1991), 1–20.

Hunt, J. D., 'The British garden and the grand tour', in G. Jackson-Stops, G. J. Schochet and L. C. Orlin eds, *The Fashioning and Functioning of the British Country House* (Winchester, 1989), 333–51.

Ireland, R. D., 'Husband and wife', in Paton ed., *Introduction to Scottish Legal History*, 82–98.

Ives, E. D., 'The bonny earl of Murray: the ballad and history', *Midwest Folklore* 9 (1959), 133–8.

Jago, C., 'The influence of debt on the relations between crown and aristocracy in 17th-century Castile', *EcHR*, second ser., 26 (1973), 218–36.

Jago, C., 'The "crisis of the aristocracy" in seventeenth-century Castile', *PP* 84 (1979), 60–90.

James, M. E., 'Two Tudor funerals', in James, *Society, Politics and Culture*, 176–87.

James, M. E., 'English politics and the concept of honour, 1485–1642', in James, *Society, Politics and Cultur*, 308–415.

Jamieson, F., 'The royal gardens of Holyroodhouse, 1500–1603', *JGH* 22 (1994), 18–36.

Jespersen, K. J. V., 'The rise and fall of the Danish nobility, 1600–1800', in Scott ed., *European Nobilities*, ii. 41–70.

Kalas, R. J., 'A noble widow's place in the patriarchal household: the life and career of Jeanne de Gontauld', *SCJ* 24 (1993), 519–39.

Kaminski, A., 'The *szlachta* of the Polish-Lithuanian Commonwealth and their government', in Banac and Bushkovitch eds, *Nobility in Russia*, 17–45.

Kemp, M. and C. Farrow, 'Humanism in the visual arts, *circa* 1530–1630', in MacQueen ed., *Humanism in Renaissance Scotland*, 32–47.

Kerridge, E., 'The movement of rent, 1540–1640', in E. M. Carus-Wilson ed., *Essays in Economic History* (London, 1962), ii. 208–26.

Kershaw, S. E., 'Power and duty in the Elizabethan aristocracy: George, earl of Shrewsbury, the Glossopdale dispute and the Council', in Bernard ed., *Tudor Nobility*, 266–95.

Kettering, S., The patronage power of early modern French noblewomen', *HJ* 32 (1989), 817–41.

Kirk, J., 'The exercise of ecclesiastical patronage by the crown, 1560–1572', in Cowan and Shaw eds, *Renaissance and Reformation*, 93–113.

Kirk, J., 'Royal and lay patronage', in Macdougall ed., *Church, Politics and Society*, 127–50.

Kirk, J., '"Melvillian" reform in the Scottish universities', in MacDonald, Lynch and Cowan eds, *Renaissance in Scotland*, 276–300.

Kooi, C., 'Popish impudence: the perseverance of the Roman Catholic faithful in Calvinist Holland, 1572–1620', *SCJ* 26 (1995), 75–85.

Kuehn, T., 'Honor and conflict in a fifteenth-century Florentine family', in Kuehn, *Law, Family and Women*, 129–42.

Kuehn, T., 'Women, marriage and *patria potestas* in late medieval Florence', in Kuehn, *Law, Family and Women*, 197–212.

Lamb, M. E., 'The countess of Pembroke and the art of dying', in M. B. Rose ed., *Women in the Middle Ages and the Renaissance* (Syracuse, 1986), 207–26.

Laslett, P., 'Characteristics of the Western family', in P. Laslett, *Family Life and Illicit Love in Earlier Generations* (Cambridge, 1978), 12–49.

Laslett, P., 'Long-term trends in bastardy in England', in P. Laslett, *Family Life and Illicit Love in Earlier Generations* (Cambridge, 1978), 102–59.

Law, R., 'The first Scottish Guinea Company, 1634–9', *SHR* 86 (1997), 185–202.

Lee, M., 'An unpublished letter of Thomas Hamilton, earl of Melrose', *SHR* 58 (1979), 175–8.

Lee, M., 'King James's popish chancellor', in Cowan and Shaw eds, *Renaissance and Reformation*, 170–82.

Lee, M., 'Scotland and the "General Crisis" of the seventeenth century', *SHR* 63 (1984), 136–54.

Lenman, B., 'The limits of godly discipline in the early modern period with particular reference to England and Scotland', in K. von Greyerz ed., *Religion and Society in Early Modern Europe 1500–1800* (London, 1984), 124–45.

Lewnlski, B. K., 'The lady in the country-house poem', in G. Jackson-Stops, G. J. Schochet and L. G. Orlin eds, *The Fashioning and Functioning of the British Country House* (Winchester, 1989), 261–73.

Llewellyn, N., 'Honour in life, death and in the memory: funeral monuments in early modern England', *TRHS*, sixth ser., 6 (1996), 179–200.

Lyall, R. J., 'Two of Dunbar's Makars: James Affleck and Sir John the Ross', *IR* 27 (1976), 99–109.

Lyall, R. J., 'Complaint, satire and invective in middle Scots literature', in Macdougall ed., *Church, Politics and Society*, 45–64.

Lythe, S. G. E., 'The union of the crowns in 1603 and the debate on economic integration', *Scottish Journal of Political Economy* v. (1958), 219–28.

MacCulloch, D., 'Catholic and Puritan in Elizabethan Suffolk', *ARH* 72 (1981), 232–87.

MacCurtain, M., 'Women, education and learning in early modern Ireland', in MacCurtain and O'Dowd eds, *Women in Early Modern Ireland*, 160–78.

Macinnes, A. I., 'Scottish Gaeldom, 1638–1651: the vernacular response to the Covenanting dynamic', in J. Dwyer, R. A. Mason and A. Murdoch eds, *New Perspectives on the Politics and Culture of Early Modern Scotland* (Edinburgh, 1982), 59–94.

Macinnes, A. I., 'Crown, clans and fine: the "civilising" of Scottish Gaeldom, 1587–1638', *NS* 13 (1993), 31–55.

Mackay, A., 'The lesser nobility in the kingdom of Castile', in Jones eds, *Gentry and Lesser Nobility*, 159–80.

Maclagan, M., 'Genealogy and heraldry in the sixteenth and seventeenth centuries', in Fox ed. *English Historical Scholarship*, 31–48.

Makey, W. H., 'Presbyterian and Canterburian in the Scottish revolution', in Macdougall ed., *Church, Politics and Society*, 151–66.

Marshall, R. K., 'Wetnursing in Scotland, 1500–1800', *Review of Scottish Culture* (1984), 43–51.

Marwick, E. W., 'Nature versus nurture: patterns and trends in seventeenth-century French child-rearing', in de Mause ed., *History of Childhood*, 259–301.

Mason, R. A., 'Covenant and commonweal: the language of politics in Reformation Scotland', in Macdougall ed., *Church, Politics and Society*, 97–126.

Mason, R. A., 'Chivalry and citizenship: aspects of national identity in Renaissance Scotland', in Mason and Macdougall eds, *People and Power*, 50–73.

McClung, W. C., 'The country house Arcadia', in G. Jackson-Stops, C. J. Schochet, and L. C. Orlin eds, *The Fashioning and Functioning of the British Country House* (Washington, 1989), 277–87.

McGrath, P., 'Elizabethan Catholicism: a reconsideration', *JEH* 35 (1984), 414–28.

McKechnie, H., 'Early land valuations', *JR* 42 (1930), 70–7.

McLaren, D., 'Marital fertility and lactation 1570–1720', in M. Prior ed., *Women in English Society 1500–1800* (London, 1985), 22–53.

McMullen, N., 'The education of English gentlewomen 1540–1640', *History of Education* 6 (1977), 87–101.

McNeill, W. A. and P. G. B. McNeill, 'The Scottish progress of James VI, 1617', *SHR* 75 (1996), 38–51.

Meikle, M., 'The invisible divide: the greater lairds and the nobility of Jacobean Scotland', *SHR* 71 (1992), 70–87.

Mettam, R., Definitions of nobility in seventeenth-century France', in Corfield ed., *Language, History and Class*, 79–100.

Mettam, R., 'The French nobility, 1610–1715', in Scott ed., *European Nobilities*, i. 114–41.

Mitchison, R., 'The movement of Scottish corn prices in the seventeenth and eighteenth centuries', *EcHR*, second ser., 18 (1965), 278–91.

Montgomery, G. A., 'Guardian and ward', in Paton ed., *Introduction to Scottish Legal History*, 125–9.

Morford, M., 'Tacitean *prudentia* and the doctrines of Justus Lipsius', in T. J. Luce and A. J. Woodman eds, *Tacitus and the Tacitean Tradition* (Princeton, 1993), 129–51.

Morford, M. P. O., 'The Stoic garden', *JGH* 7 (1987), 151–75.

Morgan, D. A. L., 'The individual style of the English gentleman', in Jones ed., *Gentry and Lesser Nobility*, 15–35.

Morgan, G., 'Dowries for daughters in west Wales, 1500–1700', *Welsh History* 17 (1995), 534–49.

Morgan, V., 'Cambridge university and "the country" 1560–1640', in L. Stone ed., *The University in Society. Volume I. Oxford and Cambridge from the 14th to the Early 19th Century* (Princeton, 1975), 183–245.

Mullan, D. G., 'Theology in the Church of Scotland, 1618–c.1640: a Calvinist consensus?', *SCJ* 26 (1995), 595–617.

Murray, A. L., 'The marriage of the earl of Sutherland, 1567', *SHR* 51 (1972), 237–41.

Neuschel, K., 'Noble households in the sixteenth century: material and human communities', *FHS* 15 (1988), 595–622.

Nevinson, J. L., 'Illustrations of costume in the *Alba Amicorum*', *Archaeologia* 106 (1979), 167–76.

Nicholls, K. W., 'Irishwomen and property in the sixteenth century', in MacCurtain and O'Dowd eds, *Women in Early Modern Ireland*, 17–31.

Nicholls, M., 'Theatre of martyrdom in the French Reformation', *PP* 121 (1988), 49–73.

O'Day, R., 'The law of patronage in early modern England', *JEH* 26 (1975), 247–60.

Olsen, I. A., 'The dreadful death of the earl of Murray: clues from the Carpenter song collection', *Folk Music Journal* 7 (1997), 281–310.

Parker, G., 'The "Kirk by law established" and the origins of "the taming of Scotland": St Andrews 1559–1600', in Leneman ed., *Perspectives in Scottish Social History*, 1–32.

Paton, G. C., 'Husband and wife', in Paton ed., *Introduction to Scottish Legal History*, 99–115.

Peck, L. L., 'Court patronage and government policy: the Jacobean dilemma', in G. F. Lytle and S. Orgel eds, *Patronage in the Renaissance* (Princeton, 1981), 27–46.

Peck, L. L., '"For a king not to be bountifull were a fault": perspectives on court patronage in early Stuart England', *JBS* 25 (1986), 31–61.

Phillips, J. E., 'George Buchanan and the Sidney circle', *Huntington Library Quarterly*, 12 (1948–9), 23–55.

Phillips, K. M., 'Maidenhood as the perfect age of a woman's life', in K. J. Lewis, N. J. Menuge and K. M. Phillips eds, *Young Medieval Women* (Stroud, 1999), 1–24.

Pollard, A. J., 'Estate management in the later Middle Ages: the Talbots and Whitchurch, 1383–1525', *EcHR*, second ser., 25 (1972), 553–66.

Pollock, L. A., 'Teach her to live under obedience: the making of women in the upper ranks of early modern England', *CC* 4 (1989), 231–58.

Pollock, L. A., 'Living on the stage of the world: the concept of privacy among the elite of early modern England', in A. Wilson ed., *Rethinking Social History. English Society 1570–1920 and its Interpretation* (Manchester, 1993), 78–97.

Potter, D., 'Marriage and cruelty among the Protestant nobility in sixteenth-century France: Diane de Barbacon and Jean de Rohan, 1561–7', *EHQ* 20 (1990), 5–38.

Powis, J. K., 'Order, religion and the magistrates of a provincial parlement in sixteenth-century France', *ARH* 71 (1980), 180–97.

Press, V., 'Adel, Reich und Reformation', in W. J. Mommsen, P. Alter and R. W. Scribner eds, *The Urban Classes, the Nobility and the Reformation* (publication of the German Historical Institute, vol. 5, 1979), 330–83.

Price, J. L., 'The Dutch nobility in the seventeenth and eighteenth centuries', in Scott ed., *European Nobilities*, i. 82–113.

Pringle, R. V., 'An early humanity class library: the gift of Sir John Scot and his friends to St Leonard's college, 1620', *Bibliotheck* 7 (1974–5), 35–54.

Queller, D. and T. F. Madden, 'Father of the bride: fathers, daughters, and dowries in late medieval and early Renaissance Venice', *RQ* 46 (1993), 685–711.

Rae, T. I., 'The historical writing of Drummond of Hawthornden', *SHR* 54 (1975), 22–62.

Reid, D., 'Royalty and self-absorption in Drummond's poetry', *SSL* 22 (1987), 115–31.

Reid, D., 'Prose after Knox', in Jack ed., *History of Scottish Literature*, vol. 1, 183–95.

Reid, D., 'Hume of Godscroft's "The origine and descent of the most noble and Illustre familie and name of Douglas" as humanist historiography', *SLJ* 22 (1995), 35–45.

Roberts, A., 'Popery in Buchan and Strathbogie in the early seventeenth century', *RSCHS* 27 (1997), 127–55.

Roelker, N., 'The appeal of Calvinism to French noblewomen in the sixteenth century', *JIH* 2 (1972), 391–418.

Roelker, N., 'The role of noblewomen in the French Reformation', *ARH* 63 (1972), 168–95.

Rosenthal, J. T., 'Fifteenth-century widows and widowhood: bereavement, reintegration and life choices', in Walker, *Wife and Widow in Medieval England*, 33–58.

Roughead, W., 'Centenary of the entail', *JR* 35 (1923), 1–38.

Sanderson, M. H. B., 'Catholic recusancy in Scotland in the sixteenth century', *IR* 31 (1970), 87–107.

Sanderson, M. H. B., 'The Edinburgh merchants in society, 1570–1603', in Cowan and Shaw eds, *Renaissance and Reformation*, 183–99.

Sawday, J., 'The fate of Marsayas: dissecting the Renaissance body', in L. Gent and N. Llewelyn eds, *Renaissance Bodies. The Human Figure in English Culture* (London, 1990), 111–35.

Scanlan, J. D., 'Husband and wife. Pre-Reformation canon law of marriage of the officials' court', in Paton ed., *Introduction to Scottish Legal History*, 69–81.

Schimert, P., 'The Hungarian nobility in the seventeenth and eighteenth centuries', in Scott ed., *European Nobilities*, ii. 144–82.

Schindler, N., 'Guardians of disorder: rituals of youthful disorder at the dawn of the modern age', in Levi and Schmitt eds, *Young People in the West*, 240–82.

Scott, H. M. and C. Storrs, 'Introduction: the consolidation of noble power in Europe, c.1600–1800', in Scott ed., *European Nobilities*, i. 1–52.

Seddon, P. R., 'Robert Carr, earl of Somerset', *Renaissance and Modern Studies* 14 (1970), 48–68.

Sellar, D., 'Marriage, divorce and concubinage in Gaelic society', *TGSI* 51 (1978–80), 464–93.

Sellar, D., 'Highland family origins: pedigree making and pedigree faking', in MacLean ed., *The Middle Ages in the Highlands*, 103–16.

Sellar, D., 'Marriage, divorce and the forbidden degrees: canon law and Scots law', in W. N. Osborough ed., *Explorations in Law and History. Irish History Discourses, 1988–1994* (Dublin, 1995), 59–82.

Sellar, W., 'The earliest Campbells: Norman, Briton or Gael?', *Stair Society* 17 (1973), 109–25.

Sharpe, J. A., 'Domestic homicide in early modern England', *HJ* 24 (1981), 29–48.

Sharpe, J. A., '"Last dying speeches": religion, ideology and public execution in seventeenth-century England', *PP* 107 (1985), 144–67.

Shaw, D., 'Adam Bothwell, a conserver of the Renaissance in Scotland', in Cowan and Shaw eds, *Renaissance and Reformation*, 141–69.

Shaw, F. J., 'Landownership in the Western Isles in the seventeenth century', *SHR* 56 (1977), 34–43.

Simpson, A. W. B., 'Entails and perpetuities', *JR*, new ser., 24 (1979), 1–20.

Smart, I. M., 'Monarchy and toleration in Drummond of Hawthornden's works', *Scotia* 4 (1980), 44–50.

Smith, D. B., 'The reformers and divorce: a study on consistorial jurisdiction', *SHR* 9 (1911), 10–36.

Smith, L. B., 'English treason trials and confessions in the sixteenth century', *JHI* 15 (1954), 471–98.

Smith, T. S., 'Persecution of Staffordshire Roman Catholic recusants, 1625–1660', *JEH* 30 (1979), 327–51.

Smout, T. C., 'Scottish marriage, regular and irregular, 1500–1940', in R. B. Outhwaite ed., *Marriage and Society: Studies in the Social History of Marriage* (London, 1981), 204–36.

Spence, R. T., 'A noble funeral in the great civil war', *Yorkshire Archaeological Journal* 65 (1993), 115–23.

Spiller, M., 'Poetry after the union, 1603–1660', in Jack ed., *History of Scottish Literature*, i. 141–60.

Squib, G. D., 'The end of the name of arms clause?', *LQR* 69 (1953), 219–25.

Stevenson, D., 'The king's Scottish revenues and the Covenanters, 1625–1651', *HJ* 17 (1974), 17–41.

Stevenson, D., 'The English devil of keeping state: elite manners and the downfall of Charles I in Scotland', in Mason and Macdougall eds, *People and Power*, 126–44.

Stone, L., 'The residential development of the West End of London in the seventeenth century', in B. C. Malament ed., *After the Reformation. Essays in Honor of J. H. Hexter* (Manchester, 1980), 177–86.

Stringer, K. J., 'The early lords of Lauderdale, Dryburgh abbey and St Andrews at Northampton', in Stringer ed., *Nobility of Medieval Scotland*, 44–61.

Styles, P., 'Politics and historical research in the early seventeenth century', in Fox ed., *English Historical Scholarship*, 49–72.

Supple, J. J., 'François de la Noue and the education of the French "noblesse d'épée"', *FHS* 36 (1982), 270–81.

Thirsk, J., 'The European debate on customs of inheritance, 1500–1700', in Goody, Thirsk and Thomson eds, *Family and Inheritance*, 177–91.

Thomas, K. V., 'Age and authority in early modern England', *Proceedings of the British Academy* 62 (1976), 205–48.

Thompson, I. A. A., '*Hidalgo* and *pechero*: the language of "estates" and "classes" in early modern Castile', in Corfield ed., *Language, History and Class*, 53–78.

Thompson, I. A. A., 'The nobility in Spain, 1600–1800', in Scott ed., *European Nobilities*, i. 174–236.

Tudor, P., 'Religious instruction for children and adolescents in the early English Reformation', *JEH* 35 (1984), 391–413.

Underdown, D. E., 'The taming of the scold: the enforcement of patriarchal authority in early modern England', in A. Fletcher and J. Stevenson eds, *Order and Disorder in Early Modern England* (Cambridge, 1985), 116–35.

Upton, A. F., 'The Swedish nobility, 1600–1772', in Scott ed., *European Nobilities*, i. 11–40.

Van Winter, J. M., 'Knighthood and nobility in the Netherlands', in Jones ed., *Gentry and Lesser Nobility*, 81–94.

Waite, G., 'The Dutch nobility and anabaptism, 1535–1545', *SCJ* 23 (1992), 458–85.

Walker, J., 'Gambling and the Venetian noblemen c.1500–1700', *PP* 162 (1999), 28–69.

Wall, A., 'For love, money, or politics? A clandestine marriage and the court of arches', *HJ* 38 (1995), 511–33.

Ward, J. C., 'English noblewomen and the local community in the later Middle Ages', in D. Watt ed., *Medieval Women in Their Communities* (Cardiff, 1997), 186–201.

White, A., 'The regent Morton's visitation: the Reformation of Aberdeen, 1574', in MacDonald, Lynch and Cowan eds, *Renaissance in Scotland*, 246–63.

Willen, D., 'Godly women in early modern England: Puritanism and gender', *JEH* 43 (1992), 561–80.

Williamson, A. H., A patriot nobility?', *SHR* 72 (1993), 1–21.

Williamson, A. H., 'Number and national consciousness: the Edinburgh mathematicians and Scottish political culture at the union of the crowns', in R. A. Mason ed., *Scots and Britons. Scottish Political Thought and the Union of 1603* (Cambridge, 1994), 187–212.

Wilson, R. D., 'The Skelmorlie aisle and monuments at Largs', in *AHCAW*, vi. 58–76.

Wilson, S., 'The myth of motherhood a myth: the historical view of European child-rearing', *SH* 9 (1984), 181–98.

Wood, J. B., 'Endogamy and mésalliance: the marriage patterns of the nobility in the election of Bayeaux 1430–1669', *FHS* 10 (1978), 375–92.

Woolf, S. J., 'Economic problems of the nobility in the early modern period: the example of Piedmont', *EcHR* 17 (1964), 267–83.

Wormald, J. M., 'Bloodfeud, kindred and government in early modern Scotland', *PP* 87 (1980), 54–97.

Wormald, J. M., 'James VI and I: two kings or one?', *History* 68 (1983), 187–209.

Wormald, J. M., '"Princes" and the regions in the Scottish Reformation', in Macdougall ed., *Church, Politics and Society*, 65–84.

Wormald, J. M., 'Lords and lairds in fifteenth-century Scotland: nobles and gentry?', in Jones ed., *Gentry and Lesser Nobility*, 181–200.

Wrightson, K., 'The nadir of English illegitimacy in the seventeenth century', in P. Laslett, K. Oosterveen and R. M. Smith eds, *Bastardy and its Comparative History* (London, 1980), 176–91.

Wrightson, K., 'Estates, degrees, and sorts: changing perceptions of society in Tudor and Stuart England', in Corfield ed., *Language, History and Class*, 30–52.

Wunderlie, R. and G. Broce, 'The final moment before death in early modern England', *SCJ* 20 (1989), 259–75.

Yates, F. A., 'The hermetic tradition in Renaissance science', in F. A. Yates ed., *Ideas and Ideals in the North European Renaissance* (London, 1984), 227–46.

Yule, G., 'James VI and I: furnishing the churches in his two kingdoms', in A. Fletcher and P. Roberts eds, *Religion, Culture and Society in Early Modern Britain* (Cambridge, 1994), 182–204.

Zell, M. L., 'The use of religious preambles as a measure of religious belief in the sixteenth century', *BIHR* 50 (1977), 256–9.

## (v) Unpublished Theses

Brown, J. J., 'The social, political and economic influences of the Edinburgh merchant elite, 1600–38' (University of Edinburgh Ph.D., 1986).

Macinnes, A. I., 'The origin and organisation of the covenanting movement during the reign of Charles I, 1625–41' (University of Glasgow Ph.D., 1987).

Macpherson, R., 'Francis Stewart, 5th earl of Bothwell, c.1562–1612: lordship and politics in Jacobean Scotland' (University of Edinburgh Ph.D., 1999).

Mann, A., 'The book trade and public policy in early modern Scotland c.1500–1720' (University of Stirling Ph.D., 1997).

Meikle, M., 'Lairds and gentlemen: a study of the landed families of the eastern Anglo-Scottish borders c.1540–1603' (University of Edinburgh Ph.D., 1989).

Scally, J., 'The political career of James, Third Marquis and First Duke of Hamilton (1606–1649) to 1643' (University of Cambridge Ph.D., 1992).

Seddon, P. R., 'Patronage and officers in the reign of James I' (University of Manchester Ph.D., 1967).

Wells, V. T., 'The origins of covenanting thought and resistance c.1580–1638' (University of Stirling Ph.D., 1998).

Zulager, R. R., 'A study of the middle-rank administrators in the government of King James VI of Scotland, 1580–1603' (University of Aberdeen Ph.D., 1991).

# Index

Numbers in *italics* refer to Plates